# Algorithms Sequential and Parallel:

## A Unified Approach

# Algorithms Sequential and Parallel: A Unified Approach

## Third Edition

Russ Miller
Laurence Boxer

CENGAGE Learning

Australia • Brazil • Japan • Korea • Mexico • Singapore • Spain • United Kingdom • United States

CENGAGE Learning

**Algorithms Sequential and Parallel: A Unified Approach, Third Edition**
**Russ Miller and Laurence Boxer**

Editor-in-Chief: Marie Lee

Senior Product Manager: Alyssa Pratt

Associate Product Manager Stephanie Lorenz

Art and Design Direction, Production Management, and Composition: Integra Software Services Pvt. Ltd.

Senior Print Buyer: Julio Esperas

Cover Image: ©Spectral-Design/Shutterstock



Library of Congress Control Number: 2012947455

ISBN-13: 978-1-133-36680-5
ISBN-10: 1-133-36680-5

**Cengage Learning**
20 Channel Center Street
Boston, MA 02210
USA

Cengage Learning is a leading provider of customized learning solutions with office locations around the globe, including Singapore, the United Kingdom, Australia, Mexico, Brazil and Japan. Locate your local office at **international.cengage.com/region**

Cengage Learning products are represented in Canada by Nelson Education, Ltd.

For your course and learning solutions, visit **www.cengage.com**
Purchase any of our products at your local college store or at our preferred online store **www.cengagebrain.com**
**Instructors:** Please visit **login.cengage.com** and log in to access instructor-specific resources.

Printed in the United States of America
1 2 3 4 5 6 17 16 15 14 13 12

*To my wife, Celeste, and my children, Amanda, Brian, and Melissa.*

*—Russ Miller*

*To my wife, Linda; our daughter and son-in-law, Robin and Mark Waldman, and their magnificent multiprocessing multiplications, Ella, Lilah, and Gabriel; and our son, Matthew.*

*—Laurence Boxer*

# Contents

# Preface

Effective computing requires the design, analysis, implementation, and evaluation of algorithms to solve problems of interest. Computational problems come from a wide variety of areas including science, engineering, business, athletics, architecture, medicine, management, economics, psychology, anthropology, and entertainment, to name a few. In addition, exciting new challenges exist in the field of *computational science and engineering*, which is the "third science," complementing both theoretical and laboratory science. Computational science and engineering unites computer science and mathematics with disciplinary expertise in biology, chemistry, physics, and other applied scientific and engineering fields. Multidisciplinary efforts in these STEM (Science, Technology, Engineering, and Mathematics) areas typically require efficient algorithms that run on high-performance computers in order to perform simulation and modeling of physical and human environments.

With current technology, it is difficult to increase significantly the density of computer chips, and, hence, the inherent speed of a traditional computer processor. Since there continues to be a demand for increased computing power, state-of-the-art computer systems are now being designed around architectures that consist of multiple processing units. That is, computing systems are currently being constructed based on multiple processors and/or processors with multiple cores. In fact, it is quite difficult to find even a consumer-based compute system that does not consist of multiple processing units. This includes desktops, laptops, netbooks, tablets, smart phones, gaming systems, and high-end computing systems. In fact, many of these systems contain Graphics Processing Units (GPUs) that consist of numerous processors targeted at enhancing a gaming and visualization environment.

Since mainstream computing consists of multiprocessor units, whether it is within a local system or in a remotely accessed "cloud," it is critical for scientists, engineers, and users of this 21st century computational infrastructure to have a working knowledge of multiprocessor algorithms and architectures. For historical reasons and due to legacy and "dusty deck" computer programs, it is also important that the reader have a basic understanding of how to manipulate uniprocessor systems efficiently.

Due to the state of current technology, the focus of this book is on parallel and sequential algorithms and architectures, including clouds, grids, clusters, fine-grained network models, shared- and distributed-memory machines, and the traditional von Neumann architecture. We discuss algorithms and their analysis for a variety of compute models in a unified approach by presenting a solution strategy, and then discussing a comparison of resources for the implementation of the high-level solution strategy on such architectures. Analyses of these resources consider the number of computational units (processors or cores), the amount of memory, interconnection networks, and running time, to name a few.

**Computer Science Courses in Algorithms:** Many computer science departments offer courses in "Analysis of Algorithms," "Algorithms," "An Introduction to Algorithms," or "Data Structures and their Algorithms" at the junior or senior level. In addition, a course in "Analysis of Algorithms" is required of most graduate students pursuing an advanced degree in computer science. Throughout the 1980s, the vast majority of these course offerings focused on algorithms for sequential (von Neumann) computers. In fact, not until the late 1980s did courses covering an introduction to parallel algorithms begin to appear in research-oriented departments. Furthermore, these courses in parallel algorithms were typically presented to advanced graduate students. However, by the early 1990s, courses in parallel computing began to emerge at the undergraduate level, especially at progressive 4-year colleges.

Throughout much of the 1990s, traditional algorithms-based courses changed very little. Gradually, such courses began to incorporate a component of parallel algorithms, typically one to three weeks near the end of the semester. During the later part of the 1990s, however, it was not uncommon to find algorithms courses that contained as much as 1/3 of the material devoted to parallel algorithms.

In this book, we take a very different approach to an algorithms-based course. Parallel computing has moved into the mainstream, with clusters of commodity-off-the-shelf (COTS) machines dominating the list of top supercomputers in the world (www.top500.org), and smaller versions of such machines being exploited in many research laboratories. Therefore, the time is right to teach a fundamental course in algorithms that covers paradigms for both sequential and parallel models.

**This Book's Approach to Presenting Algorithms:** The approach we take in this book is to integrate the presentation of sequential and parallel algorithms. Specifically, we employ a philosophy of presenting a paradigm, such as divide-and-conquer, and then discussing implementation issues for both sequential and parallel models. Due to the fact that we present design and analysis of paradigms for sequential and parallel models, the reader might notice that the number of paradigms we can treat within a semester is limited when compared to a traditional sequential algorithms text.

This book has been used successfully at a wide variety of colleges and universities.

**Prerequisites:** We assume a basic knowledge of data structures and mathematical maturity. The reader should be comfortable with notions of a stack, queue, list, and binary tree, at a level that is typically taught in a CS2 course. The reader should also be familiar with fundamentals of Discrete Mathematics and Calculus. Specifically, the reader should be comfortable with limits, summations, and integrals.

## Overview of Chapters

Background material for the course is presented in Chapters 1, 2, and 3. Chapter 1 introduces the concept of asymptotic analysis. While the reader might have seen some of this material in a course on data structures, we present this material in a fair amount of detail. The reader who is uncomfortable with some of the fundamental material from a freshman-level Calculus sequence might want to brush up on notions such as limits, summations and integrals, and derivatives, as they naturally arise in the presentation and application of asymptotic analysis. Chapter 2 focuses on fundamentals of induction and recursion. While many students have seen this material in previous courses in computer science and/or mathematics, we have found it important to review this material briefly and to provide the students with a reference for performing the necessary review. In Chapter 3, we present the Master Method, a very useful cookbook-type of system for evaluating recurrence equations that are common in an algorithms-based setting.

Chapter 4 introduces fundamental models of computation, including the RAM (a formal sequential architecture) and a variety of parallel architectures. We introduce multiprocessor systems that include the PRAM, linear array, ring, mesh, tree, pyramid, mesh-of-trees, hypercube, and the Coarse-Grained Multicomputer. Chapter 4 also introduces computational systems that are abundantly available in standard academic and industrial settings, including a Network of Workstations, Cluster, Grid, and Cloud, as well as some standard terminology in the field of parallel computing. In Chapter 5, we present an overview of combinational circuits and sorting networks. This work is used to motivate the natural use of parallel models and to demonstrate the blending of architectural and algorithmic approaches.

The focus of Chapter 6 is the important problem of matrix multiplication, which is considered for a variety of models of computation. In Chapter 7, we introduce the parallel prefix operation. This is a very powerful operation with a wide variety of applications. We discuss implementations and analysis for a number of the models presented in Chapter 5 and give sample applications. In Chapter 8, we introduce *pointer jumping* techniques and show how some list-based algorithms can be efficiently implemented in parallel.

In Chapter 9, we introduce the powerful divide-and-conquer paradigm. We discuss applications of divide-and-conquer to problems involving data movement, including sorting, concurrent reads/writes, and so forth. Algorithms and their analysis are presented for a variety of models.

Chapters 10 and 11 focus on two important application areas, respectively, Computational Geometry and Image Processing. In these chapters, we focus on interesting problems chosen from these important domains as a way of solidifying the approach of this book in terms of developing machine independent solution strategies, which can then be tailored for specific models, as required.

Chapter 12 focuses on fundamental graph theoretic problems. Initially, we present standard traversal techniques, including breadth-first search and depth-first search. Finally, we couple these techniques with greedy algorithms to solve problems, such as labeling the connected components of a graph, determining a minimal spanning forest of a graph, and problems involving shortest or minimal-weight paths in a graph.

Chapter 13 is an optional chapter concerned with some fundamental numerical problems. A focus of the chapter is on sequential algorithms for polynomial evaluation and approximations of definite integrals.

There are several appendices in which we give proofs of theorems that will be difficult for many readers. We believe that only those with the interest and mathematical aptitude to make the experience worthwhile should read these appendices. We recommend that instructors allow students to use the results discussed in the appendices whether they understand the material or not, in the fashion of computer programmers who often use library routines developed by others.

## Recommended Use

This book has been successfully deployed in both elective and required courses, with students typically ranging from sophomores (2nd-year undergraduate students) to 3rd-year graduate students. A student in a course using this book need not have an advanced understanding of mathematics. A fundamental background in mathematics will suffice.

## Correspondence

Please feel free to contact the authors directly with any comments or criticisms of this book. Russ Miller may be reached at miller@buffalo.edu and Laurence Boxer may be reached at boxer@niagara.edu. In addition, a Web site for the book can be found from http://www.cse.buffalo.edu/faculty/miller/papers.shtml. This Web site contains information related to the book, including pointers to education-based pages, relevant parallel computing links, and errata.

## Instructor Resources

Teaching tools are available for this book. When this book is used in a classroom setting, the following materials are available for download at *login.cengage.com*.

**PowerPoint Presentations.** A set of PowerPoint slides is available for each chapter. Slides may be used to guide classroom presentation, to make available to students for review, or to print as classroom handouts. Instructors are welcome to customize the slides to suit their course needs.

**Figure Files.** The complete set of images from the text is available for use in classroom presentations.

**Solution Files.** A detailed set of solutions to all exercises is available to instructors.

## Acknowledgments

The authors would like to thank Stefano Basagni, Kian L. Pokorny, and Don Kraft, as well as a variety of anonymous reviewers, for providing insightful comments that have been used to improve the presentation of this book. We would like to thank the students at SUNY-Buffalo who used early drafts and previous editions of this book in their classes and provided valuable feedback. We would like to thank the team at Cengage, especially Alyssa Pratt, Senior Product Manager and Sreejith Govindan, Project Manager at Integra for their tremendous attention to detail. We would also like to thank our families for providing us the support necessary to complete this time-consuming project.

Russ Miller & Laurence Boxer, 2013

# Reference Guide

## Asymptotic Relationships

Assume $f$ and $g$ are positive functions of $n$. Then the following relationships exist.

1. $f(n) = O(g(n)) \Leftrightarrow g(n) = \Omega(f(n))$.
2. $f(n) = \Theta(g(n)) \Leftrightarrow g(n) = \Theta(f(n))$.
3. $f(n) = \Theta(g(n)) \Leftrightarrow f(n) = O(g(n))$ and $f(n) = \Omega(g(n))$.
4. $f(n) = o(g(n)) \Leftrightarrow g(n) = \omega(f(n))$.
5. $f(n) = o(g(n)) \Leftrightarrow \lim_{n \to \infty} \frac{f(n)}{g(n)} = 0$.
6. $f(n) = \omega(g(n)) \Leftrightarrow \lim_{n \to \infty} \frac{f(n)}{g(n)} = \infty$.
7. $f(n) = o(g(n)) \Rightarrow f(n) = O(g(n))$, but the converse is false.
8. $f(n) = \omega(g(n)) \Rightarrow f(n) = \Omega(g(n))$, but the converse is false.
9. $f(n)$ is bounded above and below by positive constants *if and only if* $f(n) = \Theta(1)$.

## Limits and Asymptotic Relationships

In order to determine the relationship between functions $f$ and $g$, it is often useful to examine

$$\lim_{n\to\infty} \frac{f(n)}{g(n)} = L.$$

The possible outcomes of this relationship, and their implications, are given below.

1. $L = 0$. This means that $g(n)$ grows at a faster rate than $f(n)$. Therefore, $f(n) = O(g(n))$, $f(n) \neq \Theta(g(n))$, and $f(n) = o(g(n))$.
2. $L = \infty$. This means that $f(n)$ grows at a faster rate than $g(n)$. Therefore, $f(n) = \Omega(g(n))$, $f(n) \neq \Theta(g(n))$, and $f(n) = \omega(g(n))$.
3. $L \neq 0$ is finite. This means that $f(n)$ and $g(n)$ grow at the same *rate*, to within a constant factor. Therefore, $f(n) = \Theta(g(n))$ and $g(n) = \Theta(f(n))$. Notice that this also means that $f(n) = O(g(n))$, $g(n) = O(f(n))$, $f(n) = \Omega(g(n))$, $g(n) = \Omega(f(n))$, $f(n) \neq o(g(n))$, and $f(n) \neq \omega(g(n))$.
4. There is no limit. In the case where

$$\lim_{n\to\infty} \frac{f(n)}{g(n)}$$

does not exist, this technique cannot be used to determine the asymptotic relationship between $f(n)$ and $g(n)$.

## Logarithmic Properties and Notation

Several properties of logarithms that are useful in the analysis of algorithms are given below.

- $\log_a 1 = 0$
- $\log_a a = 1$
- $\log_a xy = \log_a x + \log_a y$
- $\log_b a = \dfrac{\log_c a}{\log_c b}$
- $\log_a x^y = y \log_a x$
- $\log_a \dfrac{x}{y} = \log_a x - \log_a y$

In the scientific literature, the following are common abbreviations for logarithms of the given base.

- $\log_e x$ is written as $\ln x$
- $\log_2 x$ is written as $\lg x$
- $\log_{10} x$ is written as $\log x$

## Standard Terminology

These terms are fairly standard, appearing in many texts and the scientific literature.

| An algorithm with running time | is said to run in |
|---|---|
| $\Theta(1)$ | *constant time* |
| $\Theta(\log n)$ | *logarithmic time* |
| $O(\log^k n)$, $k$ a positive integer | *polylogarithmic time* |
| $o(\log n)$ | *sublogarithmic time* |
| $\Theta(n)$ | *linear time* |
| $o(n)$ | *sublinear time* |
| $\Theta(n^2)$ | *quadratic time* |
| $O\big(f(n)\big)$, where $f(n)$ is a polynomial | *polynomial time* |

## Master Theorem

Let $a \geq 1$ and $b \geq 1$ be constants. Let $f(n)$ be a positive function defined on the positive integers. Let $T(n)$ be defined on the positive integers by

$$T(n) = aT\left(\frac{n}{b}\right) + f(n), \tag{3.1}$$

where we can interpret $n/b$ as meaning either $\lfloor n/b \rfloor$ or $\lceil n/b \rceil$. Then the following hold.

1. Suppose $f(n) = O\left(n^{\log_b a - \varepsilon}\right)$ for some constant $\varepsilon > 0$. Then $T(n) = \Theta\left(n^{\log_b a}\right)$.
2. Suppose $f(n) = \Theta\left(n^{\log_b a}\right)$. Then $T(n) = \Theta\left(n^{\log_b a} \log n\right)$.
3. Suppose $f(n) = \Omega(n^{\log_b a + \varepsilon})$ for some constant $\varepsilon > 0$, and there are constants $c$ and $N$, $0 < c < 1$ and $N > 0$, such that $n/b > N \Rightarrow af(n/b) \leq cf(n)$. Then $T(n) = \Theta\left(f(n)\right)$.

## Common Recurrence Equations

| Representative Algorithm | Recurrence Equation | Asymptotic Solution |
|---|---|---|
| **Binary Search** | $T(n) = T(n/2) + \Theta(1)$ | $T(n) = \Theta(\log n)$ |
| **Sequential Search** | $T(n) = T(n-1) + \Theta(1)$ | $T(n) = \Theta(n)$ |
| **Tree Traversal** | $T(n) = 2T(n/2) + \Theta(1)$ | $T(n) = \Theta(n)$ |
| **Selection Sort** | $T(n) = T(n-1) + \Theta(n)$ | $T(n) = \Theta(n^2)$ |
| **Merge Sort** | $T(n) = 2T(n/2) + \Theta(n)$ | $T(n) = \Theta(n \log n)$ |
| **Parallel Merge Sort** | $T(n) = T(n/2) + \Theta(n)$ | $T(n) = \Theta(n)$ |
| **Bitonic Sort** | $T(n) = 2T(n/2) + \Theta(n \log n)$ | $T(n) = \Theta(n \log^2 n)$ |
| **Hypercube Bitonic Sort** | $T(n) = T(n/2) + \Theta(\log n)$ | $T(n) = \Theta(\log^2 n)$ |
| **Mesh Divide-and-Conquer** | $T(n) = T(n/4) + \Theta(n^{1/2})$ | $T(n) = \Theta(n^{1/2})$ |

## Common Summations

Sum of Constant Terms: $\sum_{i=1}^{n} 1 = n$

Arithmetic Series: $\sum_{i=1}^{n} a_i = n\left[a_1 + \frac{(n-1)d}{2}\right]$, where $a_{i+1} = a_i + d$, for some constant $d$.

Example of an arithmetic series: $\sum_{i=1}^{n} i = \frac{n(n+1)}{2}$

Geometric Series: $\sum_{i=1}^{n} a_0 r^{i-1} = \frac{a_0(1-r^n)}{(1-r)}$, where $r = \frac{a_{i+1}}{a_i}$ is a constant, $r \neq 1$.

Example of a geometric series: $\sum_{i=1}^{\log_2 n} {}^{n}/_{2^i} = n - 1$

Sum of Consecutive Squares: $\sum_{i=1}^{n} i^2 = \frac{n(n+1)(2n+1)}{6}$

Sum of Consecutive Integers Raised to a Power: $\sum_{i=1}^{n} i^k = \Theta\left(n^{k+1}\right)$, for $k > 0$ a constant.

Sum of Consecutive Reciprocals:

$$\sum_{i=1}^{n} \frac{1}{i} = 1 + \frac{1}{2} + \cdots + \frac{1}{n} \approx \ln n + \gamma,\text{ where } \gamma \approx 0.5772\ldots\text{ (Euler's constant)}$$

Bounding a Sum for a Nondecreasing Function $f(x)$:

$$\int_{l-1}^{u} f(x)dx \leq \sum_{i=l}^{u} f(i) \leq \int_{l}^{u+1} f(x)dx$$

Bounding a Sum for a Nonincreasing Function $f(x)$:

$$\int_{l}^{u+1} f(x)dx \leq \sum_{i=l}^{u} f(i) \leq \int_{l-1}^{u} f(x)dx$$

## Models of Computation

| Model | Communication diameter | Bisection width |
|---|---|---|
| RAM | $\Theta(1)$ | - |
| PRAM of size $n$ | equivalent to $\Theta(1)$ | equivalent to $\Theta(n^2)$ |
| Linear array of size $n$ | $\Theta(n)$ | $\Theta(1)$ |
| Mesh of size $n$ | $\Theta(n^{1/2})$ | $\Theta(n^{1/2})$ |
| Hypercube of size $n$ | $\Theta(\log n)$ | $\Theta(n)$ |
| Pyramid of base size $n$ | $\Theta(\log n)$ | $\Theta(n^{1/2})$ |
| Mesh of trees of base size $n$ | $\Theta(\log n)$ | $\Theta(n^{1/2})$ |

Note that for the RAM, $n$ represents the size of the memory.

Note that for the other models, which are multiprocessor models, $n$ represents the number of processors, where each processor is assumed to have some (small) finite amount of memory.

## Asymptotic Running Times

| | Broadcast a unit of data | Semigroup operation on *n* data evenly distributed | Parallel prefix on *n* data evenly distributed | Sort *n* data evenly distributed (comparison-based algorithm) |
|---|---|---|---|---|
| RAM | N/A | $\Theta(n)$ | $\Theta(n)$ | $\Theta(n \log n)$ |
| CR PRAM of size $n$ | $\Theta(1)$ | $\Theta(\log n)$ | $\Theta(\log n)$ | $\Theta(\log n)$ |
| ER PRAM of size $n$ | $\Theta(\log n)$ | $\Theta(\log n)$ | $\Theta(\log n)$ | $\Theta(\log n)$ |
| Linear array of size $n$ | $\Theta(n)$ | $\Theta(n)$ | $\Theta(n)$ | $\Theta(n)$ |
| Mesh of size $n$ | $\Theta(n^{1/2})$ | $\Theta(n^{1/2})$ | $\Theta(n^{1/2})$ | $\Theta(n^{1/2})$ |
| Hypercube of size $n$ | $\Theta(\log n)$ | $\Theta(\log n)$ | $\Theta(\log n)$ | $O(\log^2 n)$ |
| Pyramid of base size $n$ | $\Theta(\log n)$ | $\Theta(\log n)$ | $\Theta(n^{1/2})$ | $\Theta(n^{1/2})$ |
| Mesh-of-Trees of base size $n$ | $\Theta(\log n)$ | $\Theta(\log n)$ | $\Theta(\log n)$ | $\Theta(n^{1/2})$ |
| $CGM(n,q)$ – coarse grained multicomputer of $q$ processors with enough memory for $n$ data | $O(q)$ | $\Theta(n/q)$ | $\Theta(n/q)$ | Not discussed in this book |

# 1

# Asymptotic Analysis

A comprehensive study of algorithms includes the design, analysis, implementation, and scientific evaluation through experimentation of algorithms to solve important problems. In this chapter, we introduce some basic tools and techniques that are required in order to evaluate effectively both a theoretical and an experimental analysis of algorithms. It is important to realize that without analysis, it is often difficult to justify the choice of one algorithm over another or to justify the need for developing a new algorithm. Therefore, a critical aspect of most courses covering *advanced data structures* or *algorithms* is on the development of techniques for estimating resources for a given algorithm. Such resources include the running time, disk space, memory, and number of processors utilized by an efficient implementation of the algorithm under consideration.

While we often focus on the running time of an algorithm, it is critical that the algorithm under consideration produce correct results. In fact, it is not uncommon for one to develop computer programs that run very fast and produce incorrect results. Such programs can be extremely harmful. However, for pragmatic reasons, nontrivial proofs of correctness are not covered in this text.

There are other goals when one is developing computer algorithms and programs to solve problems. Such goals include maximizing the use of human and computer resources. Human resources include current and future staff time for understanding the problems to be solved, devising efficient solutions, providing theoretical analyses of resources required by such solutions, implementing appropriate solutions, and performing empirical evaluations of such solutions on representative data sets. It is important to note that there is evidence to support the claim that efficiency of human resources is often a function of the clarity of code written.

Computer resources include processing time, computer memory, communication latency and bandwidth, number of processors, and the manner in which the processors communicate, to name a few. It is not unusual for there to be a conflict in the utilization of some of these resources. In particular, we will discuss a number of examples in this book where there is a tradeoff in asymptotic running time and the asymptotic amount of additional memory and/or processors required by an algorithm. That is, there are times when one can devise an algorithm that runs faster if additional memory and/or processors are available.

Throughout this book, we will focus on resources associated with a given algorithm. Specifically, we will be concerned with quantities that include the number of processors, the size of the memory, and the running time of the algorithm under consideration. A comparison of such quantities will allow for a reasonable comparison between algorithms, typically resulting in an informed choice as to the appropriate algorithm to use. For example, such analyses will allow us to make a more informed decision as to which sorting algorithm to use on a sequential machine given data with certain properties that are maintained in specific data structures.

In practice, it often is the case that the most important computer resource is running time. This may surprise students who have been exposed primarily to relatively small homework projects that, once freed of compiler errors and infinite loops, begin printing results almost immediately. However, many important applications require massive processing of large data sets, where a world-class computer may run for hours or even days before determining a solution. Examples of such applications are found in areas such as simulating disasters and responses as well as the spread and containment of infectious disease. Additional examples include data mining, traffic simulation, molecular modeling, weather forecasting, global warming, image analysis, geographical surveying, and modeling new physical structures, such as buildings, bridges, and roads, to name a few. Aside from the financial cost of computer time, human impatience or serious deadlines may limit the use of such applications. For example, it only helps to have a weather forecast if it is made available in advance of the forecast period. By contrast, it is not uncommon to be able to devise algorithms and their associated data structures such that the memory requirements are quite reasonable.

Consider, for example, the prominence of simulation and modeling in modern science and engineering. In fact, discovery in our digital data-driven society relies increasingly on simulation and modeling. A U.S. National Science Foundation report on "Simulation-based Engineering Science" echoes the following important statements.

- Simulation is typically less expensive and safer than conducting experiments with a physical prototype for many scientific and engineering devices. As a result, some of the most powerful computing systems in the world are used to simulate the detonation of nuclear devices and their effects. Others are used to simulate natural catastrophes including hurricanes, tornadoes, and tsunamis.
- Simulation often provides a more realistic result than a traditional physical experiment, as it can be set up to allow for ease of configuration of environmental parameters found in the final product. Examples include simulation of environmental systems, including ground-water flow, weather, oceans, and lakes.
- Simulations can often be constructed and evaluated much more efficiently than physical simulators. Furthermore, computer simulation can often run much faster than a real-time simulation on a physical simulator, allowing for many more parameters to be evaluated in the same amount of time.

Simulation and modeling are typically data driven, often requiring high-end computing systems. Simulation and modeling of natural systems occur in various scientific and engineering disciplines, including physics, chemistry, and biology, as well as in human systems including economics and the social sciences.

Currently, the generation and storage of data is increasing at an astonishing rate. In part, this is due to very high-end scientific devices that have come on-line recently. It is also due to consumer consumption of available technology, specifically various data-intensive multimedia forms of networked-based entertainment. So, in order to compete effectively in a knowledge-based economy, scientists, engineers, and technologists need to be proficient at the collection, organization, maintenance, analysis, and visualization of data.

Let's begin our journey into the design and analysis of algorithms for sequential and multiprocessor systems by developing mathematical tools for the analysis of resources required by computer algorithms. Because running time is more often the subject of our analysis than computer memory, we will use time-related terminology while presenting introductory material. However, the same tools may naturally be applied to the analysis of memory requirements or error tolerance.

## Notation and Terminology

In this section, we introduce some notation and terminology that will be used throughout the text. The notation and terminology that we introduce is standard in the literature.

In this book, we use the term *algorithm* to mean a procedure for correctly solving a problem in a finite number of steps. The focus of this book is on the analysis of resources for a reasonable implementation of a given algorithm to solve a given problem correctly. Specifically, the analysis of an algorithm is concerned with estimating resources, such as running time and computer memory, used by the efficient implementation of an algorithm. In general, we will remove the awkwardness of stating "an efficient implementation of an algorithm" and simply assume that the implementation is efficient. Thus, we will simply refer to the analysis of an algorithm.

A *sequential algorithm* is an algorithm designed to run on a sequential, *i.e.*, single-processor computer, while a *parallel algorithm* is an algorithm designed to run on a parallel computer, *i.e.*, a multiprocessor system. In general, an efficient parallel algorithm utilizes multiple processors working in a cooperative fashion to solve a given problem significantly faster than it could be solved on a sequential computer.

Typically, we use the positive integer $n$ to denote the size of the data set processed by an algorithm. We may process an array of $n$ entries, for example, or a linked list, tree, or graph of $n$ nodes. We will use $T(n)$ to represent the running time of an algorithm operating on a data set of size $n$.

An algorithm can be implemented on a variety of hardware/software platforms. We expect that the same algorithm operating on the same data values will execute faster if implemented in the assembly language of a supercomputer than if implemented in an interpreted language on a personal computer from, say, the 1980s. Thus, it rarely makes sense to analyze an algorithm in terms of actual CPU time. Rather, we want our analysis to reflect the intrinsic efficiency of the algorithm without regard to such factors as the speed of the hardware/software environment in which the algorithm is to be implemented. That is, we seek to measure the efficiency of our programming methods, not their actual implementations.

Thus, the analysis of algorithms generally adheres to the following principles.

1. **Ignore machine-dependent constants.** We will not be concerned with how fast an individual processor executes a machine instruction.
2. **Look at *growth* of resources as $n \to \infty$.** Even an inefficient algorithm will often finish its work in acceptable time when operating on a small data set. Thus, we are usually interested in $T(n)$, the running time of an algorithm for large $n$, where $n$ is typically the size of the data input to the algorithm.

Asymptotic analysis implies that we are interested in the general behavior of the function $T(n)$ as the input parameter gets large. That is, we are interested in the behavior of $T(n)$ as $n \to \infty$. Therefore, since we are interested in the *growth rate* of the function as $n$ gets large, we may ignore low-order terms as well as multiplicative constant factors when expressing asymptotic analysis. This is not to say that these terms are irrelevant in practice, just that they are not useful in terms of considering the growth *rate* of a function. So, for example, we say that the function $3n^3 + 10n^2 + n + 17$ grows as $n^3$. That is, for large values of $n$, the quadratic, linear, and constant terms, respectively, $10n^2$, $n$, and 17, are insignificant compared with

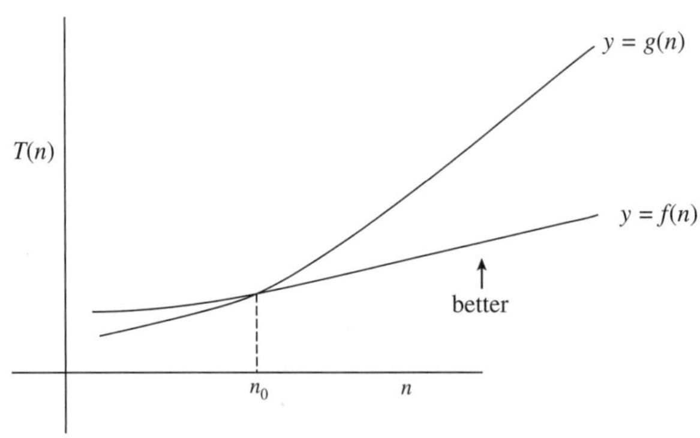


**FIGURE 1-1** *An illustration of the growth rate of two functions, $f(n)$ and $g(n)$. Notice that for large values of n, an algorithm with an asymptotic running time of $f(n)$ is typically more desirable than an algorithm with an asymptotic running time of $g(n)$. In this illustration, "large" is defined as $n \geq n_0$. The value $n_0$ represents a point beyond which the "eventually larger" function $g(n)$ dominates the "eventually smaller" $f(n)$.*

the cubic term when considering growth *rate* of the function. Consider another example. As $n$ gets large, would you prefer to use an algorithm with running time $95n^2 + 405n + 1997$ or one with a running time of $2n^3 + 12$? We hope you chose the former, which has a growth rate of $n^2$, as opposed to the latter, which has a growth rate of $n^3$. Naturally, though, if $n$ were small, one *would* prefer $2n^3 + 12$ to $95n^2 + 405n + 1997$. In fact, you should be able to determine the value of $n$ that is the breakeven point. Figure 1-1 presents an illustration of this situation.

### Asymptotic Notation

In this section, we introduce some standard notation that is useful in expressing the asymptotic behavior of a function of $n$. That is, the behavior of a function as $n$ approaches infinity. Since we often have a function that we wish to express in terms of a "simpler" function, we introduce this notation in terms of functions $f$ and $g$, both of which are positive functions of $n$.

1. $f(n) = \Theta(g(n))$, to be read as "$f$ of $n$ is ***theta*** of $g$ of $n$," *if and only if* there exist positive constants $c_1$, $c_2$, and $n_0$ such that $c_1 g(n) \leq f(n) \leq c_2 g(n)$ whenever $n \geq n_0$. That is, $f$ grows at the same asymptotic rate as $g$. See Figure 1-2.
2. $f(n) = O(g(n))$, to be read as "$f$ of $n$ is ***oh*** of $g$ of $n$" or "$f$ of $n$ is **big *oh*** of $g$ of $n$," *if and only if* there exist positive constants $c$ and $n_0$ such that $f(n) \leq cg(n)$ whenever $n \geq n_0$. That is, $f$ grows at no more than the same asymptotic rate as $g$. Equivalently, $f$ is asymptotically bounded from above by $g$. See Figure 1-3.

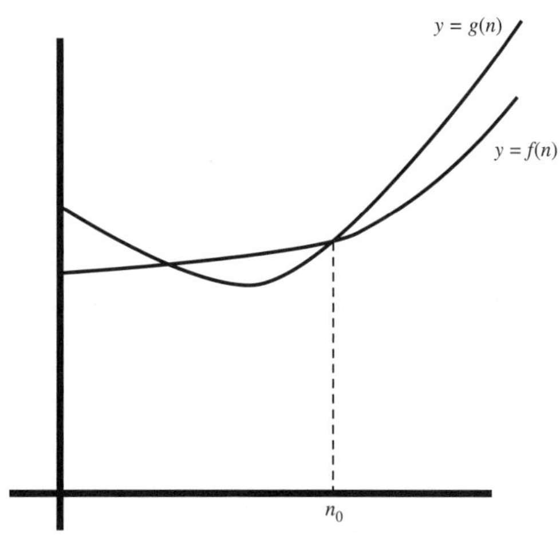


**FIGURE 1-2** *An illustration of Θ-notation. $f(n) = \Theta(g(n))$ since functions $f(n)$ and $g(n)$ grow at the same rate for all $n \geq n_0$.*

3. $f(n) = \Omega(g(n))$, to be read as "*f* of *n* is ***omega*** of *g* of *n*" or "*f* of *n* is **capital *omega*** of *g* of *n*" or "*f* of *n* is **big *omega*** of *g* of *n*," *if and only if* there exist positive constants *c* and $n_0$ such that $cg(n) \leq f(n)$ whenever $n \geq n_0$. That is, *f* grows at least at the same asymptotic rate as *g*. Equivalently, *f* is asymptotically bounded from below by *g*. See Figure 1-4.
4. $f(n) = o(g(n))$, to be read as "*f* of *n* is ***little oh*** of *g* of *n*," *if and only if* for every positive constant *C* there is a positive integer $n_0$ such that $f(n) < Cg(n)$ whenever $n \geq n_0$. That is, *f* is strictly bounded from above by *g*, where *f* and *g* do not have the same growth rate. See Figure 1-5.

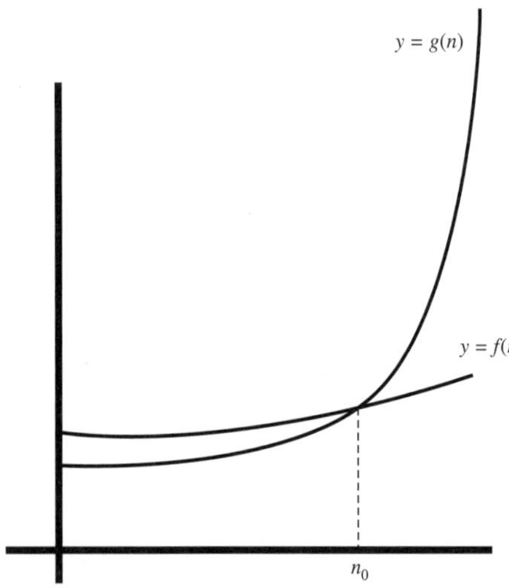


**FIGURE 1-3** *An illustration of O-notation. $f(n) = O(g(n))$ since function $f(n)$ is bounded from above by $g(n)$ for all $n \geq n_0$.*

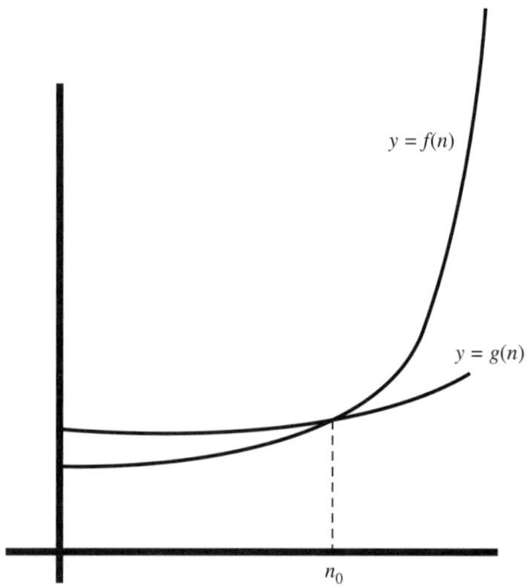


**FIGURE 1-4** *An illustration of Ω-notation. $f(n) = \Omega(g(n))$ since function $f(n)$ is bounded from below by $g(n)$ for all $n \geq n_0$.*

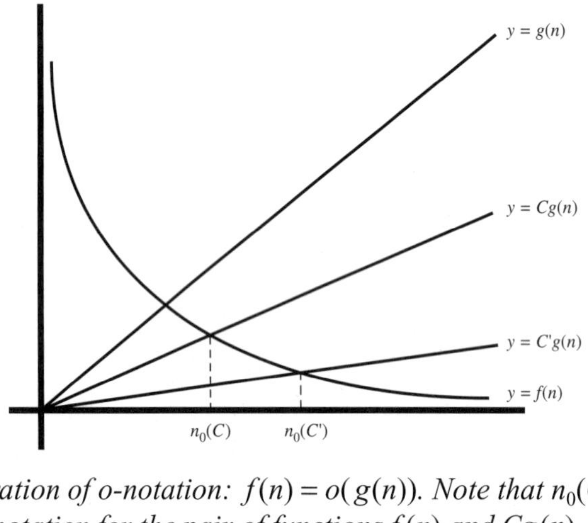


**FIGURE 1-5** *An illustration of o-notation: $f(n) = o(g(n))$. Note that $n_0(C)$ corresponds to $n_0$ in the definition of o-notation for the pair of functions $f(n)$ and $Cg(n)$. Similarly, $n_0(C')$ corresponds to $n_0$ in the definition of o-notation for the pair of functions $f(n)$ and $C'g(n)$.*

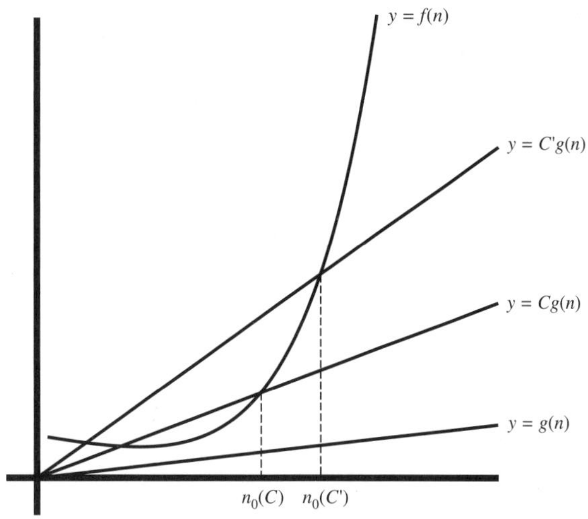


**FIGURE 1-6** *An illustration of $\omega$-notation: $f(n) = \omega(g(n))$. $n_0(C)$ is the value of $n_0$ in the definition of $\omega$-notation for the pair $(f(n), Cg(n))$. Similarly, $n_0(C')$ is the value of $n_0$ in the definition of $\omega$-notation for the pair $(f(n), C'g(n))$.*

5. $f(n) = \omega(g(n))$, to be read as "*f* of *n* is ***little omega*** of *g* of *n*," *if and only if* for every positive constant $C$ there is a positive integer $n_0$ such that $f(n) > Cg(n)$ whenever $n \geq n_0$. That is, *f* is strictly bounded from below by *g*, where *f* and *g* do not have the same growth rate. See Figure 1-6.

Strictly speaking, $\Theta$, $O$, $\Omega$, $o$, and $\omega$ are set-valued functions. Therefore, it would be appropriate to write $(3n^2 + 2) \in \Theta(n^2)$. In fact, some authors have tried to use this membership notation, but it is not the standard. In the literature, this idea is typically expressed as $3n^2 + 2 = \Theta(n^2)$. While not correct in the mathematical sense, such an expression is the standard in the field of algorithms when expressing the growth rate of a resource such as running time, memory, number of processors, and so forth. The expression $3n^2 + 2 = \Theta(n^2)$ is read as "3 *n* squared plus 2 *is* **theta** of *n* squared." Note that one *does not write* $\Theta(n^2) = 3n^2 + 2$.

The set-valued functions $\Theta$, $O$, $\Omega$, $o$, and $\omega$ are referred to as *asymptotic notation*. Recall that we use asymptotic notation to simplify analysis and capture *growth rate*. Therefore, we want the *simplest* and *best* function as a representative of each $\Theta$, $O$, $\Omega$, $o$ and $\omega$ expression. Some examples follow.

**EXAMPLE**

Given $f(t) = 5 + \sin t$ and $g(t) = 1$, then $5 + \sin t = \Theta(1)$ since $4 \leq 5 + \sin t \leq 6$. (See Figure 1-7.) Note also that $f(t) = O(1)$ and $f(t) = \Omega(1)$, but the best choice for notation is to write $f(t) = \Theta(1)$ since $\Theta$ conveys more information than either $O$ or $\Omega$.

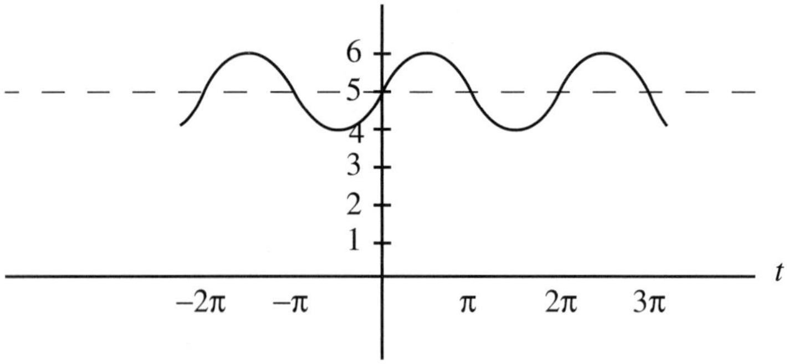


**FIGURE 1-7** *Graph of* $f(t) = 5 + \sin t$.

### Additional Notation

**Floor and Ceiling Functions.** We will often find the *floor* and *ceiling* functions useful. Given a real number $x$, there is a unique integer $n$ such that

$$n \leq x < n + 1.$$

We say that $n$ is the "floor of $x$", denoted

$$\lfloor x \rfloor = n.$$

In other words, $\lfloor x \rfloor$ is the largest integer that is less than or equal to $x$.

Similarly, given a real number $x$, there is a unique integer $n$ such that

$$n < x \leq n + 1.$$

Then $n + 1$ is the "ceiling of $x$," denoted

$$\lceil x \rceil = n + 1.$$

In other words, $\lceil x \rceil$ is the smallest integer that is greater than or equal to $x$.

For example, $\lfloor 3.2 \rfloor = 3$, $\lceil 3.2 \rceil = 4$, and $\lfloor 18 \rfloor = \lceil 18 \rceil = 18$.

Notice for all real numbers $x$ we have

$$x - 1 < \lfloor x \rfloor \leq x \leq \lceil x \rceil < x + 1.$$

It follows that $\lfloor x \rfloor = \Theta(x)$ and $\lceil x \rceil = \Theta(x)$.

**Variable Assignment.** In describing the assignment of a value to a variable, we will use either the equal sign or the left arrow, as both are widely used in computer science. That is, either of the notations

$$\textit{left} = \textit{right}$$

or

$$\textit{left} \leftarrow \textit{right}$$

will mean "assign the value of *right* as the new value of *left*."

**EXAMPLE**

Show that

$$\sum_{k=1}^{n} k^p = \Theta\left(n^{p+1}\right),$$

for $p > 1$ a fixed constant. First, we consider an upper bound on the summation. We know that

$$\sum_{k=1}^{n} k^p \le n \times n^p$$

since the summation contains $n$ terms, the largest of which is $n^p$. Therefore, we know that

$$\sum_{k=1}^{n} k^p = O\left(n^{p+1}\right).$$

Next, we consider a lower bound on the summation. Notice that it is easy to derive a trivial lower bound of $\Omega(n)$, since there are $n$ terms in the summation, the least of which is equal to 1. However, we can derive a more useful, larger, lower bound as follows. Notice that

$$\sum_{k=1}^{n} k^p = \sum_{k=1}^{\lfloor n/2 \rfloor} k^p + \sum_{k=\lfloor n/2 \rfloor+1}^{n} k^p \ge \sum_{k=\lfloor n/2 \rfloor+1}^{n} k^p.$$

Looking closely at

$$\sum_{k=\lfloor n/2 \rfloor+1}^{n} k^p,$$

notice that there are $n - \lfloor n/2 \rfloor$ terms for which $(\lfloor n/2 \rfloor + 1)^p$ is the smallest term. Therefore, we have

$$\sum_{k=1}^{n} k^p > (n/2)(n/2)^p = \frac{n^{p+1}}{2^{p+1}}.$$

Since $2^{p+1}$ is a constant, we have

$$\sum_{k=1}^{n} k^p = \Omega\left(n^{p+1}\right).$$

In fact, we have shown that

$$\frac{n^{p+1}}{2^{p+1}} \le \sum_{k=1}^{n} k^p \le n^{p+1}.$$

That is,

$$\sum_{k=1}^{n} k^p = \Theta\left(n^{p+1}\right).$$

## Asymptotic Relationships

Useful relationships exist among $\Theta$, $O$, $\Omega$, $o$, and $\omega$, some of which are given in the proposition below. The reader might wish to try to prove some of these.

**Proposition:** *Let f and g be positive functions of n. Then we have the following relationships.*

1. $f(n) = O(g(n)) \Leftrightarrow g(n) = \Omega(f(n))$.
2. $f(n) = \Theta(g(n)) \Leftrightarrow g(n) = \Theta(f(n))$.
3. $f(n) = \Theta(g(n)) \Leftrightarrow f(n) = O(g(n))$ and $f(n) = \Omega(g(n))$.
4. $f(n) = o(g(n)) \Leftrightarrow g(n) = \omega(f(n))$.
5. $f(n) = o(g(n)) \Leftrightarrow \lim_{n\to\infty} \frac{f(n)}{g(n)} = 0$.
6. $f(n) = \omega(g(n)) \Leftrightarrow \lim_{n\to\infty} \frac{f(n)}{g(n)} = \infty$.
7. $f(n) = o(g(n)) \Rightarrow f(n) = O(g(n))$, but the converse is false.
8. $f(n) = \omega(g(n)) \Rightarrow f(n) = \Omega(g(n))$, but the converse is false.
9. $f(n)$ is bounded above and below by positive constants *if and only if* $f(n) = \Theta(1)$.

### Asymptotic Analysis and Limits

In order to determine the relationship between functions $f$ and $g$, it is often useful to examine

$$\lim_{n\to\infty} \frac{f(n)}{g(n)} = L.$$

The possible outcomes of this relationship, and their implications, are given below.

1. $L = 0$. This means that $g(n)$ grows at a faster rate than $f(n)$, and hence that $f(n) = O(g(n))$. Indeed, $f(n) = o(g(n))$ and $f(n) \neq \Theta(g(n))$.
2. $L = \infty$. This means that $f(n)$ grows at a faster rate than $g(n)$, and hence that $f(n) = \Omega(g(n))$. Indeed, $f(n) = \omega(g(n))$ and $f(n) \neq \Theta(g(n))$.
3. $L \neq 0$ is finite. This means that $f(n)$ and $g(n)$ grow at the same *rate*, to within a constant factor, and hence that $f(n) = \Theta(g(n))$, or equivalently, $g(n) = \Theta(f(n))$. Notice that this also means that $f(n) = O(g(n))$, $g(n) = O(f(n))$, $f(n) = \Omega(g(n))$, $g(n) = \Omega(f(n))$, $f(n) \neq o(g(n))$, and $f(n) \neq \omega(g(n))$.

4. There is no limit. In the case where $\lim_{n\to\infty} \frac{f(n)}{g(n)}$ does not exist, this technique cannot be used to determine the asymptotic relationship between $f(n)$ and $g(n)$.

We now give some examples of how to determine asymptotic relationships based on taking limits of a quotient.

**EXAMPLE**

Let

$$f(n) = \frac{n(n+1)}{2} \text{ and } g(n) = n^2.$$

Then we can show that $f(n) = \Theta(g(n))$ since

$$\lim_{n\to\infty} \frac{f(n)}{g(n)} = \lim_{n\to\infty} \frac{n^2+n}{2n^2} =$$

(dividing both numerator and denominator by $n^2$)

$$\lim_{n\to\infty} \frac{1+\frac{1}{n}}{2} = \frac{1}{2}.$$

**EXAMPLE**

If $P(n)$ is a polynomial of degree $d > 0$, then $P(n) = \Theta(n^d)$. This can be seen as follows. The hypothesis implies $P(n) = \sum_{i=0}^{d} a_i n^i$ for some set of coefficients $\{a_i\}_{i=0}^{d}$ with $a_d \neq 0$. Therefore,

$$\lim_{n\to\infty} \frac{P(n)}{n^d} = \lim_{n\to\infty} \frac{\sum_{i=0}^{d} a_i n^i}{n^d} = \lim_{n\to\infty}\left[\left(\sum_{i=0}^{d-1} \frac{a_i}{n^{d-i}}\right) + a_d\right] = a_d.$$

The assertion follows.

**EXAMPLE**

Compare $n^{100}$ and $2^n$. We remind the reader that

$$\frac{d}{dx}e^{f(x)} = e^{f(x)}f'(x).$$

We have

$$\lim_{n\to\infty}\frac{2^n}{n^{100}} = \lim_{n\to\infty}\frac{e^{\ln 2^n}}{n^{100}} = \lim_{n\to\infty}\frac{e^{n\ln 2}}{n^{100}}.$$

We can apply L'Hopital's Rule to the numerator and denominator of this limit 100 times, which yields

$$\lim_{n\to\infty}\frac{2^n}{n^{100}} = \lim_{n\to\infty}\frac{e^{n\ln 2}}{n^{100}} = \lim_{n\to\infty}\frac{(\ln 2)^{100}2^n}{100!} = \infty.$$

The result of this limit yields $n^{100} = O(2^n)$ and $2^n = \Omega(n^{100})$. In addition, using some of the properties previously presented, we have $n^{100} = o(2^n)$ and $2^n = \omega(n^{100})$. Further, these results yield $n^{100} \neq \Theta(2^n)$.

At this point, we take a slight detour to discuss logarithmic notation, as logarithms play an important role in asymptotic analysis. As appropriate, we will use fairly standard terminology in referring to logarithms. In particular, we write

- $\log_e x$ as $\ln x$,
- $\log_2 x$ as $\lg x$, and
- $\log_{10} x$ as $\log x$.

We now continue with an example that uses logarithms.

**EXAMPLE**

Let $f(n) = \ln n$ and $g(n) = n$. Then, by applying L'Hopital's Rule, we have

$$\lim_{n\to\infty}\frac{n}{\ln n} = \lim_{n\to\infty}\frac{1}{1/n},$$

which evaluates as

$$\lim_{n\to\infty}\frac{1}{1/n} = \lim_{n\to\infty} n = \infty.$$

Therefore, $\ln n = O(n)$.

We remind the reader that $\log_b n = (\log_b a)(\log_a n)$, for positive $a$, $b$, and $n$ with $a \neq 1 \neq b$. Therefore, we have $\log_b n = C \log_a n$, for the constant $C = \log_b a$. More importantly, this yields $\log_b x = \Theta(\log x)$. Since we generally assume that $a$ and $b$ are greater than 1, the latter can be interpreted as showing that the base of a logarithm is irrelevant in asymptotic relationships.

### Summations and Integrals

Since many algorithms involve looping and/or recursion, it is not uncommon for the analysis of an algorithm to include a dependence on some function $f(n)$ that is best expressed as the sum of simpler functions. For example, it may be that the dominant term in an analysis of an algorithm can be expressed as $f(n) = h(1) + h(2) + \cdots + h(n)$. When we consider the worst-case number of comparisons in the insertion sort routine later in this chapter, we will find that the total number of comparisons can be computed as $f(n) = 1 + 2 + 3 + \cdots + n = n(n+1)/2 = \Theta(n^2)$.

We first consider the case where the function $h(i)$ is nondecreasing. Notice that the worst-case number of comparisons used in Insertion Sort, as mentioned above, uses the nondecreasing function $h(i) = i$. Specifically, let

$$f(n) = \sum_{i=1}^{n} h(i),$$

where $h$ is nondecreasing. An illustration of this situation is presented in Figure 1-8.

In order to evaluate $f(n)$, we can consider summing $n$ unit-width rectangles. Specifically, the $i^{\text{th}}$ rectangle has height $h(i)$ and width 1. In Figure 1-8, we present these rectangles in two ways in order to obtain tight bounds on the asymptotic behavior of the total area of the rectangles, *i.e.*, on the value of $f(n)$. On the left, we draw the rectangles so that the $i^{\text{th}}$ rectangle is anchored on the left. That is, the left edge of the unit-width rectangle with height $h(i)$ has its left edge at value $i$ on the $x$-axis and its right edge at value $i + 1$ on the $x$-axis. In this way, you will notice that each rectangle is below the curve of $h(t)$, where $t$ takes on values between 1 and $n + 1$, where, for simplicity, we are assuming 1 is the value of the lower bound and $n$ is the value of the upper bound in the sum.

Conversely, on the right of Figure 1-8, we draw the rectangles so that the $i^{\text{th}}$ unit-width rectangle is anchored on the right. That is, the right edge of the unit-width rectangle with height $h(i)$ has its right edge at value $i$ on the $x$-axis and its left edge at value $i - 1$ on the $x$-axis. This allows us to use the rectangles to bound the area of the curve, between 0 and $n$, assuming as before that 1 is the value of the lower bound and $n$ is the value of the upper bound, from above. Notice that in Figure 1-8, we give the relationships of the area under the curve bounding the total area of the rectangles (Figure 1-8 left side) and the total area of the rectangles bounding the area under the curve (Figure 1-8 right side). In addition, we show how to combine these relationships to obtain a bound on the summation by related integrals.

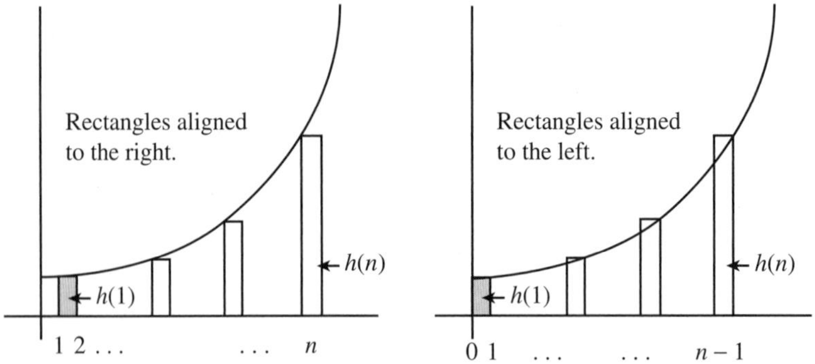


**FIGURE 1-8** *An illustration of bounding the summation* $\sum_{i=1}^{n} h(i)$ *by the integral of the nondecreasing function* $h(t)$*. On the left, we demonstrate how to use the integral* $\int_1^{n+1} h(t)dt$ *to derive an upper bound on the summation by aligning the unit-width rectangles to the right. Note that a "unit-width rectangle" has a width of* 1*. Therefore,* $\sum_{i=1}^{n} h(i) \le \int_1^{n+1} h(t)dt$*. On the right, we show how to use the integral* $\int_0^{n} h(t)dt$ *to derive a lower bound on the summation by aligning the unit-width rectangles to the left. This yields* $\int_0^{n} h(t)dt \le \sum_{i=1}^{n} h(i)$*. Therefore, we have* $\int_0^{n} h(t)dt \le \sum_{i=1}^{n} h(i) \le \int_1^{n+1} h(t)dt$*.*

The method of determining asymptotic analysis of a summation by integration is quite powerful. Next, we give several examples, and in doing so, illustrate a variety of techniques and review some basic principles of integration.

**EXAMPLE**

Find the asymptotic complexity of

$$f(n) = \sum_{i=1}^{n} i.$$

First, we consider the integral bounding principles that were given above. Since the function $h(i) = i$ is nondecreasing, we can apply the conclusion directly and arrive at the bound

$$\int_0^{n} t\,dt \le \sum_{i=1}^{n} i \le \int_1^{n+1} t\,dt.$$

Evaluating both the left-hand side and right-hand side simultaneously yields

$$\left.\frac{t^2}{2}\right|_0^n \le \sum_{i=1}^{n} i \le \left.\frac{t^2}{2}\right|_1^{n+1},$$

which can be evaluated in a fairly routine fashion, resulting in

$$\frac{n^2}{2} \le \sum_{i=1}^{n} i \le \frac{(n+1)^2}{2} - \frac{1}{2}.$$

Working with the right-hand side of this inequality, we can obtain

$$\frac{(n+1)^2}{2} - \frac{1}{2} = \frac{1}{2}n^2 + n.$$

Further simplification of the right-hand side can be used to give

$$\frac{1}{2}n^2 + n \le \frac{1}{2}n^2 + n^2$$

for $n \ge 1$. Therefore,

$$\frac{1}{2}n^2 \le \sum_{i=1}^{n} i \le \frac{3}{2}n^2.$$

Since the function

$$f(n) = \sum_{i=1}^{n} i$$

is bounded by a multiple of $n^2$ on both the left- and right-hand sides, we can conclude that

$$f(n) = \sum_{i=1}^{n} i = \Theta(n^2).$$

**EXAMPLE**

Find the asymptotic complexity of

$$f(n) = \sum_{k=1}^{n} \frac{1}{k}.$$

First, it is important to realize that the function $\frac{1}{k}$ is a *nonincreasing* function. This requires an update in the analysis presented for nondecreasing functions. In Figure 1-9, we present a figure that illustrates the behavior of a nonincreasing function over the interval $[a,b]$. Notice that with the proper analysis, you should be able to show that

$$\sum_{k=a+1}^{b} f(k) \le \int_a^b f(x)dx \le \sum_{k=a}^{b-1} f(k).$$

Based on this analysis, we can now attempt to produce an asymptotically tight bound on the function $f(n)$. First, we consider a lower bound on $f(n)$. Our analysis shows that

$$\int_1^{n+1} \frac{1}{x}dx \le \sum_{k=1}^{n} \frac{1}{k}.$$

Since

$$\int_1^{n+1} \frac{1}{x}dx = \ln x\Big|_1^{n+1} = \ln(n+1) - \ln 1 = \ln(n+1),$$

we know that $f(n)$ is bounded from below by $\ln(n+1)$.

Next, we consider an upper bound on $f(n)$. Notice that if we blindly apply the result of our analysis for a nonincreasing function, we obtain

$$\sum_{k=1}^{n} \frac{1}{k} \le \int_0^n \frac{1}{x}dx = \ln x\Big|_0^n = \infty.$$

Unfortunately, this result, while providing some information, does not yield a tight enough upper bound. However, notice that the cause of the upper bound resulting in $\infty$ is evaluation of the integral at the specific point of 0. This problem can be alleviated by carefully rewriting the equation to avoid the problematic point. Let's consider the more restricted inequality

$$\sum_{k=2}^{n} \frac{1}{k} \le \int_1^n \frac{1}{x}dx.$$

Notice that the integral evaluates to $\ln n$. Therefore, if we now add back in the problematic term, we arrive at

$$\sum_{k=1}^{n} \frac{1}{k} = 1 + \sum_{k=2}^{n} \frac{1}{k} \le 1 + \int_1^n \frac{1}{x}dx = 1 + \ln n.$$

Combining the results of both the upper and lower bounds on $f(n)$, we arrive at

$$\ln n < \ln(n+1) \le \sum_{k=1}^{n} \frac{1}{k} \le 1 + \ln n \le 2 \ln n$$

for $n$ large enough, a conclusion we suggest that the reader verify. Therefore,

$$\sum_{k=1}^{n} \frac{1}{k} = \Theta(\ln n).$$

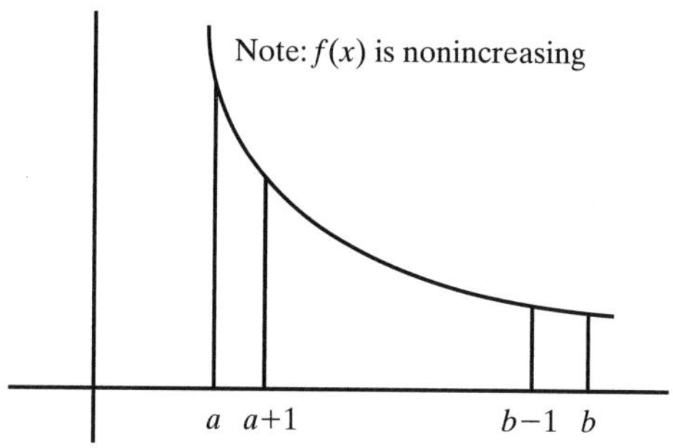


**FIGURE 1-9** *An illustration of bounding the summation* $\sum_{i=1}^{n} f(i)$ *for a nonincreasing function f. For f nonincreasing, we can derive the relationship* $\sum_{k=a+1}^{b} f(k) \le \int_a^b f(x)dx \le \sum_{k=a}^{b-1} f(k)$ *in a straightforward fashion by considering rectangles to the left and right as we did for nondecreasing functions. This translates into a bound on the summation as* $\int_a^{b+1} f(t)dt \le \sum_{i=a}^{b} f(i) \le \int_{a-1}^{b} f(t)dt.$

**EXAMPLE**

As our final example of evaluating the asymptotic behavior of a summation by integrals, we consider the function

$$f(n) = \sum_{k=1}^{n} k^p$$

for $p > 0$. Recall that we showed earlier in this chapter that

$$f(n) = \sum_{k=1}^{n} k^p = \Theta\left(n^{p+1}\right).$$

However, the purpose of this example is to show how to obtain this result by the method we have been considering that relates summations to integrals. Recall that a function $f$ is *increasing* if $u < v \Rightarrow f(u) < f(v)$. Consider the derivative of $k^p$. For $k > 0$, we have

$$\frac{d}{dk} k^p = pk^{p-1} > 0.$$

Therefore, the function $k^p$ is an increasing function of $k$. A quick sketch of an increasing function, in a setting more general than illustrated earlier, appears in Figure 1-10.

Using the analysis associated with Figure 1-10, we have both

$$\int_0^n x^p dx \le \sum_{k=1}^{n} k^p \quad \text{and} \quad \sum_{k=1}^{n} k^p \le \int_1^{n+1} x^p dx.$$

Thus,

$$\left.\frac{x^{p+1}}{p+1}\right|_0^n \le \sum_{k=1}^{n} k^p \le \left.\frac{x^{p+1}}{p+1}\right|_1^{n+1}, \quad \text{or}$$

$$\frac{n^{p+1}}{p+1} \le \sum_{k=1}^{n} k^p \le \frac{(n+1)^{p+1}-1}{p+1} < \frac{(n+1)^{p+1}}{p+1}.$$

Since $n + 1 \le 2n$ for $n \ge 1$,

$$\frac{n^{p+1}}{p+1} \le \sum_{k=1}^{n} k^p \le \frac{(n+1)^{p+1}}{p+1} \le \frac{(2n)^{p+1}}{p+1} = \frac{2^{p+1}n^{p+1}}{p+1}, \quad \text{or}$$

$$\frac{1}{p+1} n^{p+1} \le \sum_{k=1}^{n} k^p \le \frac{2^{p+1}}{p+1} n^{p+1},$$

which, based on asymptotic properties given earlier in this chapter, yields the expected solution of

$$\sum_{k=1}^{n} k^p = \Theta\left(n^{p+1}\right).$$

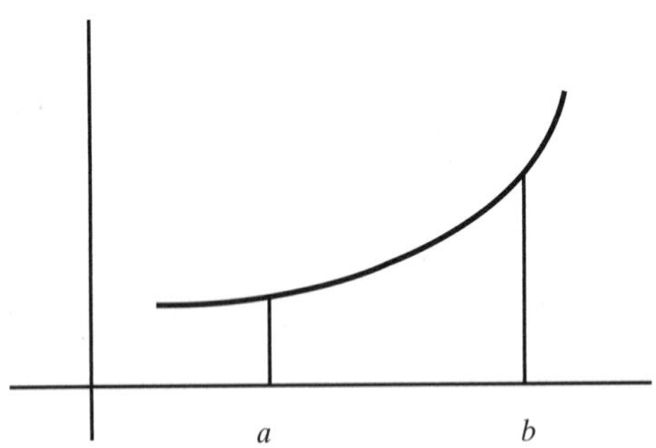


**FIGURE 1-10** *An increasing function in the range* $[a, b]$. *We have*

$$\sum_{k=a}^{b-1} f(k) < \int_a^b f(x)dx < \sum_{k=a+1}^{b} f(k).$$

## Rules for Analysis of Algorithms

The application of asymptotic analysis is critical in order to provide an effective means of evaluating both the running time and space of an algorithm as a function of the size of the input and number of processors. In this section, we present fundamental information related to the analysis of algorithms and give several examples to illustrate the major points of emphasis.

**Fundamental operations execute in Θ(1) time.** Traditionally, it is assumed that "fundamental" operations require a constant amount of time to execute, *i.e.*, a fixed number of computer "clock cycles." We assume that the running time of a fundamental operation is bounded by a constant, irrespective of the data being processed. These operations include the following.

- Arithmetic operations, *including* +, −, ×, /, as applied to a constant number of fixed-size operands.
- Comparison operators, *including* <, ≤, >, ≥, =, ≠, as applied to 2 fixed-size operands.
- Logical operators, *including* AND, OR, NOT, XOR, as applied to a constant number of fixed-size operands.
- Bitwise operations, as applied to a constant number of fixed-size operands.
- Conditional/branch operations.
- The evaluation of certain elementary functions. Notice that such functions need to be considered carefully. For example, when the function $\sin\theta$ is to be evaluated for "moderate-sized" values of $\theta$, it is reasonable to assume that $\Theta(1)$ time is required for each application of the function. However, for very large values of $\theta$, a loop dominating the calculation of $\sin\theta$ may require a significant number of operations before stabilizing at an accurate approximation. In this case, it may not be reasonable to assume $\Theta(1)$ time for this operation.
- Input and output, or I/O, operations that are used to read or write a constant number of fixed-size data items. Note this does not include input from a keyboard, mouse, or other human-operated device, as the user's response time is unpredictable.

Additional fundamental properties follow.

- Suppose the running times of operations $A$ and $B$ are, respectively, $O(f(n))$ and $O(g(n))$. Then the sequence of operations consisting of $A$ followed by $B$ runs in $O(f(n)+g(n))$ time. Note that this analysis holds for $\Theta$, $\Omega$, $o$ and $\omega$, as well.
- Suppose that each iteration of the body of a loop runs in $O(f(n))$ time, and the loop executes its body $O(g(n))$ times. Then the time required to execute the loop is $O(f(n)g(n))$. A similar property holds for $\Theta$, $\Omega$, $o$ and $\omega$.

**EXAMPLE (INSERTION SORT)**

As an example, we consider the analysis of *Insertion Sort*, a simple sorting technique that is introduced in many first-semester computer science courses.

Suppose we are given a set of data arbitrarily distributed in an array and we wish to rearrange the data so that it appears in increasing order. We give pseudocode for the algorithm and then present an analysis of both its time and space requirements. Note that later in this book, we compare more advanced algorithms to Insertion Sort, and also show how Insertion Sort can be effectively exploited in restricted situations, *e.g.*, where the set of data presented to Insertion Sort is such that no item is very far from where it belongs.

**Subprogram InsertionSort($X$)**
**Input:** an array $X$ of $n$ entries
**Output:** the array $X$ with its entries in ascending order
**Algorithm:** Insertion Sort
**Local Variables:** indices *current*, *insertPlace*

**Action:**

```
For current = 2 to n do
  {Current is initially set to 2 as the first
  current - 1 entries of X are ordered.}
  a. Search X[1...current - 1] to determine the index
     where X[current] should be inserted. This index
     will be denoted as insertPlace, which has a
     value in the range of 1,...,current.
     If insertPlace < current then
       b. Make a copy of X[current].
       c. Shift the elements X[insertPlace,...,
          current - 1] by one position into elements
          X[insertPlace + 1,...,current]. The details
          of this shift are discussed below in our
          Insert routine.
       d. Place the copy of X[current] made in step b)
          into its proper position at X[insertPlace].
     End If
End For
```

The description above presents a top-level view of Insertion Sort. An example is given in Figure 1-11. We observe that the search called for in the first step of the loop can be performed by a straightforward sequential search that runs in $O(k)$ time, where $k$ is the value of *current*. The reader should verify that this step runs in $\Theta(k)$ time on average. Alternately, an $O(\log k)$ time binary search can be performed, as will be discussed in the chapter on Induction and Recursion, though this will not improve the overall asymptotic running time in the expected or worst case.

For illustrative purposes, let us consider the total time required to perform all $n$ searches. That is, we consider the time to perform the searches and only the searches. At this point, we do not yet consider the time required to move the data. If sequential searches are used, then the running time for the $n - 1$ searches is

$$O\left(\sum_{k=2}^{n} k\right) = O\left(n^2\right).$$

If binary searches are used during each of the $n - 1$ iterations, then the time for the searches is given by

$$O\left(\sum_{k=2}^{n} \log k\right) = O\left(n \log n\right).$$

Notice that $O$-notation is used, as both results represent upper bounds on the search time since the time taken by any individual search is a function of the search value and the data values being searched.

Now, we consider the time to move the data. Once *insertPlace* is determined, *current*/2 data moves are required, on average, in order to move the data so as to free up position *insertPlace* in order to be able to place a copy of the data at the *current* there. In fact, in the worst case, the insert step always requires $X[current]$ to be moved to position number 1, requiring *current* – 1 data items in the array to be moved out of the way. Therefore, the running time of the algorithm is dominated by the data movement, which is given by

$$T(n) = \sum_{k=2}^{n} shift_k,$$

where $shift_k$, the length of the segment for which members are shifted, is 0 in the best case, $k - 1$ in the worst case, and $(k - 1)/2$ in the average case. Hence, the running time of Insertion Sort is $\Theta(n)$ in the best case, when data is already sorted and a sequential search from (*current* – 1) downto 1 is used. Insertion Sort runs in $\Theta(n^2)$ time in the average or expected case, and $\Theta(n^2)$ time in the worst case. The reader should verify these results by substituting the appropriate values into the summation and simplifying the equation. Notice that since the average- and worst-case running times are dominated by the data movement operations, in terms of the asymptotic running time, it is irrelevant as to whether a sequential or binary search is used to determine position *insertPlace*.

Finally, notice that $\Theta(n)$ space is required for the algorithm to store the $n$ data items. More importantly, the amount of extra space required for this algorithm is constant, *i.e.*, $\Theta(1)$. An insertion routine is presented below.

**Subprogram Insert(*X, current, insertPlace*)**
*Insert* $X[current]$ *into the ordered*
*subarrary* $X[1\ldots \text{current}-1]$ *at position*
insertPlace.
*We assume* $1 \le insertPlace \le current \le n$
**Local variables:** index *j*, entry-type *hold*

**Action:**

```
If current ≠ insertPlace, then {there's work to do}
  hold = X[current]
  For j = current - 1 downto insertPlace, do
    X[j + 1] = X[j]
  End For
    X[insertPlace] = hold
End If
```

For completeness, we present an efficient implementation of the Insertion Sort algorithm based on the analysis we have presented.

**Subprogram InsertionSort(*X*, *n*)**
**Input:** an array *X* of *n* entries
**Output:** the array *X* with its entries in ascending order
**Algorithm:** Insertion Sort
{This is a simple version of the Insertion Sort algorithm
with sequential search.}

```
For i = 2 to n, do
  hold = x[i]
  position = 1
  While hold > x[position], do
    position = position + 1
  End While
  If position < i, then
    For j = i downto position, do
      x[j] = x[j - 1]
    End For
    x[position] = hold
  End If
End For
End InsertionSort
```

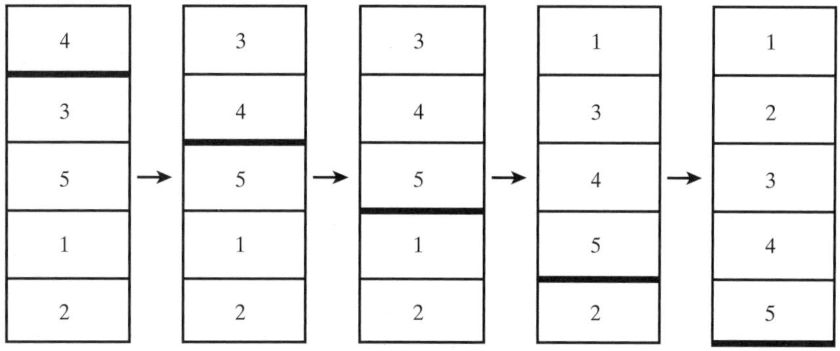


**FIGURE 1-11** *An example of the Insertion Sort algorithm, as given in Subprogram InsertionSort. It is initially assumed that the first item,* 4, *is in the correct position. Then the second item,* 3, *is placed into position with respect to all of the items in front of it, resulting in* (3,4) *being properly ordered. The algorithm continues until the last item,* 2, *is placed in its proper position with respect to the items* (1,3,4,5) *that are in front of it.*

It is often possible to modify an algorithm designed for one data structure to accommodate a different data structure. In the exercises, we ask the reader to adapt Insertion Sort to linked lists.

**EXAMPLE: BIN SORT**

Sorting is a fundamental operation as a major use of computers is to maintain order within large collections of data. Perhaps for this reason, the computer science community has developed numerous algorithms for ordering data. Some of these algorithms are considerably faster than others in the abstract. Yet, under certain conditions an asymptotically slower algorithm might be significantly more efficient than an asymptotically faster algorithm due to the characteristics or size of the input data set. For this reason, we will present and discuss a variety of sorting algorithms in this book.

In the previous section, we presented an analysis of Insertion Sort. In one of the exercises at the end of this chapter, we present Selection Sort, another straightforward and useful sorting routine that runs in the same worst-case $\Theta(n^2)$ time as Insertion Sort. Later in the book, we present alternative comparison-based sorting algorithms that exhibit an asymptotically optimal $\Theta(n \log n)$ worst-case running time. In fact, many of you may already be familiar with a result that states that *comparison-based* sorting algorithms run in $\Omega(n \log n)$ time. That is, in order to sort a collection of $n$ elements by a *comparison-based* sorting routine, $\Omega(n \log n)$ time is required.

It is quite important to note, however, that *not all sorting algorithms are based on comparisons*. In fact, when one knows detailed and specific information about the input data, it is not unusual to be able to construct a sorting algorithm that runs in $o(n \log n)$ time. An important theme that runs through this book is that we should attempt to use a sorting algorithm that runs in $o(n \log n)$ time if we have constraints on the input data that will be used.

For example, suppose we are required to sort data that is chosen from a restricted set. Further, suppose we know that the $n$ keys take on no more than $n$ values. In such a situation, we can employ an asymptotically optimal algorithm based on Bin Sort. This is an algorithm that is based on the process of placing labeled items, such as machine parts, directly into an ordered list of bins that only contain items with the same label. Alternatively, we might think about sorting a deck of cards by going through the deck once, tossing all the Aces in one pile, all the 2s in another, and so on. Once we have gone through all the cards and created 13 bins, then we simply need to pile the bins one on top of another, *i.e.*, concatenate the bins, in order to create the final sorted set. Notice that if we sort more than one deck of cards, we still need only 13 bins. Given one complete deck of cards, each bin will wind up with exactly 4 cards in it. An example of Bin Sort is presented in Figure 1-12.

Below, we present BinSort, an implementation of the Bin Sort algorithm, where we assume that the data values to be ordered are in the range from 1 to $n$. It is known that $\Omega(n \log n)$ comparisons are required to sort an arbitrary set of data by a comparison-based sort, so the reader should note that Bin Sort is not a comparison-based sorting algorithm. That is, Bin Sort does not rely on comparing data items to each other. In fact, the algorithm never compares two data items.

**Subprogram BinSort(*X*)**
**Input:** an array $X$ of $n$ entries
**Output:** the array $X$ with its entries in ascending order
**Algorithm:** Bin Sort
**Caveat:** The entries of X are integers in $[1,\ldots, n]$
**Local variables:** indices *entry*, *stack_index*
*stack*, an array of pointers, each representing a stack

**Action:**

```
For entry=1 to n, do
  {make stack[entry] an empty stack}
  stack[entry] = null
For entry=1 to n, do
  push(X[entry], stack[X[entry].key])
End For
stack_index=1
```

```
For entry=1 to n, do
  while emptyStack(stack[stack_index])
      stack_index ← stack_index+1
  end while
  pop(stack[stack_index], X[entry])
end For
```

An analysis of the algorithm follows. It is easy to see that the first two For-loops each run in $\Theta(n)$ time, after which each element is in one of the $n$ bins. The initialization of each stack runs in $\Theta(1)$ time. The final For-loop requires that every item be examined once. Therefore, the final For-loop runs in $\Theta(n)$ time. Hence, the entire algorithm runs in $\Theta(n)$ time. Further, notice that the algorithm utilizes $\Theta(n)$ space to store the items and only $\Theta(n)$ additional space for indices, stack pointers, and the like. We observe that the linear amount of additional space requires only a small constant of proportionality, since the items themselves are placed on the stacks, and no copies of the items are ever made. Later in this chapter, we make precise the notion of an *optimal* algorithm. Our algorithm for Bin Sort is optimal as any asymptotically faster algorithm would require not examining all of the items, in which case the data might not wind up sorted.

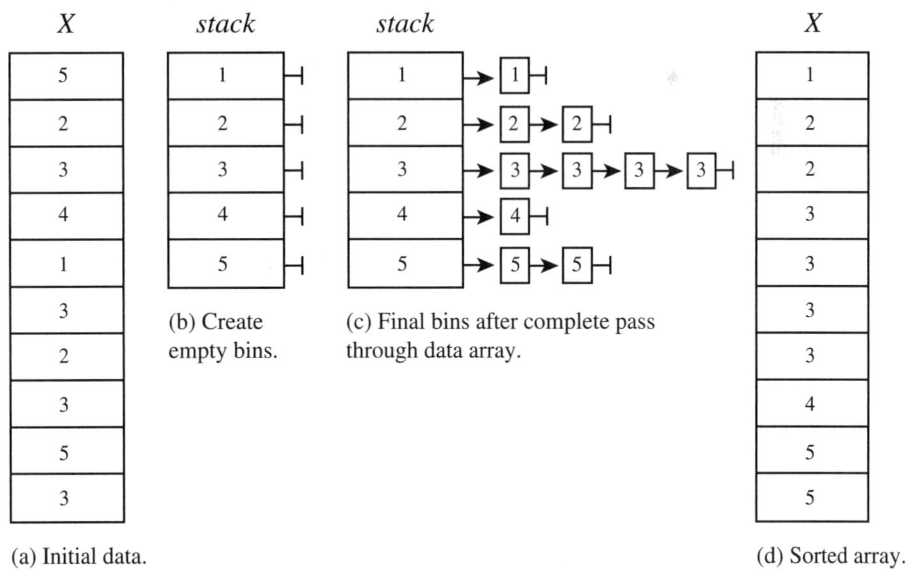


**FIGURE 1-12** *Bin Sort applied to an array of* 10 *items chosen from* [1…5]. *In* (a), *the initial array of data is given. In* (b), *the set of empty bins is created. In* (c), *the bins are shown after a complete pass through the array. In* (d), *the array is recreated by "concatenating" the bins.*

## Limitations of Asymptotic Analysis

Suppose a given problem has two equally acceptable solution strategies. Further, suppose both of these algorithms have the same asymptotic running times and the same asymptotic space requirements. This might make it difficult to choose between the two algorithms.

Asymptotic analysis provides some guidelines for behavior, but we are aware that asymptotic analysis also hides high-order constants and low-order terms. In fact, suppose that algorithm $A$ is 5 times faster than algorithm $B$ for problems of a given size. Since 5 is just a constant, this will be hidden in the $O$-notation. Similarly, since low-order terms are masked with $O$-notation, it may be that one algorithm is superior for "small" data sets, where the low-order terms are important, but not for "large" data sets, where these low-order terms are, appropriately, masked.

Since your application might be used predominantly for "small" data sets or for data sets with special properties, it is always advisable to perform some basic experimental verification in terms of which algorithm is the best fit for your particular application rather than for a generic application.

Consider the problem of sorting a set of data, and assume that based on knowledge of the input, you decide that a general, comparison-based sorting algorithm is required. Among your choices are algorithms that copy data and algorithms that do not copy data. For example, sorting can be done by using pointer manipulation as well as by copying data. Suppose, for example, we consider three algorithms with running times dominated by the following steps.

a. Algorithm $A$: $\Theta(n^2)$ comparisons, $\Theta(n^2)$ copying operations
b. Algorithm $B$: $\Theta(n^2)$ comparisons, $\Theta(n)$ copying operations
c. Algorithm $C$: $\Theta(n^2)$ comparisons, $\Theta(n)$ pointer manipulation operations

All three algorithms run in $\Theta(n^2)$ time, yet we should expect $A$ to be slower than $B$, and $B$ to be slower than $C$. For example, suppose the data being sorted consists of 10,000-byte data records. Then at the machine level, every copying operation, an assignment statement of the form $x \leftarrow y$, can be thought of as a loop of the form

For *byteNumber* = 1 to 10000, do

$$x[byteNumber] \leftarrow y[byteNumber]$$

Therefore, a data-copying operation takes time proportional to the size of the data entity being copied. Thus, given data entries of significant size, where *significant* is machine-dependent, we expect Algorithm $A$ to be slower than Algorithm $B$, even though the two algorithms have the same asymptotic running time.

Pointers of four bytes, *i.e.*, 32 bits, can theoretically be used to address $2^{32}$ bytes or four Gigabytes of memory. A sorting algorithm that uses $\Theta(n)$ pointer manipulations, might involve three to four pointer assignments, which might result in 12 to 16 bytes of assignments, per data movement. Therefore, such an algorithm would typically be more efficient than an algorithm that copies data, so long as the data items are sufficiently long. Of course, on real machines, some of these conjectures must be tested experimentally, as instruction sets and compilers can play a major role in choosing the most efficient algorithm.

## Asymptotic Relationships and Common Terminology

We first gather material from earlier in the chapter so that this section can be used as a reference guide. The reader should note that a Reference Guide is presented immediately preceding this chapter. The Reference Guide contains the following information, as well as additional information that the reader will find useful in the context of Algorithms and their Analysis.

Let $f$ and $g$ be positive functions of $n$. Then the following hold.

1. $f(n) = O(g(n)) \Leftrightarrow g(n) = \Omega(f(n))$.
2. $f(n) = \Theta(g(n)) \Leftrightarrow g(n) = \Theta(f(n))$.
3. $f(n) = \Theta(g(n)) \Leftrightarrow f(n) = O(g(n))$ and $f(n) = \Omega(g(n))$.
4. $f(n) = o(g(n)) \Leftrightarrow g(n) = \omega(f(n))$.
5. $f(n) = o(g(n)) \Leftrightarrow \lim_{n\to\infty} \dfrac{f(n)}{g(n)} = 0$.
6. $f(n) = \omega(g(n)) \Leftrightarrow \lim_{n\to\infty} \dfrac{f(n)}{g(n)} = \infty$.
7. $f(n) = o(g(n)) \Rightarrow f(n) = O(g(n))$, but the converse is false.
8. $f(n) = \omega(g(n)) \Rightarrow f(n) = \Omega(g(n))$, but the converse is false.
9. $f(n)$ is bounded above and below by positive constants *if and only if* $f(n) = \Theta(1)$.

We conclude this chapter by giving some common terminology that will be used throughout the text. These terms are fairly standard, appearing in many texts and the scientific literature.

| An algorithm with running time | is said to run in |
|---|---|
| $\Theta(1)$ | *constant time* |
| $\Theta(\log n)$ | *logarithmic time* |
| $O(\log^k n)$, $k$ a positive integer | *polylogarithmic time* |
| $o(\log n)$ | *sublogarithmic time* |
| $\Theta(n)$ | *linear time* |
| $o(n)$ | *sublinear time* |
| $\Theta(n^2)$ | *quadratic time* |
| $O(f(n))$, where $f(n)$ is a polynomial | *polynomial time* |

An algorithm is said to run in *optimal time* for the given computer architecture if its running time $T(n) = O(f(n))$ is such that $\Omega(f(n))$ time is required to solve the problem on that architecture. It is important to note that when we use terms such as *optimality* or *efficiency*, we compare the running time of a given *algorithm* to the lower bound on the running time to solve the *problem* being considered on a given architecture. For example, any algorithm to compute the minimum entry of an unsorted array of $n$ entries must examine every item in the array, because any item skipped could be the minimal item. Therefore, any sequential algorithm to solve this problem requires $\Omega(n)$ time. So, an algorithm for this problem that runs in $\Theta(n)$ time is optimal.

Notice that we use the term *optimal* to mean *asymptotically optimal*. An optimal algorithm need not be the fastest possible algorithm to give a correct solution to its problem, but it must be within a constant factor of being the fastest possible algorithm to solve the problem. Proving optimality is often difficult, and there are many problems for which optimal running times are not known. There are, however, problems for which proof of optimality is fairly easy, some of which will appear in this book.

## Summary

In this chapter, we introduce fundamental techniques, strategies, notions, and terminologies related to the analysis of algorithms. We discuss and give examples of a variety of techniques from algebra and calculus, including limits, L'Hopital's Rule, summations, and integrals, by which algorithms are analyzed. We also discuss the limitations of asymptotic analysis.

## Chapter Notes

The notion of applying asymptotic analysis to algorithms is often credited to Donald E. Knuth, whose Web site is at www-cs-faculty.Stanford.EDU/~knuth/.

Although it served as the foundation for part of his seminal series *The Art of Computer Programming*, Knuth, in fact, traces $O$-notation back to a number theory textbook by Bachmann in 1892. The $O$-notation was apparently first introduced by Landau in 1909, but the modern use of this notation in algorithms is attributed to the paper by D.E. Knuth, "Big omicron and big omega and big theta," *ACM SIGACT News*, 8(2)(1976): 18–23.

Historical developments of the asymptotic notation in computer science can be found in reviews by D.E. Knuth and in *Algorithmics: Theory and Practice* by Brassard and Bratley (Prentice Hall, 1988). One of the early books that earned "classic" status was *The Design and Analysis of Computer Algorithms*, by A.V. Aho, J.E. Hopcroft, and J.D. Ullman, which was released by Addison-Wesley in 1974. More recent books that focus on algorithms and their analysis include *Introduction to Algorithms*, by T.H. Cormen, C.E. Leiserson, R.L. Rivest, and C. Stein (3rd ed.: MIT Press, Cambridge, MA, 2009), and *Computer Algorithms/ C++* by E. Horowitz, S. Sahni, and S. Rajasekaran (Computer Science Press, New York, 1996).

## Exercises

**1.** Rank the following by growth rate: $n$, $n^{1/2}$, $\log n$, $\log(\log n)$, $\log^2 n$, $(1/3)^n$, 4, $(3/2)^n$, $n!$

**2.** Prove or disprove each of the following.

a. $f(n) = O(g(n)) \Rightarrow g(n) = O(f(n))$

b. $f(n) + g(n) = \Theta(\max\{f(n), g(n)\})$

c. $f(n) = O([f(n)]^2)$

d. $f(n) = O(g(n)) \Rightarrow g(n) = \Omega(f(n))$

e. $f(n) + o(f(n)) = \Theta(f(n))$

**3.** Use $O$, $o$, $\Omega$, $\omega$, and $\Theta$ to describe the relationship between the following pairs of functions.

a. $\log^k n$, $n^\varepsilon$, where $k$ and $\varepsilon$ are positive constants

b. $n^k$, $c^n$, where $k$ and $c$ are constants, $k > 0$, $c > 1$

c. $2^n$, $2^{n/2}$

**4.** Prove that $17n^{1/6} = O(n^{1/5})$.

**5.** Prove that $\sum_{k=1}^{n} k^{1/6} = \Theta(n^{7/6})$.

6. Given a set of $n$ **integer** values in the range of [1, …, 100], give an efficient sequential algorithm to sort these items. Discuss the time, space, and optimality of your solution.

7. **(Total function)** Determine the asymptotic running time of the following algorithm, which is used to sum a set of values. Show that the running time is optimal.

**Function Total (*list*)**
**Input:** an array, *list*, of numeric entries indexed from 1 to $n$
**Output:** the total of the entries in the array
**Local variables:** integer *index*, numeric *subtotal*

**Action:**

```
subtotal = 0
For index = 1 to n, do
  subtotal = subtotal + list[index]
Return subtotal
```

8. **(Selection Sort)** Determine the asymptotic running time of the following algorithm, which is used to sort a set of data. See Figure 1-13. Determine the total asymptotic space and the additional asymptotic space required.

**FIGURE 1-13** *An example of Selection Sort. A complete pass is made through the initial set of data in order to determine the item that belongs in the front of the list* (1). *A swap is performed between this minimum element and the element currently in the front of the list. Next, a pass is made through the remaining four items to determine the minimum* (2) *of these elements. This minimum element is swapped with the current second item* (3). *The procedure continues until $n - 1$ items have been properly ordered since this forces all $n$ items to be properly ordered.*

**Subprogram SelectionSort(*List*)**
**Input:** array *List*[1, …, *n*], to be sorted in ascending order according to the *key* field of the records
**Output:** the ordered *List*
**Algorithm:** Selection Sort, as follows
For each position in the *List*, we

1. Determine the index corresponding to the entry from the unsorted portion of the *List* that is a minimum.
2. Swap the item at the position just determined with the current item.

**Local variables:** indices *ListPosition, SwapPlace*

**Action:**

```
{ListPosition is only considered for values up to
n−1, because once the first n−1 entries have been
swapped into their correct positions, the last item
must also be correct.}
For ListPosition = 1 to n−1
                {Determine the index of correct entry
              for ListPosition and swap the entries.}
   SwapPlace = MinimumIndex(List, ListPosition)
   Swap(List[SwapPlace], List[ListPosition])
End For
End Sort
```

**Subprogram Swap(*A, B*)**
**Input:** Data entities *A, B*
**Output:** The input variables with their values interchanged, *e.g.*, if on entry we have *A* = *3* and *B* = *5*, then at exit we have *A* = *5* and *B* = *3*.
**Local variable:** *temp*, of the same type as *A* and *B*

**Action:**

```
temp = A {Backup the entry value of A}
A = B {A gets entry value of B}
B = temp {B gets entry value of A}
end Swap
```

**Function MinimumIndex(*List, startIndex*)**
**Input:** *List*[1 … *n*], an array of records to be ordered by a *key* field; *startIndex*, the first index considered.

**Output:** index of the smallest *key* entry among those indexed *startIndex* ... *n* (the range of indices of the portion of the *List* presumed unordered)
**Local variables:** indices *bestIndexSoFar, at*

**Action:**

```
  bestIndexSoFar = startIndex
                                {at is used to traverse the
                                rest of the index subrange}
  For at = startIndex + 1 to n, do
    If List[at].key < List[bestIndexSoFar].key
    then bestIndexSoFar = at
  End For
  Return bestIndexSoFar
End MinimumIndex
```

**9.** Earlier in this chapter, we gave an array-based implementation of Insertion Sort. In this problem, we consider a linked list-based version of the algorithm.

**Subprogram InsertionSort(*X*)**

```
  For every current entry of the list after the first
  entry:
    Search the sublist of all entries from the first
    entry to the current entry for the proper place-
    ment, indexed insertPlace, of the current entry in
    the sublist;
    Insert the current entry into the same sublist at
    the position insertPlace.
  End For
```

Suppose we implement the Insertion Sort algorithm as just described for a linked list data structure.

a. What is the worst-case running time for a generic iteration of the Search step?

b. What is the worst-case running time for a generic instance of the Insert step?

c. Show that the algorithm has a worst-case running time of $\Theta(n^2)$.

d. Although both the array-based and linked list-based implementations of Insertion Sort have worst-case running times of $\Theta(n^2)$, in practice, we usually find that the linked list-based implementation, applied to the same data, in the same input order, is faster. Why should this be? Think in terms of entries consisting of large data records.

**10.** Array implementations of both Insertion Sort and Selection Sort have $\Theta(n^2)$ worst-case running times. Which is likely to be faster if we time both in the same hardware/software environment for the same input data? Why?

**11.** **The Stable Marriage Problem (SMP)** requires establishing a stable matching between two sets of elements given a set of preferences for each element. Suppose there are arrays $him[1 \ldots n]$ and $her[1 \ldots n]$ of identically structured *person* records, where one of the fields in the record is *partner*. Suppose the entries of these arrays represent members of couples, with the value of the *partner* field indexing the member of the opposite array that is the entry's partner. For example, if $him[5]$ and $her[8]$ are a couple, then $him[5].partner = 8$ and $her[8].partner = 5$. Suppose there is an *evaluation* function of two *person* records that executes in $\Theta(1)$ time, returning a numerical evaluation of how the *person* represented by the first parameter evaluates the *person* represented by the second parameter. There is an unstable situation if an uncoupled pair, one from the *him* array and one from the *her* array, each evaluates the other higher than his/her own *partner*.

a. Give an efficient algorithm that determines whether or not the *him* and *her* arrays represent an unstable situation, and analyze its worst-case running time.

b. Analyze the best-case running time of this algorithm.

c. If your algorithm is efficient, argue that it has optimal worst-case running time.

# 2

# Induction and Recursion

Mathematical Induction

Induction Examples

Recursion

Sequential Search

Binary Search

Additional Notes on Sequential and Binary Searches

Merging and Merge Sort

Summary

Chapter Notes

Exercises

In this chapter, we present fundamental mathematical techniques that are used throughout the book in order to derive analyses of algorithms. These techniques, including mathematical induction and recursion, are typically taught in courses such as Calculus and Discrete Mathematics. For some readers, much of this chapter will serve as a review. For other readers, a careful reading of this chapter may provide a solid understanding of induction and recursion, which is critical to the design and analysis of algorithms.

*Mathematical induction*, to which we will often refer simply as *induction*, is a technique for proving statements about sets of consecutive integers. One can view this as being done by *inducing* our knowledge of the next case from that of its predecessor.

*Recursion* is a technique of designing algorithms in which we

*i.* **divide** a large problem into smaller subproblems,

*ii.* **solve** the subproblems *recursively*, unless the problems are small enough to be solved directly, and then

*iii.* **combine** the solutions to our subproblems in order to obtain a solution to the original problem.

So, in order to solve a given problem $P_1$ by recursion, we might first divide $P_1$ into two subproblems, say $P_2$ and $P_3$. We would then recursively solve $P_2$ and $P_3$, and then combine their results in order to obtain the required result for $P_1$. Notice that in order to solve $P_2$ and $P_3$, we might continue with the recursion of dividing problem $P_2$ into subproblems $P_4$ and $P_5$, and similarly dividing problem $P_3$ into subproblems $P_6$ and $P_7$. Before combining $P_4$ and $P_5$, and similarly $P_6$ and $P_7$, these problems must first be solved, typically by way of recursion. Therefore, we might recursively divide problems $P_4$, $P_5$, $P_6$, and $P_7$ into subproblems, recursively solve them, and so on. This recursive subdivision of problems typically continues until subproblems have simple/trivial solutions, in which case they are solved directly.

Thus, recursion resembles induction in that a recursive algorithm solves a problem by making use of its capability to solve simpler problems, inducing a solution to the initial problem from solutions of these simpler problems.

## Mathematical Induction

Suppose we have a statement about positive integers, and we wish to show that the statement is always true. Formally, let $P(n)$ be a *predicate,* a statement that is true or false, depending on its argument $n$, which we assume to be a positive integer. For example, the statement "the product of the positive integers from 1 to $n$ is divisible by 10" is a predicate. This predicate is true for $n = 5$, since $1 \times 2 \times 3 \times 4 \times 5 = 120$, which is divisible by 10, and is false for $n = 4$, since $1 \times 2 \times 3 \times 4 = 24$, which is not divisible by 10. However, if we have a predicate $P(n)$ that it is true for all positive integers $n$, we often can prove the latter by using the following principle.

**Principle of Mathematical Induction:** Let $P(n)$ be a predicate, where $n$ is an arbitrary positive integer. Suppose we can accomplish the following.

1. Show that $P(1)$ is *true*.
2. Show that whenever $P(k)$ is *true*, it follows that $P(k + 1)$ is also *true.*

If we can achieve these two goals, then it follows that $P(n)$ is *true* for all positive integers $n$.

Why does this work? Suppose we have proven the two statements given above. So, we know from statement 1 that $P(1)$ is true, and thus by statement 2 that $P(1 + 1) = P(2)$ is true, and thus by statement 2 that $P(2 + 1) = P(3)$ is true, and thus by statement 2 that $P(3 + 1) = P(4)$ is true, and so forth. That is, statement 2 allows us to induce the truth of $P(n)$ for every positive integer $n$ from the truth of $P(1)$. For a mathematically stronger argument, see Appendix 1.

We often refer to the statement $P(1)$ as the *base case* of the problem being considered. The assumption in statement 2 that $P(k) =$ *true* is called the *Inductive Hypothesis* due to the fact that statement 2 is typically used to induce the conclusion that $P(k + 1)$ is true.

The *Principle of Mathematical Induction* is stated above as an assertion. Further, we have also given an informal argument as to its validity. For the sake of mathematical completeness, we prove the assertion in Appendix 1.

## Induction Examples

**EXAMPLE**

Prove that for all positive integers $n$, $\sum_{i=1}^{n} i = \frac{n(n+1)}{2}$.

Before we give a proof, we show how we might *guess* that $\sum_{i=1}^{n} i = \frac{n(n+1)}{2}$. Let $S = \sum_{i=1}^{n} i$. Then we have

$$S = 1 + 2 + \cdots + (n-1) + n. \qquad \text{(a)}$$

Now, if we write $S$ in reverse order, we have

$$S = n + (n-1) + \cdots + 2 + 1. \qquad \text{(b)}$$

*Again, note that the current exposition is not a proof, due to the imprecision of the "$\ldots$" notation.* So, if we add these two equations by combining the first terms of the right sides, the second terms of the right sides, and so on, we obtain

$$2S = (n+1) + (n+1) + (n+1) + \cdots + (n+1) + (n+1).$$

That is,

$$2S = n(n+1) \text{ or } S = \frac{n(n+1)}{2}.$$

Now, we formally prove that $\sum_{i=1}^{n} i = \frac{n(n+1)}{2}$. The equation claims that the sum of the first $n$ positive integers is $\frac{n(n+1)}{2}$. For $n = 1$, the left side of the asserted equation is

$$\sum_{i=1}^{1} i = 1$$

and the right side of the asserted equation is

$$\frac{1(1+1)}{2} = 1.$$

Thus, for $n = 1$, the asserted equation is true. That is, we have achieved the first step of an induction proof, namely, the base case.

Suppose the asserted equation is valid for $n = k$, for some positive integer $k$. Notice that we are justified in stating this assumption by our demonstration above that the case $n = k = 1$ is an instance for which the assumption is valid. Then we need to prove the asserted equation is true for the next case, namely, $n = k + 1$. That is, by using the assumption for $n = k$, we want to prove that

$$\sum_{i=1}^{k+1} i = \frac{(k+1)(k+2)}{2}.$$

Notice that we can rewrite the left side of the latter equation as

$$\sum_{i=1}^{k+1} i = \left(\sum_{i=1}^{k} i\right) + (k+1).$$

Substituting from the inductive hypothesis, we have

$$\sum_{i=1}^{k+1} i = \frac{k(k+1)}{2} + (k+1) = \frac{(k+1)(k+2)}{2},$$

as desired. Thus, our proof is complete.

**EXAMPLE**

Prove that $n! > 2^n$ for all integers $n \geq 4$. Notice that we may view this as a statement about all positive integers, not just those greater than or equal to 4, by observing that the assertion is equivalent to the statement that for all positive integers $j$, $(j+3)! > 2^{j+3}$. This observation easily generalizes so that mathematical induction can be viewed as a technique for proving the truth of predicates defined for all integers greater than or equal to some fixed integer $m$. In this generalized view of induction, the first step of an inductive proof requires showing that $P(m) = \textit{true}$. The proof of our assertion follows.

1. We first show that the assertion is true for the base case of $n = 4$. Since $4! = 24 > 16 = 2^4$, the assertion is true for the base case.
2. Now, suppose $k! > 2^k$ for some integer $k \geq 4$. This assumption is the inductive hypothesis. Based on this assertion, we must now show that $(k+1)! > 2^{k+1}$. Note that $(k+1)! = (k+1)(k!)$, which, by the inductive hypothesis and the assumption that $k \geq 4$, is an expression at least as large as $5(2^k) > 2(2^k) = 2^{k+1}$, as desired. This completes the proof.

**EXAMPLE**

Prove that $\frac{d}{dx}x^n = nx^{n-1}$, for all integers $n$.

*Proof:* Even though this is a statement about *all* integers, we can use mathematical induction to give the proof for $n$, an arbitrary positive integer, and then use fundamental rules of calculus to handle other values of $n$.

First, assume that $n$ is a positive integer. For the base case, we let $n = 1$, in which case the assertion simplifies to

$$\frac{d}{dx}x = 1,$$

which is true. Next, consider the inductive step. Suppose the assertion is true for some positive integer $k$. That is, the inductive hypothesis is the statement

$$\frac{d}{dx}x^k = kx^{k-1}.$$

Now, consider the case of $n = k + 1$. By utilizing the product rule of calculus and the inductive hypothesis, we have

$$\frac{d}{dx}x^{k+1} = \frac{d}{dx}(xx^k) = 1x^k + x\frac{d}{dx}x^k = x^k + xkx^{k-1} = (k+1)x^k,$$

as desired. Thus, the proof is complete for positive integers $n$.

For $n = 0$, the assertion simplifies to

$$\frac{d}{dx}x^0 = 0,$$

which is true.

Finally, if $n < 0$, we can apply the quotient rule to the result of applying our assertion to the positive integer $-n$. That is,

$$\frac{d}{dx}x^n = \frac{d}{dx}\frac{1}{x^{-n}} = \frac{0x^{-n} - 1(-n)x^{-n-1}}{(x^{-n})^2} = nx^{n-1},$$

as desired. Therefore, we have shown that for all integers $n$,

$$\frac{d}{dx}x^n = nx^{n-1}.$$

## Recursion

A subprogram that calls upon itself, either directly or indirectly, is called *recursive*. Formally, an algorithm exhibits recursive behavior when it can be defined by two properties.

1. A simple base case or cases.
2. A set of rules that reduce all other cases towards the base case.

To the beginner unfamiliar with this notion, it may sound like recursion is a recipe for an infinite loop in disguise, as indeed it may be if not used with care.

However, recursion is typically used in such a way that each recursive call is made only with a smaller/simpler instance of the problem. Furthermore, in order to avoid infinite recursion, it is crucial that when the program is invoked with a small enough, *i.e.*, simple enough, set of data, the subprogram will compute the required answer and return without issuing another call to itself.

So, a recursive algorithm typically exhibits the following behavior.

- Recursive calls are made with a smaller/simpler set of data.
- When a call is made with a sufficiently small/simple enough set of data, the call is resolved directly.

Notice the similarity of mathematical induction and recursion. Just as mathematical induction is a technique for inducing conclusions for "large $n$" from our knowledge of "small $n$," recursion allows us to process large or complex data sets based on our ability to process smaller or less complex data sets.

A classic example of recursion is computing the *factorial function*, which has a recursive definition. Although it can be proven that, for $n > 0$, $n!$, to be read as "*n factorial*," is the product of the integers from 1 to $n$, and, therefore, can be computed using a tight loop, the definition of $n!$ is recursive and lends itself to a recursive calculation.

**Definition of *n* Factorial:** Let $n$ be a nonnegative integer. Then $n!$ is defined as

$$n! = \begin{Bmatrix} 1 & \text{if } n = 0; \\ n[(n-1)!] & \text{if } n > 0. \end{Bmatrix}$$

For example, we use the Definition of $n$ Factorial to compute 3! as follows. From the recursive definition, we know that $3! = 3 \times 2!$. Thus, we need the value of 2!. Using the second line of the recursive definition, we know that $3! = 3 \times 2! = 3 \times 2 \times 1! = 3 \times 2 \times 1 \times 0!$. Notice that the first line of the Definition of $n$ Factorial tells us that $0! = 1$. This is the simplest case of $n$ considered by the definition of $n!$, a case that does not require further use of recursion and therefore is a *base case.* A recursive definition or algorithm may have more than one base case. It is the existence of one or more base cases, and logic that drives the computation toward base cases, that prevent recursion from producing an infinite loop.

In our example, we substitute 1 for 0! in order to resolve our calculations. If we proceed in the typical fashion of a person calculating with pencil and paper, we would make this substitution in the above and complete the multiplication,

$$3! = 3 \times 2 \times 1 \times 0! = 3 \times 2 \times 1 \times 1 = 6.$$

A typical computer implementation of this example's recursion follows. Substitute $0! = 1$ to resolve the calculation of $1!$, obtaining $1! = 1 \times 0! = 1 \times 1 = 1$. Next, substitute the result of $1!$ in the calculation of $2!$, obtaining $2! = 2 \times 1! = 2 \times 1 = 2$. Finally, substitute the result for $2!$ into the calculation of $3!$, which yields $3! = 3 \times 2! = 3 \times 2 = 6$.

Below, we give a recursive algorithm for computing the factorial function. It is important to note that this algorithm is given for illustrative purposes only. If one really wants to write an efficient program to compute the factorial function, a simple tight loop would typically be much more efficient.

**Integer function factorial (integer *n*)**
**Input:** $n$ is assumed to be a nonnegative integer.
**Algorithm:** Produce the value of $n!$ by using recursion.

**Action:**

```
If n=0, then return 1
Else return n× factorial(n-1)
```

How do we analyze the running time of such an algorithm? Notice that while the size of the data set does not decrease with each invocation of the procedure, the value of $n$ decreases monotonically with each successive call. Therefore, let $T(n)$ denote the running time of the procedure with input value $n$. We see from the base case of the recursion that $T(0) = \Theta(1)$, since the time to compute $0!$ is constant. From the recurrence given above, we can define the time to compute $n!$, for $n > 0$, as $T(n) = T(n-1) + \Theta(1)$. The conditions

$$\left\{ \begin{array}{c} T(0) = \Theta(1); \\ T(n) = T(n-1) + \Theta(1) \end{array} \right\} \tag{1}$$

form a *recursive relation*. We wish to evaluate $T(n)$ in such a way as to express $T(n)$ without recursion. A naïve approach uses repeated substitution of the recursive relation. This results in

$$T(n) = T(n-1) + \Theta(1) =$$
$$T(n-2) + \Theta(1) + \Theta(1) = T(n-2) + 2\Theta(1) =$$
$$T(n-3) + \Theta(1) + 2\Theta(1) = T(n-3) + 3\Theta(1).$$

It is important to note the pattern that is emerging is $T(n) = T(n-k) + k\Theta(1)$. Such a pattern will lead us to conjecture that $T(n) = T(0) + n\Theta(1)$, which, by the base case of the recursive definition, yields $T(n) = \Theta(1) + n\Theta(1) = (n+1)\Theta(1) = \Theta(n)$.

Indeed, the conjecture that we have arrived at is correct. However, the "proof" given is *not* correct. Although naïve arguments are often useful for recognizing patterns, they do not serve as proofs. In fact, whenever one detects a pattern and uses such a conjecture as a proof, there is a logical hole in the proof. After all, such an argument fails to rule out the possibility that the pattern is incorrect for some case that wasn't considered. Such an approach reminds us of the well-known Sidney Harris cartoon in which a difficult step in the derivation of a formula is explained with the phrase "THEN A MIRACLE OCCURS" (see http://www.sciencecartoons plus.com/gallery.htm). Thus, once we think that we have recognized a solution to a recursive relation, it is still necessary to give a solid mathematical proof.

In the case of the current example, the following proof can be given. We observe that the Θ-notation in condition (1) is a generalization of proportionality. Suppose we consider the simplified recursive relation

$$\left\{ \begin{array}{c} T(0) = 1; \\ T(n) = T(n-1) + 1. \end{array} \right\} \tag{2}$$

Our previous observations lead us to suspect that this turns out to be $T(n) = n + 1$, which we can prove by mathematical induction, as follows.

- For $n = 0$, the assertion is $T(0) = 1$, which is true.
- Suppose the assertion $T(n) = n + 1$ is true for some positive integer $k$. Thus, our inductive hypothesis is the equation $T(k) = k + 1$. We need to show $T(k+1) = k + 2$. Now, using the recursive relation (2) and the inductive hypothesis, we have $T(k+1) = T(k) + 1 = (k+1) + 1 = k + 2$, as desired.

Thus, we have completed an inductive proof that our recursive relation (2) simplifies as $T(n) = n + 1$. Since condition (1) is a generalization of (2), in which the Θ-interpretation is not affected by the differences between (1) and (2), it follows that condition (1) satisfies $T(n) = \Theta(n)$. Thus, our recursive algorithm for computing $n!$ runs in $\Theta(n)$ time.

## Sequential Search

A *sequential search* is efficiently implemented in an iterative fashion. We present the traditional non-recursive sequential search algorithm so that it can be compared to the recursive implementation of binary search that is given in the following section.

Consider the problem of searching an arbitrarily ordered set of data by a traditional sequential search. Notice that in the worst case, every item must be examined, since the item we are looking for *i*) might not exist or *ii*) might be the last item listed. So, without loss of generality, let's assume that our sequential search starts at the beginning of the unordered data set and concludes based on one of the following conditions.

- The search succeeds when the required item is located.
- The search fails after every item has been examined without finding the item being sought.

Since the data is not known to be ordered, the sequential examination of data items is necessary, because were we to skip over any item, the skipped item could be the one that we wanted (see Figure 2-1).

| | | | | | | |
|---|---|---|---|---|---|---|
| 5 | 7 | 9 | 3 | 4 | 6 | 8 |

**FIGURE 2-1** *An example of sequential search. Given the array of data, a search for the value* 4 *requires five key comparisons. A search for the value* 9 *requires three key comparisons. A search for the value* 1 *requires seven key comparisons in order to determine that the requested value is not present.*

Thus, we give the following algorithm for a sequential search.

**Subprogram SequentialSearch (*X, searchValue, success, foundAt*)**
**Algorithm:** Perform a sequential search on the array $X[1\ldots n]$ for *searchValue*. If an element with a key value of *searchValue* is found, then return *success* = *true* and *foundAt*, where *searchValue* = *X*[*foundAt*].*key*, and where *X*[*foundAt*].*key* is the first instance of *searchValue*.
Otherwise, return *success* = *false*.
**Local variable:** index *position*

**Action:**

```
  position = 1
  Do
    success = (searchValue = X[position].key)
    If success, then foundAt = position
    Else position = position + 1
  While (Not success) and (position ≤ n)          {End Do}
  Return success, foundAt
End Search
```

**Analysis:** The set of instructions inside the Do-While loop runs in $\Theta(1)$ time since each instruction runs in constant, *i.e.*, $\Theta(1)$, time. In the worst case, the body of the loop will be executed $n$ times. This occurs when either the search is unsuccessful or when the item we are searching for is the last item in the array $X$.

Thus, one can say that the worst-case sequential search runs in $\Theta(n)$ time. Assuming that the data is ordered in a truly random fashion, then a successful search will, on average, succeed after examining half of the entries. That is, a successful search of an unordered data set in which the items are randomly distributed, requires examining $n/2$ items on average. Indeed, the expected-case or average-case running time of a successful sequential search is $\Theta(n)$. Finally, since the data is presented in a random fashion, it is possible that we find the item we are searching for immediately, which means that the time required for the best-case search is $\Theta(1)$.

## Binary Search

In contrast with our recursive algorithm for computing $n!$, recursion is more commonly used when every recursive call involves a significant reduction in the *size* of the current instance of the problem. An example of such a recursive algorithm is *Binary Search.* Searching for a data value is a fundamental operation, in which efficiency is crucial. For example, consider searching for an entry of a phone book, a sorted listing of names and telephone numbers, or for an entry of a dictionary, a sorted listing of words and their definitions. Since hardcopy phone books and dictionaries are examples of sorted databases, we can take advantage of the fact that the data is ordered when we attempt to find an element. For example, when searching a hardcopy phone book for "Miller," we would not start at the very beginning of the book and search entry by entry, page by page, in hopes of finding "Miller". Instead, we would likely open the book to the middle and decide whether "Miller" appears on the page(s) before, after, or on the page being examined.

We now consider the impact of performing a search on a sorted set of data. Think about designing an algorithm that mimics what you would do to find "Miller" in a hardcopy phone book. That is, grab a bunch of pages and flip back and forth, each time grabbing fewer and fewer pages, until the desired item is located. Notice that this method considers very few data values relative to the number considered by the sequential search. A question we need to consider is whether or not this algorithm is asymptotically faster than the sequential search algorithm, since it may be faster by just a high-order constant or low-order term. Before we consider a proper analysis of this binary search, we present a detailed description of the algorithm.

**Subprogram BinarySearch (*X, searchValue, success, foundAt, minIndex, maxIndex*)**
**Algorithm:** Binary search algorithm to search ordered subarray $X[minIndex \ldots maxIndex]$ for a *key* field equal to *searchValue.*
The algorithm is recursive. In order to search the entire array $X[1, \ldots, n]$, the initial call is of the form *Search(X, searchValue, success, foundAt,* 1, *n*).
If *searchValue* is found, return *success = true* and *foundAt* as an index at which *searchValue* is found; otherwise, return *success = false.*

**Local variable:** index *midIndex*

**Action:**

```
If minIndex > maxIndex, then          {The subarray is empty}
  success = false, foundAt = 0
Else                                  {The subarray is nonempty}
  midIndex = ⌊(minIndex + maxIndex) / 2⌋
  If searchValue = X[midIndex].key, then
    success = true, foundAt = midIndex
  Else {searchValue ≠ X[midIndex].key}
    If searchValue < X[midIndex].key, then
      BinarySearch(X, searchValue, success, foundAt,
                   minIndex, midIndex − 1)
    Else {searchValue > X[midIndex].key}
      BinarySearch(X, searchValue, success, foundAt,
                   midIndex + 1, maxIndex)
  End {searchValue ≠ X[midIndex].key}
End {Subarray is nonempty}
Return success, foundAt
End Search
```

See Figure 2-2. Notice that the running time, $T(n)$, of our binary search algorithm satisfies the recursive relation

$$T(1) = \Theta(1);$$
$$T(n) \le T(n/2) + \Theta(1).$$

| | | | | | | |
|---|---|---|---|---|---|---|
| 3 | 4 | 5 | 6 | 7 | 8 | 9 |

**FIGURE 2-2** *An example of binary search. Given the array of data, a search for the value* 4 *requires two key comparisons* (6,4). *A search for the value* 9 *requires three key comparisons* (6,8,9). *A search for the value* 1 *requires three key comparisons* (6,4,3) *in order to determine that the value is not present.*

To analyze the worst-case running time implied by this recursive relation, we can again use the naïve approach of repeated substitution into this recursive relation to try to find a pattern, interpret the pattern for a non-recursive base case, then try to prove the resulting assertion by mathematical induction. This results in an expansion that looks like

$$T(n) = T(n/2) + \Theta(1) =$$
$$T(n/4) + \Theta(1) + \Theta(1) = T(n/4) + 2 \times \Theta(1) =$$
$$T(n/8) + \Theta(1) + 2 \times \Theta(1) = T(n/8) + 3 \times \Theta(1).$$

Notice that the pattern beginning to emerge is $T(n) = T(n/2^k) + k \times \Theta(1)$, where the argument of $T$ reaches the base value $1 = n/2^k$ when $k = \log_2 n$. Such a pattern leads us to the conjecture that

$$T(n) = T(1) + \log_2 n \times \Theta(1) = \Theta(\log n).$$

Based on this "analysis," we believe that a binary search exhibits a worst-case running time of $\Theta(\log n)$.

Notice that in our "analysis" above, we made the simplifying assumption that $n$ is a positive integer that is a power of 2. It turns out that this assumption only simplifies the analysis of the running time without changing the result of the analysis (see the Exercises).

As before, it is important to realize that once we have recognized what *appears* to be the pattern of the expanded recursive relation, we must prove our conjecture. To do this, we can use mathematical induction. We leave the proof of the running time of binary search as an exercise for the reader.

The term *binary*, when applied to this search procedure, is used to suggest that during each iteration of the algorithm, the search is being performed on roughly 1/2 the number of items that were used during the preceding iteration. Although such an assumption makes the analysis more straightforward, it is important for the reader to note that the asymptotic running time holds so long as at the conclusion of each recursion, some fixed fraction of the data is removed from consideration.

## Additional Notes on Sequential and Binary Searches

It is important to recall that a sequential search can be used on a list, whether or not the list is known to be ordered. By contrast, a binary search requires an *ordered* list, assuming the user wants to be assured of a correct result. Notice that Binary Search correctly solves the search problem for an ordered list with a $\Theta(\log n)$ worst-case running time, while Sequential Search solves the search problem on an arbitrarily ordered list in $\Theta(n)$ worst-case running time.

## Merging and Merge Sort

Many efficient sorting algorithms are based on a recursive paradigm in which the list of data to be sorted is split into sublists of approximately equal size, each of the resulting sublists is sorted recursively, and then the sorted sublists are combined into a completely sorted list (see Figure 2-3).

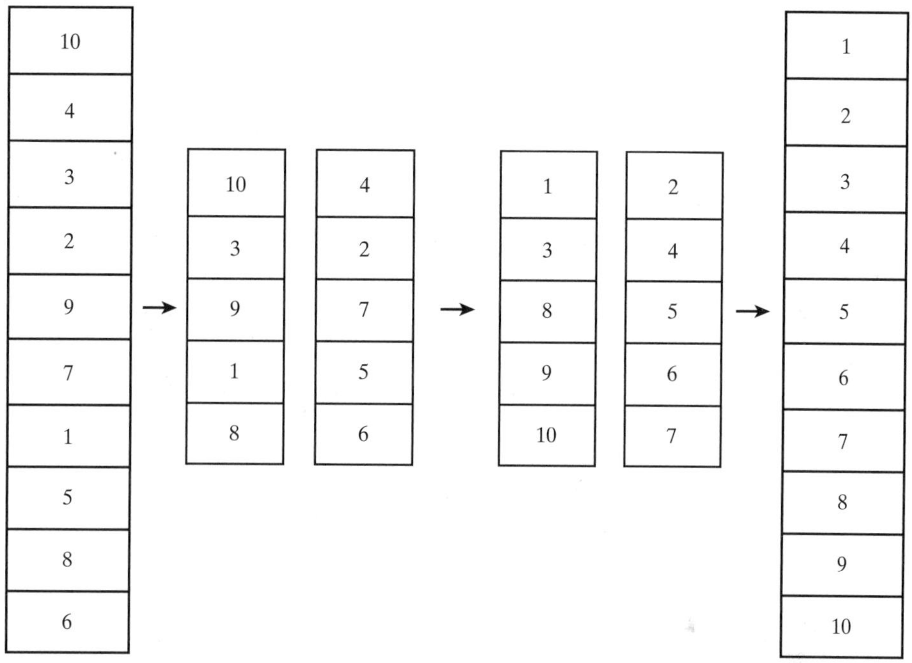


**FIGURE 2-3** *Recursively sorting a set of data. Take the initial list and divide it into two lists, each roughly half the size of the original list. Recursively sort each of the sublists. Merge these sorted sublists to create the final sorted list.*

The recursive relation that describes the running time of such an algorithm is given by

$$T(1) = \Theta(1);$$
$$T(n) = S(n) + 2T(n/2) + C(n),$$

where $S(n)$ is the time used by the algorithm to split a list of $n$ entries into two sublists of approximately $n/2$ entries apiece, and $C(n)$ is the time used by the algorithm to combine two sorted lists of approximately $n/2$ entries apiece into a single sorted list. An example of such an algorithm is *Merge Sort*, discussed below.

Merging two ordered lists $A$ and $B$ into a single ordered list $C$ requires properly intermingling the members of $A$ and $B$ in order to produce $C$. Think of it as having half a deck of cards in each hand, both of which are ordered, and combining them to get a final ordered list.

This operation is most natural to describe when the lists are maintained as *linked lists*, *i.e.*, pointer-based lists. In the following discussion, we consider our data to be arranged as a singly linked list in which each data record has the following.

*i.* A field called *sortkey*, which is used as the basis for sorting.
*ii.* Zero or more other fields, denoted *otherinfo* in Figure 2-4, that are used to store information pertinent to the record but are not used by the sort routine.
*iii.* A field called *next*, which is a pointer to the next element in the list.

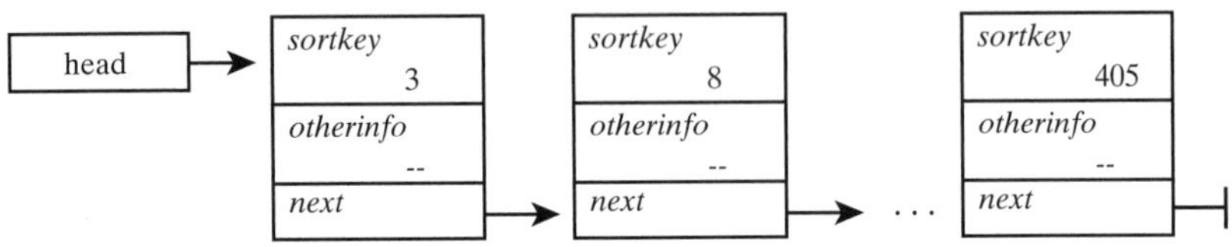


**FIGURE 2-4** *An illustration of a linked list in a language that supports dynamic allocation of elements. Notice that the head of the list is simply a pointer and not a complete record, and that the last item in the list has its next pointer set to NULL. An algorithm to merge two ordered linked lists containing a total of n elements in O(n) time is given below. An example of merging is shown in Figure 2-5.*

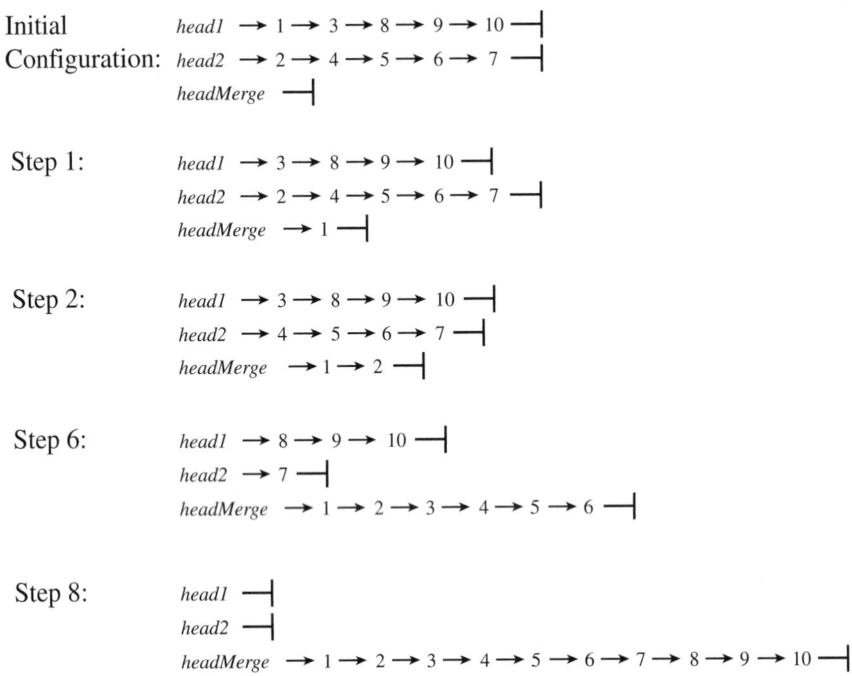


**FIGURE 2-5** *An example of merging two ordered lists, initially indexed by head1 and head2, to create an ordered list headMerge. Snapshots are presented at various stages of the algorithm. As the merge progresses, head1 and head2 each indexes the first unmerged node in their respective list.*

Note that a programming language typically has a special pointer constant that is defined to point to no element, *e.g.*, "NULL" or "nil". This value is typically used to mark boundaries of pointer-based data structures, *e.g.*, the last member of a linked list typically has a *next* field with this special value. Figure 2-4 presents a representation of such a data structure. Notice that in Figure 2-4, we assume the *sortkey* data is of type *integer.*

**Subprogram Merge(*head1*, *head2*, *headMerge*)**
**Input:** *head1* and *head2* point to two distinct ordered lists that are to be merged with respect to field *sortkey.* We assume all ordered lists are in ascending order.
**Output:** This routine produces a merged list addressed by *headMerge.*
**Local variable:** *atMerge*, a pointer to a link of the merged list

**Action:**

```
If head1 = null, then return headMerge = head2
Else                    {The first input list is nonempty}
  If head2 = null, then return headMerge = head1
  Else                       {Both input lists are nonempty}
    If head1.sortkey ≤ head2.sortkey, then
         {Start merged list with 1st element of 1st list}
       headMerge = head1; head1 = head1.next
    Else {Start merged list with 1st element of 2nd list}
       headMerge = head2; head2 = head2.next
    End                          {Decide first merge element}
    atMerge = headMerge
    While (head1 ≠ null and head2 ≠ null), do
      If head1.sortkey ≤ head2.sortkey then
                                 {Merge element of 1st list}
        atMerge.next = head1
        atMerge = head1
        head1 = head1.next
      Else                       {Merge element of 2nd list}
        atMerge.next = head2
        atMerge = head2
        head2 = head2.next
      End If
    End While
                    {Now, one of the lists is exhausted, but
                         the other isn't. So concatenate the
                         unmerged portion of the unexhausted
                                    list to the merged list.}
```

```
      If head1 = null, then atMerge.next = head2
      Else atMerge.next = head1
     End Else                    {Both input lists are nonempty}
    End Else                      {First input list is nonempty}
    Return headMerge
   End Merge
```

It is useful to examine the merge algorithm above in terms of both the *best-case*, *i.e.*, minimal running time, and the *worst-case*, *i.e.*, maximal running time. In the best case, one of the input lists is empty, and the algorithm finishes its work in $\Theta(1)$ time. In the worst-case, when one of the input lists is exhausted, only one item remains in the other list. In this case, since each iteration of the While-loop requires a constant amount of work to merge one element into the merged list that is being constructed, the running time for the entire procedure is $\Theta(n)$. We note also that the algorithm processes every element of one of its input lists. Therefore, the running time of this simple merge algorithm is $\Theta(k)$, where $k$ is the number of nodes from both input lists that have been merged when the first input list is exhausted. So, if the total length of both lists combined is $\Theta(n)$, *e.g.*, if we are merging two lists of length $n/2$ each, then the worst-case running time of this merge algorithm is $\Theta(n)$.

In addition to being able to merge two ordered lists, the Merge Sort algorithm requires a routine that will split a list into two sublists of roughly equal size. Suppose we are given a deck of cards and don't know how many cards are in the deck. A reasonable way to divide the deck into two piles so that each pile had roughly the same number of cards in it is to deal the cards alternately between the two piles. We give such an algorithm for splitting a list below.

**Subprogram Split(*headIn*, *headOut*)**
**Algorithm:** Split an input list indexed by *headIn*, a pointer to the first element, into two output lists by alternating the output list to which an input element is assigned.
The output lists are indexed by *headOut*[0…1].
**Local variables:** *current_list*, an index alternating between output lists *temp*, a temporary pointer to current link of input list

**Action:**

```
                                {Initialize output lists as empty.}
  headOut[0] = headOut[1] = null
  current_list = 0
  While headIn ≠ null, do
    temp = headIn
```

```
        headIn = headIn.next
        temp.next = headOut[current_list]
        headOut[current_list] = temp
        current_list = 1 - current_list
                                   {Switch value between 0, 1}
      End While
      Return headOut
    End Split
```

In the Split algorithm above, every iteration of the loop takes one element from the input list and places it at the head of one of the output lists. This operation runs in $\Theta(1)$ time. Thus, if the initial list has $n$ elements, the algorithm runs in $\Theta(n)$ time.

Since we have introduced and analyzed the tools necessary for Merge Sort, we now present an implementation of the algorithm in Subprogram MergeSort.

**Subprogram MergeSort(*head*)**
**Algorithm:** Sort a linked list by using the Merge Sort algorithm
**Input:** a linked list indexed by *head*, a pointer to the first element
**Output:** an ordered list
**Local variables:** *temp*[0…1], an array of two pointers

**Action:**

```
  If head ≠ null, then              {Input list is nonempty}
    If head.next ≠ null, then
                          {There's work to do, as the list
                                 has at least 2 elements.}
      Split(head, temp)
      MergeSort(temp[0])
      MergeSort(temp[1])
      Merge(temp[0], temp[1], head)
    End If
  End If
  Return head
End Sort
```

Before we analyze the Merge Sort algorithm given above in Subprogram MergeSort, we make the following observations. The algorithm is recursive, so a question that should be raised is, “what condition represents the base case?” Actually, two base cases are present, but they are both so simple that they are easily missed.

1. Consider the statement "If $head \neq null$, then" in Subprogram MergeSort. The consequent action does not seem like the simple case we expect in a base case of recursion. It does, however, suggest that we consider the opposite case, $head = null$. The latter case is not mentioned at all in the algorithm, yet clearly it can happen. This, in fact, is a base case of recursion. Notice that if $head = null$, then there is no work to be done, as the list is empty. It is tempting to say that when this happens, no time is used, but we should attribute to this case the $\Theta(1)$ time necessary to recognize that $head = null$.
2. Consider the inner "If" clause, "If $head.next \neq null$." Notice that this condition is only tested when the outer If-condition is true, and therefore represents the condition of having a list with at least one element beyond the head element. That is, the list must have at least two elements. Thus, negation of the inner If-condition represents the condition of having a list with exactly one node, since the outer If's condition being true means there is at least one node. As above, the condition $head.next = null$ results in no listed action, corresponding to the fact that a list of one element must be ordered. As above, we analyze the case $head.next = null$ as using $\Theta(1)$ time.

   It is important to observe that a piece of code of the form

```
If A, then
  actionsForA
End If A
```

is logically equivalent to

```
If not A, then        {no action}
Else                  {A is true}
  actionsForA
End Else A
```

We usually prefer the former form for its brevity, but in discussing Merge Sort, the latter form helps us distinguish base cases that require no action from recursive cases.

**Analysis:** Let $T(n)$ be the running time of the Merge Sort algorithm, which sorts a linked list of $n$ items. Based on the analysis above, we know that the splitting time is $S(n) = \Theta(n)$. We also know that the time to merge is $M(n) = O(n)$. Given the time for splitting and merging, we can construct a recurrence equation for the running time of the entire algorithm, as follows.

$$T(1) = \Theta(1);$$

$$T(n) = S(n) + 2T(n/2) + M(n) = 2T(n/2) + \Theta(n). \quad \text{(a)}$$

Before we proceed further, notice that the latter equation, in the worst case, could have been written as

$$T(n) = 2[T(n/2) + \Theta(n)]. \quad \text{(b)}$$

Roughly, equations (a) and (b) are equivalent because $2\Theta(n) = \Theta(2n) = \Theta(n)$. In order to proceed with the analysis, we again consider using repeated substitution as a means of obtaining a conjecture about the running time. Therefore, we have, from equation (a),

$$T(n) = 2T(n/2) + \Theta(n) =$$
$$2[2T(n/4) + \Theta(n/2)] + \Theta(n) = 4T(n/4) + 2 \times \Theta(n) =$$
$$4[2T(n/8) + \Theta(n/4)] + 2 \times \Theta(n) = 8T(n/8) + 3 \times \Theta(n).$$

The emerging pattern is $T(n) = 2^k T(n/2^k) + k \times \Theta(n)$, reaching the base case $1 = n/2^k$ for $k = \log_2 n$. This pattern results in a conjecture that

$$T(n) = nT(1) + \Theta(n \log n) = \Theta(n) + \Theta(n \log n) = \Theta(n \log n).$$

If we are still not comfortable by the remark above that equations (a) and (b) are equivalent, notice that had we based our search for a conjecture on repeated substitution into equation (b), we would have obtained

$$T(n) = 2[T(n/2) + \Theta(n)]$$
$$2\{2[T(n/4) + \Theta(n/2)]\} + 2\Theta(n) = 4T(n/4) + 4\Theta(n) =$$
$$4\{2[T(n/8) + \Theta(n/4)]\} + 4\Theta(n) = 8T(n/8) + 6\Theta(n).$$

The emerging pattern is $T(n) = 2^k T(n/2^k) + 2k\Theta(n)$, reaching its base case for $k = \log_2 n$, substitution of which into the pattern equation yields the conjecture $T(n) = nT(1) + (2 \log_2 n)\Theta(n) = \Theta(n \log n)$, as above.

Our conjecture can be proved using mathematical induction on $k$ for $n = 2^k$ (see Exercises). Therefore, the running time of our Merge Sort algorithm is $\Theta(n \log n)$.

## Common Recurrence Equations

In this section, we give some common recurrence equations, several of which were derived in this chapter.

| Representative Algorithm | Recurrence Equation | Asymptotic Solution |
|---|---|---|
| **Binary Search** | $T(n) = T(n/2) + \Theta(1)$ | $T(n) = \Theta(\log n)$ |
| **Sequential Search** | $T(n) = T(n-1) + \Theta(1)$ | $T(n) = \Theta(n)$ |
| **Tree Traversal** | $T(n) = 2T(n/2) + \Theta(1)$ | $T(n) = \Theta(n)$ |
| **Insertion Sort** | $T(n) = T(n-1) + \Theta(n)$ | $T(n) = \Theta(n^2)$ |
| **Merge Sort** | $T(n) = 2T(n/2) + \Theta(n)$ | $T(n) = \Theta(n \log n)$ |

## Summary

In this chapter, we introduce the related notions of mathematical induction and recursion. Mathematical induction is a technique for proving statements about sets of successive integers. Often, the set of concern takes the form of all integers greater than or equal to an initial integer. This is done by proving a base case and then proving that the truth of a successor case follows from the truth of its predecessor. Recursion is a technique of solving problems by dividing the original problem into multiple smaller problems, solving these smaller problems, and combining the solutions to the smaller problems in order to obtain the desired solution to the original problem. Note that the step of "solving these smaller problems" is done recursively unless a simple base case is reached where the problem can be solved directly. Examples of both of these powerful tools are presented, including applications to fundamental data processing operations such as searching and sorting.

## Chapter Notes

A classic reference for the material presented in this chapter is *Fundamental Algorithms*, volume 1 of *The Art of Computer Programming*, by Donald Knuth. The book, published by Addison-Wesley, originally appeared in 1968, and, along with the companion volumes, is a classic that should be on every computer scientist's desk. An excellent book on discrete mathematics is *Discrete Algorithmic Mathematics* by S.B. Maurer & A. Ralston (Addison-Wesley Publishing Company, Reading, Massachusetts, 1991). An interesting book, combining discrete and continuous mathematics, is *Concrete Mathematics* by R.L. Graham, D.E. Knuth, & O. Patashnik (Addison-Wesley Publishing Company, Reading, Massachusetts, 1989). Finally, we should mention an excellent book, *Introduction to Algorithms*, by T.H. Cormen, C.E. Leiserson, R.L. Rivest, and C. Stein (3rd ed.: MIT Press, Cambridge, MA, 2009). This book covers fundamental mathematics for algorithmic analysis in a thorough fashion.

## Exercises

Note: Some of our exercises are based on the sequence of *Fibonacci numbers* $f_1, f_2, f_3, \ldots$, defined recursively as

$$f_1 = f_2 = 1;$$

$$f_{n+2} = f_n + f_{n+1}.$$

**1.** Suppose we have a positive number $c$ and define a sequence $g_1, g_2, g_3, \ldots$, recursively by

$$g_1 = g_2 = c;$$

$$g_{n+2} = g_n + g_{n+1}.$$

Show that for every positive integer $n$, we have $g_n = cf_n$, where $f_n$ is the $n^{\text{th}}$ Fibonacci number.

The next two exercises may be completed with non-recursive algorithms. These algorithms may be used in subsequent exercises.

**2.** Devise a $\Theta(n)$ time algorithm that takes as input an array $X$ and produces as output a singly linked list $Y$ such that the $i$th element of $Y$ has the same data as the $i$th entry of $X$. Prove that the algorithm runs in $\Theta(n)$ time.

**3.** Devise a $\Theta(n)$ time algorithm that takes as input a singly linked list $X$ and produces as output an array $Y$ such that the $i$th entry of $Y$ has the same data as the $i$th element of $X$. Prove that the algorithm runs in $\Theta(n)$ time.

**4.** Show that $\sum_{i=1}^{\infty} \frac{1}{2^i} = 1$. This can be done by showing that for all positive integers $n$, $\sum_{i=1}^{n} \frac{1}{2^i} = 1 - \frac{1}{2^n}$, which can be shown by mathematical induction.

**5.** (Arithmetic progression.) Show that a recursive algorithm, where the running time is given as a function of items

$$T(1) = \Theta(1);$$
$$T(n) = T(n-1) + \Theta(n),$$

satisfies $T(n) = \Theta(n^2)$.

**6.** (Geometric progression.) Show that a recursive algorithm, where the running time is given as a function of items

$$T(1) = \Theta(1);$$
$$T(n) = T(n/r) + \Theta(n),$$

where $r > 1$ is a constant, satisfies $T(n) = \Theta(n)$.

**7.** (Binary search.)

a. Show that the recursive relation used with the binary search algorithm,

$$T(1) = \Theta(1);$$
$$T(n) \le T(n/2) + \Theta(1),$$

satisfies $T(n) = O(\log n)$ when $n = 2^k$ for some nonnegative integer $k$. *Hint*: Your proof should use mathematical induction on $k$ to show that

$$T(1) = 1;$$
$$T(n) \le T(n/2) + 1,$$

satisfies $T(n) \le 1 + \log_2 n$.

b. Even if $n$ is not an integer power of 2, the recursive relation above satisfies $T(n) = O(\log n)$. Prove this assertion, using the result for the case of $n$ being a power of 2. *Hint*: Start with the assumption that $2^k < n < 2^{k+1}$ for some positive integer $k$. One approach is to show that only one more item need be examined, in the worst case, than in the worst case for $n = 2^k$. Another approach is to prove that we could work instead with the recursive relation

$$T(1) = 1;$$

$$T(n) \leq T\left(\left\lceil \frac{n-1}{2} \right\rceil\right) + 1,$$

then show how this, in turn, yields the desired conclusion.

**8.** Prove that Subprogram MergeSort has a running time of $\Theta(n \log n)$ by showing that the recursive relation used in its partial analysis above,

$$T(1) = \Theta(1);$$

$$T(n) = S(n) + 2T(n/2) + C(n) = 2T(n/2) + \Theta(n),$$

satisfies $T(n) = \Theta(n \log n)$. As above, this can be done by an argument based on the assumption that $n = 2^k$, for some nonnegative integer $k$, using mathematical induction on $k$.

**9.** Show that an array of $n$ entries can be sorted in $\Theta(n \log n)$ time by an algorithm that makes use of the Merge Sort algorithm given above. *Hint*: see Exercises 2 and 3.

**10.** More on Fibonacci numbers

a. Develop a nonrecursive $\Theta(n)$ time algorithm to return the $n^{\text{th}}$ Fibonacci number.

b. Below, we state a recursive algorithm to produce the $n^{\text{th}}$ Fibonacci number, based on the definition above. Show that this algorithm has a running time that is $\omega(n)$. This shows that the naïve use of recursion isn't always a good idea.

**integer function fibonacci(*n*)**
Outputs the $n^{\text{th}}$ Fibonacci number
**Input:** $n$, a nonnegative integer

**Action:**

```
If n≤2, then return 1
Else return fibonacci(n−2) + fibonacci(n−1)
```

*Hint*: The analysis can be achieved by the following steps.

- Show that the running time $T(n)$ can be analyzed by using the recursive relation $T(n) = T(n-1) + T(n-2) + \Theta(1)$.
- Show the recursive relation obtained above implies $T(n) > 2T(n-2)$.
- Use the above to show that $T(n) = \omega(n)$. Note it is not necessary to find an explicit formula for either $f_n$ or $T(n)$ to achieve this step.

**11.** A certain method for computing the determinant of an $n \times n$ matrix has running time $T(n^2)$ described, to within constants of proportionality, by

$$T(n^2) = \begin{cases} nT\big((n-1)^2\big) & \text{for } n > 1; \\ 1 & \text{for } n = 1. \end{cases}$$

Show this recursion resolves as $T(n^2) = n!$, the factorial function.

# 3

# The Master Method

The *Master Method* is an important tool that can provide solutions to a large class of recursion relations. This is important, for example, when we try to solve equations that provide the time, space, or memory requirements of an algorithm. Further, recurrence equations can often be used to suggest solution strategies, *i.e.*, algorithms, to solve problems of interest.

Consider a recurrence of the form

$$T(n) = aT\left(\frac{n}{b}\right) + f(n),$$

where $a \geq 1$ and $b > 1$ are constants, and $f(n)$ is a positive function. In addition, we assume a base case of $T(c) = \Theta(1)$, for $c \leq 1$ unless explicitly stated otherwise.

If $T(n)$ is the running time of a problem of size $n$, we can interpret this recurrence as defining $T(n)$ to be the time to solve $a$ subproblems of size $n/b$, plus $f(n)$, which is the sum of the following.

- The time to divide the original problem into the $a$ subproblems.
- The time to combine the subproblems' solutions in order to obtain the solution to the original problem.

Consider the problem of sorting a linked list of data using the Merge Sort algorithm described in the previous chapter (see Figure 3-1). Assume that we split a list of length $n$ into two lists, each of length $n/2$, recursively sort these new lists, and then merge them together. In terms of developing a recurrence equation, we have 2 subproblems to solve, each of size $n/2$. That is, we have $a = 2$ subproblems, each of size $n/b$, for $b = 2$.

Further, the interpretation is that $f(n)$ is the time to split the list of length $n$ into two lists of length $n/2$ each, plus the time to merge two ordered lists of length $n/2$ each into an ordered list of length $n$. See Figure 3-2.

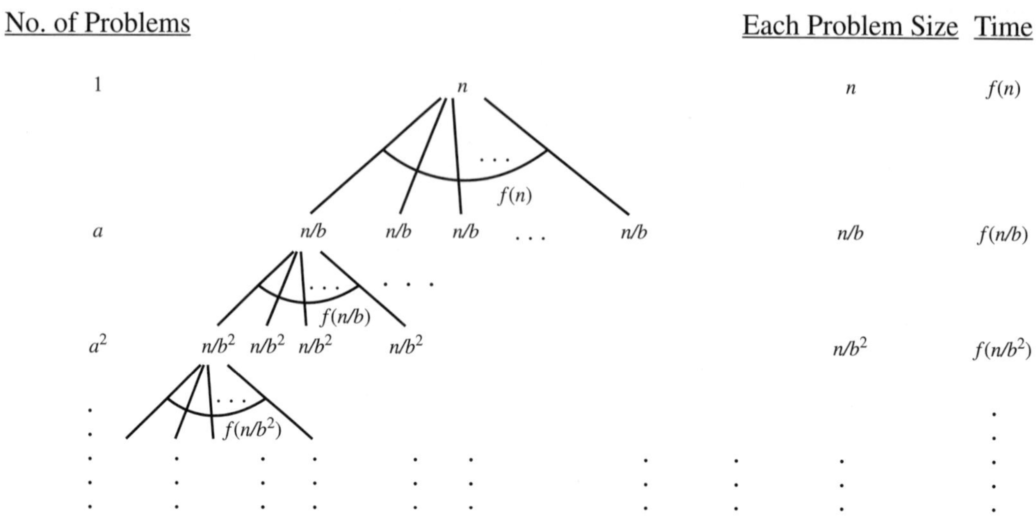


**FIGURE 3-1** *A recursion tree representing the recurrence equation $T(n) = aT(n/b) + f(n)$. The number of problems to be solved at each horizontal level of recursion is listed, along with the size of each problem at that level. "Time" is used to represent the time per problem, not counting recursion, at each level.*

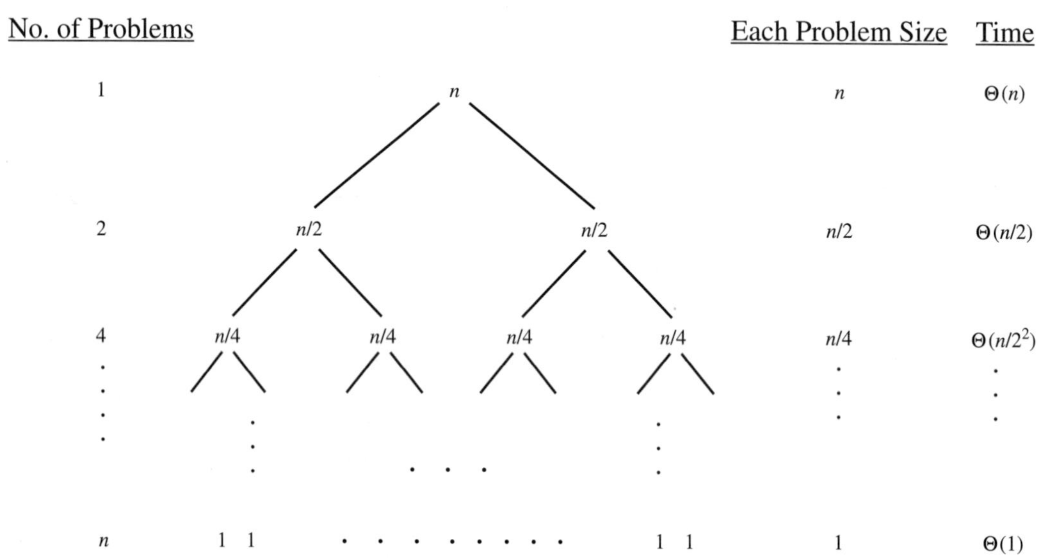


**FIGURE 3-2** *A recursion tree for Merge Sort, as represented by $T(n) = 2T(n/2) + \Theta(n)$. Notice that level i of the recursion tree, for $i \in \{1, 2, \ldots, \log_2 n\}$, runs in $2^i \times \Theta(n/2^i) = \Theta(n)$ time. This resolves as $T(n) = \Theta(n \log n)$.*

## Master Theorem

The *Master Method* is summarized in the following **"Master Theorem."**

**Master Theorem:** Let $a \geq 1$ and $b \geq 1$ be constants. Let $f(n)$ be a positive function defined on the positive integers. Let $T(n)$ be defined on the positive integers by

$$T(n) = aT\left(\frac{n}{b}\right) + f(n), \tag{3.1}$$

where we can interpret $n/b$ as meaning either $\lfloor n/b \rfloor$ or $\lceil n/b \rceil$. Then the following hold.

1. Suppose $f(n) = O\left(n^{\log_b a-\varepsilon}\right)$ for some constant $\varepsilon > 0$. Then $T(n) = \Theta\left(n^{\log_b a}\right)$.
2. Suppose $f(n) = \Theta\left(n^{\log_b a}\right)$. Then $T(n) = \Theta\left(n^{\log_b a} \log n\right)$.
3. Suppose $f(n) = \Omega(n^{\log_b a+\varepsilon})$ for some constant $\varepsilon > 0$, and there are constants $c$ and $N$, $0 < c < 1$ and $N > 0$, such that $(n/b) > N \Rightarrow af(n/b) \leq cf(n)$. Then $T(n) = \Theta\left(f(n)\right)$.

The reader should observe that the **Master Theorem** does not cover all instances of equation (3.1).

In Appendix 2, we sketch a proof for the **Master Theorem.** The proof is provided as a convenience to those who have the mathematical skills, interest, and background to appreciate it, but should be skipped by other readers.

## Examples

**EXAMPLE**

**(Geometric progression)** Consider the recurrence

$$T(c) = \Theta(1) \text{ for } c \leq 1,$$

$$T(n) = T(n/r) + \Theta(n) \text{ for } c > 1,$$

for some constant $r > 1$. Notice that this geometric series was presented in an Exercise of Chapter 2, where it was to be resolved by mathematical induction. Many of you have been exposed to the case of $r = 2$, which is equivalent to $T(n) = \Theta(n + n/2 + n/4 + \ldots) = \Theta(n)$.

If, instead, we use the **Master Theorem** to resolve the general recurrence, we have $a = 1$, $b = r$, and $\log_b a = \log_r 1 = 0$. This yields

$$f(n) = n = n^{\log_b a+1}$$

Further,

$$af(n/b) = n/r = \frac{1}{r}f(n)$$

From the third case of the **Master Theorem,** it follows that even in the general case, $T(n) = \Theta(n)$.

**EXAMPLE**

Consider the recurrence

$$T(n) = 4T\left(\frac{n}{4}\right) + n^{1/2}$$

that occurs in the analysis of some image processing algorithms. We have

$$a = 4, b = 4, \ \log_b a = \ \log_4 4 = 1, \text{and } f(n) = n^{1/2} = n^{\log_b a - 1/2}.$$

By case 1 of the **Master Theorem,** $T(n) = \Theta(n)$.

**EXAMPLE**

Consider the recurrence

$$T(n) = T\left(\frac{n}{2}\right) + 1$$

that occurs in the analysis of Binary Search. Corresponding to the notation used in our statement of the **Master Theorem,** we have $f(n) = 1 = n^{\log_2 1}$, so by case 2 of the **Master Theorem,** $T(n) = \Theta(\log n)$.

**EXAMPLE**

Consider the recurrence

$$T(n) = 2T\left(\frac{n}{2}\right) + n$$

that occurs in the analysis of Merge Sort. Corresponding to the notation used in our statement of the **Master Theorem,** we have $a = 2$, $b = 2$, and $f(n) = n = n^{\log_b a}$. So, by case 2 of the **Master Theorem,** $T(n) = \Theta(n \log n)$.

**EXAMPLE**

Consider the recurrence

$$T(n) = T\left(\frac{n}{4}\right) + n^{1/2}$$

that occurs in the analysis of many mesh computer algorithms that will be presented later in the text. Corresponding to the notation used in our statement of the **Master Theorem,** we have

$$a = 1, b = 4, f(n) = n^{1/2} = \Omega(n^{\log_b a + 0.5}),$$

and

$$af(n/b) = (n/4)^{1/2} = n^{1/2}/2 = 0.5f(n).$$

So, by case 3 of the **Master Theorem,** $T(n) = n^{1/2}$.

## Summary

In this chapter, we present the Master Theorem, which provides solutions to many, although not all, types of recursive relationships. A proof of this theorem is given in Appendix 2. We show how to use this theorem with several examples.

## Chapter Notes

In this chapter, we focus on the Master Method, a cookbook approach to solving certain recurrences of the form $T(n) = aT(n/b) + f(n)$. This approach has been well utilized in texts by E. Horowitz and S. Sahni, including *Computer Algorithms/C++*, by E. Horowitz, S. Sahni, and S. Rajasekaran (Computer Science Press, New York, 1996). The paper, "A general method for solving divide-and-conquer recurrences," by J.L. Bentley, D. Haken, and J.B. Saxe, *SIGACT News*, 12(3): 36–44, 1980, appears to serve as one of the earliest references to this technique.

## Exercises

For each of the following recurrences, either solve by using the Master Theorem, or show it is not applicable, as appropriate. If the Master Theorem is not applicable, try to solve the recurrence by another means.

1. $T(n) = 2T\left(\frac{n}{2}\right) + 1$
2. $T(n) = T(n-2) + 1$
3. $T(n) = 4T\left(\frac{n}{2}\right) + n^2$
4. $T(n) = 4T\left(\frac{n}{2}\right) + n^{3/2}$
5. $T(n) = 3T\left(\frac{n}{2}\right) + n^2$
6. $T(n) = 8T\left(\frac{n}{2}\right) + \frac{n^2}{\log_2 n}$
7. $T(n) = 16T\left(\frac{n}{4}\right) + \frac{n^3}{\log_2 n}$
8. $T(n) = 2T\left(\frac{n}{2}\right) + 2^n$

# 4

# Models of Computation

In this chapter, we introduce a variety of models of computation that will be used throughout the book. Initially, we introduce the *random access machine* (*RAM*), which is the traditional sequential model of computation, *i.e.*, the *von Neumann model*. The RAM has been an extremely successful model in terms of the design and analysis of sequential algorithms targeted at traditional sequential computers.

Next, we introduce the *parallel random access machine* (*PRAM*), which is the most popular model for the theoretical study of parallel computation, largely because the PRAM allows for the design and analysis of parallel algorithms without concern for communication of data. That is, when designing an algorithm for the PRAM, one may assume that any two processors can communicate in constant time and that any processor can access any memory location in constant time. For the PRAM, we present a variety of algorithms to perform essential operations and use these algorithms to solve a number of fundamental problems.

After introducing the RAM and PRAM, we introduce parallel models of computation that rely on specific interconnection networks. Each interconnection network consists of a set of direct connections between pairs of processors that contain on-board memory. The reader might picture a chessboard in which every square is a processor with memory and every generic processor is connected to its two horizontal neighbors and its two vertical neighbors. Such *network models* include the mesh, tree, pyramid, mesh-of-trees, and hypercube, many of which have been built and sold by a variety of companies.

For these network models, we first present fundamental algorithms, including broadcasting, semigroup operations, and parallel prefix, to name a few. These fundamental algorithms are used throughout the book to build efficient solutions to higher-level problems. This method of building efficient solutions to higher-level problems from fundamental algorithms provides us with the opportunity to point out the relative positives and negatives of these models with respect to each other, as well as with respect to the RAM and PRAM.

We will then present the *Coarse-Grained Multicomputer*, a theoretical model that is designed to represent a simple, practical parallel computing system. Finally, we introduce modern production systems that are widely deployed. These include the *cloud, grid, cluster, and Network of Workstations* (*NOW*). Such multiprocessor systems are currently used by tens of thousands of companies, educational institutions, and government laboratories. These systems are typically used to solve large-scale computationally-intensive or data-intensive problems and/or to provide solutions to problems that are large in the aggregate.

Algorithms that take advantage of high-end systems, including clusters and NOWs, typically address problems that come from areas of computational science and engineering. In addition, numerous solutions to problems on such systems also involve the manipulation of large databases. These high-end computational systems, which dominate the list of top 500 most powerful computing systems[1] in the world, will be included in discussions throughout the remainder of the text as we present the design and analysis of multiprocessor algorithms to solve disciplinary problems.

We conclude the chapter by presenting some standard terminology that is used in the literature and throughout the remainder of the text.

---

[1] The reader is encouraged to review www.top500.org, which lists the 500 most powerful supercomputers in the world. At that website, the reader will also find interesting analysis and trends in supercomputing.

## RAM (Random Access Machine)

The random access machine, or RAM, is the traditional sequential model of computation, as shown in Figure 4-1. It has proved to be quite successful since algorithms designed for the RAM tend to perform as predicted on a single processing element, which is often referred to as a "core" on the processor of a standard multi-core desktop, laptop, tablet, or even cellular phone system.

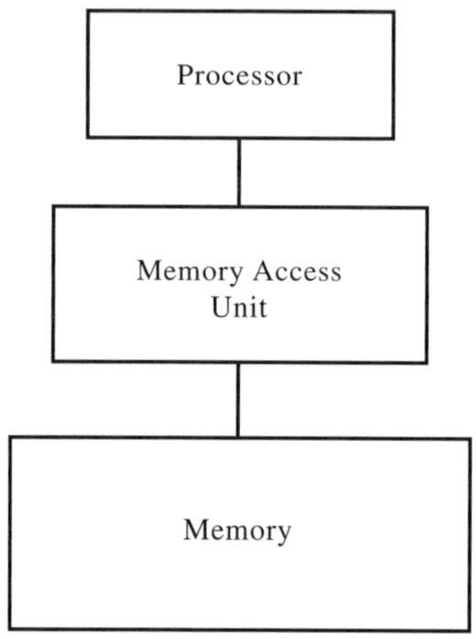


**FIGURE 4-1** *The random access machine (RAM) is a traditional sequential model of computation. It consists of a single processing element and local memory. The processor is able to access any location of memory in* $\Theta(1)$ *time through the memory access unit.*

The RAM has the following characteristics.

**Memory:** Assume that the RAM has $M$ memory locations, where $M$ is a large finite number. Each memory location has a unique address and is capable of storing a single piece of data. The memory locations can be accessed in a direct fashion. That is, there is a constant $C > 0$ such that given any memory address $A$, the data stored at address $A$ can be accessed in at most $C$ units of time. Thus, memory access on a RAM is assumed to take $\Theta(1)$ time, regardless of the number of memory locations or the particular location of a memory cell.

**Processor:** The RAM contains a single processor, without multiple cores, and executes a sequential algorithm. That is, the processor issues one instruction at a time and each instruction is performed to completion before continuing with the next instruction. We assume that the processor can perform a variety of fundamental operations. These operations include loading and storing data between memory and the processor's registers, as well as performing basic arithmetic and logical operations on the contents of the data in the registers.

**Memory Access Unit:** The memory access unit is used to create a direct connection between the processor and a memory location.

**Execution:** Each step of an algorithm consists of three phases, namely, a *read phase*, a *compute phase*, and a *write phase*. In the read phase, the processor can read data from memory into one of its registers. In the compute phase, the processor can perform basic operations on the contents of its registers. Finally, during the write phase, the processor can send the contents of one of its registers to a specific memory location. This is a high-level interpretation of a single step/cycle of an algorithm, corresponding typically to several low-level assembly or machine instructions. There is no distortion of analysis in such an interpretation, as several low-level instructions can be executed in $\Theta(1)$ time.

**Running Time:** We now consider running times for the read, process, and write phases that comprise each step of an algorithm. It is important to note that each register in the processor must be of size greater than or equal to $\log_2 M$ bits in order to accommodate $M$ distinct memory locations. Due to the fan-out of "wires" between the processor and memory, any access to memory will require $O(\log M)$ time. Notice, however, that it is often possible for $k$ consecutive memory accesses to be pipelined to run in $O(k + \log M)$ time on a slightly enhanced model of a RAM. Based on this analysis, and the fact that many computations are amenable to pipelining for memory access, we assume that both the read and the write phase of an execution cycle are performed in $\Theta(1)$ time.

Now consider the compute phase of the execution cycle. Given a set of $k$-bit registers, many of the fundamental operations can be performed in $\Theta(\log k)$ time. *The reader unfamiliar with these results might wish to consult a basic book on computer architecture and read about carry-lookahead adders, which provide an excellent example.* Therefore, since each register has $k = \Theta(\log M)$ bits, the compute phase of each execution cycle can be performed in $O(\log \log M)$ time.

Historically, one assumes that every cycle of a RAM algorithm requires $\Theta(1)$ time. This is due to the fact that neither the $O(k + \log M)$ time required for memory access nor the $O(\log \log M)$ time required to perform fundamental operations on registers typically affects the comparison of running time between algorithms. Further, these two asymptotic terms are relatively small and negligible in practice, so much so that the running time of an algorithm is typically dominated by other considerations, including the following.

- The amount of data being processed.
- The instructions executed.
- The error tolerance.

It is important to note that this $\Theta(1)$ time model is the standard, and that most authors do not go into the analysis or justification of it. However, this model is properly referred to as the *uniform analysis* variant of the RAM. This is the model that we will assume throughout the book when we refer to the RAM and, as mentioned, it is the model that is used in all standard algorithms and data structures books.

## PRAM (Parallel Random Access Machine)

The parallel random access machine, or PRAM, is the most widely utilized theoretical parallel model of computation. The PRAM was developed with the intention that it would do for parallel computing what the RAM did for sequential computing. That is, the PRAM was developed so that parallel algorithms would run on real parallel computers using resources such as running time, memory, and number of processors, as predicted by analysis on the PRAM. The advantage of the PRAM is that it ignores communication and allows the user to focus on the potential parallelism available in the design of an efficient solution to the given problem. The PRAM has the following characteristics. (See Figure 4-2.)

**Processors:** The PRAM consists of $n$ identical processors, say $P_1, P_2, \ldots, P_n$, each of which is a RAM. These processors are often referred to as *processing elements*, *PEs*, or simply *processors.*

**Memory:** As with the RAM, there is a common/shared/global memory. All processors have access to this shared memory. It is typically assumed that there are $m \geq n$ memory locations.

**Memory Access Unit:** The memory access unit of the PRAM is similar to the memory access unit of the RAM in that it assumes that every processor can access any memory location in $\Theta(1)$ time.

It is important to note that *the processors are not directly connected to each other*. So, if two processors wish to communicate in their effort to solve a problem, they must do so through the common memory. That is, PRAM algorithms often treat the common memory as a *blackboard*, to borrow a term from *Artificial Intelligence*. For example, suppose processor $P_1$ maintains the value $X$ in one of its registers. Then, in order for another processor to access this value, $P_1$ must write $X$ to a location in the global memory. Once it is there, other

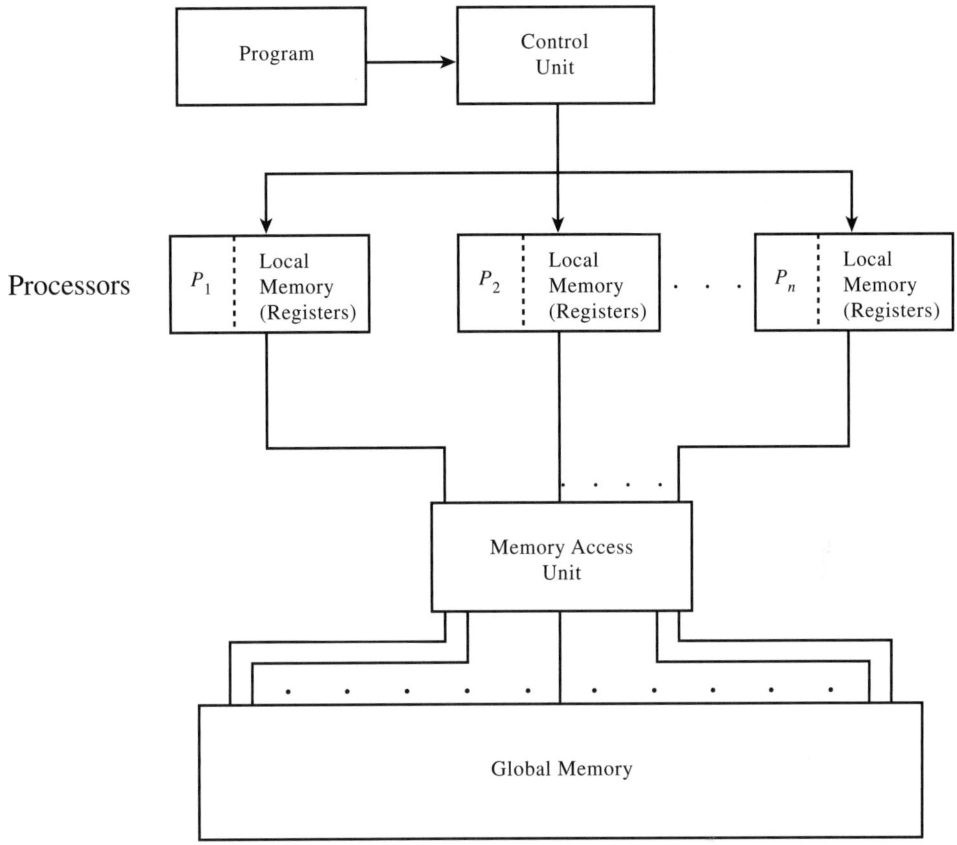


**FIGURE 4-2** *Characteristics of a parallel random access machine (PRAM). The PRAM consists of a set of identical processing elements connected to a global memory through a memory access unit. All memory accesses are assumed to take* $\Theta(1)$ *time.*

processors that know the location can read this value. Therefore, even though processors are not directly connected, a pair of processors can share a unit of data in $\Theta(1)$ time.

**Execution:** As with the RAM, each step of an algorithm consists of three phases, namely, a *read phase*, a *compute phase*, and a *write phase*. During the read phase, all $n$ processors can read simultaneously a piece of data from a, not necessarily unique, memory location. Each processor places the data item into one of its registers. In the compute phase, every processor can perform a fundamental operation on the contents of its registers. This phase is identical to that of the RAM. However, $n$ independent compute operations, one per processor, can be performed simultaneously. During the write phase, every processor can simultaneously write an item from one of its registers to the global memory. Again, the write stage is very similar to the write stage of the RAM, with the exception that $n$ simultaneous writes, one per processor, can occur.

It is important to note that conflicts can occur during both the read and write phases. We will consider resolutions to such conflicts shortly.

**Running Time:** As with the RAM, we consider the time to perform the read, compute, and write phases of a cycle. An analysis of the read and write phases will again show that the time required for each processor to access any of the $m$ memory locations, due to constraints in fan-in, is $O(\log m)$. As discussed previously, this can be improved by pipelining to allow $k$ consecutive requests from all $n$ processors to be handled in $O(k + \log m)$ time. Similarly, every processor can perform fundamental operations on its own $k$-bit registers in $O(\log k)$ time. Finally, by assuming a *uniform access* model, we can assume that every cycle can be performed in $\Theta(1)$ time. Although this uniform access model is not perfect, it suits most of our needs and is the standard model used in the literature.

**Memory Access (resolving data access conflicts):** Conflicts in memory access can arise during both the read phase and the write phase of a cycle. How should one handle this? For example, if two processors are simultaneously trying to read from the same memory location, should only one succeed? If so, which one? If two processors are simultaneously trying to write to the same memory location, *i.e.*, the classic "race condition," which one, if either, succeeds? Further, should a processor be notified if it didn't succeed? After we define the traditional PRAM variants of read and write access options, we will discuss ways in which they can be combined in order to produce common PRAM models.

**Read Conflicts:** Handling read conflicts is fairly straightforward. Two basic models exist.

1. **Exclusive Read (ER).** The definition of an *ER PRAM* states that only one processor is allowed to read from a given memory location during a cycle. That is, it is considered an *illegal instruction* if at any point during the execution of a procedure, two or more processors attempt to read from the same memory location. One might alternately think of this as a run-time error. So, while $n$ reads may occur simultaneously during a read phase, no two simultaneous reads are permitted to be from the same memory location.

2. **Concurrent Read (CR).** The definition of a *CR PRAM* states that multiple processors are allowed to read from the same memory location during a clock cycle. So, while $n$ reads may occur simultaneously during a read phase, there is no restriction on the memory locations from which the processors may read.

**Write Conflicts:** Handling write conflicts is much more complex than handling read conflicts. A variety of options exist.

1. **Exclusive Write (EW).** The *exclusive write* model permits only one processor to write to a given memory location during a clock cycle. That is, it is considered to be a run-time error if a piece of code results in two or more processors attempting to write to the same memory location during the same clock cycle. So, while *n* write operations may occur during the write phase, no two processors can write to the same memory location.

2. **Concurrent Write (CW).** The *concurrent write* model allows multiple processors to attempt to write to the same memory location simultaneously. That is, as many as *n* write operations occur during the write phase with no restriction on which processors write to which memory locations. This brings up an interesting point. How should one resolve write conflicts? A variety of arbitration schemes have been used in the literature. We list some of the popular ones.

   a. **Priority CW.** The *priority CW* model assumes that if two or more processors attempt to write to the same memory location during the same clock cycle, the processor with the highest priority succeeds. In this case, it is assumed that processors have been assigned priorities in advance of such an operation, and that the priorities are unique. Notice that there is no feedback to the processors as to which processor succeeds and which processor(s) fail.

   b. **Common CW.** The *common CW* model assumes that all processors attempting a simultaneous write to a given memory location during the same clock cycle will write the same value. A run-time error occurs otherwise.

   c. **Arbitrary CW.** The *arbitrary CW* model is quite interesting. This model assumes that if multiple processors try to write simultaneously to a given memory location during the same clock cycle, then one of them, arbitrarily, will succeed.

   d. **Combining CW.** The *combining CW* model assumes that when multiple processors attempt to write simultaneously to the same memory location during the same clock cycle, the values written by these multiple processors are "magically" combined, and this combined value will be written to the memory location in question. Popular operations for the combining CW model include arithmetic functions such as **sum** and **product,** logical functions such as **and, or,** and **xor,** and higher-level fundamental operations such as **min** and **max.**

**Standard PRAM Models.** Now that we have defined some of the common ways in which reads and writes are arbitrated during the read and write phases of an operation, respectively, on a PRAM, we will discuss the three popular PRAM models.

1. **CREW (Concurrent Read, Exclusive Write).** The *CREW PRAM* is one of the most popular models because it is intuitively appealing to assume that concurrent reads may occur, but concurrent writes may not occur.

2. **CRCW (Concurrent Read, Concurrent Write).** The *CRCW PRAM* allows for both concurrent reads and concurrent writes. When we use such a model, the details of the concurrent write must be specified. Several choices of CW were discussed above.

3. **EREW (Exclusive Read, Exclusive Write).** The *EREW PRAM* is the most restrictive form of a PRAM in that it forbids both concurrent reads and concurrent writes. Since only exclusive reads and writes are permitted, it is much more of a challenge to design efficient algorithms for this model. Further, due to the severe restrictions placed on the EREW PRAM model, notice that any algorithm designed for the EREW PRAM will run on the CREW and CRCW models. Note, however, that an optimal EREW algorithm may not be optimal on the CREW or CRCW PRAM.

One might also consider an *ERCW* (Exclusive Read, Concurrent Write) *PRAM* to round out the obvious combinations of options for PRAM reads and writes. However, the ERCW model is rarely mentioned in the literature. Notice that intuitively, if one assumes that hardware can perform concurrent writes, it is not intellectually satisfying to assume that concurrent reads cannot be performed.

**Discussion.** The PRAM is one of the earliest and most widely studied parallel models of computation. However, it is important to realize that the PRAM is not a physically realizable machine. That is, while a machine with PRAM-type characteristics can be built with relatively few processors, such a machine could not be built with an extremely large number of processors. In part, this is due to current technological limitations in connecting processors and memory. Regardless of the practical implications, the PRAM is a powerful model for studying the logical structure of parallel computation under conditions that permit theoretically optimal communication. Therefore, the PRAM offers a model for exploring the limits of parallel computation, in the sense that the asymptotic running time of an optimal PRAM algorithm should be at least as fast as that of an optimal algorithm on any other architecture with the same number of processors. It is worth noting that there are some exceptions to this last statement, but they are outside the scope of this book.

The great speed that is available through an efficient use of a PRAM is primarily due to the fact that the PRAM ignores processor-to-memory communication costs. This is because any two processors can communicate in $\Theta(1)$ time through the shared memory, as follows.

a. A source processor writes a data value to a predetermined memory location.
b. A destination processor reads the data value from the predetermined memory location.

By contrast, parallel computers based on other architectures may require a non-constant amount of time for communication between certain pairs of processors, as the data must be passed step-by-step between neighboring processors as it travels from a source processor to a destination processor.

**EXAMPLES: FUNDAMENTAL ALGORITHMS**

Now that we have introduced many of the critical aspects of the PRAM, it is appropriate to present several fundamental algorithms, along with some basic analysis of time and space. The first operation we consider is that of *broadcasting* a piece of information. For example, suppose a particular processor contains a piece of information in one of its registers that is required by all other processors. We can use a broadcast operation to distribute this information from the given source processor to all destination processors. The first broadcast algorithm we present is targeted at Concurrent Read PRAMs. Note that this algorithm will not work on Exclusive Read PRAM models.

**Concurrent Read (CR) PRAM Broadcast Algorithm**
**Initial Condition:** One processor, $P_i$, stores a value $d$ in its $j^{\text{th}}$ register, $r_{i,j}$, that is to be broadcast to all processors.
**Exit Condition:** All processors store the value $d$ in one of their registers.

**Action:**

```
1. Processor Pi writes the value d from register
   ri,j to shared memory location X.
2. In parallel, all processors read d from shared
   memory location X.
End Broadcast
```

Step 1 runs in $\Theta(1)$ time, assuming that each processor knows whether or not it is the one broadcasting the data. Step 2 runs in $\Theta(1)$ time by using a concurrent read operation. Therefore, the running time of this algorithm is $\Theta(1)$, regardless of the number of processors.

Now, consider the broadcast problem for an Exclusive Read PRAM. A simple modification to the previous algorithm could be made to allow each processor, in sequence, to read the data item from shared memory location $X$. However, this would result in an algorithm that runs in time linear in the number of processors, which is an inefficient use of the PRAM. That is, given an Exclusive Read PRAM with $n$ processors, such an algorithm would run in $\Theta(n)$ time. Alternately, we could make multiple copies of the data, one for each processor, and then allow all processors to read their respective copies simultaneously. We will take this approach. The algorithm follows.

**Exclusive Read (ER) PRAM Broadcast Algorithm**
**Assumption:** The ER PRAM has $n$ processors.
**Initial Condition:** One processor, $P_i$, has the data value $d$ stored in its $j^{\text{th}}$ register, $r_{i,j}$, that is to be broadcast to all processors.
**Exit Condition:** All processors have the value $d$.

**Action:**

```
1. Processor P_i writes the value d from register r_{i,j}
   to shared memory location X_1.
2. For i = 1 to ⌈log_2 n⌉, do
      In parallel, processors P_j, j ∈ {1,...,2^{i-1}}, do
         read d from X_j
         If j + 2^{i-1} ≤ n then P_j writes d to x_{j+2^{i-1}}
      End Parallel
   End For
3. Every processor P_i, i ∈ {1,...,n}, reads d from X_i.
End Broadcast
```

This is an example of a *recursive doubling* procedure. Note that during every iteration of the For-loop, the number of copies of the item to be broadcast doubles, either exactly or approximately. In general, such a procedure also implies that the number of processors that maintain a copy of the data item doubles from one step of the algorithm to the next. Note that for a PRAM, the number of memory locations associated with processors that contain a copy of the data doubles during each successive step. Since each step of reading and writing can be performed in $\Theta(1)$ time, regardless of the number of processors participating in the operation, an ER PRAM with $n$ processors can perform a broadcast operation in $\Theta(\log n)$ time.

Next, we consider PRAM algorithms to perform fundamental operations involving arrays of data. Let's assume that the input to these problems consists of an array $X = [x_1, x_2, \ldots, x_n]$, where each entry $x_i$ might be a record containing multiple fields. When there is no confusion, we will make references to the key fields simply by referring to an entry $x_i$.

A *semigroup operation* is a *binary associative operation.* The term *binary* implies that the operator $\otimes$ takes two operands, say $x_i$ and $x_j$, as input, and $\otimes$ is a well-defined operation for any values of its operands. The result of a semigroup operation $\otimes$ on $x_i$ and $x_j$ is denoted as $x_i \otimes x_j$. The term *associative* means that $(x_i \otimes x_j) \otimes x_k = x_i \otimes (x_j \otimes x_k)$. Note that we do not assume that $\otimes$ is commutative. That is, $x_i \otimes x_j$ may or may not be equal to $x_j \otimes x_i$. Popular semigroup operators include **max, min, sum, product,** and **OR.** Sometimes we find it easier to present a concrete example. Therefore, we will choose **min** as our operator for several of the semigroup operations that follow. We first consider an efficient algorithm on a RAM to compute the minimum of a set *X*.

**RAM Minimum Algorithm**
**Input:** Array *X*.
**Output:** Minimum entry of *X*.
**Local variables:** *i*, *min_so_far*

**Action:**

```
    min_so_far = x1
    For i = 2 to n, do
      If xi < min_so_far then min_so_far = xi
    End For
    return min_so_far
End Minimum
```

The analysis of this algorithm's running time is fairly straightforward. Given an array of size *n*, each entry is examined exactly once, utilizing $\Theta(1)$ time per entry. Therefore, the running time of the algorithm is $\Theta(n)$. Further, given an unordered set of data, this is optimal since if we fail to examine any of the *n* elements, we may miss the minimal value and thus produce an incorrect result. Next, we consider the space requirements of this algorithm. Notice that $\Theta(n)$ space is used to store the array of data, and that the algorithm uses $\Theta(1)$ additional space.

Now consider a semigroup operation for the PRAM. The first algorithm we present is fairly intuitive. The algorithm uses a bottom-up, level by level, tree-like computation, as shown in Figure 4-3. The algorithm computes the minimum of disjoint pairs of items, then the minimum of these disjoint pairs, and so on until the global minimum has been determined. In Figure 4-4, we show how the processors cooperate in order to compute the minimum. The reader should note that the processing presented in Figure 4-4 performs the computations that are presented in Figure 4-3. To simplify our presentation, we assume the size of the problem, *n*, is a power of 2.

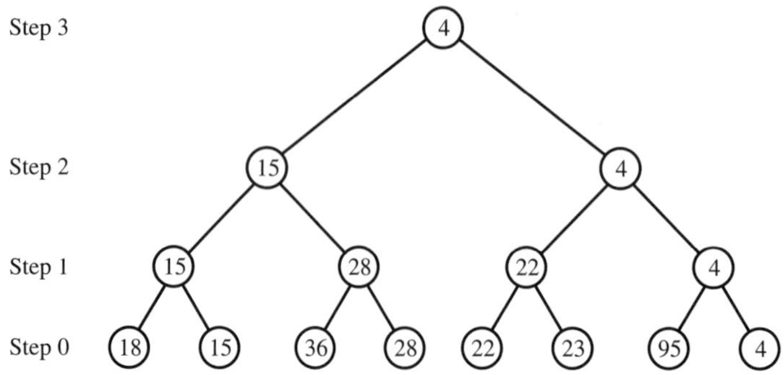


**FIGURE 4-3** *A bottom-up tree-like computation to compute the minimum of eight values. The global minimum can be computed in 3 parallel steps. Each step reduces the total number of candidates by half since computations are performed in a simultaneous fashion throughout one level of processors at a time, from leaves to root.*

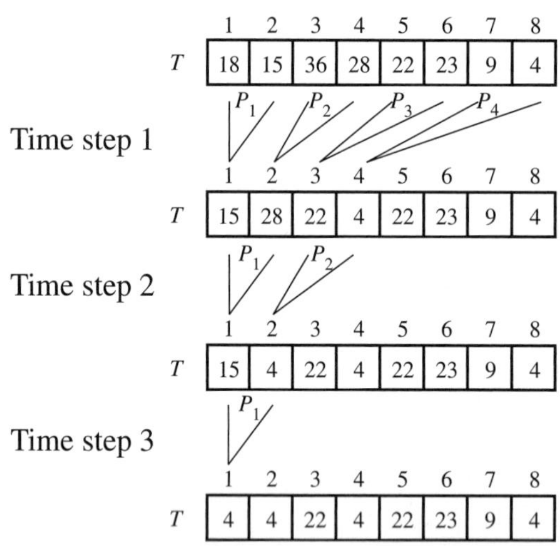


**FIGURE 4-4** *Another view of the minimum operation presented in Figure 4-3. This shows the action of a set of 4 processors. The data is presented as residing in a horizontal array. The processors that operate on data are shown for each of the three time steps.*

**PRAM Minimum Algorithm (initial attempt)**
**Assumption:** The CR or ER PRAM has $n$ processors.
**Input:** An array $X=[x_1, x_2, \ldots, x_n]$, in which the entries are drawn from a linearly ordered set.
**Output:** A smallest entry of $X$.

**Action:**

```
1. Copy X to a temporary array T = [t₁, t₂, ..., tₙ].
2. For i = 1 to log₂ n, do
       In parallel, processors Pⱼ, j ∈ {1, ..., n/2^i}, do
            a. Read t_{2j-1} and t_{2j}
            b. Write min {t_{2j-1}, t_{2j}} to tⱼ
       End Parallel
   End For
3. If desired, broadcast t₁ = min {x₁, x₂, ..., xₙ}
End Minimum
```

Step 1 of the algorithm runs in constant time since all processors $P_j$ can, in parallel, copy an element in $\Theta(1)$ time. That is, every processor can execute a statement of the form $t_j \leftarrow x_j$ in constant time. Notice that if we do not care about preserving the input data, then we could omit Step 1. Step 2 runs in $\Theta(\log n)$ time. This step performs the bottom-up, tree-type operation of computing pairwise minima, then minima of minima, and so forth. The broadcast operation can be performed in $\Theta(1)$ time on a CR PRAM and in $\Theta(\log n)$ time on an ER PRAM. Thus, the algorithm runs in $\Theta(\log n)$ total time.

However, time is not the only measure of the quality of an algorithm. Sometimes we care about the efficient utilization of additional resources. We define a measure that considers both running time and productivity of the processors, as follows.

**Definition:** Let $T_{par}(n)$ be the time required for an algorithm on a parallel machine with $n$ processors. The *cost* of such an algorithm is defined as cost $= n \times T_{par}(n)$, which represents the total number of cycles *available* during the execution of the given algorithm.

Since $n$ processors are available in the preceding PRAM algorithm to determine the minimum value of an array, the cost of the algorithm is $n \times \Theta(\log n) = \Theta(n \log n)$. That is, during the time that the algorithm is executing, the machine has the *capability* of performing $\Theta(n \log n)$ operations, regardless of how many operations it actually performs. Since the machine has the capability of performing $\Theta(n \log n)$ operations, and the *problem* can be solved with $\Theta(n)$ operations on a RAM, we know that this PRAM algorithm is *not cost-optimal*.

Let's consider how we might improve this algorithm. In order to improve the cost of the algorithm, we might consider either reducing the number of processors, reducing the running time, or both. We might argue that with the model we have defined, we cannot combine more than a fixed number of data values in a processor during one clock cycle. Therefore, it must take a logarithmic number of clock cycles to combine the input data. Since our argument suggests that $\Theta(\log n)$ time is required, let's consider reducing the number of processors. So, consider the question of how many processors are required in order to obtain a cost-optimal algorithm without sacrificing the running time. That is, assuming that the running time remains at $\Theta(\log n)$, what is the value of $P$, the number of processors, that will yield $P \times \Theta(\log n) = \Theta(n)$? The answer to this query is that the number of processors must be $P = \Theta(n/\log n)$.

The algorithm that follows shows how to utilize $P = \Theta(n/\log n)$ processors in order to determine the global minimum of $n$ values in $\Theta(\log n)$ time on a PRAM. Given a parallel architecture, where the processors can store more than a constant amount of data, the algorithm that follows will serve as an illustration of a heterogeneous fine-grained/coarse-grained algorithmic paradigm. Specifically, such an approach typically includes the following steps.

- An initial RAM algorithm that is run simultaneously on all processors.
- A "fine-grained" algorithm that operates on a single value per processor.

In addition, at times there is a final pass that executes a RAM algorithm simultaneously on all processors. See Figures 4-5 and 4-6. To simplify our presentation, we assume that $n = 2^k$ for some positive integer $k$. Note that if this assumption is not true, minor modifications can be made to the algorithm that do not affect the asymptotic running time.

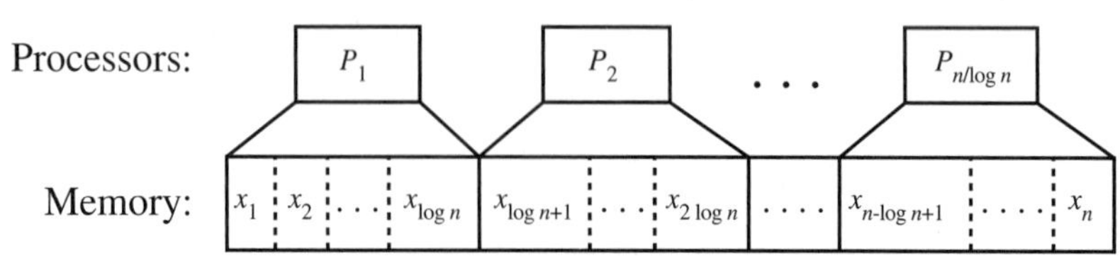


**FIGURE 4-5** *Improving the performance of a PRAM algorithm by requiring each of n/log n processors to be responsible for* log *n data items.*

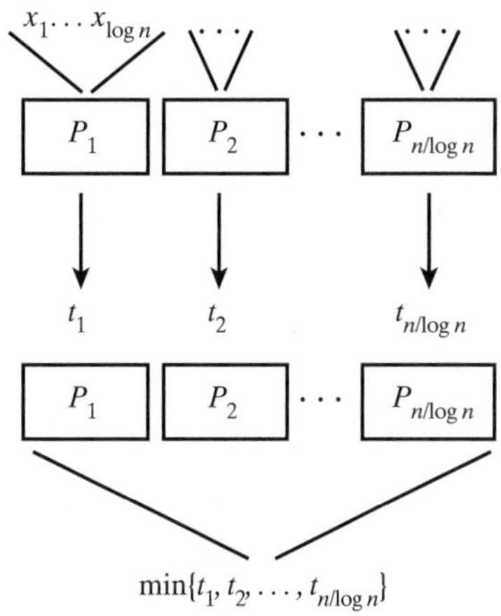


**FIGURE 4-6** *An algorithm for computing the minimum of n items with $n/\log_2 n$ processors on a PRAM. Initially, every processor sequentially determines the minimum of the $\log_2 n$ items that it is responsible for. Once these $n/\log_2 n$ results are known, then the minimum of these values can be determined in* $\Theta(\log(n/\log n)) = \Theta(\log n - \log\log n) = \Theta(\log n)$ *time on a PRAM with $n/\log_2 n$ processors.*

**PRAM Minimum Algorithm (efficient and cost-*optimal*)**
**Assumption:** The ER or CR PRAM has $n/\log_2 n$ processors.
**Input:** An array $X = [x_1, x_2, \ldots, x_n]$, drawn from a linearly ordered set.
**Output:** A smallest entry of $X$.

**Action:**

1. Conceptually partition the data into $n/\log_2 n$ disjoint sets of $\log_2 n$ items each. In parallel, every processor $P_j$ computes $t_j = \min\{x_i\}_{i=(j-1)\log_2 n+1}^{j\log_2 n}$ using an optimal RAM algorithm, given previously. Since the data set operated on by $P_j$ has size $\Theta(\log n)$, this operation runs in $\Theta(\log n)$ time.
2. Use the previous PRAM algorithm to compute $\min\{t_1, t_2, \ldots, t_{n/\log_2 n}\}$ with $n/\log_2 n$ processors in $\Theta(\log(n/\log n)) = \Theta(\log n)$ time.

End Minimum

The algorithm just described uses asymptotically fewer processors than there are data items of concern. This is an approach that we utilize throughout the text when considering cost-optimal or cost-efficient algorithms. In particular, we divide the data items over the number of processors. For example, suppose there are $P$ processors and $D$ data items. Then we assume every processor is responsible for approximately $D/P$ items. Each processor first works on its set of $D/P$ items in a sequential manner. After the sequential phase of the algorithm completes, each processor has reduced its information to only one item of concern, which in this case is the minimum of the items for which the processor is responsible. Finally, one item per processor is used as input into the simple, non-optimal parallel algorithm to complete the task. This may seem to be a contradiction, but we will see several times in this book that a non-optimal algorithm can be a key tool in designing an optimal algorithm. Notice that this final parallel operation uses $P$ items with $P$ processors. Therefore, this PRAM algorithm runs in $\Theta(\log n)$ time on $n/\log_2 n$ processors. This results in a cost of $n/\log_2 n \times \Theta(\log n) = \Theta(n)$, which is optimal. Therefore, we have a cost-optimal PRAM algorithm for computing the minimum entry of an array of size $n$ that also runs in time-optimal $\Theta(\log n)$ time.

Now, let's consider the problem of searching an *ordered* array on a PRAM. That is, given an array $X = [x_1, x_2, \ldots, x_n]$ in which the elements are in some predetermined order, construct an efficient algorithm to determine if a given query element $q$ is present. Without loss of generality, let's assume that our array $X$ is given in nondecreasing order. If $q$ is present in $X$, we will return an index $i$ such that $x_i = q$. Notice that $i$ is not necessarily unique.

First, let's consider a traditional binary search on a RAM. Given an ordered set of data, we have previously discussed how to perform a binary search in worst-case $\Theta(\log n)$ time (see Chapter 2, "Induction and Recursion"). Using this result as the base case for the parallel models, we know that we are aiming for algorithms with a worst-case total *cost* of $\Theta(\log n)$, which is an extremely tight bound. The first model we consider is the CRCW PRAM.

**CRCW PRAM Algorithm to Search an Ordered Array (initial attempt)**
**Assumption:** We use an *arbitrary* CRCW PRAM of $n$ processors.
**Input:** An ordered array, $X = [x_1, x_2, \ldots, x_n]$, and *search_value*, the value sought
**Output:** *succeeds*, a flag indicating whether or not the search succeeds, and *location*, an index at which the search succeeds, if it does

**Action:**

```
Processor P_1 initializes succeeds = false
In parallel, every processor P_i does the following.
  1. read search_value and x_i {Note that CR is used
     to read search_value.}
  2. If x_i = search_value then
```

```
            succeeds = true
            location = i
          End If
      End Parallel
    End Search
```

When this CRCW algorithm terminates, the value of the Boolean variable *succeeds* will be *true* if and only if *search_value* is found in the array. In the event that the item is found, the variable *location* is set to a position in the array where *search_value* exists. This position need not be unique, as there might be duplicate data values in the array. Now let's consider the running time of the algorithm. Notice that the initial concurrent read runs in $\Theta(1)$ time. The time for every processor simultaneously to compare its element to the query element is $\Theta(1)$. Finally, the two concurrent write operations run in $\Theta(1)$ time. Notice that the concurrent writes exploit the arbitrary property of the CRCW PRAM. Therefore, the total running time of the algorithm is $\Theta(1)$. Consider the cost of the algorithm on this architecture. Since $\Theta(1)$ time is required on a machine with $n$ processors, the total cost is a less-than-wonderful $\Theta(n)$. Next, we present an alternative algorithm that is somewhat slower but more cost-efficient than the previous algorithm.

**CRCW PRAM Algorithm to Search an Ordered Array (cost efficient)**
**Assumption:** The *arbitrary* CRCW PRAM has $f(n) = O(n)$ processors. For simplicity, we assume that $f(n)$ is a factor of $n$.
**Input:** An ordered array $X = [x_1, x_2, \ldots, x_n]$, and *search_value*, the item to search for

**Action:**

Processor $P_1$ initializes *succeeds* = *false*.
In parallel, every processor $P_i$ conducts a binary search on the subarray $\left[x_{\frac{(i-1)n}{f(n)}+1}, x_{\frac{(i-1)n}{f(n)}+2}, \ldots, x_{\frac{in}{f(n)}}\right]$
End Search

The algorithm above is interesting in that it presents the user with a continuum of options in terms of the number of processors utilized and the effect that this number will have on the running time and total cost. So, if a primary concern is minimizing cost, notice that by using one processor, the worst case running time will be $\Theta(\log n)$ and the cost will be $\Theta(\log n)$, which is optimal. In fact, with the number of processors set to one, notice that this is the RAM binary search algorithm.

Now, suppose we are concerned with minimizing the running time. Then the more processors we use, the better off we are, although using more than $n$

processors has no positive effect on the running time. In the case of an $n$ processor system, we have already seen that the running time is $\Theta(1)$. In general, the worst-case running time of this algorithm is $\Theta(\log(n/f(n)))$, and the cost is $\Theta(f(n)\log(n/f(n)))$. In particular, notice that if we use $f(n) = \Theta(\log n)$ processors, the worst-case running time will be $\Theta(\log n)$, as in the case of the RAM, but presumably with a smaller constant of proportionality. In other words, this PRAM implementation should run significantly faster if other factors such as chip speed, optimized code, and so on, are the same. The cost of $\Theta(\log^2 n)$ will be very good, though not quite optimal.

## Distributed-Memory vs. Shared-Memory Machines

Multiprocessor machines, *i.e.*, parallel computing systems, are typically constructed with some combination of shared and distributed memory. When we discuss such memory, it is important to note that we are discussing traditional, off-chip, main memory. This memory is sometimes referred to as secondary memory to differentiate it from the various on-chip or near-chip cache memories.

A *shared-memory machine* provides physically shared memory for the processors, as shown on the left side of Figure 4-7. For small shared-memory machines,

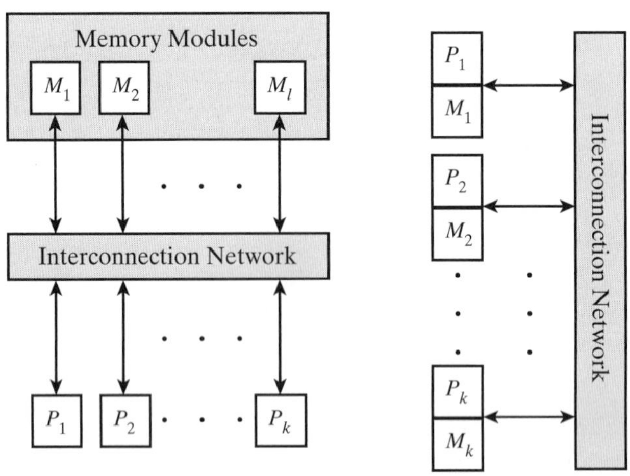


**FIGURE 4-7** *A traditional shared-memory machine is presented on the left, in which all k processors operate through an interconnection network and have equal unit-time access to all l memory modules. A traditional distributed-memory machine is presented on the right in which each of the k processing elements, i.e., processor and memory pairs, communicates with every other processing element through an interconnection network.*

networks can be constructed so that every processor can access every memory location in the same amount of time. Unfortunately, such machines cannot currently scale to large numbers of processors while preserving uniformly fast access time to memory.

In a *distributed-memory machine*, each processing element only has access to its own private/local memory, as shown on the right side of Figure 4-7. That is, in terms of the models discussed in this book, *distributed-memory machines do not have global memory*. Instead, one can think of the total memory of a distributed-memory multiprocessor system as being *distributed* among the processors. On such machines, communication links are provided in order to allow processors to communicate with each other. This set of communication links defines the architecture's *interconnection network*. So, in order for two processors that are not directly connected by a communication link to communicate, they must send data through intermediate processors that form a path between the two processors of interest. That is, processors that need to communicate must send messages to each other through their architecture's interconnection network, which consists of the processing elements and their processor-to-processor bidirectional communication links.

Specifically, a distributed-memory parallel computer consists of a set of processing elements, *i.e.,* processor-memory pairs, and a well-defined set of bidirectional interconnections between these processing elements. So, if processor $P_i$ needs a copy of some information stored in the memory of processor $P_j$, then this information must be transported from processor $P_j$ to processor $P_i$. This operation can be performed by having $P_i$ initiate a request for information, which is sent through the interconnection network to processor $P_j$, followed by $P_j$ sending the requested information back through the interconnection network to processor $P_i$. Such a communication can also be performed by a well thought-out algorithm in which processor $P_j$ simply sends the information through the interconnection network to $P_i$ without receiving such a request.

In particular, it is very important to note that transporting a message from $P_i$ to $P_j$ might involve sending the message from $P_i$ to $P_a$ to $P_b$ to $P_c$ to ... to $P_j$, where consecutive pairs of processors in the sequence are directly connected by communication links. That is, it is important to recognize that there is no guarantee that $P_i$ and $P_j$ are directly connected by the interconnection network, though there is a guarantee that in a distributed-memory parallel computer there exists at least one path between every pair of processors.

## Interconnection Networks

In this section, we consider distributed-memory machines, which are constructed as processor-memory pairs connected by communication links to each other in a well-defined pattern. As stated in the previous section, a distributed-memory machine consists of a set of processors, where every pair of processors need not be connected, but in which there must exist a *path* between every pair of processors.

These machines also have a global control unit, which is used to broadcast instructions *simultaneously to all* processors in the network. Once an instruction is broadcast, it is executed by every processor simultaneously before the next instruction is issued. An important form of an instruction is a *conditional instruction*, which might act as a mask in terms of which processors perform operations of substance. For example, an instruction might be of the form "if the contents of register $A$ is even, then add the contents of register $B$ to the contents of register $C$ and put the result in register $D$." So, given a distributed-memory system with $n$ processors, then all $n$ processors will execute that instruction during the same clock cycle. However, only a processor with an even value stored in register $A$ will add the contents of its register $B$ to the contents of its register $C$ and put the result in its register $D$. So, if $1 \leq m \leq n$ processors have an even value stored in register $A$, then $m$ processors will simultaneously update the contents of their respective registers $D$. That is, $m$ updates will occur simultaneously and depending on the values of registers $B$ and $C$ in each of these $m$ processors, this might result in $m$ different values being computed and stored throughout the distributed-memory machine.

These processor-memory pairs are often referred to as *processing elements*, or *PEs*, or sometimes just as *processors*, when this term will not cause confusion. The efficient use of an interconnection network to route data on a multiprocessor machine is often critical in the development of an efficient parallel algorithm. Interconnection networks can be characterized in a variety of ways. Some of the terminology used for this purpose follows.

1. **Degree of the network:** The term *degree* comes from graph theory. The *degree of a processor* is defined to be the number of bidirectional communication links attached to the processor. That is, the degree of processor $A$ is the number of other processors to which processor $A$ is *directly* connected. If we think of processors as corresponding to vertices and the communication links as corresponding to edges in an undirected graph, the degree of a processor is the degree of the corresponding vertex. Similarly, the *degree of a network* is the maximum degree of any processor in the network. Naturally, networks of high degree become very difficult to manufacture, even though high degree networks can be constructed to increase the efficiency of large data movement. From a practical point of view, with current technology, it is desirable to use networks of low degree whenever possible. In fact, if we are concerned with scaling the network to extremely large numbers of processors, then a small fixed degree is highly desirable.
2. **Communication diameter:** The *communication diameter* of a network is defined to be the maximum of the minimum distance between any pair of processors. That is, the communication diameter represents the longest path between any two processors, assuming that a shortest path between processors

is always chosen. Therefore, a distributed-memory machine with a low communication diameter is highly desirable, in that it allows for efficient communication between arbitrary pairs of processors.

3. **Bisection width:** The *bisection width* of a network is defined to be the minimum number of wires that have to be removed in order to disconnect the network into two approximately equal size subnetworks. In general, machines with a high bisection width are more costly to build, but they provide the possibility of moving large amounts of data efficiently.
4. **I/O bandwidth:** The input/output bandwidth is not a primary concern in terms of the algorithms we consider in this book, as we typically assume that the data is already in the machine before our algorithms are initiated. However, when considering the construction of a real machine, I/O bandwidth is certainly important.
5. **Running time:** When comparing models of computation, it is often enlightening to consider the time required to perform *fundamental* operations. Such operations include the following.
   - Semigroup computations, such as **min, max, sum,** and so forth.
   - Prefix computations, which will be defined later.
   - Fundamental data movement operations, such as broadcast and sort.

   In fact, as we introduce some of the network models below, we will consider the efficiency of such routines.

To summarize, we want to design the interconnection network, *i.e.*, network of processors, of a distributed-memory machine with certain characteristics. In order to reduce the cost of building a processor, we would like to minimize the degree of the network. In order to minimize the time necessary for individual messages to be sent long distances, we want to minimize the communication diameter. Finally, in order to reduce the probability of contention between multiple messages in the system, we want to maximize the bisection width. Unfortunately, it is often difficult to balance these design criteria, which may be in conflict. For example, a small network degree tends to result in a small bisection width and a large communication diameter. In fact, we also would prefer to use a simple design, as simplicity reduces the hardware and software design costs. Further, we would like the network embedded in the machine to be scalable, so that machines of various sizes can be manufactured in an economically feasible fashion.

Note that for the majority of parallel models of computation, it is assumed that all processors in a given model are identical. That is, all processors in a given parallel model have the identical register/cache/memory structure, internal bus, speed of computation, and so forth. It is also assumed that all processors have the same number of interconnection ports, even if they are not all used for some processors. In addition, it is assumed that the time it takes for data to travel across all communication links is identical.

## Processor Organizations

In this section, we introduce a variety of distributed-memory network models. A *network model* consists of a set of processing elements and a well-defined set of links that connect the processors so that there are no isolated processors. These network models are characterized by *i*) the interconnection scheme between the processors, and *ii*) the fact that the memory is distributed among the processors. Again, it is very important to recognize that *these network models are distributed-memory systems and do not have any shared memory*. In particular, it is the interconnection pattern that distinguishes these distributed-memory architectures from one another.

As we introduce several such network models, we will consider some of the measures discussed in the previous section. Notice, for example, that the communication diameter often serves as a limiting factor in the running time of an algorithm. This measure serves as an upper bound on the time required for an arbitrary pair of processors to exchange information, and therefore as a lower bound on the running time of any algorithm that requires global exchanges of information.

**Terminology:** We say that two processors in a network are *neighbors* if and only if they are directly connected by a communication link. We assume these communication links are *bidirectional*. That is, if processor $A$ and processor $B$ are connected by a communication link, we assume that using this link, processor $A$ can send data to processor $B$ and, simultaneously, processor $B$ can send data to processor $A$. Since sorting is a critical operation in network-based parallel machines, we need to define what it means to sort on such architectures. Suppose we have a list, $X = [x_1, x_2, \ldots, x_n]$, with entries stored in the processors of a distributed-memory machine. In order for the members of $X$ to be considered ordered, there must be a meaningful ordering not only of those entries that are stored in the same processor, but also of entries in different processors. We assume that there is an ordering of the processors. The notation $R(i)$ is used to denote the ranking function for the processor labeled $i$. We say the list $X$ is in ascending order if $i < j$ implies

1. $x_i \leq x_j$, and
2. if $x_i$ is stored in $P_r$ and $x_j$ is stored in $P_s$, then either $r = s$ or $R(r) < R(s)$.

Similar statements can be made for data stored in descending order.

### Linear Array

A *linear array of size n* consists of a string of $n$ processors, $P_1, P_2, \ldots, P_n$, where every generic processor is connected to its one or two neighbors (see Figure 4-8). Specifically, processor $P_i$ is connected to its two neighbors, processors $P_{i-1}$ and $P_{i+1}$, for all $2 \leq i \leq n - 1$. However, the two end processors, $P_1$ and $P_n$, are each only connected to one neighbor. Given a linear array of size $n$, let's consider some of the basic measures.

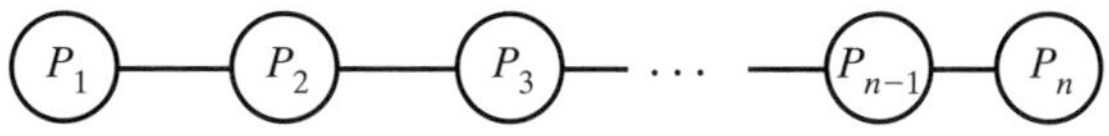

**FIGURE 4-8** *A linear array of size n.*

Since $n - 2$ processors have degree 2 and two processors have degree 1, the degree of the network is 2.

Now consider the communication diameter, *i.e.,* the maximum over the minimum distances between any two processors. Consider the minimum number of communication links that need to be traversed in order for processors $P_1$ and $P_n$ to exchange information. The only way that a piece of data originating in $P_1$ can reach processor $P_n$ is by traversing through the other $n - 2$ processors. Therefore, the communication diameter is $\Theta(n)$. This is important in that it tells us that time linear in the number of processors is required to compute any function for which all processors may need to know the final answer. Now consider the minimum time required for a computation to be performed on two arbitrary pieces of data. Notice that information from processors $P_1$ and $P_n$ could meet in processor $P_{\lceil n/2 \rceil}$. However, this still requires $\lceil n/2 \rceil - 1$ communication steps. Therefore, time linear in the number of processors is required, even in the best case, to solve a problem that requires arbitrary pairs of data to be combined.

Finally, we consider the bisection width of a linear array of size $n$. The bisection width of a linear array of size $n$ is 1, as the communication link between processors $P_{n/2}$ and $P_{(n/2)+1}$ can be severed, and the result would be two linear arrays, each of size $n/2$. This is important when one considers an operation, such as sorting, that might require data to move from one side of the linear array to the other. The bisection width tells us that there is only one line to carry data between each half of the linear array. This is similar to thinking about moving everyone as efficiently as possible from exotic island $A$ to exotic island $B$ *and* everyone from exotic island $B$ to exotic island $A$ if there exists only a one lane bridge between $A$ and $B$. So, if there are $n/2$ people on island $A$ and $n/2$ people on island $B$, then regardless of the algorithm, it must take at least time proportional to $n$ to accomplish this task.

It is important to note that some of the terminology introduced in the last section can be used to determine lower bounds on time required to solve a problem. *The distinction between a lower bound on the time to solve a problem and the lower bound on the running time of an algorithm is critical.*

A lower bound on the time to solve a particular problem requires one to prove that a solution to the *problem* requires a minimum amount of time. When attempting to prove a lower bound on the time to solve a problem, one should not consider particular algorithms for solving the problem. One should consider properties of the problem, including input, output, required computations, number of processors, interconnection network, and so forth.

A lower bound on the running time of an algorithm requires a proof that the *algorithm* requires a certain amount of time.

Understanding this distinction is important when one is considering efficient solutions to a problem. So, if we are able to construct an algorithm with a running time that matches the lower bound on the time to solve a problem, then we know that this algorithm is asymptotically optimal. That is, no other algorithm could possibly be asymptotically faster. Conversely, if the best algorithm we can construct to solve a problem does not match the lower bound for the running time to solve the problem, then we cannot state that the algorithm is asymptotically optimal. It may be that we are just not bright enough to provide an asymptotically superior algorithm. Then again, it may be that we are not bright enough to prove a higher lower bound on the running time to solve the problem.

Now let's consider some basic operations on a linear array of size $n$. Assume that a set of data, $X = [x_1, x_2, \ldots, x_n]$, is distributed so that data element $x_i$ is stored in processor $P_i$. First, we consider the problem of determining the minimum element of array $X$. This can be done in several ways.

Our first approach is one in which all the data march left in lockstep fashion, and as each data item reaches processor $P_1$, this leftmost processor updates the running minimum, as shown in Figure 4-9. That is, during the first step of the algorithm,

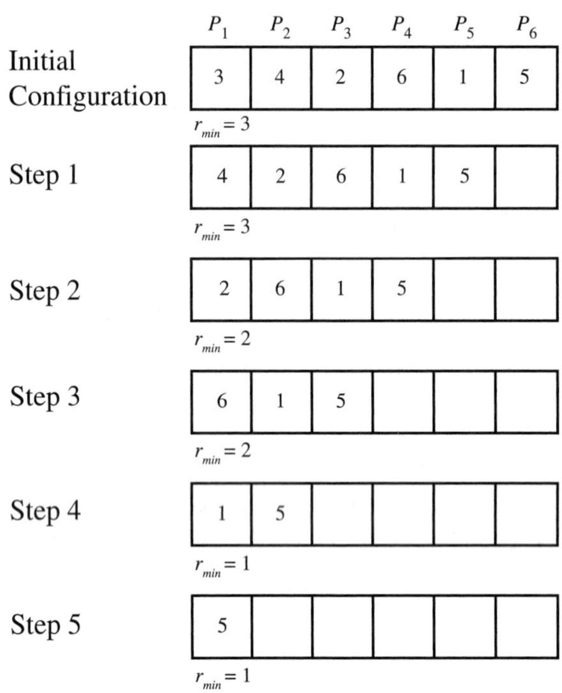


**FIGURE 4-9** *Computing the minimum of n items initially distributed one per processor on a linear array of size n. Notice that the data is passed in lockstep fashion to the left during every time step. The leftmost processor, $P_1$, keeps the running minimum.*

processor $P_1$, viewed as the leftmost processor in the linear array, sets a register that we call *running_min* to $x_1$. During the second step of the algorithm, simultaneously and in lockstep fashion, processors $P_2, \ldots, P_n$ each send their data elements to the left. Now processor $P_1$ sets *running_min* = min $\{running\_min, x_2\}$. The procedure continues so that after $i$ steps, processor $P_1$ has the value of min $\{x_1, \ldots, x_i\}$. Therefore, after $n$ steps, the minimum of $X$ is stored in processor $P_1$.

Now, let's assume that every processor needs to know this minimum value, which is currently stored in processor $P_1$. Initially, processor $P_1$, viewed as the leftmost processor in the linear array, can send this value to processor $P_2$, its right neighbor. If this value continues to move to the right during each step, then after a total of $n - 1$ such steps, all $n$ processors will know the minimum of $X$. Therefore, the minimum can be determined and distributed to all processors in $\Theta(n)$ time on a linear array of size $n$. Note that this result holds true, in fact, for any semigroup operation.

Notice that computing and distributing the result of a semigroup operation on a linear array of size $n$ runs in $\Theta(n)$ time, which results in a cost of $n \times \Theta(n) = \Theta(n^2)$. This is not very appealing, considering that such problems can be easily solved in $\Theta(n)$ time on a RAM. Therefore, we should consider whether or not it is possible to do better on a linear array of size $n$. Notice that we simply cannot do better, due to the $\Theta(n)$ communication diameter.

Next, consider whether or not we can reduce the communication diameter by reducing the number of processors and arrive at a cost-optimal algorithm. We have seen that if we use only one processor, given that all $n$ data items are stored in the processor, then computing the minimum of $n$ items can be performed in $\Theta(n)$ time, which would yield an optimal cost of $\Theta(n)$. However, this is not desirable if we wish to use a parallel computer, since the running time has not been reduced over that of the RAM. So, while we have considered the two extremes in terms of numbers of processors, *i.e.*, both 1 and $n$, let's now consider some intermediate value.

What value should we consider? We would like to balance the amount of work performed by each processor with the work performed by the network. That is, we would like to balance the number of data elements per processor, since the local minimum algorithm runs in time linear in the number of elements, with the number of processors, since the communication diameter is linear in the number of processors. Therefore, we consider a linear array of size $n^{1/2}$, where each processor is responsible for $n^{1/2}$ items, as shown in Figures 4-10 and 4-11.

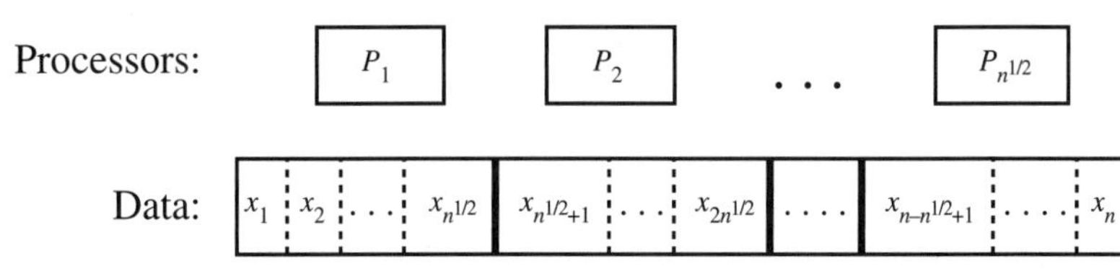


**FIGURE 4-10** *Partitioning the data in preparation for computing the minimum of n items initially distributed on a linear array of size $n^{1/2}$ in such a fashion that each of the $n^{1/2}$ processors stores $n^{1/2}$ items.*

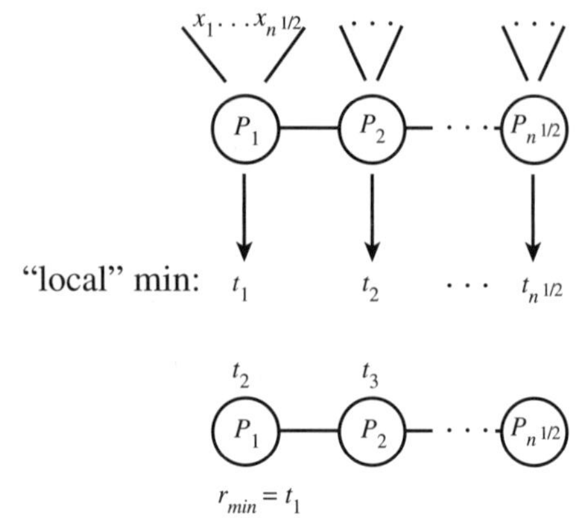


**FIGURE 4-11** *Computing the minimum of n items initially distributed on a linear array of size $n^{1/2}$ in such a fashion that each of the $n^{1/2}$ processors stores $n^{1/2}$ items. In the first step, every processor sequentially computes the minimum of the $n^{1/2}$ items that it is responsible for. In the second step, the minimum of these $n^{1/2}$ minima is computed on the linear array of size $n^{1/2}$ by the typical lockstep algorithm.*

An algorithm to compute the minimum of $n$ data items, evenly distributed on a linear array of size $n^{1/2}$, can be constructed with two major steps. First, each processor runs the standard sequential semigroup algorithm on its own set of data. This step runs in time linear in the number of data elements stored in the processor. Next, the previous linear array semigroup algorithm is run on these $n^{1/2}$ partial results. At the end of the parallel algorithm, the final global result will be known. Note that the final result is the minimum of the $n^{1/2}$ local minima. Therefore, the running time of this hybrid algorithm is dominated by the $\Theta(n^{1/2})$ time to perform the RAM algorithm simultaneously on all processors, followed by the $\Theta(n^{1/2})$ time to determine the minimum of these $n^{1/2}$ local minima, distributed one per processor on a linear array of size $n^{1/2}$. Hence, the running time of the algorithm is $\Theta(n^{1/2})$, which results in an optimal cost of $\Theta(n)$.

Note that utilizing more processors does not always result in a faster algorithm. This medium-grained algorithm that processes $n$ data items with $n^{1/2}$ processors is actually faster than the earlier, fine-grained algorithm that processes $n$ data items with $n$ processors for computing the minimum on a linear array.

Suppose we have a linear array of size $n$, but that the data does not initially reside in the processors. That is, suppose we have to input the data as part of the problem. For lack of a better term, we will call this model an *input-based linear array*. Assume that the data is input to the leftmost processor, *i.e.*, processor $P_1$, and only one piece of data can be input per unit time. Assume that the data is input in reverse order and that at the end of the operation, every processor $P_i$

must know both $x_i$ and the minimum of $X$. This can be accomplished by the following algorithm.

In the first step, processor $P_1$ takes as input $x_n$ and initializes *running_min* to $x_n$. In the next step, processor $P_1$ sends $x_n$ to processor $P_2$, inputs $x_{n-1}$, and assigns *running_min* = min{*running_min*, $x_{n-1}$}. In general, during each step of the algorithm, the data continues to march in lockstep fashion to the right, and the leftmost processor continues to store the running minimum, as shown in Figure 4-12. After $n$ steps, all processors have their data element, and the leftmost processor stores the minimum of all $n$ elements of $X$. As before, processor $P_1$ can then broadcast

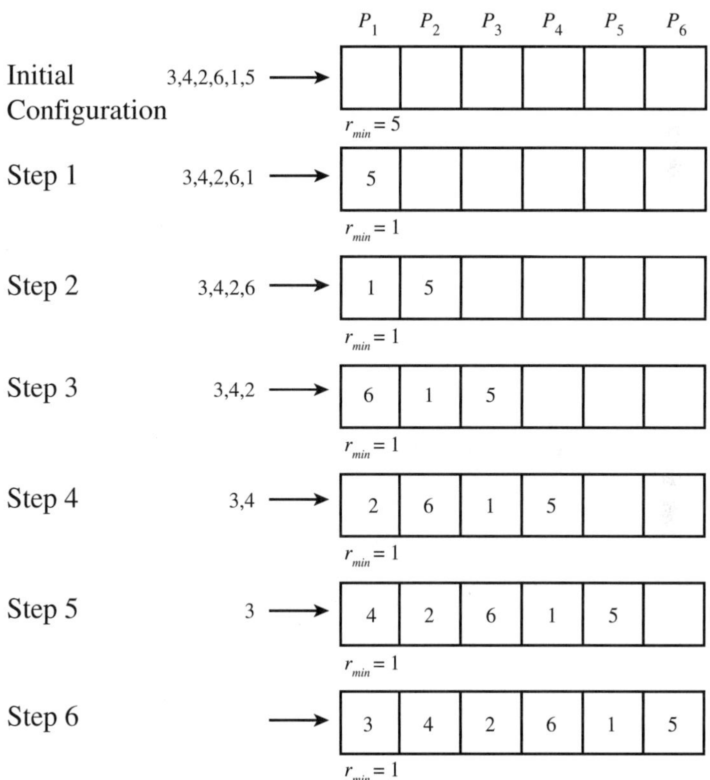


**FIGURE 4-12** *Computing the minimum on an input-based linear array of size 6. During Step 1, processor $P_1$ takes as input $x_6 = 5$ and initializes running_min to 5. During Step 2, processor $P_1$ sends $x_6$ to processor $P_2$, inputs $x_{n-1} = 1$, and assigns running_min = min(running_min,$x_{n-1}$) which is the minimum of 5 and 1. The algorithm continues in this fashion as shown, sending data to the right in lockstep fashion while the first processor keeps track of the minimum value of the input data.*

the minimum to all other processors in $n - 1$ additional steps. Therefore, we have an optimal $\Theta(n)$ time algorithm for the input-based linear array to take in all input and have every processor $P_i$ store both $x_i$ and the minimum of $X$.

We introduced this input-based variant of the linear array so that we could extrapolate an algorithmic strategy. Suppose we wanted to emulate this input-based linear array algorithm on a traditional linear array of size $n$, in which the data is initially stored in the array.

This could be done with a *tractor-tread* algorithm, where the data moves as one might observe on the tractor-tread of many large construction vehicles or tanks. In the initial phase, view the data as marching to the right, *i.e.*, riding the top of the tractor tread, so that when a data element hits the right wall, it turns around and begins its march along the bottom of the tractor tread to the left (see Figure 4-13).

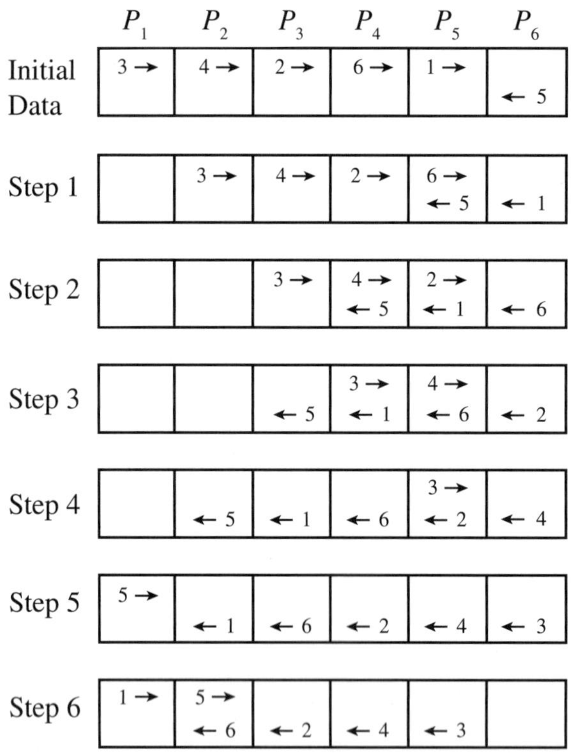


**FIGURE 4-13** *A tractor-tread algorithm. Data in the linear array moves to the right until it hits the right wall, where it reverses itself and starts to march to the left. Once the data hits the left wall, it again reverses itself. A revolution of the tractor-tread algorithm is complete once the initial data resides in its original set of processors. Given a linear array of size n, this algorithm allows every processor to view all n data items in Θ(n) time.*

That is, every processor initially starts by sending its data to the right, with the exception of the rightmost processor. When the rightmost processor receives data, during the next step, the rightmost processor will send the data to the left so that the data item can begin its journey to the left. When a data element hits the left wall, *i.e.*, a data element is taken into the leftmost processor, it will again reverse direction and begin its journey to the right.

In general, every processor will continue to pass all the data that it receives in the direction it is going, with the exception of the first and last processors, which emulate the walls in a goalless game of air hockey, and serve to reverse the direction of data. So, after the initial $n - 1$ steps, notice that processor $P_1$ will store a copy of $x_n$, processor $P_2$ will store a copy of $x_{n-1}$, and so forth. That is, the data is now positioned so that processor $P_1$ is prepared to accept as "input" $x_n$, as in the input-based linear array algorithm. In fact, the input-based linear array algorithm can now be emulated with a loss in running time of these initial $n - 1$ steps. Therefore, the asymptotic running time of the algorithm remains as $\Theta(n)$.

Notice that this tractor-tread algorithm is quite powerful. It can be used, for example, to rotate all of the data through all of the processors of the linear array. This gives every processor an opportunity to view all of the data. Therefore, such an approach can be used to allow every processor to compute the result of a semigroup operation in parallel. Notice that we have traded off an initial setup phase for the postprocessing broadcast phase. However, as we shall soon see, this approach is even more powerful than it might initially appear.

We now consider the very important problem of sorting data. The communication diameter of a linear array of size $n$ tells us that $\Omega(n)$ time is necessary to sort $n$ pieces of data distributed in an arbitrary fashion one item per processor. Alternately, by considering the bisection width, we know that in the worst case, if the $n/2$ items on the left side of the linear array belong on the right side of the array, and vice versa, then in order for $n$ items to cross the single middle wire, $\Omega(n/1) = \Omega(n)$ time is required.

We will now construct such a time-optimal sorting algorithm for this model. We first consider a simple algorithm for the input-based linear array of size $n$. Notice that the leftmost processor $P_1$ will view all $n$ data items as they come in. If that processor retains the smallest data item and never passes it to the right, then at the end of the algorithm, processor $P_1$ will store the minimum data item. Further, if processor $P_2$ performs the same minimum-keeping algorithm, then at the end of the algorithm, processor $P_2$ will store the minimum data item of all $n - 1$ items that it viewed (see Figure 4-14). That is, processor $P_2$ would store the minimum of all items with the exception of the smallest item, which processor $P_1$ never passed along. Therefore, at the end of the algorithm, processor $P_2$ would store the second smallest data item.[2]

[2] This algorithm can be illustrated quite nicely in the classroom. Each row of students can simulate this algorithm running on such a machine, where the input comes from the instructor standing in the aisle.

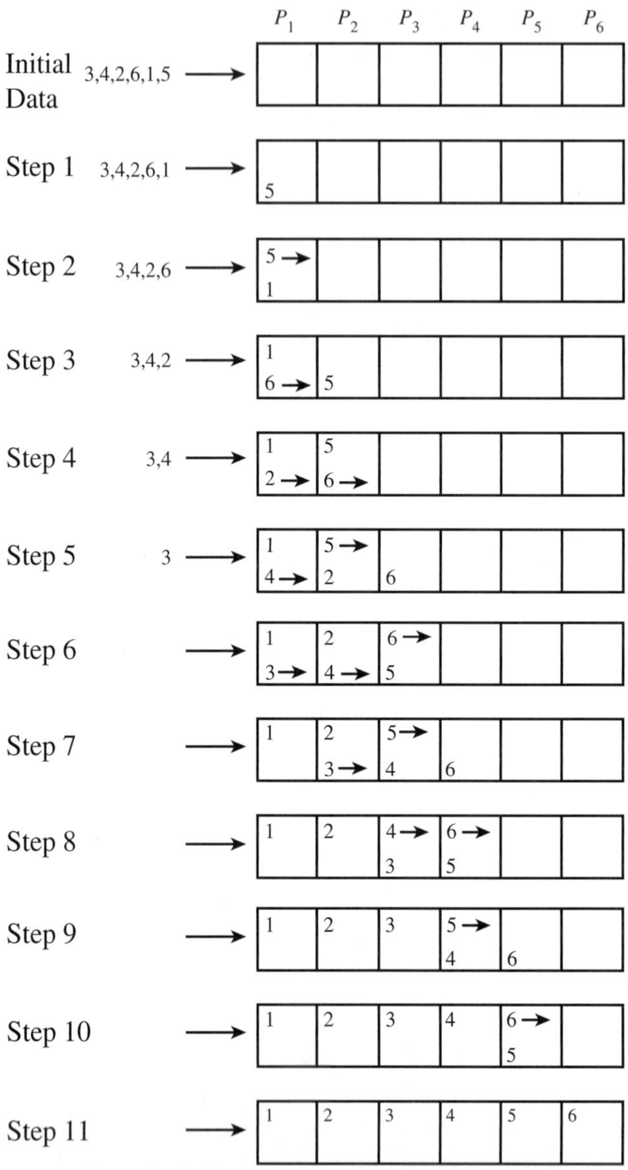


**FIGURE 4-14** *Sorting data on an input-based linear array. Every processor simply retains the item that represents the minimum value it has seen to date. All other data continues to pass in lockstep fashion to the right. Notice that this is a minor generalization of the minimum algorithm illustrated in Figure 4-12.*

We now have an optimal $\Theta(n)$ time algorithm for the input-based linear array of size $n$. By using the tractor-tread method, we can emulate this algorithm to produce a time-optimal $\Theta(n)$ time algorithm for a linear array of size $n$. As an aside, we should mention that this sorting algorithm can be viewed as a parallel version of Selection Sort. That is, the first processor views all of the data and selects the minimum. The next processor views all of the remaining data and selects the minimum, and so forth.

The final algorithm we consider for the linear array is that of computing the parallel prefix of $X = [x_1, x_2, \ldots, x_n]$. Assume that initially, every processor $P_i$ stores data element $x_i$. When the algorithm terminates, $P_i$ must store the $i^{\text{th}}$ prefix, $x_1 \otimes \ldots \otimes x_i$, where $\otimes$ is a binary associative operator. The algorithm follows.

First, we note that processor $P_1$ initially stores $x_1$, which is its final value. During the first step, processor $P_1$ sends a copy of $x_1$ to processor $P_2$, which computes and stores the second prefix, $x_1 \otimes x_2$. During the second step, processor $P_2$ sends a copy of its prefix value to processor $P_3$, which computes and stores the third prefix value, $x_1 \otimes x_2 \otimes x_3$. The algorithm continues in this fashion for $n - 1$ steps, after which every processor $P_i$ stores the $i^{\text{th}}$ prefix, as required. It is important to note that during step $i$, the $i^{\text{th}}$ prefix is passed from processor $P_i$ to processor $P_{i+1}$. That is, processor $P_i$ passes a single value, which is the result of $x_1 \otimes \ldots \otimes x_i$, to processor $P_{i+1}$. If processor $P_i$ passed all of the components of this result, $x_1, \ldots, x_i$, to processor $P_{i+1}$, the running time for the $i^{\text{th}}$ step would be $\Theta(i)$, and the total running time for the algorithm would therefore be $\Theta\left(\sum_{i=1}^{n-1} i\right) = \Theta(n^2)$. However, since only one data item is passed during every step, the running time of this algorithm is $\Theta(n)$. Notice that this is optimal for a linear array of size $n$ since the data entries stored at maximum distance must be combined. In this case, no argument can be made with respect to the bisection width, since this problem does not require large data movement.

### Ring

A ring is a linear array of processors in which the two end processors are connected to each other, as shown in Figure 4-15. That is, a *ring of size n* consists of a linear array of $n$ processors, $P_1, \ldots, P_n$, where processors $P_1$ and $P_n$ are connected. Specifically, processor $P_i$ is connected to its two neighbors, $P_{i-1}$ and $P_{i+1}$, for $2 \le i \le n - 1$, and processors $P_1$ and $P_n$ are connected to each other.

Let's examine some of our measures to see what advantages the ring provides over the linear array. The degree of both networks is 2. The communication diameter of a ring of size $n$ is approximately $n/2$, which compares favorably with the $n - 1$ of the linear array. However, notice that this factor of approximately 1/2 is only a multiplicative constant. Thus, both architectures have the same asymptotic communication diameter of $\Theta(n)$. Although the bisection width does not really make sense in this model, if one assumes that the ring

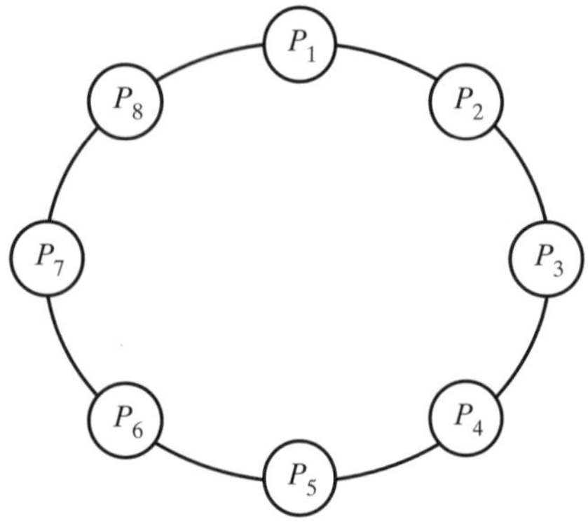


**FIGURE 4-15** *A ring of size 8. All processors in a ring are connected to 2 neighbors.*

could be broken and then each subring sealed back up, this would require severing/patching $\Theta(1)$ communication links, which is the same as the linear array. In fact, when we consider the ring compared to the linear array, the best we could hope for is a multiplicative factor of two improvement in the running time of algorithms.

In practice, being able to perform a task twice as fast is often a most welcome improvement. However, since this book is concerned primarily with the design and *asymptotic* analysis of algorithms, *i.e.*, growth *rate* of the running time of algorithms, the ring presents an uninteresting variant of the linear array, and will not be discussed further.

### Mesh

In this book, we will use the term *mesh* to refer to a 2-dimensional, checkerboard-type, mesh-based computer, except where stated otherwise. A variety of 2-dimensional meshes have been proposed in the literature. In a traditional mesh, each generic processor has four neighbors, namely, the closest processor to its north, south, east, and west. The mesh itself is constructed either as a rectangular or square array of processors, as shown in Figure 4-16.

A simple variant of the four-connected mesh is an eight-connected mesh in which each generic processor is connected to its north, south, east, and west neighbors, as well as to its northeast, northwest, southwest, and southeast neighbors. Meshes have also been proposed in which each processor has six neighbors, *i.e.*, a hexagonal mesh. Again, in this text, we use the term mesh to refer to a traditional 4-connected square array of processors. Generally, the 6-connected and 8-connected variants do not have asymptotically different running times for algorithms to solve fundamental problems than are exhibited by the 4-connected mesh.

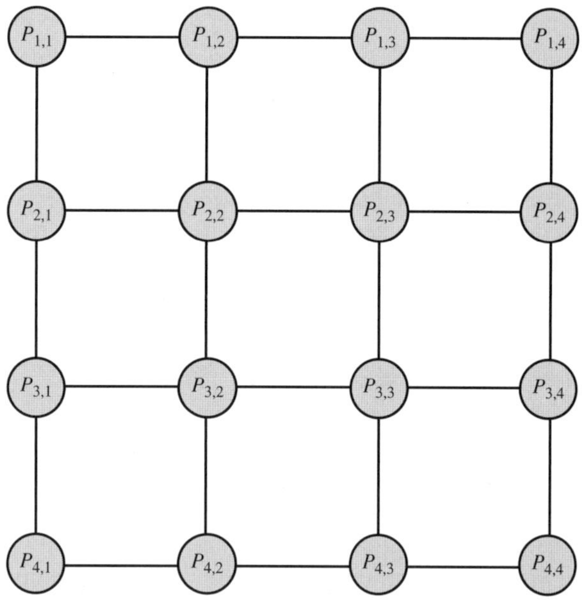


**FIGURE 4-16** *A mesh of size* 16. *Each generic processor in a traditional mesh is connected to its four nearest neighbors. Notice that there are no wraparound connections and that the processors located along the edges of the mesh have fewer than four neighbors. Processors are labeled by row and column, as shown.*

In particular, we restrict our attention to a traditional 2-dimensional square mesh, which will be referred to as a *mesh of size n*, where $n = 4^k$, for $k$ a positive integer. Throughout the text, we will show how to utilize effectively a divide-and-conquer solution strategy on the mesh. This will be done by showing how to divide a problem into either two or four independent subproblems, map each of these subproblems to a submesh, recursively solve the smaller subproblems on each submesh, and then stitch the results together.

Now, let's consider several of the measures that we have discussed. Given a mesh of size $n$, the interior processors have degree 4, the four corner processors have degree 2, and the remaining edge processors have degree 3. Therefore, the degree of a mesh of size $n$ is 4. That is, the mesh is a fixed degree network.

Consider the communication diameter, *i.e.*, the maximum distance over every pair of shortest paths in the network. Notice that on a mesh of size $n$, there are $n^{1/2}$ rows and $n^{1/2}$ columns. So, transporting a piece of data from the northwest processor to the southeast processor requires traversing $n^{1/2} - 1$ rows and $n^{1/2} - 1$ columns. That is, a message originating in one corner of the mesh and traveling to the opposite corner of the mesh requires traversing a minimum of $2n^{1/2} - 2$ communication links. Therefore, the communication diameter of a mesh of size $n$ is $\Theta(n^{1/2})$.

Notice that if we are interested in *combining* information from two processors at opposite corners of a mesh of size $n$, such information could be sent to one of the middle processors in less than $2n^{1/2} - 2$ steps. While the time to combine distant data may be an improvement over the time to transmit such data, notice that the improvement is only by a constant factor.

Determining the bisection width of a mesh of size $n$ is straightforward. If we cut the links between the middle two columns, then we are left with two rectangular meshes of size $n/2$. If this is not intellectually satisfying, then we could sever the links between the middle two rows and the middle two columns and be left with four square meshes, each of size $n/4$. In any event, the bisection width of a mesh of size $n$ is $\Theta(n^{1/2})$. Before considering some fundamental operations, we should note that the bisection width can be used to provide a lower bound on the worst-case time to sort a set of data distributed one piece per processor.

For example, suppose all data elements initially stored in the leftmost $n/2$ columns need to move to the rightmost $n/2$ columns and vice versa. Moving $n$ pieces of data between the middle two columns, which are joined by $n^{1/2}$ communication links, requires $\Theta(n/n^{1/2}) = \Theta(n^{1/2})$ time.

We now turn our attention to some fundamental mesh operations. Since the mesh can be viewed as a collection of linear arrays stacked one on top of the other and interconnected in a natural fashion, we start by observing that the mesh can implement linear array algorithms independently in every row and/or column of the mesh. Of immediate interest is the fact that the mesh can perform a row (column) rotation simultaneously in every row (column), so that every processor will have the opportunity to view all information stored in its row (column).

Recall that a row rotation consists of sending data from every processor in lockstep fashion to the right. When data reaches the rightmost processor, that rightmost processor will reverse the direction of travel of the data so that it marches to the left. When the data reaches the leftmost processor, that processor again reverses the direction of movement of the data so that it moves to the right until it reaches the processor where it originated, at which point the row rotation terminates.

Notice that at any point during the rotation algorithm, a processor is responsible for at most two pieces of data that are involved in the rotation, one that is moving from left to right, which is viewed as the top of the tractor tread, and the other that is moving from right to left, which is viewed as the bottom of the tractor tread. A careful analysis will show that exactly $2n^{1/2} - 2$ steps are required to perform a complete rotation. Recall that this operation is asymptotically optimal for the linear array.

Since a rotation allows every processor in a row (column) to view all other pieces of information in its row (column), this operation can be used to solve a variety of problems. For example, if it is required that all processors determine the result of applying some semigroup operation to a set of values distributed over all the processors in its row/column, a rotation can be used to provide a time-optimal solution.

In the following, it is useful to refer to a processor of a mesh by the notation $P_{i,j}$. The first subscript $i$ represents the $i^{th}$ row of processors, $1 \le i \le n^{1/2}$, where the rows are numbered from top to bottom. Similarly, the second subscript $j$ represents the $j^{th}$ column of processors, $1 \le j \le n^{1/2}$, where the columns are numbered from left to right. See Figure 4-16.

We now provide an algorithm for performing a semigroup operation over a set $X = [x_1, \ldots, x_n]$, initially distributed one item per processor on a mesh of size $n$. This operation consists of performing a sequence of rotations. First, a row rotation is performed in every row so that every processor knows the result of applying the operation to the data elements in its row. Next, a column rotation is performed so that every processor can determine the final result, which is a combination of every row-restricted result. Notice that if the operation $\otimes$ is *commutative, i.e.*, $u \otimes v = v \otimes u$ for all operands $u, v$, then we need not worry about which data value is in which processor. However, if the operation is not commutative, then we assume the data is distributed in *row-major* fashion, where we mean that the first $n^{1/2}$ items are distributed from left to right by index, one per processor, in the first row, while the next $n^{1/2}$ items are distributed from left to right by index, one per processor, in the second row, and so on.

**Mesh Semigroup Algorithm**
**Input:** An input set $X$, consisting of $n$ elements, such that every processor $P_{i,j}$ initially stores data value $x_{i,j}$.
**Output:** Every processor stores the result of applying the semigroup operation $\otimes$ to all of the input values.

**Action:**

a. Simultaneously, every row $i$ performs a row rotation so that every processor in row $i$ knows the product $r_i = \otimes_{j=1}^{n^{1/2}} x_{i,j}$.

b. Simultaneously, every column $j$ performs a column rotation so that every processor in column $j$ knows the product $p = \otimes_{i=1}^{n^{1/2}} r_i$. Notice that this is the desired product of $\otimes_{i=1}^{n^{1/2}} \otimes_{j=1}^{n^{1/2}} x_{i,j}$.

End *Semigroup Algorithm*

This algorithm runs in $\Theta(n^{1/2})$ time, which is optimal for a mesh of size $n$. However, on a RAM, a simple scan through the data will solve the problem in $\Theta(n)$ time. Since our $\Theta(n^{1/2})$ time algorithm on a mesh of size $n$ has a cost of $\Theta(n \times n^{1/2}) = \Theta(n^{3/2})$, it is not cost-optimal.

So, let's try to construct a cost-optimal semigroup algorithm for a mesh. In order to balance the local computation time with communication time based on the communication diameter, consider an $n^{1/3} \times n^{1/3}$ mesh, in which each processor stores $n^{1/3}$ of the data items. Initially, every processor can perform a sequential semigroup operation on its set of $n^{1/3}$ data items. Next, the $n^{2/3}$ partial results, one per processor on an $n^{1/3} \times n^{1/3}$ mesh, can be used as input to the fine-grained mesh algorithm just presented. Notice that the sequential component of the algorithm, which operates on $n^{1/3}$ data items, can be performed in $\Theta(n^{1/3})$ time. The parallel semigroup component also runs in $\Theta(n^{1/3})$ time. Therefore, the algorithm is complete in $\Theta(n^{1/3})$ time on a mesh of size $n^{2/3}$, which results in an optimal cost of $\Theta(n^{2/3} \times n^{1/3}) = \Theta(n)$.

Row and column rotations are also important components of a broadcast operation for the mesh. Suppose a data item $x$ is stored in an arbitrary processor $P_{i,j}$ of a mesh of size $n$, and we need to broadcast $x$ to all of the other $n - 1$ processors. Then a single row rotation, followed by $n^{1/2}$ simultaneous column rotations, can be used to solve this problem, as follows. (See Figure 4-17.)

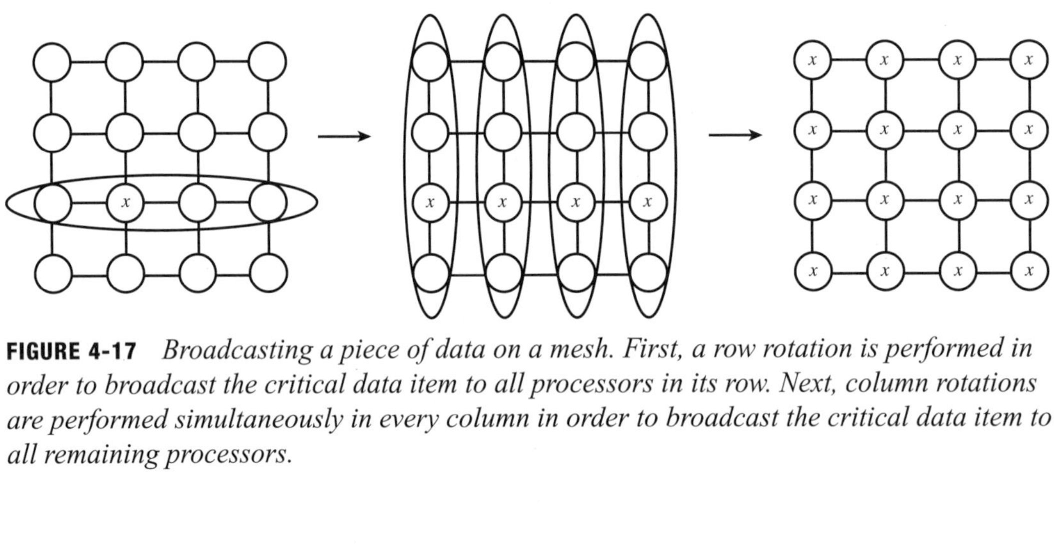

**FIGURE 4-17** *Broadcasting a piece of data on a mesh. First, a row rotation is performed in order to broadcast the critical data item to all processors in its row. Next, column rotations are performed simultaneously in every column in order to broadcast the critical data item to all remaining processors.*

**Mesh Broadcast Algorithm**
**Procedure:** Broadcast the data value $x$, initially stored in processor $P_{i,j}$, the processor in row $i$ and column $j$, to all processors of the mesh.

**Action:**

```
1. Use a row rotation in row i to broadcast x to all
   processors in row i.
```

```
2. Simultaneously, for all columns j ∈ {1,2,...,n^(1/2)},
   use a column rotation to broadcast x to every
   processor in column j.
End Broadcast
```

An analysis of the running time of the broadcast operation is straightforward. It consists of two $\Theta(n^{1/2})$ time rotations. Based on the communication diameter of a mesh of size $n$, we know that the running time for the algorithm is optimal for this architecture.

### Tree

A *tree of base size n* is constructed as a full binary tree with $n$ processors at the base level. In graph terms, this is a tree with $n$ leaves. Therefore, a tree of base size $n$ has $2n - 1$ total processors (see Figure 4-18). The root processor is connected to its two children. Each of the $n$ leaf processors is connected only to its parent. All other processors are connected to three other processors, namely, one parent and two children. Therefore, the degree of a tree network is 3. Notice that a tree with $n$ leaves contains nodes at $1 + \log_2 n$ levels. Thus, any processor in the tree can send a piece of information to any other processor in the tree by traversing $O(\log n)$ communication links. This is done by moving the piece of information along the unique path between the two processors involving their least common ancestor. That is, information flows from one processor up the tree to their least common ancestor and then down the tree to the other processor. Therefore, the $O(\log n)$ communication diameter of a tree of base size $n$ is far superior to the other network models that we have considered.

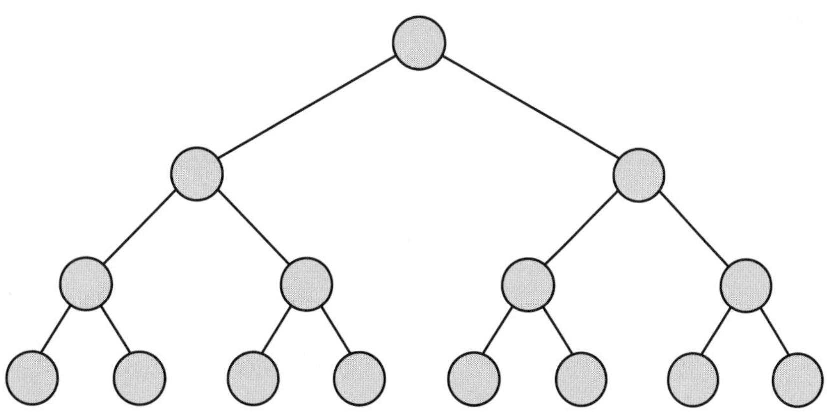

**FIGURE 4-18** *A tree of base size 8. Notice that base processors have only a single neighbor, i.e., their parent processors, the root only has two neighbors, i.e., its children processors, and the remaining processors have three neighbors, namely, one parent and two children processors.*

Now, let's consider the bisection width of a tree of base size $n$. The bisection width of a tree of base size $n$ is $\Theta(1)$, since if the two links are cut between the root and its children, a tree of base size $n$ will be partitioned into two trees, each of base size $n/2$.

A tree yields a nice (low) communication diameter, but a less than desirable (low) bisection width. So, the good news is that fundamental semigroup operations can be performed in $\Theta(\log n)$ time, but the bad news is that $\Theta(n)$ data items cannot be moved efficiently between both halves of the tree.

Consider a semigroup operation on a tree of base size $n$. Assume that $n$ pieces of data are initially distributed one per base processor. Then in order to compute a semigroup operation over this set of data, the semigroup operator can be applied to disjoint pairs of partial results in parallel as data moves up the tree level by level. Notice that after $\Theta(\log n)$ steps, the final result will be known in the root processor. Naturally, if all processors need to know the final result, it can be broadcast from the root to all processors in a straightforward top-down fashion in $\Theta(\log n)$ time. So, semigroup, broadcast, and combine-type operations can be performed in $\Theta(\log n)$ time and with $\Theta(n \log n)$ cost on a tree of base size $n$. Notice that the running time of $\Theta(\log n)$ is optimal for a tree of base size $n$, and that the cost of $\Theta(n \log n)$, while not optimal, is only a factor of $\Theta(\log n)$ from optimal since a RAM can perform these operations in $\Theta(n)$ time.

Now, consider the problem of sorting or any routing operation that requires moving data from the leftmost $n/2$ base processors to the rightmost $n/2$ processors and vice versa. Unfortunately, the root serves as a bottleneck, since it can only process a constant amount of traffic during each clock cycle. Therefore, we need $\Omega(n)$ time in order to move $n$ pieces of data from one side of the tree to the other.

Hence, the tree provides a major benefit over the linear array and mesh in terms of combining information, but is not well equipped to deal with situations that require extensive data movement.

Based on the advantages of a tree over a mesh in terms of communication diameter, and the advantages of a mesh over a tree in terms of bisection width, we will consider architectures that combine the best features of these two architectures.

### Pyramid

A *pyramid of base size n* combines the advantages of both the tree and the mesh architectures (see Figure 4-19). It can be viewed as a set of processors connected as a 4-ary tree. That is, a pyramid of base size $n$ can be viewed as a tree in which every generic node has one parent and four children, where at each level, the processors are connected as a 2-dimensional mesh. Alternately, the pyramid can be viewed as a tapering array of meshes, in which each mesh level is connected to the preceding and succeeding levels with 4-ary tree-type connections. Thus, the base level of the pyramid of base size $n$ is a mesh of size $n$, the next level up is a mesh of size $n/4$, and so on until we reach the single processor at the root.

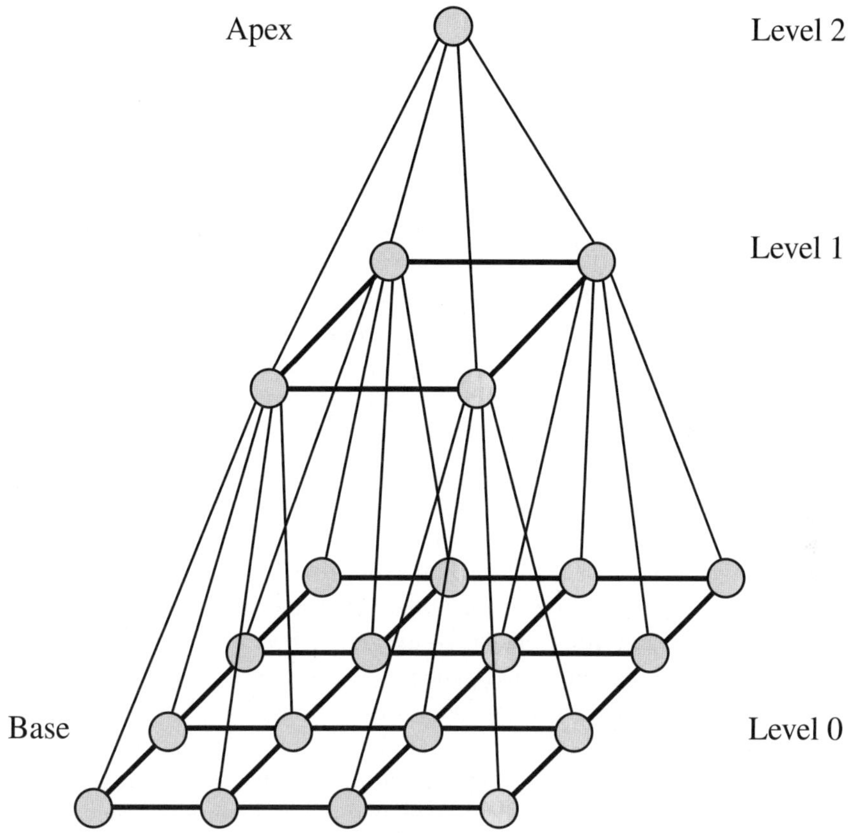


**FIGURE 4-19** *A pyramid of base size n can be viewed as a set of processors connected as a 4-ary tree, where at each level in the pyramid, the processors at that level are connected as a 2-dimensional mesh. Alternately, it can be viewed as a tapering array of meshes. The root of a pyramid only has links to its four children. Each base processor has links to its four base-level mesh neighbors and an additional link to a parent. In general, a generic processor somewhere in the middle of a pyramid is connected to one parent, four children, and has four mesh-connected neighbors.*

A careful count of the number of processors reveals that a pyramid of base size $n$ contains $(4n - 1)/3$ processors. (An exercise at the end of this chapter asks the reader to prove the latter claim.)

The root of a pyramid only has links to its four children. Each base processor has links to its four base-level mesh neighbors and an additional link to a parent. A generic processor in the middle of a pyramid has nine connections, namely, one parent, four children, and four mesh-connected neighbors. Therefore, the degree of the pyramid network is nine. The communication diameter of a pyramid of base size $n$ is $\Theta(\log n)$, since a message can be sent from the northwest base processor to the southeast base processor by traversing $2 \log_4 n$ links, which represents a worst-case scenario. This data movement can be performed by sending a piece of data upwards from the base to the root and then downwards from the root to the base.

Consider the bisection width of a pyramid of base size $n$. The reader might picture a plane, *i.e.*, a flat geometric object, passing through the pyramid, positioned so that it passes just next to the root and winds up severing connections between the middle two columns of the base. We now need to count the number of links that have been broken. There are $n^{1/2}$ at the base, $n^{1/2}/2$ at the next level, and so on up the pyramid, for a total of $\Theta(n^{1/2})$ such links. Consider passing two planes through the root, one that passes between the middle two rows of the base and the other that passes through the middle two columns of the base. This will result in four pyramids, each of base size $n/4$, with roots that were originally the children of the root processor. Therefore, as with the mesh of size $n$, the bisection width of a pyramid of base size $n$ is $\Theta(n^{1/2})$.

Now consider fundamental semigroup and combination-type operations. Such operations can be performed on a pyramid of base size $n$ in $\Theta(\log n)$ time by using tree-type algorithms, as previously described. However, for algorithms that require extensive data movement, such as moving $\Theta(n)$ data between halves of the pyramid, the mesh lower bound of $\Omega(n^{1/2})$ applies. So, the pyramid combines the advantages of both the tree and mesh architectures without a net asymptotic increase in the number of processors. Note that one of the reasons that the pyramid has not been more popular in the commercial marketplace is that laying out a *scalable* pyramid in hardware is a difficult process.

### Mesh-of-Trees

We now consider another interconnection network that combines advantages of tree and mesh connections. The mesh-of-trees is a standard mesh computer with a tree above every row and a tree above every column, as shown in Figure 4-20. Specifically, a *mesh-of-trees of base size n* consists of a mesh of size $n$ at the base with a tree above each of the $n^{1/2}$ base columns and a tree above each of the $n^{1/2}$ base rows. Notice that these $2n^{1/2}$ trees are completely disjoint except at the base. That is, row tree $i$ and column tree $j$ only have base processor $P_{i,j}$ in common. So, the mesh-of-trees of base size $n$ has $n$ processors in the base mesh, $2n^{1/2} - 1$ processors in each of the $n^{1/2}$ row trees, and $2n^{1/2} - 1$ processors in each of the $n^{1/2}$ column trees. Since the $n$ base processors appear both in the row trees and the column trees, the mesh-of-trees has a total of $2n^{1/2}(2n^{1/2} - 1) - n = 3n - 2n^{1/2}$ processors. Therefore, as with the pyramid, the number of processors in the entire machine is linear in the number of base processors.

Consider the degree of a mesh of trees of base size $n$. A generic base processor is connected to four mesh neighbors, one parent in a row tree, and one parent

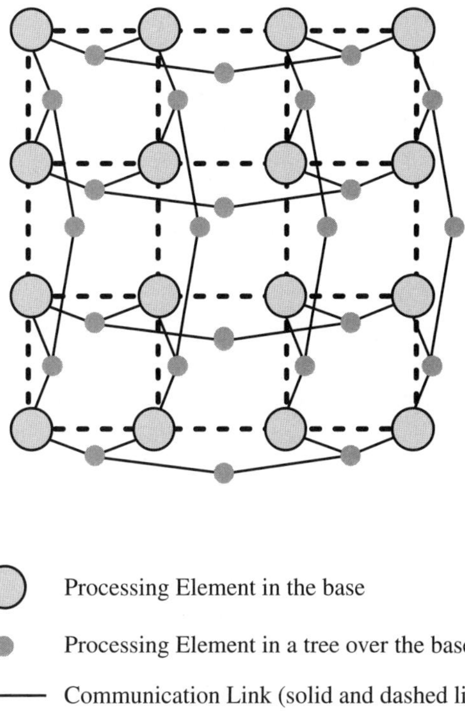


**FIGURE 4-20** *A mesh-of-trees of base size n consists of a mesh of size n at the base, with a tree above each of the* $n^{1/2}$ *base columns, and a tree above each of the* $n^{1/2}$ *base rows. Notice that the trees are completely disjoint except at the base. The mesh-of-trees of base size n has n processors in the base mesh,* $2n^{1/2} - 1$ *processors in each of the* $n^{1/2}$ *row trees, and* $2n^{1/2} - 1$ *processors in each of the* $n^{1/2}$ *column trees.*

in a column tree. Notice that processors along the edge of the mesh have fewer mesh connections. The root processor of every tree is connected to two children, and interior tree nodes are connected to one parent and two children. Note that leaf processors are mesh processors, which have already been discussed. Therefore, the degree of the mesh-of-trees of base size $n$ is six as defined by a generic base processor. Such a processor has four mesh connections and serves as a leaf processor in each of two distinct trees, namely, one column tree and one row tree.

Next, consider the communication diameter of a mesh-of-trees of base size $n$. Without loss of generality, assume that base processor $P_{a,b}$ needs to send a piece of information $x$ to base processor $P_{c,d}$. Notice that processor $P_{a,b}$ can use the tree over row $a$ to send $x$ to base processor $P_{a,d}$ in $O(\log n^{1/2}) = O(\log n)$ time. Now, processor $P_{a,d}$ can use the tree over column $d$ to send $x$ to base processor $P_{c,d}$ in $O(\log n^{1/2}) = O(\log n)$ time. Therefore, any two base processors can communicate by exploiting one row tree and one column tree in $O(\log n)$ time.

The bisection width of a mesh-of-trees can be determined by passing a plane through the middle two rows or columns, or both, of the base mesh. The analysis is similar to the pyramid, where the total number of links severed is $\Theta(n^{1/2})$.

Therefore, some of the objective measures of the pyramid and mesh-of-trees are similar. A difference between the two is that in a pyramid, the root of the pyramid serves as a bottleneck, while for the mesh-of-trees, there is no such bottleneck. In fact, the mesh-of-trees offers more paths between processors. So, one might hope that more efficient algorithms can be designed for the mesh-of-trees than for the pyramid. However, the bisection width tells us that this is not possible for problems that require significant data movement. For example, for problems such as sorting, in which all data on the left half of the base mesh might need to move to the right half, and vice versa, a lower bound of $\Omega(n/n^{1/2}) = \Omega(n^{1/2})$ still holds. One can only hope that problems which require a moderate amount of data movement can be solved faster than on the pyramid.

Let's first consider the problem of computing a semigroup operation on a set $X = [x_1, x_2, \ldots, x_n]$, initially distributed one item per base processor in some reasonable fashion. Within each row simultaneously, use the row tree to compute the operation over the set of data that resides in the row. Once the result is known in the root of a tree, it can be passed down to all base processors in the row. So, in $\Theta(\log n)$ time, every base processor will know the result of applying the semigroup operation to the elements of $X$ that are stored in its row. Next, perform a semigroup operation on this data simultaneously within each column by using the tree above each column. Notice that when the root processors of the column trees have their respective results, they all in fact have the identical final result, which they can again pass back down to the base processors. Therefore, after two $\Theta(\log n)$ time tree-based semigroup operations, all processors know the final answer. As with the tree and pyramid, this is a time-optimal algorithm. However, the cost of the algorithm is again $\Theta(n \log n)$, which is a factor of $\Theta(\log n)$ from optimal.

Next, we consider a very interesting problem of sorting a reduced amount of data. This problem surfaces at times in the middle of a solution strategy. Formally, we are given a unique set of data, $D = [d_1, d_2, \ldots, d_{n^{1/2}}]$, distributed one per processor along the first row of the base mesh in a mesh-of-trees such that processor $P_{1,i}$ stores $d_i$. We wish to sort the data so that the $i^{\text{th}}$ largest element in $D$ will be stored in processor $P_{1,i}$.

The method we use will be that of *Counting Sort*. That is, for each element $d \in D$, we will count the number of elements smaller than $d$ in order to determine the final position of $d$. In order to use Counting Sort, we first create a cross-product of the data so that each pair $(d_i, d_j)$ is stored in some processor, as shown in Figure 4-21.

$(d_1,d_1)$ — $(d_1,d_2)$ — $(d_1,d_3)$ — $(d_1,d_4)$
| | | |
$(d_2,d_1)$ — $(d_2,d_2)$ — $(d_2,d_3)$ — $(d_2,d_4)$
| | | |
$(d_3,d_1)$ — $(d_3,d_2)$ — $(d_3,d_3)$ — $(d_3,d_4)$
| | | |
$(d_4,d_1)$ — $(d_4,d_2)$ — $(d_4,d_3)$ — $(d_4,d_4)$

**FIGURE 4-21** *Creating a cross-product of items* $<d_1, d_2, d_3, d_4>$. *Notice that processor* $P_{i,j}$ *will store a copy of* $d_i$ *and* $d_j$. *That is, every processor in row i will store a copy of* $d_i$ *and every processor in column j will store a copy of* $d_j$.

Notice that since the number of elements in $D$ is $n^{1/2}$, we have room in the base mesh to store all $n^{1/2} \times n^{1/2} = n$ such pairs. This cross-product is created as follows (see Figure 4-22). First, use the column trees in parallel to broadcast $d_j$ in column $j$. At the conclusion of this $\Theta(\log n)$ time step, every base processor $P_{i,j}$ will store a copy of $d_j$. Now, using the row trees in parallel, in every row $i$, broadcast item $d_i$ from processor $P_{i,i}$ to all processors in row $i$. This operation also runs in $\Theta(\log n)$ time. Therefore, after a row and column broadcast, every processor $P_{i,j}$ will store a copy of $d_j$, which was obtained from the column broadcast, and a copy of $d_i$, which was obtained from the row broadcast. At this point, the creation of the cross-product is complete.

Let row $i$ be responsible for determining the rank of element $d_i$. Simultaneously for every processor $P_{i,j}$, set register *count* to 1 if $d_j < d_i$, and to 0 otherwise. Now use the row trees to sum the *count* registers in every row. Notice that in every row $i$, this sum, which we call $r(i)$, corresponds to the *rank* of $d_i$, the number of elements of $D$ that precede $d_i$. Finally, a column broadcast is used within every column to broadcast $d_i$ from processor $P_{i,r(i)+1}$ to processor $P_{1,r(i)+1}$, completing the procedure.

The time to create the cross-product is $\Theta(\log n)$, as is the time to determine the rank of every entry and the time to broadcast each entry to its final position. Therefore, the running time of the algorithm is $\Theta(\log n)$, which is worst-case optimal for the mesh-of-trees, due to the $\Theta(\log n)$ communication diameter and the fact that $d_1$ and $d_{n^{1/2}}$ might need to change places, *i.e.*, processors $P_{1,1}$ and $P_{1,n^{1/2}}$ might need to exchange information. The cost of the algorithm is $\Theta(n \log n)$. Notice that the cost is not optimal since $\Theta(n^{1/2})$ items can be sorted in $\Theta(n^{1/2} \log n)$ time on a RAM.

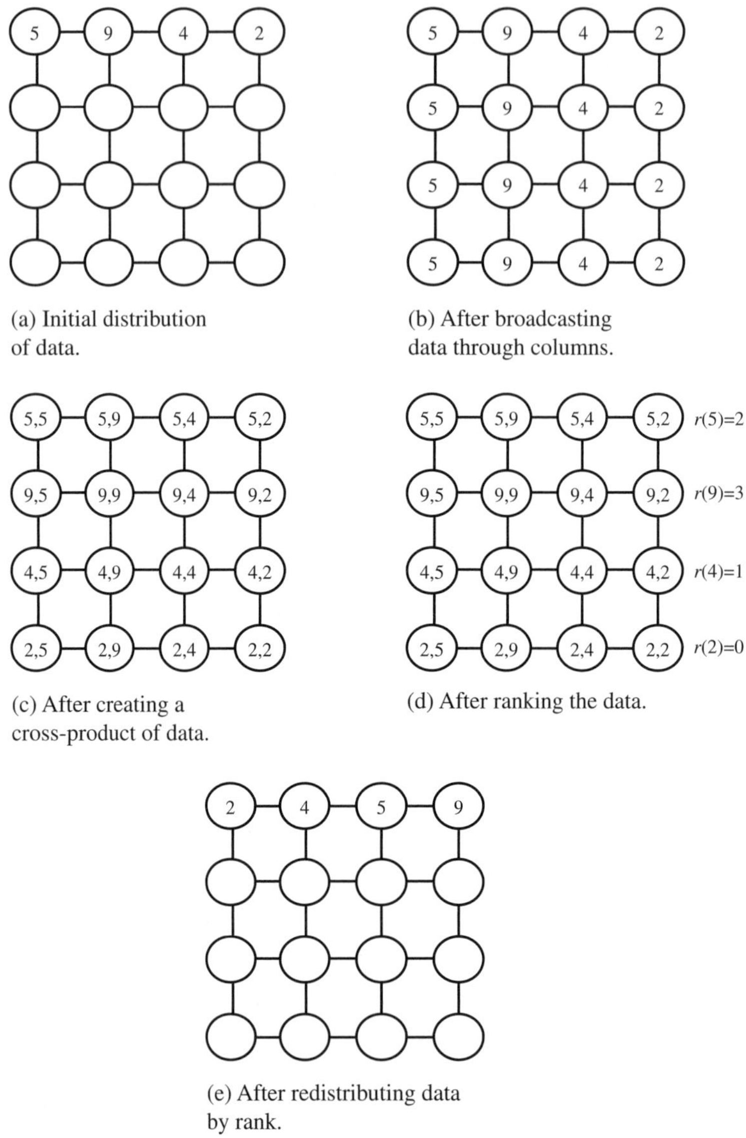


**FIGURE 4-22** *Sorting a reduced set of data on a mesh-of-trees* (*only the base mesh is shown*). (a) *The initial distribution of data consists of a single row of elements.* (b) *The data after using the column trees to broadcast the data element in every column.* (c) *The result after using the row trees to broadcast the diagonal elements along every row. At this point, a cross-product of the initial data exists in the base mesh of the mesh-of-trees.* (d) *The result of performing row-rankings of the diagonal element in each row. This step is accomplished by performing a comparison in the base mesh followed by a semigroup operation in every row tree.* (e) *The result after performing the final routing step of the diagonal elements to their proper positions according to the rankings.*

### Hypercube

The final network model we consider is the hypercube, as shown in Figure 4-23. The hypercube presents a topology that provides a desirable combination of a low communication diameter and a high bisection width. The communication diameter is logarithmic in the number of processors, which allows for fast semigroup and combination-based algorithms. This is the same as for the tree, pyramid, and mesh-of-trees. However, the bisection width of the hypercube is linear in the number of processors, which is a significant improvement over the bisection width for the mesh, pyramid, and mesh-of-trees. Therefore, there is the possibility of moving large amounts of data quite efficiently.

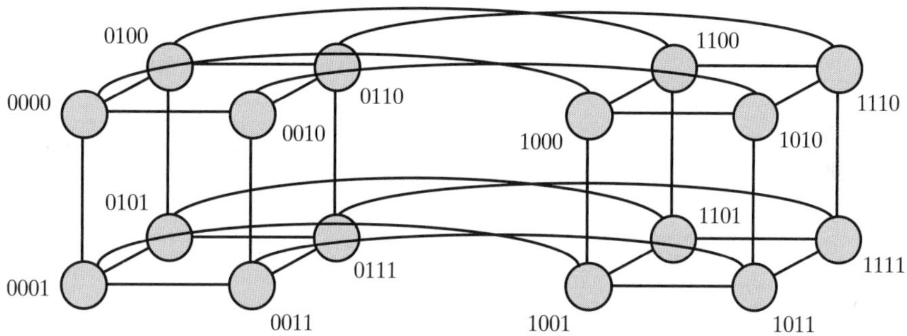


**FIGURE 4-23** *A hypercube of size* 16 *with the processors indexed by the integers* $\{0,1,\ldots,15\}$. *Pairs of processors are connected if and only if their unique* $\log_2 16 = 4$ *bit strings differ in exactly* 1 *position.*

Formally, *a hypercube of size n* consists of $n$ processors indexed by the integers $\{0,1,\ldots,n-1\}$, where $n > 0$ is an integral power of 2. Processors $A$ and $B$ are connected *if and only if* their unique $\log_2 n$-bit strings differ in *exactly* one position. For example, suppose that $n = 8$. Then the processor with binary index 011 is connected to three other processors, namely those with binary indices 111, 001, and 010.

It is often useful to think of constructing a hypercube in a recursive fashion, as shown in Figure 4-24. A hypercube of size $n$ can be constructed from two hypercubes of size $n/2$, which we refer to as $H_0$ and $H_1$, as follows. Place $H_0$ and $H_1$ side by side, with every processor labeled according to its $\log_2(n/2)$-bit string. Notice that there are now two copies of every index, one associated with $H_0$ and one associated with $H_1$. We need to resolve these conflicts and also to connect $H_0$ and $H_1$ in order to form a hypercube of size $n$. So, that we may distinguish the labels of $H_0$ from those of $H_1$, we will add a leading zero to every index of $H_0$ and add a leading 1 to every index of $H_1$. Finally, we need to connect the corresponding nodes of $H_0$ and $H_1$. That is, we need to connect those nodes that differ only in their (new) leading bit. This completes our construction of a hypercube of size $n$.

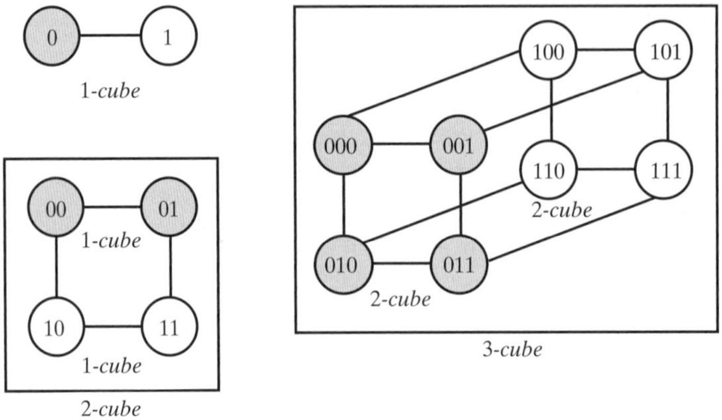


**FIGURE 4-24** *Constructing a hypercube of size n from two subcubes each of size n/2. First, attach elements of subcube A to elements of subcube B with the same index. Then prepend, i.e., add to the beginning, a 0 to the indices of subcube A and prepend a 1 to all indices of subcube B. Subcube A is shaded in each diagram for ease of presentation.*

Based on this construction scheme, the reader should note that the number of communication links affiliated with every processor must increase as the size of the network increases. In particular, unlike the mesh, tree, pyramid, and mesh-of-trees, the hypercube *is not a fixed degree network.* Specifically, notice that a processor in a hypercube of size $n$ is labeled with a unique index of $\log_2 n$ bits and is therefore connected to exactly $\log_2 n$ other processors. So, the degree of a hypercube of size $n$ is $\log_2 n$. This value is also called the *dimension* of the hypercube. Further, in contrast to the mesh, pyramid, tree, and mesh-of-trees, all nodes of a hypercube are identical with respect to the number of attached neighboring nodes.

Next, we consider the communication diameter of a hypercube of size $n$. Notice that if processor 011 needs to send a piece of information to processor 100, then one option is for the piece of information to move systematically along the path of processors with the labels $011 \rightarrow 111 \rightarrow 101 \rightarrow 100$. Note that the piece of information could just as easily move along the path $011 \rightarrow 010 \rightarrow 000 \rightarrow 100$. Such traversal schemes work by "correcting," if necessary, each bit in the processor labels between the source processor to the destination processor, specifically from the leftmost bit to the rightmost bit, in the first case, and from the rightmost bit to the leftmost bit, in the second case. Indeed, one could "correct," if necessary, the logarithmic number of bits in any order and this would represent a valid path between neighboring processors.

The important point is that one can send a message from any processor to any other by visiting a sequence of nodes that *must be connected*, by definition of a hypercube, since they differ in exactly one bit position. Therefore, the communication diameter of a hypercube of size $n$ is $\log_2 n$. However, unlike the tree and pyramid, multiple minimal-length paths traverse $O(\log n)$ communication links between many pairs of processors. This is an appealing property in that the hypercube shows promise of avoiding some of the bottlenecks that occurred in the previously defined network architectures.

Now consider the bisection width of a hypercube of size $n$. From the construction procedure described near the beginning of this section, it is clear that any two disjoint subcubes of size $n/2$ are connected by exactly $n/2$ communication links. That is, the bisection width of a hypercube of size $n$ is $\Theta(n)$. Therefore, we now have the *possibility* of being able to sort $n$ pieces of data in $\Theta(\log n)$ time, which would be cost-optimal. In fact, in Chapter 5, "Combinational Circuits," we present a Bitonic Sort algorithm that demonstrates that $n$ pieces of data, initially distributed one piece per processor on a hypercube of size $n$, can be sorted in $\Theta(\log^2 n)$ time. This result represents a significant improvement over the mesh, tree, pyramid, and mesh-of-trees.

Of course, a major drawback to the hypercube is that it does not maintain a fixed interconnection network. Therefore, one cannot design and produce a generic scalable hypercube processor.

We should note that the hypercube is both node- and edge-symmetric in that nodes can be relabeled so that we can map one index scheme to a new index scheme and preserve connectivity. This is a very nice property and also means that unlike some of the other architectures, there are no special nodes. That is, there are no special root nodes, edge nodes, or leaf nodes, and so forth. And yet, we can often use algorithms designed for other architectures such as meshes or trees, since if we merely ignore the existence of some of a hypercube's interprocessor connections, we may find the remaining connections form a mesh, tree, or other parallel architecture, or in some cases, an "approximation" of another interesting architecture.

In terms of fundamental operations, we will consider an efficient algorithm to perform a semigroup computation, which will also serve to illustrate a variety of algorithmic techniques for the hypercube. We will use the term *k-dimensional edge* to refer to a set of communication links in the hypercube that connect processors that differ in the $k^{th}$ bit position of their indices. Without loss of generality, suppose we want to compute the minimum of $X = [x_0, x_1, \ldots, x_{n-1}]$, where $x_i$ is initially stored in processor $P_i$.

Consider the simple case of a hypercube of size 16, as shown in Figure 4-25. In the first step, we send entries from all processors with a 1 in the most significant bit to their neighbors that have a 0 in the most significant bit. That is, we use the 1-dimensional edges to pass information. The processors that receive information, compute the minimum of the received value and their element, and store this result as a running minimum. In the next step, we send running minima from all processors with a 1 in their next most significant bit and that received data during the previous step, to their neighbors with a 0 in that bit position, using the

Initial Configuration

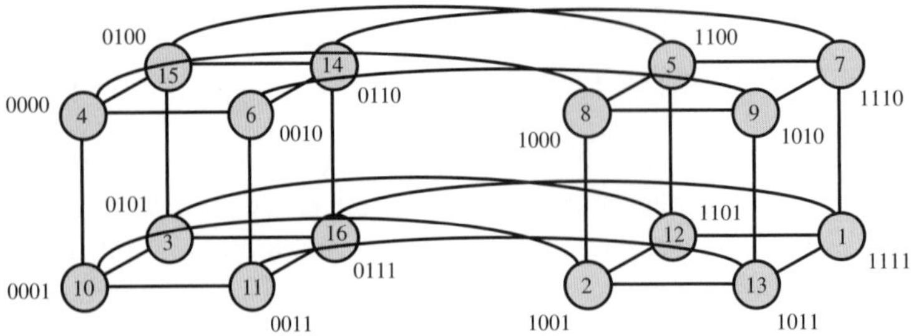


(a) Initial distribution of data. Data values are presented inside the processors. Processor labels are given as binary numbers that are positioned beside the processors.

(b) Step 1: Transmit-and-compare along 1-dimensional edges (*i.e.,* processors that differ in the most significant bit).

Step 1

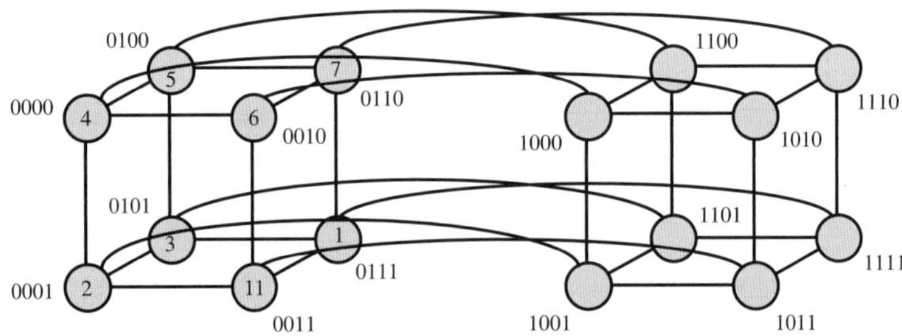


Step 2

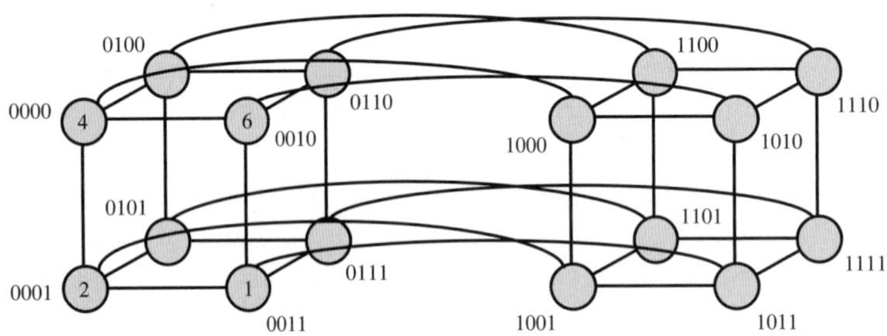


(c) Step 2: Transmit-and-compare along 2-dimensional edges.

(d) Step 3: Transmit-and-compare along 3-dimensional edges.

Step 3

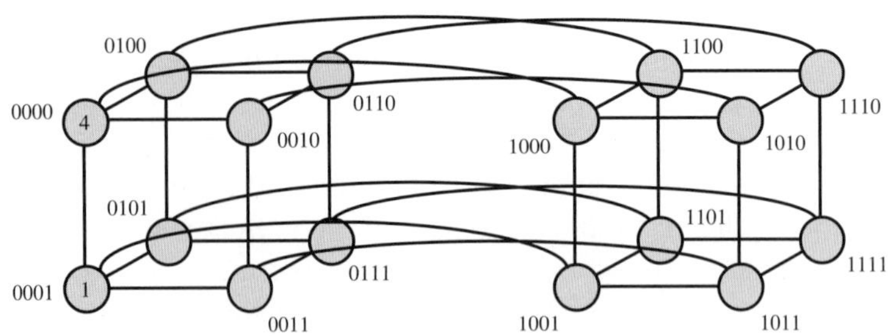

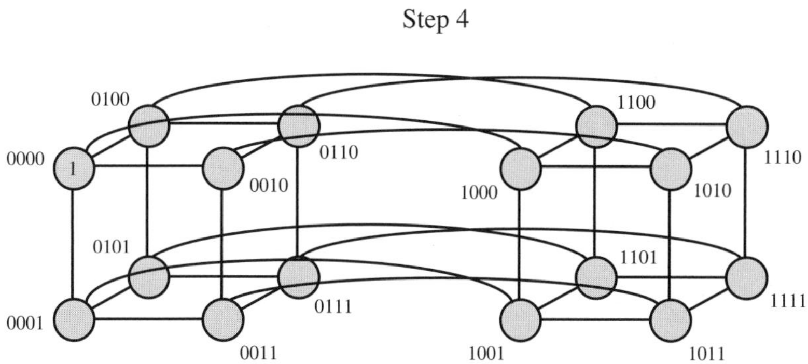


(e) Step 4: Transmit-and-compare along 4-dimensional edges. The result is the global minimum stored in processor 0000.

**FIGURE 4-25** *An example of computing a semigroup operation on a hypercube of size n. For this example, we use minimum as the semigroup operation. In the first step, we send entries from all processors with a* 1 *in the most significant bit to their neighbors that have a* 0 *in the most significant bit. That is, elements from the right subcube of size* 8 *are sent to their neighboring nodes in the left subcube of size* 8. *The receiving processors compare the two values and keep the minimum. The algorithm continues within the left subcube of size* 8. *After* $\log_2 16 = 4$ *transmission-and-compare operations, the minimum value* (1) *is known in processor* 0000.

2-dimensional edges. The receiving processors again compute the minimum of the value received and the value stored. The third step consists of sending data along the 3-dimensional edges and determining the minima. That is, in the third step, data is sent from processor 0011 to processor 0001 and simultaneously from processor 0010 to processor 0000, where processors 0001 and 0000 each determine their running minimum. The final step consists of sending the running minimum along the 4-dimensional edge from processor 0001 to processor 0000, which computes the final global minimum. Therefore, after $\log_2 n = \log_2 16 = 4$ steps, the final result is known in processor $P_0$ (see Figure 4-26).

If we now wish to distribute the final result to all processors, we can simply reverse the process and in the $i^{\text{th}}$ step, send the final result along $(\log_2 n - i + 1)$-dimensional edges from processors with a 0 in the $i^{\text{th}}$ bit to those with a 1 in the $i^{\text{th}}$ bit. Again, this takes $\log_2 n = \log_2 16 = 4$ steps. Clearly, a generalization of this algorithm simply requires combining data by cycling through the bits of the indices and sending data appropriately in order to determine the final result. If desired, this result can be distributed to all processors by reversing the communication mechanism just described. Therefore, semigroup, reporting, broadcasting, and general combination-based algorithms can be performed on a hypercube of size $n$ in $\Theta(\log n)$ time.

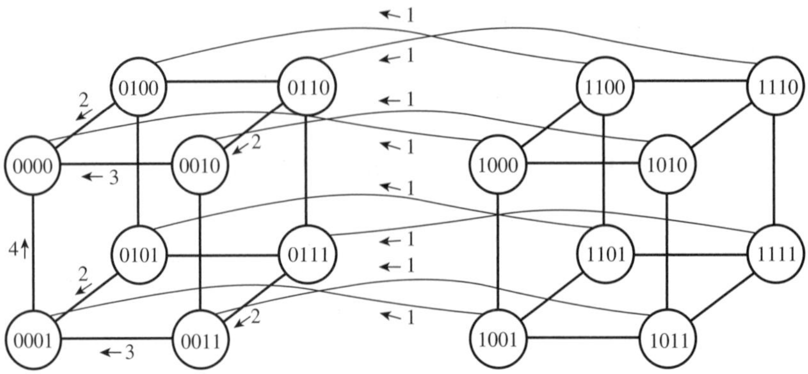


**FIGURE 4-26** *Data movement in a semigroup operation on a hypercube. The links of the hypercube of size* 16 *are labeled based on the step in which they are used to move data in the semigroup operation shown in Figure 4-25.*

## Coarse-Grained Multiprocessors

In much of the discussion above, we have made the theoretically pleasant, but often unrealistic, assumption that we can scale the number of processors in a fine-grained parallel computer, much as we assume we can scale the size of the memory in a RAM. For example, in many problems, we assumed $n$ data items were processed by $n$ processors. For several decades, this was simply not practical with the technology of the day. However, as of the writing of this text, *General Purpose Graphic Processing Units* (*GPGPUs*) are providing critical value to the high-performance computing market. As such, the fine-grained paradigms and algorithms that are discussed in this text are extremely important in terms of utilizing such machines to their fullest potential.

Current technology also provides for relatively small, yet cost-effective, computational systems configured as *coarse-grained* parallel computers, where the number of processors $q$ is much smaller than the number of data items $n$. Small or moderately sized coarse-grained multiprocessors are frequently used to solve medium-scale problems in computational science and engineering. In fact, such architectures are typically found on desktop workstations or in racks of multicore nodes, where a processor/node might contain 32 or more "cores," *i.e.*, compute elements. One can utilize coarse-grained algorithms that combine efficient sequential pre-processing steps with an overall fine-grained algorithmic approach, assuming a large collection of such multi-core systems that can be programmed as a single system.

A common strategy for the development of efficient coarse-grained algorithms follows cost-effective strategies we have discussed earlier in this chapter, namely, that of reducing the number of processors, where there is a significant amount of data per processor, and combining efficient sequential algorithms intertwined with parallel communication strategies. Recall that for a problem where the solution consists of $\Theta(1)$ data, the following strategy may be efficient.

1. Each processor runs an efficient sequential algorithm on its share of the data to obtain a partial solution.
2. The processors combine their partial solutions to obtain the problem's solution.
3. If desired, broadcast the problem's solution to all processors.

For problems in which the first step's partial solutions consist of $\Theta(1)$ data per processor, the second step can use a fine-grained algorithm to combine the partial solutions.

The *Coarse-Grained Multicomputer CGM*$(n, q)$ is a model for coarse-grained parallel computing, for processing $n$ data items on $q$ processors. Thus, each processor must have $\Omega(n/q)$ memory locations, sufficient to store the data for the problem at hand. It is customary to take $q \leq n/q$ (equivalently, $q^2 \leq n$). This assumption facilitates many operations. For example, a *gather* operation, in which one data item from each processor is gathered into a designated processor $P_i$, requires that the number of items gathered, $q$, not exceed the storage capacity $\Omega(n/q)$ of $P_i$. Note that the description we give of a gather operation in Appendix 3 is more general than the above.

The processors of a CGM make up a connected graph. That is, any processor can communicate with any other processor, although exchanging data between processors may take more than one communication step. This graph could be in the form of a linear array, mesh, hypercube, pyramid, and so forth. The CGM model can also be realized on a PRAM, in which case we assume that each processor is directly connected, by means of the shared memory, to every other processor.

Suppose for a given problem, the best sequential solution runs in $T_{seq}(n)$ time. In light of our discussion of speedup in the next section, the reader should conclude that an optimal solution to this problem on a *CGM*$(n, q)$ runs in time

$$T_{par}(n) = \frac{T_{seq}(n)}{q}.$$

For many fundamental problems, CGM solutions make use of *gather* and *scatter* operations. As discussed in Appendix 3, a gather operation collects a set $S$ of data items that are distributed among the processors of the CGM into one processor $P_j$. That is, for each $x \in S$, we bring a copy of $x$ to $P_j$. A *scatter* operation may be used to reverse a gather by returning each $x \in S$ from $P_j$ to the $P_i$ that originally contained $x$. This is useful, for example, when $x$ is a record with components that have been written into by $P_j$.

Results of Appendix 3 imply that gather and scatter operations on sets of size $q$ can be performed on a $CGM(n, q)$ in $O(q)$ time. In the following discussion, we make use of this fact. Consider the following algorithm for a minimum (or, more generally, semigroup) computation on a $CGM(n, q)$.

**$CGM(n, q)$ Minimum Algorithm**
**Input:** Array $X$, stored with the subarray $\{x_i\}_{i=(j-1)\frac{n}{q}+1}^{\frac{jn}{q}}$ in $P_j$, $j \in \{1, \ldots q\}$
**Output:** Minimum entry of $X$, known to each processor.

**Action:**

```
1. In parallel, each processor P_j computes m_j =
   min{x_i}_{i=(j-1)n/q+1}^{jn/q}, using the sequential algorithm
   discussed above. This step runs in Θ(n/q) time.
2. Gather{m_j}_{j=1}^{q} into P_1. This step runs in O(q) time.
3. P_1 computes the desired minimum value, M =
   min{m_j}_{j=1}^{q}, using the sequential algorithm
   discussed above, in Θ(q) time.
4. If desired, broadcast M to all processors. This can
   be done by a "standard" broadcast operation in O(q)
   time (see Exercises) or by attaching the value of M
   to each m_j record in Θ(q) time and scattering the
   m_j records to the processors from which they came,
   in O(q) time.
End Minimum
```

Since $q \le n/q$, the algorithm runs in $\Theta(n/q)$ time. This is optimal, since an optimal sequential solution runs in $\Theta(n)$ time.

Notice that if we assume a particular architecture, such as a PRAM, mesh, hypercube, or other traditional models, for our $CGM(n, q)$, the last three steps of the algorithm above can be replaced by faster fine-grained computations of the minimum that do not use gather/scatter operations. For example, on a mesh, the last three steps of the algorithm can be replaced by fine-grained mesh semigroup and broadcast operations that run in $\Theta(q^{1/2})$ time. Doing so, however, is likely to yield little improvement in the performance of the algorithm, which would still run in $\Theta(n/q)$ time. An advantage of our presentation above is that it covers all parallel architectures that might be used for a CGM.

#### Network of Workstations (NOW)

Beginning in the 1970s and 1980s, commodity workstations were deployed with some regularity. Some of these systems were relatively high-end Unix workstations, which were typically used to solve scientific and engineering problems. In addition, personal computers were deployed in order to improve the efficiency of daily office-type activities like word processing, maintaining spreadsheets, creating overheads for presentations, and so forth. During this time, labs of workstations started to emerge as a way for students or scientists to have shared access to such systems.

Scientists who relied on computation to perform leading-edge research, started to consider ways in which the aggregate compute power of a collection of workstations found in such a laboratory could be harnessed in order to provide a cost-effective system for solving computationally intensive problems. At the time, the only real alternative for scientists to access high-end computational systems was to expend a significant effort to gain access to supercomputers, which were typically located at national labs and eventually at public government supported sites. This required either knowing the right people and/or submitting a proposal to be reviewed by a peer-reviewed committee. Once access was granted, these machines were typically very difficult to program.

By contrast, in order to use a laboratory of Sun™ workstations, for example, one could write computer programs in traditional programming languages and use a vendor-supplied system software package called Remote Procedure Call (RPC) in order to allow the workstations to communicate with one another. Typically, RPC was used to create a master/worker system where one workstation would be designated as the master and would distribute jobs to available worker systems. Each worker would report back to the master when its job was complete. Such a configuration of workstations was ideal for computations that required many individual jobs to be processed.

For example, in the late 1980s, the *Shake-and-Bake* algorithm for molecular structure determination was deployed in a graduate student laboratory of Sun workstations at the State University of New York at Buffalo. This procedure required starting with a representation of a random set of atoms, applying constraints to update the set of atoms continually, and then produce a potential solution to the molecular structure in question. *Shake-and-Bake* belongs to a family of multi-trial algorithms, where a large number of random starts is used and the aggregate final results are evaluated in order to determine if a solution to the problem was produced by any of the random starts. Additional Monte Carlo-type calculations were also deployed in such a fashion.

One concern was that sometimes a worker node would fail or that a user would reboot such a machine. Therefore, such networks of workstations were best used when the solution strategy could tolerate failures in some of the jobs that were deployed.

For some problems where the specific random starting set of data was critical, the master would keep track of the jobs and if a job did not complete after a certain amount of time, it would simply re-deploy it. In other cases, such as *Shake-and-Bake*, the master would just continue to deploy jobs with random starts until the requisite number of jobs was complete.

Simultaneously and independently, a group in the Computer Science Department at the University of Wisconsin, led by Miron Livny, recognized that such a computing methodology could be more generally applied to a wide variety of computational requirements. The result of the work by one group in distributed resource management and another in remote Unix systems led to the development of a project called *Condor*.

According to the current Condor Web site, Condor is a specialized workload management system for compute-intensive jobs. Like other full-featured batch systems, Condor provides a job queueing mechanism, scheduling policy, priority scheme, resource monitoring, and resource management. Users submit their jobs to Condor, Condor places them into a queue, chooses when and where to run the jobs based upon a policy, carefully monitors their progress, and ultimately informs the user upon completion. It is important to note that in a traditional implementation of Condor on a NOW, it is perfectly acceptable for a program to fail on a worker node and that the system was typically used as a compute farm where individual jobs would be farmed out to available nodes that had cycles available. Finally, Condor has been successfully implemented on a network consisting of many thousands of workstations to serve as a compute farm in order to solve a wide variety of problems.

### Cluster

A *compute cluster*, also called a *cluster* for short, typically consists of a set of compute nodes that are capable of working together in a highly integrated fashion. The form factor of the nodes in a cluster can be standard desktop PCs, but they are more often than not a set of nodes designed to be placed in a rack. At this writing, a relatively standard rack is 42U high (~80 inches high), 19 internal inches wide (~24 inches in terms of the external width), and ~40 inches deep. Note that 1U (*i.e.,* one *rack unit*) is 1.75 inches high and nodes typically range in size from 1U-6U, with 1U and 2U units being the most common. Larger units (3U-6U) are currently more common for storage units, power distribution units, UPS units, or fairly specialized compute units. See Figures 4-27 and 4-28.

A cluster is typically viewed as a single system that consists of the following.

1. A head node, which typically is the single-point-of-contact to the outside world and is used for debugging, maintains access to the external storage system, and manages the batch queuing system.
2. A set of heterogeneous worker nodes, which may differ in the number of processors per node, the number of cores per processor, the amount of memory per node/processor, the existence or lack thereof of an attached device, like a GPGPU unit, and so forth.

**FIGURE 4-27** *One of the authors, R. Miller, standing next to several racks of a computational cluster. Notice the racks on the right side of the image consist of a large number of 2U computational units. The three racks on the left and behind R. Miller consist primarily of networking equipment and cables that provide connectivity within the cluster.*

**FIGURE 4-28** *One aisle showing a number of racks of a very large computational cluster. Notice that the floor consists of perforated tiles, which provide cooling from beneath the raised floor. Note that the nodes in the rack take cooling in from the front and export warm air out of the back. Therefore, in most computer rooms, you will notice alternating cool and hot aisles, where each aisle consists of either fronts (cool aisle; perforated tiles) of two sets of racks, or backs (warm aisle; no perforated tiles) of two sets of racks.*

3. A storage system, which in its simplest form is connected solely to the head node, but in a highly data intensive environment, might be connected as a parallel I/O system to a subset of the worker nodes.
4. A very high speed interconnection network.

In fact, a cluster may be composed of subclusters with different processor architectures, different interconnection networks, different versions of the operating system, and so forth, but is still managed by the same head node(s).

Compute clusters emerged as a result of convergence of trends, including the availability of the following.

1. Low-cost microprocessors, which are often referred to as *commodity off-the-shelf systems*, or COTS.
2. Affordable very high speed networks, which currently include Gigabit Ethernet, InfiniBand, Myrinet, and others.
3. Software for high-performance distributed computing, including MPI (Message Passing Interface), which is currently the most common means of programming clusters consisting of tens or hundreds of thousands of nodes. MPI is an Application Programming Interface (API), that consists of a set of

subroutines or procedures that are easily invoked within standard programming languages. For example, MPI contains a set of routines for sending and receiving data between nodes, as well as a set of routines for performing fundamental communications within a multiprocessor system.

Clusters are usually deployed in an effort to provide significant compute power in a cost-effective fashion to solve very large leading-edge problems. More often than not, however, they are actually used as high-throughput devices that provide a compute farm to a large community that runs large numbers of sequential codes. The compute farm model is obviously quite similar to how a NOW is typically used.

In order to visualize the difference between a NOW and a cluster, consider the following.

1. A NOW may consist of a set of workstations situated throughout an entire campus. These workstations include those on faculty desks, in laboratories, in student dorms, and so forth. In fact, some of the larger CONDOR systems contain thousands of such workstations.
2. A cluster might consist of between one and one thousand racks of very thin horizontal nodes stacked one on top of the other in each rack with a dedicated interconnection, a set of cables, behind the racks. The large cables typically use a large router to connect racks together, where each rack typically has a smaller router that connects the nodes within the rack.

Finally, the reader should note that for the past couple of decades, the vast majority of the world's most powerful systems have been clusters. More recently, the fastest systems contain GPGPU systems attached to the compute nodes. The reader might find a look at the top500 list, along with some of the analysis and associated data, to be quite interesting and insightful. The top500 list and related materials, which is updated twice a year, may be found at www.top500.org.

#### Grid

A grid, as shown in Figure 4-29, allows a heterogeneous set of geographically distributed and independently operated resources to be linked together in a transparent fashion. Such resources include clusters, NOWs, data storage, sensors, visualization devices, and a wide variety of Internet-ready instruments, to name a few. The power of the grid lies in its ability to bring a variety of resources to bear on a particular problem while hiding details of utilization and location of resources from the user. For example, a user should be able to connect to a grid from any Internet-ready device, *e.g.*, a cell phone, and through a simple interface, initiate a scientific experiment that requires applying an algorithm to a data set that is being constructed from a set of sensors, the result of which will be rendered and then returned to the user as an easy-to-evaluate image without knowledge of where the computation is performed, where the data is stored, or where the image/video is rendered.

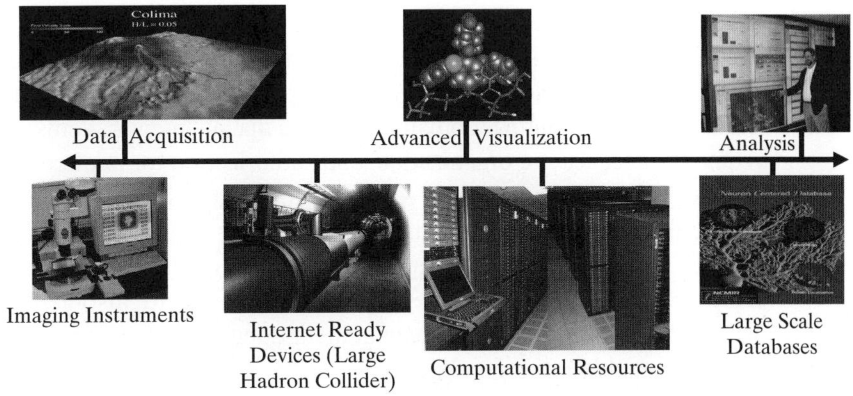


**FIGURE 4-29** *A schematic representation of a grid. A grid provides a user with seamless access to sensors, visualization devices, imaging systems, computational resources, databases, applications, and a wide variety of Internet-ready devices. A user need not know or care where all of these components are physically located.*

The term "grid" comes from an analogy to the electric grid, where a user can simply plug a device into an outlet and get power without knowledge of where or how the power is supplied from some source to the outlet. Grids are now a viable solution to certain computationally- and data-intensive computing problems for reasons that include the following.

1. The Internet is reasonably mature and able to serve as fundamental infrastructure for network-based computing.
2. Network bandwidth, which recently has been doubling approximately every 12 months, has increased to the point of being able to provide efficient and reliable services.
3. Storage devices have reached commodity levels, where one can purchase a terabyte of disk for roughly the same price as a commodity PC.
4. Many instruments are Internet-aware.
5. Clusters, NOW, storage, and visualization devices are mainstream.
6. Major applications, including critical scientific community codes, have been parallelized.

Limited and controlled grids have moved out of the research laboratories and are used as production systems. However, the focus of grid deployment continues to be on the difficult issue of developing high quality middleware in order to develop a general-purpose grid that coordinates resource sharing and problem solving in a dynamic, multi-institutional scenario using standard, open, general-purpose protocols and interfaces that deliver a high quality of service.

Many types of computational tasks are naturally suited to grid environments, including data-intensive applications. Grid-based research and development activities have generally focused on applications where data is stored in files. However, in many scientific and commercial domains, database management systems play a central role in data storage, access, organization, and authorization for numerous applications.

As grid computing initiatives move forward, issues of interoperability, security, performance, management, and privacy must be carefully considered. In fact, security is concerned with various issues relating to authentication in order to insure application and data integrity. Grid initiatives are also generating best practice scheduling and resource management documents, protocols, and API specifications to enable interoperability.

### Cloud

The standard joke is that what some companies call a "cloud" is what the rest of us call the "Internet." On a serious note, while a cloud (*c.f.*, Figure 4-30) has similarities to clusters and grids, one distinguishing definition of a cloud is that it is used to deliver computing as a *service* rather than as a product.

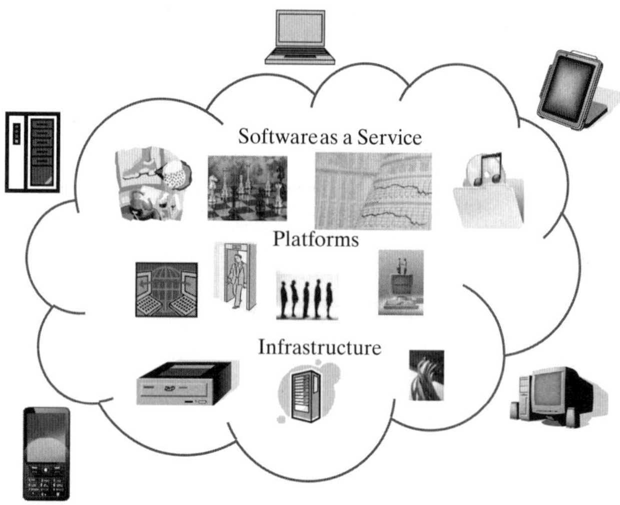


**FIGURE 4-30** *Software as a service includes application software including popular media applications and proprietary software, which sits on top of traditional software platforms (communication protocols, security, queueing systems, communication systems, operating systems), which sit on top of hardware platforms (storage, compute systems, networking). One accesses a cloud through cell phones, workstations, tablets, laptops, and servers, to name a few.*

Cloud computing is often a term that refers to systems that provide computation, applications, storage, access to data, visualization, and so forth, to users without providing knowledge of the physical location and configuration of the system that delivers the services to the user. That is, one of the standard definitions of a cloud is the Internet while another definition of a cloud is that it is a grid. Finally, many so-called clouds offered to the public are essentially special purpose clusters. This includes cloud services for data backups, cloud services to store your media, *e.g.,* photos, videos, movies, and music, cloud services that provide access to computer programs and associated data, cloud services that provide access to software, hardware, and data for performing computational experiments, and so forth.

In an academic/research environment, one critical distinguishing feature of a cloud is that it is a system, ranging from a simple processor to a small cluster to a large grid, which typically involves provisioning of dynamically scalable and virtualized resources. Like a grid, a cloud must provide ease of access to users, typically through a browser.

In the case of a physically small compute system, a cloud requires virtualization in order to move systems and application software in and out of the compute system easily in order to satisfy a wide variety of user demands.

In fact, the tremendous impact of cloud computing on business has resulted in the reorganization of the IT infrastructure at organizations in order to decrease IT budgets.

Since NOW, clusters, grids, and clouds are not generally restricted to using a particular architecture or processors with uniform performance characteristics, it is not possible to give a "one-size-fits-all" analysis of an algorithm executed on such an environment. Tools developed in this book may help a user develop analysis of an algorithm on a particular NOW, cluster, grid, or cloud.

## Additional Terminology

In this chapter, we present an introduction to models of computation that will be used throughout the book. We also present fundamental algorithms for these models so that the reader can appreciate some of the similarities and differences among the models. We have intentionally avoided using too much terminology throughout this chapter and will continue that practice throughout the book. However, we feel it would be a disservice not to define some commonly used terminology, definitions, and conjectures that are found in the scientific literature.

**Flynn's Taxonomy:** In 1966, M.J. Flynn defined a taxonomy of computer architectures based on the concepts of both instruction stream and data stream. Briefly, an *instruction stream* is defined to be a sequence of instructions performed by the computer, while a *data stream* is defined to be the sequence of data items that are operated on by the instructions. Flynn defines the instruction stream as being either single or multiple, and also defines the data stream as being either single or multiple. In particular, he defines the following.

A *single instruction stream, single data stream* (*SISD*) machine consists of a single set of instructions executed one per cycle on a single set of data. The RAM model is an SISD model, where most individual cores fall into this category. This is the "von Neumann" model of computing.

A *single instruction stream, multiple data stream* (*SIMD*) machine consists of a set of processors with local memory, a control unit, and an interconnection network. The control unit stores the program and broadcasts the instructions, one per clock cycle, to all processors simultaneously. All processors execute the same instruction at the same time, but on the contents of their own local memory. However, through the use of a *mask*, processors can be in either an active or inactive state at any time during the execution of a program. Further, these masks can be determined dynamically. Networks of processors, such as the mesh, pyramid, and hypercube, can be built as SIMD machines. In fact, the algorithms that we have described so far for these network models have been described in an SIMD fashion. When one thinks about SIMD systems, one typically thinks of fine-grained synchronous systems.

A *multiple instruction stream, single data stream* (*MISD*) machine is a model that doesn't make much sense. One might argue that systolic arrays fall into that category, but such a discussion is not productive within the context of this book.

A *multiple instruction stream, multiple data stream* (*MIMD*) machine typically consists of a set of processors with local memory and an interconnection network. In contrast to the SIMD model, the MIMD model allows each processor to store and execute its own program. However, in reality, in order for multiple processors to cooperate to solve a given problem, these programs must at least occasionally synchronize and cooperate. In fact, it is quite common for an algorithm to be implemented in such a fashion that all processors execute the same program. This is referred to as the *single-program multiple-data* (*SPMD*) programming style. Notice that this style is popular since it is typically infeasible to write a large number of different programs that will be executed simultaneously on different processors. Most commercially available multiprocessor machines fall into the MIMD category, including clusters, NOW, departmental servers, and so on. These systems contain multiple processors and either a physically or virtually "shared memory." Further, most large codes implemented on such systems fall into the SPMD category.

**Granularity:** Machines can also be classified according to their *granularity*. That is, machines can be classified according to the number and/or complexity of their processors. For example, a commercial machine with a dozen or so very fast and complex processors would be classified as a *coarse-grained machine*, while a machine with hundreds of thousands of very simple processors would be classified as a *fine-grained machine*. Most commercially available multiprocessor machines fall into the coarse-grained MIMD category. Of course, such terminology is quite subjective and may change with time.

This terminology is also used to characterize the relationship between the amount of data being processed, $n$, and the number of processors, $q$. When $n/q = \Theta(1)$, we consider the machine to be fine-grained. When the ratio $n/q$ is larger, we speak of *medium-grained* or coarse-grained parallel computers. We usually call a computer medium-grained if $n/q = \omega(1)$ and $q > n/q$, and we call a computer coarse-grained if $q \leq n/q$.

We now define some general performance measures. These are common terms that the user is likely to come across while reading the scientific literature.

**Throughput:** The term *throughput* refers to the number of results produced per unit time. This is a critical measure of the effectiveness of our problem-solving environment, which includes not only algorithms used to solve problems, the computing system, *i.e.*, processors, interconnection network, memory, disk, access to disk, and so forth, but also the quality of any queueing system and other operating system features.

**Cost/Work:** Let $T_{par}(n, q)$ represent the length of time that an algorithm operating on $n$ data items with $q$ processors takes to solve a problem. Then the *cost* of such a parallel algorithm, as previously discussed, can be defined as $C(n, q) = q \times T_{par}(n, q)$. That is, the cost of an algorithm is defined as the number of *potential* instructions that *could* be executed during the running time of the algorithm, which is clearly the product of the running time and the number of processors. A term that is related to cost is *work*, which is typically defined to be the *actual* number of instructions performed regardless of the wall-clock time it takes to perform these operations.

**Speedup:** We define *speedup* as the ratio between the time taken for the *most efficient* sequential algorithm to perform a task and the time taken for the *most efficient* parallel algorithm to perform the same task on a machine with $n$ processors, which we denote as $S_{n,q} = T_{seq}(n)/T_{par}(n, q)$. The term *linear speedup* refers to a speedup of $S_{n,q} = q$. In general, linear speedup cannot be achieved since the coordination and cooperation of processors to solve a given problem must take some time. However, we have seen that it is often possible to achieve a speedup within a constant factor of linear, *i.e.*, $S_{n,q} = \Theta(q)$. An interesting debate concerns the concept of *superlinear speedup*, or the situation where $S_{n,q} > q$.

For example, if we consider asymptotic analysis, then it would seem that a sequential algorithm could always be written to emulate the parallel algorithm with $O(q)$ slowdown, which implies that superlinear speedup is not possible. However, assume that the algorithms are chosen in advance. Then several situations could occur. First, in a nondeterministic search-type algorithm, a multiprocessor search might simply get lucky and discover the solution before such an emulation of the algorithm might. That is, the parallel algorithm has an increased probability of getting lucky in certain situations. Second, effects of memory hierarchy might come into play. For example, a set of very lucky or unlucky cache hits could have a drastic effect on running time.

**Efficiency:** The *efficiency* of an algorithm is a measure of how well utilized the processors are. That is, efficiency is the ratio of sequential running time and the cost on a $q$-processor machine, which is equivalent to the ratio between the $q$-processor speedup and $q$. So, efficiency is given as $E_{n,q} = T_{seq}(n)/C(n, q) = S_{n,q}/q$.

**Amdahl's Law:** While discussing speedup, we should define *Amdahl's Law*, which states that the maximum speedup achievable by an $n$-processor machine is given by $S_n \leq 1/\left[f + (1 - f)/n\right]$, where $f$ is the fraction of operations in the computation that must be performed sequentially. So, for example, if five percent of the operations in a given computation must be performed sequentially, then the speedup can never be greater than 20, *regardless of how many processors are used.* That is, a small number of sequential operations can significantly limit the speedup of an algorithm on a parallel machine.

Fortunately, what Amdahl's Law overlooks is the fact that for many algorithms, the percentage of required sequential operations decreases as the size of the *problem* increases. Further, it is often the case that as one scales up a parallel machine, scientists often want to solve larger and larger problems, and not just the same problems more efficiently. That is, it is common enough to find that for a given machine, scientists will want to solve the largest problem that fits on that machine, and complain that the machine isn't just a bit bigger so that they could solve the larger problem they really want to consider.

**Scalability:** We say that an algorithm is *scalable* if the level of parallelism increases at least linearly with the problem size. We say that an architecture is scalable if the machine continues to yield the same performance per processor as the number of processors increases. In general, scalability is important in that it allows users to solve larger problems in the same amount of time by purchasing a machine with more processors.

## Summary

In this chapter, we discuss a variety of models of computation. These include the classical RAM model for single-processor computers, as well as several models of parallel computation, including the PRAM, linear array, mesh, tree, pyramid, hypercube, and others. For each model of computation, we discuss solutions to fundamental problems and give analysis of our solutions' running times. We also discuss, for parallel models, factors that can limit the efficiency of the model, such as the communication diameter and the bisection width. Finally, we discuss current coarse-grained systems, including Network of Workstations (NOW), clusters, grids, and clouds, as well as some standard terminology and definitions.

## Chapter Notes

The emphasis of this chapter is on introducing the reader to a variety of parallel models of computation. A nice, relatively concise presentation is given in "Algorithmic Techniques for Networks of Processors," by R. Miller and Q.F. Stout in the *Handbook of Algorithms and Theory of Computation*, M. Atallah, ed., CRC Press, Boca Raton, FL, 1994–1998. A general text targeted at undergraduates that covers algorithms, models, real machines, and some applications, is *Parallel Computing Theory and Practice* by M.J. Quinn (McGraw-Hill, Inc., New York, 1994). For a book that covers PRAM algorithms at a graduate level, the reader is referred to *An Introduction to Parallel Algorithms* by J. Já Já (Addison-Wesley, Reading, MA., 1992), while advanced undergraduate students or graduate students interested primarily in mesh and pyramid algorithms might refer to *Parallel Algorithms for Regular Architectures: Meshes and Pyramids* by R. Miller and Q.F. Stout (The MIT Press, Cambridge, MA., 1996). For the reader interested in a text devoted to hypercube algorithms, see *Hypercube Algorithms for Image Processing and Pattern Recognition* by S. Ranka and S. Sahni (Springer-Verlag, 1990). A parallel algorithms book that focuses on models related to those presented in this chapter is *Introduction to Parallel Algorithms and Architectures: Arrays, Trees, Hypercubes* by F.T. Leighton (Morgan Kaufmann Publishers, San Mateo, CA., 1992).

While Amdahl's law is discussed or mentioned in most texts on parallel algorithms, it is worth mentioning the original paper, "Validity of the single processor approach to achieving large scale computing capabilities" by G. Amdahl, *AFIPS Conference Proceedings*, vol. 30, Thompson Books, pp. 483–485, 1967. Similarly, Flynn's taxonomy is a standard in texts devoted to parallel computing. The original articles by Flynn are "Very high-speed computing systems" by M.J. Flynn, *Proceedings of the IEEE,* 54 (12), pp. 1901–1909, 1966, and "Some computer organizations and their effectiveness" by M.J. Flynn, *IEEE Transactions on Computers*, C-21, pp. 948–960, 1972.

The coarse-grained multicomputer, $CGM(n,q)$, was introduced in F. Dehne, A. Fabri, and A. Rau-Chaplin, "Scalable parallel geometric algorithms for multicomputers," *Proceedings 9$^{th}$ ACM Symposium on Computational Geometry* (1993), pp. 298–307, and has been used in many subsequent papers (see, *e.g.*, F. Dehne, ed., special edition of *Algorithmica* 24, no. 3–4, 1999, devoted to coarse grained parallel algorithms). The proof that we give in Appendix 3 that gather and scatter algorithms can be performed on a $CGM(n,q)$ in time approximately proportional to the amount of data being gathered or scattered appears in L. Boxer and R. Miller, "Coarse grained gather and scatter operations with applications," *Journal of Parallel and Distributed Computing* 64 (2004), 1297–1320.

For more about multiprocessor systems, see http://www.cloudbus.org/, a Web site for the *IEEE/ACM International Symposium on Cluster, Cloud and Grid Computing* (*CCGrid*), and also the book edited by P. Kacsuk, T. Fahringer and Z. Nemeth, entitled *Distributed and Parallel Systems: From Cluster to Grid Computing*, Springer Science+Business Media, New York, 2007.

The reader interested in additional information about a Network of Workstations (NOW) is referred to the Condor Web site, which is maintained at http://research.cs.wisc.edu/condor/.

Two good references for additional information about clusters include the Web site for IEEE Cluster, which is http://www.ieeecluster.org/, as well as the Web site for an annual IEEE conference on cluster computing, at http://www.clustercomp.org/.

The reader interested in additional information about a grid might consider the book *Introduction to Grid Computing,* by F. Magoules, J. Pan, K.-A. Tan and A. Kumar, CRC Press, London, England, 2009, as well as the book by B. Wilkinson, entitled *Grid Computing: Techniques and Applications*, Chapman & Hall/CRC, Boca Raton, FL, 2010.

For more about cloud computing, see the following.

- *IEEE Cloud: International Conference on Cloud Computing*. http://www.thecloudcomputing.org/
- G. Reese, *Cloud Application Architectures: Building Applications and Infrastructure in the Cloud*, O'Reilly Media, Sebastopol, CA, 2009.
- B. Sosinsky, *Cloud Computing Bible*, Wiley Publishing, Inc., Indianapolis, IN, 2011.

The reader interested in additional information about programming GPGPU systems might consider *Programming Massively Parallel Processors: A Hands-on Approach* (Applications of GPU Computing Series), by D. B. Kirk and W.-m. W. Hwu, Morgan-Kaufmann Publishers, Burlington, Massachusetts, 2010. The reader interested in programming NVIDIA GPGPUs should consider the book *CUDA by Example: An Introduction to General-Purpose GPU Programming*, by J. Sanders and E. Kandrot, Addison-Wesley, Reading, Massachusetts, 2011.

For more general books focused on multicore systems, the reader is referred to the following.

- J. Kurzak, D.A. Bader, and J. Dongarra, *Scientific Computing with Multicore and Accelerators*, CRC Press, Boca Raton, FL, 2010.
- T. Rauber and G. Rünger, *Parallel Programming for Multicore and Cluster Systems*, Springer-Verlag Berlin Heidelberg, New York, 2010.

## Exercises

**1.** Consider the "star-shaped" architecture shown in Figure 4-31, which consists of $n$ processors, labeled from 0 to $n - 1$, where processor $P_0$ is directly connected to all other processors, but for $i, j > 0$, $i \neq j$, processors $P_i$ and $P_j$ are not directly connected.

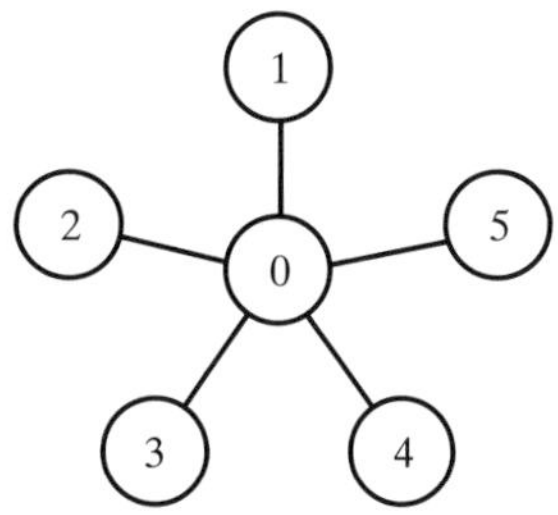


**FIGURE 4-31** *A star-shaped computer of size* 6.

a. Explain why this architecture has a "serial bottleneck" at processor $P_0$.

b. How much time is required to compute a semigroup operation $\otimes_{i=0}^{n-1} x_i$ on this architecture, where $x_i$ is stored in processor $P_i$?

c. Does the star-shaped configuration seem to be a useful arrangement of processors for parallel computation?

**2.** Consider an architecture consisting of $n$ processors partitioned into two disjoint subsets, $A$ and $B$, each with $n/2$ processors. Further, assume that each processor in $A$ is joined to each processor in $B$, but no pair of processors having both members in $A$ or both members in $B$ are joined. See Figure 4-32 for an example.

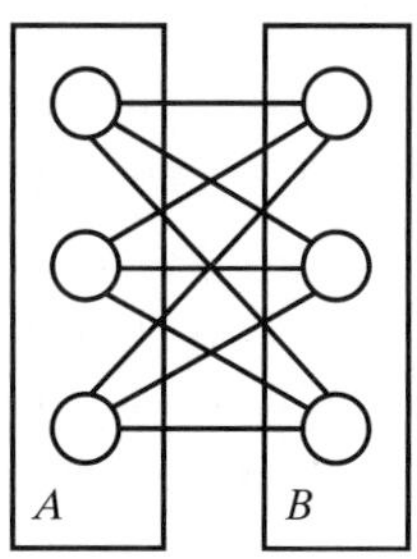


**FIGURE 4-32** *An architecture in which n processors are partitioned into two disjoint subsets of n*/2 *processors each.*

a. Design and analyze an efficient parallel algorithm for computing a semigroup operation on this architecture that is faster than that possible for a star-shaped architecture. Assume the semigroup operation is given as $\otimes_{i=0}^{n-1} x_i$, where $x_i$ is stored in processor $P_i$.

b. What is the bisection width of this architecture? What does this imply about the practicality of this architecture?

**3.** Define an X-tree to be a tree machine in which neighboring processors on a level are connected. That is, each interior processor has two additional links, one to each of its left and right neighbors. Processors on the outer edge of the tree, with the exception of the root, have one additional link, to its neighboring node in its level.

a. What is the communication diameter of an X-tree? Explain.
b. What is the bisection width of an X-tree? Explain.
c. Give a lower bound on sorting for the X-tree. Explain.

**4.** Suppose that we have constructed a CRCW PRAM algorithm to solve problem $A$ in $O(t(n))$ time. When we begin to consider solutions to problem $A$ on a CREW PRAM, what information will help us bound the running time to solve this problem on a CREW PRAM? Justify your answer.

**5.** Suppose that problem $A$ can be solved on a CREW PRAM in $\Theta(t(n))$ time. If we now consider a solution to the same problem $A$ on an EREW PRAM, how does the CREW PRAM algorithm help us in determining a lower bound on the running time to solve this problem on an EREW PRAM?

**6.** Give an asymptotically optimal algorithm to sum $n$ values on a 3-dimensional mesh. Discuss the running time and cost of your algorithm. Give a precise definition of your model.

**7.** Give an efficient algorithm to sum $n$ values on a hypercube.

**8.** Define a *linear array of size n with a bus* to be a 1-dimensional mesh of size $n$ augmented with a single global bus. Every processor is connected to the bus, and in each unit of time, one processor can write to the bus and all processors can read from the bus. That is, the bus may be thought of as a CREW bus.

a. Give an efficient algorithm to sum $n$ values, initially distributed one per processor. Discuss the time and cost of your algorithm.
b. Give an efficient algorithm to compute the parallel prefix of $n$ values, initially distributed one per processor. Discuss the time and cost of your algorithm.

**9.** Show that a pyramid computer with base size $n$ contains $(4n - 1)/3$ processors. *Hint*: Let $n = 4^k$ for integer $k \geq 0$, and use mathematical induction on $k$.

**10.** Why is it unrealistic to expect to solve an *NP*-complete problem on the PRAM in polylogarithmic time using a polynomial number of processors?

**11.** a. Show that a gather operation, in which one data item is collected from each processor of a linear array of $q$ processors, runs in $\Omega(q)$ time in the worst case.
b. Devise an algorithm to gather one data item from each processor of a linear array of $q$ processors into any one of the processors. Analyze the running time of your algorithm. *Hint*: an efficient algorithm will run in $\Theta(q)$ time. Note this shows that $\Theta(q)$ is optimal for such an operation, and the $O(q)$ time we have claimed for a gather of $q$ data items on a $CGM(n, q)$ is optimal in the worst case, *i.e.*, with respect to the worst case architecture.

12. Given a set of $q$ data items, assume that algorithms for gather and scatter operations are available to apply to a set of $q$ data items that run in $\Theta(q)$ time on a $CGM(n, q)$. State and analyze the running time of an efficient algorithm to broadcast a value from one processor of a $CGM(n,q)$ to all processors.

13. The model of computation for this problem is a fine-grained SIMD parallel computer configured as a master set of $n^{1/4} \times n^{1/4}$ mesh of $n^{1/4} \times n^{1/4}$ base meshes, as illustrated in Figure 4-33. That is, each processor of the master $n^{1/4} \times n^{1/4}$ mesh serves as a communications processor for its $n^{1/4} \times n^{1/4}$ base mesh. Each communications processor is connected to every processor of its base mesh. For the sake of simplicity, assume all processors, master or base, run at identical speed, and all communications links between any two processors carry a unit of data in the same constant amount of time.
    a. Give an efficient algorithm to broadcast a unit of data from a processor in a base mesh to all processors in this architecture in optimal time.
    b. Suppose a list of numbers is distributed one member per base processor of this architecture. Give an efficient algorithm to compute the total of these numbers, and show its running time is optimal for this architecture. You may make use of the fact that addition is commutative.
    c. Suppose a list of data records is distributed one member per base processor of this architecture. Give a lower bound for the running time of any algorithm to sort this list.

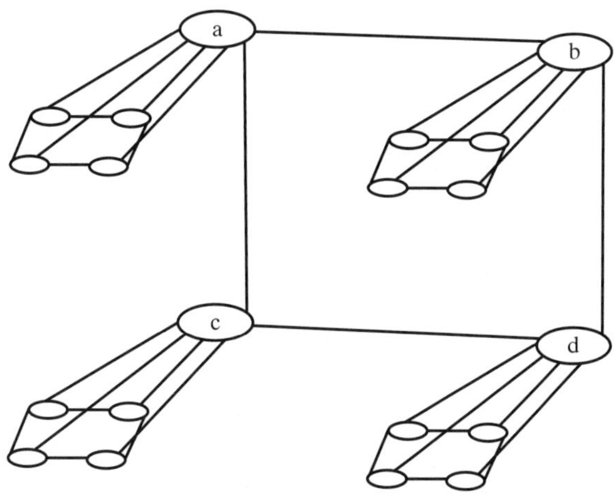


**FIGURE 4-33** *A cluster made up of a $2 \times 2$ mesh of $2 \times 2$ meshes. The processors labeled a, b, c, and d, are communications processors for each of the processors in a base mesh.*

# 5

# Combinational Circuits

In this chapter, we present efficient algorithms to sort data on a PRAM and on a hypercube. In addition, the methodology presented in this chapter is used later in the book to provide sorting algorithms for mesh-based architectures.

A significant portion of the computing cycles in the 1960s and 1970s was devoted to sorting/ordering data. As a result, a substantial effort has been put into developing efficient sorting techniques.

The focus of this chapter is on a then-revolutionary Bitonic Sort algorithm introduced in 1968 by Ken Batcher. The algorithm was proposed for a simple hardware model, which we will present. We will also discuss implementations of Bitonic Sort on several models of computation that we introduced in Chapter 4.

It is important to note that using hardware to sort data also provides an efficient way to route data on circuit boards, which was one of Batcher's motivations. In fact, in his seminal 1968 paper, Batcher actually proposed two hardware-based sorting algorithms, namely, *Bitonic Sort* and *Odd-Even Merge Sort*. Both of these algorithms are based on a Merge Sort framework. Both algorithms are also presented for a simple hardware model. Further, in the case of Bitonic Sort, Batcher makes the insightful observation that such an algorithm would be very efficient on a parallel computer with the interconnection properties of a hypercube.

## Combinational Circuits and Sorting Networks

We begin this chapter with a presentation of combinational circuits. A *combinational circuit* is a hardware model that consists of a unidirectional flow of data from input to output through a series of basic functional units. We present illustrations of combinational circuits that show the flow of information. The input data flows along communication lines, through functional units that perform basic operations, and the results are finally presented as output. The functional units are represented by boxes. It is understood that, in these diagrams, the *information flows from left to right.*

After this introduction, we discuss Batcher's Bitonic Merge Unit, as applied to combinational circuits. We then present an in-depth analysis of the running time of the Bitonic Merge routine on this model. Finally, we conclude with a combinational circuit implementation and analysis of Bitonic Sort, which takes advantage of this very interesting Bitonic Merge Unit.

*Combinational circuits* were among the earliest models developed in terms of providing a systematic study of parallel algorithms. They have the advantage of being simple, and many algorithms that are developed for combinational circuits serve as the basis for algorithms presented elsewhere in this book for other models of parallel computing.

A combinational circuit can be thought of as taking input from the left, allowing data to flow through a series of functional units in a systematic fashion, and producing output at the right. The functional units in the circuit are quite simple. Each such unit performs a single operation in $\Theta(1)$ time. These operations include logical operations such as **and, or,** and **not,** comparisons such as $<$, $>$, and $=$, and fundamental arithmetic operations such as addition, subtraction, minimum, and maximum.

These functional units are connected to each other by *unidirectional* links, which serve to transport the data. These units are assumed to have constant *fan-in* and constant *fan-out*. That is, the number of links entering a functional unit and the number of links exiting a functional unit are both bounded by a constant.

In this chapter, we restrict our attention to comparison-based combinational networks in which each functional unit simply takes two values as input and presents these values ordered on its output lines. Finally, it should be noted that there are no cycles in these circuits.

### Sorting Networks

We consider a comparison-based combinational circuit that can be used as a general-purpose sorting network. Such *sorting networks* are said to be *oblivious* to their inputs since this model fixes the sequence of comparisons in advance. That is, the sequence of comparisons is not a function of the input values. Notice that some traditional sorting routines, such as Quicksort or Heapsort, are not oblivious in that they perform comparisons that are dependent on the input data.

While Bitonic Sort was originally defined in terms of sorting networks, it was intended to be used not only as a sorting network, but as a simple switching network for routing multiple inputs to multiple outputs. The basic element of a sorting network is the *comparison element*, which receives two inputs, say, $A$ and $B$, and produces both the minimum of $A$ and $B$ and the maximum of $A$ and $B$ as output, as shown in Figure 5-1.

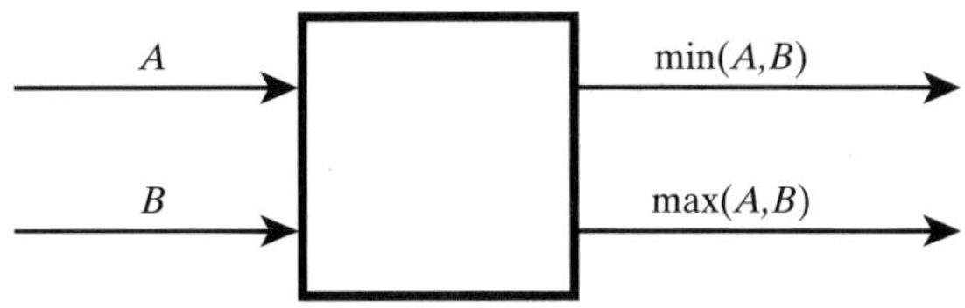


**FIGURE 5-1** *An illustration of a comparison element. This is the fundamental element of a sorting network. The comparison element receives inputs A and B and produces outputs min(A,B) and max(A,B).*

**Definition:** A sequence $a = \langle a_1, a_2, \ldots, a_p \rangle$ of $p$ numbers is said to be *bitonic* if and only if

1. $a_1 \leq a_2 \leq \ldots \leq a_k \geq \ldots \geq a_p$, for some $k$, $1 < k < p$, or
2. $a_1 \geq a_2 \geq \ldots \geq a_k \leq \ldots \leq a_p$, for some $k$, $1 < k < p$, or
3. $a$ can be split into two parts that can be interchanged to give either of the first two cases.

The reader should notice that by including the third case in the **Definition,** the first two cases become equivalent, and thus redundant. The third case can be interpreted as stating that a circular rotation of the members of the sequence yields an example of one of the first two cases. For example, the sequence $\langle 3, 2, 1, 6, 8, 24, 15, 10 \rangle$ is bitonic, since there is a circular rotation of the sequence that yields $\langle 6, 8, 24, 15, 10, 3, 2, 1 \rangle$, which satisfies case 1.

A bitonic sequence can therefore be thought of as a circular list that obeys the following.

- Start a traversal at the entry in the list of minimal value, which we will refer to as $x$.
- Traverse the list in either direction. During a traversal, we will encounter elements in nondecreasing order until we reach a maximum element in the list, after which we will encounter elements in nonincreasing order until we return to $x$. Notice that if there are duplicate elements in the sequence, then there will be plateaus in the traversal where multiple items of the same value appear contiguously.

Before introducing a critical theorem about bitonic sequences, we make an important observation about two *monotonic* sequences. Given one ascending sequence and one descending sequence, they can be concatenated to form a bitonic sequence. Therefore, a network that sorts a bitonic sequence into monotonic order can be used as a *merging* network. That is, such a network will take as input a bitonic sequence and produce as output a sorted sequence. In particular, given any of *i*) the concatenation of ordered list $A$ and the reverse of ordered list $B$, *ii*) the ordered list $B$ concatenated to the reverse of ordered list $A$, *iii*) the reverse of ordered list $A$ concatenated to ordered list $B$, or *iv*) the reverse of ordered list $B$ concatenated to ordered list $A$, a bitonic *merge* network will produce a sorted list of $A \cup B$.

The proof of the theorem that follows is critical to an understanding of bitonic sequences and bitonic merge units. More importantly, the proof is constructive in that it can be used to devise a combinational circuit of a bitonic merge unit or an algorithm for performing Bitonic Merge. We urge the reader to comprehend fully the intricacies of the proof in order to understand and appreciate the construction of a wide variety of parallel sorting methods that will be presented in this text.

**Theorem:** Given a bitonic sequence $a = \langle a_1, a_2, \ldots, a_{2n} \rangle$, the following hold.

a. $d = \langle \min\{a_i, a_{n+i}\} \rangle_{i=1}^{n} = \langle \min\{a_1, a_{n+1}\}, \min\{a_2, a_{n+2}\}, \ldots, \min\{a_n, a_{2n}\} \rangle$ is bitonic.

b. $e = \langle \max\{a_i, a_{n+i}\} \rangle_{i=1}^{n} = \langle \max\{a_1, a_{n+1}\}, \max\{a_2, a_{n+2}\}, \ldots, \max\{a_n, a_{2n}\} \rangle$ is bitonic.

c. $\max(d) \le \min(e)$.

**Proof:** Let $d_i = \min\{a_i, a_{n+i}\}$ and $e_i = \max\{a_i, a_{n+i}\}$, $1 \le i \le n$. We must prove that *i*) $d$ is bitonic, *ii*) $e$ is bitonic, and *iii*) $\max(d) \le \min(e)$. Without loss of generality, we can assume that $a_1 \le a_2 \le \ldots \le a_{j-1} \le a_j \ge a_{j+1} \ge \ldots \ge a_{2n}$, for some $j$ such that $n \le j \le 2n$.

- Suppose $a_n \le a_{2n}$. For $1 \le i \le n$, if $n + i < j$ then the choice of $j$ implies $a_i \le a_{n+i}$, while if $n + i \ge j$ then $a_i \le a_n \le a_{2n} \le a_{n+i}$. (See Figure 5-2.) Therefore, if $a_n \le a_{2n}$, we have $d_i = a_i$ and $e_i = a_{n+i}$. Further, since $\max(d) = a_n$ and $\min(e) = \min(a_{n+1}, a_{2n})$, we also have $\max(d) \le \min(e)$. This completes the proof for the case where $a_n \le a_{2n}$.
- Now consider the case where $a_n > a_{2n}$. Since $a$ is nondecreasing for $i \le j$ and nonincreasing for $i \ge j$, and since $a_{j-n} \le a_j$, then there is an index $k$, $j \le k < 2n$, for which $a_{k-n} \le a_k$ and $a_{k-n+1} > a_{k+1}$. This is illustrated in Figure 5-3.

First, consider the sequence $d$. For $1 \le i \le k - n$, we have either

- $i + n \le j$, which implies $a_i \le a_{i+n}$, or
- $i + n > j$, in which case $a_i \le a_{k-n} \le a_k \le a_{i+n}$, the last inequality in the chain following from

$$(i \le k - n) \Rightarrow (j < i + n \le k).$$

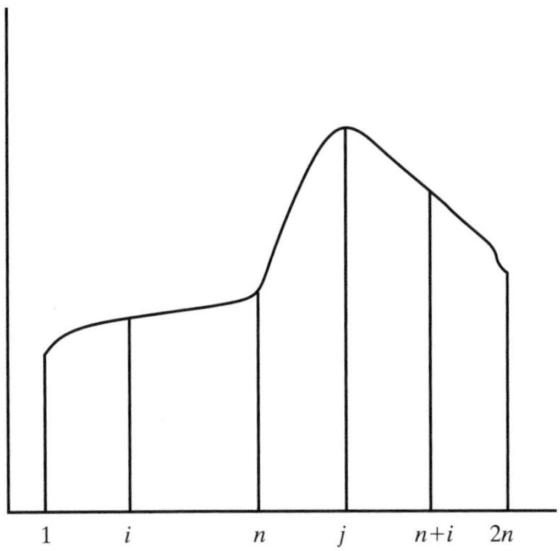


**FIGURE 5-2** *An illustration of a bitonic sequence <a> in which* $a_n \le a_{2n}$ *and* $a_j$ *is a maximal element of <a>, where* $n \le j \le 2n$.

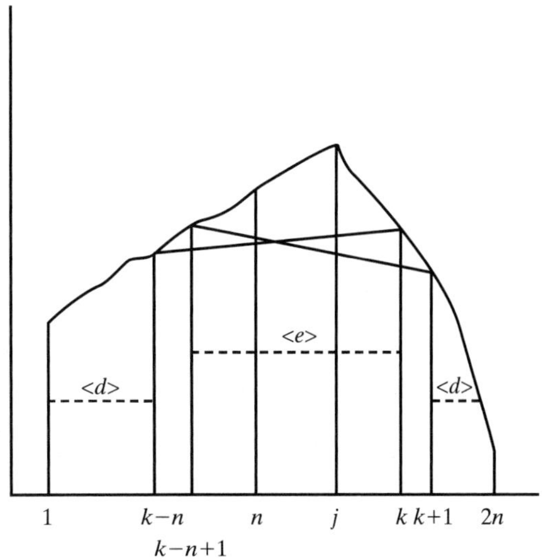


**FIGURE 5-3** *An illustration of a bitonic sequence <a> in which* $a_n > a_{2n}$, $a_j$ *is a maximal element of <a>, where* $n \le j \le 2n$, *and there exists a pivot element k such that* $a_{k-n} \le a_k$ *and* $a_{k-n+1} > a_{k+1}$.

Thus, for $1 \le i \le k - n$, we have $d_i = a_i$. Further, this subsequence of $d$ is nondecreasing. Next, notice that $d_i = a_{n+i}$ for $k - n < i \le n$, since for such $i$,

$$a_i \ge a_{k-n+1} \text{ (since } k - n + 1 \le i \le n \le j)$$

$$\ge a_{k+1} \text{ (by choice of } k)$$

$$\ge a_{i+n} \text{ (since } j < k + 1 \le i + n).$$

Further, this subsequence of $d$ is nonincreasing. Therefore, $d$ is made of a nondecreasing subsequence followed by a nonincreasing subsequence. By the first part of the bitonic sequence definition, we know that $d$ is bitonic.

Now consider the sequence $e$. Notice that $e_i = a_{n+i}$ for $1 \le i \le j - n$. Further, this subsequence of $e$ is nondecreasing. Next, notice that $e_i = a_{n+i}$ for $j - n \le i \le k - n$. Further, this subsequence is easily seen to be nonincreasing. Finally, notice that $e_i = a_i$ for $k - n < i \le n$. This final subsequence of $e$ is nondecreasing. Therefore, $e$ is bitonic by case three from the definition since we also have that $e_n = a_n \le a_{n+1} = e_1$. See Figure 5-3.

Now, consider the relationship between bitonic sequences $d$ and $e$. Notice that $\max(d) = \max\{a_{k-n}, a_{k+1}\}$ and $\min(e) = \min\{a_k, a_{k-n+1}\}$. It follows easily that $\max(d) \le \min(e)$, completing the proof for the case of $a_n > a_{2n}$.

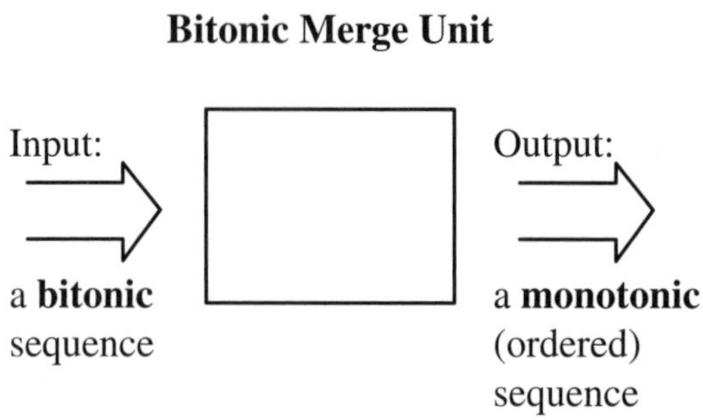


**FIGURE 5-4** *Input and output for a bitonic merge unit.*

## Bitonic Merge

The theorem above gives the iterative rule for constructing a bitonic merge unit. That is, a unit that will take a bitonic sequence as input and produce a monotonic sequence as output. (See Figure 5-4.) It is important to note that this is only a merge step, and that this merge step works only on bitonic sequences. After we finish our discussion and analysis of the *merge* unit, we will show how to utilize this merge unit to sort data in the Bitonic Sort algorithm.

We now present the Bitonic Merge algorithm. The input to the routine is a bitonic sequence $A$ and direction, *i.e.*, ascending or descending, into which $A$ will be sorted. Notice this is unlike the merge algorithm used in Merge Sort, for which two lists are input. The routine will produce a monotonic sequence $Z$, ordered as requested.

**Subprogram BitonicMerge(*A, Z, direction*)**
**Procedure:** Merge bitonic list $A$, assumed at top level of recursion to be of size $2n$, to produce list $Z$, where $Z$ is ordered according to the *function* ***direction,*** which can be viewed as a $\Theta(1)$-time function with values "<" or ">".
**Local variables:** $i$: list index
$Z_d, Z'_d, Z_e, Z'_e$: lists, initially empty

**Action:**

```
If |A| < 2 then return Z = A            {This is a base case
                                          of recursion}
Else
  For i = 1 to n, do
    If direction(A_i, A_{n+i}), then
      append A_i to Z_d and append A_{n+i} to Z_e
    Else append A_{n+i} to Z_d and append A_i to Z_e
  End For
```

```
      BitonicMerge(Z_d, Z'_d direction)
      BitonicMerge(Z_e, Z'_e, direction)
      Concatenate(Z'_d, Z'_e, Z)
    End Else |A| ≥ 2
  End BitonicMerge
```

Notice the strong resemblance in algorithmic structure between Bitonic Merge and both Merge Sort and Quicksort, *c.f.*, Chapter 9.

- Bitonic Merge is similar to Merge Sort in that it requires a list of elements to be split into two even sublists, recursively sorted, and then concatenated. Be aware, though, that Merge Sort takes as input an *unordered* list, which is sorted to produce an ordered list, while Bitonic Merge takes as input a bitonically ordered list and produces an ordered list.
- Bitonic Merge is similar to Quicksort in that it splits a list into sublists, recursively solves the problem on the sublists, and then concatenates the sublists into the final list. In fact, notice that for each of Bitonic Merge and Quicksort, the two intermediate sublists that are produced both have the property that every element in one of the lists is greater than or equal to every element in the other list. As above, we observe that Quicksort is less restrictive than Bitonic Merge, in that the input to Quicksort is a list that need not have any order, while the input to Bitonic Merge must be a bitonically ordered list.

As described, a Bitonic Merge unit for $2n$ numbers is constructed from $n$ comparitors and two $n$-item Bitonic Merge units. Two items can be merged with a single comparison unit. In fact, $n$ pairs of items can be simultaneously merged using one level of merge units. That is, if $L(x)$ is the number of levels of comparitors required to merge simultaneously $x/2$ pairs of items, we know that the base case is $L(2) = 1$. In general, to merge two bitonic sequences, each of size $n$, requires $L(2n) = L(n) + 1 = \log_2 2n$ levels.

In terms of our analysis of running time, we assume that a comparison unit performs its operation in $\Theta(1)$ time. So, each level of a sorting network contributes $\Theta(1)$ time to the total running time. Therefore, a bitonic merge unit for $2n$ numbers performs a Bitonic Merge in $\Theta(\log n)$ time.

Now consider implementing Bitonic Merge on a sequential machine. The algorithm employs $\Theta(\log n)$ iterations of a procedure that makes $n$ comparisons. Therefore, the total running time for this *merge* routine on a sequential machine is $\Theta(n \log n)$. As a means of comparison, recall that *i*) the time for Merge Sort to merge two lists with a total of $n$ items is $\Theta(n)$, and *ii*) the time for Quicksort to partition a set of $n$ items is, as we show later in the book, $\Theta(n)$.

In Figure 5-5, we present a $2n$-item bitonic merge unit. It is important to note that the input sequence, $a$, is bitonic and that the output sequence, $c$, is sorted. The

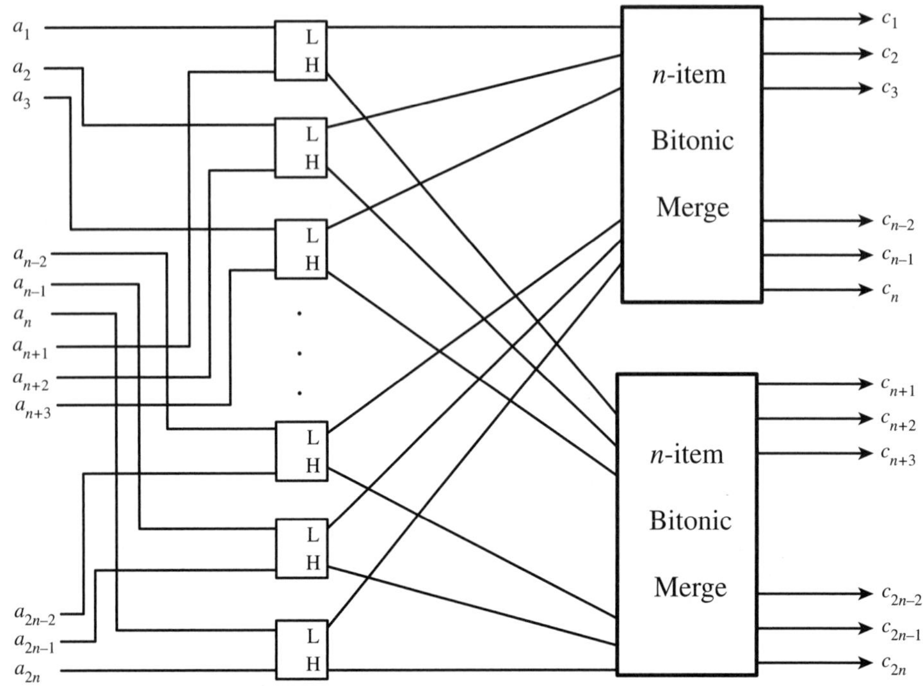


**FIGURE 5-5** *The iterative rule for constructing a bitonic merge unit. The input sequence* <a> *consists of* 2n *items and is bitonic. The* 2n *item output sequence* <c> *is sorted.*

boxes represent the comparitors that accept two inputs and produce two outputs, namely, *L*, which represents the minimum of the two input values, and *H*, which represents the maximum of the two input values. The reader might think of *L* as being the "lower" value of the pair of inputs and *H* as being the "higher" value of the pair.

Figures 5-6 and 5-7 present examples of a four-element bitonic merge unit and an eight-element bitonic merge unit, respectively. The input sequence <*a*> in both figures is assumed to be bitonic. Further, as in Figure 5-5, we let *L* denote the minimum result of the comparison, and we let *H* represent the maximum result. As mentioned in the text, the reader might think of *L* as being the "lower" value of the pair of inputs and *H* as being the "higher" value of the pair.

## Bitonic Sort

Bitonic Sort is a sorting routine based on Merge Sort. Given a list of $n$ elements, Merge Sort can be viewed in a bottom-up fashion as first merging $n$ single elements into $n/2$ pairs of ordered elements. The next step consists of pair-wise merging these $n/2$ ordered pairs of elements into $n/4$ ordered quadruples. This process continues until the last stage, which consists of merging 2 ordered groups of

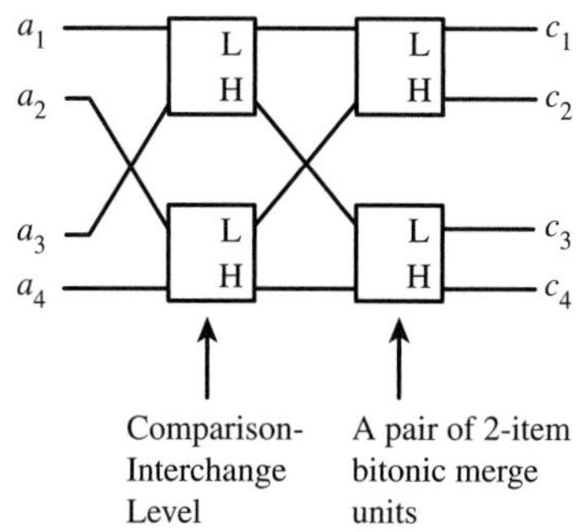


A 4-item bitonic merge unit performs a comparison-interchange on items 2 apart (comparing $a_1$ and $a_3$ and simultaneously $a_2$ and $a_4$) and then sends the minima into a 2-item bitonic merge unit and the maxima into a 2-item bitonic merge unit.

**FIGURE 5-6** *A four-item bitonic merge unit. Note that* $\langle a_1, a_2, a_3, a_4 \rangle$ *is the bitonic input sequence and* $\langle c_1, c_2, c_3, c_4 \rangle$ *is the sorted output sequence. The number of levels* $L(2n)$ *can be determined as* $L(2n) = L(2 \times 2) = 1 + L(n) = 1 + L(2) = 2 = \log_2 (2n)$.

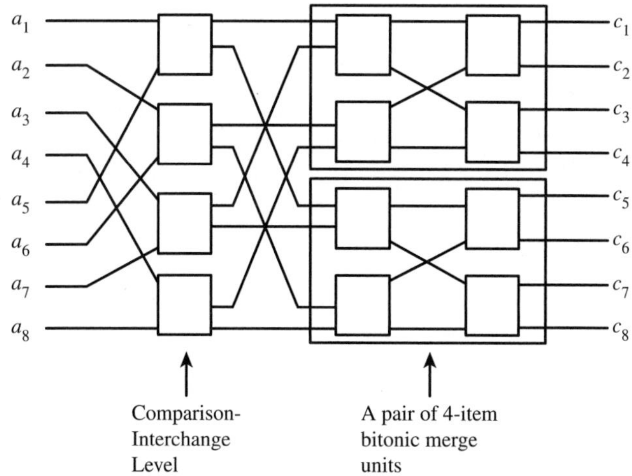


An 8-item bitonic merge unit performs a comparison-interchange on items 4 apart (comparing $a_1$ and $a_5$, $a_2$ and $a_6$, $a_3$ and $a_7$, and simultaneously $a_4$ and $a_8$) and then sends the minima into a 4-item bitonic merge unit and the maxima into a 4-item bitonic merge unit.

**FIGURE 5-7** *An 8-item bitonic merge unit. Note that the input sequence* $\langle a_1, \ldots, a_8 \rangle$ *is bitonic and the output sequence* $\langle c_1, \ldots, c_8 \rangle$ *is sorted. The number of levels* $L(2n)$ *can be determined as* $L(2n) = L(2 \times 4) = 1 + L(4) = 1 + 2 = 3 = \log_2 8 = \log_2 (2n)$.

elements, each of size $n/2$, into a single ordered list of size $n$. Bitonic Sort works in much the same way.

Given an initial input list of random elements, notice that every pair of elements is bitonic. Therefore, in the first stage of Bitonic Sort, bitonic sequences of size 2 are merged to create ordered lists of size 2. Notice that if these lists alternate between being ordered into increasing and decreasing order, then at the end of this first stage of merging, we actually have $n/4$ bitonic sequences of size 4. In the next stage, bitonic sequences of size 4 are merged into sorted sequences of size 4, alternately into increasing and decreasing order, so as to form $n/8$ bitonic sequences of size 8. Given an unordered sequence of size $2n$, notice that exactly $\log_2 2n$ stages of merging are required to produce a completely ordered list. Note that we have assumed, for the sake of simplicity, that $2n = 2^k$, for some positive integer $k$. See Figure 5-8.

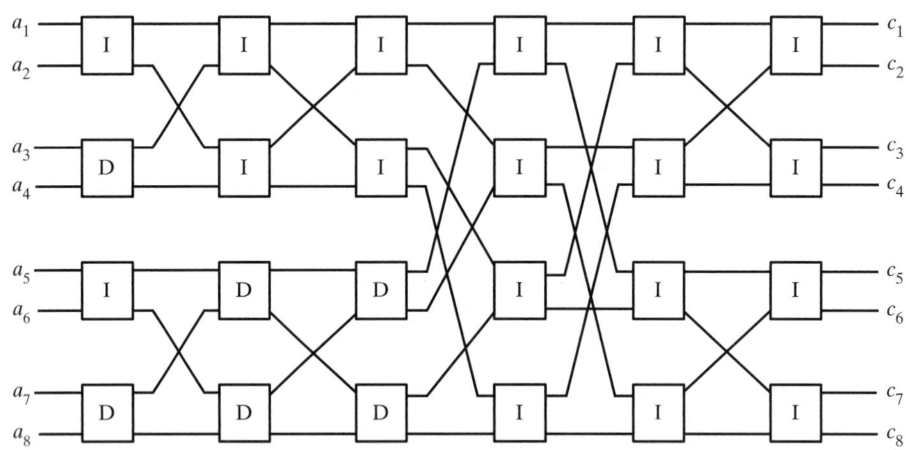


**FIGURE 5-8** *An example of Bitonic Sort on 8 data items. Note that the input sequence <a> is initially unordered, and the output sequence <c> is sorted into nondecreasing order. The symbol "I" means that the comparison is done so that the items appear in increasing order. That is, the top output item is less than or equal to the bottom output item. The symbol "D" represents that the comparison is done so that the items appear in decreasing order. That is, the top output item is greater than or equal to the bottom output item.*

Now consider the merging stages. Each of the $\log_2 2n$ stages of Bitonic Sort utilizes a different number of comparitors. In fact, notice that in stage 1, each bitonic list of size 2 is merged with one comparitor. In stage 2, each bitonic sequence of size 4 is merged with two *levels* of comparitors, as per our previous example. In fact, at stage $i$, the Bitonic Merge requires $i$ levels of comparitors.

We now consider the total number of levels of comparitors required to sort an *arbitrary* set of $2n$ input items with Bitonic Sort. Again, there are $\log_2 2n$ stages of merging, and each stage $i$ requires $i$ levels of comparisons. Therefore, the number of levels of comparitors is given by

$$\sum_{i=1}^{\log_2 2n} i = \frac{(\log_2 2n)(\log_2 2n + 1)}{2} = \frac{\log_2^2 (2n)}{2} + \frac{\log_2 (2n)}{2}.$$

So, $\Theta(\log^2 n)$ levels of comparitors are required to sort completely an initially unordered list of size $2n$. That is, an input list of $2n$ values can be sorted under this combinational circuit model with $\Theta(\log^2 n)$ delay.

Now, consider how this algorithm compares to traditional sorting algorithms operating on a RAM. Notice that for $2n$ input values, each of the $\Theta(\log^2 n)$ levels of comparitors actually uses $n$ comparitors. That is, a total of $\Theta(n \log^2 n)$ comparitors is required to sort $2n$ input items with Bitonic Sort. Therefore, this algorithm runs in $\Theta(n \log^2 n)$ time on a sequential machine.

**Subprogram BitonicSort($X$)**
**Procedure:** Sort the list $X[1, \ldots, 2n]$, using the Bitonic Sort algorithm.
**Local variables:** integers *segmentLength, i*

**Action:**

```
segmentLength = 2
Do
  For i = 1 to n/segmentLength, do in parallel
    BitonicMerge(
        X[(2i − 2) × segmentLength + 1, ..., 2i ×
        segmentLength],
        X[(2i − 2) × segmentLength + 1, ..., 2i ×
        segmentLength],
        ascending = odd(i))
  End For
  segmentLength = 2 × segmentLength
While segmentLength < 2n {End Do}
End BitonicSort
```

There is an alternative view of sorting networks that some find easier to grasp. We present such a view in Figure 5-9 for Bitonic Sort, as applied to an eight-element unordered sequence. The input elements are given on the left of the diagram. Each line is labeled with a unique three-bit binary number. Please do not confuse these labels with the values that are contained on the lines, which are not shown in this figure. Horizontal lines are used to represent the flow of data from left to right. A vertical line is used to illustrate a comparison between the elements on the endpoints of its line. In particular, the vertical line will compare the two elements and either leave them on their current lines or swap them so as to place them in the required order. This is called a *comparison-exchange* operation. The letters next to the vertical lines indicate whether the comparison being performed is ≤, represented as I, giving the intuition of *increasing*, or ≥, represented as D, giving the intuition of *decreasing*. Note that dashed vertical lines are used to separate the $3 = \log_2 8$ merge stages of the algorithm. The reader might want to draw a diagram of an eight-element bitonic sorting network using the lines and comparitors that have been used previously in this chapter and verify that such a diagram is consistent with this one.

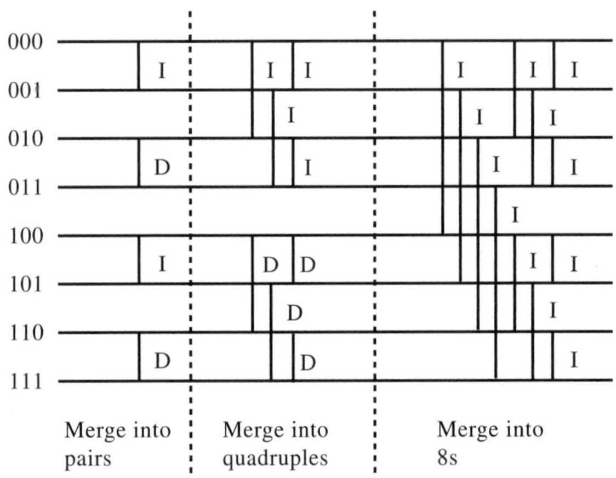


**FIGURE 5-9** *An alternative view of Bitonic Sort for 8 elements. The horizontal lines represent wires and the vertical lines represent comparison-exchange elements. That is, the vertical lines represent points in time at which two items are compared and ordered according to the label I or D. Notice that the* $\log_2 8 = 3$ *bitonic merge stages are separated by dotted vertical lines.*

## Bitonic Sort on Parallel Computers

Finally, Batcher made a very interesting observation in his seminal 1968 paper that included Bitonic Sort and Odd-Even Merge Sort. Consider the alternative view of Bitonic Sort just presented. Batcher noticed that at each stage of the algorithm, the only elements ever compared are those on lines that differ in exactly one bit of their line labels. Suppose that we are given a parallel machine consisting of a set of $2n$ processors and we have one item per processor that we wish to sort. Batcher noted that if every processor were connected to all other processors that differ in exactly one bit position, the sorting would be performed in $\Theta(\log^2 n)$ time. In fact, such a model corresponds to the interconnection of a hypercube, which was introduced in Chapter 4.

| Processor | Entry | Neighbor processors |
|---|---|---|
| 000 | $a_0$ | 001, 010, and 100 |
| 001 | $a_1$ | 000, 011, and 101 |
| 010 | $a_2$ | 011, 000, and 110 |
| 011 | $a_3$ | 010, 001, and 111 |
| 100 | $a_4$ | 101, 110, and 000 |
| 101 | $a_5$ | 100, 111, and 001 |
| 110 | $a_6$ | 111, 100, and 010 |
| 111 | $a_7$ | 110, 101, and 011 |

Naturally, in addition to being able to sort efficiently on a hypercube, the Bitonic Sort algorithm can be applied to a PRAM, where "neighboring" processors can communicate directly through the shared memory. As we discuss later in the text, the communication pattern and general algorithmic strategy of Bitonic Sort can be applied to medium- and coarse-grained machines, including hypercubes, meshes, clusters, and networks of workstations, to name a few. In such cases, each processor has a packet of $m$ fundamental data items. After an initial sort of the $m$ data items in $O(m \log m)$ time, exchanges of packets between processors run in a total of $\Theta(m)$ time instead of $\Theta(1)$ time, and a merge, for example, of 2 data packets is performed in asymptotically optimal $\Theta(m)$ time by using a standard merge.

**Concluding Remarks.** We have shown the following.

- Bitonic Sort will sort $n$ items in $\Theta(\log^2 n)$ time using a sorting network.
- Bitonic Sort will sort $n$ items in $\Theta(\log^2 n)$ time on a hypercube of size $n$.
- Bitonic Sort will sort $n$ items in $\Theta(\log^2 n)$ time on a parallel machine with $n$ processors that allows any two processors to communicate in constant time. That is, Bitonic Sort will sort $n$ items on a PRAM of size $n$.
- Bitonic Sort will sort $n$ items in $\Theta(n \log^2 n)$ time on a sequential machine (RAM).

## Summary

In this chapter, we present one of Batcher's sorting networks for combinational circuits and their natural extension to parallel machines with certain well-defined interconnection networks. These are pioneering ideas in the history of parallel computing, illustrating the time efficiencies that are possible by using an appropriate combination of architectures and algorithms. We illustrate Batcher's Bitonic Merge and Bitonic Sort algorithms and analyze their running times on hardware networks, as well as sequential and parallel architectures. We also observe that Batcher's algorithms are easily modified to other parallel architectures, as will be discussed later in the book.

## Chapter Notes

In 1968, Ken Batcher presented a short paper that introduced Bitonic Sort and Odd-Even Merge Sort, and made the insightful observation that both sorting networks would operate efficiently on a hypercube network of processors. The work from this paper, "Sorting networks and their applications," (K.E. Batcher, *Proceedings of the AFIPS Spring Joint Computer Conference* 32, 1968, 307–314) has been covered in traditional courses on data structures and algorithms by many instructors in recent decades. The material has become more integral for such courses as parallel computing has reached the mainstream. This material has recently been incorporated into textbooks. A nice presentation of this material can be found in *Introduction to Algorithms*, by T.H. Cormen, C.E. Leiserson, R.L. Rivest, and C. Stein (3rd ed.: MIT Press, Cambridge, MA, 2009).

## Exercises

**1.** Define a **transposition network** to be a comparison network in which comparisons are only made between elements on adjacent lines. Prove that sorting $n$ input elements on a transposition network requires $\Omega(n^2)$ comparison units.

**2.** What is the smallest number of elements for which you can construct a sequence that is not bitonic? Prove your result.

**3.** Consider a comparison network $C$ that takes a sequence of elements $X = \{x_1, x_2, \ldots, x_n\}$ as input. Further, suppose that the output of $C$ is the same set of $n$ elements, but in some predetermined order. Let the output sequence be denoted as $\{y_1, y_2, \ldots, y_n\}$.

a. Given a monotonically increasing function $F$, prove that if $C$ is given the sequence $\{F(x_1), F(x_2), \ldots, F(x_n)\}$ as input, it will produce $\{F(y_1), F(y_2), \ldots, F(y_n)\}$ as output.

b. Suppose that input set $X$ consists only of 0's and 1's. That is, the input is a set of $n$ bits. Further, suppose that the output produced by $C$ consists of all the 0's followed by all the 1's. That is, $C$ can be used to sort any permutation of 0's and 1's. Prove that such a circuit (one that can sort an arbitrary sequence of $n$ bits) can correctly sort any sequence of arbitrary numbers (not necessarily 0's and 1's). This result is known as the *0–1 sorting principle*.

**4.** Use the *0–1 sorting principle* to prove that the following *odd-even merging network* correctly merges sorted sequences $\{x_1, x_2, \ldots, x_n\}$ and $\{y_1, y_2, \ldots, y_n\}$.

- The odd-indexed elements of the input sequences, that is $\{x_1, x_3, \ldots, x_{n-1}\}$ and $\{y_1, y_3, \ldots, y_{n-1}\}$, are merged to produce a *sorted* sequence $\{u_1, u_2, \ldots, u_n\}$.
- Simultaneously, the even-indexed elements of the input sequences, $\{x_2, x_4, \ldots, x_n\}$ and $\{y_2, y_4, \ldots, y_n\}$, are merged to produce a *sorted* sequence $\{v_1, v_2, \ldots, v_n\}$.
- Finally, the output sequence $\{z_1, z_2, \ldots, z_{2n}\}$ is obtained from $z_1 = u_1$, $z_{2n} = v_n$, $z_{2i} = \min(u_{i+1}, v_i)$, $z_{2i+1} = \max(u_{i+1}, v_i)$, for all $1 \leq i \leq n - 1$.

# 6

# Matrix Operations

*Computational science and engineering* (*CS&E*) is a discipline that utilizes high-end computing and mathematics to solve problems in science and engineering. Computational science and engineering is the third scientific paradigm, complementing *theoretical science* and *laboratory science.* Academic programs in computational science and engineering are widespread at universities, colleges, and even in the kindergarten through high-school (*i.e.,* K–12) curriculum.

The thrust of computational science and engineering is on simulation and modeling, which has led to breakthroughs in a wide variety of scientific and engineering disciplines. In fact, numerical simulation has been used to study complex systems that would be too expensive, time-consuming, or dangerous to study by direct, physical, experimentation. The importance of simulation can be found in "grand challenge" problems in areas such as structural biology, materials science, high-energy physics, economics, fluid dynamics, and global climate change, to name a few. For example, designers of automobiles and airplanes rely heavily on simulation in an effort to reduce the costs of prototypes, to test models, and as an alternative to expensive wind tunnels.

Computational science and engineering is an interdisciplinary subject, uniting computing, which includes hardware, software, algorithms, and a wide variety of computational tools, with mathematics and disciplinary efforts in biology, chemistry, physics, and other applied scientific and engineering fields. Computationally intensive operations such as matrix multiplication and solving systems of linear or differential equations are at the heart of many problems in computational science and engineering. In this chapter, we consider the problems of matrix multiplication and Gaussian elimination on a variety of models of computation.

## Matrix Multiplication

Suppose matrix $A$ has $p$ rows and $q$ columns. We will alternately denote this matrix as $A_{p,q}$ or $A_{p\times q}$. Given matrices $A_{p,q}$ and $B_{q,r}$, the matrix product of $A$ and $B$ is written informally as $C = A \times B$ and more formally as $C_{p,r} = A_{p,q} \times B_{q,r}$. The element $c_{i,j}$, which represents the element of $C$ in the $i^{\text{th}}$ row and $j^{\text{th}}$ column, for $1 \le i \le p$ and $1 \le j \le r$, is defined as the dot product of the $i^{\text{th}}$ row of $A$ and the $j^{\text{th}}$ column of $B$. That is,

$$c_{i,j} = \sum_{k=1}^{q} a_{i,k} b_{k,j}.$$

Notice that the number of columns of $A$ must be the same as the number of rows of $B$, since each entry of the product corresponds to the *dot product* of one row of $A$ and one column of $B$. In fact, in order to determine the product of $A$ and $B$, the dot product of every row of $A$ with every column of $B$ is typically computed. See Figure 6-1.

$$\underset{A_{3\times 4}}{\begin{bmatrix} 1 & 2 & 3 & 4 \\ 5 & 6 & 7 & 8 \\ 9 & 10 & 11 & 12 \end{bmatrix}} \times \underset{B_{4\times 5}}{\begin{bmatrix} 1 & 0 & 2 & 0 & 4 \\ 0 & 1 & 0 & 2 & 0 \\ 1 & 0 & 2 & 0 & 4 \\ 0 & 1 & 0 & 2 & 0 \end{bmatrix}} = \underset{C_{3\times 5}}{\begin{bmatrix} 4 & 6 & 8 & 12 & 16 \\ 12 & 14 & 24 & 28 & 48 \\ 20 & 22 & 40 & 44 & 80 \end{bmatrix}}$$

**FIGURE 6-1** *An example of matrix multiplication. For example,* $c_{2,3}$ *is the dot product of the second row of A,* (5, 6, 7, 8), *and the third column of B,* (2, 0, 2, 0), *which is computed as* $c_{2,3} = 5 \times 2 + 6 \times 0 + 7 \times 2 + 8 \times 0 = 24$.

A traditional, sequential dot product of two vectors, each of length $q$, requires $q$ multiplications and $q - 1$ additions. Therefore, such a sequential operation can be performed in $\Theta(q)$ time. Hence, the $p \times r$ dot products, each of length $q$, used to perform a traditional matrix multiplication can be computed in a straightforward fashion in $\Theta(prq)$ time on a RAM. So, the total number of operations performed in a brute-force matrix multiplication on a RAM, as described, is $\Theta(prq)$. Such an algorithm follows.

**Input:** A $p \times q$ matrix $A$ and a $q \times r$ matrix $B$.
**Output:** The matrix product $C_{p,r} = A_{p,q} \times B_{q,r}$.

**Action:**

```
For i = 1 to p, do                    {Loop through rows of A}
  For j = 1 to r, do               {Loop through columns of B}
                 {Perform the dot product of a row of A and
                                             a column of B}
    C[i,j] = 0
    For k = 1 to q, do
        C[i,j] = C[i,j] + A[i,k] × B[k,j]
    End For k
  End For j
End For i
```

We now consider matrix multiplication on a variety of models of computation. For simplicity, we will assume that all matrices are of size $n \times n$.

**RAM:** A traditional sequential algorithm, as given above, will multiply $A_{n\times n} \times B_{n\times n}$ to produce $C_{n\times n}$ in $\Theta(n^3)$ time. The importance of matrix multiplication and its relatively large running time led to Strassen's 1968 breakthrough of a divide-and-conquer algorithm to perform matrix multiplication in $O(n^{2.81})$ time. Subsequently, algorithms have been developed that run in $o(n^{2.81})$ time. We give a reference to Strassen's algorithm at the end of this chapter as the details of this highly advanced algorithm are beyond the scope of this book.

**PRAM:** Consider the design of an efficient matrix multiplication algorithm for a CR PRAM. Suppose we are given a PRAM with $n^3$ processors, where each processor has a unique label, $(i, j, k)$, where $1 \leq i, j, k \leq n$ are integers. That is, we assume that the $n$ processors are given as $P_{1,1,1}, \ldots, P_{n,n,n}$.

We associate processor $P_{i,k,j}$ with $a_{i,k}b_{k,j}$, the $k^{\text{th}}$ product between the $i^{\text{th}}$ row of $A$ and the $j^{\text{th}}$ column of $B$. Notice that this product is one of the terms that contributes to $c_{i,j}$. So, suppose that initially every processor $P_{i,k,j}$ computes the result of $a_{i,k}b_{k,j}$. After this $\Theta(1)$ time parallel step, notice that all $\Theta(n^3)$ multiplications have been performed.

Now we must compute the summation of each dot product's $\Theta(n)$ terms. This can be done in $\Theta(\log n)$ time by performing $\Theta(n^2)$ independent and simultaneous semigroup operations, where the operator is addition. So, in $\Theta(\log n)$ time, processors $P_{i,k,j}$, $k \in \{1, 2, \ldots, n\}$, can perform a semigroup operation to determine the value of $c_{i,j}$. Therefore, the running time of the algorithm is $\Theta(\log n)$ and the total cost is $\Theta(n^3 \log n)$.

Unfortunately, while efficient, this algorithm is not cost-optimal. Therefore, we can consider trying to reduce the running time by a factor of $\Theta(\log n)$ or the number of processors by a factor of $\Theta(\log n)$. Since reducing the running time is a difficult challenge, let's consider a CR PRAM with $n^3/\log_2 n$ processors. First, let each processor be responsible for a unique set of $\Theta(\log n)$ multiplications. For example, processor $P_1$ can perform the multiplication operations that processors $P_1, \ldots, P_{\log_2 n}$ performed in the previous algorithm, processor $P_2$ can perform the multiplication operations that processors $P_{1+\log_2 n}, \ldots, P_{2\log_2 n}$ performed in the previous algorithm, and so on. Next, each processor can sum the products it computed above in $\Theta(\log n)$ time. Finally, in $\Theta(\log n)$ time, each of the $n^2$ values $c_{i,j}$ can be computed by parallel semigroup operations (addition), with each semigroup operation performed by a group of $\Theta(n/\log n)$ of the $\Theta(n^3/\log n)$ processors associated with $c_{i,j}$. The algorithm follows.

**PRAM Matrix Product Algorithm using $\Theta(n^3/\log n)$ processors**
**Input:** A $p \times q$ matrix $A$ and a $q \times r$ matrix $B$.
**Output:** The matrix product $C_{p,r} = A_{p,q} \times B_{q,r}$.

**Action:**

To simplify our analysis, we assume $p = q = r = n$.

1. For each processor, determine the logarithmic number of products for which it is responsible. That is, logically determine a partition of the triples $(i,k,j)$, $1 \le i \le n$, $1 \le j \le n$, $1 \le k \le n$, so each processor knows the subset of $\Theta(\log n)$ products for which it is responsible. This determination can be done by a programmer in advance, and therefore does not utilize any computing time.
2. In parallel, each processor computes its $\Theta(\log n)$ products $p_{i,j,k} = a_{i,j} \times b_{j,k}$. This computation can be performed in $\Theta(\log n)$ time.
3. Compute each of the $n^2$ values $c_{i,j} = \sum_{k=1}^{n} p_{i,k,j}$ by parallel semigroup operations, as described above. This computation can be performed in $\Theta(\log n)$ time.

Therefore, the running time of the algorithm is $\Theta(\log n)$ and the cost of the algorithm is $\Theta(n^3)$, which is optimal when compared to the traditional matrix multiplication algorithm.

Finally, we consider a CR PRAM with $n^2$ processors. The algorithm is straightforward. Every processor simultaneously computes the result of a distinct entry in matrix $C$. Notice that every processor implements a traditional sequential algorithm for multiplying a row of $A$ by a column of $B$. This is performed in $\Theta(n)$ time, simultaneously for every row and column. Therefore, the $n^2$ entries of $C$ are determined in $\Theta(n)$ time with $n^2$ processors, which results in a cost-optimal $\Theta(n^3)$ operations algorithm, with respect to the traditional matrix multiplication algorithm.

**Mesh:** Consider the problem of determining $C = A \times B$ on a mesh computer, where $A$, $B$, and $C$ are $n \times n$ matrices. Initially, we will consider a $2n \times 2n$ mesh, where matrix $A$ is stored in the lower-left quadrant of the mesh, matrix $B$ is stored in the upper-right quadrant, and matrix $C$ will be produced in the mesh's lower-right quadrant, as shown in Figure 6-2. Let's consider the operations necessary to compute the entries of $C$ in place. That is, let's design an algorithm so that the entries of $A$ and $B$ flow through the lower-right quadrant of the $2n \times 2n$ mesh and arrive in processors where they can be of use at an appropriate time.

Consider the first step of the algorithm. Notice that if all processors containing an element of the first row of $A$ send their entries to the right and all processors containing an entry of the first column of $B$ simultaneously send their entries down, the processor responsible for $c_{1,1}$ will have entries $a_{1,n}$ and $b_{n,1}$ (see Figures 6-3a and 6-3b). Since $a_{1,n} \times b_{n,1}$ is one of the terms necessary to compute $c_{1,1}$, this partial result can be used to initialize the running sum for $c_{1,1}$ in the northwest processor of the lower-right quadrant. Notice that initially, $a_{1,n}$ and $b_{n,1}$ represent the only pair of elements that could meet during the first step and produce a useful result.

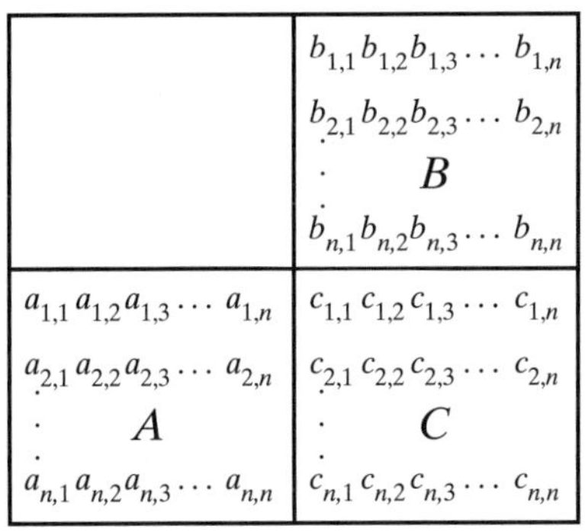


**FIGURE 6-2** *Matrix multiplication on a $2n \times 2n$ mesh. Matrix $A_{n\times n}$ initially resides in the lower-left quadrant and matrix $B_{n\times n}$ initially resides in the upper-right quadrant of the mesh. The matrix product $C_{n\times n} = A_{n\times n} \times B_{n\times n}$ is stored in the lower-right quadrant of the mesh.*

Now, consider the second step of such an algorithm. Notice that if the elements in row 1 of $A$ move to the right again, and that if the elements of column 1 of $B$ move down again, then $a_{1,n-1}$ and $b_{n-1,1}$ will meet in the processor responsible for $c_{1,1}$, which can add $a_{1,n-1} \times b_{n-1,1}$ to its running sum. In addition, notice that if the second row of $A$ and the second column of $B$ begin to move to the right and down, respectively, during this second time step, then the processors responsible for entries $c_{2,1}$ and $c_{1,2}$ can begin to initialize their running sums with a partial result (see Figure 6-3c).

In general, notice that we can extrapolate this process so that at time $i$, the $i^{\text{th}}$ row of $A$ and the $i^{\text{th}}$ column of $B$ initiate their journeys to the right and down, respectively. Further, at time $i$, rows $1 \dots i-1$ and columns $1 \dots i-1$ will continue on their respective journeys. Eventually, all of the elements of $C$ will be computed.

Now, let's consider the running time of the algorithm. Notice that at time $n$, the last row of $A$ and the last column of $B$ begin their journeys. During every subsequent time step, the last row of $A$ will continue to move one position to the right, and the last column of $B$ will continue to move one position down. At time $3n-2$, elements $a_{n,1}$ and $b_{1,n}$ will finally meet in the processor responsible for computing $c_{n,n}$, the last element to be computed. Therefore, the running time for this algorithm is $\Theta(n)$. Is this good? Consider that in the sequential matrix multiplication algorithm that is the basis of our current algorithm, every pair of elements $(a_{i,k}, b_{k,j})$ must be combined. Therefore, it is easy to see that this algorithm is asymptotically optimal in terms of running time on a mesh of size $4n^2$. This is due to the $\Theta(n)$ communication diameter of a mesh of size $4n^2$. Now, consider the total cost of the algorithm. Since this algorithm runs in $\Theta(n)$ time on a machine with $\Theta(n^2)$ processors, the total cost of the

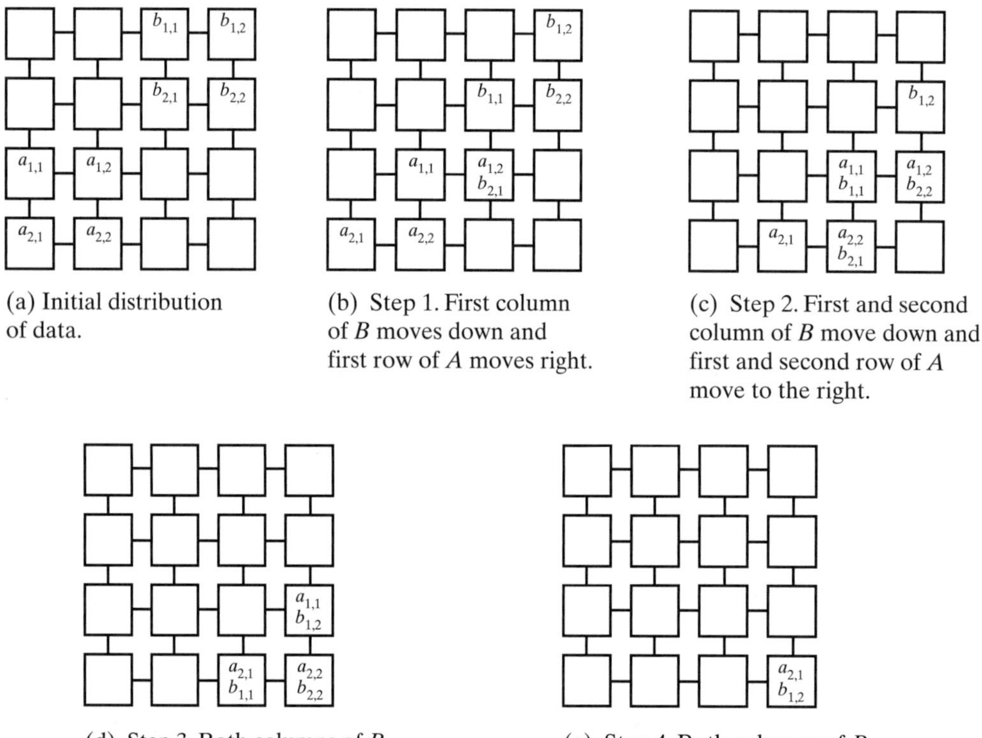


(a) Initial distribution of data.

(b) Step 1. First column of $B$ moves down and first row of $A$ moves right.

(c) Step 2. First and second column of $B$ move down and first and second row of $A$ move to the right.

(d) Step 3. Both columns of $B$ continue to move down while both rows of $A$ continue to move right.

(e) Step 4. Both columns of $B$ continue to move down while both rows of $A$ continue to move right.

**FIGURE 6-3** *Data flow for matrix multiplication on a $2n \times 2n$ mesh.*

algorithm is $\Theta(n^3)$. Therefore, this algorithm is cost-optimal with respect to the traditional sequential algorithm.

While the previous algorithm is time- and cost-optimal on a $2n \times 2n$ mesh computer, let's consider a matrix multiplication algorithm targeted at an $n \times n$ mesh. Assume that processor $P_{i,j}$ initially stores element $a_{i,j}$ of matrix $A$ and element $b_{i,j}$ of matrix $B$. When the algorithm terminates, processor $P_{i,j}$ will store element $c_{i,j}$ of the product matrix $C$. Since we already have an optimal algorithm for a slightly expanded mesh, we consider adapting the algorithm just presented to an $n \times n$ mesh. To do this, we simply use row and column rotations, as we did when we adapted the Selection Sort algorithm from the input-based linear array to run on the traditional linear array. Specifically, in order to prepare to simulate the previous algorithm, start by performing a row rotation so that processor $P_{i,j}$ contains element $a_{i,n-j+1}$ of matrix $A$, followed by a column rotation so that processor $P_{i,j}$ contains element $b_{n-i+1,j}$ of matrix $B$ (see Figure 6-4).

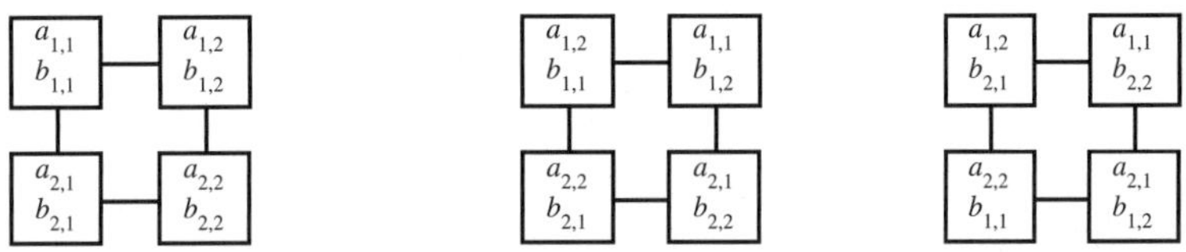


(a) Initial distribution of data.

(b) Result of row rotation of A.

(c) Result of column rotation of B.

**FIGURE 6-4** *Row and column rotations, which are used as preprocessing steps for matrix multiplication on an $n \times n$ matrix.*

At this point, the strategy described in the previous algorithm can be followed while we make the natural adjustments to accommodate the rotations that are necessary to continue moving the data properly, as well as the fact that data is starting in the first row and the first column. Notice that the additional rotations, which can be thought of as serving as a "preprocessing" step, run in $\Theta(n)$ time. Therefore, the asymptotic analysis of this algorithm results in the same time- and cost-optimal results as previously discussed.

***CGM*($n^2$, $q$):** Notice that we need $\Omega(n^2)$ memory to store $n \times n$ factor and product matrices, so we use a $CGM(n^2, q)$ rather than a $CGM(n, q)$. The basic strategy of the algorithm we present is to imitate the RAM algorithm given above. Notice, however, that the lower bound for each processor's memory is $\Omega(n^2/q)$, so a processor may not be able to store the factor matrices $A_{n\times n}$ and $B_{n\times n}$. Therefore, to achieve our target running time of $\Theta(n^3/q)$, we must be able to move data among the processors efficiently. In particular, we need to rotate blocks of, say, rows of $A$ among the processors. We will show this can be done efficiently by a *permutation exchange* operation.

A *permutation* is a one-to-one and onto function from a finite set of integers to itself. We say a function $f: X \to Y$ is *one-to-one* if for every $x_0, x_1 \in X$, $x_0 \neq x_1$ implies $f(x_0) \neq f(x_1)$. A function $f: X \to Y$ is *onto* if for every $y \in Y$ there exists $x \in X$ such that $f(x) = y$. For example, let $X = \{-1, 0, 1\}$, and consider the functions $F: X \to X$ and $G: X \to X$ defined by $F(x) = x$ and $G(x) = |x|$. It is easy to show that $F(x)$ is both one-to-one and onto. $G(x)$ is not one-to-one, since $G(-1) = G(1)$. Also, $G(x)$ is not onto, since there is no $x \in X$ such that $G(x) = -1$.

If we use the set of indices of the processors $S = \{0, 1, \ldots, q-1\}$ as the domain of concern, a permutation of $S$ is a one-to-one, onto function $f: S \to S$. Let's define the $n$-fold composition of such a function inductively, as follows. For each $s \in S$,

$$f^{(n)}(s) = \begin{cases} s & \text{for } n = 0; \\ f\left(f^{(n-1)}(s)\right) & \text{for } n > 0. \end{cases}$$

A circular permutation is a permutation $f$ such that for each $s \in S$,

$$\left\{f^{(n)}(s)\right\}_{n=0}^{q-1} = S.$$

For example, the function defined by $f(s) = (s + 1) \bmod q$ is a circular permutation. The function $g: \{0,1,2,3\} \to \{0,1,2,3\}$ defined by

$$g(0) = 1, g(1) = 0, g(2) = 3, g(3) = 2$$

is a permutation, but is not circular.

In a parallel computer of $q$ processors, suppose there is an array $list[1,\ldots,n]$ whose members are evenly distributed among the processors, *i.e.*, each processor has $\Theta(n/q)$ members of *list*. For convenience, we will abbreviate by assuming each processor has $n/q$ members of *list*. In a permutation exchange operation, for some permutation $f: S \to S$, we have each processor $P_i$ send copies of its members of *list* to $P_{f(i)}$. We have the following algorithm for a permutation exchange.

**Input:** An array, $list[1,\ldots,n]$, distributed such that processor $P_i$ has $list\left[\frac{in}{q} + 1, \ldots, \frac{(i+1)n}{q}\right]$, and a permutation $f: S = \{0,1,\ldots,q-1\} \to S$.

**Output:** copies of *list* elements are redistributed among the processors in realization of a permutation exchange.

**Action:**

For $i=0$ to $q-1$, processor $P_{f(i)}$ gathers
$list\left[\frac{in}{q}+1,\ldots,\frac{(i+1)n}{q}\right]$ from processor $P_i$.
End algorithm

It follows from our discussion of the gather operation in Appendix 3 that this algorithm runs in $\Theta(n)$ time.

Another tool useful in our calculation of a matrix product on a coarse-grained parallel computer is an algorithm for computing the transpose $B^T$ of a matrix $B$. $B^T$ is the matrix obtained from $B$ by interchanging the roles of rows and columns. For example,

$$\begin{bmatrix} 1 & 2 & 3 \\ 4 & 5 & 6 \\ 7 & 8 & 9 \end{bmatrix}^T = \begin{bmatrix} 1 & 4 & 7 \\ 2 & 5 & 8 \\ 3 & 6 & 9 \end{bmatrix}.$$

This operation is important for computing a matrix product, for the following reason. We might initially have both $n \times n$ matrices $A$ and $B$ stored in a $CGM(n^2, q)$ such that processor $P_i$ holds the rows indexed $\frac{in}{q}+1,\ldots,\frac{(i+1)n}{q}$ of both $A$ and $B$. However, we want the *columns* of $B$, *i.e.*, the rows of $B^T$, with indices $\frac{in}{q}+1,\ldots,\frac{(i+1)n}{q}$, in $P_i$ to compute entries of the matrix product $A \times B$. An algorithm for $CGM(n^2, q)$ computation of $B^T$ is given below.

***CGM(n²,q)* algorithm for computing $B^T$**

**Input:** $n \times n$ matrix $B$ such that processor $P_i$ holds the rows indexed $\frac{in}{q}+1,\ldots,\frac{(i+1)n}{q}$ of $B$.

**Output:** matrix $B^T$ such that processor $P_i$ holds the rows indexed $\frac{in}{q}+1,\ldots,\frac{(i+1)n}{q}$ of $B^T$.

**Action:**

For $i=0$ to $q-1$
  Processor $P_i$ gathers the columns of $B$ indexed

```
$\frac{in}{q}+1,\ldots,\frac{(i+1)n}{q}$, i.e., the rows of $B^T$ indexed
$\frac{in}{q}+1,\ldots,\frac{(i+1)n}{q}$.
  End For
End algorithm
```

Each gather operation in the loop body gathers $n/q$ columns of $n$ items apiece, for a total of $n^2/q$ matrix entries. It follows from our discussion of gather operations in Appendix 3 that the algorithm runs in $\Theta(n^2)$ time.

We can now give our $CGM(n^2, q)$ algorithm for computing the product $A \times B$ of two $n \times n$ matrices. Assume each of $A$ and $B$ is initially distributed so that processor $P_i$ holds the rows of both $A$ and $B$ indexed $\frac{in}{q}+1,\ldots,\frac{(i+1)n}{q}$. Assume $f: S \to S$ is any circular permutation of the processor indices. Let $R_i$ be the set of rows of $A$ indexed $\frac{in}{q}+1,\ldots,\frac{(i+1)n}{q}$. Do the following.

**Begin matrix product algorithm for $CGM(n^2, q)$**

Let $f: \{0,1,\ldots,q-1\} \to \{0,1,\ldots,q-1\}$ be a circular permutation.

```
1. Compute $B^T$. As described above, this takes $\Theta(n^2)$
   time. Now, each processor $P_i$ holds the columns of $B$
   indexed $\frac{in}{q}+1,\ldots,\frac{(i+1)n}{q}$.
2. For blockNum = 1 to q
   a. In parallel, each processor $P_j$ does the following.
      Let $R_i$ be the set of rows of A currently in $P_j$.
      Then $R_i$ was originally in $P_i$, so we know the
      indices of its rows, and can proceed as follows.
        For $a=\frac{in}{q}+1$ to $\frac{(i+1)n}{q}$
          For $b=\frac{jn}{q}+1$ to $\frac{(j+1)n}{q}$
            Compute $c_{a,b}$ as the dot product of row a of A
            and column b of B. This operation can be
            performed in $\Theta(n)$ time.
          End For b. This loop runs in $\Theta(n^2/q)$ time.
        End For a. This loop runs in $\Theta(n^3/q^2)$ time.
      End parallel. This step runs in $\Theta(n^3/q^2)$ time.
```

```
      b. If blockNum < q, perform a permutation exchange so
         that for each processor P_j, the set of rows R_i
         currently in P_j is sent to P_f(j). Since this means
         the entire n×n matrix A is shuffled, the running
         time is Θ(n²).
      End For blockNum. Since f is a circular permutation,
      each set of rows R_j visits every processor, so all
      the necessary dot products are computed. Since, for a
      CGM(n², q) we have q ≤ n, it follows that n² ≤ n³/q.
      Hence, this loop runs in Θ(n³/q + n²q) time.
   End algorithm
```

The running time for this algorithm is $\Theta(n^3/q + n^2q)$. In order to realize our target running time of $\Theta(n^3/q)$, it suffices for $n^2q \leq n^3/q$, or $q \leq n^{1/2}$. Thus, we achieve our target running time of $\Theta(n^3/q)$ for $1 < q \leq n^{1/2}$. Although this is not the full range of the number of processors for a *CGM*$(n^2, q)$, this is still a very useful result, as in practice, $n$ will grow more rapidly than $q$.

We also observe that the algorithm discussed above is for an arbitrary *CGM*$(n^2, q)$. If a *CGM*$(n^2, q)$ is implemented by a PRAM, mesh, or hypercube, it is possible to obtain a $\Theta(n^3/q)$ running time for a larger range of processors.

## Gaussian Elimination

The technique of *Gaussian elimination* is widely used for applications such as finding the inverse of a matrix and solving a system of $n$ linear equations in $n$ unknowns. In this section, we focus on the problem of finding the inverse of an $n \times n$ matrix.

The $n \times n$ matrix $I_n$, called the *identity matrix*, is the matrix in which the entry in row $i$ and column $j$ is

$$\begin{array}{ll} 1 & \text{if } i = j, \text{ and} \\ 0 & \text{otherwise.} \end{array}$$

Fundamentals from Linear Algebra include the following. Given an $n \times n$ matrix $A$, we know that $A \times I_n = A$ and $I_n \times A = A$. We say an $n \times n$ matrix $A$ is *invertible* if there is an $n \times n$ matrix $B$ such that $A \times B = B \times A = I_n$. If such a matrix $B$ exists, it is called the *inverse* of $A$, and we write $B = A^{-1}$.

The following are called *elementary row operations* on an $n \times n$ matrix $A$.

- Interchange distinct rows of $A$ (see Figure 6-5).
- Multiply a row of $A$ by a nonzero constant. That is, for some $c \neq 0$, replace each element $a_{i,j}$ of row $i$ by $ca_{i,j}$ (see Figure 6-6).
- Add a constant multiple of row $i$ to row $j$ for $i \neq j$. That is, for some constant $c$, replace each element $a_{j,k}$ of row $j$ by $a_{j,k} + ca_{i,k}$ (see Figure 6-7).

$$\begin{bmatrix} 5 & 0 & 6 & -2 \\ 0 & -2 & 4 & 5 \\ 1 & 1 & -3 & 7 \\ 2 & -4 & 9 & 15 \end{bmatrix} \longrightarrow \begin{bmatrix} 1 & 1 & -3 & 7 \\ 0 & -2 & 4 & 5 \\ 5 & 0 & 6 & -2 \\ 2 & -4 & 9 & 15 \end{bmatrix}$$

**FIGURE 6-5** *Interchange of row* 1 *and row* 3.

$$\begin{bmatrix} 5 & 0 & 6 & -2 \\ 0 & -2 & 4 & 5 \\ 1 & 1 & -3 & 7 \\ 2 & -4 & 9 & 15 \end{bmatrix} \longrightarrow \begin{bmatrix} 1 & 0 & 1.2 & -0.4 \\ 0 & -2 & 4 & 5 \\ 1 & 1 & -3 & 7 \\ 2 & -4 & 9 & 15 \end{bmatrix}$$

**FIGURE 6-6** *Replace row* 1 *by* 0.2 × *row* 1.

$$\begin{bmatrix} 1 & 6 & -8 \\ -5 & 20 & 10 \\ 3 & 8 & 15 \end{bmatrix} \longrightarrow \begin{bmatrix} 1 & 6 & -8 \\ 0 & 50 & -30 \\ 3 & 8 & 15 \end{bmatrix}$$

**FIGURE 6-7** *Replace row* 2 *by row* 2 + 5 × *row* 1.

Again, from Linear Algebra, we know that if a sequence $\sigma$ of elementary row operations applied to an $n \times n$ matrix $A$ transforms $A$ into $I_n$, then the same sequence $\sigma$ of elementary row operations applied to $I_n$ transforms $I_n$ into $A^{-1}$. Thus, we can implement an algorithm to find $A^{-1}$ by finding a sequence $\sigma$ of elementary row operations that transforms the "augmented matrix" $[A|I_n]$ to $[I_n|A^{-1}]$.

Consider an example. Let

$$A = \begin{bmatrix} 5 & -3 & 2 \\ -3 & 2 & -1 \\ -3 & 2 & -2 \end{bmatrix}.$$

We can find $A^{-1}$ as follows. Start with the augmented matrix

$$[A|I_3] = \left[\begin{array}{ccc|ccc} 5 & -3 & 2 & 1 & 0 & 0 \\ -3 & 2 & -1 & 0 & 1 & 0 \\ -3 & 2 & -2 & 0 & 0 & 1 \end{array}\right].$$

The first phase of our procedure is the "Gaussian elimination" phase. One column at a time from left to right, we perform elementary row operations to create entries of 1 along the *diagonal*, the set of entries for which the row and column indices have the same value, and 0s below the diagonal. In this example, we use row operations to transform column 1 so that $a_{1,1} = 1$ and $a_{2,1} = a_{3,1} = 0$. Next, we use row operations that do not change column 1 but result in $a_{2,2} = 1$ and $a_{2,3} = 0$. Finally, we use a row operation that does not change columns 1 or 2 but results in $a_{3,3} = 1$. More generally, after Gaussian elimination on $A_{n \times n}$, all $a_{i,i} = 1$, $1 \leq i \leq n$, and all $a_{i,j} = 0$, $1 \leq j < i \leq n$. That is, there are 1's along the diagonal and 0's below the diagonal, as shown below.

1. Divide row 1 by 5 to obtain

$$\left[\begin{array}{ccc|ccc} 1 & -0.6 & 0.4 & 0.2 & 0 & 0 \\ -3 & 2 & -1 & 0 & 1 & 0 \\ -3 & 2 & -2 & 0 & 0 & 1 \end{array}\right].$$

2. Add 3 times row 1 to row 2, and 3 times row 1 to row 3, to obtain

$$\left[\begin{array}{ccc|ccc} 1 & -0.6 & 0.4 & 0.2 & 0 & 0 \\ 0 & 0.2 & 0.2 & 0.6 & 1 & 0 \\ 0 & 0.2 & -0.8 & 0.6 & 0 & 1 \end{array}\right].$$

   Notice column 1 now has the desired form. We continue with Gaussian elimination steps on column 2.

3. Divide row 2 by 0.2 to obtain

$$\left[\begin{array}{ccc|ccc} 1 & -0.6 & 0.4 & 0.2 & 0 & 0 \\ 0 & 1 & 1 & 3 & 5 & 0 \\ 0 & 0.2 & -0.8 & 0.6 & 0 & 1 \end{array}\right].$$

4. Subtract 0.2 times row 2 from row 3 to obtain

$$\left[\begin{array}{ccc|ccc} 1 & -0.6 & 0.4 & 0.2 & 0 & 0 \\ 0 & 1 & 1 & 3 & 5 & 0 \\ 0 & 0 & -1 & 0 & -1 & 1 \end{array}\right].$$

   Note column 2 now has the desired form.

5. Divide row 3 by −1 to obtain

$$\left[\begin{array}{ccc|ccc} 1 & -0.6 & 0.4 & 0.2 & 0 & 0 \\ 0 & 1 & 1 & 3 & 5 & 0 \\ 0 & 0 & 1 & 0 & 1 & -1 \end{array}\right].$$

This completes the Gaussian elimination phase of the procedure.

Now we proceed with the "back substitution" phase, in which, for one column at a time from right to left, we use elementary row operations to eliminate nonzero entries above the diagonal. In a sense, this is more Gaussian elimination, as we use similar techniques, now creating 0's above the diagonal. We proceed as follows.

1. Subtract 0.4 times row 3 from row 1, and 1 times row 3 from row 2, to obtain

$$\left[\begin{array}{ccc|ccc} 1 & -0.6 & 0 & 0.2 & -0.4 & 0.4 \\ 0 & 1 & 0 & 3 & 4 & 1 \\ 0 & 0 & 1 & 0 & 1 & -1 \end{array}\right].$$

2. Add 0.6 times row 2 to row 1, to obtain

$$\left[\begin{array}{ccc|ccc} 1 & 0 & 0 & 2 & 2 & 1 \\ 0 & 1 & 0 & 3 & 4 & 1 \\ 0 & 0 & 1 & 0 & 1 & -1 \end{array}\right].$$

Since the left side of the augmented matrix is now $I_3$, the right side is the desired inverse, namely, $A^{-1} = \begin{bmatrix} 2 & 2 & 1 \\ 3 & 4 & 1 \\ 0 & 1 & -1 \end{bmatrix}$. This can be verified easily by showing that the products $A \times A^{-1}$ and $A^{-1} \times A$ both coincide with $I_3$.

The example given above illustrates our general algorithm for finding the inverse of an $n \times n$ matrix $A$. In the algorithm presented below, we assume that array $A[1 \ldots n, 1 \ldots n]$ is used to represent the matrix we wish to invert, and the matrix $I[1 \ldots n, 1 \ldots n]$ is initialized to represent the $n \times n$ identity matrix. Here we state a procedure for either finding the inverse of $A$ or determining that such an inverse does not exist.

1. {Gaussian elimination phase: create in $A$ an upper triangular matrix, a matrix with 1 on every diagonal entry and 0 on every entry below the diagonal.}
   For $i = 1$ to $n$, do
   a. If $A[i,i] = 0$ and $A[m,i] = 0$ for all $m > i$, conclude that $A^{-1}$ does not exist and halt the algorithm.

b. If $A[i,i] = 0$ and $A[m,i] \neq 0$ for some smallest $m > i$, interchange rows $i$ and $m$ in the array $A$ and in the array $I$.

c. Due to the previous step, we assume $A[i,i] \neq 0$. Divide row $i$ of $A$ and row $i$ of $I$ by $A[i,i]$. That is, let $scale = A[i,i]$ and then for $j = 1$ to $n$, replace $A[i,j]$ by $A[i,j]/scale$. Note that it suffices to make these replacements for $j = i$ to $n$, since the Gaussian elimination has caused $A[i,j] = 0$ for $j < i$. Similarly, for $j = 1$ to $n$, replace $I[i,j]$ by $I[i,j]/scale$. Note we now have $A[k,k] = 1$ for $k \leq i$, and $A[m,j] = 0$ if $j < i, j < m$ (0 below the diagonal in columns indexed less than $i$).

d. Now we have $A[i,i] = 1$. If $i < n$, then for $r > i$, subtract $A[r,i]$ times row $i$ from row $r$ in both the arrays $A$ and $I$. This zeroes out the entries in $A$ of column $i$ below the diagonal without destroying the 0s below the diagonal in columns further to the left. That is,

```
    If i < n, then
      For row = i + 1 to n
        factor ← A[row, i]
        For col = 1 to n
          A[row, col] ← A[row, col] - factor × A[i, col]
          I[row, col] ← I[row, col] - factor × I[i, col]
        End For col
      End For row
    End If
    {Note we now have A[k, k] = 1 for k ≤ i, and A[m, j] = 0
    if j ≤ i, j < m (0 below the diagonal in columns
    indexed ≤ i).}
End For i
```

2. {Back substitution phase: eliminate the nonzero entries above the diagonal of $A$. We use *zeroingCol* as both a row and column index; it represents both the column we are "zeroing" off the diagonal, and the row combined with the current *row* to create the desired matrix form.}

```
For zeroingCol = n downto 2
  For row = zeroingCol - 1 downto 1
    factor ← A[row, zeroingCol]
    For col = 1 to n
      A[row, col] ← A[row, col] - factor × A[zeroingCol, col]
      I[row, col] ← I[row, col] - factor × I[zeroingCol, col]
    End For col
  End For row
End For zeroingCol
```

We now discuss the analysis of Gaussian elimination on sequential and parallel models of computation.

**RAM:** A straightforward implementation of the algorithm given above on a RAM runs in $\Theta(n^3)$ time in the worst case, when the matrix inverse exists and is determined. The best case running time is $\Theta(n)$, when it is determined by examining the first column that an inverse does not exist.

**Parallel models:** We must be careful. For example, it is easy to see how some of our inner loops may be parallelized, but some of the outer loops appear to be inherently sequential. Thus, on a PRAM it is easy to see how to obtain significant speedup over the RAM. However, it is not clear how to obtain optimal performance. Further, on distributed memory models such as the mesh, some of the advantages of parallelism may seem negated by delays needed to broadcast key data values throughout rows or columns of the mesh. Below, we discuss how the basic algorithm we have presented can be implemented efficiently on various parallel models.

**PRAM of $n^2$ processors:** Let's assume we are using a PRAM with the EW property. Then each decision on whether or not to halt, as described in the algorithm, can be performed by a semigroup operation in $\Theta(\log n)$ time. This is performed by a semigroup AND operation across all entries of the current column to determine if the column has only 0 entries. Now, consider the situation when the algorithmic decision is to continue, which leads to the results that $a_{i,i} = 1$ and $a_{i,j} = 0$ for $j < i$. A row interchange can be performed in $\Theta(1)$ time. Scalar multiplication or division of a row can be performed on a CR PRAM in $\Theta(1)$ time. However, scalar multiplication or division of a row on an ER PRAM runs in $\Theta(\log n)$ time, since a broadcast of the scalar to all processors associated with a row is required. Notice that the row subtraction of the last step of the Gaussian elimination phase may be done in parallel. That is, the outer For-*row*-loop can be parallelized as there is no sequential dependence between the rows in its operations. Further, the inner For-*col*-loop parallelizes. As in the scalar multiplication step, the outer For-*row*-loop executes its operations in $\Theta(1)$ time on a CR PRAM and in $\Theta(\log n)$ time on an ER PRAM. Thus, a straightforward implementation of the Gaussian elimination phase runs in $O(n \log n)$ time on a PRAM (CR or ER).

For the back substitution phase, we can similarly parallelize the inner and the intermediate-nested loop to conclude this phase, which runs in $\Theta(n)$ time on a CR PRAM and in $\Theta(n \log n)$ time on an ER PRAM. Thus, a straightforward implementation of this algorithm runs in $\Theta(n \log n)$ time on an EW PRAM of size $n^2$. The total cost is $\Theta(n^3 \log n)$. Note that relative to the cost of our RAM implementation, the PRAM implementation of Gaussian elimination to invert a matrix is not optimal.

**Mesh of size $n^2$:** Assume that entries of the arrays $A$ and $I$ are distributed among the processors of the mesh so that the processor $P_{i,j}$ in row $i$ and column $j$ of the mesh contains both $A[i, j]$ and $I[i, j]$.

Several of the steps of our general algorithm require communication of data across a row or column of the mesh. For example, scalar multiplication of a row requires communication of the scalar across the row. If every processor in the row waits for this communication to finish, the scalar multiplication step would run in $\Theta(n)$ time. This would yield a running time of $\Theta(n^2)$, which is not optimal, since the total cost is then $\Theta(n^2 \times n^2) = \Theta(n^4)$.

We obtain better mesh performance by *pipelining* and *pivoting*. The following is true of each of the steps of the inner loops of our algorithm. Once a processor has the data it needs to operate upon, its participation in the current step runs in $\Theta(1)$ additional time, after which the processor can proceed to its participation in the next step of the algorithm, regardless of whether other processors have finished their work for the current step. Therefore, if we could be sure that every processor experiences a total of $O(n)$ time waiting for data to reach it, it would follow that the algorithm runs in $\Theta(n)$ time, as each processor would run in $O(n)$ time for waits and in $\Theta(n)$ time for the "active" execution of instructions.

However, there is one place where the algorithm as described above could have processors that experience $\omega(1)$ delays of $O(n)$ time apiece to receive data. That is, the step that calls conditionally for exchanging a row of $A$ having a 0 diagonal entry with a row below it having a nonzero entry in the same column. In order to ensure this situation does not cost us too much time due to frequent occurrence, we modify our algorithm by the technique of *pivoting*, which we describe now. If processor $P_{i,i}$ detects that $A[i,i] = 0$, then $P_{i,i}$ sends a message down column $i$ to search for the first nonzero $A[j,i]$ with $j > i$. If such a $j$ is found, row $j$ is called the *pivot row*, and plays the role similar to that otherwise played by row $i$. That is, in this situation, row $j$ is used for Gaussian elimination in the rows below it, which creates 0 entries in the $i^{\text{th}}$ column of each such row. In rows between row $i$ and row $j$, if there exist entries of 0 in column $i$, then no row combination is required at this stage. Finally, row $j$ "bubbles up" to row $i$ in a wave-like fashion, using both vertical and horizontal pipelining, while row $i$ bubbles down to row $j$, executing the row interchange.

On the other hand, if no such $j$ is found, then processor $P_{i,n}$ broadcasts a message to halt throughout the mesh.

In this fashion, we pipeline the row interchange step with the following steps of the algorithm in to order ensure that each processor spends $O(n)$ time awaiting data. It follows, as described above, that we can compute the inverse of an $n \times n$

matrix or decide, when appropriate, that it is not invertible, through Gaussian elimination on an $n \times n$ mesh in $\Theta(n)$ time, which is optimal relative to our RAM implementation.

## Roundoff Error

It should be noted that the Gaussian elimination algorithm is sensitive to roundoff error. Roundoff error occurs whenever an exact calculation requires more decimal places, or, equivalently, binary bits, than are actually used for storage of the result. Occasionally, roundoff error can cause an incorrect conclusion with respect to whether or not the input matrix has an inverse, or with respect to which row should be the pivot row. Such a situation could be caused by an entry that should be 0, computed as having a small nonzero absolute value. Also, a roundoff error in a small nonzero entry could have a powerfully distorting effect if the entry becomes a pivot element, since the pivot row is divided by the pivot element and combined with other rows.

It is tempting to think such problems could be corrected by selecting a small positive number $\varepsilon$ and establishing a rule that whenever a step of the algorithm computes an entry with absolute value less than $\varepsilon$, the value of the entry is set to 0. However, such an approach can create other problems since a nonzero entry in the matrix with an absolute value less than $\varepsilon$ may be correct.

Measures used to prevent major errors due to roundoff errors in Gaussian elimination are beyond the scope of this book. However, a crude test of the accuracy of the matrix $B$ computed as the inverse of $A$ is to determine the matrix products $A \times B$ and $B \times A$. If all entries of both products are sufficiently close to the respective entries of the identity matrix $I_n$ to which they correspond, then $B$ is likely a good approximation of $A^{-1}$.

## Summary

In this chapter, we study the implementation of the fundamental matrix operations, matrix multiplication and Gaussian elimination, the latter a popular technique for solving an $n \times n$ system of linear equations and for finding the inverse of an $n \times n$ matrix. We give algorithms to solve these problems and discuss their implementations on several models of computation.

## Chapter Notes

A traditional sequential algorithm to multiply $A_{n \times n} \times B_{n \times n}$ runs in $\Theta(n^3)$ time. This algorithm is suggested by the definition of matrix multiplication. However, in 1968, the paper "Gaussian elimination is not optimal," by V. Strassen, *Numerische Mathematik* 13(4), 1969, pp. 354–356, showed that a divide-and-conquer algorithm could be exploited to perform matrix multiplication in $O(n^{2.81})$ time. The mesh matrix algorithm presented in this chapter is derived from the one presented in *Parallel Algorithms for Regular Architectures* by R. Miller and Q.F. Stout (The MIT Press, Cambridge, Mass., 1996). The algorithm we present for matrix multiplication on a $CGM(n^2, q)$ comes from the paper "Efficient Coarse Grained Permutation Exchanges and Matrix Multiplication," by L. Boxer, *Parallel Processing Letters* 19, 2009, 477–484.

The algorithm we present for Gaussian elimination is a traditional algorithm found in many introductory textbooks for the mathematical discipline of Linear Algebra. Its presentation is similar to that found in *Parallel Algorithms for Regular Architectures*.

Two additional books that concentrate on algorithms for problems in computational science are G.S. Almasi and A. Gottlieb's *Highly Parallel Computing* (The Benjamin/Cummings Publishing Company, New York, 1994) and G.W. Stout's *High Performance Computing* (Addison-Wesley Publishing Company, New York, 1995).

## Exercises

1. The PRAM algorithms presented in this chapter for matrix multiplication are simpler under the assumption of the CR property. Why? In other words, in what step or steps of the algorithms presented in this chapter is there a computational advantage in assuming the CR property as opposed to the ER property?
2. Give an algorithm for a CR PRAM with $n$ processors that solves the matrix multiplication problem in $\Theta(n^2)$ time.
3. In this chapter, we present a mesh algorithm for computing the product of two $n \times n$ matrices on an $n \times n$ mesh. A somewhat different algorithm for an $n \times n$ mesh can be given, in which we more closely simulate the algorithm given above for a $2n \times 2n$ mesh. If we compress matrices $A$ and B into $\frac{n}{2} \times \frac{n}{2}$ submeshes, it becomes easy to simulate the $2n \times 2n$ mesh algorithm given in this chapter.
   a. Give an algorithm that runs in $\Theta(n)$ time to compress the matrix $A$, where $A$ is initially stored so that $a_{i,j}$ is in processor $P_{i,j}$, $1 \leq i \leq n$, $1 \leq j \leq n$. At the end of the compression, $A$ should be stored so that processor $P_{i,j}$, $1 \leq i \leq n/2$, $1 \leq j \leq n/2$, stores $a_{k,m}$, for $k \in \{2i-1, 2i\}$, $m \in \{2j-1, 2j\}$. Show that your algorithm is correct.
   b. Give an algorithm that runs in $\Theta(n)$ time to inflate the matrix $C$, where the initial storage of the matrix is such that processor $P_{i,j}$, $\frac{n}{2} < i \leq n$, $\frac{n}{2} < j \leq n$,

contains $c_{k,m}$, for $k \in \{2i-n-1, 2i-n\}$, $m \in \{2j-n-1, 2j-n\}$. At the end of the inflation, processor $P_{i,j}$ should store $c_{i,j}$ for $1 \le i \le n$, $1 \le j \le n$. Show that your algorithm is correct.

4. Show how our algorithm for Gaussian elimination to invert an $n \times n$ matrix can be implemented on a PRAM of $n^2/\log n$ processors in $\Theta(n \log n)$ time.
5. Show how the array changes (as determined by pipelining, pivoting, and replacement computations) via our matrix inversion algorithm as implemented on a $3 \times 3$ mesh for the matrix

$$A = \begin{bmatrix} 0 & 2 & 5 \\ 4 & -1 & 1 \\ -8 & 2 & 1 \end{bmatrix}.$$

That is, you should show the appearance of $A$ at each time step, in which a processor performs any of the following operations:

- Send a unit of data to an adjacent processor (if necessary, after a $\Theta(1)$ time decision).
- Receive a unit of data from an adjacent processor (if necessary, after a $\Theta(1)$ time decision).
- Calculate in $\Theta(1)$ time and store a new value of its entry of $A$ (if necessary, after a $\Theta(1)$ time decision).

6. Devise an efficient algorithm for computing the matrix multiplication $C_{n\times n} = A_{n\times n} \times B_{n\times n}$ on a linear array of $n$ processors, and analyze its running time. You should make the following assumptions.

- The processors $P_1, \ldots, P_n$ of the linear array are numbered from left to right.
- For each $j$, $1 \le j \le n$, the $j^{\text{th}}$ column of $A$ and the $j^{\text{th}}$ column of $B$ are initially stored in $P_j$.
- At the end of the algorithm, for each $j$, $1 \le j \le n$, the $j^{\text{th}}$ column of $C$ is stored in $P_j$.

Your algorithm may take advantage of the fact that addition is commutative. For example, if $n = 4$, your algorithm may compute

$$c_{1,2} = a_{1,2}b_{2,2} + a_{1,1}b_{1,2} + a_{1,4}b_{4,2} + a_{1,3}b_{3,2}$$

rather than using the "usual" order

$$c_{1,2} = a_{1,1}b_{1,2} + a_{1,2}b_{2,2} + a_{1,3}b_{3,2} + a_{1,4}b_{4,2}.$$

**7.** In order to implement Gaussian elimination efficiently on a $CGM(n^2, q)$, we should be able to implement each of the three types of elementary row operations efficiently. Suppose $A$ is an $n \times n$ matrix such that each processor has $n/q$ columns (not rows) of $A$. Suppose also that $1 < q \leq n^{1/2}$. Show that

a. Interchanging distinct rows of $A$ can be done in $\Theta(n/q)$ time.

b. Multiplying a row of $A$ by a non-zero constant can be done in $\Theta(n/q)$ time.

c. Adding a constant multiple of row $u$ to row $v$ can be done in $\Theta(n/q)$ time.

# 7

# Parallel Prefix

Parallel prefix is a powerful operation that can be used to sum elements, find the minimum or maximum of a set of data, broadcast values, compress data, and perform numerous seemingly complex tasks. We will find many uses for the parallel prefix operation as we go through the remaining chapters of this book. In fact, parallel prefix is such an important operation that it has been implemented at the lowest levels on many machines and is typically available to the user as a library call. In this chapter we will *i*) develop efficient algorithms to perform the parallel prefix computation and *ii*) demonstrate the power of parallel prefix by using it in a variety of applications.

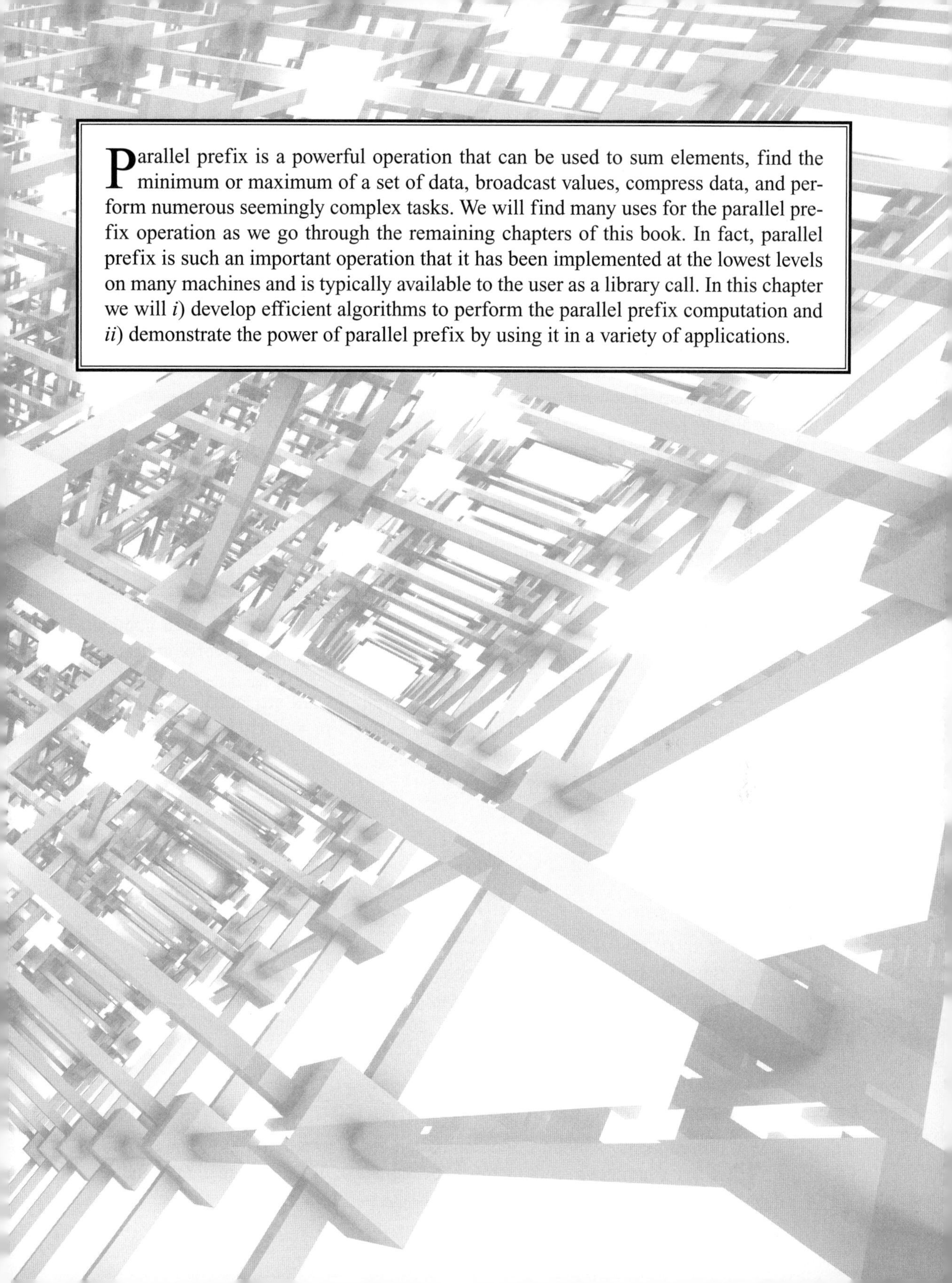

## Parallel Prefix

First, we review the definition of parallel prefix. Let $X = \{x_1, x_2, \ldots, x_n\}$ be a set of elements contained in a set *Y*. Let $\otimes$ be a *binary associative* operator that is *closed* with respect to *Y*. Recall that the term *binary* means that the operator $\otimes$ takes two operands, say $x_i$ and $x_j$, as input. The term *associative* means that the operator $\otimes$ obeys the relation

$$(x_i \otimes x_j) \otimes x_k = x_i \otimes (x_j \otimes x_k).$$

The term *closed* means that the result of $x_i \otimes x_j$ is a member of *Y*. Note there is no requirement for $\otimes$ to be *commutative*. That is, we do *not* require $x_i \otimes x_j$ to be equal to $x_j \otimes x_i$.

The result of $x_1 \otimes x_2 \otimes \ldots \otimes x_k$ is referred to as the $k^{\text{th}}$ prefix. The computation of all $n$ prefixes, $x_1, x_1 \otimes x_2, x_1 \otimes x_2 \otimes x_3, \ldots, x_1 \otimes x_2 \otimes \ldots \otimes x_n$, is the result of the *parallel prefix computation.* Since parallel prefix can be performed by making a straightforward pass through the data, it is sometimes referred to as a *scan* or *sweep* operation. The operator $\otimes$ is typically a unit-time operator. That is, $\otimes$ is an operation that can be computed in $\Theta(1)$ time. Sample operators include addition, multiplication, minimum, maximum, **and, or,** and **xor.**

**Lower Bound:** The number of operations required to perform a complete parallel prefix computation is $\Omega(n)$, since the value of the $n^{\text{th}}$ prefix is based on all $n$ values.

**RAM Algorithm:** Let's consider a straightforward sequential algorithm for computing the $n$ prefix values $p_1, p_2, \ldots, p_n$, where $p_1 = x_1$ and $p_{i+1} = p_i \otimes x_{i+1}$, for $i \in \{1, 2, \ldots, n-1\}$. The algorithm follows.

```
p1 = x1                        {A constant time assignment}
For i = 1 to n-1, do            {A linear time scan through
                                 the elements}
    pi+1 = pi ⊗ xi+1             {A constant time operation}
End For
```

Since the running time of the sequential parallel prefix algorithm is dominated by the work performed within the loop, it is easy to see that this algorithm runs in $\Theta(n)$ time. Further, this algorithm is asymptotically optimal since parallel prefix requires $\Omega(n)$ operations (see Figures 7-1 and 7-2).

### Parallel Algorithms

For shared-memory models of computation, it is common for the input data to be stored in a contiguous set of memory locations. For distributed-memory models of computation, this is not necessarily the case.

| | | | | | | |
|---|---|---|---|---|---|---|
| X | 4 | 3 | 6 | 2 | 1 | 5 |
| P | 4 | 7 | 13 | 15 | 16 | 21 |

**FIGURE 7-1** *An example of parallel prefix on a set X of 6 items. The operation ⊗ is **addition**. The resulting prefix sums are given in array P.*

| | | | | | | |
|---|---|---|---|---|---|---|
| X | 4 | 3 | 6 | 2 | 1 | 5 |
| P | 4 | 3 | 3 | 2 | 1 | 1 |

**FIGURE 7-2** *An example of parallel prefix on a set X of 6 items. The operation ⊗ is **minimum**. The resulting prefixes are given in array P.*

### Parallel Prefix on the CREW PRAM

The first parallel model of computation we consider is the CREW PRAM. In this section, we will use the term *segment* to refer to a nonempty subset of consecutively indexed entries of an array. We denote a segment covering entries $i$ through $j$, $i \leq j$, as $s_{i,j}$. Using this notation, the parallel prefix problem can be defined as computing the prefix of $s_{1,k}$, for all $k \in \{1,2,\ldots,n\}$. We also use the notation $S_{i,j}$ to represent the final prefix value over the segment $s_{i,j}$. So, we have $S_{i,j} = x_i \otimes x_{i+1} \otimes \ldots \otimes x_j$ and $p_k = S_{1,k}$.

The algorithm we present is reminiscent of Merge Sort in terms of its overall flow of combining single items into pairs, then pairs into pairs of pairs, and so on. We initialize single prefix values $<x_1,x_2,\ldots,x_n>$. Next, we combine the single prefix values to determine prefix values of pairs, resulting in the determination of $<S_{1,2},S_{3,4},\ldots,S_{n-1,n}>$. Then we combine pairs of prefix values in order to determine prefix values of pairs of pairs, which results in the determination of $<S_{1,4},S_{5,8},\ldots,S_{n-3,n}>$, and so forth. The algorithm continues for $\lceil \log_2 n \rceil$ iterations, at which point all prefix values have been determined for segments that have lengths that are powers of 2 or that end at $x_n$. See Figure 7-3 for an example.

In an additional $\Theta(\log n)$ time, in parallel every processor $P_i$ can build up the prefix $p_i$ by a process that mimics the construction of the value $i$ as a string of binary bits, from the prefix values computed in previous steps. For example, processor $P_7$ computes $p_7 = S_{1,4} \otimes S_{5,6} \otimes S_{7,7}$ while processor $P_{12}$ computes $p_{12} = S_{1,4} \otimes S_{5,8}$. These examples show the use of the Concurrent Read property of the CREW PRAM, as $P_7$ and $P_{12}$ will simultaneously read $S_{1,4}$ for their calculations.

| | Initial data | Step 1 | Step 2 | Step 3 | Step 4 |
|---|---|---|---|---|---|
| $x_1$ | 1 | 1 | 1 | 1 | 1 |
| $x_2$ | 2 | 3 | 3 | 3 | 3 |
| $x_3$ | 3 | 3 | 6 | 6 | 6 |
| $x_4$ | 4 | 7 | 10 | 10 | 10 |
| $x_5$ | 5 | 5 | 5 | 15 | 15 |
| $x_6$ | 6 | 11 | 11 | 21 | 21 |
| $x_7$ | 7 | 7 | 18 | 28 | 28 |
| $x_8$ | 8 | 15 | 26 | 36 | 36 |
| $x_9$ | 9 | 9 | 9 | 9 | 45 |
| $x_{10}$ | 10 | 19 | 19 | 19 | 55 |
| $x_{11}$ | 11 | 11 | 30 | 30 | 66 |

**FIGURE 7-3** *An example of computing parallel prefix by continually combining results of disjoint pairs of items. The operation ⊗ used in this example is* ***addition***. *Notice that the algorithm requires* $\lceil \log_2 11 \rceil = 4$ *steps. At the conclusion of Step* 1, *we have computed* $S_{1,2}$, $S_{3,4}$, $S_{5,6}$, $S_{7,8}$, $S_{9,10}$, *and* $S_{11,11}$. *At the end of Step* 2, *we have computed* $S_{1,4}$, $S_{5,8}$, *and* $S_{9,11}$. *At the end of Step* 3, *we have computed* $S_{1,8}$ *and* $S_{9,11}$. *At the end of Step* 4, *we have computed* $p_{11} = S_{1,11}$.

Notice that the cost of this algorithm, which is a product of the running time and number of available processors, is $\Theta(n \log n)$. Unfortunately, this is not cost-optimal since we know from the running time of the RAM algorithm that this problem can be solved with $\Theta(n)$ operations.

Now, let's consider options for developing a time- and cost-optimal CREW PRAM algorithm for computing a parallel prefix. With respect to the algorithm just introduced, we can either try to reduce the running time from $\Theta(\log n)$ to $\Theta(1)$, which is unlikely, or reduce the number of processors from $n$ to $\Theta(n/\log n)$ while retaining the $\Theta(\log n)$ running time. The latter approach is the one we will take. This is similar to the approach we took earlier in the book when we introduced a time- and cost-optimal PRAM algorithm for computing a semigroup operation.

That is, we let every processor assume responsibility for a logarithmic number of data items. Initially, every processor sequentially computes the parallel prefix over its set of $\Theta(\log n)$ items. A global prefix is then computed over these $\Theta(n/\log n)$ final, local prefix results. Finally, each processor uses the global prefix associated with the previous processor to update each of its $\Theta(\log n)$ prefix values. The algorithm follows. (See the example shown in Figure 7-4.)

| | $P_1$ | | | | $P_2$ | | | | $P_3$ | | | | $P_4$ | | | |
|---|---|---|---|---|---|---|---|---|---|---|---|---|---|---|---|---|
| $x_i$ | 1 | 2 | 3 | 4 | 5 | 6 | 7 | 8 | 9 | 10 | 11 | 12 | 13 | 14 | 15 | 16 |
| $p_i$ (step 1) | 1 | 3 | 6 | 10 | 5 | 11 | 18 | 26 | 9 | 19 | 30 | 42 | 13 | 27 | 42 | 58 |
| $r_i$ (step 2) | | | | 10 | | | | 36 | | | | 78 | | | | 136 |
| $p_i$ (step 3) | 1 | 3 | 6 | 10 | 15 | 21 | 28 | 36 | 45 | 55 | 66 | 78 | 91 | 105 | 120 | 136 |

**FIGURE 7-4** *An example of computing the parallel prefix on a CREW PRAM with* $\Theta(n/\log n)$ *processors. In this example, we are given* $n = 16$ *data items, the operation is addition, there are* $\log_2 n = 4$ *processors, and each processor is responsible for* $n/\log_2 n = 16/4 = 4$ *data items.*

**Step 1:**

For $i = 1$ to $\dfrac{n}{\log_2 n}$, every processor $P_i$ does in parallel

$p_{[(i-1)\log_2 n]+1} = x_{[(i-1)\log_2 n]+1}$

For $j = 2$ to $\log_2 n$, do

$p_{[(i-1)\log_2 n]+j} = p_{[(i-1)\log_2 n]+j-1} \otimes x_{[(i-1)\log_2 n]+j}$

End For $i$

**Comment:** After Step 1, processor $P_1$ has the correct final prefix values stored for the first $\log_2 n$ prefix terms. Similarly, processor $P_2$ now knows the local prefix values of the $\log_2 n$ entries stored in processor $P_2$, and so forth. In fact, every processor $P_i$ stores $p_{[(i-1)\log_2 n]+j}$, the prefix computed over the segment of the array $X$ indexed by $[(i-1)\log_2 n + 1, \ldots, (i-1)\log_2 n + j]$, for all $j \in \{1, 2, \ldots, \log_2 n\}$.

**Step 2:** Compute the global prefixes over the $n/\log_2 n$ final prefix values, currently stored one per processor. Let

$$r_1 = p_{\log_2 n},$$

$$r_i = r_{i-1} \otimes p_{i \log_2 n}, i \in \left\{2, 3, \ldots, \frac{n}{\log_2 n}\right\}.$$

**Comment:** Note that $r_i$ is a prefix over the segment of the array $X$ indexed by $1 \ldots i \log_2 n$. This prefix computation over $n/\log_2 n$ terms is computed in $\Theta(\log(n/\log n)) = \Theta(\log n)$ time by the fine-grained CREW PRAM algorithm presented above, since the step uses one piece of data stored in each of the $n/\log_2 n$ processors.

**Step 3:** The final stage of the algorithm consists of distributing, within each processor, the final prefix value determined by the previous processor.

For $i = 2$ to $\frac{n}{\log_2 n}$, processors $P_i$ do in parallel
  For $j = (i - 1)\log_2 n + 1$ to $i \log_2 n$, do
    $p_j = r_{i-1} \otimes p_j$
  End For $i$
End Parallel

**Comment:** Note that $p_j$ has the desired final value, as it is now calculated over the segment $s_{1,j}$ of $X$.

### Mesh

In this section, we consider the problem of computing the parallel prefix on a mesh computer. As discussed earlier, when considering an operation that involves an ordering imposed on the data, we must first consider an ordering of the processors. In this section, we will consider a simple *row-major ordering* of the processors. Formally, the row-major index of processor $P_{i,j}$, $i, j \in \{1, 2, \ldots, n^{1/2}\}$, is $(i - 1)n^{1/2} + j$ (see Figure 7-5).

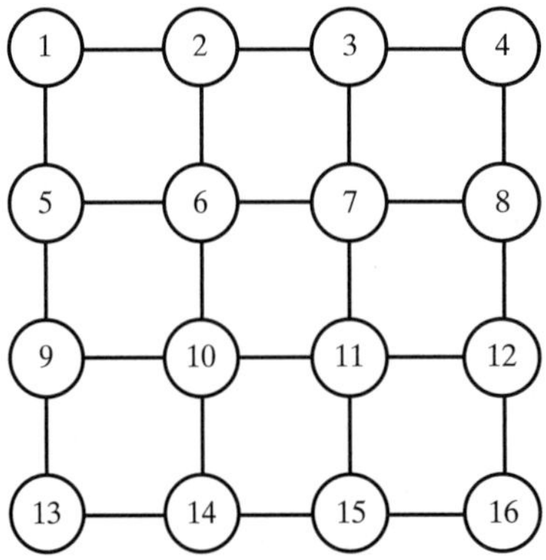


**FIGURE 7-5** *The row-major index scheme imposed on a mesh of size* 16.

The input to our parallel prefix problem consists of a data set $X = \{x_1, x_2, \ldots, x_n\}$, distributed one item per processor on an $n^{1/2} \times n^{1/2}$ mesh. That is, processor $P_i$, denoted by its row-major index, initially contains $x_i$, $1 \le i \le n$. When the algorithm terminates, processor $P_i$ should contain the $i^{th}$ prefix $x_1 \otimes \ldots \otimes x_i$. We describe the algorithm in terms of mesh operations that we developed earlier in the book. Note that in this example, the data items need *not* be in adjacent processors. That is, there are items $x_i$ and $x_{i+1}$ that are not in adjacent processors, when $x_i$ is in the rightmost processor of its row in the mesh and $x_{i+1}$ is in the leftmost processor of the next row.

First, perform a row rotation within every row. At the conclusion of this rotation, the rightmost processor in every row knows the final prefix value of the contiguous subset of $n^{1/2}$ elements of $X$ in its row. Notice that this step is similar to Step 1 of the algorithm just described for a PRAM with a reduced number of processors, in which every processor computes the prefix of entries initially stored in its processor. Next, using only the processors in the rightmost column, perform a column rotation to determine the parallel prefix of these row-restricted final prefix values. Again, note that this step is similar to Step 2 of the PRAM algorithm, which computes the global parallel prefix of the partial results determined in Step 1.

At this point, notice that the rightmost processors in every row contain their correct final answers. Furthermore, the value stored in the rightmost processor of row $i$, denoted as $r_i$, must be prepended to all of the partial prefix values determined by the processors in row $i + 1$ during Step 1. This can be done by first moving, in parallel, the appropriate prefix values $r_i$ determined at the end of Step 2 down one processor, from the rightmost processor in row $i$, $1 \le i \le n^{1/2} - 1$, to the rightmost processor in row $i + 1$. Once this is done, every row with index greater than 1 can perform a broadcast from the rightmost processor in its row to all other processors in its row. Finally, all processors in row $i + 1$ can prepend $r_i$ to their respective current prefix values.

Therefore, the algorithm consists of a row rotation, a column rotation, a communication step between neighboring processors, and a final row broadcast. Each of these steps can be performed in $O(n^{1/2})$ time on a mesh of size $n$. In fact, since the rotations run in $\Theta(n^{1/2})$ time, the running time of the algorithm is $\Theta(n^{1/2})$. Of course, we are now presented with what is becoming a routine question, namely, "How good is this algorithm?" Since the mesh of size $n$ has a $\Theta(n^{1/2})$ communication diameter, and since every pair of data elements is required for the determination of the $n^{\text{th}}$ prefix, we can conclude that the running time is optimal for this architecture. Now, consider the cost. The algorithm has a running time of $\Theta(n^{1/2})$, using a set of $\Theta(n)$ processors, which results in a cost of $\Theta(n^{3/2})$. Since we know that only $\Theta(n)$ operations are required, we can conclude that this is not cost-optimal.

So, this brings us to one of our favorite questions. Can we design an algorithm that is more cost-effective than our current algorithm? The major limitation for the mesh, in this case, is the communication diameter. That is, there is no inherent problem with the bisection width. In order to reduce the communication diameter, we must reduce the size of the mesh. This will have the effect of increasing the number of data elements that each processor is responsible for, including the number of input elements, the number of final results, and the number of intermediate results.

Notice that at the extreme, we could consider a mesh of size 1, *i.e.,* a RAM. The algorithm would run in a very slow $\Theta(n)$ time, but would also have an optimal cost of $\Theta(n)$. However, this is not quite what we envisioned when we thought about reducing the size of a mesh. Instead, consider keeping the cost of the mesh optimal, but improving the running time from that of a fine-grained mesh. In such a case, we want to balance the communication diameter with the amount of work each processor must perform. Given an $n^{1/3} \times n^{1/3}$ mesh, notice that each of these $n^{2/3}$ processors would store $n^{1/3}$ elements of $X$ and would be responsible for storing $n^{1/3}$ final prefix results. This is similar to the PRAM algorithm in which we required every processor to be responsible for $\Theta(\log n)$ input elements and final results.

So, let's consider an $n^{1/3} \times n^{1/3}$ mesh, where each processor initially stores $n^{1/3}$ entries of $X$. The algorithm follows the time- and cost-optimal PRAM algorithm presented in the last section, combined with the global operations and techniques presented in the non-optimal $n^{1/2} \times n^{1/2}$ mesh algorithm just presented. First, every processor computes the prefix of its $n^{1/3}$ entries in $\Theta(n^{1/3})$ time by the standard sequential algorithm. Now, consider the final restricted prefix value in each of the $n^{2/3}$ processors. The previous mesh algorithm can be applied to these $n^{2/3}$ entries, stored one per processor on the $n^{1/3} \times n^{1/3}$ mesh. Since this mesh algorithm runs in time proportional to the communication diameter of the mesh, this step runs in $\Theta(n^{1/3})$ time. At the conclusion of this step, every processor will now have to obtain the previous prefix value and go through and determine each of its final $n^{1/3}$ results, as we did in the PRAM algorithm. Clearly, this can be performed in $\Theta(n^{1/3})$ time. Therefore, the running time of the algorithm is $\Theta(n^{1/3})$.

This is due to the fact that we balanced the time required for data movement with the time required for sequential computing. Since the algorithm runs in $\Theta(n^{1/3})$ time on a machine with $\Theta(n^{2/3})$ processors, the cost of the algorithm is $\Theta(n^{1/3} \times n^{2/3}) = \Theta(n)$, which is optimal.

### Hypercube

In this section, we consider the problem of computing the parallel prefix on a hypercube computer. As with the mesh, when considering an operation that involves an ordering imposed on the data, we must first consider an ordering of the processors. In this section, we assume that the data set $X = \{x_0, x_1, \ldots, x_{n-1}\}$ is distributed so that processor $P_i$ initially contains data item $x_i$. Notice that we have changed the indexing of the set $X$ from $[1, \ldots, n]$, which was used for the RAM, Mesh, and PRAM, to $[0, 1, \ldots, n-1]$ for the hypercube. This change of indexing allows us to accommodate the natural indexing of a hypercube of size $n$, in which the $\log_2 n$-bit indices are in the range of $[0, 1, \ldots, n-1]$. So we assume that every processor $P_i$ initially contains data item $x_i$, and at the conclusion of the algorithm, every processor $P_i$ will store the $i^{\text{th}}$ prefix, $x_0 \otimes \ldots \otimes x_i$, $0 \le i \le n-1$.

The procedure we present is similar to the recursive doubling algorithm we presented for broadcasting on a hypercube. The algorithm operates by cycling through the $\log_2 n$ bits of the processor indices. At iteration $i$, every processor determines the prefix for the subhypercube that it is in with respect to the $i$ least significant bits of its index. In addition, every processor uses this partial information, as appropriate, to compute its required prefix value. The algorithm follows (see Figure 7-6).

**Input:** Processor $P_i$ contains data element $x_i$, $0 \leq i \leq n - 1$.
**Output:** Processor $P_i$ contains the $i^{th}$ prefix $x_0 \otimes \ldots \otimes x_i$.

```
In Parallel, every processor Pi does the following.
  subcube_prefix = xi              {prefix for current subcube}
  processor_prefix = xi              {prefix of desired result}
                                {lsb = least significant bit and
                                     msb = most significant bit}
  For b = lsb to msb, do
                           {In this loop, we consider the binary
                            processor indices from the rightmost
                                      bit to the leftmost bit.}
    send subcube_prefix to b-neighbor
    receive temp_prefix from b-neighbor
    If the bth bit of processor Pi is a 1, then
      processor_prefix = temp_prefix ⊗ processor_prefix
      subcube_prefix = temp_prefix ⊗ subcube_prefix
    Else
      subcube_prefix = subcube_prefix ⊗ temp_prefix
                         {We compute subcube_prefix differently
                         than in the previous case, since ⊗ need
                                           not be commutative.}
    End If
  End For
End Parallel
```

### Analysis

The analysis of this algorithm is fairly straightforward. Notice that the $n$ processors are uniquely indexed with $\log_2 n$ bits. The algorithm iterates over these bits, each time performing $\Theta(1)$ operations, which include sending/receiving data over a link and performing a fixed number of unit-time operations on the contents of local memory. Therefore, given $n$ elements initially distributed one per processor on a hypercube of size $n$, the running time of the algorithm is $\Theta(\log n)$. Since the communication diameter of a hypercube of size $n$ is $\Theta(\log n)$, the algorithm is optimal for this architecture. However, the cost of the algorithm is $\Theta(n \log n)$, which is not optimal. In order to reduce the cost to $\Theta(n)$, we might consider reducing the

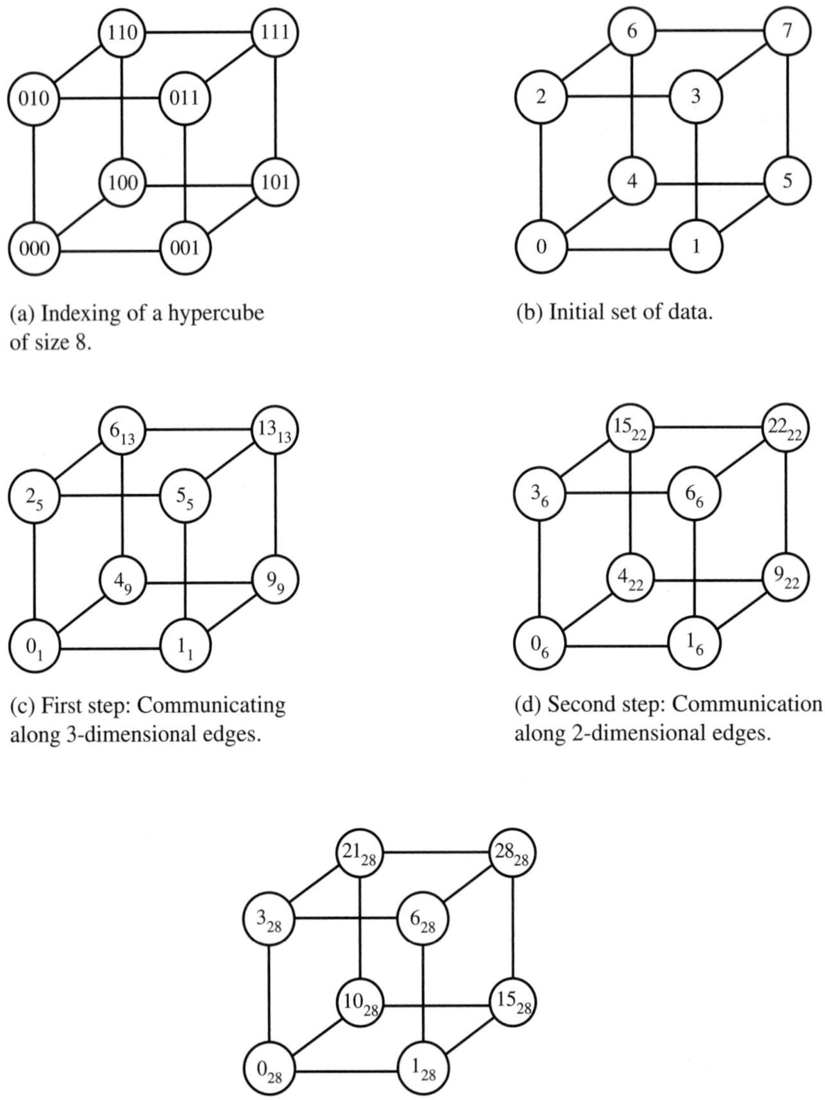


(a) Indexing of a hypercube of size 8.

(b) Initial set of data.

(c) First step: Communicating along 3-dimensional edges.

(d) Second step: Communication along 2-dimensional edges.

(e) Third step: Communicating along 1-dimensional edges.

**FIGURE 7-6** *An example of computing the parallel prefix on a hypercube of size 8 with the operation of addition. Processor prefix values are shown large in* (c), (d), *and* (e), *and subcube prefix values are small.*

number of processors from $n$ to $n/\log_2 n$ while still maintaining a running time of $\Theta(\log n)$. We leave this problem as an exercise.

### Coarse Grained Multicomputer

By making use of efficient gather and scatter operations, one may modify the algorithm presented above for the CREW PRAM with $n/\log_2 n$ processors or for the $n^{1/3} \times n^{1/3}$ mesh in order to obtain an algorithm for the parallel prefix computation on a $CGM(n,q)$ that runs in optimal $\Theta(n/q)$ time. See the Exercises, where a more precise statement of the problem is given.

## Maximum Sum Subsequence

In this section, we consider an application of the parallel prefix computation. The problem we consider is that of determining a *subsequence* of a data set that sums to the maximum value with respect to any subsequence of the data set. Formally, we are given a sequence $X = \langle x_0, x_1, \ldots, x_{n-1} \rangle$, and we are required to find a set of indices $u$ and $v$, $u \leq v$, such that the subsequence $\langle x_u, x_{u+1}, \ldots, x_v \rangle$ has the largest possible sum, $x_u + x_{u+1} + \cdots + x_v$, among all possible subsequences of $X$. Note that by a *subsequence* of $X$ we mean a subset of $X$ made up of *consecutively* indexed entries. Note also that while the largest sum is unique, there may be multiple subsequences that correspond to the same largest sum.

If all the elements of $X$ are nonnegative, then the problem is trivial, as the entire sequence represents the solution. Similarly, if all elements of $X$ are nonpositive, an empty subsequence is the solution, since, by convention, the sum of the elements of an empty set of numbers is 0. So, this problem is interesting only when both positive and negative values are present. This is the case we now consider for several models of computation.

### RAM

The lower bound to solve this problem on a RAM is $\Omega(n)$, since if any one element is not examined, it is possible that an incorrect solution may be obtained. We will now attempt to develop an optimal $\Theta(n)$ time solution to this problem. Consider the situation of scanning the list from the first element to the last while maintaining some basic information about the maximum subsequence observed and the contribution that the current element can make to the current subsequence under investigation. A first draft of the algorithm follows.

1. Solve the problem for $\langle x_0, x_1, \ldots, x_{i-1} \rangle$.
2. Extend the solution to include the next element, $x_i$. Notice that the maximum sum in $\langle x_0, x_1, \ldots, x_i \rangle$ is the maximum of
   a. the sum of a maximum sum subsequence in $\langle x_0, x_1, \ldots, x_{i-1} \rangle$, which we refer to as *Global_Max*, and
   b. the sum of a subsequence ending with $x_i$, which we refer to as *Current_Max*.

The details of the algorithm are straightforward. (Also see the example presented in Figure 7-7.)

```
Global_Max ← x_0
u ← 0                  {Start index of global max subsequence}
v ← 0                    {End index of global max subsequence}
Current_Max ← x_0
q ← 0              {Initialize index of current subsequence}
For i = 1 to n−1, do                          {Traverse list}
  If Current_Max ≥ 0 Then
    Current_Max ← Current_Max + x_i
  Else
    Current_Max ← x_i
    q ← i                {Reset index of current subsequence}
  End Else
  If Current_Max > Global_Max Then
    Global_Max ← Current_Max
    u ← q
    v ← i
  End If
End For
```

| *i* | *x* | *Global_Max* | *u* | *v* | *Current_Max* | *q* |
|---|---|---|---|---|---|---|
| 0 | 5 | 5 | 0 | 0 | 5 | 0 |
| 1 | 3 | 8 | 0 | 1 | 8 | 0 |
| 2 | –2 | 8 | 0 | 1 | 6 | 0 |
| 3 | 4 | 10 | 0 | 3 | 10 | 0 |
| 4 | –6 | 10 | 0 | 3 | 4 | 0 |
| 5 | –5 | 10 | 0 | 3 | –1 | 0 |
| 6 | 1 | 10 | 0 | 3 | 1 | 6 |
| 7 | 10 | 11 | 6 | 7 | 11 | 6 |
| 8 | –2 | 11 | 6 | 7 | 9 | 6 |

**FIGURE 7-7** *An example of the maximum sum subsequence problem.*

The five initialization steps each run in $\Theta(1)$ time. Each pass through the For-loop also runs in $\Theta(1)$ time. Since the loop is performed $\Theta(n)$ times, it follows that the running time of the algorithm is $\Theta(n)$, which is optimal, as all $n$ entries of the input array $X$ must be examined.

### CREW PRAM

Consider an efficient solution to the maximum sum subsequence problem for the CREW PRAM. Let's attempt to design a CREW PRAM algorithm that is efficient in its running time and cost-optimal. Based on our previous experience with designing cost-effective PRAM algorithms, it makes sense to target a $\Theta(\log n)$ time algorithm on a machine with $\Theta(n/\log n)$ processors. Such an algorithm would be time- and cost-optimal.

Suppose we first compute the parallel prefix sums $S=\{p_0,p_1,\ldots,p_{n-1}\}$ of $X=\{x_0,x_1,\ldots,x_{n-1}\}$, where $p_i = x_0 \otimes \ldots \otimes x_i$. This can be performed in $\Theta(\log n)$ time by the cost-optimal parallel prefix algorithm presented in the previous section.

Next, compute the *parallel postfix maximum* of $S$ so that for each index $i$, the maximum $p_j$, $j \geq i$, is determined, along with the value $j$. Given data values $\{y_0,\ldots,y_{n-1}\}$, we define the parallel postfix computation as an algorithm that determines the $n$ values $y_0 \otimes y_1 \otimes \ldots \otimes y_{n-1}$, $y_1 \otimes y_2 \otimes \ldots \otimes y_{n-1}$, $y_2 \otimes \ldots \otimes y_{n-1}$, $\ldots$, $y_{n-2} \otimes y_{n-1}$, $y_{n-1}$. Notice that when computing the desired parallel postfix maximum, one can simply compute parallel prefix maximum on $\{p_{n-1},p_{n-2},\ldots,p_0\}$ since the maximum operation is commutative.

Let $m_i$ denote the value of the postfix-max at position $i$, and let $a_i$ be the associated index, *i.e.*, $p_{a_i} = \max\{p_i,p_{i+1},\ldots,p_{n-1}\}$. This parallel postfix is computed in $\Theta(\log n)$ time by the algorithm presented in the previous section.

Next, for each $i$, compute $b_i = m_i - p_i + x_i$, the maximum prefix value of anything to the right minus the prefix sum plus the current value. Note that $x_i$ must be added back in since it appears in term $m_i$ as well as in term $s_i$. This operation can be performed in $\Theta(\log n)$ time by having each processor compute the value of $b$ for each of its $\Theta(\log n)$ entries. Finally, the solution corresponds to the maximum of the $b_i$'s, where $u$ is the index of the position where the maximum of the $b_i$'s is found and $v = a_u$. This final step can be computed by a semigroup operation in $\Theta(\log n)$ time.

Therefore, the algorithm runs in optimal $\Theta(\log n)$ time on a CREW PRAM with $n/\log_2 n$ processors, which yields an optimal cost of $\Theta(n)$.

We now give an example for this problem. Consider the input sequence $X = \langle -3,5,2,-1,-4,8,10,-2 \rangle$. The parallel prefix sum of $X$ is $S = \langle -3,2,4,3,-1,7,17,15 \rangle$.

| | | |
|---|---|---|
| $m_0 = 17$ | $a_0 = 6$ | $b_0 = 17-(-3)+(-3) = 17$ |
| $m_1 = 17$ | $a_1 = 6$ | $b_1 = 17-2+5 = 20$ |
| $m_2 = 17$ | $a_2 = 6$ | $b_2 = 17-4+2 = 15$ |
| $m_3 = 17$ | $a_3 = 6$ | $b_3 = 17-3+(-1) = 13$ |
| $m_4 = 17$ | $a_4 = 6$ | $b_4 = 17-(-1)+(-4) = 14$ |
| $m_5 = 17$ | $a_5 = 6$ | $b_5 = 17-7+8 = 18$ |
| $m_6 = 17$ | $a_6 = 6$ | $b_6 = 17-17+10 = 10$ |
| $m_7 = 15$ | $a_7 = 7$ | $b_7 = 15-15+(-2) = -2$ |

As the example shows, we have a maximum subsequence sum of $b_1 = 20$. This corresponds to $u = 1$ and $v = a_1 = 6$, or the subsequence $\langle 5,2,-1,-4,8,10 \rangle$. It is also interesting to observe that the maximum sum subsequence for this example is a subsequence that contains positive and negative terms.

### Mesh

We now consider a mesh. Notice that an optimal CREW PRAM algorithm for solving the maximum sum subsequence problem relies on a parallel prefix operation, a parallel postfix operation, a semigroup operation, and some local unit-time computations. Also notice that a semigroup computation can be implemented by a parallel prefix computation. Therefore, the maximum sum subsequence problem can be solved by using three parallel prefix operations and some local computations. Recall that one of these parallel prefix operations is actually a parallel postfix operation, which performs parallel prefix from the end to the beginning of the list of data. Therefore, in designing an algorithm for the mesh, we can simply follow the general guidelines of the CREW PRAM algorithm while implementing the appropriate mesh steps in an efficient manner. So, we know that we can solve the maximum sum subsequence problem in $\Theta(n^{1/3})$ time on an $n^{1/3} \times n^{1/3}$ mesh. Since this algorithm runs in $\Theta(n^{1/3})$ time on a machine with $n^{2/3}$ processors, the cost is $\Theta(n^{1/3} \times n^{2/3}) = \Theta(n)$, which is optimal. Further, as discussed previously, this is the minimal running time on a mesh for a cost-optimal solution.

## Array Packing

In this section, we consider an interesting problem, the result of which is a global rearrangement of data. The problem consists of taking an input data set, in which a subset of the items are *marked*, and rearranging the data set so that all of the marked items precede all of the unmarked items. Formally, we are given an array $X$ of items. Each item has an associated label field that is initially set to one of two values, namely, *marked* or *unmarked*. The task is to *pack* the items so that all of the *marked* items appear before all of the *unmarked* items in the array. Notice that this problem is equivalent to sorting a set of 0s and 1s. In fact, if we consider 0 to represent *marked* and 1 to represent *unmarked*, then this problem is equivalent to sorting a set of 0s and 1s into nondecreasing order.

### RAM

The first model of computation that we consider is the RAM. Since this problem is equivalent to sorting a set of 0's and 1's, we could solve this problem quite simply in $O(n \log n)$ time by any one of a number of $\Theta(n \log n)$ worst-case running time sorting routines. However, since we know something about the input data, we should consider the possibility of constructing a RAM sorting algorithm that runs in $o(n \log n)$ time. In this case, we know that the sort field consists of a restricted set of values. In fact, the keys used to sort the data can only take on one of two values. Using this information, we can consider scan-based sorts such as *Counting Sort* or *Radix Sort.*

Consider Counting Sort. If we are sorting an array of $n$ entries, we could simply make one pass through the array and count the number of 0's and the number of 1's. Suppose we count $X$ zeros and $Y$ ones. Then we could simply write out the value zero $X$ times followed by writing out the value one $Y$ times. However, the situation we are presented with is slightly more complicated since each key is part of a larger record.

In such a case, we could initialize two linked lists, one for those records with a zero as key and one for those records with a one as key, and then traverse the array element by element. As we encounter each element in the array, we create and initialize a record with the pertinent information and add it in $\Theta(1)$ time to either the 0's list or the 1's list, as appropriate. This traversal is complete in $\Theta(n)$ time.

We can then scan through the 0's list, element by element, and overwrite the pertinent information into the next available place in the array. After exhausting the 0's list, we continue similarly with the 1's list. Again, this step of writing the lists onto the array is done in $\Theta(n)$ time, and hence the algorithm is complete in asymptotically optimal $\Theta(n)$ time. The reader should observe that this algorithm is closely related to the Bin Sort algorithm discussed in Chapter 1, "Asymptotic Analysis."

Suppose we are given an array of $n$ records, and we are required to perform array packing in place. That is, suppose that the space requirements in the machine are such that we cannot duplicate more than some fixed number of items. In this case, we can use the array-based Partition routine from Quicksort (see Chapter 9, "Divide-and-Conquer") to rearrange the items. This partition routine is implemented by considering one index $L$ that moves from the beginning toward the end of the array, *i.e.*, from left to right, and another index $R$ that moves from the end toward the beginning of the array, *i.e.*, from right to left. Index $L$ stops when it encounters an *unmarked* item, while index $R$ stops when it encounters a *marked* item. When both $L$ and $R$ have found an out-of-place item, and $L$ precedes $R$ in the array, then the items are swapped and the search continues. When $L$ does not precede $R$, the algorithm terminates. The running time of the algorithm is linear in the number of items in the array. That is, the running time is $\Theta(n)$.

### CREW PRAM

Now consider the CREW PRAM. As with the maximum sum subsequence problem, we realize that in order to obtain an efficient and cost-effective algorithm, we should try to develop an algorithm that runs in $\Theta(\log n)$ time using only $\Theta(n/\log n)$ processors. This problem is easily solved using a parallel prefix sum to determine the rank of each 0 with respect to all 0's and the rank of each 1 with respect to all 1's.

That is, suppose we first determine for each 0 the number of 0's that precede it. Similarly, suppose we determine for each 1 the number of 1's that precede it. Further, assume that the total number of 0's is computed as part of the process of ranking the 0's. Then during a write stage, every 0 can be written to its proper location, the index of which is one more than the number of 0's that precede it. Also, during this write state, every 1 can be written to its proper location, the index of which is one plus the number of 1's that precede it plus the number of 0's that also precede it.

Let's consider the running time of such an algorithm. Given a CREW PRAM with $\Theta(n/\log n)$ processors, the parallel prefix computation can be performed in $\Theta(\log n)$ time, as previously described. Along with this computation, the total number of 0's is easily determined in an additional $\Theta(\log n)$ time. Therefore, the write stage of the algorithm runs in $\Theta(\log n)$ time. Note that each processor is responsible for writing out $\Theta(\log n)$ items. Hence, the total running time of the algorithm is $\Theta(\log n)$, and the cost of the algorithm on a machine with $\Theta(n/\log n)$ processors is $\Theta(\log n \times n/\log n) = \Theta(n)$, which is optimal. It is important to note that this algorithm can be easily adapted to sort a set of values chosen from a constant size set. In fact, the algorithm can be easily adapted to sort records, where all keys are chosen from a set of constant size.

### Network Models

Now, let's consider the problem of array packing for the general network model. Suppose one simply cares about sorting the data set, which consists of 0's and 1's. Then the algorithm is straightforward. Using either a semigroup operation or a parallel prefix computation, determine the total number of 0's and 1's. These values are then broadcast to all processors. Assume there are $k$ 0's in the set. Then all processors $P_i$, $i \le k$, record their final result as 0, while all other processors record their final result as 1. This results in all 0's appearing before all 1's in the final sorted list. Notice that this is a simple implementation of the Counting Sort algorithm we have used previously.

Suppose that instead of simply sorting keys, one needs the actual data to be rearranged. That is, assume that we are performing array packing on labeled records where all records that are marked are to appear before all records that are not marked. This is a fundamentally different problem from sorting a set of 0's and 1's. Notice that for this variant of the problem, it may be that all of the records are on the "wrong" half of the machine under consideration. Therefore, the lower bound for solving the problem is a function of the bisection width. For example, on a mesh of size $n$, if all $n$ records need to move across the links that connect the middle two columns, a lower bound on the running time is $\Omega(n/n^{1/2}) = \Omega(n^{1/2})$. On a hypercube of size $n$, the bisection width gives us a lower bound of $\Omega(n/(n/2)) = \Omega(1)$. However, the communication diameter yields a better lower bound of $\Omega(\log n)$. The reader should consider bounds on other machines, such as the pyramid and mesh-of-trees.

Since the record-based variant of the array packing problem reduces to sorting, the solution can be obtained by performing an efficient general-purpose sorting algorithm on the architecture of interest. Such algorithms will be discussed later in this book.

## Interval Broadcasting

In this section, we consider a variant of the parallel prefix problem. Assume that we are given a sequence of data items. Further, we assume that some subset of these items is "marked." For example, given a list of 20 items, we might find that items 3, 7, 9, 15, and 18 are marked.

We can view these marked data items as separating the complete sequence of data items into logical subsequences, where the first item of every subsequence is a marked data item. The problem we consider is that of broadcasting a marked data item to all of the records in its subsequence. It is important to note that in each subsequence, there is one and only one marked data item, and, in fact, it is the first item of the subsequence. So, in the example given above, the data in item 3 would be broadcast to items 4, 5, and 6. The data in item 7 would be broadcast to item 8. The data in item 9 would be broadcast to items 10 through 14, and so forth. For this reason, the marked data items are often referred to as "leaders." We now give a more concise description of the problem.

Suppose we are given an array *X* of *n* data items with a subset of the elements marked as "leaders." We then broadcast the value associated with each leader to all elements that follow it in *X* up to but not including the next leader. Another example, which is slightly more visual, is given below.

The top table in Figure 7-8 gives the information before the segmented broadcast. The leaders are those entries for which the "Leader" component is equal to 1. In the table at the bottom of Figure 7-8, we show the information after this segmented broadcast. At this point, every entry knows its leader and the information broadcast from its leader.

| Processor Index: | 0 | 1 | 2 | 3 | 4 | 5 | 6 | 7 | 8 | 9 |
|---|---|---|---|---|---|---|---|---|---|---|
| Leader | 1 | 0 | 0 | 1 | 0 | 1 | 1 | 0 | 0 | 0 |
| Data | 18 | 22 | 4 | 36 | -3 | 72 | 28 | 100 | 54 | 0 |

| Processor Index: | 0 | 1 | 2 | 3 | 4 | 5 | 6 | 7 | 8 | 9 |
|---|---|---|---|---|---|---|---|---|---|---|
| Leader | 1 | 0 | 0 | 1 | 0 | 1 | 1 | 0 | 0 | 0 |
| Data | 18 | 22 | 4 | 36 | -3 | 72 | 28 | 100 | 54 | 0 |
| LeaderIndex | 0 | 0 | 0 | 3 | 3 | 5 | 6 | 6 | 6 | 6 |
| LeaderData | 18 | 18 | 18 | 36 | 36 | 72 | 28 | 28 | 28 | 28 |

**FIGURE 7-8** *An example of segmented broadcast. The top table shows the initial state, i.e., the information before the segmented broadcast. Thus, by examining the Leader field in each processor, we know the interval leaders are processors* 0, 3, 5, *and* 6. *In the bottom table, we show the information after the segmented broadcast. Information from each leader has been propagated to all processors to the right, up to, but not including, the next leader.*

### Solution Strategy

The interval broadcasting problem can be solved in a fairly straightforward fashion by exploiting a parallel prefix computation, as follows. For each leader $x_i$ in $X$, create the record $(i,x_i)$. For each data item $x_i$ that does not correspond to a leader in $X$, create the record $(-1,x_i)$. Now define our prefix operator $\otimes$ as

$$(i,a) \otimes (j,b) = \begin{cases} (i,a) \text{ if } i > j; \\ (j,b) \text{ otherwise.} \end{cases}$$

The reader should verify that $\otimes$ has all properties necessary to be an operator for parallel prefix. That is, the reader should verify that this operator is binary, closed, and associative. Recall that $\otimes$ need not be commutative. Notice that a straightforward application of a parallel prefix will now serve to broadcast the data associated with each leader to the members of its interval.

### Analysis

Consider the RAM. A parallel prefix is implemented as a linear time scan operation, making a single pass through the data. So given an array $X$ of $n$ elements, the running time of the algorithm on a RAM is $\Theta(n)$, which is asymptotically optimal. Notice that the solution to the interval broadcasting problem simply consists of a careful definition of the prefix operator $\otimes$, coupled with a straightforward implementation of parallel prefix. Therefore, the analyses of running time, space, and cost on the CREW PRAM and network models are consistent with those for parallel prefix computations that were presented earlier in this chapter for these respective models. Similarly, as a consequence of an Exercise at the end of this chapter, the running time, space, and cost of this algorithm on the Coarse Grained Multicomputer are consistent with those for parallel prefix computations.

## Point Domination Query

In this section, we consider an interesting problem from *computational geometry*, a branch of computer science concerned with designing efficient algorithms to solve geometric problems. Such problems typically involve points, lines, polygons, and other geometric figures. Consider a set of $n$ data items, where each item consists of $m$ fields. Further, suppose that each field is drawn from some linearly ordered set. That is, within each field, one can compare two entries and determine whether the first entry is less than, equal to, or greater than the second entry.

We consider the point domination problem in two-dimensional space. That is, we say that a point $q_1 = (x_1, y_1)$ *dominates* a point $q_2 = (x_2, y_2)$ *if and only if* $x_1 > x_2$ **and** $y_1 > y_2$. A solution to this problem is useful, for example, if one wants to determine for a given set of points $Q = \{q_1, q_2, \ldots, q_n\}$, which points are **not** dominated by any point in $Q$.

Suppose we are interested in performing a study to identify the set of students for which no other student has both a higher grade point average (GPA) *and* has sent more tweets. An example is given in Figure 7-9, where the $x$-axis represents the number of tweets sent and the $y$-axis represents GPA. Exactly three points from this set of nine students satisfy our query.

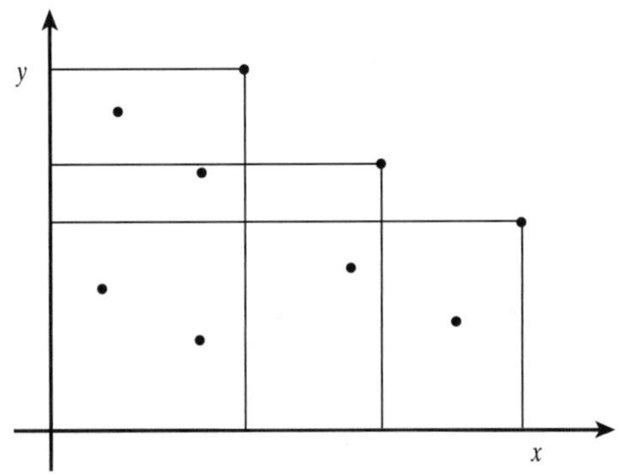


**FIGURE 7-9** *An example of the point domination problem. In this example, exactly three points have no other point both above and to the right. The remainder of the points are dominated by at least one of these three points.*

Suppose that the input to our problem consists of a set of $n$ points, $Q = \{q_1, q_2, \ldots, q_n\}$, where each point $q_i = (x_i, y_i)$ is such that no two members of $Q$ have the same $x$-coordinates or the same $y$-coordinates. Further, suppose that $Q$ is initially ordered with respect to the $x$-coordinate of the records. Given such input, we now consider an algorithm to solve the point domination query.

***Solution Strategy***

Since the records are initially ordered with respect to the $x$-coordinate, the points can be thought of as lying ordered along the $x$-axis. The first step of the algorithm is to perform a *parallel postfix* operation, where the operator is *maximum-y-value.* Since the *maximum* operation is commutative, this is equivalent to performing a parallel prefix operation on the sequence of data $\langle q_n, q_{n-1}, \ldots, q_1 \rangle$. Let $p_i$ denote the parallel prefix value associated with record $q_i$. Notice that at the conclusion of the parallel prefix algorithm, the desired set of points consists of all $q_i$ for which

$i < n$ and $p_i > p_{i+1}$. Also, $q_n$ is one of the desired points. We now consider the time- and space-complexity of the algorithm on the RAM, CREW PRAM, and network models.

### RAM

Given an ordered array of data, a prefix operation can be performed on the $n$ entries in $\Theta(n)$ time using a constant amount of additional space. A final pass through the data can be used to identify the desired set of records. We should note that this second pass could be avoided by incorporating the logic to recognize points that are not dominated into the parallel prefix operation. Note that it is easy to argue that the running time is optimal since the only way to complete the algorithm faster would be not to examine all of the entries, which could result in an incorrect result.

### CREW PRAM and Network Models

Notice that the solution to the 2-dimensional point domination query, where the input is given ordered by $x$-axis, is dominated by a parallel prefix operation. Therefore, the running time, space, and cost analyses are consistent with those of parallel prefix computations for these respective models given earlier in this chapter.

## Computing Overlapping Line Segments

In this section, we consider other simple problems from computational geometry. These problems involve a set of *line segments* that lie along the same *line.* We can think of this as a set of line segments that lie along the $x$-axis, as shown in Figure 7-10, where the segments are shown raised above the $x$-axis for clarity. The line segments are allowed to overlap in any possible combination.

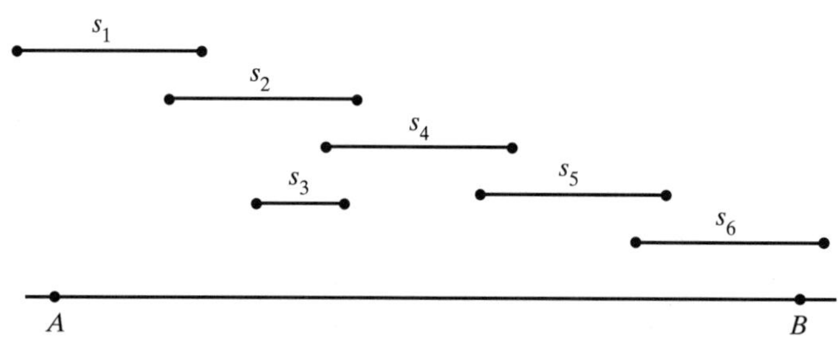


**FIGURE 7-10** *An example of problems involving overlapping line segments. The line segments are all assumed to lie on the x-axis, though they are drawn superimposed for viewing purposes.*

In particular, we assume that the input consists of a set $S = \{s_1, s_2, \ldots, s_n\}$ of $n$ uniquely labeled line segments, all of which lie along the same horizontal line. Each member of $S$ is represented by two records, one corresponding to each endpoint. Each such record consists of the $x$-coordinate of the endpoint, the label of the line segment, and a flag indicating whether the point is the left or right endpoint of the line segment.

In addition, we assume that these $2n$ records are ordered with respect to the $x$-coordinate of the records, and if there is a tie, *i.e.*, two records with the same $x$-coordinate, the tie is broken by having a record with a Left endpoint precede a record with a Right endpoint.

**Coverage Query:** The first problem we consider is determining whether or not the $x$-axis is completely covered by the set $S$ of $n$ line segments between two given $x$-coordinates, $A$ and $B$, where $A < B$.

**Solution:** We give a machine-independent solution strategy and then discuss the analysis for a variety of models.

1. Determine whether or not $left\ (s_1) \leq A$ and $B \leq \max\{right\ (s_i)\}_{i=1}^{n}$. If this is the case, then we can proceed. If not, we can halt with the answer that the coverage query is false.
2. For each of the $2n$ records, create a fourth field that is set to 1 if the record represents a left endpoint, and is set to $-1$ if the record represents a right endpoint. We will refer to this field as the *operand field.*
3. Considering all $2n$ records, perform a parallel prefix sum operation on the values in this operand field. The result of the $i^{\text{th}}$ prefix will be stored in a fifth field of the $i^{\text{th}}$ record, for each of the $2n$ records.
4. Notice that any parallel prefix sum of 0 must correspond to a right endpoint. Suppose that such a right endpoint is at $x$-coordinate $c$. Then all line segments with a left endpoint in $(-\infty, c]$ must also have their right endpoint in $(-\infty, c]$. Recall that in case of a tie in the $x$-coordinate, the left endpoint precedes the right endpoint, so the record that follows must be either a right endpoint with $x$-coordinate equal to $c$, or a left endpoint with $x$-coordinate strictly greater than $c$. Either way, the ordered sequence cannot have a right endpoint with $x$-coordinate strictly greater than $c$ until after another left endpoint with $x$-coordinate strictly greater than $c$ occurs in the sequence. Thus, there is a break in the coverage of the $x$-axis at point $c$. So, we determine the first record with parallel prefix sum equal to 0. If the $x$-coordinate of the endpoint is greater than or equal to $B$, then the answer to the coverage query is true, while otherwise it is false (see Figure 7-11).

## RAM

Consider an implementation of this algorithm on a RAM. The input consists of an array $S$ with $2n$ entries and the values of $A$ and $B$. Step 1 requires the comparison

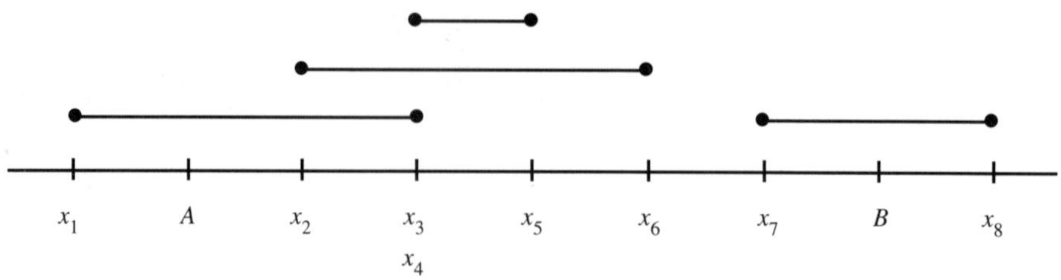


| Key | Operand | Prefix |
|---|---|---|
| $x_1$ | 1 | 1 |
| $x_2$ | 1 | 2 |
| $x_3$ | 1 | 3 |
| $x_4$ | –1 | 2 |
| $x_5$ | –1 | 1 |
| $x_6$ | –1 | 0 |
| $x_7$ | 1 | 1 |
| $x_8$ | –1 | 0 |

**FIGURE 7-11** *Transforming the coverage query problem to the parentheses matching problem. For this example, notice that there is a break in coverage between* $x_6$ *and* $x_7$*, as indicated by the* 0 *in the prefix value of* $x_6$.

of the first element of *S* with the scalar quantity *A* and, since the records are ordered, a comparison of *B* with the last point. Therefore, Step 1 can be performed in Θ(1) time. Step 2 is completed with a simple Θ(*n*) time scan through the array. In Step 3, a parallel prefix computation is performed on an array of 2*n* items with a scan that runs in Θ(*n*) time. In Step 4, a final scan is used to determine the first break in the coverage of the line segments before determining in Θ(1) time whether or not this endpoint precedes *B*. Therefore, the running time of the RAM algorithm is Θ(*n*), which is optimal.

### CREW PRAM

In order to attempt to derive a cost-optimal algorithm for this problem on the CREW PRAM, we will consider a CREW PRAM with Θ(*n*/log *n*) processors. In the first step, the values of *A* and *B* can be broadcast to all processors in Θ(1) time, as shown previously. This is followed by a Θ(log *n*) time OR semi-group operation to compute the desired comparison for *A* and then *B*, and a broadcast of the decision concerning halting that runs in $\Theta(1)$ time. Step 2 runs in $\Theta(\log n)$ time since every processor must examine all $\Theta(\log n)$ of the records for which it is responsible. Step 3 is a straightforward parallel prefix, which can be performed on a CREW PRAM with $\Theta(n/\log n)$ processors in $\Theta(\log n)$ time, as discussed previously. In Step 4, a $\Theta(\log n)$ time semigroup operation can be used to determine the first endpoint that breaks coverage, and a $\Theta(1)$ time comparison can be used to resolve the final query. Therefore, the running time of the algorithm is $\Theta(\log n)$ on a CREW PRAM with $\Theta(n/\log n)$ processors, resulting in an optimal cost of $\Theta(n)$.

### Mesh

As we have done previously when attempting to derive an algorithm with $\Theta(n)$ cost on a mesh, we consider an $n^{1/3} \times n^{1/3}$ mesh, in which each of the $n^{2/3}$ processors initially contains the appropriate set of $n^{1/3}$ contiguous items from $S$. If we follow the flow of the PRAM algorithm, as implemented on a mesh of size $n^{2/3}$, we know that the broadcasts and parallel prefix operations can be performed in $\Theta(n^{1/3})$ time. Since these operations dominate the running time of the algorithm, we have a $\Theta(n^{1/3})$ time algorithm on a mesh with $n^{2/3}$ processors, which results in an optimal cost of $\Theta(n)$.

### Maximal Overlapping Point

The next variant of the overlapping line segments problem that we consider is the problem of determining a point on the $x$-axis that is covered by the most line segments. The input to this problem consists of the set $S$ of $2n$ ordered endpoint records, as discussed above.

#### *Solution*

The solution we present for the maximal overlapping point problem is very similar to the solution just presented for the coverage query problem.

1. For each of the $2n$ records, create a fourth field that is set to 1 if the record represents a left endpoint, and is set to $-1$ if the record represents a right endpoint. We will refer to this field as the *operand field.*
2. Considering all $2n$ records, perform a parallel prefix sum operation on the values in this operand field. For each of the $2n$ records, the result of the $i^{\text{th}}$ prefix will be stored in the fifth field of the $i^{\text{th}}$ record.
3. Determine the maximum value of these prefix sums, denoted as $M$. All points with a prefix sum of $M$ in the fifth field of their record correspond to points that are overlapped by a maximal number of line segments.

### Analysis

The analysis of this algorithm follows that of the coverage query problem quite closely. Both problems are dominated by operations that are efficiently performed by parallel prefix computations. Therefore, the RAM algorithm is optimal at $\Theta(n)$ time. A CREW PRAM algorithm can be constructed with $\Theta(n/\log n)$ processors that runs in $\Theta(\log n)$ time, yielding an optimal cost of $\Theta(n)$. Finally, a mesh algorithm can be constructed with $\Theta(n^{2/3})$ processors, running in $\Theta(n^{1/3})$ time, which also yields an algorithm with optimal $\Theta(n)$ cost.

## Parallel Prefix on a NOW, Cluster, or Grid

Each of the problems considered in this chapter is often part of a solution to a much larger problem. In fact, solutions to the problems presented in this chapter are often used to solve problems for which one might use a NOW, Cluster, or Grid. That is, many of the larger problems that require solutions to the problems presented in this section require access to machines with significant compute- and/or data-capabilities.

The solutions presented in this section rely on standard low-level parallel computing operations, including parallel prefix, broadcast, and semigroup operations. Some of these operations are either enhanced or restricted, but are still important operations with wide applicability.

For this reason, such operations are typically part of a set of pre-defined routines that come standard with the machines in question. That is, such routines will be part of standard data movement operations packages, numerical methods packages, or message passing packages, as appropriate. Therefore, the reality is that when designing solutions to such problems, it is critical to understand fundamental sequential and parallel solution strategies, objectives of efficiency or optimality, and alternative strategies.

However, when it comes time to implement such solutions, it is often best to use predefined routines that have been tuned at very low levels for the specific architectures in question. That is, it is in the best interest of a hardware or architecture vendor to produce not only machines with efficient and desirable hardware subsystems, but also to supply software libraries that will make efficient use of the available hardware, including processors, memory, interconnection networks, storage, and so forth.

## Summary

In this chapter, we study parallel prefix computations. Roughly, a parallel prefix computation on $n$ data items $x_1, \ldots, x_n$ is the result of applying a binary operator $\otimes$ when we wish to preserve not only the result $x_1 \otimes \ldots \otimes x_n$, but also the sequence of partial results $x_1, x_1 \otimes x_2, x_1 \otimes x_2 \otimes x_3, \ldots, x_1 \otimes \ldots \otimes x_{n-1}$. We discuss efficient to optimal implementation of parallel prefix on a variety of computational models. We show the power of this computation by presenting several applications.

## Chapter Notes

In this chapter, we study the implementation and application of parallel prefix, an extremely powerful operation, especially on parallel computers. Parallel prefix-based algorithms are presented in R. Miller's and Q.F. Stout's *Parallel Algorithms for Regular Architectures* (The MIT Press, Cambridge, 1996), to solve fundamental problems as well as to solve application-oriented problems from fields including image processing and computational geometry for mesh and pyramid computers. A similar treatment is presented for the PRAM in J. Já Já's *An Introduction to Parallel Algorithms* (Addison-Wesley Publishing Company, New York, 1992). Parallel prefix is presented in a straightforward fashion in the introductory text by M.J. Quinn, *Parallel Computing Theory and Practice* (McGraw-Hill, Inc., New York, 1994). Finally, the Ph.D. thesis by G.E. Blelloch, *Vector Models for Data-Parallel Computing* (The MIT Press, Cambridge, 1990), considers a model of computation that includes parallel prefix as a fundamental unit-time operation.

Efficient gather and scatter algorithms for coarse grained multicomputers are demonstrated in L. Boxer's and R. Miller's paper, "Coarse Grained Gather and Scatter Operations with Applications," *Journal of Parallel and Distributed Computing*, 64 (2004), 1297–1320. These algorithms are discussed in Appendix 3, and are referred to in the Exercises for this chapter.

## Exercises

1. Show that a hypercube with $\Theta(n/\log n)$ processors can perform a parallel prefix operation for a set of $n$ data, $\{x_0, x_1, \ldots, x_{n-1}\}$, distributed $\Theta(\log n)$ items per processor, in $\Theta(\log n)$ time.
2. The *interval prefix computation* is defined as performing a parallel prefix within predefined disjoint subsequences of the data set. Give an efficient solution to this problem for the RAM, CREW PRAM, and Mesh. Discuss the running time, space, and cost of your algorithm.
3. Show how a parallel prefix operation can be used to broadcast $\Theta(1)$ data to all the processors of a parallel computer in the asymptotic time of a parallel prefix operation. This should be done by giving a generic parallel algorithm, where the running time of the algorithm is dominated by a parallel prefix operation.

4. Define **Insertion Sort** in terms of parallel prefix operations for the RAM and PRAM. Give an analysis of running time, space, and cost of the algorithm.

5. Give an *optimal* $\Theta(\log n)$ time EREW PRAM algorithm to compute the parallel prefix of $n$ values $x_1, x_2, \ldots, x_n$.

6. Give an efficient algorithm to perform *Carry-Lookahead Addition* of two $n$-bit numbers on a CREW PRAM. *Hint*: Keep track of whether each one-bit subaddition stops (`s`) a carry, propagates (`p`) a carry, or generates (`g`) a carry. See the example below. Notice that if the $i^{th}$ carry indicator is `p`, then the $i^{th}$ carry is a 1 if and only if the leftmost non-`p` to the right of the $i^{th}$ position is a `g`.

```
0100111010110010010
0110010110101011100
-------------------
sgpspgppgsgppsgppps
```

7. Give an efficient algorithm for computing the parallel prefix of $n$ values, initially distributed one per processor on a $q$-dimensional mesh of size $n$. Discuss the time and cost of your algorithm.

8. Suppose that you are given a set of $n$ pairwise disjoint line segments in the first quadrant of the Euclidean plane, each of which has one of its endpoints on the $x$-axis. Think of these points as representing the skyline of a city. Give an efficient algorithm for computing the piece of each line segment that is observable from the origin. You may assume that the viewer does not have $x$-ray vision. That is, the viewer cannot see through any piece of a line segment. You may also assume the input is ordered from left to right. Discuss the time, space, and cost complexity of your algorithms for each of the following models of computation.

   a. CREW PRAM

   b. Mesh

   c. Hypercube

9. Give an efficient algorithm for computing the parallel prefix of $n$ values stored one per processor in

   a. the leaves of a tree machine and

   b. the base of a mesh-of-trees of base size $n$.

   Discuss the time- and cost-complexity of your algorithms.

10. Consider the array packing algorithms presented in this chapter. Which of the routines is stable? That is, given duplicate items in the initial list, which of the routines will preserve the initial ordering with respect to duplicate items?

**11.** Suppose a set of $n$ data, $X = \{x_0, x_1, \ldots, x_{n-1}\}$, is evenly distributed among the processors of a coarse grained multicomputer *i.e.*, a $CGM(n,q)$, such that processor $P_i$ has the data $\{x_j\}_{j=\frac{(i-1)n}{q}+1}^{\frac{in}{q}}$.

Give the steps of an efficient algorithm to perform a parallel prefix computation on the $CGM(n,q)$, and analyze its running time. *Hint*: you should be able to obtain an algorithm that runs in $\Theta(n/q)$ time. In order to do this, you may find useful the algorithms for gather and scatter operations that are presented in Appendix 3.

# 8

# Pointer Jumping

In this chapter, we consider algorithms for manipulating linked lists, which we assume are arbitrarily distributed throughout the memory of the computational model under consideration. Each element of the list consists of a data record and a *next* field. The *next* field contains the memory address of the next element in the list. In addition, we assume that the *next* field of the last entry in the list is set to **null.**

On a RAM, the list is arbitrarily distributed throughout the memory, and we assume that the location in memory of the first element is known. On a PRAM, we assume that the list is arbitrarily distributed throughout the shared memory. If the list has $n$ elements on a PRAM of size $n$, we assume that every processor knows *i*) the location in memory of a unique list element and *ii*) the memory location of the first element in the list. In addition, if we are given a PRAM with $m \leq n$ processors, then we assume that each processor is responsible for $\Theta(n/m)$ such list elements.

**RAM:** A linked list of $n$ elements stored in the memory of a sequential machine provides a model for traversing the data elements that is inherently sequential. Therefore, given a list of size $n$ on a RAM, problems including search, traversal, parallel prefix, and performing a semigroup operation, to name a few, can be solved in $\Theta(n)$ time by a linear search.

**PRAM:** The most interesting parallel model to discuss in terms of linked list operations is the PRAM. This is due to the fact that the communication diameter is $\Theta(1)$ and the bisection width of a PRAM with $n$ processors is equivalent to $\Theta(n^2)$. It was long believed by the parallel computing community that list-based operations were inherently sequential. However, some clever techniques have been used to circumvent this notion. We demonstrate some of these *pointer jumping* techniques in the context of two problems, namely, *list ranking* and *parallel prefix*. A description of the problems, along with PRAM implementations and analyses, follow.

## List Ranking

Suppose that we are given a linked list $L$ of size $n$, and we wish to determine the distance from each data element to the end of the list. That is, for every list element $L(i)$, we want to compute the distance to the end of the list. We denote this distance as $d(i)$. Without loss of generality, we will assume that the first element in the list is marked. Note that, if necessary, the first element can be marked in $\Theta(1)$ time by the unique processor that has an identical memory location for its element and for the first element of its list. Note also that the only other element that knows its position is the last element of a list, since it has a *next* value of *null*. We define the distance, $d(i)$, as follows.

$$d(i) = \begin{cases} 0 & \text{if } next(i) = null; \\ 1 + d\big(next(i)\big) & \text{if } next(i) \neq null. \end{cases}$$

The PRAM algorithm we present operates by a recursive doubling procedure. Initially, every processor finds the next element in the list. That is, the first step consists of every element finding the element that succeeds it in a traversal of the list from beginning to end. In the next step, every element locates the element two places away from it, if such an element exists. In the following step, every element locates the element four places away from it, if such an element exists. Notice that in the first step, every element has a pointer to the next element. During the course of the algorithm, these pointers are updated. During every step of the algorithm, each element $L(i)$ can easily determine the element twice as far as away from it as $L(next(i))$ is. Notice that the element twice as far from $L(i)$ as $L(next(i))$ is simply $L(next(next(i)))$, as shown in Figure 8-1. As the process progresses, every element needs to keep track of the number of such links traversed in order to determine its distance to the end of the list. In fact, some care needs to be taken for computing distances at the end of the list. The details follow.

**Input:** A linked list $L$ consisting of $n$ elements, arbitrarily stored in the shared memory of a PRAM with $n$ processors.
**Output:** For every element $L(i)$, determine the distance $d(i)$ from that element to the end of the list.

**Action:**

```
                {First, initialize the distance entries.}
For all L(i) do
```

$$d(i) \leftarrow \begin{cases} 0 & \text{if } next(i) = null; \\ 1 & \text{if } next(i) \neq null. \end{cases}$$

```
End For all
                        {Perform pointer-jumping algorithm.
                           The actual pointer jumping step
                              is next(i) ← next(next(i)).}
```

```
In parallel, each processor Pi does the following.
  While next(i) ≠ null, do
    d(i) ← d(i) + d(next(i))
    next(i) ← next(next(i))
  End While
End parallel
```

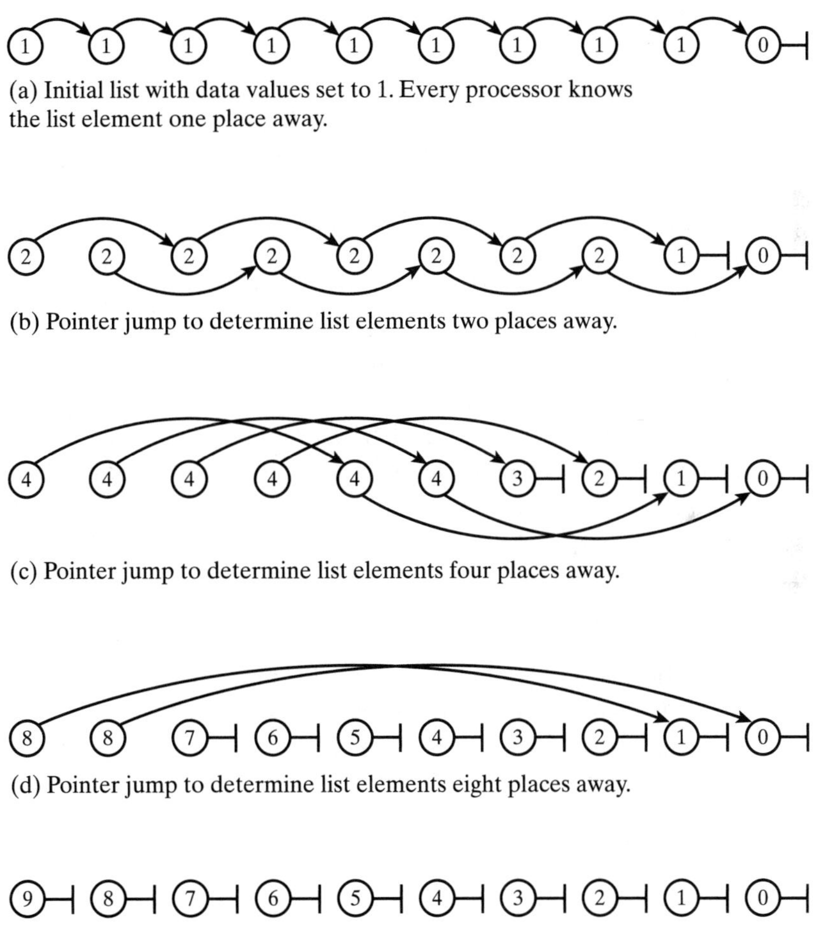

(a) Initial list with data values set to 1. Every processor knows the list element one place away.

(b) Pointer jump to determine list elements two places away.

(c) Pointer jump to determine list elements four places away.

(d) Pointer jump to determine list elements eight places away.

(e) Final data values after recursive doubling.

**FIGURE 8-1** *An example of list ranking. Given a linked list, determine for each element the number of elements in the list that follow it. The algorithm follows a recursive doubling procedure. Initially, every processor finds the next element in the list. Given a list with* 10 *elements, the number of iterations required is* $\lceil \log_2 10 \rceil = 4$.

**Analysis:** Given a PRAM of size $n$, the running time of this algorithm is $\Theta(\log n)$. This can be seen by the fact that the first element in the list must traverse $\lceil \log_2 n \rceil + 1$ links in order to reach the end of the list. Since the time for a PRAM of size $n$ to solve the list ranking problem for a list of size $n$ is $\Theta(\log n)$, the total cost is $\Theta(n \log n)$, which we know is suboptimal.

In order to reduce this cost, we can consider a PRAM with $n/\log_2 n$ processors. In this case, we can attempt to make modifications to this algorithm as we have done previously. That is, we can attempt to create a hybrid algorithm in which each processor first solves the problem locally in $\Theta(\log n)$ time, and then the algorithm just described is run on this set of partial results. Finally, in $\Theta(\log n)$ time, we can make a final local pass through the data.

However, consider this proposal carefully. It is important to note that if each processor were responsible for $\Theta(\log n)$ items, there is no guarantee that these items form a contiguous segment of the linked list. Therefore, there is no easy way to consider merging the $\Theta(\log n)$ items that a processor is responsible for into a single partial result that can be used during the remainder of the computation. In this case, such a transformation fails, and we are left with a cost-suboptimal algorithm.

## Linked List Parallel Prefix

Now let's consider the parallel prefix problem. Although the problem is the same as we have considered earlier the book, the input is of a significantly different form. Previously, whenever we considered the parallel prefix problem, we had the advantage of knowing that the data was ordered in a random access structure, that is, an array. Now, we have to consider access to the data in the form of a linked list. Notice that if we simply perform a scan on the data, then the running time will be $\Theta(n)$, which is equivalent to the RAM algorithm. Instead, we consider applying techniques of pointer jumping so that we can make progress simultaneously on multiple prefix results. For completeness, recall that we are given a set of data $X = \{x_1, \ldots x_n\}$ and a binary associative operator $\otimes$, from which we are required to compute prefix values $p_1, p_2, \ldots, p_n$, where the $k$-th prefix is defined as

$$p_k = \begin{cases} x_1 & \text{if } k = 1; \\ p_{k-1} \otimes x_k & \text{if } 2 \le k \le n. \end{cases}$$

We now present an algorithm for computing the parallel prefix of a linked list of size $n$ on a PRAM of size $n$, based on the concept of pointer jumping.

```
                        {p_i is used to store the i-th prefix.}
For all i, p_i ← x_i
                        {Perform a pointer-jumping algorithm.}
In parallel, each processor P_i does the following.
  While next(i) ≠ null, do
    p_next(i) ← p_i ⊗ p_next(i)
    next(i) ← next(next(i))
  End While
End parallel
```

An example of this algorithm is given in Figure 8-2, where we show the application of a parallel prefix on a PRAM to a linked list of size 6. While going through the algorithm, it is important to implement the update steps presented inside of the "In parallel" statement in lockstep fashion across the processors.

**Analysis:** This algorithm is similar to that of the list ranking algorithm just presented. That is, given a PRAM of size $n$, the running time of this algorithm is $\Theta(\log n)$. This can be seen by the fact that the first element in the list must traverse $\lceil \log_2 n \rceil$ links in order to propagate $x_1$ to all $n$ prefix values. Since the time for a PRAM of size $n$ to compute the parallel prefix on a list of size $n$ is $\Theta(\log n)$, the total cost of the algorithm is $\Theta(n \log n)$. As with the list ranking algorithm, the cost of the parallel prefix computation is suboptimal.

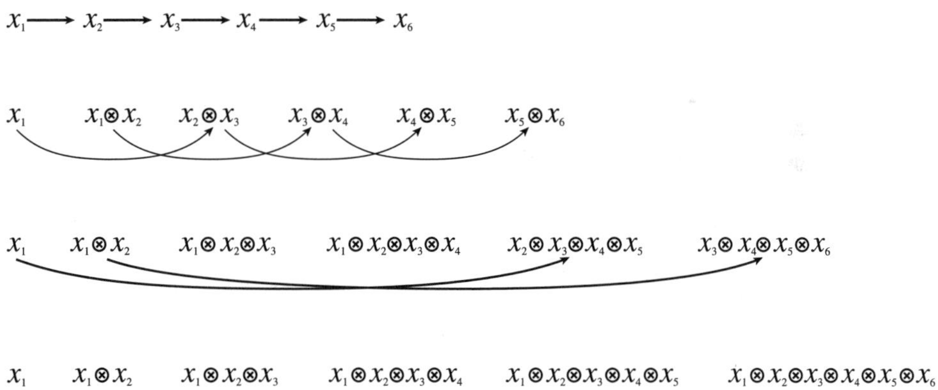


**FIGURE 8-2** *An example of parallel prefix on a PRAM with linked list input. Given a list of size* 6, *the recursive doubling procedure requires three iterations* ($\lceil \log_2 6 \rceil = 3$).

## Summary

In this chapter, we consider pointer jumping computations on a PRAM for the linked list data structure. The techniques presented allow us to double, in each parallel step, the portion of a list "known" to each node of the list, so that in logarithmic time, each node can know its relationship with all other nodes between its own position and the end of the list. The problems we consider are those of list ranking and parallel prefix (for linked lists). Our solutions are efficient, although not optimal.

## Chapter Notes

The focus of this chapter is on pointer-jumping algorithms and efficient solutions to problems involving linked lists, an inherently sequential structure. An excellent chapter was written on this subject by R.M. Karp and V. Ramachandran, entitled "A survey of parallel algorithms and shared memory machines," which appeared in the *Handbook of Theoretical Computer Science: Algorithms and Complexity* (A.J. vanLeeuwen, ed., Elsevier, New York, 1990, pp. 869–941). It contains numerous techniques and applications to interesting problems. In addition, pointer jumping algorithms are discussed in *An Introduction to Parallel Algorithms*, by J. Já Já (Addison-Wesley Publishing Company, New York, 1992).

## Exercises

1. Consider a set of linked lists $L_1, L_2, \ldots, L_k$ on a CREW PRAM with $n$ processors. Assume these lists have a total of $n$ elements. Initially, each processor $P_i, 1 \leq i \leq n$, knows the location of a unique list element, but not necessarily what list the element is in. Suppose that in every list, there is a unique element that is marked. Further, suppose that in each list, the uniquely marked element has a data value that must be broadcast to all elements of its list. Give an efficient algorithm to complete this distinct multi-list broadcast.
2. Describe an efficient algorithm to solve the following problem. Given a collection of linked lists with a total of $n$ elements, let every element know the number of elements in its list and how far the element is from the front of the list. Analyze the algorithm for the RAM and the CREW PRAM.
3. Give an efficient algorithm to solve the following problem. For a linked list with $n$ links, report the number of links with a given data value $x$. Analyze your algorithm for the RAM and the PRAM.
4. Give an efficient algorithm to solve the following problem. Given a set of ordered linked lists with a total of $n$ elements, record in every element the median value of the element's list. Note that in an ordered list of length $k$, for even $k$, the median value can be taken either as the value in element $(k/2 - 1)$ or element $k/2$ with respect to distance from the head of the list. Do not assume that it is known at the start of the algorithm how many elements are in any of the lists. Analyze the running time of your algorithm on the RAM and on the CREW PRAM.

# 9

# Divide-and-Conquer

The phrase "divide-and-conquer" is used in the study of algorithms to refer to a method of solving a problem that typically involves *i*) partitioning a problem into smaller subproblems, *ii*) recursively solving these subproblems, and then *iii*) stitching these partial solutions together in order to obtain a solution to the original problem. The divide-and-conquer strategy is summarized below.

1. *Divide* the problem into subproblems, each of which is smaller than the original.
2. *Conquer* the subproblems by recursively solving them, unless a subproblem is small enough to be solved directly.
3. *Combine* or *stitch* the solutions to the subproblems together in order to obtain a solution to the original problem.

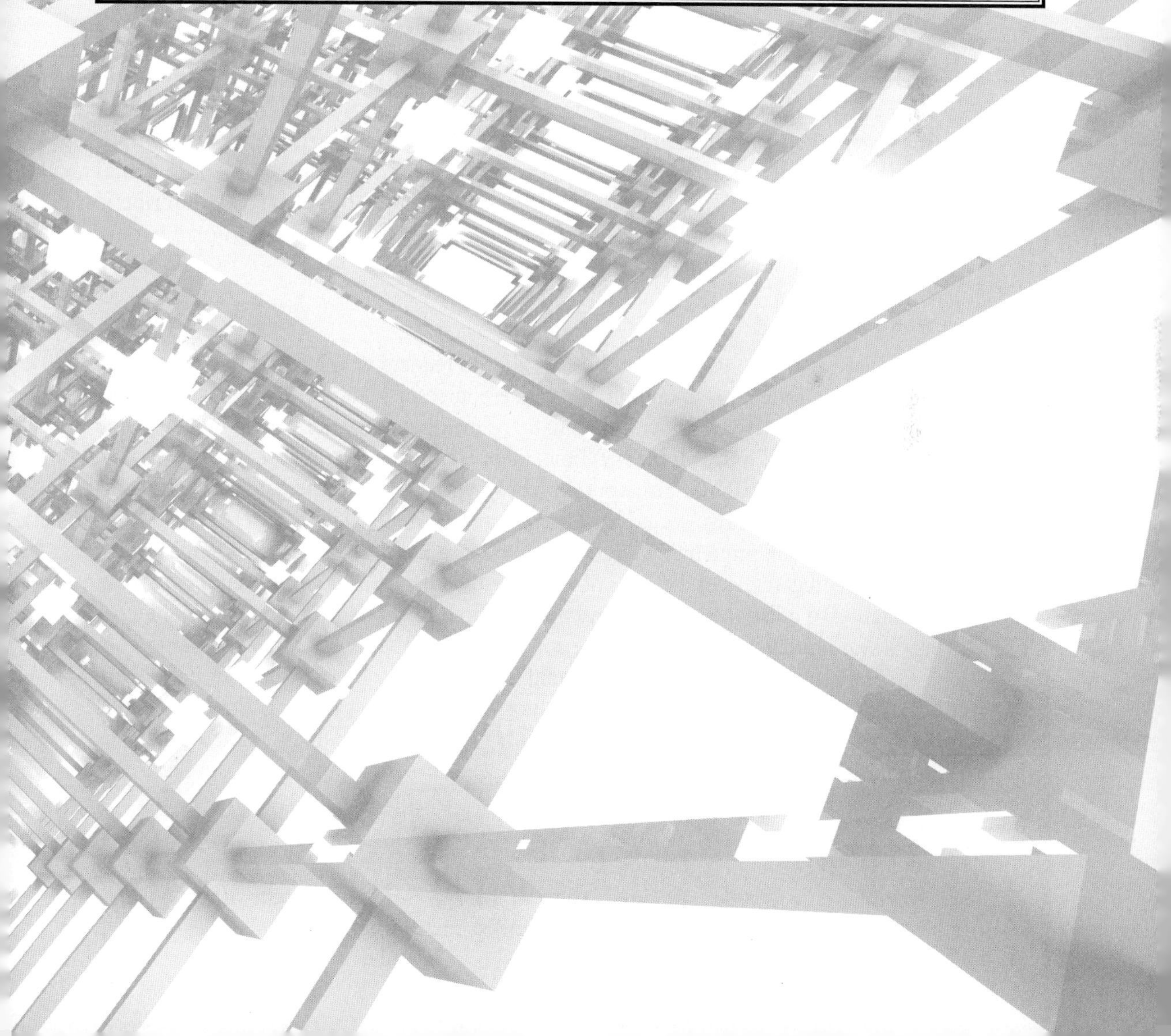

## Merge Sort (Revisited)

The divide-and-conquer paradigm is exhibited in *Merge Sort*, a sorting algorithm that we have previously discussed (see Chapter 2, "Induction and Recursion"). Recall that the input to the Merge Sort routine consists of an unordered list of $n$ elements, and the output consists of an ordered list of the $n$ elements. A high-level divide-and-conquer description of a basic Merge Sort follows.

1. **Divide:** Divide the unordered $n$-element input sequence into two unordered subsequences, each containing $n/2$ items.
2. **Conquer:** Recursively sort each of the two subsequences, unless a subsequence has only one item, in which case the subsequence is already sorted.
3. **Stitch:** Combine the two sorted sequences by *merging* them into the sorted result.

We should point out that this "top-down" divide-and-conquer description of Merge Sort is in contrast to a "bottom-up" description that students typically see in their early courses. A bottom-up description of Merge Sort might state that one should merge pairs of sequences of length 1 into ordered sequences of length 2, then merge ordered sequences of length 2 into ordered sequences of length 4, and so on. While these two descriptions differ significantly, the work they describe is identical. We now consider the time and space analysis of Merge Sort on a variety of models of computation.

### RAM

The analysis for the RAM should be familiar to readers who have taken a traditional year-long introduction to computer science course or a course that focuses on data structures. Let's first consider a schematic of the operations performed by the Merge Sort algorithm on a RAM. In $\Theta(n)$ time, the $n$ elements in the list are initially divided into two sublists, each of size approximately $n/2$. Both of these lists are then recursively sorted. These two sorted lists are then merged into a single ordered list. Notice that a traditional, sequential *merge* of two ordered lists with a total of $n$ items runs in $O(n)$ time, regardless of the sizes of the individual lists. So, assuming a typical implementation of a list, the total running time for both the initial split and the final merge is $\Theta(n)$. Figure 9-1 demonstrates the computation of the running time of Merge Sort.

The top-down description and analysis of a basic Merge Sort can be used to derive the running time of the algorithm in the form of the recurrence $T(n) = 2T(n/2) + \Theta(n)$. From the *Master Method*, we know that this recurrence has a solution of $T(n) = \Theta(n \log n)$. This is not surprising considering the *recursion tree* presented in Figure 9-1.

### Linear Array

We now consider an implementation of Merge Sort on a linear array. Assume that the elements of the list are arbitrarily distributed one per processor on a

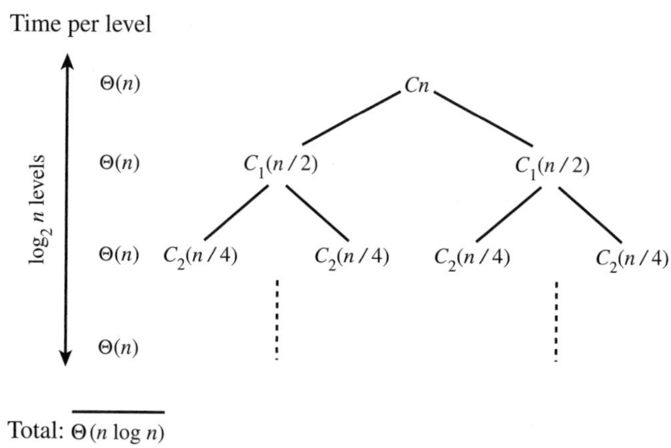


**FIGURE 9-1** *A recursion tree giving insight into the time required to perform a traditional Merge Sort algorithm on a RAM. Without loss of generality, assume that the time required to perform a split and a merge routine on n items is Cn, for some constant C.*

linear array of size $n$, where for simplicity of presentation, we assume that $n$ is a power of 2. Let's consider the stitch step of the algorithm. That is, assume that processors $P_1, \ldots, P_{n/2}$ contain an ordered subset of the data and that processors $P_{(n/2)+1}, \ldots, P_n$ contain the remaining elements in sorted order (see Figure 9-2). By knowing its processor ID, every processor knows the rank of its element with respect to its subsequence of size $n/2$ (see Figure 9-3). That is, processor $P_i$, $1 \leq i \leq n/2$, knows that the element it currently contains is the $i^{\text{th}}$ element with respect to those elements stored in processors $P_1, \ldots, P_{n/2}$. Similarly, processor $P_i$, $(n/2) + 1 \leq i \leq n$, knows that the element it currently contains has a rank of $i - n/2$ with respect to those elements stored in processors $P_{(n/2)+1}, \ldots, P_n$. Based on

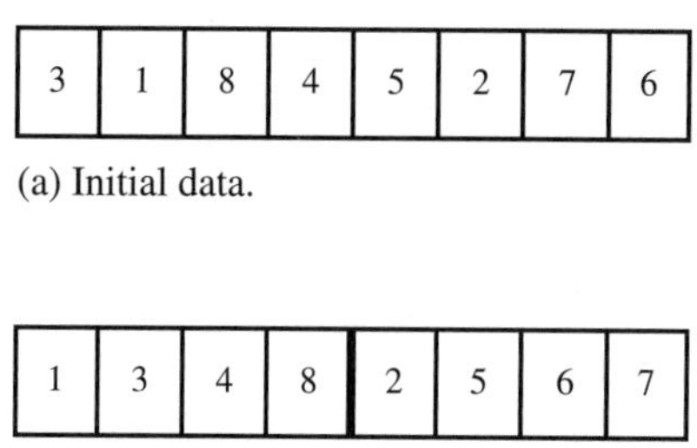


(a) Initial data.

(b) Independently sorted subarray data.

**FIGURE 9-2** *A snapshot of Merge Sort on a linear array of size* 8.

| | | | | | | | | |
|---|---|---|---|---|---|---|---|---|
| Data | 1 | 3 | 4 | 8 | 2 | 5 | 6 | 7 |
| Local Rank | 1 | 2 | 3 | 4 | 1 | 2 | 3 | 4 |

**FIGURE 9-3** *A snapshot of Merge Sort on a linear array of size* 8, *using the data from Figure 9-2. The snapshot shows the data and local ranks that are determined after the independent sorts on both the left and right subarrays.*

| | | | | | | | | |
|---|---|---|---|---|---|---|---|---|
| Data | 1 | 3 | 4 | 8 | 2 | 5 | 6 | 7 |
| Local Rank | 1 | 2 | 3 | 4 | 1 | 2 | 3 | 4 |
| Rank in Other Subarray | 0 | 1 | 1 | 4 | 1 | 3 | 3 | 3 |

**FIGURE 9-4** *A snapshot of Merge Sort on a linear array of size* 8 *after the independent sorts on both the left and right subarrays. The data, local ranks, and ranks with respect to the opposite subarray are all given. The data is from Figure 9-2.*

this information and knowledge of where an element ranks in the other subsequence, every processor will know the final position of the element it contains. That is, if the element in processor $P_i$, $1 \le i \le n/2$, is such that $s$ elements in processors $P_{(n/2)+1}, \ldots, P_n$ are less than it, then the final position for the element in processor $P_i$ is $i + s$. Similarly, if the element in processor $P_i$, $n/2 + 1 \le i \le n$, is such that $t$ elements in processors $P_1, \ldots P_{n/2}$ are less than or equal to it, then the final position for the element in processor $P_i$ is $i - (n/2) + t$ (see Figure 9-4).

In order to determine the rank of an element with respect to the other subsequence, simply perform a rotation of the data and allow every processor to count the number of elements from the other subsequence that rank ahead of the element that the processor is currently maintaining. Specifically, the following occur during the rotation.

- Every processor $P_i$, $1 \le i \le n/2$, counts the number of elements in processors $P_j$, $n/2 + 1 \le j \le n$, that are less than the entry maintained in $P_i$.
- Every processor $P_j$, $n/2 + 1 \le j \le n$, counts the number of elements in processors $P_i$, $1 \le i \le n/2$, that are less than or equal to the entry maintained in $P_j$.

A final rotation can then be used to send every element to its correct sorted position. The running time of such an algorithm is given by the recurrence

$T(n) = T(n/2) + \Theta(n)$. This recurrence has a solution of $T(n) = \Theta(n)$, which is optimal for the linear array. We make two critical observations.

1. The algorithm, as described, requires that during each recursive step, a rotation is *only performed within the pairs of subsequences of processors being merged.* That is, a complete rotation over the entire linear array of size $n$ is *not* performed during each recursive merge step. If a complete $\Theta(n)$ time rotation of the data through all $n$ processors were performed during each of the $\Theta(\log n)$ merge steps, then the running time of the algorithm would be $\Theta(n \log n)$.
2. Although the $\Theta(n)$ time algorithm is asymptotically equivalent in running time to the tractor-tread/rotation-based sorting algorithm for the linear array, the high order constants for this Merge Sort routine are significantly larger than those of the tractor-tread algorithm. This is clear from the fact that the last iteration of the Merge Sort procedure requires two complete rotations, whereas the rotation-based sort requires only one rotation in total.

Finally, consider the cost of this Merge Sort algorithm. The running time is $\Theta(n)$ on a linear array with $n$ processors, which yields a total cost of $\Theta(n^2)$. Notice that this is significantly larger than the $\Theta(n \log n)$ lower-bound result on the number of operations required for comparison-based sorting. Due to the $\Theta(n)$ communication diameter of the linear array, we know that it is not possible to reduce the running time of Merge Sort on a linear array of $n$ processors. Therefore, our only reasonable option for developing a Merge Sort-based algorithm that is cost-optimal on a linear array is to reduce the number of processors. If we reduce the number of processors to one, then the cost-optimal RAM algorithm can be executed. Since this yields no improvement in running time, we would like to consider a linear array with more than a fixed number of processors but less than a linear number of processors in the size of the input, in an asymptotic sense. We leave this problem as an exercise.

### Cluster

Assume that the $n$ elements to be sorted are stored in the master processor of a cluster of size $N$. We can use a recursive doubling technique to distribute the $n$ items to the $N$ processors. Once distributed, each of the processors in the cluster will sort its initial set of $n/N$ items. We then use a recursive halving technique to gather and merge pairs of sorted sublists continually until the final sorted list lands in the master processor.

The time to split the $n$ data items in half, send each half to the "tree-based" children, receive the data back from the children, and merge the two sorted subsets of data is $\Theta(n)$. The base level of the recursion is invoked when each of the $N$ processors receives its $n/N$ pieces of data. Once this occurs, each processor sorts its data and sends it back to the processor that sent it the data. The time for the base of the recursion is $B(n/N) = \Theta(n/N \log n/N)$. Therefore, the total running time to sort $n$ data items initially stored in the master processor of a cluster of size $N$ is given by $T(n) = \Theta(n + n/2 + n/4 + \cdots + n/N) + B(n/N)$, or

$$T(n) = \Theta(n) + B\left(\frac{n}{N}\right) = \Theta\left(n + \frac{n}{N}\log\frac{n}{N}\right).$$

So, given data in a single processor of a cluster, it is asymptotically more efficient to distribute the data to all processors, have each processor sort a reduced amount of data, and then combine the data. However, experience shows that due to the overhead of communication on existing clusters, if one needs to sort data that already resides in a single processor, it is much more efficient to have that processor sort the data locally rather than performing a distributed Merge Sort algorithm.

## Selection

In this section, we consider the *selection* problem, which requires the identification of the $k^{\text{th}}$ smallest element from a list of $n$ elements, where the integer $k$ is given as input to the procedure and where we assume that $1 \le k \le n$. Notice that this problem serves as a generalization of a number of problems, three of which are given below.

- The *minimum problem* corresponds to $k = 1$.
- The *maximum problem* corresponds to $k = n$.
- The *median problem* corresponds to either $k = \lfloor n/2 \rfloor$ or $k = \lceil n/2 \rceil$.

A naïve algorithm to solve the selection problem consists of sorting the data, and then reporting the entry that resides in the $k^{\text{th}}$ position of the ordered list.

If we assume that on the given model of computation, the running time for the sort step dominates the running time for the report step, then the asymptotic running time for selection is bounded by the running time for sorting. So, on a RAM, our naïve algorithm has a running time of $O(n \log n)$. Further, a solution to the problem has a worst-case lower bound of $\Omega(n)$ since every element might need to be examined.

In fact, for the restricted problem of finding the minimum or maximum element, we know that an optimal $\Theta(n)$ time algorithm can be obtained by a semigroup operation. This suggests the possibility of solving the more general selection problem in $o(n \log n)$ time.

We first consider an efficient $\Theta(n)$ time algorithm for the RAM, which is followed by a discussion of selection on parallel machines.

### RAM

We present an efficient algorithm based on the semigroup operation to solve the general selection problem. Assume that the $n$ data items are initially stored in arbitrary order in an array. For ease of explanation, we assume that $n$, the number of elements in the array, is a multiple of 5.

Initially, we take the unordered array as input and sort disjoint subsequences of five items (see Figure 9-5). That is, given an array $S$, we sort $S[1 \ldots 5]$, $S[6 \ldots 10], \ldots, S[n-4 \ldots n]$. Notice that this requires the application of $n/5$ sorting routines. However, since each of the $n/5$ sorting routines is working on a constant number of items, each of these $n/5$ sorts can be performed in constant time. Once these segments of size 5 are sorted within the array, we gather the medians of each of these $n/5$ segments. Notice that after the initial local sort step, the first median is in $S[3]$, the next median is in $S[8]$, and so on.

| | | | | | | | | | | | | | | | | | | | | | | | | |
|---|---|---|---|---|---|---|---|---|---|---|---|---|---|---|---|---|---|---|---|---|---|---|---|---|
| 10 | 18 | 23 | 17 | 5 | 11 | 16 | 1 | 9 | 4 | 6 | 15 | 22 | 8 | 3 | 14 | 20 | 24 | 2 | 19 | 7 | 12 | 21 | 25 | 13 |

(a) Initial array of size 25.

| | | | | | | | | | | | | | | | | | | | | | | | | |
|---|---|---|---|---|---|---|---|---|---|---|---|---|---|---|---|---|---|---|---|---|---|---|---|---|
| 5 | 10 | 17 | 18 | 23 | 1 | 4 | 9 | 11 | 16 | 3 | 6 | 8 | 15 | 22 | 2 | 14 | 19 | 20 | 24 | 7 | 12 | 13 | 21 | 25 |

(b) Array after independent sorts.

**FIGURE 9-5** *Using the Partition routine to solve the Selection Problem.*

Next, we recursively find the median of these $n/5$ median values. This median of medians, which we denote as $AM$, serves as an approximate median of the entire set $S$. Once we have this approximation, we compare all elements of $S$ with $AM$ and create three buckets, namely, those elements less than $AM$, those elements equal to $AM$, and those elements greater than $AM$ (see Figure 9-6). Finally, we determine which of these three buckets contains the $k^{\text{th}}$ element and solve the problem on that bucket, recursively if necessary. Notice that if the $k^{\text{th}}$ element falls in the second bucket, then, since all elements in this bucket have equal value, we have identified the requested element.

*smallList* → 12 → 7 → 2 → 8 → 6 → 3 → 11 → 9 → 4 → 1 → 10 → 5 ⊣

*equalList* → 13 ⊣

*bigList* → 25 → 21 → 24 → 20 → 19 → 14 → 22 → 15 → 16 → 23 → 18 → 17 ⊣

**FIGURE 9-6** *Creating three buckets based on* $AM = 13$*, the median of the five medians* (17, 9, 8, 19, 13) *given in Figure 9-5b. The data given in Figure 9-5b is traversed from the beginning to the end of the array, with every element less than* 13 *being placed in smallList, every item equal to* 13 *being placed in equalList, and every item greater than* 13 *being placed in bigList. Notice that the items should be placed in these lists in a manner that allows for* $\Theta(1)$ *time insertion. This can be done either by placing a new item at the head of the list, as shown, or by placing items at the end of a list if a tail pointer is maintained.*

**Function Selection(*k, S, lower, upper*)**
**Input:** An array *S*, positions *lower* and *upper*, and a value *k*.
**Output:** The $k^{\text{th}}$ smallest item in *S*[*lower*...*upper*].
**Local variables:**
*n*, the size of the subarray;
*M*, an array used for medians of certain subarrays of *S*;
*smallList, equalList, bigList*: lists used to partition *S*;
*j*, an index variable;
*AM*, an approximation of the median of *S*.

**Action:**

```
If |upper - lower| < 50, then  {The base case of recursion.
                                The value of the constant, in this
                                  case 50, is typically determined
                                    experimentally in terms of the
                                         target computing system.}
   SelectionSort(S, lower, upper)
   return S[lower + k - 1]
End If
Else                                          {The recursive case.}
   1. n = upper - lower + 1
   2. Sort disjoint subarrays of size 5 or less. That is,
      independently sort S[lower, ..., lower + 4], ...,
      S[lower + 5(⌈n/5⌉ - 1), ..., upper].
   3. For j = 1 to ⌈n/5⌉, do
        Assign the j^th median to M[j]. That is,
        M[j] = S[lower + 5j - 3].
   4. AM = Selection(⌈|M|/2⌉, M, 1, ⌈n/5⌉), the median of M.
   5. Create empty lists smallList, equalList, and
      bigList.
```

```
6. For j=1 to n, do
   Copy S[lower+j-1] to
                    { smallList  if S[lower+j-1] < AM;
                    { equalList  if S[lower+j-1] = AM;
                    { bigList    otherwise.
   End For
7. If k≤|smallList|, then
     CreateArray(smallList, smallList_array)
     return Selection(k,smallList_array,1,|smallList|)
   Else If k≤|smallList|+|equalList| then return AM
        Else {find result in bigList}
          CreateArray(bigList, bigList_array)
          return Selection(k-|smallList|-|equalList|,
                           bigList_array,1,|bigList|)
        End Else {find result in bigList}
End Else recursive case
```

#### Correctness of Algorithm

Consider the lists *smallList, equalList,* and *bigList.* These lists contain members of $S$ such that if $x \in smallList$, $y \in equalList$, and $z \in bigList$, then $x < y < z$. Therefore, we have the following.

- If $k \leq |smallList|$, then the entries of *smallList* include the $k$ smallest entries of $S$, so the algorithm correctly returns $Selection(k,\ smallList\_array,\ 1,\ |smallList|)$.
- If $|smallList| < k \leq |smallList| + |equalList|$, then the $k^{\text{th}}$ smallest entry of S belongs to *equalList*, each entry of which has a key value equal to *AM,* so the algorithm correctly returns *AM.*
- If $|smallList| + |equalList| < k$, then the $k^{\text{th}}$ smallest member of $S$ must be the $(k - |smallList| - |equalList|)^{\text{th}}$ smallest member of *bigList,* so the algorithm correctly returns $Selection(k - |smallList| - |equalList|, bigList\_array, 1,\ |bigList|)$.

#### Analysis of Running Time

The base case of the recursive algorithm calls for sorting a list with some experimentally determined constant. Therefore, the running time of the base case is $\Theta(1)$. This is due to the fact that any polynomial time algorithm, such as the $\Theta(n^2)$ time Selection Sort, will run in constant time on a fixed number of input items. Again, note that the choice of 50 is arbitrary, as any fixed positive integer will suffice.

We now consider the remainder of the algorithm.

- Step 1 runs in $\Theta(1)$ time.
- Step 2 calls for sorting $\Theta(n)$ sublists of the input list, where each sublist has at most five entries. Since 5 is a constant, we know that each sublist can be sorted

in constant time. Therefore, the time to complete these $\Theta(n)$ sorts, each of which runs in $\Theta(1)$ time, is $\Theta(n)$.

- Step 3 gathers the medians of each sublist, which requires making a copy of $\lceil n/5 \rceil$ elements, each of which can be retrieved in $\Theta(1)$ time. Therefore, the running time for this step is $\Theta(n)$.
- Step 4 requires the application of the entire procedure on an array with $\lceil n/5 \rceil$ elements. Therefore, this step runs in $T(\lceil n/5 \rceil)$ time.
- Step 5 calls for the creation of a fixed number of lists, which runs in $\Theta(1)$ time in most modern programming languages.
- Step 6 consists of copying each of the $n$ input elements to exactly one of the three lists created in Step 4. Therefore, the running time for this step is $\Theta(n)$.
- Step 7 determines which of the three lists needs to be inspected and, in two of the three cases, a recursive call is performed. The running time for this step is a function of the input value $k$ as well as the order of the initial set of data. Due to these complexities, analysis of the running time of this step is a bit more involved. Three basic cases must be considered, each of which we evaluate separately. Namely, the requested element could be in *smallList*, *equalList*, or *bigList*.
    - We first consider the case where the requested element is in *smallList*, which occurs when $k \le |smallList|$. Let's consider just how large *smallList* can be. That is, what is the maximum number of elements that can be in *smallList*? The maximal size of *smallList* can be determined as follows.
        - Consider the maximum number of elements that can be less than $AM$, the median of the medians. At most $\lfloor |M|/2 \rfloor = \lfloor \lceil n/5 \rceil /2 \rfloor$ members of $M$ are less than $AM$. For simplicity, and since our analysis is based on asymptotic behavior, let's say that at most $n/10$ median elements are less than $AM$.
        - Notice that each $m \in M$ is the third smallest entry of an ordered 5-element sublist of the input list $S$. In the $n/10$ sublists for which we have $m < AM$, possibly all 5 members could be less than AM. However, in the $n/10$ sublists for which we have $m \ge AM$, at most 2 members apiece are less than $AM$.
        - Therefore, at most $5n/10 + 2n/10 = 7n/10$ elements of the input list $S$ can be sent to *smallList*. Thus, the recursive call to *Selection* $(k, smallList\_array, 1, |smallList|)$ runs in at most $T(7n/10)$ time.
    - If $|smallList| < k \le |smallList| + |equalList|$, then the required element is in *equalList,* and this step runs in $\Theta(1)$ time, since the required element is equal to $AM$.
    - If $|smallList| + |equalList| < k$, then the required element is in *bigList*. Consider the maximum number of elements that can appear in *bigList*.

An argument similar to the one given above for the size of *smallList* can be used to show that *bigList* has at most $7n/10$ entries. Thus, the recursive call of the *Selection* routine in this case runs in at most $T(7n/10)$ time.

Finally, consider the total running time $T(n)$ for the selection algorithm we have presented. There are positive constants $c$, $c_0$ such that the running time of this algorithm is given by

$$\begin{aligned} &T(n) \le cn && \text{for } 1 \le n \le 50; \\ &T(n) \le T(n/5) + T(7n/10) + c_0 n && \text{for } n > 50. \end{aligned}$$

By taking $C = \max\{c, 10c_0\}$, the previous statement yields

$$\begin{aligned} &T(n) \le Cn && \text{for } 1 \le n \le 50; \\ &T(n) \le T(n/5) + T(7n/10) + Cn/10 && \text{for } n > 50. \end{aligned}$$

Thus, for $1 \le n \le 50$ we have $T(n) \le Cn$. This statement serves as the base case for an induction proof. Suppose we have $T(n) \le Cn$ for all positive integer values $n < m$. Then we have

$$T(m) \le T(m/5) + T(7m/10) + Cm/10 \le$$

(by the inductive hypothesis)

$$Cm/5 + C(7m/10) + Cm/10 = Cm.$$

This completes the induction proof that $T(n) \le Cn$. Therefore, $T(n) = O(n)$. Since we also must examine every entry of the input list, we know that any selection algorithm must run in $\Omega(n)$ time. Therefore, our algorithm runs in optimal $\Theta(n)$ time on a RAM.

#### PRAM

Consider applying the algorithm we have just presented to a PRAM. Notice that the independent sorting of Step 2 can be performed in parallel in $\Theta(1)$ time. Step 3 requires that the median elements are placed in their proper positions, which can be done quite simply on a PRAM in $\Theta(1)$ time. Step 4 is a recursive step that runs in time proportional to $T(n/5)$. Step 5 runs in constant time. Step 6 can be performed by a parallel prefix operation and an exclusive write. The parallel prefix operation is used to determine the position of each element in the appropriate list of *smallList, equalList,* or *bigList* and the exclusive write is used to copy the element into its assigned position. Therefore, this step can be performed in $O(\log n)$ time. Now consider the recursion in Step 7. Again, the running time of this step is no more than $T(7n/10)$. So, the running time for the algorithm can be expressed as $T(n) = T(7n/10) + T(n/5) + O(\log n)$, which is asymptotically equivalent to $T(n) = T(7n/10) + O(\log n)$, which resolves to $T(n) = O(\log^2 n)$. It should be noted that the running time of this algorithm can be reduced to $O(\log n \log \log n)$ by applying some techniques that are outside the scope of this text. In addition, the problem can also be solved by first sorting the elements in $\Theta(\log n)$ time and then selecting the required element in $\Theta(1)$ time. This $\Theta(\log n)$ time sorting routine is also outside the scope of this book. In fact, $\Theta(n)$ optimal-cost algorithms for the selection problem on a PRAM are known. These algorithms are also outside the scope of this text.

### Mesh

Consider the selection problem on a mesh of size $n$. Since the communication diameter of a mesh of size $n$ is $\Theta(n^{1/2})$, and since it will be shown later in this chapter that sorting can be performed on the mesh in $\Theta(n^{1/2})$ time, we know that the problem of selection can be solved in optimal $\Theta(n^{1/2})$ time on a mesh of size $n$.

## Quicksort (Partition Sort)

*Quicksort* is an efficient and popular sorting algorithm that was originally designed by C.A.R. Hoare for the RAM. It is a beautiful algorithm that serves as an excellent example of the divide-and-conquer paradigm. Quicksort also serves as a good example of an algorithm without a deterministic running time, in the sense that its best-, expected-, and worst-case running times are not the same. Depending on the arrangement of the $n$ input items on a RAM, Quicksort has a $\Theta(n)$ best-case running time, a $\Theta(n \log n)$ expected-case running time, and a $\Theta(n^2)$ worst-case running time. In particular, the reason that Quicksort is so popular on the RAM is due to its very fast $\Theta(n \log n)$ expected-case running time, where "fast" is relative to other popular $\Theta(n \log n)$ time and $\Theta(n^2)$ time algorithms, including Merge Sort, Selection Sort, and Insertion Sort, to name a few.

One must be quite careful when invoking Quicksort since for certain datasets that are relatively common, Quicksort can run in $\Theta(n^2)$ time. In fact, Quicksort's worst-case $\Theta(n^2)$ running time is often slower in practice than a "simple sort" such as Selection Sort. This may occur, for example, when trying to sort common datasets that include nearly ordered or nearly reverse ordered data.

The importance of Quicksort motivates us to study this algorithm carefully. Our discussion includes the following.

- An outline of the Quicksort algorithm as an example of divide-and-conquer.
- Examples.
- A more detailed description of the algorithm that is especially geared for implementation using linked lists.

- Analysis of running time for various cases of input.
- A comparison of Quicksort and Merge Sort.
- A description of how Quicksort can be implemented for data given in an array.
- Analysis of memory usage.
- Discussion of ways to improve the performance of the basic Quicksort algorithm.
- Modifications of the Quicksort algorithm for efficient implementation on parallel computers.

Note that in Appendix 4, we prove that the expected running time of Quicksort for a list of $n$ entries is $\Theta(n \log n)$. The proof is challenging and should only be read by those with the patience and mathematical skills to make the experience worthwhile.

The basic Quicksort algorithm can be expressed as follows.

- **Divide:** Divide the $n$ input items into three lists, denoted as *smallList*, *equalList*, and *bigList*, where all items in *smallList* are less than all items in *equalList*, all items in *equalList* have the same value, and all items in *equalList* are less than all items in *bigList*.
- **Conquer:** Recursively sort *smallList* and *bigList*. Note that a list need not be sorted if it contains no more than one element.
- **Stitch:** Concatenate *smallList*, *equalList*, and *bigList*.

The reader should note the similarity of the Divide step with the Divide step of the Selection algorithm discussed earlier in this chapter (see Figure 9-7). Also, note the Conquer step does not require processing *equalList*, as its members are sorted, since all have the same value. Finally, one should note that Quicksort does not rely on comparing list elements to each other for the purpose of determining an ordering of the elements.

Typically, the input data is divided into three lists by first using a small amount of time to determine an element that has a high probability of being a good approximation to the median element. We use the term *splitValue* to refer to the element that is selected for this purpose. This value is then used much in the same way as *AM* was used during the selection algorithm. Every element is sent to one of three lists. The list *smallList* contains those elements less than *splitValue*. The list *equalList* contains those elements equal to *splitValue*. The list *bigList* contains those elements larger than *splitValue*. After recursively sorting *bigList* and *smallList*, the three lists can simply be concatenated.

$q \to 5 \to 8 \to 1 \to 2 \to 6 \to 7 \to 4 \to 9 \to 3 \dashv$

(a) Initial unsorted list.

*smallList* $\to 1 \to 2 \to 4 \to 3 \dashv$

*equalList* $\to 5 \dashv$

*bigList* $\to 8 \to 6 \to 7 \to 9 \dashv$

(b) Three lists after the partitioning based on the value of 5.

*smallList* $\to 1 \to 2 \to 3 \to 4 \dashv$

*equalList* $\to 5 \dashv$

*bigList* $\to 6 \to 7 \to 8 \to 9 \dashv$

(c) The three lists after *smallList* and *bigList* are recursively sorted.

$q \to 1 \to 2 \to 3 \to 4 \to 5 \to 6 \to 7 \to 8 \to 9 \dashv$

(d) Completed list after the three sorted sublists are concatenated.

**FIGURE 9-7** *An example of Quicksort on a linked list. Notice that an item can be placed into the appropriate list either at the front or the back of the list in* $\Theta(1)$ *time since efficient concatenation at the end of Quicksort requires the use of tail pointers. We show lists built using* $\Theta(1)$ *time insertion at the back of the list, simply as a contrast to* $\Theta(1)$ *time insertion at the front of a list as shown in Figure 9-6.*

Naturally, we hope that the splitting item is chosen at every level of the recursion to be close to the median of the data under consideration. Such a choice of *splitValue* would result in a running time given by $T(n) = 2T(n/2) + \Theta(n)$, which gives $T(n) = \Theta(n \log n)$.

We now present details of a list-based Quicksort algorithm on a RAM. We start with a top-down description of the algorithm.

**Subprogram QuickSort($q$)**
**Input:** A list $q$.
**Output:** The list $q$, with the elements sorted.
**Procedure:** Use Quicksort to sort the list.
**Local variables:**
*splitValue*, key used to partition the list;
*smallList, equalList, bigList,* sublists for partitioning.

**Action:**

```
  If q has at least two elements, then          {do work}
    Create empty lists smallList, equalList, and bigList.
                              {Divide: Partition the list.}
    splitValue = findSplitValue(q);
    splitList(q, splitValue, smallList, equalList, bigList);
                    {Conquer: Recursively sort sublists.}
    QuickSort(smallList);
    QuickSort(bigList);
                            {Stitch: Concatenate sublists.}
    Concatenate(smallList, equalList, bigList, q)
  End If
End Sort
```

Now let's consider the running time of Quicksort.

- In $\Theta(1)$ time, we can determine whether or not a list has at least two items. Notice that a list having fewer than two items serves as the base case of recursion, requiring no further work since such a list is already sorted.
- Constructing three empty lists can be performed in $\Theta(1)$ time using a modern programming language.
- Consider the time it takes to find *splitValue*. Ideally, we want this splitter to be the median element, so that *smallList* and *bigList* will be of approximately the same size. If *smallList* and *bigList* are of approximately the same size, then the running time of the algorithm will be minimized. The splitter can be chosen in as little as $\Theta(1)$ time, if one utilizes an easily accessible item such as the first item of the list. The splitter can also be chosen in as much as $\Theta(n)$ time by the Selection algorithm if one wants to determine the precise median. Initially, we will consider using a unit-time algorithm to determine the splitter. We realize that this could lead to a bad split and, if this continues through too many levels of recursion, to a very slow algorithm. Later in the chapter we will discuss improvements in choosing the splitter and the effect that such improvements have on the overall algorithm.

- Splitting the list is performed in $\Theta(1)$ time per item. Dividing the $n$ elements into the three aforementioned lists can be performed in $\Theta(n)$ time. This can be done by a straightforward traversal of the list, comparing each element to the splitter and tossing each element into the appropriate list. The algorithm follows.

**Subprogram splitList(*A, splitValue, smallList, equalList, bigList*)**
**Input:** List *A,* partition element *splitValue.*
**Output:** Three sublists corresponding to items of *A* less than, equal to, and greater than *splitValue*, respectively.
**Local variable:** *temp*, a pointer used for removing an entry from one list and moving the entry onto another list.

**Action:**

```
While not empty(A), do
  getfirst(A, temp)
  If temp.key < splitValue, then
    putelement(temp, smallList)
  Else If temp.key = splitValue, then
        putelement(temp, equalList)
      Else putelement(temp, bigList)
End While
End splitList
```

Notice that for the sake of efficiency, it is important to be able to add an element to a list in $\Theta(1)$ time. That is, suppose that the elements of a list are maintained as a singly linked list in which the list is identified by a pointer that points to the first element, which contains data and a pointer to the second element, which contains data and a pointer to the third element, and so on, with the last element of a list having a pointer set to *null*. One may add an element to such a list in $\Theta(1)$ time by adding a new element as the first item of such a list. Alternately, if a *tail* pointer is kept to the last item in the list, then by taking advantage of the tail pointer, a new item may be added in $\Theta(1)$ time at the end of the list. Many programmers make the mistake of adding an element to a list of size $m$ by starting at the head of the list and traversing the list until the end and adding the new element to the end of the list. Notice that such an approach runs in $\Theta(m)$ time and will adversely affect the running time of the algorithm. Finally, notice that in order to concatenate two lists in $\Theta(1)$ time, one will typically keep a *tail* pointer.

Since both inserting and removing a data item from a list can be done in $\Theta(1)$ time, the split procedure can be implemented to run in $\Theta(n)$ time.

In the *best case*, every element of the input list goes into *equalList*, with *smallList* and *bigList* remaining empty. If this is the case, then the algorithm makes one pass through the data, places all of the items in a single list, performs two recursive calls that are completed in $\Theta(1)$ time, and concludes with a concatenation of the two empty lists to the one list containing all of the identical items in $\Theta(1)$ time. This results in a total running time of $T(n) = 2T(0) + \Theta(n) = \Theta(n)$.

Without loss of generality, let's now consider the case where all of the elements are distinct. Given this scenario, the *best-case* running time will occur when an even split occurs. That is, when one item is placed in *equalList*, $\lfloor n/2 \rfloor$ items in either *smallList* or *bigList*, and $\lceil n/2 \rceil - 1$ items in *bigList* or *smallList*, respectively. In this situation, the running time of the algorithm, $T(n)$, is approximately given as

$$T(1) = \Theta(1);$$
$$T(n) = 2T(n/2) + \Theta(n).$$

Recall that this recurrence results in a running time of $T(n) = \Theta(n \log n)$. So, in the best case, the running time of Quicksort is asymptotically optimal. We show in Appendix 4 that the expected, *i.e.*, average, running time of Quicksort is $\Theta(n \log n)$, which has important practical implications. In fact, its $\Theta(n \log n)$ average running time is one of the reasons that Quicksort comes packaged with so many computing systems.

Now consider the worst-case scenario of Quicksort. Suppose that at every level of recursion, either the maximum or minimum element in the list is chosen as *splitValue*. Examples of how this can occur are input lists that are already sorted, in either ascending or descending order. Therefore, after assigning elements to the three lists, one of the lists will have $n - 1$ items in it, one will be empty, and *equalList* will have only the splitter in it. In this case, the running time of the algorithm obeys the recurrence $T(n) = T(n - 1) + \Theta(n)$, which has a solution of $T(n) = \Theta(n^2)$. That is, if one gets very unlucky at each stage of the recursion, the running time of Quicksort could be as bad as $\Theta(n^2)$.

One should be concerned about this problem in the event that such a running time is not acceptable. Further, if one anticipates data sets that have large segments of ordered data, one may want to avoid a straightforward implementation of Quicksort. The scenario of a bad split at every stage of the recursion could also be realized with an input list that does not have large segments of ordered data (see the Exercises). Later in this chapter, we discuss techniques for minimizing the possibility of a $\Theta(n^2)$-time Quicksort algorithm.

### Quicksort vs. Merge Sort

Quicksort and Merge Sort are most naturally implemented with data stored in linked lists. Consider a comparison of these two popular sorting techniques. Merge Sort requires a straightforward division of the elements into two lists of equal size, while Quicksort partitions its input list using some intelligent reorganization of the data.

Conversely, Merge Sort requires an intricate combination of the recursively sorted sublists, while Quicksort merely requires concatenation of three lists. Therefore, Merge Sort is referred to as an *easy split, hard join* algorithm, while Quicksort is referred to as a *hard split, easy join* algorithm. That is, Merge Sort is more efficient than Quicksort in the divide stage, but less efficient than Quicksort in the stitch stage.

Notice that in Merge Sort, comparisons are made between items in different lists during the merge operation. In Quicksort, however, comparisons are made between elements during the divide stage. The reason that no comparisons are made during the stitch step in Quicksort is because the divide step guarantees that if element $x$ is sent to list *smallList*, element $y$ is sent to list *equalList*, and element $z$ is sent to *bigList*, then $x < y < z$.

### Array Implementation

In this section, we discuss the application of Quicksort to a set of data stored in an array. The astute reader might note that with modern programming languages, one rarely encounters a situation where the data to be sorted is maintained in a static array. However, there are certain "dusty deck" codes that must be maintained in the original style of design and implementation for various reasons. This includes vintage scientific software written in languages such as FORTRAN. In addition, there are other reasons why we present this *unnatural implementation of Quicksort*. The first is historic. When algorithms texts first appeared, the major data structure was a static array. For this reason, Quicksort has been presented in many texts predominantly from the array point of view. Although this is unfortunate, we do believe that for historic reasons, it is worth including an array implementation of Quicksort in this text. Finally, while the linked list implementation that we presented in the preceding section is straightforward in its design, implementation, and analysis, the array implementation is quite complex and somewhat counterintuitive. The advantage of this is that it allows us to present some interesting analysis techniques and to discuss some interesting algorithmic issues in terms of optimization.

Assume that the input to the Quicksort routine consists of an array $A$ containing $n$ elements to be sorted. For simplicity, we will assume that $A$ contains only the keys of the data items. Note that the data associated with each element could more generally be maintained in other fields if the language allows an array of records or could be maintained in other related arrays. The latter situation was common in the 1960s and 1970s, especially with languages such as FORTRAN.

Notice that a major problem with a static array is partitioning the elements. We assume that additional data structures cannot be allocated in a dynamic fashion. For historical reasons, let's assume that all rearrangement of data is restricted to the array(s) that contain the initial data plus a constant number of temporary data cells. While this situation may seem strange to current students of computer science who have learned modern, *i.e.*, post-1980s, programming languages, we reiterate that there are situations and languages for which this scenario is critical.

So, let's consider the basic Quicksort algorithm as implemented on an array $A$, where we wish to sort the elements $A[left \ldots right]$, where $left \leq right$ are integers that serve as pointers into the array. Typically, the first call on this recursive procedure would have $left = 1$ and $right = n$ if indexing begins with 1, or $left = 0$ and $right = n - 1$ if indexing begins with 0.

**Subprogram QuickSort (*A, left, right*)**
**Input:** An array $A$.
**Output:** The array $A$ with elements sorted by the Quicksort method.

```
If left < right, then
  Partition(A, left, right, partitionIndex)
  QuickSort(A, left, partitionIndex)
  QuickSort(A, partitionIndex + 1, right)
End If
End QuickSort
```

Notice that a concatenation step comes for free since concatenating two adjacent subarrays does not require any work. Therefore, no concatenation step is listed in our description of the array implementation of Quicksort above. The basic algorithm is similar to the linked list version of Quicksort presented previously. That is, we need to partition the elements and then sort each of the subarrays. For purposes of our discussion in this section, we view the array as being horizontal. In order to work more easily with an array, we will partition it into only two "subarrays" under a relaxed criterion that requires all elements in the left subarray to be *less than or equal to* all elements in the right subarray. It is critical to note that if the keys are not unique, then copies of the split element could appear in both the left and right subarrays. We then recursively sort the left subarray and the right subarray. Specifically, we have the following.

1. **Divide:** $A[left \ldots right]$ is partitioned into two *nonempty* subarrays $A[left \ldots p]$ and $A[p + 1 \ldots right]$ such that all elements in $A[left \ldots p]$ are less than *or equal to* all elements in $A[p + 1 \ldots right]$.
2. **Conquer:** Recursively sort subarray $A[left \ldots p]$, if $left < p$, and $A[p + 1 \ldots right]$, if $p + 1 < right$.
3. **Stitch:** Requires no work since the data is in an array that is already correctly joined.

So, given the basic algorithm, we only need to provide an algorithm for the partition routine (see Figure 9-8). We need to point out that this routine is specific to array implementations. Over the years, we have watched numerous programmers try to implement this routine on a linked list because they did not understand the fundamentals of Quicksort and did not realize that this array implementation is

| | | | | | | | | |
|---|---|---|---|---|---|---|---|---|
| 5 | 8 | 1 | 2 | 6 | 7 | 4 | 9 | 3 |

(a) The initial unordered array is given.

| | | | | | | | | |
|---|---|---|---|---|---|---|---|---|
| 3 | 4 | 1 | 2 | 6 | 7 | 8 | 9 | 5 |

(b) The data is shown after partitioning has been performed with respect to the value of 5. Notice that <3,4,1,2> are all less than or equal to 5 and <6,7,8,9,5> are all greater than or equal to 5.

| | | | | | | | | |
|---|---|---|---|---|---|---|---|---|
| 1 | 2 | 3 | 4 | 5 | 6 | 7 | 8 | 9 |

(c) The array is presented after the recursive sorting on each of the two subarrays. Notice that this results in the entire array being sorted.

**FIGURE 9-8** *An example of Quicksort on an array of size* 9.

unnatural. The standard partition routine that we are about to present *should only be used with an array.*

This partition routine works as follows. First, choose a partition value. Next, partition the array into two subarrays so that all elements in the left subarray are less than or equal to the partition value, while all elements in the right subarray are greater than or equal to this value. This is done by marching through the array from left to right in search of an element that is *greater than or equal to* the partition value, and similarly, from right to left in search of an element that is *less than or equal to* the partition value. In other words, we march through the array from the outside in, looking for misplaced items. If such elements are found, they are swapped, and the search continues until the elements discovered are in their proper subarrays. Refer again to Figure 9-8. Pseudo-code follows.

**Subprogram Partition(*A, left, right, partitionIndex*)**
**Input:** A subarray $A[left,\ldots,right]$.
**Output:** An partition index, *pIndex*, and the subarray $A[left,\ldots,right]$ partitioned so that all elements in $A[left,\ldots,pIndex]$ are less than or equal to all elements in $A[pIndex+1,\ldots,right]$.
**Local variables:** *splitValue*; indices *i, j*

**Action:**

```
splitValue ← A[left]        {A simple choice of splitter}
i ← left − 1
j ← right + 1
While i < j, do
  Repeat i ← i + 1 until A[i] ≥ splitValue
  Repeat j ← j − 1 until A[j] ≤ splitValue
  If i < j, then Swap(A[i], A[j])
  Else pIndex ← j
End While
End Partition
```

We now present an example of the partition routine. Notice that the marching from left to right is accomplished by the movement of index $i$, while the marching from right to left is accomplished by the movement of index $j$. It is important to note that each is looking for an element that could be located in the other subarray. That is, $i$ will stop at any element *greater than or equal to* the splitter element, and $j$ will stop at any element *less than or equal to* the splitter element. The reader should note that the condition for reiteration of the While-loop body, $i < j$, guarantees the algorithm will terminate without allowing either index to move off of the end of the array, so there is no infinite loop or out-of-bounds indexing.

**EXAMPLE**

Initially, *splitValue* is chosen to be $A[1] = 5$, $i$ is set to $left - 1 = 0$ and $j$ is set to $right + 1 = 9$, as shown in Figure 9-9a.

Since $i < j$, the algorithm proceeds by incrementing $i$ until an element is found that is greater than or equal to 5. Next, $j$ is decremented until an element is encountered that is less than or equal to 5. At the end of this first pair of index updates, we have $i = 1$ and $j = 7$, as shown in Figure 9-9b.

Since $i < j$, we swap elements $A[i] = A[1]$ and $A[j] = A[7]$. This results in the configuration of the array shown in Figure 9-9c.

Since $i < j$, the algorithm proceeds by incrementing $i$ until an element is found that is greater than or equal to 5. Next, $j$ is decremented until an element is encountered that is less than or equal to 5. At the end of this pair of index updates, we have $i = 4$ and $j = 6$, as shown in Figure 9-9d.

Since $i < j$, we swap elements $A[i] = A[4]$ and $A[j] = A[6]$. This results in the configuration of the array shown in Figure 9-9e.

Since $i < j$, the algorithm continues. First, we increment $i$ until an element (6) is found that is greater than or equal to 5. Next, we decrement $j$ until an element (4) is found that is less than or equal to 5. At the end of this pair of index updates, we have $i = 6$ and $j = 5$ (see Figure 9-9f).

Since $i \geq j$, the procedure terminates with the *partitionIndex* set to $j = 5$. This means that Quicksort can be called recursively on $A[1\ldots5]$ and $A[6\ldots8]$.

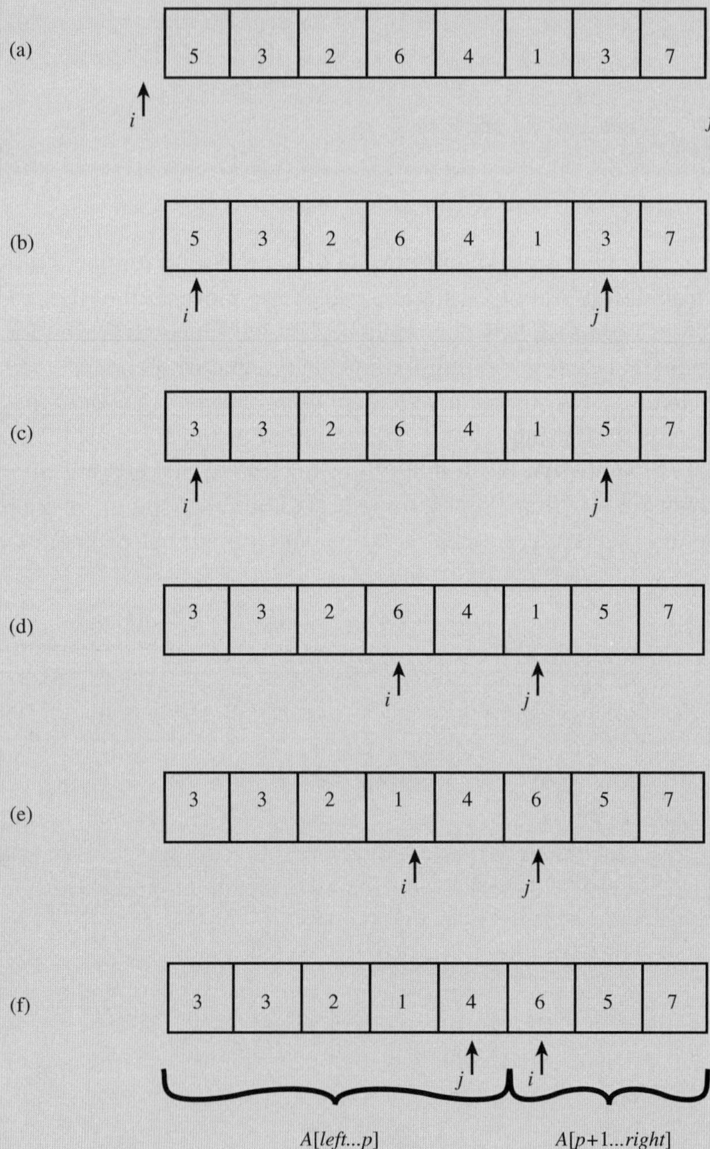


**FIGURE 9-9** *An example of the Partition routine of Quicksort on an array of 8 items.*

### Analysis of Quicksort

In this section, we consider the time and space requirements for the array version of Quicksort, as implemented on a RAM.

#### *Time*

Notice that the running time is given by $T(n) = T(n_L) + T(n_R) + \Theta(n)$, where $\Theta(n)$ is the time required for the partition and concatenation operations, $T(n_L)$ is the time required to sort recursively the left subarray of size $n_L$, and $T(n_R)$ is the time required to sort recursively the right subarray of size $n_R$, where $n_L + n_R = n$.

Consider the best-case running time. That is, consider the situation that will result in the minimum running time of the array version of Quicksort as presented. Notice that in order to minimize the running time, we want $T(n_L) = \Theta(T(n_R))$, which occurs if $n_L = \Theta(n_R)$. In fact, it is easy to see that the running time is minimized if we partition the array into two approximately equally sized pieces at every step of the recursion. An ideal partition with an appropriate number of elements results in the recurrence $T(n) = 2T(n/2) + \Theta(n)$, which has a solution of $T(n) = \Theta(n \log n)$. This situation will occur if every time the partition element is selected, it is the median of the elements being sorted.

Consider the worst-case running time. Notice that the running time is maximized if either $n_L$ or $n_R$ is equal to $n - 1$. That is, the running time is maximized if the partition is such that the subarrays are of size 1 and $n - 1$. This would yield a recurrence of $T(n) = T(n - 1) + \Theta(n)$, which resolves to $T(n) = \Theta(n^2)$. While this situation can occur in a variety of ways, notice that this situation easily occurs for data that is ordered or reverse-ordered. The user should be very careful of this since sorting data that is nearly ordered can occur frequently in a number of important situations.

Finally, consider the expected running time. As it turns out, the expected-case running time is asymptotically equivalent to the best-case running time. That is, given a set of elements with distinct keys arbitrarily distributed throughout the array, we expect the running time of Quicksort to be $\Theta(n \log n)$. The proof of this running time is a bit complex, though very interesting. We present this proof in Appendix 4.

A summary of the running times for the array version of Quicksort is presented in the table below.

| Scenario | Running Time |
|---|---|
| Best-Case | $\Theta(n \log n)$ |
| Worst-Case | $\Theta(n^2)$ |
| Expected-Case | $\Theta(n \log n)$ |

#### *Space*

In this section, we consider the *additional space* used by the array version of Quicksort as implemented on a RAM. This may seem like a trivial issue since the routine does not use anything more than a few local variables. That is, there are no additional arrays, no dynamic allocation of memory, and so on. However, since the routine is recursive, the system will create a system stack entry for each procedure call pushed onto the system stack.

Consider the best-case space scenario. This occurs when both procedure calls are placed on the system stack, the first is popped off and immediately discarded, and the second is popped off and evaluated. In this case, there will never be more than three items on the system stack, which include the initial call to Quicksort and at most two additional recursive calls. Notice that this situation occurs when the array is split into pieces of size 1 and $n - 1$. Furthermore, the recursive calls must be pushed onto the system stack so that the subarray of size 1 is sorted first. This procedure call terminates immediately since sorting an array of size 1 represents the base case of the Quicksort routine. Next, the system stack is popped and the procedure is invoked to sort the subarray of size $n - 1$. What we have described may seem to imply that the system stack will grow to have $\Theta(n)$ recursive calls. However, the system stack can be prevented from growing to more than three calls by a minor modification in the code that replaces a tail-end recursive call by either an increment to *left* or a decrement to *right*, and a branch.

Now let's consider the worst-case space scenario. This situation is almost identical to the best-case space scenario. The only difference is that the procedure calls are pushed onto the system stack in the reverse order. In this situation, the procedure will first be invoked to evaluate the subarray of size $n - 1$, which in turn generates other recursive procedure calls, and after that routine is complete, the system stack will be popped and the subarray of size 1 will be sorted. In this situation, the chain of recursive calls generated by the call to evaluate the subarray of size $n - 1$ requires the system stack to store $\Theta(n)$ procedure calls. Demonstration of this claim is left as an exercise.

It is interesting to note that both the best-case and worst-case space situations occur with the $\Theta(n^2)$ worst-case running time.

Consider the expected-case space scenario. This occurs with the expected-case $\Theta(n \log n)$ running time, where no more than $\Theta(\log n)$ procedure calls are ever on the system stack at any one time. Again, this can be seen in conjunction with the expected-case analysis that appears in Appendix 4.

A summary of space requirements for the array version of Quicksort is presented in the table below.

| Scenario | Extra Space |
|---|---|
| Best-Case | $\Theta(1)$ |
| Worst-Case | $\Theta(n)$ |
| Expected-Case | $\Theta(\log n)$ |

In Appendix 4, we show that the expected running time of Quicksort is $\Theta(n \log n)$. The proof is rather long and requires a level of mathematical sophistication that will be beyond some readers. Therefore, we recommend that only those with strong mathematical abilities and interests read the proof.

### Improving Quicksort

In this section, we discuss some improvements that can be made to Quicksort. First, we consider modifications targeted at improving the running time. It is important to note that the modifications we discuss should be evaluated experimentally on the systems under consideration. One way to reduce the probability of a bad splitter is to sample more than one element. For example, quickly choosing the splitter as the median of more than one key should result in a small percentage improvement in overall running time for large input sets.

When considering the asymptotic running time of Quicksort, one might use the Selection algorithm presented earlier in this chapter to choose the splitter as the median value in the list. Notice that this raises the time to choose the splitter from $\Theta(1)$ to $\Theta(n)$. However, this increased running time has no effect on the asymptotic expected-case running time of Quicksort. Further, because such a selection guarantees good splits, choosing the split value in this fashion lowers the worst-case running time of Quicksort to $\Theta(n \log n)$.

If one is really concerned about trying to avoid the worst-case running time of Quicksort, it might be wise to reduce the possibility of having to sort mostly ordered or reverse-ordered data. As strange as it may seem, a reasonable way to do this is first to randomize the input data. That is, *take the set of input data and randomly permute it*. This will have the effect of significantly reducing the possibility of taking ordered sequences of significant length as input.

After experimentation, the reader will note that Quicksort is very fast for large values of $n$, but relatively slow when compared to $\Theta(n^2)$ time algorithms such as Selection Sort and Insertion Sort for small values of $n$. The reader might perform an experiment comparing Quicksort to Selection Sort, Insertion Sort, and other sorting methods for various values of $n$. One of the reasons that Quicksort is slow for small $n$ is that there is significant overhead to recursion. This overhead does not exist for straight-sorting methods, like Insertion Sort and Selection Sort, which are constructed as tight, doubly nested loops.

Therefore, one might consider a *hybrid* approach to Quicksort that exploits an asymptotically inferior routine, which is only applied in a situation where it is better in practice. Such a hybrid sort can be constructed in several ways. The most obvious is to use Quicksort only as long as $right - left \geq m$, for some experimentally determined $m$. That is, one uses the basic Quicksort routine of partitioning and calling Quicksort recursively on both the left and right subarrays. However, the base case changes from a simple evaluation of $left < right$ to $right - left < m$. In the case that $right - left < m$, then one applies the straight-sorting routine that was used to determine the cutoff value of $m$. Possibilities include Selection Sort and Insertion Sort, with Selection Sort typically being favored.

Consider an alternative approach. Sort the data recursively, so long as $right - left \geq m$. Whenever a partition is created such that $right - left < m$, simply ignore that partition. That is, leave that partition in an unsorted state whenever a partition exists such that $right - left < m$. Notice that at the end of the entire Quicksort procedure, every element will be within $m$ places of where it really belongs. At this point, one could run Insertion Sort on the entire set of data. Notice that Insertion Sort runs in $O(mn)$ time, where $n$ is the number of elements in the array, and $m$ is the maximum distance any element must move. Therefore, for $m$ small, Insertion Sort is a very fast routine. In fact, for $m$ constant, this implementation of Insertion Sort runs in only $\Theta(n)$ time. Further, compared to the previous hybrid approach, this approach has an advantage in that only one additional procedure call is made, compared to the $O(n)$ procedure calls that could be made if small subarrays are immediately sorted. Hence, this version of a hybrid Quicksort is generally preferred.

Note that similar remarks apply to Merge Sort. Keeping track of the number of elements in a list will not raise the asymptotic cost of Merge Sort in either time or memory usage. By doing so, we can modify the base case of Merge Sort so that when the list to be sorted has length less than some constant determined experimentally, then this base case is handled by, say Selection Sort. This does not raise the asymptotic cost of the Merge Sort algorithm, since the lists to be sorted in this fashion have length of $\Theta(1)$. The fact that we have presented Selection Sort using an array data structure and Merge Sort using a pointer-based linked list structure is not a barrier to this proposal. One can bridge this difference in data structures by using either of the following approaches.

- Our array-based presentation of Selection Sort is easily mimicked in a pointer-based linked list.
- Alternately, the data of the pointer-based list can be copied to an array and sorted using the array-based implementation of Selection Sort, and then the sorted array can be copied back to a pointer-based linked list. Exercises at the end of Chapter 2 discuss efficient transformations between array and pointer-based linked list data structures.

We now consider improvements in the space requirements of Quicksort. Recall that the major space consideration is the additional space required for the system stack. One might consider unrolling the recursion and rewriting Quicksort in a nonrecursive fashion, which requires maintaining your own stack. This can be used to save some real space, but it does not have a major asymptotic benefit and causes the code to become more complex. Another improvement we might consider is to maintain the stack only with jobs that need to be done and not jobs representing tail-end recursion that are simply waiting for another job to terminate. However, in terms of saving significant space, one should consider pushing the jobs onto the stack in an intelligent fashion. That is, one should always push the jobs onto the stack so that the smaller job is evaluated first. This helps to avoid or lessen the $\Theta(n)$ worst-case additional space problem, which can be quite important if you are working in a relatively small programming environment.

## Modifications of Quicksort for Parallel Models

There have been numerous attempts to parallelize Quicksort for a variety of machines and models of computation. One parallelization that is particularly interesting is the extension of Quicksort, by Bruce Wagar, to *Hyperquicksort*, a Quicksort-based algorithm targeted at medium- and coarse-grained parallel computers. In this section, we first describe the *Hyperquicksort* algorithm for a medium-grained hypercube and then present an analysis of its running time.

### Hyperquicksort

1. Initially, it is assumed that the $n$ elements are evenly distributed among the $2^d$ nodes of a hypercube so that every node contains $N = n/2^d$ elements.
2. Each node sorts its $N$ items independently using a $\Theta(N \log N)$ time algorithm.
3. Node 0 determines the median of its $N$ elements, denoted as *Med*. This is performed in $\Theta(1)$ time since the elements in the node have just been sorted.
4. Node 0 broadcasts *Med* to all $2^d$ nodes in $\Theta(d)$ time.
5. Every node logically partitions its local set of data into two groups, $X$ and $Y$, where $X$ contains those elements less than or equal to *Med* and $Y$ contains those elements greater than *Med*. This step runs in $\Theta(\log N)$ time by way of a binary search for *Med* among the values of the node's data.
6. Consider two disjoint subcubes of size $2^{d-1}$, denoted as $L$ and $U$. For simplicity, let $L$ consist of all nodes with a 0 as the most significant bit of the node's address and let $U$ consist of all nodes with a 1 as the most significant bit of the node's address. Note that the union of $L$ and $U$ is the entire hypercube of size $2^d$. So every node of the hypercube is a member of either $L$ or $U$. Each node that is a member of $L$ sends its set $Y$ to its adjacent node in $U$. Likewise, each node in $U$ sends its set $X$ to its adjacent node in $L$. Notice that when this step is complete, all elements less than or equal to *Med* are in $L$, while all elements greater than *Med* are in $U$. The expected time for the transmission of data, as described, is $\Theta(N)$. Note this is not the worst-case time, since the sets $X$ and $Y$ are not restricted to a size of $\Theta(N)$.
7. Each node now *merges* the set of data just received with the one it has kept. That is, a node in $L$ merges its own set $X$ with its $U$-neighbor's set $X$ and a node in $U$ merges its own set $Y$ with its $L$-neighbor's set $Y$. Therefore, after an expected $\Theta(N)$ time for merging two sets of data, every node again has a sorted set of data.

8. Repeat Steps 3-7 on each of $L$ and $U$ simultaneously, recursively, and in parallel until the subcubes consist of a single node, at which point the data in the entire hypercube is sorted.

The time analysis embedded in the presentation above does not coincide with the analysis for the worst-case running time as the algorithm continues to iterate over Steps 3-7 due to the fact that the data may become quite unbalanced. That is, pairs of processors may utilize $\omega(N)$ time to transmit and merge data. As a consequence, when the algorithm terminates, all processors may not necessarily have $N$ items.

Assuming that the data is initially distributed in a random fashion, Wagar has shown that the expected-case running time of this algorithm is

$$\Theta\left(N \log N + \frac{d(d+1)}{2} + dN\right).$$

The $N \log N$ term represents the sequential running time from Step 2. The $d(d+1)/2$ term represents the broadcast step used in Step 4. The $dN$ term represents the time required for the exchanging and merging of the sets of elements. We leave discussion of the efficiency of this running time as an exercise.

In the next section, we will consider a medium-grained implementation of Bitonic Sort. We will see that Bitonic Sort offers the advantage that, throughout the algorithm, all nodes maintain the same number of elements per processor. However, given good recursive choices of splitting elements, Hyperquicksort offers the advantage that it is more efficient than Bitonic Sort.

## Bitonic Sort (Revisited)

In Chapter 5, we presented some motivation, history, and a detailed description of Bitonic Sort. In addition, we presented an analysis of the algorithm for several models of computation. To recap, given a set of $n$ elements, we showed that Bitonic Sort will run in $\Theta(\log^2 n)$ time on a PRAM of size $n$, in $\Theta(\log^2 n)$ on a fine-grained hypercube of size $n$, and in $\Theta(n \log^2 n)$ time on a RAM.

In this section, we consider Bitonic Sort on a medium-grained hypercube as a means of comparison to the Hyperquicksort routine presented in the last section. We then consider Bitonic Sort on a fine-grained mesh of size $n$.

Our initial assumptions are the same as they were for Hyperquicksort. Assume that we are initially given $n$ data elements evenly distributed among the $2^d$ processors so that each processor contains $N = n/2^d$ items. Suppose that each processor sorts its initial set of data in $\Theta(N \log N)$ time. Once this is done, we simply follow the data movement and general paradigm of the fine-grained Bitonic Sort algorithm, as previously presented. The major modification is to accommodate the difference between processors performing a comparison and exchange of two items for the fine-grained model, and a comparison and exchange of $2N$ items for the medium-grained model.

Suppose processor $A$ and processor $B$ need to order their $2N$ items so that the $N$ smaller items will reside in processor $A$ and the $N$ larger items will reside in processor $B$. This can be accomplished as follows. In $\Theta(N)$ time, processors $A$ and $B$ exchange data so that each processor has the complete set of $2N$ items. Each processor now merges the two sets of items in $\Theta(N)$ time, simultaneously and independently. Finally, processor $A$ "retains" the $N$ smallest items by discarding the $N$ largest items, and processor $B$ "retains" the $N$ largest items by discarding the $N$ smallest items.

The running time of Bitonic Sort on a medium-grained hypercube consists of the simultaneous initial set of $\Theta(N \log N)$ time sequential sorts, followed by the $d(d+1)/2$ steps of Bitonic Sort, each of which runs in $\Theta(N)$ time, resulting in a total running time of

$$\Theta\left(N \log N + \frac{d(d+1)}{2} N\right).$$

As mentioned previously, the reader should note two major differences when considering whether to use Bitonic Sort or Hyperquicksort on a medium-grained hypercube.

1. The expected-case running time of Hyperquicksort is more efficient than the running time of Bitonic Sort by a relatively small factor.
2. When Bitonic Sort terminates, the data is distributed evenly among the processors, while this is not the case with Hyperquicksort.

### Bitonic Sort on a Mesh

In this section, we present a straightforward implementation of the fine-grained Bitonic Sort algorithm on a fine-grained mesh computer. After the presentation of the algorithm, we discuss details of the implementation and the effect that such details have on the running time of the algorithm.

Initially, let's assume that a set of $n$ data elements is given, arbitrarily distributed one per processor on a mesh of size $n$. In order to perform sorting on a distributed-memory parallel machine, we must define the ordering of the processors, since the elements are sorted with respect to the ordering of the processors. Initially, we assume that the processors are ordered with respect to *shuffled row-major* indexing scheme, as shown in Figure 9-10. Note that for a machine with more than 16 processors, this ordering holds recursively within each quadrant.

| | | | |
|---|---|---|---|
| 0 | 1 | 4 | 5 |
| 2 | 3 | 6 | 7 |
| 8 | 9 | 12 | 13 |
| 10 | 11 | 14 | 15 |

**FIGURE 9-10** *The shuffled-row major index scheme as applied to a mesh of size* 16. *It is important to note that on a mesh of size n, this indexing continues recursively within each quadrant.*

At the end of this section, we will discuss a simple way to adapt Bitonic Sort to whatever predefined processor ordering is required/utilized. Recall that Bitonic Sort is a variant of Merge Sort. Viewed in a bottom-up fashion, initially bitonic sequences of size 2 are bitonically merged into sorted sequences of size 4. Then bitonic sequences of size 4 are bitonically merged into sorted sequences of size 8, and so on. At each stage, the sequences being merged are independent and the merging is performed in parallel on all such sequences. In addition, recall that the concatenation of an increasing sequence with a decreasing sequence forms a bitonic sequence. Therefore, we must be careful when merging a bitonic sequence into a sorted sequence as to whether it is merged into an increasing or a decreasing sequence. The reader may wish to review the section on Bitonic Sort before proceeding with the remainder of this section.

In the example presented below, notice that we exploit the shuffled row-major indexing scheme. Therefore, sequences of size 2 are stored as $1 \times 2$ strings, sequences of size 4 are stored as $2 \times 2$ strings, sequences of size 8 are stored as $2 \times 4$ strings, and so on. A critical observation is that if a comparison and possible exchange must be made between data that reside in two processors, then those processors always *reside in either the same row or in the same column*. This is due to the properties of the shuffled row-major indexing scheme coupled with the fact that Bitonic Sort only compares entries that differ in one bit of their indexing.

Consider the example of Bitonic Sort on a mesh of size 16, as presented in Figure 9-11. This example shows how to sort the initial set of arbitrarily distributed data into increasing order with respect to the shuffled row-major ordering of the processors. The first matrix shows the initial set of arbitrarily distributed data. Notice that a sequence of size 1 is, by default, sorted into both increasing and decreasing order. Therefore, initially, there are $n/2$ bitonic sequences of size 2, in

**Example:**

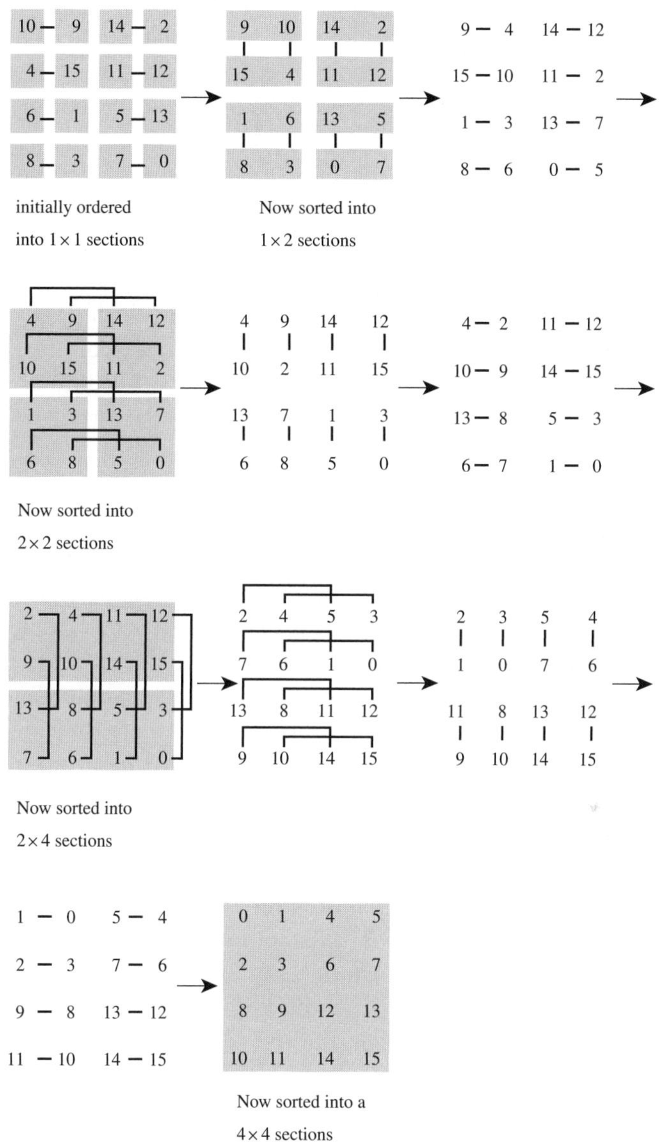


**FIGURE 9-11** *An example of Bitonic Sort on a mesh of size* 16. *The elements are sorted into shuffled-row major order, as given in Figure 9-10. The initial data is given in the top-left matrix. After applying a comparison-exchange operation between indicated elements, e.g.,* 10-9, 14-2, 4-15, *and so forth, the matrix has been ordered into disjoint* $1 \times 2$ *segments, as indicated in the next matrix. The interpretation of the figure continues in this manner. Note up until the final stage, half the sorted sections are in ascending order, and the other half are in descending order.*

the form of $1 \times 2$ strings, each of which must be bitonically merged. This is accomplished by a single comparison, representing the base case of the Bitonic Sort, resulting in the second matrix. Notice that some of the sequences are sorted into increasing order and some into decreasing order. Next, we take this matrix and wish to merge bitonic sequences of size 4, in the form of $2 \times 2$ strings, into sorted order. This is accomplished by first performing a comparison-exchange operation between items that are two places apart in the indexing, followed by recursively sorting each of the $1 \times 2$ strings independently. The fourth matrix shows the result of this sorting. Notice that each of the four quadrants has data in sorted order with respect to the shuffled row-major indexing. In particular, notice that the northwest and southwest quadrants are sorted into increasing order, while the northeast and southeast quadrants are sorted into decreasing order. The example continues, showing the details of combining $2 \times 2$ strings into sorted $2 \times 4$ strings, and finally combining the two $2 \times 4$ strings into the final sorted $4 \times 4$ string.

#### *Analysis of Running Time*

Recall from the detailed analysis of Bitonic Sort presented in Chapter 5 that Bitonic Sort is based on Merge Sort. As such, it uses $\Theta(\log n)$ parallel merge operations, merging lists of size 1 into lists of size 2, then lists of size 2 into lists of size 4, and so forth. However, the merge operation is not the standard merge routine that one learns in a second semester computer science course, but rather the more complex bitonic merge. Further, the time for each bitonic merge requires a slightly more complex analysis than that of determining the time for a traditional merge. For example, merging pairs of elements into ordered lists of size 2 requires one level of comparison-exchange operations, which can be thought of as one parallel comparison-exchange operation. This is the base case. Merging bitonic sequences of size 2 into ordered lists of size 4 requires an initial comparison-exchange level, that is, $n/2$ comparison-exchange operations, followed by applying the Bitonic Sort routine for sequences of size 2 to each of the resulting subsequences. Therefore, the total number of comparison-exchange levels is $1 + 1 = 2$. The time to merge bitonic sequences of size 4 into ordered sequences of size 8 requires one comparison-exchange level to divide the data, followed by two parallel comparison-exchange levels to sort each of the bitonic subsequences of size 4. Therefore, the total number of comparison-exchange levels to merge a bitonic sequence of size 8 into an ordered sequence is three $(1 + 2 = 3)$. In general, the time to merge two bitonic sequences of size $n/2$ into an ordered sequence of size $n$ is $\Theta(\log n)$.

Recall that in order to use the bitonic merge unit to create a sorting routine/network, we apply the basic Merge Sort scenario. That is, sorting an arbitrary sequence of $n$ items requires us first to sort two subsequences of size $n/2$ in parallel, then to perform a comparison-exchange on items $n/2$ apart, and then to merge recursively each subsequence of size $n/2$. Therefore, the total number of comparison-exchange levels, *i.e.*, parallel comparison-exchange operations, is

$$\sum_{i=1}^{\log_2 n} i = \frac{(\log_2 n)(\log_2 n + 1)}{2} = \frac{1}{2}\left(\log^2 n + \log n\right).$$

The reader should refer to the section on Bitonic Sort for the original presentation of this analysis.

Now consider a mesh implementation. Suppose that each of the $\Theta(\log^2 n)$ comparison-exchange levels is implemented by a column or row rotation, as appropriate. Such an implementation leads to a $\Theta(n^{1/2} \log^2 n)$ running time on a mesh of size $n$. However, if we look closely at the data movement operations that are required in order to perform the comparison-exchange operations, we notice that during the first iteration, when creating the $1 \times 2$ lists, the data items are only one link apart. When creating the $2 \times 2$ lists, the data items are again only one link apart. When creating the $2 \times 4$ and $4 \times 4$ lists, the data items are either one or two links apart, and so forth. Therefore, if we are careful to construct modified row and column rotations that allow for simultaneous and disjoint rotations within segments of a row or column, respectively, the running time of Bitonic Sort operations can be improved significantly. With this optimized rotation scheme, the time to sort $n$ items on a mesh of size $n$ is given by the recurrence $T(n) = T(n/2) + \Theta(n^{1/2})$, where $T(n/2)$ is the time to sort each of the subsequences of size $n/2$, and the $\Theta(n^{1/2})$ term represents the time required to perform a set of $n/2$ comparison-exchange operations. Therefore, the running time of the Bitonic Sort algorithm is $\Theta(n^{1/2})$, which is optimal for a mesh of size $n$. While the algorithm is optimal for this architecture, notice that the cost of the algorithm is $\Theta(n^{3/2})$, which is far from optimal. We leave as an exercise the possibility of modifying this architecture and algorithm to achieve a cost-optimal sorting algorithm on a mesh.

### Sorting Data with Respect to Other Orderings

How would we handle the situation of sorting a set of data on a fine-grained mesh into an ordering other than shuffled row-major? For example, given a set of $n$ data items, initially distributed in an arbitrary fashion one per processor on a mesh of size $n$, how would the data be sorted into row-major or snake-like order? If one is only concerned about asymptotic complexity, the answer is quite simple: perform two sorting operations. The first operation will sort data in terms of a known sorting algorithm into the indexing order required by that algorithm. For example, one could use Bitonic Sort and sort data into shuffled row-major order. During the second sort, each processor would generate a *sort key* that corresponds to the desired destination address with respect to the desired indexing scheme, such as row major or snake-like ordering.

Suppose that one wants to sort the 16 data items from the previous example into row-major order. One could first sort the data into shuffled row-major order and then resort the items so that they are appropriately ordered. For example, during the second sort, keys would be created so that processor 0 would send its data to processor 0, processor 1 would send its data to processor 1, processor 2 would send its data to processor 4, processor 3 would send its data to processor 5, processor 4 would send its data to processor 2, and so forth (see Figure 9-12). The combination of these two sorts would result in the data being sorted according to row-major order in the same asymptotically optimal $\Theta(n^{1/2})$ time. Notice that this algorithm assumes that the destination addresses can be determined in $O(n^{1/2})$ time, which is sufficient for most well-defined indexing schemes.

| | | | |
|---|---|---|---|
| 5 | 2 | 10 | 6 |
| 12 | 8 | 4 | 0 |
| 14 | 1 | 11 | 13 |
| 15 | 7 | 3 | 9 |

(a) Initial data.

| | | | |
|---|---|---|---|
| $0_0$ | $1_1$ | $4_2$ | $5_3$ |
| $2_4$ | $3_5$ | $6_6$ | $7_7$ |
| $8_8$ | $9_9$ | $12_{10}$ | $13_{11}$ |
| $10_{12}$ | $11_{13}$ | $14_{14}$ | $15_{15}$ |

(b) Sorted data with keys for resorting.

| | | | |
|---|---|---|---|
| $0_0$ | $1_1$ | $2_4$ | $3_5$ |
| $4_2$ | $5_3$ | $6_6$ | $7_7$ |
| $8_8$ | $9_9$ | $10_{12}$ | $11_{13}$ |
| $12_{10}$ | $13_{11}$ | $14_{14}$ | $15_{15}$ |

(c) Resorted data with keys.

**FIGURE 9-12** *An example of sorting data on a mesh into row-major order by two applications of sorting into shuffled-row major order. The initial unordered set of data is given in* (a). *After applying a shuffled-row major sort, the data appears as in* (b). *Note that in the lower right corner of each item is the index for where that item should be placed with respect to shuffled-row major order so that the data will be in row-major order. The items are then sorted into shuffled-row major order with respect to these indices, with the results in row-major order as shown in* (c).

### Sorting on a Cluster

Ordering data on a cloud or a cluster is an important operation. Many corporations and agencies require data to be ordered at various stages of operation. Since a cluster or network of workstations, which may or may not be used to implement a cloud, typically has a reasonably fast interconnect between the various nodes, sorting is typically performed on such systems by using one of the aforementioned algorithms with the node labels mapped onto the cluster/NOW. Note that in some cases, nodes may contain multiple processors and each processor may contain multiple cores or have an attached processor, for example, a General Purpose Graphics

Processing Unit, or GPGPU. Regardless, while the interprocessor communication time may be dramatically different between on-node processors and processors connected by an external interconnection network, Hyperquicksort, Bitonic Sort, or a modified Merge Sort are the standard options. In such a case, one's time is often best spent in performing in-depth timing studies to determine the most efficient algorithm for the particular data under consideration.

## Concurrent Read/Write

In this section, we discuss an important application of sorting that allows for the efficient and straightforward porting of PRAM algorithms to other architectures. The PRAM is the most widely studied parallel model of computation. As a result, a significant body of algorithmic literature exists for that architecture. Therefore, when one considers developing an efficient algorithm for a non-PRAM-based parallel machine, it is often constructive to consider first the algorithm that would result from a direct simulation of the PRAM algorithm on the target architecture. In order to simulate the PRAM, it is critical to be able to simulate the concurrent read and concurrent write capabilities of the PRAM on the target machine.

A **concurrent read,** or, in its more general form, an **associative read,** can be used in a situation where a set of processors must obtain data associated with a set of keys, but where there need not be *a priori* knowledge as to which processor maintains the data associated with any particular key.

For example, processor $P_i$ might need to know the data associated with the key "blue," but might not know which processor $P_j$ in the system is responsible for maintaining the information associated with the key "blue." In fact, all processors in the system might be requesting one or more pieces of data associated with keys that are not necessarily distinct.

A **concurrent write,** or in its more general form, an **associative write,** may be used in a situation where a set of processors $P_i$ must update the data associated with a set of keys, but again $P_i$ does not necessarily know which processor is responsible for maintaining the data associated with the key.

As one can see, these concurrent read/write operations generalize the CR/CW operations of a PRAM by making them *associative*, in other words, by locating data with respect to a key rather than by an address. In order to maintain consistency during concurrent read and concurrent write operations, we will assume that there is at most one *master record*, stored in some processor, associated with each unique key. In a concurrent read, every processor generates one *request record* corresponding to each of a small fixed number of keys that it wishes to receive information about. A concurrent read permits multiple processors to request information about the same key. A processor requesting information about a nonexistent key will receive a null message at the end of the operation.

#### Implementation of a Concurrent Read

A relatively generic implementation of a concurrent read operation on a parallel machine with $n$ processors follows.

1. Every processor creates $C_1$ *master records* of the form [Key, Return Address, data, "MASTER"], where $C_1$ is the maximum number of keyed master records maintained by any processor, and Return Address is the index of the processor that is creating the record. Processors maintaining less than $C_1$ master records will create dummy records so that all processors create the same number of master records.
2. Every processor creates $C_2$ *request records* of the form [Key, Return Address, data, "REQUEST"], where $C_2$ is the maximum number of request records generated by any processor, and Return Address is the index of the processor that is creating the record. Processors requesting information associated with less than $C_2$ master records will create dummy records so that all processors create the same number of request records. Notice that the data fields of the request records are presently undefined.
3. *Sort* all $(C_1 + C_2)n$ records together by the Key field. In case of ties, place records with the flag "MASTER" before records with the flag "REQUEST."
4. Use a *broadcast* within ordered intervals to propagate the data associated with each master record to the request records with the same Key field. This allows all request records to find and store their required data.
5. Return all records to their original processors by *sorting* all records on the Return Address field.

Therefore, the time to perform a concurrent read, as described, is bounded by the time to perform a fixed number of sort and interval operations. See Figure 9-13.

#### Implementation of Concurrent Write (overview)

The implementation of the concurrent write is quite similar to that of the concurrent read. In general, it consists of a sort step to group records with similar keys together, followed by a semigroup operation within each group to determine the value to be written to the master record, followed by a sort step to return the records to their original processors. Again, it is assumed that there is at most one *master record*, stored in some processor, associated with each unique key. When processors generate *update records*, they specify the key of the record and the piece of information they wish to update. If two or more update records contain the same key, then a master record will be updated with the minimum data value of these records. In other circumstances, one could replace the minimum operation with any other commutative, associative, binary operation. Therefore, one can see that the implementation of the concurrent write is nearly identical to the implementation just described for the concurrent read.

| | | | |
|---|---|---|---|
| [red,0,10,M],[blue,0,?,R] | [–,1,–1,M],[blue,1,?,R] | [blue,2,30,M],[red,2,?,R] | [green,3,40,M],[blue,3,?,R] |

(a) The initial data is given where each processor maintains one master record (signified by an "M" in the fourth field) and generates one request record (with an "R" in the fourth field).

| | | | |
|---|---|---|---|
| [blue,2,30,M],[blue,0,?,R] | [blue,1,?,R],[blue,3,?,R] | [green,3,40,M],[red,0,10,M] | [red,2,?,R],[–,1,–1,M] |

(b) After sorting all of the data together based on the key (first) field, with ties broken in favor of master records, we arrive at the situation shown here.

| | | | |
|---|---|---|---|
| [blue,2,30,M],[blue,0,30,R] | [blue,1,30,R],[blue,3,30,R] | [green,3,40,M],[red,0,10,M] | [red,2,10,R],[–,1,–1,M] |

(c) A segmented broadcast is then performed so that the information maintained in the master records is propagated to the appropriate request records.

| | | | |
|---|---|---|---|
| [red,0,10,M],[blue,0,30,R] | [–,1,–1,M],[blue,1,30,R] | [blue,2,30,M],[red,2,10,R] | [green,3,40,M],[blue,3,30,R] |

(d) The data is resorted based on the return address (second) field.

**FIGURE 9-13** *An example of a concurrent read on a linear array of size* 4.

### Concurrent Read/Write on a Mesh

A mesh of size $n$ can simulate any PRAM algorithm that works with $n$ data items on $n$ processors by using a concurrent read and concurrent write to simulate every step of the PRAM algorithm. Suppose that a given PRAM algorithm runs in $T(n)$ time. Then by simulating every read step and every write step of the PRAM algorithm in a systematic fashion by a $\Theta(n^{1/2})$ time concurrent read and concurrent write, respectively, the running time of the PRAM algorithm as ported to a mesh of size $n$ will be $O(T(n)n^{1/2})$, which is often quite good. In fact, it is often not more than some polylogarithmic factor from optimal.

## Summary

In this chapter, we examine the recursive divide-and-conquer paradigm for solving problems. We show the power of this paradigm by illustrating its efficient usage in several algorithms for sorting, including sequential versions of Merge Sort and Quicksort and their adaptations to several parallel models; also, reconsideration of

Bitonic Sort and its implementations on a coarse-grained hypercube and on a fine-grained mesh. Efficient to optimal divide-and-conquer algorithms for selection and for concurrent read and write operations on parallel computers are also given.

## Chapter Notes

Divide-and-conquer is a paradigm central to the design and analysis of both parallel and sequential algorithms. An excellent reference, particularly for sequential algorithms, is *Introduction to Algorithms* by T.H. Cormen, C.E. Leiserson, R.L. Rivest, and C. Stein (3rd ed.: The MIT Press, Cambridge, MA, 2009). A nice text focusing on algorithms for the hypercube, which includes some divide-and-conquer algorithms, is *Hypercube Algorithms for Image Processing and Pattern Recognition* by S. Ranka & S. Sahni (Springer-Verlag, New York, 1990). More general references for theoretical parallel algorithms that exploit the divide-and-conquer paradigm are *Parallel Algorithms for Regular Architectures* by R. Miller and Q.F. Stout (The MIT Press, 1996), and *Introduction to Parallel Algorithms and Architectures: Arrays, Trees, Hypercubes,* by F.T. Leighton (Morgan Kaufmann Publishers, San Mateo, CA, 1992). Details of advanced PRAM algorithms, including a $\Theta(\log n)$ time sorting algorithm, can be found in *An Introduction to Parallel Algorithms* by J. JáJá, (Addison-Wesley, 1992).

Optimal-cost PRAM algorithms for the Selection Problem are given in R.J. Cole's paper, "An optimally efficient selection algorithm," *Information Processing Letters* 26 (1987/88), 295–299.

The Quicksort algorithm was originally presented by in "Quicksort," by C.A.R. Hoare, *Computer Journal*, 5(1):10–15, 1962. Wagar's Hyperquicksort algorithm was originally presented in, "Hyperquicksort: A fast sorting algorithm for hypercubes," by B. Wagar in *Hypercube Multiprocessors 1987*, 292–299.

## Exercises

1. We have shown that Quicksort has a $\Theta(n^2)$ running time if its input list is sorted or nearly sorted. Other forms of input can also produce a $\Theta(n^2)$ running time. For example, let $n = 2^k$ for some positive integer $k$ and suppose
   - the input list has key values $x_1, x_2, \ldots, x_n$,
   - the subsequence $O = \{x_1, x_3, \ldots, x_{n-1}\}$ of odd-indexed keys is decreasing,
   - the subsequence $E = \{x_2, x_4, \ldots, x_n\}$ of even-indexed keys is increasing,
   - $x_{n-1} > x_n$,
   - queues are used for the lists, with the partitioning process enqueueing new items to *smallList*, *equalList*, and *bigList*, and
   - the split value is always taken to be the first key in the list.

   Show that under these circumstances, the running time of Quicksort is $\Theta(n^2)$.

2. In our sequential implementation of Quicksort, the "conquer" stage of the algorithm consists of two recursive calls. The order of these calls clearly does not matter in terms of the correctness and running time of the algorithm. However, the order of these recursive calls does affect the size of the stack needed to keep track of the recursion. Show that if one always pushes the jobs onto the stack so that the larger job is processed first, then the stack must be able to store $n$ items.
3. Suppose that on a parallel computer with $n$ processors, processor $P_i$ has data value $x_i$, $i \in \{1,\ldots,n\}$. Further, suppose that $i \neq j \Rightarrow x_i \neq x_j$. Describe an efficient algorithm so that every processor $P_i$ can determine the rank of its data value $x_i$. That is, if $x_i$ is the $k^{\text{th}}$ largest member of $\{x_j\}_{j=1}^{n}$, then processor $P_i$ will store the value $k$ at the end of the algorithm. Analyze the running time of your algorithm in terms of operations discussed in this chapter. Your analysis may be quite abstract. For example, you may express the running time of your algorithm in terms of the running times of the operations you use.
4. Suppose that we implement a linked-list version of Quicksort on a RAM using predefined abstract data types. Further, suppose that inserting an element into a list is actually written so that it traverses the list from the front to the end and then inserts the new element at the end of the list. Give an analysis of the running time of Quicksort under this situation.
5. Suppose we are given a singly-linked list on a RAM and mistakenly implement the array version of Quicksort to perform the partition step. Give the running time of the partition step and use this result to give the running time of the resulting version of the Quicksort algorithm.
6. Describe and analyze the running time of Bitonic Sort given a set of $n$ data items arbitrarily distributed $n/p$ per processor on a hypercube with $p$ processors where $n \gg p$, *i.e.*, where $n$ is $\omega(p)$.
7. Prove that algorithm Partition is correct.
8. Modify Quicksort so that it recursively sorts as long as the size of the subarray under consideration is greater than some constant $C$. Suppose that if a subarray of size $C$ or less is reached, then the subarray is not sorted. As a final post-processing step, suppose that this subarray of size at most $C$ is then sorted by one of the following simple sorts.

   a. Insertion Sort

   b. Bubble Sort

   c. Selection Sort

   Given the total running time of the modified Quicksort algorithm. Prove that the algorithm is correct.
9. Let $S$ be a set of $n$ distinct real numbers and let $k$ be a positive integer with $1 < k < n$. Give a $\Theta(n)$ time RAM algorithm to determine the middle $k$ entries of $S$. The input entries of $S$ should not be assumed ordered; however, if the

elements of $S$ are such that $s_1 < s_2 < \ldots < s_n$, then the output of the algorithm is the set $\{s_{(n-k)/2}, s_{((n-k)/2)+1}, \ldots, s_{((n+k)/2)-1}\}$, not necessarily sorted. Since the running time of the algorithm should be $\Theta(n)$, sorting $S$ should not be part of the algorithm.

10. Analyze the running time of the algorithm you presented in response to the previous query as adapted in a straightforward fashion

    a. for a PRAM and

    b. for a mesh.

11. Develop a version of Merge Sort for a linear array of $\Theta(\log n)$ processors to sort $n$ data items, initially distributed $\Theta(n/\log n)$ items per processor. Show that your algorithm runs in $\Theta(n)$ time and that it is cost-optimal.

12. Analyze the running time of a concurrent read operation involving $\Theta(n)$ items on a mesh of size $n$.

13. Given a set of $n$ data items distributed on a mesh of size $m$, $m \leq n$, so that each processor contains $n/m$ items, what is the best lower bound for the time to sort these items? Justify your answer. Provide an algorithm that matches these bounds.

14. Given a set of $n$ input elements, arbitrarily ordered, prove that any sorting network has a depth of at least $\log_2 n$.

15. Prove that the number of comparison units in any sorting network on $n$ inputs is $\Omega(n \log n)$.

16. Suppose that we are given a sequence of arcs of a circle $R = \langle r_1, r_2, \ldots, r_n \rangle$, and are required to find a point on the circle that has maximum overlap. That is, we are required to determine a, not necessarily unique, point $q$ that has a maximum number of arcs that overlap it. Suppose that no arc is contained in any other arc, that no two arcs share a common endpoint, and that the endpoints of the arcs are given completely sorted in clockwise order. Further, suppose that the tail point of an arc only appears following the head of its arc. Give efficient algorithms to solve this problem on the following architectures. In addition, discuss the time-, space-, and cost complexity.

    a. RAM

    b. PRAM

    c. Mesh

17. Give an efficient algorithm to compute the parallel prefix of $n$ values, initially distributed one per processor in the base of a pyramid computer. Discuss the time- and cost-complexity of your algorithm. You may assume processors in the base mesh are in shuffled row major order, with data distributed accordingly.

**18.** Show that the expected time $\Theta(N \log N + (d(d+1)/2) + dN)$ of Wagar's Hyperquicksort algorithm achieves the ideal $T_{par}(n) = \Theta(T_{seq}(n)/q)$ for a coarse grained hypercube. Recall $q = 2^d$ is the number of processors, $N = n/q = n/2^d$ is the initial number of data items in each processor, and in the coarse-grained model we assume $q^2 \le n$.

**19.** Suppose a foundation wishes to award scholarships to the students who score in the top 5% of applicants according to their scores on a competitive exam. Devise an efficient RAM algorithm, that does not sort the data, to determine which students receive the awards.

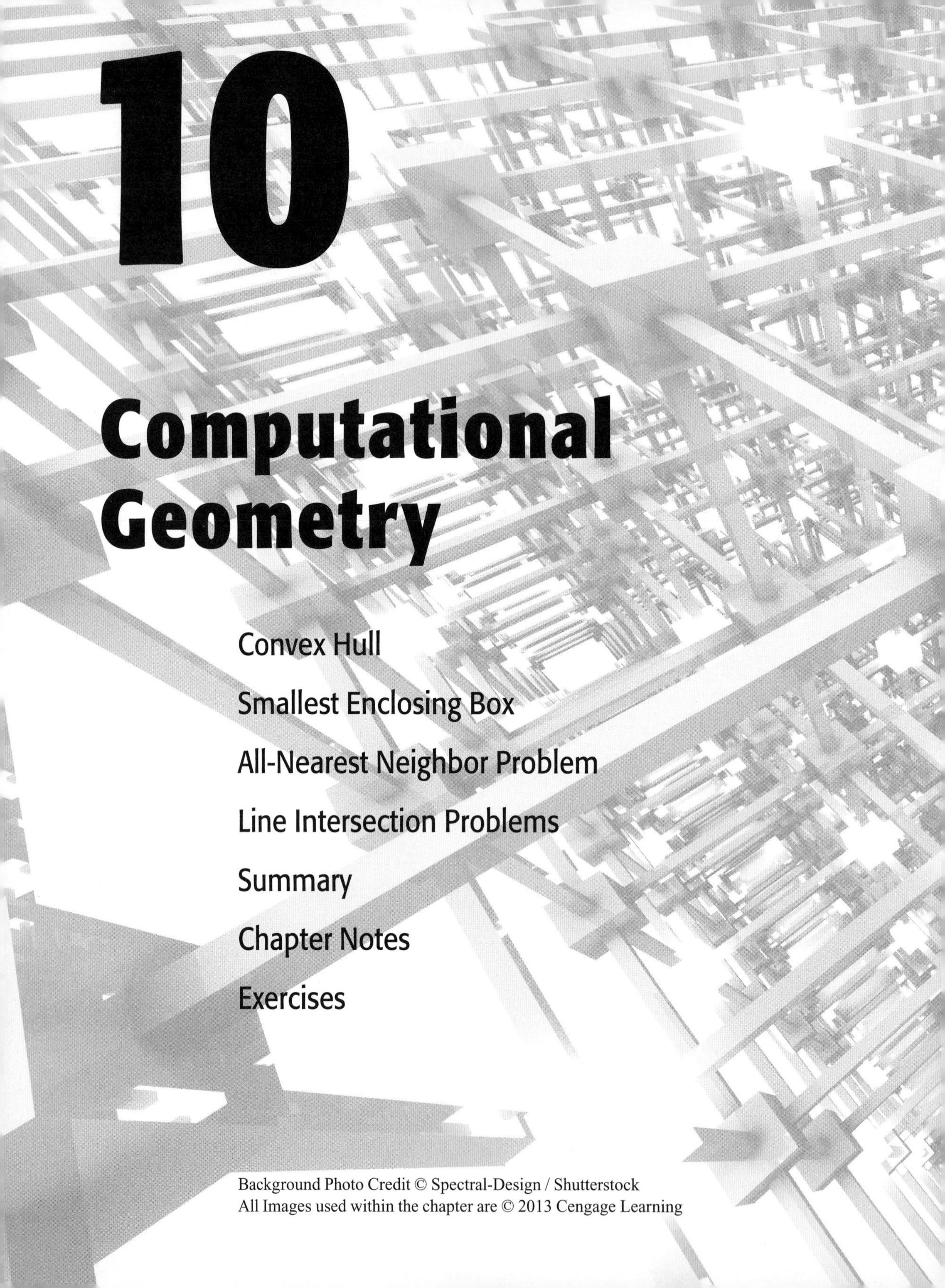

# 10

# Computational Geometry

The field of computational geometry focuses on the design, analysis, and implementation of efficient algorithms to solve problems involving geometric objects, including points, lines, and polygons. Problems in computational geometry are derived from a variety of areas, including computer graphics, computer-aided design and manufacturing, visualization, robotics, and geographic information systems, to name a few. Fundamental problems in computational geometry involve relationships among points, line segment intersection, proximity of objects, shortest paths, the convex hull, and the Voronoi Diagram, to name a few.

In fact, in Chapter 7, "Parallel Prefix," we presented a solution to *dominance*, a fundamental problem in computational geometry. In this chapter, we consider additional problems from this important and interesting field. Note that many of the problems in this chapter were chosen so that we could continue our exploration of the divide-and-conquer solution strategy.

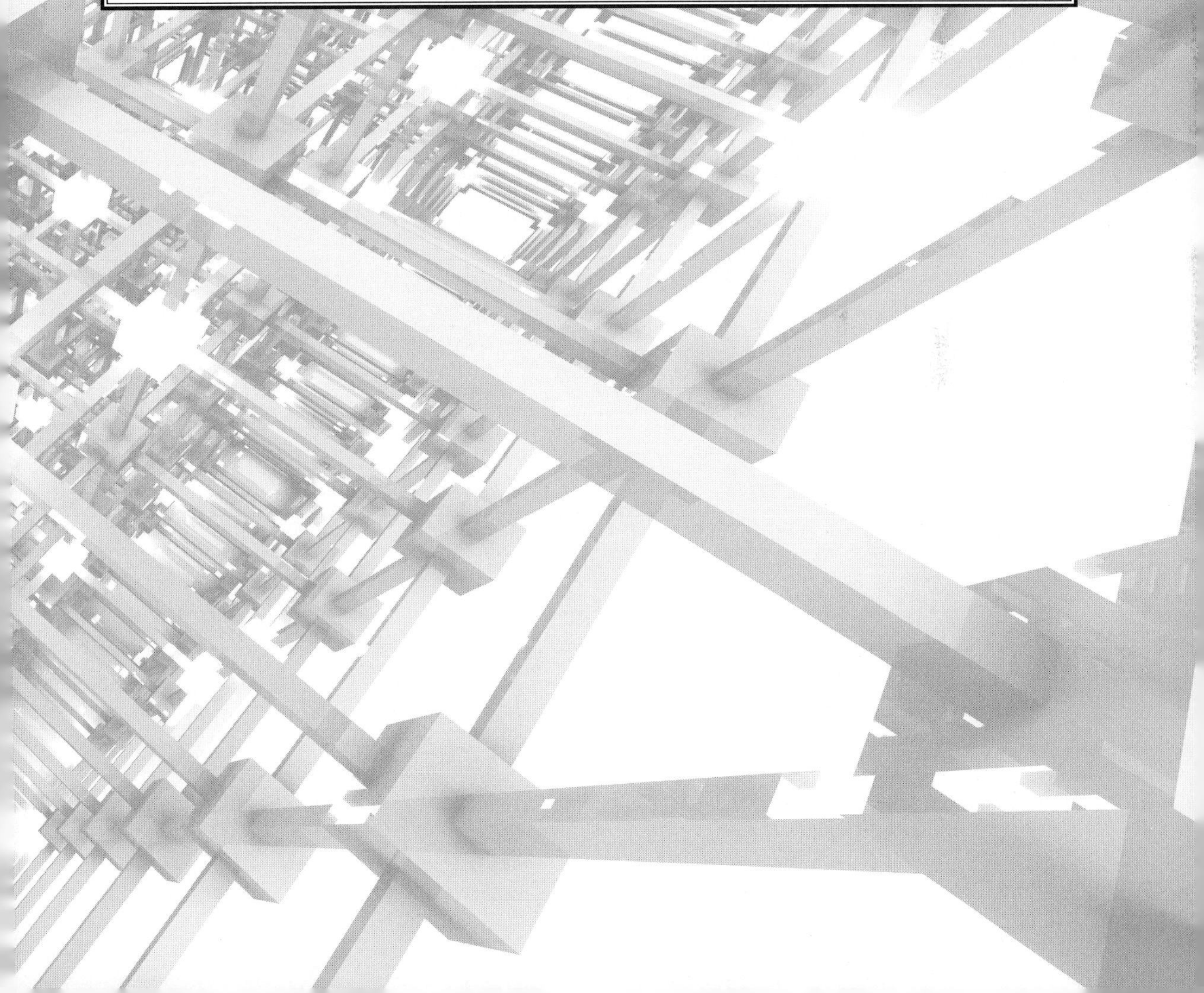

## Convex Hull

The first problem we consider is that of determining the *convex hull* of a set of points in the plane. The convex hull is an important geometric structure that has been extensively studied. The convex hull of an object can be used to solve problems in numerous fields, including image processing, feature extraction, layout and design, molecular biology, and geographic information systems. Further, the convex hull of a set $S$ of points often gives a good approximation of $S$, while providing a significant reduction in the volume of data used to represent or approximate $S$. Finally, the convex hull of a set $S$ is often used as an intermediate step in order to obtain additional geometrical information about $S$.

**Definitions:** A set of planar points $R$ is *convex* if and only if for every pair of points $x, y \in R$, the line segment $\overline{xy}$ is contained in $R$ (see Figure 10-1). Let $S$ be a set of $n$ points in the plane. The *convex hull* of $S$ is defined to be the smallest convex polygon $P$ containing all $n$ points of $S$. A solution to the *convex hull problem* consists of determining an ordered list of points of $S$ that define the boundary of the convex hull of $S$. This ordered list of points is referred to as *hull*($S$). Each point in *hull*($S$) is called an *extreme point* of the convex hull and a pair of adjacent extreme points is referred to as an *edge* of the convex hull (see Figure 10-2), or a *hull edge*, as appropriate.

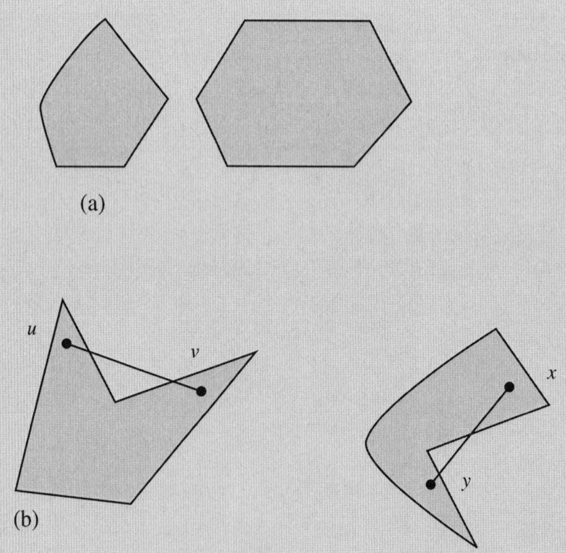


**FIGURE 10-1** *Examples of convex and non-convex regions. The regions in* (a) *are convex. The regions in* (b) *are not convex, as the line segments* $\overline{uv}$ *and* $\overline{xy}$ *are not contained in their respective regions.*

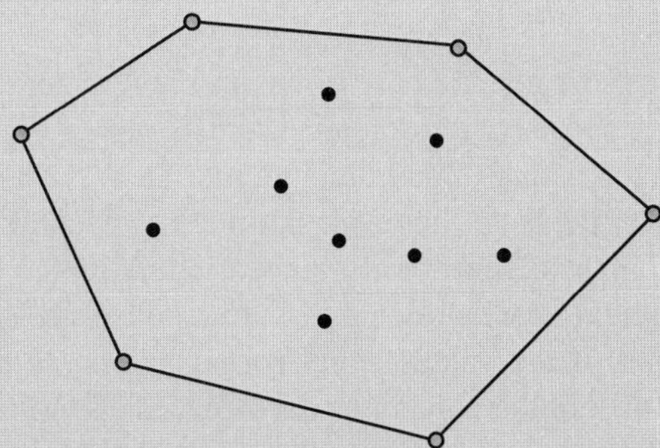

**FIGURE 10-2** *The convex hull. The set S of n points in the plane is represented by circles, some of which are black and some of which are gray. The extreme points of S are represented by the gray points. The set of such extreme points is denoted by hull(S). Each pair of adjacent extreme points represents an edge of the convex hull.*

The reader may wish to consider an intuitive construction of the convex hull. Suppose that each of the planar points in $S$ is represented as a headless nail perpendicular to and sticking out of a wooden board. Now, take a sufficiently elastic rubber band and stretch it to its maximum in all directions. Lower the rubber band over the nails so that all the nails are enclosed within the rubber band. Finally, release the rubber band so that it is restricted from collapsing only by the nails in $S$ that it touches. The rubber band can be thought of as forming a polygon. This polygon $P$, along with its interior, represents the convex hull of $S$. The nails that cause the rubber band to change direction are the *extreme points* of the convex hull. Note that there may be some nails that are touched that do not cause the rubber band to change direction if they are in between two nails that do force a change of direction. Finally, the adjacent extreme points of $P$ are defined as the *edges* of the convex hull.

Notice that a solution to the convex hull problem requires presenting a set of points in a predefined order. Therefore, we first consider the relationship between the convex hull problem and sorting.

**Theorem:** Sorting is linear-time transformable to solving the convex hull problem. That is, in $\Theta(n)$ time, we can transform the problem of sorting $n$ real numbers to the problem of finding the convex hull of $n$ points in the Euclidean plane.

**Proof:** Without loss of generality, suppose we are given a set of $n$ unique real numbers, $X = \{x_1, \ldots, x_n\}$. Then a convex hull algorithm can be used to sort the points in $X$ with only linear overhead, as follows. Corresponding to each number $x_i$ is the point $p_i = (x_i, x_i^2)$. Notice that these $n$ points all lie on the parabola $y = x^2$.

The convex hull of this set consists of a list of all the distinct points $p_i$ sorted by $x$-coordinate.

In the more general case of the problem, there might be duplicate entries in $X$. That is, suppose that for some $i$ and $j$, $p_i = p_j$. Then at most one of these will appear in the listing of members of $hull(X)$. We can modify the algorithm given for unique data items so that every unique representative $p \in hull(X)$ can keep track of the number of times that $p$ appears in $X$. One $\Theta(n)$-time pass through the list representing $hull(X)$ will enable us to read off the values of the $x_i$ in order.

Further, if the values being sorted belong to larger records, then instead of keeping track of the number of occurrences of duplicated values, the representative of a value can maintain a list of records with the same value. This would not change the asymptotic running time of the algorithm.

**Implications of Theorem:** Based on this theorem, we know the convex hull problem cannot be solved asymptotically faster than we can sort a set of points presented in arbitrary order. So, given an arbitrary set of $n$ points in the Euclidean plane, solving the convex hull problem requires $\Omega(n \log n)$ time on a RAM.

### Graham's Scan

In this section, we present a traditional sequential solution to the convex hull problem, known as *Graham's Scan*, which was developed by Ron Graham in 1972. The reader may notice that this algorithm is dominated by sort and scan operations and does not rely on a divide-and-conquer solution strategy. The *Graham Scan* procedure is quite simple and is presented for completeness. A description follows (see Figure 10-3).

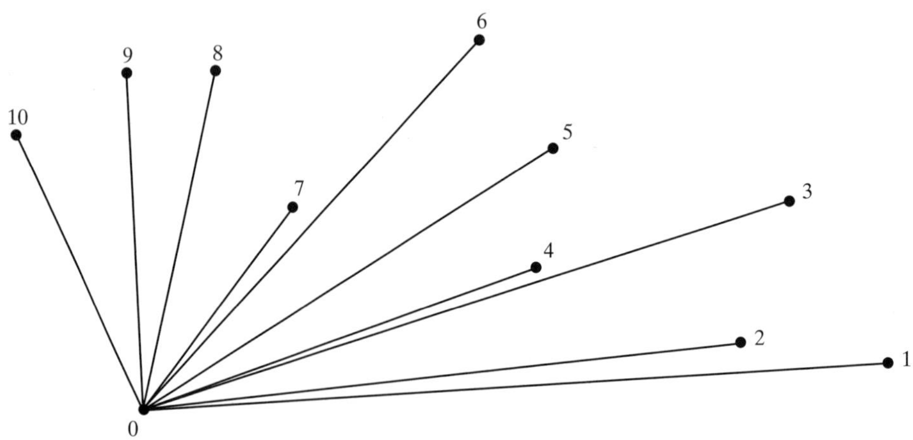


**FIGURE 10-3** *Graham's Scan is a technique for determining the convex hull of a set of points. The lowest point is chosen as point* 0 *and the remaining points are sorted into counterclockwise order with respect to the angles they make to a horizontal line through point* 0. *Graham's Scan examines the points in the order listed.*

1. Select the lowermost point in $S$ and label this point 0. If there is more than one lowermost point in $S$, choose the leftmost such point to label 0.
2. Sort the remaining $n - 1$ points of $S$ by angle in $[0, \pi)$ with respect to the origin, *i.e.,* point 0. Specifically, do the following.
   a. For each of the points $p = (x, y) \in S$ other than the point $(x_0, y_0)$ marked as point 0, compute the associated angle $\phi$ by
   $$\phi = \cos^{-1} \frac{(x - x_0)}{\sqrt{(x - x_0)^2 + (y - y_0)^2}}.$$
   b. Sort $S \backslash \{(x_0, y_0)\}$ by the angles computed in the previous step.
   c. For any angle that includes multiple points, remove all duplicates, retaining only the point at the maximum distance from point 0. Without loss of generality, we will proceed under the assumption that the set $S$ has $n$ distinct points.
3. Now consider the points $[1,\ldots,n - 1]$ in sequence. We build the convex hull up in an iterative fashion. At the $i^{\text{th}}$ iteration, we consider point $S(i)$. For $i = 1$, we have point $S(1)$ initially considered an "active point," *i.e.*, it is an extreme point of the two element set $S(0,\ldots,1)$. For $1 < i < n$, we proceed as follows. Assume the active points prior to the $i^{\text{th}}$ iteration are $S(0), S(j_1),\ldots, S(j_k)$, where $0 < j_1 < \ldots < j_k < i$.
   a. Suppose that the path from $S(j_{k-1})$ to $S(j_k)$ to $S(i)$ turns toward the left at $S(j_k)$ in order to reach $S(i)$, as shown in Figure 10-4. Then the point $S(i)$ is an extreme point of the convex hull with respect to the set of points $S(0,\ldots,i)$, and it remains active. Further, all of the currently active points in $S(0,\ldots,i - 1)$ remain active. That is, those points that were extreme points of $S(0,\ldots,i - 1)$ will remain extreme points of $S(0,\ldots,i)$.

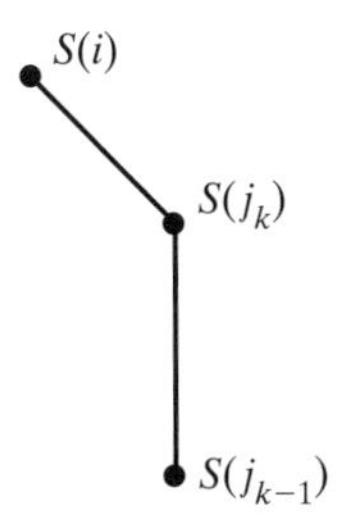


**FIGURE 10-4** *A path from $S(j_{k-1})$ to $S(j_k)$ to $S(i)$ that makes a left turn at $S(j_k)$.*

   b. Suppose that the path from $S(j_{k-1})$ to $S(j_k)$ to $S(i)$ turns toward the right at $S(j_k)$ in order to reach $S(i)$, as shown in Figure 10-5. Then the point $S(i)$ is an extreme point of the convex hull with respect to the set of points $S(0,\ldots,i)$, and it remains active. However, we now know that some of the currently active points in $S(0,\ldots,i-1)$ are not extreme points in $S(0,\ldots,i)$ and must be eliminated from consideration as extreme points. This elimination is performed by working backwards through the ordered list of currently active points and eliminating each point that continues to cause point $S(i)$ to be reached by a right turn with respect to the currently active points in $S(0,\ldots,i-1)$. In fact, we only need work backwards through the ordered list of currently active points until we reach an active point that is not eliminated.

c. Suppose that $S(j_{k-1})$, $S(j_k)$, and $S(i)$ are collinear. Then the ordering of the points implies that the path from $S(j_{k-1})$ to $S(j_k)$ to $S(i)$ does not turn at $S(j_k)$ in order to reach $S(i)$. Therefore, $S(j_k)$ can be eliminated since it cannot be an extreme point in $S(0,\ldots,i)$. (See Figure 10-6.)

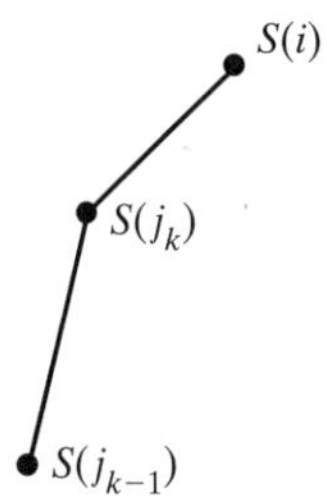


**FIGURE 10-5** *A path from $S(j_{k-1})$ to $S(j_k)$ to $S(i)$ that makes a right turn at $S(j_k)$.*

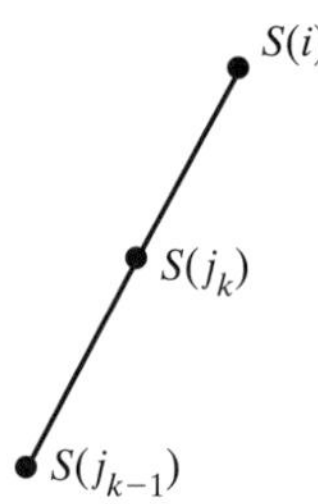


**FIGURE 10-6** *A path from $S(j_{k-1})$ to $S(j_k)$ to $S(i)$ that is straight. That is, the three points are collinear.*

Consider the example presented earlier in Figure 10-3. We are required to enumerate the convex hull of $S$, a set consisting of 11 points. Details of the algorithm, as applied to this example, are as follows.

a. Scan the list of points in order to determine the lowest point. Label this lowest point 0. Note that if there is more than one lowest point, choose the leftmost one.

b. Sort the remaining $n-1$ points by angle with respect to a horizontal line through point 0. The points are now ordered in counterclockwise fashion with respect to point 0, as shown in Figure 10-3. Initially, all $n$ points are candidates as extreme points of *hull*($S$).

c. The point labeled 0 must be an extreme point of the convex hull, as it is the lowest point in the set $S$. We proceed to visit successive points in order, applying the "right-turn test" described in the algorithm given above.

d. The first stop on our tour is point number 1, which is accepted since points 0 and 1 form a convex set.

e. Now, consider point number 2. Notice that the turn from point 0 to 1 to 2 is a left turn. Therefore, points 0, 1, and 2 are extreme points with respect to $S(0,\ldots,2)$.

f. Now, consider point number 3. Notice that the turn from point 1 to 2 to 3 is a right turn. Therefore, we begin to work backwards from the preceding point. That is, point number 2 must be eliminated. Next, consider the turn from point 0 to 1 to 3. This is a left turn. Therefore, point number 1 remains, and this backward scan to eliminate points is complete. So points 0, 1, and 3 are the extreme points representing the convex hull of $S(0,\ldots 3)$.

g. Now, consider point number 4. Notice that the turn from point 1 to 3 to 4 is a left turn. Therefore, no points are eliminated, and we know that points 0, 1, 3, and 4 are extreme points of $S(0,\ldots,4)$.

h. Now, consider point number 5. Notice that the turn from point 3 to 4 to 5 is a right turn. Therefore, we begin to work backwards from the preceding point. That is, point number 4 is eliminated. Next, consider the turn from point 1 to 3 to 5. Notice that this is a left turn. Therefore, the points 0, 1, 3, and 5 are the extreme points representing the convex hull of $S(0,\ldots,5)$.

i. Now, consider point number 6. Notice that the turn from point 3 to 5 to 6 is a right turn. Therefore, we begin to work backwards from the preceding point. That is, point number 5 is eliminated. Next, consider the turn from point 1 to 3 to 6. This is a left turn. Therefore, the points 0, 1, 3, and 6 are the extreme points representing the convex hull of $S(0,\ldots,6)$.

j. Now, consider point number 7. Notice that the turn from point 3 to 6 to 7 is a left turn. Therefore, no points are eliminated, and we know that points 0, 1, 3, 6, and 7 are extreme points of $S(0,\ldots,7)$.

k. Now, consider point number 8. Notice that the turn from 6 to 7 to 8 is a right turn. Therefore, we begin to work backwards from the preceding point. That is, point number 7 is eliminated. Now consider the turn from point 3 to 6 to 8. This is a left turn. Therefore, the points 0, 1, 3, 6, and 8 are the extreme points representing the convex hull of $S(0,\ldots,8)$.

l. Now, consider point number 9. Notice that the turn from point 6 to 8 to 9 is a right turn. Therefore, we begin to work backwards from the preceding point. That is, point number 8 is eliminated. Now consider the turn from point 3 to 6 to 9. This is a left turn. Therefore, the points 0, 1, 3, 6, and 9 are the extreme points representing the convex hull of $S(0,\ldots,9)$.

m. Now, consider point number 10. Notice that the turn from point 6 to 9 to 10 is a left turn. Therefore, no points are eliminated, and we know that points 0, 1, 3, 6, 9, and 10 are extreme points of $S(0,\ldots,10)$. The solution is now complete.

Notice that where we discuss a "right turn" or "left turn" above, these can be determined computationally in $\Theta(1)$ time. Specifically, given line segments $\overline{xy}$ and

$\overline{yz}$ in the Euclidean plane, the following cases provide the necessary information to determine the relationship between $\overline{xy}$ and $\overline{yz}$.

1. If $\overline{xy}$ and $\overline{yz}$ are both vertical or have the same slopes, then there is no turn from $x$ to $y$ to $z$ as these points are collinear.
2. If $\overline{xy}$ and $\overline{yz}$ both have positive slopes and the slope of $\overline{xy}$ is greater than the slope of $\overline{yz}$, then the turn from $x$ to $y$ to $z$ is to the right.
3. If $\overline{xy}$ and $\overline{yz}$ both have positive slopes and the slope of $\overline{xy}$ is less than the slope of $\overline{yz}$, then the turn from $x$ to $y$ to $z$ is to the left.
4. If $\overline{xy}$ is vertical and $\overline{yz}$ has a positive slope, then the turn from $x$ to $y$ to $z$ is to the right.
5. If $\overline{xy}$ has a positive slope or is vertical and $\overline{yz}$ has a negative slope, then the turn from $x$ to $y$ to $z$ is to the left.
6. If $\overline{xy}$ has a negative slope and $\overline{yz}$ is vertical or has a positive slope, then the turn from $x$ to $y$ to $z$ is to the right.
7. If $\overline{xy}$ and $\overline{yz}$ both have negative slopes and the slope of $\overline{xy}$ is greater than the slope of $\overline{yz}$, then the turn from $x$ to $y$ to $z$ is to the right.
8. If $\overline{xy}$ and $\overline{yz}$ both have negative slopes and the slope of $\overline{xy}$ is less than the slope of $\overline{yz}$, then the turn from $x$ to $y$ to $z$ is to the left.

#### *Analysis on a RAM*

Let's consider the running time and space requirements of Graham's Scan on a RAM. The first step of the algorithm consists of determining point 0, the leftmost-lowest point in the set $S$. That is, we choose a lowest point, and if there are multiple points in $S$ with the minimum y-coordinate, the one we select is the leftmost. Assuming that $S$ contains $n$ points, the leftmost-lowest point can be determined in $\Theta(n)$ time by a simple scan through the data.

In $\Theta(n)$ time, the remaining $n - 1$ points of $S$ can then have their angles computed with respect to a horizontal line through point 0. These $n - 1$ points can then be sorted with respect to these angles in $\Theta(n \log n)$ time.

Next, the algorithm considers the points in order and makes decisions about eliminating points. Notice that each time a new point $i$ is encountered during the scan, it will be an extreme point of $S(0,\ldots,i)$. This is due to the fact that we are traversing the points in order according to their angles with respect to $S(0)$, and we have eliminated, at Step 3c) above, all but one member of any set in $S \backslash \{S(0)\} = \{s \in S \mid s \neq S(0)\}$ that has the same angle with $S(0)$. Each time a new point is visited, $\Theta(1)$ work is necessary in order to

1. include the new point in the data structure if it is active, and
2. stop any backwards search that might arise.

The remainder of the time spent in the tour is accounted for when considering the total number of points that can be eliminated, since with a judicious choice of data structures, no point is ever considered once it has been eliminated. It is important to consider the analysis from a global perspective. Since no point is ever eliminated more than once, the total time required for the loop in Step 3 is $\Theta(n)$, though the analysis is a bit different than some of the straightforward deterministic analyses presented earlier in the book. Therefore, the running time of Graham's Scan on a RAM is a worst-case optimal $\Theta(n \log n)$, since the running time is dominated by the sort performed in Step 2.

Next, we consider the space required in addition to that which is necessary in order to maintain the initial set of points. Notice that this algorithm does not rely on recursion, so we need not worry about the system stack. It does, however, require a separate data structure that in the worst case might require a copy of every point. That is, it is possible to construct situations where the number of extreme points is $\Theta(n)$, *e.g.*, when the $n$ points approximate a circle. Therefore, if an additional stack or array is used, the additional space will be $\Theta(n)$. However, if one maintains the points in a pointer-based data structure, it is possible to avoid making copies of the points. Of course, the penalty one pays for this is the additional $\Theta(n)$ pointers.

#### *Parallel Implementation*

Consider parallel implementations of Graham's Scan. Steps 1 and 2 require computing a semigroup operation and sorting the data. These steps can be performed efficiently on most parallel models. However, Step 3 does not appear easily amenable to a parallel implementation. One might try to remove concave regions in parallel and hope that, reminiscent of our pointer jumping algorithms, the number of such parallel removals will be polylogarithmic in the number of points. However, consider the situation where the first $n - 1$ points form a convex set, but when the last point is added to this set, then $\Theta(n)$ points must be removed. It is not clear that such a situation can be easily parallelized.

### Jarvis' March

Another important sequential algorithm for solving the convex hull problem was developed in 1973 by R.A. Jarvis. This algorithm, which is referred to as *Jarvis' March*, works by a *package wrapping* technique. To illustrate this technique, consider a piece of string with one end fixed at the lowest point, which we again refer to as point number 0. Next, wrap the string around the nails representing the points in a counterclockwise fashion. This can be done by iteratively adding the point with the least polar angle with respect to a horizontal line through the most recently added point. Since all the remaining points are considered at each iteration, the total running time of this algorithm is $O(nh)$, where $h$ is the number of extreme points on *hull*($S$). Therefore, when the number of extreme points is $o(\log n)$, Jarvis' March is asymptotically superior to Graham's Scan in terms of running time.

### Divide-and-Conquer Solutions to the Convex Hull Problem

In this section, we focus on divide-and-conquer solutions to the convex hull problem. Initially, we present a generic divide-and-conquer solution. The analysis is then presented based on an implementation for the RAM and mesh. At the conclusion of this section, we present a divide-and-conquer algorithm, complete with analysis, targeted at the PRAM.

#### *Generic Divide-and-Conquer Solution to the Convex Hull Problem*

Assume that we are required to enumerate the extreme points of a set $S$ of $n$ planar points. We will enumerate the points so that the rightmost point is labeled 1, where in the case of ties, the lowest of the rightmost points is labeled 1. At the conclusion of the algorithm, the numbering of the extreme points will be given in counterclockwise fashion, starting with a rightmost point. Notice that for algorithmic convenience and in order to remain consistent with the literature, the first enumerated extreme point determined by this algorithm differs in position from the first enumerated extreme point derived from Graham's Scan or Jarvis' March, where we used the leftmost-lowest point. A generic divide-and-conquer algorithm to determine the extreme points of the convex hull of a set of $n$ planar points follows.

1. If $n = 2$, then **return**. In this case, both of the points are extreme points of the given set. If $n = 1$, then **return**. In this case, the point is an extreme point of the given set. If $n > 2$, then we continue with Step 2.
2. *Divide* the $n$ points by $x$-coordinate into two sets, $A$ and $B$, each of size approximately $n/2$. The division of points is done so that all points in $A$ are to the left of all points in $B$. That is, $A$ is linearly separable from $B$ by a vertical line (see Figure 10-7).
3. *Recursively* compute *hull*($A$) and *hull*($B$). See Figure 10-8.
4. *Stitch* *hull*($A$) and *hull*($B$) together to determine *hull*($S$). This is done as follows (see Figure 10-9).
   a. Find the upper and lower common tangent lines, which are often referred to as the *lines of support*, between *hull*($A$) and *hull*($B$).
   b. Discard the points inside the quadrilateral formed by the four points that determine these two lines of support.
   c. Renumber the extreme points so that they remain ordered with respect to the defined enumeration scheme. This is necessary since the algorithm is recursive in nature.

Notice that Step 2 requires us to divide the input points into disjoint sets $A$ and $B$ in such a fashion that

- every point of $A$ is to the left of every point of $B$, and
- both $A$ and $B$ have "approximately" $n/2$ members.

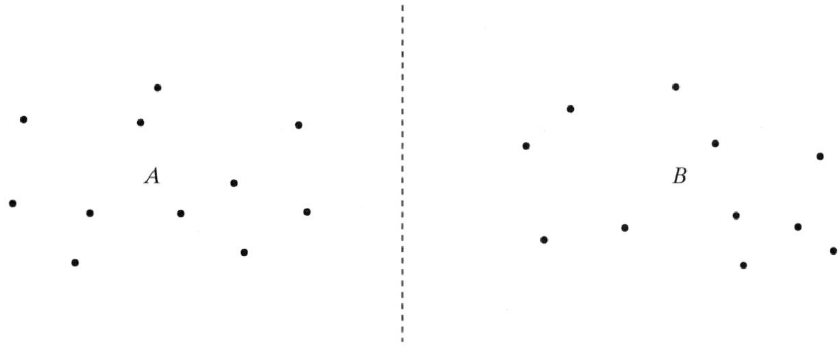


**FIGURE 10-7** *A set of n planar points evenly divided into two sets A and B by x-coordinate. All points in A lie to the left of every point in B.*

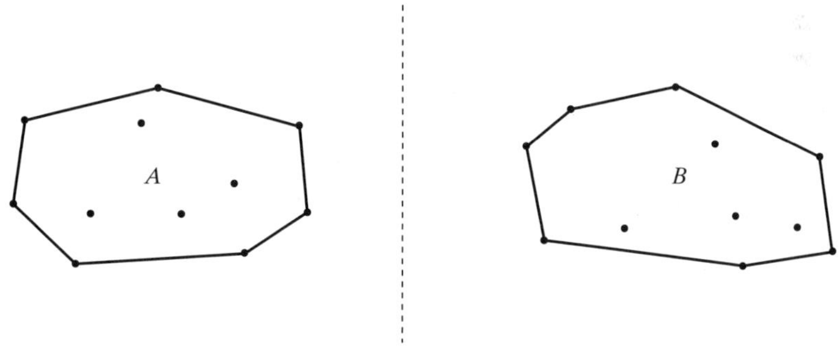


**FIGURE 10-8** *An illustration of the situation after hull(A) and hull(B) have been determined from input shown in Figure 10-7.*

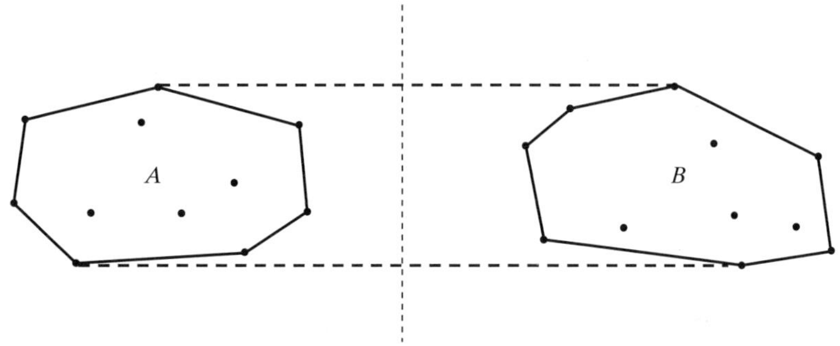


**FIGURE 10-9** *The stitch step. In order to construct hull(S) from hull(A) and hull(B), the upper common tangent line and lower common tangent line between hull(A) and hull(B) are determined.*

Unfortunately, if we are overly strict in our interpretation of "approximately," these requirements might not be met. Such a situation might occur when the median $x$-coordinate is shared by a large percentage of the input points. For example, suppose five of 100 input points have $x$-coordinate less than 0, 60 input points have $x$-coordinate equal to 0, and 35 input points have $x$-coordinate greater than 0. The requirement that every point of $A$ is to the left of every point of $B$ results in either $|A| = 5$ and $|B| = 95$, or $|A| = 65$ and $|B| = 35$. This is not really a problem since the recursion will quickly rectify the imbalance due to the fact that at most two points with the same $x$-coordinate can be extreme points of a convex hull. Thus, when we determine the vertical line of separation between $A$ and $B$, we can arbitrarily assign any input points that fall on this line to $A$.

This algorithm is a fairly straightforward adaptation of divide-and-conquer.

An interesting step is that of determining the lines of support. Note that lines of support are not necessarily determined by easily identified points. For example, the lines of support are not necessarily determined by the topmost and bottommost points in the two convex hulls, as illustrated in Figure 10-10. Considerable thought is required in order to construct an efficient algorithm to determine these four points and hence the two tangent lines.

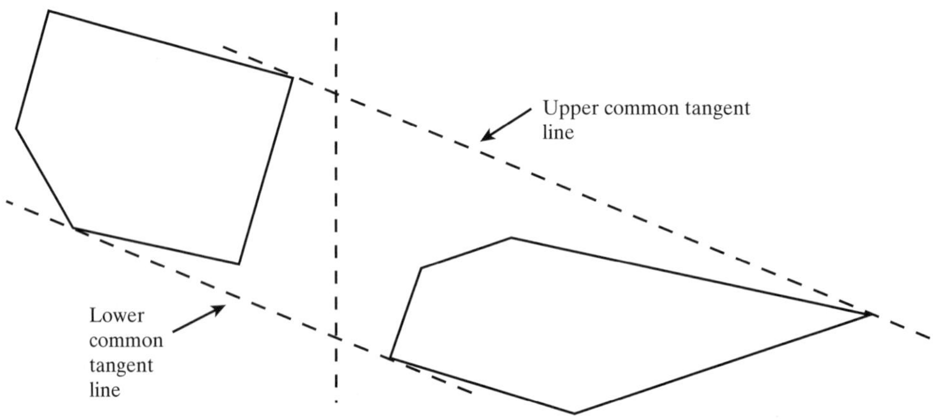


**FIGURE 10-10** *An illustration of the common tangent lines between linearly separable convex hulls. The upper common tangent line between hull(A) and hull(B) does not necessarily include the topmost extreme points in either set. A similar remark can be made about the lower common tangent line.*

Since the convex hulls of $A$ and $B$ are linearly separable by a vertical line, there are some restrictions on possibilities of points that determine the upper tangent line. For example, consider $a_l$, a leftmost point of $A$ and $a_r$, a rightmost point of $A$. Similarly, consider $b_l$, a leftmost point of $B$, and $b_r$, a rightmost point of $B$. It is then easy to show that the upper common tangent line is determined by an extreme point of *hull*($A$) on or above $\overline{a_l a_r}$, where the edges of *hull*($A$) on or above $\overline{a_l a_r}$ are referred to as the *upper envelope* of $A$, and an extreme point of $hull(B)$ on or above $\overline{b_l b_r}$, the upper envelope of $B$. Similarly, the lower common tangent line is determined by an extreme point of $hull(A)$ on or below $\overline{a_l a_r}$ and an extreme point of $hull(B)$ on or below $\overline{b_l b_r}$. Therefore, without loss of generality, we focus on determining the upper common tangent line, and note that determining the lower common tangent line is similar.

The extreme point $p \in hull(A)$ that determines the upper common tangent line has the property that if $x$ and $y$ are, respectively, its left and right neighbors among the extreme points of $hull(A)$, where one or both of $x$ and $y$ may not exist, then every extreme point of $hull(B)$ lies on or below $\overleftrightarrow{xp}$, while at least one extreme point of $hull(B)$ lies on or above $\overleftrightarrow{py}$ (see Figure 10-11). Notice that the mirror image scenario is valid in terms of identifying the right common tangent point, that is, the upper common tangent point in $hull(B)$.

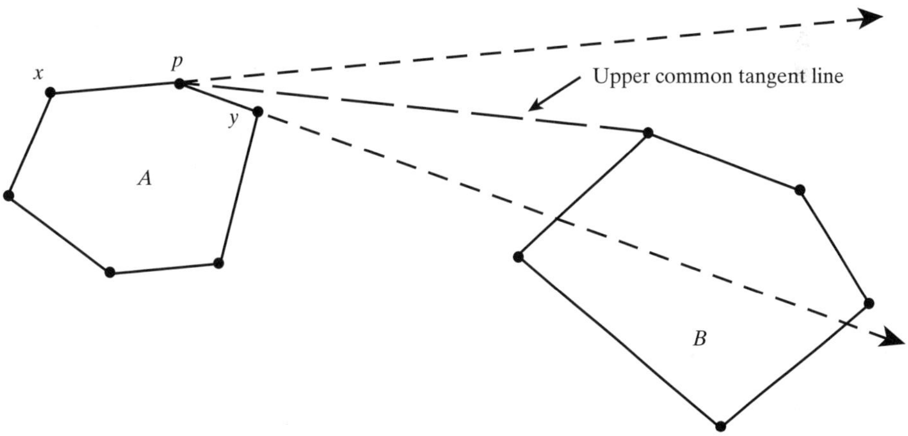


**FIGURE 10-11** *Constructing the upper common tangent lines. The upper common tangent line includes the extreme point $p \in hull(A)$ with the following properties. Let the next extreme point in counterclockwise order be called $x$ and the previous extreme point in counterclockwise order be called $y$. Then every extreme point of $hull(B)$ lies on or below $\overleftrightarrow{xp}$ while at least one extreme point of $hull(B)$ lies on or above $\overleftrightarrow{py}$.*

### *Convex Hull Algorithm on a RAM*

In this section, we consider the implementation details and running time of the divide-and-conquer algorithm just presented for the RAM. In order to partition the points with respect to $x$-coordinates, a $\Theta(n \log n)$ time sorting procedure can be used. In fact, it is important to notice that this single sort will serve to handle the partitioning that is required at every level of the recursion. That is, sorting is only performed once for partitioning, not at every level of recursion. Now let's consider the stitch step. The necessary points can be identified in $\Theta(\log n)$ time by a clever "teeter-totter" procedure. Basically, the procedure performs a type of binary search in which endpoints of a line segment, one from *hull*($A$) and the other from *hull*($B$), are adjusted in a binary search-type iterative fashion. Once the extreme points are identified, then with an appropriate choice of data structures, the points can be reordered and renumbered in $\Theta(n)$ time. This eliminates the points inside the quadrilateral determined by the lines of support. Therefore, the running time of the algorithm is given by $T(n) = \Theta(n \log n) + R(n)$, where $\Theta(n \log n)$ is the time required for the initial sort, and $R(n)$ is the time required for the recursive procedure. Notice that $R(n) = 2R(n/2) + \Theta(n)$, where $\Theta(n)$ time is required to stitch two convex hulls. The latter is because $\Theta(\log n)$ time is required to identify the tangent line, and $\Theta(n)$ time is required to reorder the points. Therefore, $R(n) = \Theta(n \log n)$, and it follows that the running time of the entire algorithm is $\Theta(n \log n)$, which is asymptotically optimal.

#### *Convex Hull Algorithm on a Mesh*

In this section, we discuss a mesh implementation and provide an analysis of the divide-and-conquer solution to the convex hull problem. Specifically, given $n$ points, arbitrarily distributed one point per processor on a mesh of size $n$, we will show that the convex hull of the set $S$ of planar points can be determined in optimal $\Theta(n^{1/2})$ time.

The basic algorithm follows. First, sort the points into shuffled row-major order. This results in the first $n/4$ points, with respect to $x$-coordinate ordering, being mapped to the northwest quadrant, the next $n/4$ points being mapped to the northeast quadrant, and so forth, as shown in Figure 10-12. Notice that with this indexing scheme, the partitioning holds recursively within each quadrant.

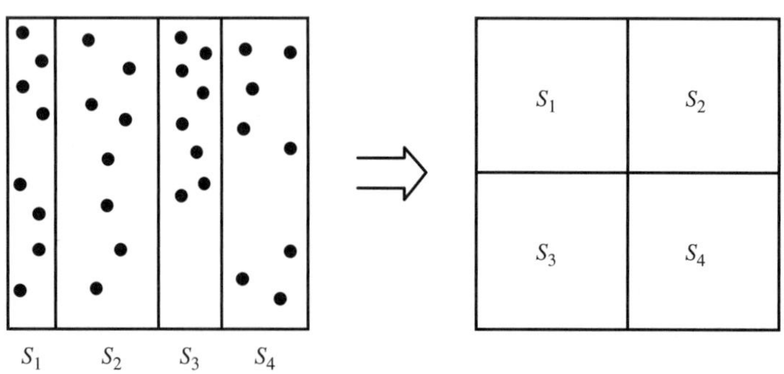


**FIGURE 10-12** *Dividing the n planar points in S so that each of the four linearly separable sets of points is stored in a different quadrant of the mesh. Notice that the vertical slabs of points in the plane need not cover the same area of space. They simply must contain the same number of points.*

Since this algorithm is recursive, we now need only discuss the binary search routine. Notice that due to the mesh environment and the way in which we have partitioned the data, we will perform simultaneous binary searches between $S_1$ and $S_2$, as well as between $S_3$ and $S_4$. We will then perform a binary search between $S_1 \cup S_2$ and $S_3 \cup S_4$. Therefore, we only need to describe the binary search between $S_1$ and $S_2$, with the others being similar. In fact, we will only describe the binary search that will determine the upper common tangent line between $S_1$ and $S_2$.

Notice that it takes $\Theta(n^{1/2})$ time to broadcast a query from $S_1$ to $S_2$ and then report the result back to all processors in $S_1$. So, in $\Theta(n^{1/2})$ time, we can determine whether or not some line from $S_1$ goes above all of the points in $S_2$ or whether there is at least one point in $S_2$ that is above the query line. If we continue performing this binary search in a natural way, the running time of this convex hull algorithm will be $\Theta(n^{1/2} \log n)$.

However, if we first perform a query from $S_1$ to $S_2$, and then one from $S_2$ to $S_1$, notice that half of the data from $S_1$ and half the data from $S_2$ can be logically eliminated. The reader should note that while logically eliminating points during this back-and-forth binary search, reducing the total number of points under consideration by at least half during each iteration, the points representing the common tangent line segments remain in the active sets.

So, if the logically active data is compressed into a smaller submesh after the binary search, then each iteration of the binary search, including the compression, will take time proportional to the square root of the number of items remaining. Therefore, such a dual binary search with compression will run in $B(n) = B(n/2) + \Theta(n^{1/2}) = \Theta(n^{1/2})$ time. Hence, the total running time of the divide-and-conquer-based binary search on a mesh of size $n$ is the $\Theta(n^{1/2})$ time for the initial sort plus

$$T(n) = T(n/4) + B(n) = T(n/4) + \Theta(n^{1/2}) = \Theta(n^{1/2})$$

time for the remainder of the algorithm. Therefore, the total running time to determine the convex hull on a mesh of size $n$ is $\Theta(n^{1/2})$, which is optimal for this architecture.

#### ***Convex Hull Algorithm on a PRAM***

In this section, we present a divide-and-conquer algorithm to solve the convex hull problem on a PRAM. The algorithm follows the spirit of the divide-and-conquer algorithm that we have presented. However, the individual steps have been optimized for the PRAM. The algorithm follows.

1. *Partition* the set $S$ of $n$ planar points into $n^{1/2}$ sets, denoted $R_1, R_2, \ldots, R_{n^{1/2}}$. The partitioning is done so that all points in region $R_i$ are to the left of all points in region $R_{i+1}$ for $1 \le i \le n^{1/2} - 1$ (see Figure 10-13). This partitioning is most simply accomplished by sorting, as previously described.

2. *Recursively*, and in parallel, solve the convex hull problem for every $R_i$, $i \in \{1,2,\ldots,n^{1/2}\}$. At this point, *hull*($R_i$) is now known for every $R_i$.
3. *Stitch* the $n^{1/2}$ convex hulls together in order to determine *hull*(*S*). This is done by the **combine** routine that we define below.

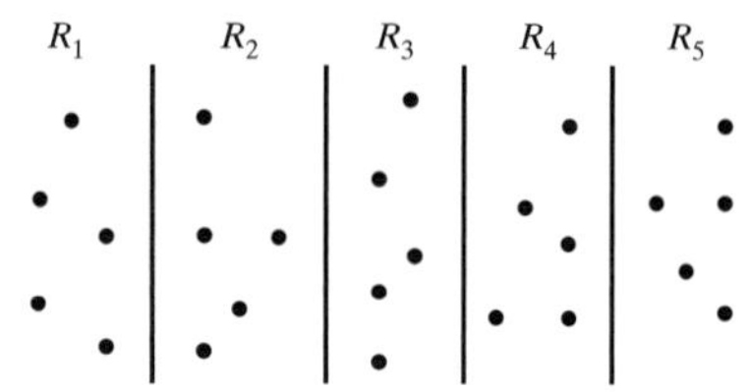


**FIGURE 10-13** *An illustration of partitioning the set S of n planar points into $n^{1/2}$ linearly separable sets, each with $n^{1/2}$ points. The sets are denoted as $R_1, R_2, \ldots, R_{n^{1/2}}$.*

### *Combine*

The input to the combine routine is the set of convex hulls, *hull*($R_1$), *hull*($R_2$), ..., *hull*($R_{n^{1/2}}$), each represented by $O(n^{1/2})$ extreme points. Notice that *hull*($R_1$) ≤ *hull*($R_2$) ≤ ... ≤ *hull*($R_{n^{1/2}}$), where we use "$A \le B$" to mean that "all points in *A* are to the left of all points in *B*." The combine routine will produce *hull*(*S*). As we have done previously, we will only consider the upper envelopes of *hull*($R_i$), $1 \le i \le n^{1/2}$, and we will describe an algorithm to merge these $n^{1/2}$ upper envelopes in order to produce the upper envelope of *hull*(*S*). The procedure for determining the lower envelope is analogous. The algorithm follows.

1. Assign $n^{1/2}$ processors to each set $R_i$ of points. For each $R_i$, determine the $n^{1/2} - 1$ tangent lines between *hull*($R_i$) and every distinct *hull*($R_j$). Notice that a total of $n^{1/2} \times (n^{1/2} - 1) = O(n)$ such upper tangent lines are determined. These tangent lines are computed as follows.
   a. Let $T_{i,j}$ be used to denote the upper common tangent line between *hull*($R_i$) and *hull*($R_j$), $i \ne j$.
   b. For each $R_i$, use the $k^{\text{th}}$ processor that was assigned to it to determine the upper tangent line between *hull*($R_i$) and *hull*($R_k$), $i \ne k$. Each of these upper tangent lines can be determined by a single processor in $O(\log n)$ time by invoking the "teeter-totter" algorithm outlined above. In fact, all $\Theta(n)$ tangent lines can be determined simultaneously in $O(\log n)$ time on a CREW PRAM.
2. Let $V_i$ be the tangent line with the smallest slope in $\{T_{i,1}, T_{i,2}, \ldots, T_{i,i-1}\}$. That is, with respect to $R_i$, $V_i$ represents the tangent line of minimum slope that "comes from the left." Let $v_i$ be the point of contact of $V_i$ with *hull*($R_i$).

3. Let $W_i$ be the tangent line with largest slope in $\{T_{i,i+1}, T_{i,i+2}, \ldots, T_{i,n^{1/2}}\}$. That is, with respect to $R_i$, $W_i$ represents the tangent line of maximum slope that "comes from the right." Let $w_i$ be the point of contact of $W_i$ with *hull*($R_i$).
4. Notice that both $V_i$ and $W_i$ can be found in $O(\log n)$ time by the $n^{1/2}$ processors assigned to $R_i$. This only requires that the $n^{1/2}$ processors perform a minimum or maximum operation, respectively.
5. Since neither $V_i$ nor $W_i$ can be vertical, they intersect and form an angle, with the interior point upward. If this angle is $\leq 180°$, or if $w_i$ is to the left of $v_i$, then none of the points of the upper envelope of *hull*($R_i$) belong to *hull*($S$). Otherwise, all points from $v_i$ to $w_i$, inclusive, belong to *hull*($S$) (see Figures 10-14, 10-15, 10-16, and 10-17). Notice that this determination is performed in $\Theta(1)$ time.
6. Finally, compress all of the extreme points of *hull*($S$) into a compact region in memory in $O(\log n)$ time by performing parallel prefix computations.

The running time of the **combine** routine is dominated by the time required to determine the common tangent lines and the time required to organize the final results. Therefore, the running time for the combine routine is $O(\log n)$.

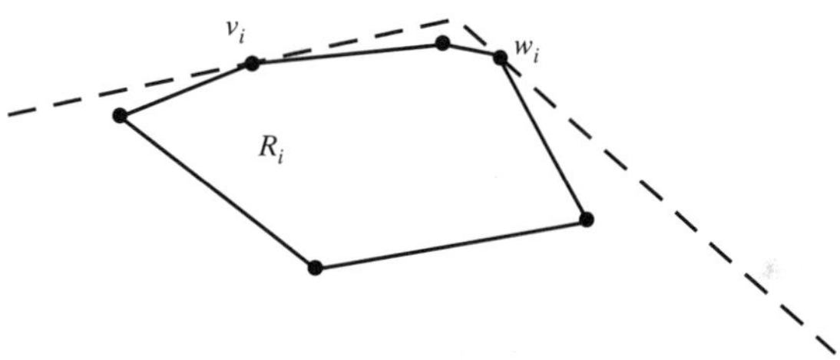


**FIGURE 10-14** *Suppose that $v_i$ is to the left of $w_i$ and that the angle above the intersection of their tangents exceeds 180°. Then all of the extreme points of $R_i$ between (and including) $v_i$ and $w_i$ are extreme points of S.*

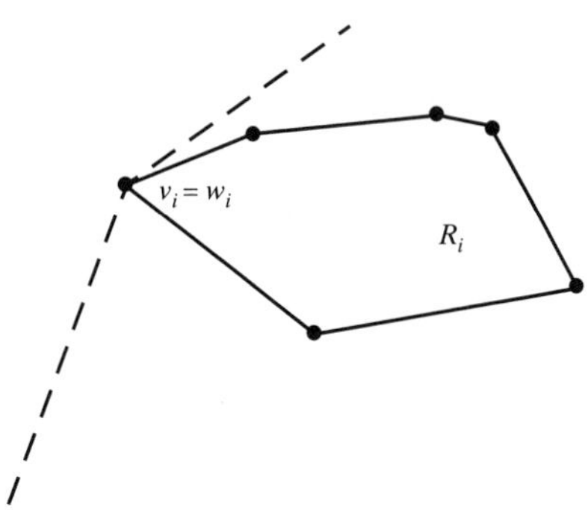


**FIGURE 10-15** *Suppose that $v_i = w_i$ and that the angle above the intersection of their tangents exceeds 180°. Then $v_i$ is an extreme point of S.*

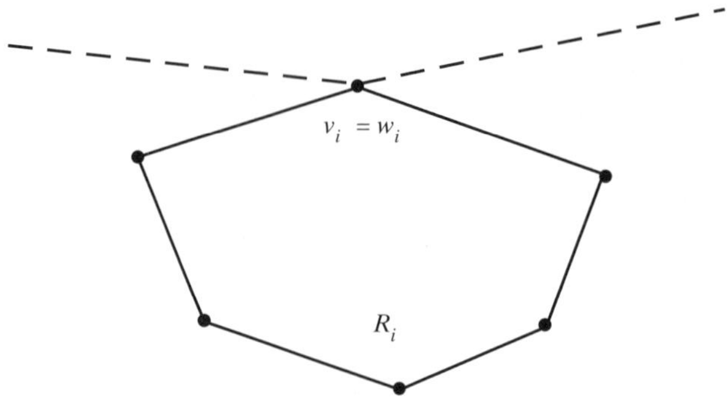


**FIGURE 10-16** *Suppose that $v_i = w_i$ and that the angle above the intersection of their tangents does not exceed 180°. In this case, no extreme point on the upper envelope of $R_i$ is an extreme point of S.*

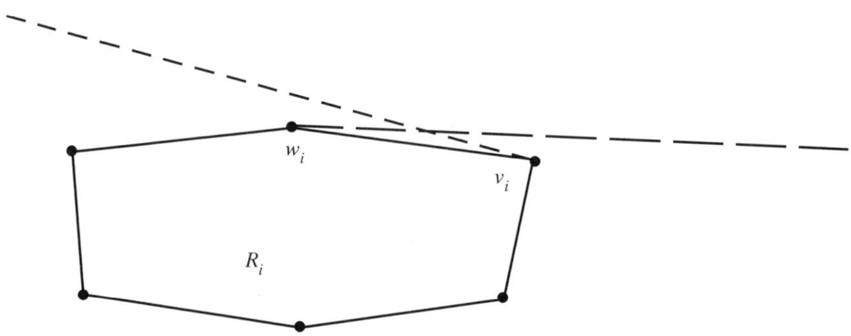


**FIGURE 10-17** *Suppose that $w_i$ is to the left of $v_i$. Then no extreme point on the upper envelope of $R_i$ is an extreme point of S.*

#### *PRAM Analysis*

While it is beyond the scope of this text, we have mentioned that sorting can be performed on a PRAM in $\Theta(\log n)$ time. Therefore, the running time of this convex hull algorithm is given by $T(n) = S(n) + R(n)$, where $S(n) = \Theta(\log n)$ is the time required for the initial sort, and $R(n) = R(n^{1/2}) + C(n)$ is the time required for the recursive part of the algorithm, including the $C(n) = O(\log n)$ time combine routine. Hence, the running time for this convex hull algorithm is $\Theta(\log n)$. Further, this results in an optimal total cost of $\Theta(n \log n)$.

## Smallest Enclosing Box

In this section, we consider the problem of determining a smallest enclosing "box" of a set of points. That is, given a set $S$ of $n$ planar points, determine a, not necessarily unique, minimum-area enclosing rectangle of $S$. This problem has applications in layout and design. Since a rectangle is convex, it follows from the definition of convex hull that any enclosing rectangle of $S$ must enclose *hull*($S$). One can show that for a minimum-area enclosing rectangle, *i*) each of its edges must intersect an extreme point of *hull*($S$) and *ii*) one of the edges of the rectangle must be collinear with a pair of adjacent extreme points of *hull*($S$) (see Figure 10-18).

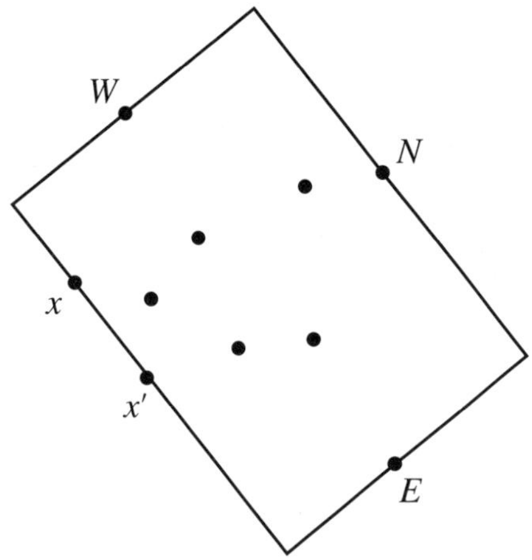


**FIGURE 10-18** *A smallest enclosing box of S. A, not necessarily unique, minimum-area enclosing rectangle of S includes three edges, each of which contains an extreme point of hull(S), and one edge that is collinear with an edge of hull(S).*

A straightforward solution to the smallest enclosing box problem consists of the following steps.

1. Identify the extreme points of the set $S$ of $n$ planar points.
2. Consider every pair of adjacent extreme points in *hull*($S$). For each such pair, find the three maximum points, as shown in Figure 10-18, and as described below.
   a. Given a line collinear with hull edge $\overline{xx'}$, the point $E$ associated with $\overline{xx'}$ is the last point of *hull*($S$) encountered as a line perpendicular to $\overline{xx'}$ passes through *hull*($S$) from left to right.
   b. The point $N$ associated with hull edge $\overline{xx'}$ is the last point encountered as a line parallel to $\overline{xx'}$, originating at $\overline{xx'}$, passes through *hull*($S$).
   c. Finally, the point $W$ associated with hull edge $\overline{xx'}$ is the last point of *hull*($S$) encountered as a line perpendicular to $\overline{xx'}$ passes through *hull*($S$) from right to left.
3. For every adjacent pair of extreme points, $x$ and $x'$, determine the area of the minimum enclosing box that has an edge collinear with hull edge $\overline{xx'}$.

4. A smallest enclosing box of $S$ is a box that yields the minimum area over all of the rectangles just determined. Therefore, identify a box that corresponds to the minimum area with respect to those values determined in Step 3.

#### RAM

We have shown that the convex hull of a set $S$ of $n$ planar points can be determined in $\Theta(n \log n)$ on a RAM. Further, given $m$ enumerated extreme points, for each pair of adjacent extreme points, one can determine the other three critical points by a binary search type of procedure in $\Theta(\log m)$ time. Therefore, the time required to determine the $m$ restricted minimum-area rectangles is $\Theta(m \log m)$. Once these $m$ rectangles have been determined, a minimum-area rectangle over this set can be determined in $\Theta(m)$ time by a simple scan. Therefore, the running time for the entire algorithm on a RAM is $\Theta(n \log n + m \log m) = \Theta(n \log n)$, since $m = O(n)$.

#### PRAM

Consider the same basic strategy as just presented for the RAM. Notice that the $m$ restricted minimum-area rectangles can be determined simultaneously in $\Theta(\log m)$ time on a PRAM. Further, a semigroup operation can be used to determine the minimum of these in $\Theta(\log m)$ time. Therefore, the running time of the entire algorithm, including the time to determine the extreme points of the convex hull, is $\Theta(\log n + \log m) = \Theta(\log n)$ on a PRAM.

#### Mesh

Given a mesh of size $n$, we have shown how to enumerate the $m$ extreme points of *hull*($S$) in $\Theta(n^{1/2})$ time. In order to arrive at an asymptotically optimal algorithm for this architecture, we need to be able to design a $\Theta(n^{1/2})$ time algorithm to generate the $m$ rectangles. Once we have generated the rectangles, we know that a straightforward $\Theta(n^{1/2})$ time semigroup operation can be used to identify one of these of minimum area. So, how do we determine all $m$ minimum-area rectangles simultaneously in $\Theta(n^{1/2})$ time?

Recall that the extreme points of *hull*($S$) have been enumerated. Each point is incident on two hull edges. Each such edge has an *angle of support* that it makes with *hull*($S$). These angles are all in the range of $[0, 2\pi)$, where the angle, in radian measure, is viewed with respect to the points of $S$ (see Figure 10-19). Consider the situation in which every edge $\overline{xx'}$ is trying to determine its point $N$. This corresponds to the situation in which every edge $\overline{xx'}$ is searching for the extreme point of *hull*($S$) that has an angle of support that differs from that of $\overline{xx'}$ by $\pi$. In order for edge $\overline{xx'}$ to determine its other two points, $E$ and $W$, it is simply searching for points bounded by hull edges with angles of support that differ from that of $\overline{xx'}$ by $\pi/2$ and $3\pi/2$, respectively. Therefore, these simultaneous searches can simply be performed by a fixed number of sort-based routines and ordered interval broadcasts. In the interest of flow of text, we have not given all of the details, but it should be clear that these operations are essentially performed in a straightforward fashion by concurrent read operations. Therefore, the running time of this algorithm, including the time to identify the extreme points of *hull*(*S*), is $\Theta(n^{1/2})$.

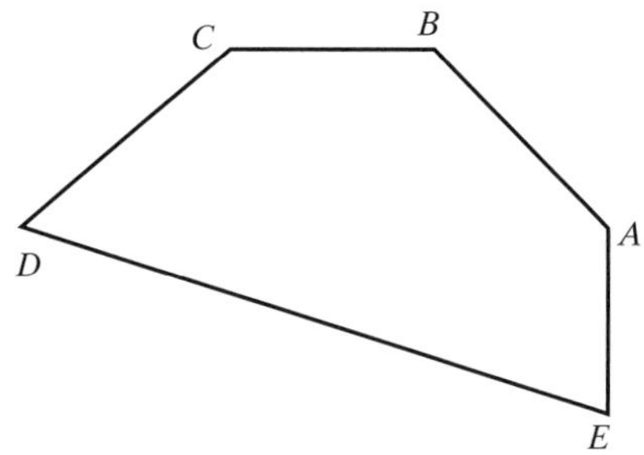


**FIGURE 10-19** *An illustration of angles of support. The angle of incidence of hull edge $\overline{EA}$ is $\pi/2$, of $\overline{AB}$ is $3\pi/4$, of $\overline{BC}$ is $\pi$, and so forth. An angle of support of extreme point A is in $[\pi/2, 3\pi/4]$. An angle of support of extreme point B is in $[3\pi/4, \pi]$, and so forth.*

## All-Nearest Neighbor Problem

In this section, we consider another fundamental problem in computational geometry. Suppose we have a set $S$ of $n$ planar points and for every point in $S$ we want to know a, not necessarily unique, nearest neighbor with respect to the other points in $S$. That is, we are required to determine for every point $p \in S$, a point $\overline{p}$, such that $dist(p, \overline{p})$ is the minimum $dist(p, q), p \neq q, q \in S$. For this reason, the problem is often referred to as the *all-nearest neighbor problem.*

An optimal $\Theta(n \log n)$-time algorithm for the RAM typically consists of constructing the *Voronoi Diagram* of $S$ and then traversing this structure. The *Voronoi Diagram* of a set of planar points consists of a collection of $n$ convex polygons, where each such polygon $C_i$ represents the region of 2-dimensional space such that any point in $C_i$ is closer to $p_i \in S$ than to any other point in $S$. The Voronoi Diagram is a very important structure in computational geometry. While a detailed discussion of the construction of the Voronoi Diagram is beyond the scope of this book, references to such algorithms are given at the end of the chapter.

In this section, we will concentrate on an interesting divide-and-conquer solution to the all-nearest neighbor problem for the mesh. Notice that an optimal $\Theta(n^{1/2})$-time algorithm on a mesh of size $n$ carries with it a cost of $\Theta(n^{3/2})$. So, while not cost-optimal, this is significantly better than a brute-force algorithm that uses $\Theta(n^2)$ operations to compute distances between all pairs of points.

We consider an algorithm that partitions the points into disjoint sets of points, solves the problem recursively within each set of points, and then stitches the partial results together in an efficient fashion. We prevent the stitching process from becoming the dominant step by partitioning in such a way that almost all of the points within each partition know their final answer after the recursive solution.

We can accomplish this as follows.

1. Partition the plane into linearly separable vertical slabs and solve the problem recursively within each vertical slab.
2. Repartition the plane into linearly separable horizontal slabs and solve the problem recursively within each horizontal slab.
3. We can then utilize a theorem from computational geometry that states that there are no more than a fixed number of points in each rectangle formed by the intersection of a horizontal and vertical slab that could have a nearest neighbor somewhere other than in its horizontal or vertical slab (see Figure 10-20).

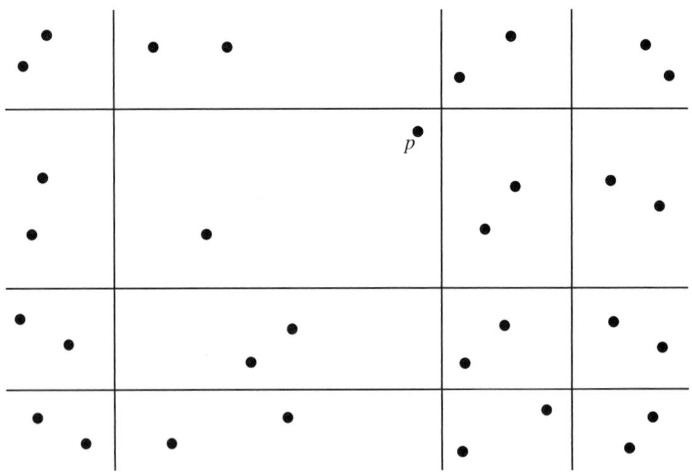


**FIGURE 10-20** *The nearest neighbor of p is neither in the same horizontal nor vertical slab as p is.*

We now give an outline of the algorithm.

1. Solve the problem recursively in vertical slabs, as follows.
   a. Sort the $n$ points in $S$ by $x$-coordinate, creating four vertical slabs.
   b. Solve the all-nearest neighbor problem recursively (Steps 1-3) within each vertical slab.
2. Solve the problem recursively in horizontal slabs, as follows.
   a. Sort the $n$ points in $S$ by $y$-coordinate, creating four horizontal slabs.
   b. Solve the all-nearest neighbor problem recursively (Steps 1-3) within each horizontal slab.

3. Sort the $n$ points of $S$ with respect to the identity of their boxes. The identity of a specific box is given as the concatenation of the label of the vertical slab and the label of the horizontal slab.
   a. For the points in each box, it is important to note that a result from computational geometry shows that at most two points closest to each corner of the box could be closer to a point outside the box than to any point found so far. Notice that there are no more than $8 \times 16 = 128$ such corner points. In fact, if we count carefully we notice that the 4 interior rectangles can each have 8 such points, the 4 corner rectangles can each have only 2 such points, and the remaining 8 edge-rectangles can each have 4 such points. That is, the total number of points that could have a closest neighbor outside of its rectangle is actually 72, though 128 and 72 are both just constants.
   b. Each of these corner points can now be passed through the mesh so that they can view, and be viewed by, all $n$ points. After this traversal, each of these corner points will know its nearest neighbor. Hence, the solution will be complete.

### Running Time

The running time of this algorithm on a mesh of size $n$ is given as $T(n) = 2T(n/4) + \Theta(n^{1/2})$. Using the *Master Method*, we can determine that this recurrence has a solution of $T(n) = \Theta(n^{1/2} \log n)$, which is within a $\log n$ factor of optimal for this architecture.

## Line Intersection Problems

Suppose we are given a set $L$ of $n$ line segments in the Euclidean plane. The segments may be arbitrary, or we may have additional knowledge, for example, that every member of $L$ is either horizontal or vertical. Common *line intersection problems* include the following.

1. **Intersection Query:** Determine if there is at least one pair of members of $L$ that intersect.
2. **Intersection Reporting:** Find and report all pairs of members of $L$ that intersect.

An easy, though perhaps inefficient, method of solving the intersection query problem is to solve the intersection reporting problem and then observe whether or not any intersections were reported. We might hope to obtain an asymptotically more efficient solution to the intersection query problem that does not require us to solve the intersection reporting problem.

An obvious approach to both problems is based on an examination of each of the $\Theta(n^2)$ pairs of members of $L$. It is easy to see how such an approach yields an $O(n^2)$ time RAM algorithm for the intersection query problem, and a $\Theta(n^2)$ time

RAM algorithm for the intersection reporting problem. In fact, other solutions are more efficient.

- **Consider the intersection query problem.** In $\Theta(n)$ time, create two records for each member of $L$, one for each endpoint. Let each record have an indicator as to whether the endpoint is a *left* or *right* endpoint, where lower corresponds to *right* in the case of a vertical segment. Sort these records into ascending order by the $x$-coordinates of their endpoints, using the *left/right* indicator as the secondary key, with *right* < *left*, and $y$-coordinates as the tertiary key. Now, perform a *plane sweep* operation, which allows us to "sweep the plane" from left to right, maintaining an ordered data structure $T$ of non-intersecting members of $L$ not yet eliminated from consideration, as possible members of an intersecting pair. Assume that $T$ is a data structure, such as a balanced tree, in which insert, retrieve, and delete operations can be performed in sequential $O(\log n)$ time. As we move the vertical "sweep line" from left to right and encounter a left endpoint of a member $s$ of $L$, we insert $s$ into $T$, then determine whether or not $s$ intersects either of its at most two neighbors in $T$. If we find an intersection, we report its existence and halt. As the sweep line encounters a right endpoint of a member $s$ of $L$, we remove $s$ from $T$, and, as above, determine whether or not $s$ intersects either of its, at most, 2 neighbors in $T$. If we find an intersection, we report its existence and halt. Otherwise, we continue the plane sweep (see Figure 10-21).

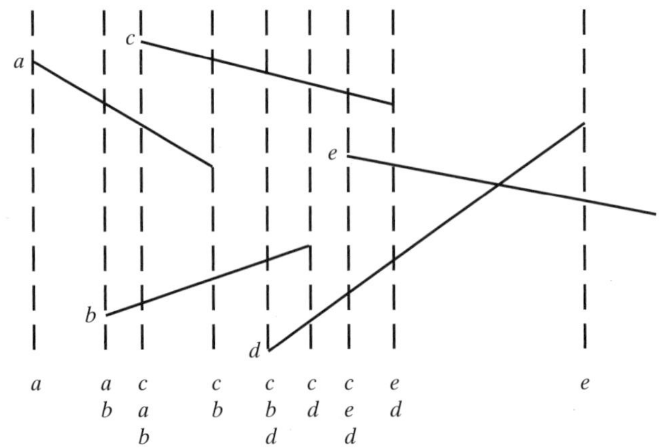


**FIGURE 10-21** *Illustration of a plane sweep operation to solve the intersection query problem. The line segments are labeled by left endpoint. As a sweep of the all endpoints is performed from left to right, when a left endpoint is encountered, the line segment is inserted into the list at the appropriate ordered, i.e., top to bottom, position, and is tested for intersection with its neighbors in the list. The currently active ordered list of line segments is shown beneath each endpoint. When a right endpoint is encountered, an evaluation of an intersection is made before removing that point from the ordering. Here, when the left endpoint of e is encountered, the d-e intersection is detected.*

- **Consider the intersection reporting problem.** We can construct an algorithm with an *output-sensitive* running time for the RAM, which is asymptotically faster under certain conditions than the straightforward $\Theta(n^2)$ time required for the brute force algorithm. The term *output-sensitive* refers to the fact that the amount of output is a parameter of the running time. That is, if there are $k$ intersections, a RAM algorithm for this problem can be constructed to run in $O((n + k)\log n)$ time. Thus, if $k = o(n^2/\log n)$, such an algorithm is asymptotically faster than one that examines all pairs. Such an algorithm can be obtained by making minor modifications to the solution above for the intersection query problem. The most important change is that instead of halting upon discovering an intersection, we list the intersection and continue the plane sweep to the right.

### Overlapping Line Segments

In Chapter 7, we examined the following problems.

- *The coverage query problem* considers the question of whether or not a given fixed interval $[a, b]$ is covered by the union of an input set of intervals.
- *The maximal overlapping point problem* determines a point of the real line that is covered by the largest number of members of an input set of intervals.

Such problems fall within the scope of computational geometry. Another problem in computational geometry that is concerned with overlapping line segments is the *minimal-cover* problem, which can be expressed as follows: Given an interval $[a, b]$ and a set of $n$ intervals $S = \{[a_i, b_i]\}_{i=1}^{n}$, find a minimal-membership subset $S'$ of $S$ such that $[a, b]$ is contained in the union of the members of $S'$, if such a set exists, or report that no such set exists. Another version of this problem uses a circle instead of an interval for the object to be covered and a set of circular arcs instead of a set of intervals.

An application of this problem is in minimizing the cost of security. The interval $[a, b]$ might represent a borderline to be guarded, and the members of $S$ might represent sectors that can be viewed by individual guards. A positive solution to the problem might represent a minimal-cost solution, including a listing of the responsibilities of the individual guards, for keeping the entire borderline or perimeter under surveillance.

Efficient solutions exist for both the interval and circular versions of these problems, which are quite similar. For the reader's convenience, we will consider the interval version of the problem as some of its steps are easier to state than their analogs in the circular version of the problem.

We discuss a *greedy* algorithm, that is, an algorithm marked by steps designed to reach as far as possible towards a solution. The algorithm is greedy in that it starts with a member of $S$ that covers $a$ and extends maximally to the right. If no such member of $S$ exists, then the algorithm terminates and reports that the requested coverage does not exist. Further, once a member $s \in S$ is selected, a maximal *successor* for $s$ is determined. That is, a successor is a member of $S$ that intersects with $s$ and extends maximally to the right. This procedure continues until either $b$ is covered, which represents a successful outcome, or a successor cannot be found, which represents an unsuccessful outcome. Thus, a high-level view of this algorithm is as follows.

- Find a member $s \in S$ that covers $a$ and has a maximal right endpoint. If no such member of $S$ exists, report *failure* and halt.
- While *failure* has not been reported and $s = [a_i, b_i]$ does not cover $b$, assign to $s$ a member of $S \backslash \{s\}$ that has a maximal right endpoint among those members of $S \backslash \{s\}$ that contain $b_i$. If no such member of $S \backslash \{s\}$ exists, report *failure* and halt.

At the end of these steps, if failure has not been reported, the selected members of $S$ form a minimal-cardinality cover of $[a, b]$. See Figure 10-22, in which the intervals of $S$ have been raised vertically in the Euclidean plane for clear viewing, but should be thought of as all belonging to the same Euclidean line.

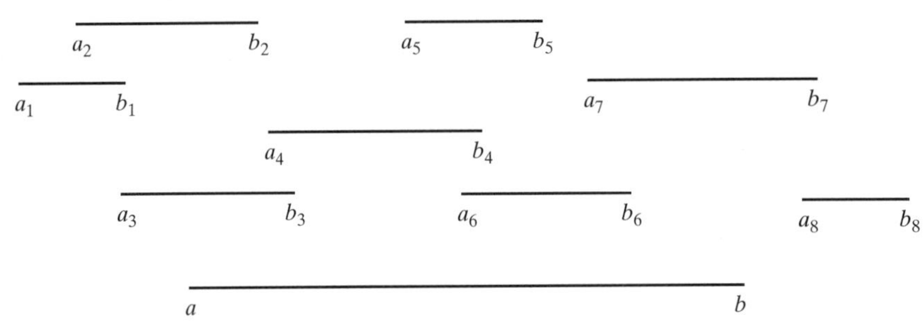


**FIGURE 10-22** *A minimal-cardinality cover of* $[a, b]$ *consists of line segments* 3, 4, 6, *and* 7.

The approach outlined above is inherently sequential. However, we can revise the algorithm so that it can be implemented on a RAM or on a variety of parallel architectures. Such an architecture-independent algorithm follows.

1. For each $t \in S$, find its successor, if one exists.
2. For each $t \in S$, take the union of $t$ and its successor as a chain of at most two connected intervals. Then take the union of this chain of at most two intervals and its final line segment's successor's chain of at most two intervals to produce a chain of at most four. Repeat this doubling until the chain starting with $t$ either does not have a successor chain or covers $b$.
3. Use a minimum operation to find a chain that covers $[a, b]$ with a minimal number of intervals.

As is so often the case, "find" operations, including those mentioned above, are typically facilitated by having the data appropriately sorted. It is useful to have the intervals ordered from left to right. However, since the data consists of intervals rather than single values, some thought must be given to what such an ordering means. Our primary concern is to order the intervals in such a way as to enable an efficient solution to the problem at hand, by enabling us to identify successor intervals efficiently. The ordering that we use is embedded in the algorithm given below, which relies on a postfix operation on the ordered intervals in order to determine maximal overlap of $[a, b]$ with a minimum number of intervals.

a. Sort the interval records by left endpoint, breaking ties in favor of maximal right endpoints.

b. We observe that if $\{[a_i, b_i], [a_j, b_j]\} \subset S$ and $[a_i, b_i] \subset [a_j, b_j]$, then any connected chain of members of $S$ of minimal-cardinality among those chains that start with $[a_i, b_i]$ and cover $[a, b]$, will have at least as many members as a connected chain of members of $S$ of minimal-cardinality among those chains that start with $[a_j, b_j]$ and cover $[a, b]$. Therefore, we can remove all such nonessential intervals $[a_i, b_i]$ by performing a simple prefix operation on the ordered set of interval data. Without loss of generality, we will proceed under the assumption that no remaining member of $S$ is a subset of another remaining member of $S$.

c. For each remaining $[a_i, b_i] \in S$, create two records. The first set of records, called *successor records*, consists of two components, namely, the index $i$ of the interval and the index $j$ of the successor of the interval. For each interval $[a_i, b_i] \in S$, we initialize its successor record to $(i, i)$, with the interpretation that initially every interval is its own successor. Notice that during the procedure, the first component of these records does not change, while the second component will eventually point to the successor of interval $[a_i, b_i]$. The second set of records, referred to as *information records*, contains connectivity information. The components of the information records include the following.

   - The first two components are the left and right endpoints, respectively, of the connected union of members of $S$ represented by the record's chain of intervals.
   - The third and fourth components represent the indices of the leftmost and rightmost members of the record's chain, respectively.
   - The fifth component is the index of the successor to the rightmost interval in the record's chain, *i.e.*, the successor to the interval indexed by the fourth component.
   - The sixth component is the number of members of $S$ in the line segment's chain.

   For each record $[a_i, b_i] \in S$, we initialize an information record to $(a_i, b_i, i, i, i, 1)$.

d. Sort the information records into ascending order by the second component.

e. In this step, we use the first four components of the information records. Determine the span of the chain of intervals starting at $a_i$ as follows, where $\circ$ is an operation defined as

$$(a_i, b_j, i, j) \circ (a_k, b_m, k, m) = \begin{cases} (a_i, b_m, i, m) & \text{if } a_i \le a_k \le b_j < b_m; \\ (a_i, b_j, i, j) & \text{otherwise.} \end{cases}$$

The result of this operation represents $[a_i, b_j] \cup [a_k, b_m]$, provided these line segments intersect and $[a_k, b_m]$ extends $[a_i, b_i]$ to the right more than does $[a_j, b_j]$. In this case, we can say the result represents $[a_i, b_m]$, and that $[a_k, b_m]$ is the successor of $[a_i, b_j]$. Otherwise, the result of this operation is its first factor, representing $[a_i, b_j]$. Note the interval we call the successor of $[a_i, b_j]$ may change as the algorithm proceeds. Use a parallel postfix operation with operation $\circ$ to compute, for each information record representing $[a_i, b_i]$, the transitive closure of $\circ$ on all records representing line segment $i$ up through and including the information record representing line segment $n$. Since the intervals are ordered by their left endpoints, it follows that the fourth component of the postfix information record representing line segment $[a_i, b_i]$ is the index of the successor of the chain initiated by $[a_i, b_i]$.

f. For all $i \in \{1,2,\ldots,n\}$, copy the fourth component of the postfix information record created in the previous step, representing $[a_i, b_i]$, to the second component of the successor record representing $[a_i, b_i]$, so that the successor record for $[a_i, b_i]$ will have the form $(i, s_i)$, where $s_i$ is the index of the successor of $[a_i, b_i]$.

g. For all $i \in \{1,2,\ldots,n\}$, compute the chain of intervals $v_i$ obtained by starting with $[a_i, b_i]$ and adding successors until either $b$ is covered or we reach an interval that is its own successor. This can be done by way of a parallel postfix computation in which we define $\bullet$ as

$$(a_i, b_j, i, j, k, c) \bullet (a_m, b_q, m, q, r, s) = \begin{cases} (a_i, b_q, i, q, r, c+s) & \text{if } k = m; \\ (a_i, b_j, i, j, k, c) & \text{otherwise.} \end{cases}$$

h. A minimum operation on $\{v_i\}_{i=1}^{n}$, in which we seek the minimal sixth component such that the interval determined by the first and second components contains $[a, b]$, determines whether or not a minimal-cardinality covering of $[a, b]$ by members of $S$ exists, and, if so, its cardinality. If $j$ is an index such that $v_j$ yields a minimal-cardinality covering of $[a, b]$ by members of $S$, the members of $S$ that make up this covering can be listed by a parallel prefix operation that marks a succession of successors starting with $[a_j, b_j]$.

## Computational Geometry on NOW, Clusters, and Grids

Many large-scale applications require the evaluation and/or construction of geometric objects as part of their solution strategy. Many such applications require the use of large-scale computing systems in order to solve problems of interest. Such systems include large-scale NOW, clusters, grids, and clouds. Algorithms to solve problems in computational geometry on such systems typically require the redistribution of data so that data on each node consists of records representing objects that are in close proximity in space. After such a redistribution of data, the algorithm is typically implemented by solving subproblems within computational nodes, followed by stitching such results together.

That is, the solutions typically mimic algorithms presented in this and previous chapters on parallel architectures when considering a cost-effective solution, *i.e.,* an architecture in which asymptotically fewer processors are utilized than the number of data to be processed. So, these geometric algorithms are typically of a hybrid nature. That is, solve the local subproblems in the nodes and then use the fine-grained communication protocols to stitch such solutions together into a final result, which is then typically distributed to all of the nodes/processors.

## Summary

In this chapter, we consider algorithms for several interesting problems from computational geometry. Problems considered include computation of the convex hull of a set of planar points, computation of a smallest enclosing box for a set of planar points, the All-Nearest Neighbor Problem, and several problems concerning line intersections and overlaps in the Euclidean plane.

## Chapter Notes

The focus of this chapter is on efficient sequential and parallel solutions to fundamental problems in the field of computational geometry. The reader interested in a more comprehensive exploration of computational geometry is referred to *Computational Geometry* by F.P. Preparata & M.I. Shamos (Springer-Verlag, 1985). In fact, the proof that sorting is linear-time transformable to the convex hull problem comes from this source. The reader interested in parallel implementations of solutions to problems in computational geometry is referred to S.G. Akl & K.A. Lyons' *Parallel Computational Geometry* (Prentice Hall, 1993).

The Graham's Scan algorithm was originally presented in "An efficient algorithm for determining the convex hull of a finite planar set," by R.L. Graham in *Information Processing Letters* **1**, 1972, 132–133. The Jarvis March algorithm was originally presented by R.A. Jarvis in the paper "On the identification of the convex hull of a finite set of points in the plane," *Information Processing Letters* **2**, 1973, 18–21. These algorithms are also presented in a thorough fashion in *Introduction to Algorithms* (3rd ed.: The MIT Press, Cambridge, MA, 2009) by T.H. Cormen, C.E. Leiserson, R.L. Rivest, and C. Stein.

The generic divide-and-conquer solution to the convex hull problem presented in this chapter is motivated by the material presented in *Parallel Algorithms for Regular Architectures* by R. Miller & Q.F. Stout (The MIT Press, 1996). The "teeter-totter" binary search algorithm referred to when describing an intricate binary search for determining common tangent lines was originally presented by M.H. Overmars and J. van Leeuwen in "Maintenance of configurations in the plane," in the *Journal of Computer and Systems Sciences*, vol. 23, 1981, 166–204. The interesting divide-and-conquer algorithm for the PRAM was first presented by M. Atallah and M. Goodrich in "Efficient parallel solutions to some geometric problems," in the *Journal of Parallel and Distributed Computing* **3**, 1986, 492–507. One might note that this algorithm exploits the CR capabilities of a CREW PRAM. We should point out that an optimal $\Theta(\log n)$ time EREW PRAM algorithm to solve the convex hull problem has been presented by R. Miller & Q.F. Stout in "Efficient parallel convex hull algorithms," in *IEEE Transactions on Computers*, 37 (12), 1988. However, the presentation of the Miller and Stout algorithm is beyond the scope of this book.

The notion of angles of support is interesting in that it allows multiple parallel searches to be implemented by a series of sort steps. Details of the mesh convex hull algorithm that relies on angles of support can be found in *Parallel Algorithms for Regular Architectures*.

The reader interested in learning more about the Voronoi Diagram and its application to problems involving proximity might consult *Computational Geometry* by F.P. Preparata & M.I. Shamos (Springer-Verlag, 1985). Details of the all-nearest neighbor algorithm for the mesh can be found in *Parallel Algorithms for Regular Architectures*.

A RAM algorithm for the circular version of the cover problem was presented by C.C. Lee and D.T. Lee in "On a Cover-Circle Minimization Problem," in *Information Processing Letters* **18** (1984), 180–185. A CREW PRAM algorithm for the circular version of this problem appears in "Parallel Circle-Cover Algorithms," by A.A. Bertossi in *Information Processing Letters* **27** (1988), 133–139. The algorithm by Bertossi was improved independently in each of the following papers:

- M.J. Atallah and D.Z. Chen, "An Optimal Parallel Algorithm for the Minimum Circle-Cover Problem," *Information Processing Letters* **32** (1989), 159–165.
- L. Boxer and R. Miller, "A Parallel Circle-Cover Minimization Algorithm," *Information Processing Letters* **32** (1989), 57–60.
- D. Sarkar and I. Stojmenovic, "An Optimal Parallel Circle-Cover Algorithm," *Information Processing Letters* **32** (1989), 3–6.

The exercises of this chapter, which appear in the next section, include questions concerning the *all maximal equally spaced collinear points problem*. This and several related problems were studied in the following papers:

- A.B. Kahng and G. Robins, "Optimal Algorithms for Extracting Spatial Regularity in Images," *Pattern Recognition Letters* **12** (1991), 757–764.
- L. Boxer and R. Miller, "Parallel Algorithms for All Maximal Equally Spaced Collinear Sets and All Maximal Regular Coplanar Lattices," *Pattern Recognition Letters* **14** (1993), 17–22.
- L. Boxer, R. Miller, and A. Rau-Chaplin, "Scalable Parallel Algorithms for Geometric Pattern Recognition," *Journal of Parallel and Distributed Computing* **58** (1999), 466–486.
- G. Robins, B.L. Robinson, and B.S. Sethi, "On Detecting Spatial Regularity in Noisy Images," *Information Processing Letters* **69** (1999), 189–195.
- L. Boxer and R. Miller, "A Parallel Algorithm for Approximate Regularity," *Information Processing Letters* **80** (2001), 311–316.

These problems have considerable practical value, as the presence of the regularity amidst seeming or expected chaos is often meaningful. For example, the members of $S$ might represent points observed in an aerial or satellite photo, and the maximal equally spaced collinear sets might represent traffic lights, military formations, property or national boundaries in the form of fence posts, and so forth. The paper of Kahng and Robins presents a RAM algorithm for the all maximal equally spaced collinear sets problem that runs in optimal $\Theta(n^2)$ time. This algorithm seems to be essentially sequential. The 1993 Boxer and Miller paper and the 1999 paper of Boxer, Miller, and Rau-Chaplin show how a rather different algorithm can be implemented in efficient to optimal time on parallel architectures. These three papers are concerned with exact solutions. The Robins *et al.* paper gives an approximate sequential solution that runs in $O(n^{5/2})$ time. The asymptotically slower running time for an approximate solution, as opposed to an exact solution, is due to the fact that an approximate solution may have more output than an exact solution. Notice, however, that an approximate solution is likely to be more useful than an exact solution, since data is generally not exact. On the other hand, the approximate solution to this problem is beyond the scope of this book. The algorithm of Robins *et al.* seems essentially sequential. A rather different algorithm appears in the 2001 Boxer and Miller paper, giving an approximate parallel solution that can be implemented on multiple platforms.

A prominent area of Computational Geometry that we have not discussed is that of "guarding an art gallery," in which a typical problem is the following. Given a polygon $P$ and a point $x$ of $P$ or its interior, determine efficiently what portions of $P$ are visible from $x$. Notice that if $P$ is known to be convex, then this problem is trivial. Sources of further information on this topic include the following.

M. DeBerg, O. Cheong, M. van Kreveld, and M. Overmars, *Computational Geometry: Algorithms and Applications*, Springer, Berlin, 2010.

J. O'Rourke, *Art Gallery Theorems and Algorithms*, Oxford University Press, New York, 1987 - available for free downloading from the author's Web site at http://maven.smith.edu/~orourke/books/ArtGalleryTheorems/Art_Gallery_Full_Book.pdf

## Exercises

Notes: Several of the exercises are concerned with polygons. Assume that by "polygon" we do not mean just the edges. Rather, we mean the union of its edges and the interior of the polygon.

Also, among the exercises are those with solutions that can use the *lexicographic order* of points in the Euclidean plane. The lexicographic order is defined as follows. If $p = (p_x, p_y)$ and $q = (q_x, q_y)$, then $p < q$ if either $p_x < q_x$ or both $p_x = q_x$ and $p_y < q_y$.

1. Given a set $S$ of $n$ planar points, construct an efficient algorithm to determine whether or not there exist three points in $S$ that are collinear. *Hint:* While there are $\Theta(n^3)$ triples of members of $S$, you should be able to construct an algorithm that runs in $o(n^3)$ sequential time.
2. Given a set of $n$ line segments in the plane, prove that there may be as many as $\Theta(n^2)$ intersections.
3. Show that the algorithm sketched in this chapter to solve the intersection query problem runs in $\Theta(n \log n)$ time on a RAM.
4. Given a set of $n$ line segments in the plane that have a total of $k$ intersections, show that a RAM algorithm can report all intersections in $O((n + k)\log n)$ time.
5. Given a convex polygon with $n$ vertices, construct an algorithm that can be implemented efficiently on a variety of architectures to determine the area of the polygon. The input to the problem consists of the circularly ordered vertices of the polygon. Analyze the running time of this algorithm for a RAM, ER PRAM with $n/\log n$ processors, hypercube of size $n/\log n$, mesh of size $n^{2/3}$, and $CGM(n, q)$.
6. Given a polygon with $n$ vertices, construct an efficient algorithm to determine whether or not the polygon is simple.
7. Given a simple polygon $P$ and a point $p$, give an efficient algorithm to determine whether or not $p$ is contained in $P$.
8. Given two simple polygons, each consisting of $n$ vertices, give an efficient algorithm to determine whether or not the polygons intersect.
9. Give an efficient algorithm to determine the convex hull of a simple polygon.
10. On a fine-grained parallel computer, a very different approach can be taken to the Intersection Reporting Problem. Suppose input to a PRAM, mesh, or

hypercube of $n$ processors consists of the $n$ line segments in the Euclidean plane. In the case of a mesh or hypercube, assume the segments are initially distributed one per processor. Give a solution to the Intersection Reporting Problem that is optimal in the worst case, and prove the optimality, for each of these architectures. *Hints*: This can be done with an algorithm that "seems" simpler to describe than the RAM algorithm described in the text. Also, the processors of a hypercube may be renumbered in a circular fashion.

**11.** In this chapter, we sketched an algorithm to solve the following problem: For a set of $n$ intervals and a range $[a, b]$, give an efficient algorithm to determine a minimal-cardinality subset of the intervals that cover $[a, b]$ or show, when appropriate, that no such cover exists. Prove the algorithm runs

- in $\Theta(n \log n)$ time on a RAM,
- in $\Theta(\log n)$ time on a CREW PRAM of size $n$, and
- in $\Theta(n^{1/2})$ time on a mesh of $n$ processors, assuming the intervals are initially distributed one per processor.

**12.** In the Graham Scan procedure given in this chapter, prove that both the point chosen as the origin, and the last point encountered in the tour, must be extreme points of the convex hull.

**13.** Given a set $S$ of $n$ planar points, prove that a pair of farthest neighbors, *i.e.*, a pair of points at maximum distance over all pairs of points in $S$, must be chosen from the set of extreme points.

**14.** Given two sets of points, $P$ and $Q$, give an efficient algorithm to determine whether $P$ and $Q$ are *linearly separable*. That is, give an efficient algorithm to determine whether or not it is possible to define a line $l$ with the property that all points of $P$ lie on one side of $l$ while all points of $Q$ lie on the other side of $l$.

**15.** In this problem, we consider the *all maximal equally spaced collinear points problem* in the Euclidean plane $\mathbb{R}^2$: Given a set $S$ of $n$ points in $\mathbb{R}^2$, identify all of the maximal equally spaced collinear subsets of $S$ that have at least three members. A collinear set $\{p_1, p_2, \ldots, p_k\}$, for which we assume in the following that the points are numbered according to their order on their common line, is *equally spaced* if all the line segments $\overline{p_i p_{i+1}}$, $i \in \{1, 2, \ldots, k-1\}$, have the same length. Assume that we are given a set $S$ of $n$ points in $\mathbb{R}^2$, where each point is represented by its Cartesian coordinates (see Figure 10-23).

a. Show that $O(n^2)$ is an upper bound for the output of this problem. *Hint*: Show that every pair of distinct points $\{p, q\} \subset S$ can be a consecutive pair of at most one maximal equally spaced collinear subset of $S$.

b. Show that $\Omega(n^2)$ is a lower bound for the worst-case output of this problem. *Hint*: Let $n$ be a square and let $S$ be the square of integer points

$$S = \left\{ (a,b) \,\middle|\, 1 \le a \le n^{1/2}, 1 \le b \le n^{1/2} \right\}.$$

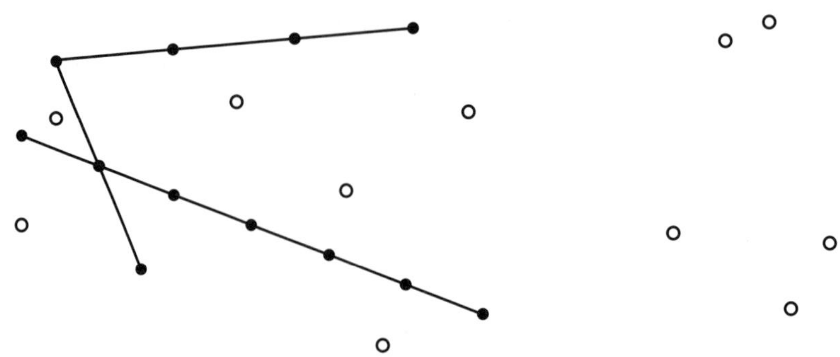

**FIGURE 10-23** *The all maximal equally spaced collinear points problem. An illustration of three equally spaced collinear line segments.*

Let $S_0 \subset S$ be defined by

$$S_0 = \left\{ (a, b) \,\middle|\, \frac{n^{1/2}}{3} \le a \le \frac{2n^{1/2}}{3},\ \frac{n^{1/2}}{3} \le b \le \frac{2n^{1/2}}{3} \right\}.$$

Show that if $\{p, q\} \subset S_0$, $p \ne q$, then $\{p, q\}$ is a consecutive pair in a maximal equally spaced collinear subset $C$ of $S$ such that $|C| \ge 3$. Together with part a) of this exercise, this shows the worst-case output for this problem is $\Theta(n^2)$.

c. Consider the following algorithm, which can be implemented on a variety of architectures, although the details of implementing some of the steps will vary with the architecture.

   i. Form the set $P$ of all ordered pairs $(p, q) \in S$ such that $p < q$ in the lexicographic order of points in $\mathbb{R}^2$.

   ii. Sort the members $(p, q)$ of $P$ in ascending order with respect to all the following keys:

   - The primary key of $(p, q)$ is the slope of the line determined by $(p, q)$, using $\infty$ as the slope of a vertical line.
   - The secondary key of $(p, q)$ is $d(p, q)$, the Euclidean distance from $p$ to $q$.
   - The tertiary key of $(p, q)$ is $(p, q)$, which is lexicographically ordered.

   iii. Use a parallel postfix operation on $P$ to identify all maximal equally spaced collinear subsets of $S$. The operation is based on the formation of quintuples and a binary operation specified as follows. Initial quintuples are of the form $(p, q, \mathit{length}, 2, \mathit{true})$, where the components are as follows. The first two components are the endpoints, *i.e.*, members of $S$, in an equally spaced collinear set. The third component is the length of segments that make up the current equally spaced collinear set. The fourth component is the number of input points in the equally spaced collinear set. The fifth component is true or false according to whether the first component is the first point in an equally spaced collinear set. The binary operation is defined by

$$(a,b,c,d,u) \otimes (e,f,g,h,v) =$$

$$\begin{cases} (a,f,c,d+h-1,u) & \text{if } b=e \text{ and } c=g \text{ and } \{a,b,f\} \text{ is collinear;} \\ (a,b,c,d,u) & \text{otherwise,} \end{cases}$$

and in the former case, set $v \leftarrow false$.

iv. A postfix operation on the members of $P$ is used to enumerate members of each equally spaced collinear set of more than two points. This operation is based on members of $P$ with a postfix quintuple having the fifth component *true* and the fourth component greater than 2.

Analyze the running time of this algorithm for each of a RAM, a CREW PRAM of $n^2$ processors, and a mesh of size $n^2$. In the case of the mesh, assume that the members of $S$ are initially distributed so that no processor has more than one member of $S$. Formation of the set $P$ can thus be done on the mesh by appropriate row and column rotations, and/or random-access write operations. The details are left to the reader.

**16.** In the chapter, an architecture-independent algorithm was given for solving the minimal-cover problem for intervals on the real line. Analyze efficient implementations of this algorithm for a mesh of size $n$ and for a hypercube of size $n$, where the input is of size $n$.

# 11

# Image Processing

In this chapter, we consider some fundamental problems in image processing, an important and challenging area of computer science. In particular, image processing, image analysis, and pattern recognition are related fields that typically fall into an area of computer science known as Artificial Intelligence. In this chapter, we present several divide-and-conquer solutions to problems in image analysis for the mesh computer. In addition, we present algorithms for the RAM, as appropriate. Finally, it is important to note that a combination of solution strategies for the mesh and RAM often serve as core strategies for solving image-based problems for large images on clusters and multicore machines.

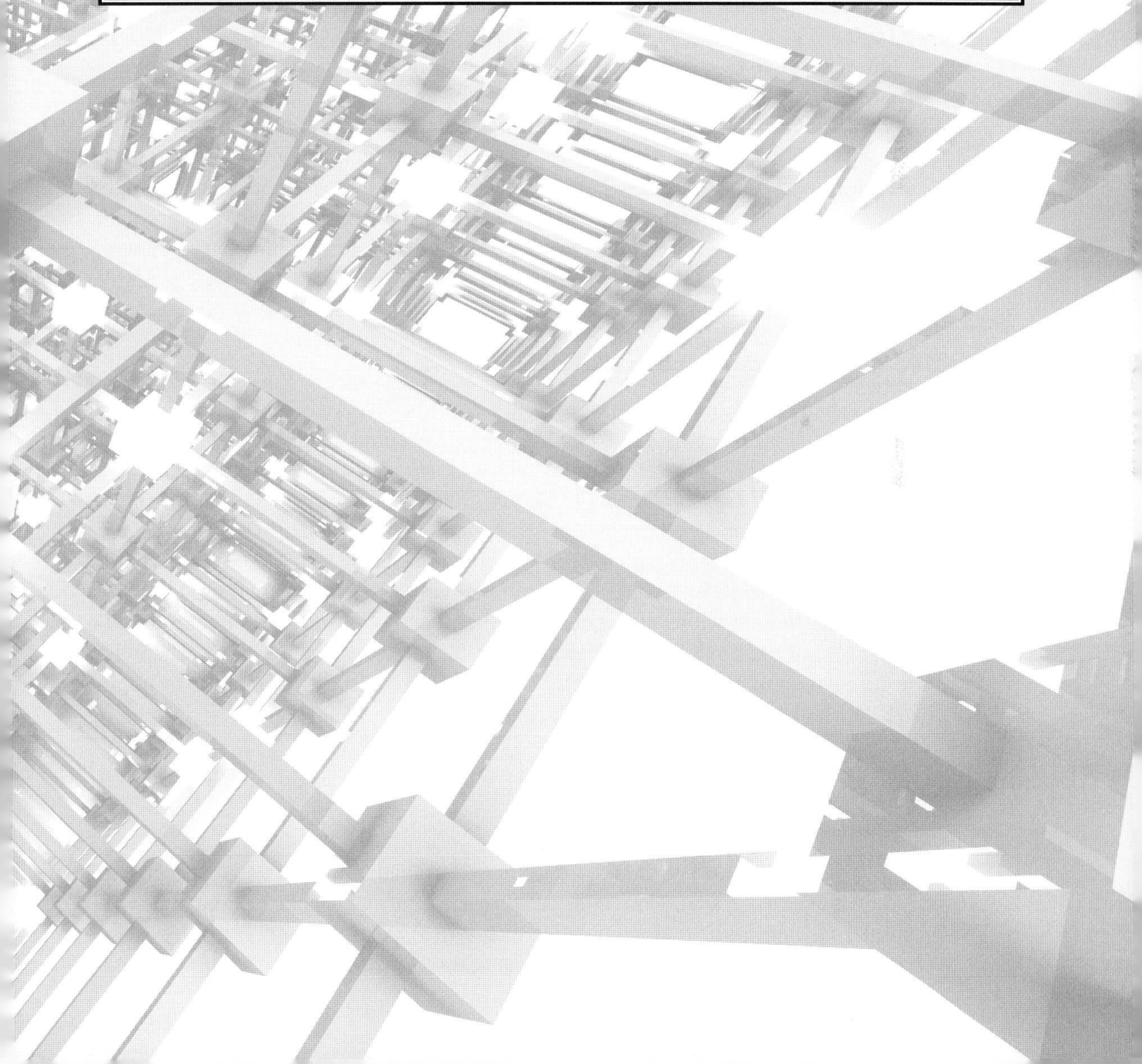

## Preliminaries

In this chapter, we consider the input to problems to be an $n \times n$ digitized black-and-white picture. That is, the input can be viewed as a matrix of data in which every data element is either a 0 or a 1, where a 0 represents a white background data item and a 1 represents a black foreground data item. These pieces of data are often referred to as "picture elements," or *pixels*, where the interpretation of the image is that it is a black image on a white background. The set of black pixels, represented by the 1s, is often referred to as a *digital image*. The terminology and assumptions that we use in this chapter represent the norm in the field of image processing.

Readers must be careful to recalibrate their expectations. In most of the preceding chapters, the input consisted of $n$ data elements, whereas in this chapter the input is of size $n^2$, *i.e.*, an $n \times n$ image. Therefore, a *linear time* sequential algorithm will run in $\Theta(n^2)$ time, not in $\Theta(n)$ time. If the input data is to be sorted on a RAM, then an optimal worst-case comparison-based sequential sorting algorithm will run in $\Theta(n^2 \log n^2) = \Theta(n^2 \log n)$ time, not in $\Theta(n \log n)$ time.

Since we want to map the $n \times n$ image directly onto a mesh of size $n^2$, we assume that pixel $p_{i,j}$ resides in mesh processor $P_{i,j}$. Again, we need to recalibrate. Given a mesh of size $n^2$, the communication diameter is $\Theta(n)$. So, for any problem that might require pixels at opposite ends of the mesh to be combined in some way, a lower bound for the running time of an algorithm to solve the problem is $\Omega(n)$. Note that the bisection width is also $\Theta(n)$.

## Transitive Closure of a Binary Matrix

There is an important result that we will use in this chapter concerned with determining the transitive closure of a matrix. Let $G$ be a directed graph with $n$ vertices, represented by an adjacency matrix $A$. That is, $A(i,j) = 1$ if and only if there is a *directed* edge in $G$ *from* vertex $i$ to vertex $j$. Otherwise, $A(i,j) = 0$. The *transitive closure* of $A$, which is written as $A^*$, is an $n \times n$ matrix such that $A^*(i,j) = 1$ if and only if there is a *directed* path in $G$ from vertex $i$ to vertex $j$. $A^*(i,j) = 0$ otherwise.

It is important to note that both $A$ and $A^*$ are binary matrices. That is, $A$ and $A^*$ are matrices in which all entries are either 0 or 1. Consider the effect of "multiplying" matrix $A$ by itself in order to obtain the matrix we denote as $A^2$, where the usual method of matrix multiplication is modified by replacing addition (+) with OR ($\vee$) and multiplication ($\times$) with AND ($\wedge$). Notice that an entry $A^2(i,j) = 1$ if and only if either

- $A(i,j) = 1$ or
- $A(i,k) = 1$ AND $A(k,j) = 1$ for some $k$.

That is, $A^2(i,j) = 1$ if and only if there exists a path of length no more than two from vertex $i$ to vertex $j$. Now, consider the matrix $A^3$, which can be computed in a similar fashion from $A^2$ and $A$. Notice that $A^3(i,j) = 1$ if and only if there exists a path from vertex $i$ to vertex $j$ that consists of three or fewer edges. Continuing this line of thought, notice that the matrix $A^n$ is such that $A^n(i, j) = 1$ if and only if there exists a path from vertex $i$ to vertex $j$ that consists of $n$ or fewer edges (see Exercises). That is, $A^n$ contains information about the *existence* of a directed path in the graph $G$ from vertex $i$ to vertex $j$, for every pair of vertices $(i, j)$. The matrix $A^n$, which is often referred to as the *connectivity matrix*, represents the transitive closure of $A$. That is, $A^n = A^*$.

Consider a sequential solution to the problem of determining the transitive closure of an $n \times n$ matrix $A$. Based on the preceding discussion, it is clear that the transitive closure can be determined by multiplying $A$ by itself $n$ times. Since the traditional matrix multiplication algorithm for two $n \times n$ matrices runs in $\Theta(n^3)$ time, we know that the transitive closure of $A$ can be determined in $O(n \times n^3) = O(n^4)$ time. So the question is, within the context of a traditional $\Theta(n^3)$ time matrix multiplication algorithm, can we do better?

Consider matrix $A^2$. Once $A^2$ has been determined, we can multiply it by $A$ to arrive at $A^3$. Alternately, we can multiply $A^2 \times A^2$ in order to obtain $A^4$. Since a matrix multiplication runs in $\Theta(n^3)$ time, then both $A^2 \times A$ and $A^2 \times A^2$ can be determined in $\Theta(n^3)$ time. Therefore, if our interest is in determining $A^n$ using the least number of matrix multiplications, it makes more sense to determine $A^2 \times A^2 = A^4$ rather than $A^2 \times A = A^3$. Continuing along this path of matrix multiplication doubling, we will either determine or overshoot $A^n$ after $\Theta(\log n)$ such matrix multiplications. It is important to note that it does not matter if we overshoot $A^n$ as $A^{n+c} = A^n$ for any positive integer $c$ (see Exercises). Therefore, if we perform $\Theta(\log n)$ matrix multiplication operations, each time squaring the most recently obtained matrix, we can determine the transitive closure in $\Theta(n^3 \log n)$ time.

In fact, we can produce the matrix $A^n$ even more efficiently, as follows. Define a binary matrix $A_k$ so that $A_k(i, j) = 1$ if and only if there is a path from vertex $i$ to vertex $j$ *using no intermediate vertex with label greater than k*. Given the matrix $A$, an algorithm can be designed that will iteratively transform $A_0 = A$ to $A_n = A^n = A^*$ through a series of intermediate matrix computations of $A_k$, $0 < k < n$.

We define $A_k(i, j) = 1$ if and only if

- there is a path from vertex $i$ to vertex $j$ using no intermediate vertex greater than $k - 1$, or
- there is a path from vertex $i$ to vertex $k$ using no intermediate vertex greater than $k - 1$ and there is a path from vertex $k$ to vertex $j$ using no intermediate vertex greater than $k - 1$.

We now present *Warshall's algorithm* to determine the transitive closure of a Boolean matrix.

```
for k=1 to n, do
  for i=1 to n, do
    for j=1 to n, do
      A_k(i, j) = A_{k-1}(i, j) ∨ [A_{k-1}(i, k) ∧ A_{k-1}(k, j)]
```

While the running time of Warshall's algorithm on a RAM is $\Theta(n^3)$, notice that the algorithm utilizes $\Theta(n^2)$ additional memory. This is due to the fact that at the $k^{th}$ iteration of the outermost loop, the previous iteration's matrix $A_{k-1}$ is retained in memory.

F.L. Van Scoy has shown that given an $n \times n$ adjacency matrix $A$ mapped onto a mesh of size $n^2$ such that $A(i, j)$ is mapped to processor $P_{i,j}$, the transitive closure of $A$ can be determined in optimal $\Theta(n)$ time. Details of this algorithm are presented in Chapter 12.

**Notes on Terminology:** Since pixels are mapped to processors of a fine-grained mesh in a natural fashion, we tend to think about pixels and processors as coupled when designing mesh algorithms. Therefore, when there is no confusion, we will use the terms "pixel" and "processor" interchangeably in describing fine-grained mesh algorithms.

## Component Labeling

In this section, we consider the problem of uniquely labeling every maximally connected component in an image. The solution to this *component labeling problem* is critical to being able to perform image analysis tasks such as recognizing shapes and developing relationships among objects.

Specifically, given a digitized black-and-white picture, viewed as a black image on a white background, we consider the problem of uniquely labeling each of the distinct figures, *i.e.*, black components, in the picture.

It is often convenient to recast the component-labeling problem in graph theoretic terms. Consider every black pixel to be a vertex. Consider that an edge exists between every pair of vertices represented by neighboring black pixels. We say that pixels $x$ and $y$ are *neighbors* if and only if $x$ is directly above, below, left of, or right of $y$. This 4-*adjacency* notion of neighbors means that pixels that are diagonally adjacent are not considered neighbors for the purpose of this problem. However, if one does consider diagonally adjacent pixels as neighbors, the asymptotic running time of our component-labeling algorithms would not be affected.

The goal of a component-labeling algorithm is to label uniquely every maximally connected set of pixels/vertices. Although the unique label chosen for every component is irrelevant, in this book we will choose to label every component with the minimum label over any pixel (vertex) in the figure (component). This is a fairly standard means of labeling components (see Figure 11-1).

### RAM

Initially, let's consider a sequential algorithm to label the maximally connected components of an $n \times n$ digitized black-and-white picture. Suppose we use a straightforward propagation-based algorithm.

(a) (b)

**FIGURE 11-1** (a) *A digitized* $4 \times 4$ *picture. The interpretation is that the picture represents a black image on a white background.* (b) *The same* $4 \times 4$ *picture with its maximally connected components labeled under 4-adjacency definition of connectedness. Every component is labeled with the minimum label of any pixel in its component. In this example, the pixel labels are given by their row-major indices, with values* $1, \ldots, 16$.

Initialize the *component label* for every pixel to *null*. Initialize the *vertex label* for every pixel to the concatenation of its row and column indices. Now traverse the image in row-major order. When a black pixel is encountered for which the component label is *null*, assign that pixel's vertex label as its component label. Next, use a backtracking procedure to propagate this component label to all of the pixel's black neighbors, which recursively propagate this label to all of their black neighbors, and so on.

Let's consider the running time of this simple propagation algorithm. Every pixel is visited once during the row-major scan. Now consider the backtracking phase of the algorithm, in which both black and white pixels can be visited. The black pixels can be visited as the propagation continues and the white pixels serve as stopping points to the backtracking. Fortunately, every component is only labeled once, and if backtracking is done properly, every black pixel is only visited a fixed number of times during a given backtracking/propagation phase. That is, when a black pixel $p$ is visited, no more than three of its neighbors need to be considered (why?) and in the recursion, control returns to the pixel $p$ three times before it returns control to its parent pixel, *i.e.*, the black pixel visited immediately prior to visiting $p$ for the first time. A white pixel can only be visited by four of its neighbors during some propagation phase, each time returning control immediately. Therefore, the running time of the algorithm is linear in the number of pixels, which is $\Theta(n^2)$.

### Mesh

Now, let's consider a mesh algorithm to solve the component-labeling problem. Assume that we are given an $n \times n$ digitized black-and-white picture mapped in a natural fashion onto a mesh of size $n^2$ so that pixel $p_{i,j}$ is mapped to processor $P_{i,j}$. The first algorithm we might consider is a direct implementation of the sequential propagation algorithm. A straightforward implementation of a propagation algorithm will yield a $\Theta(n^2)$ time algorithm, which is unacceptable for this architecture.

We now consider the natural parallel variant of a propagation-type algorithm. That is, every processor that maintains a black pixel continually exchanges its current component label with each of its, at most four, black neighbors. During each such exchange, a processor accepts the minimum of its current label and that of its black neighbors as its new component label. The effect is that the minimum vertex/processor label in a component is propagated throughout the component in the minimum time required, *i.e.*, using the minimum number of communication links required, assuming that all messages must remain within a component. In fact, this label reaches every processor in its component in the minimum time necessary to broadcast the label between them, assuming that all messages must remain within the component.

Therefore, if all the maximally connected components are relatively small, this mesh propagation algorithm is efficient. Notice that "relatively small" refers to the internal diameter of a figure, *i.e.*, the maximum of the minimum distance between any two black pixels in a figure when one is only allowed to consider distance between neighboring pixels. In fact, if every figure is enclosed in some $k \times k$ region, then the running time of the algorithm is $O(k^2)$. This is efficient if $k^2 = O(n)$. So, if we regard $k$ as constant, then the running time is $\Theta(1)$ (see Figure 11-2).

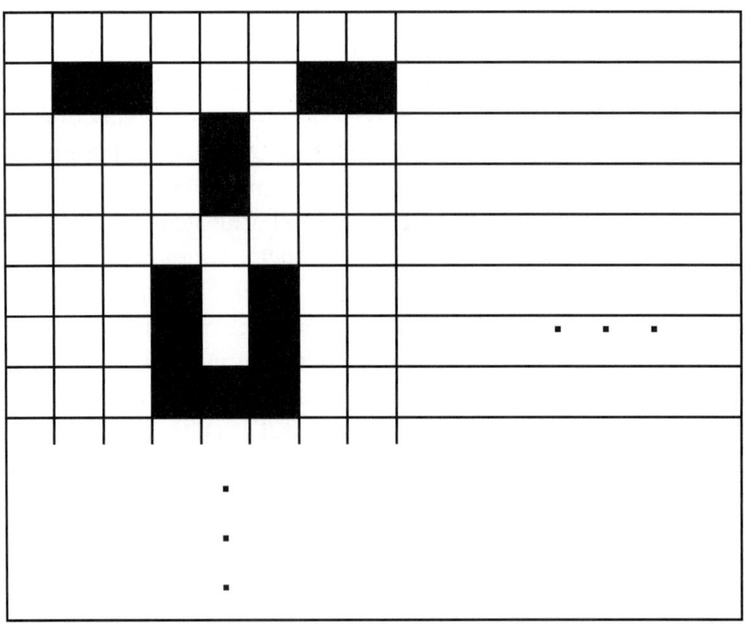

**FIGURE 11-2** *Every connected component is confined to a* $3 \times 3$ *region. In such situations, the mesh propagation algorithm will run in* $\Theta(1)$ *time.*

Now, let's consider the worst-case running time of this parallel propagation algorithm. Suppose we have a picture that consists of a single figure. Further, suppose that the internal diameter, *i.e.*, the maximum distance between two black pixels, assuming that one travels only between pixels that are members of the figure, is large. For example, consider Figure 11-3, which includes a "spiral" on the left and a "snake" on the right.

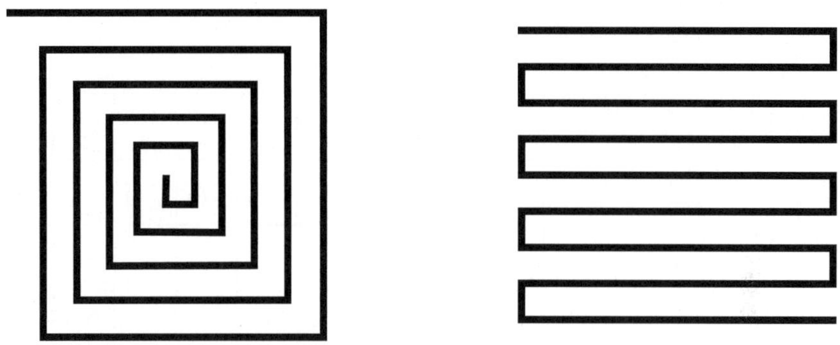

**FIGURE 11-3** *Two problematic figures. A "spiral" is shown on the left and a "snake" is shown on the right.*

We see that it is easy to construct a figure that has an internal diameter of $\Theta(n^2)$. This propagation algorithm will run in $\Theta(n^2)$ time for such a figure. So, our parallel propagation algorithm has a running time of $\Omega(1)$ and $O(n^2)$. For many situations, we might be willing to accept such an algorithm if we know that these troublesome situations, *i.e.*, those that result in the worst-case running time, will rarely occur. There may be situations in which, even if such an image might occur, we know that no figure of interest could have such characteristics, and we could then modify the algorithm so that it terminates after some more reasonable predetermined amount of time. However, there are many situations in which we care about minimizing the general worst-case running time.

We now consider a divide-and-conquer solution to the general component-labeling problem on a mesh. This divide-and-conquer algorithm should feel familiar in its implementation and has the feature of exhibiting an asymptotically optimal worst-case running time.

1. **Divide** the problem into 4 subproblems, each of size $(n/2) \times (n/2)$.
2. **Recursively** label each of the independent subproblems.
3. **Stitch** the partial solutions together to obtain a labeled image.

As with many divide-and-conquer algorithms, the Stitch step is crucial. Notice that once each $(n/2) \times (n/2)$ subproblem has been solved, there are only $O(n)$ pixels in each such submesh, those on the submesh border, that might have a neighbor with a different label. Thus, for every *local component, i.e.*, a component completely contained within its $(n/2) \times (n/2)$ region, the recursive label must be correct. Only those *global components, i.e.*, components of one of the $(n/2) \times (n/2)$ regions with at least one pixel on an edge between neighboring submeshes, might need to be relabeled (see Figure 11-4). Therefore, while the initial problem had $\Theta(n^2)$ pieces of data (pixels), after the recursive solutions were obtained, there are only $O(n)$ critical pieces of information necessary to resolve the problem. We can stitch the partial results together as follows.

| | | | | | | | |
|---|---|---|---|---|---|---|---|
| | | | | | | | |
| | 4 | 4 | | | 20 | 20 | |
| | | | | | | | |
| | | | 16 | 27 | | | 32 |
| | | | | | | | 54 |
| | | 39 | | | | | 54 |
| | | 39 | 39 | 57 | 57 | | 54 |
| | | | | | | | |

**FIGURE 11-4** *An* $8 \times 8$ *image after labeling each of its* $4 \times 4$ *quadrants. Notice that the component labels come from the shuffled row-major indexing scheme, starting the numbering of the processors with* 1. *The local components that are completely contained in a quadrant, i.e., components labeled* 4 *and* 20, *do not need to be considered further. The remaining components have pixels on the border between quadrants and are considered during the global relabeling procedure.*

First, each processor $P$ containing a black pixel on the border of one of the $(n/2) \times (n/2)$ regions examines its neighbors that are located in a distinct $(n/2) \times (n/2)$ region. For each such border processor $P$, there are either one or two such neighbors. For each neighboring black pixel in a different region, processor $P$ generates a record containing the identity and current component label of both $P$

and the neighboring pixel. Notice that there are at most two records generated by any processor containing a border vertex. However, also notice that for every record generated by one processor, a "mirror image" record is generated by its neighboring processor. Next, compress these $O(n)$ records into an $n^{1/2} \times n^{1/2}$ region within the $n \times n$ mesh. In the $n^{1/2} \times n^{1/2}$ region, use these $O(n)$ unordered edge records to solve the component-labeling problem on the underlying graph.

Notice that the stitch step can perform the compression operation by sorting the necessary records in $\Theta(n)$ time. Once the critical data is compressed to an $n^{1/2} \times n^{1/2}$ region, we can perform a logarithmic number of iterations to merge components together until they are maximally connected. Each such iteration involves a fixed number of sort-based operations, including concurrent reads and writes. Therefore, each iteration is performed in $\Theta(n^{1/2})$ time. Hence, the time required for computing maximally connected components within the $n^{1/2} \times n^{1/2}$ region is $\Theta(n^{1/2} \log n)$. Completing the stitch step involves a complete $\Theta(n)$ time concurrent read so that every pixel in the image can determine its new label. Since the compression and concurrent read steps dominate the running time of the Stitch routine, the running time of the algorithm is given by $T(n^2) = T(n^2/4) + \Theta(n)$, which sums to $T(n^2) = \Theta(n)$. It should be noted that the solution to this recurrence can be obtained by substituting $N$ for $n^2$ and applying the Master Theorem. Notice that this is a time-optimal algorithm for a mesh of size $n^2$. However, the total cost of such an algorithm is $\Theta(n^3)$, while the problem has a lower bound of $\Omega(n^2)$ total cost.

We now consider an interesting alternative to the stitch step. In the approach that we presented, we reduced the amount of data from $\Theta(n^2)$ to $O(n)$, compressed the $O(n)$ data, and then spent time leisurely working on it. Instead, we can consider creating a cross-product with the reduced amount of critical data. That is, once we have reduced the data to $O(n)$ critical pieces, representing an undirected graph, we can create an adjacency matrix. Notice that the adjacency matrix will easily fit into the $n \times n$ mesh. Once the adjacency matrix is created, we can perform the $\Theta(n)$ time transitive closure algorithm of Van Scoy mentioned at the beginning of the chapter in order to determine maximally connected components. The minimum vertex label can be chosen as the label of each connected component, and a concurrent read by all pixels can be used for the final relabeling. Although the running time of this algorithm remains at $\Theta(n)$, it is instructive to show different approaches to dealing with a situation in which one can drastically reduce the size of the set of data under consideration.

## Convex Hull

In this section, we consider the problem of marking the extreme points of the convex hull for each *labeled set of pixels* in a given image. Notice that a labeled set of pixels need not be a connected component. In fact, the sets might be intertwined and their convex hulls might overlap, as shown in Figure 11-5.

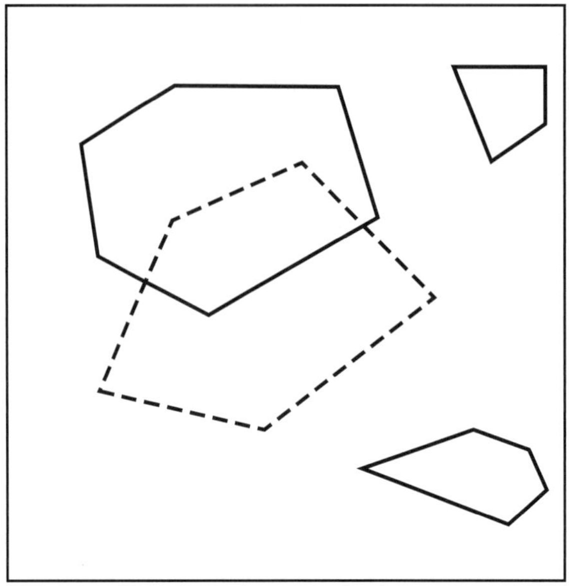

**FIGURE 11-5** *An illustration of overlapping convex hulls of, not necessarily connected, labeled sets of pixels.*

For this problem, it is useful to order the processors of a mesh by *snake-like indexing*. This indexing uses a labeling of the processors that follows the pattern on the right side of Figure 11-3. So, the top-left processor in the mesh is labeled 1. The rightmost processor on the first row is labeled $n$. The rightmost processor on the second row is labeled $n + 1$. The leftmost processor on the second row is labeled $2n$, and so forth. That is, the first row is labeled $1 \ldots n$ in a left to right fashion, the second row is labeled $n + 1 \ldots 2n$ in a right to left fashion, and so on. In general, rows with odd indices have processors numbered from left to right, and rows with even indices have processors number from right to left. See Figure 11-6.

Suppose that we have a mesh of size $n^2$ and that we associate every processor $P_{i,j}$ with the lattice point $(i,j)$. Suppose that every processor contains a label in the range of $0 \ldots n^2$, where the interpretation is that 0 represents the background and that values $1 \ldots n^2$ represent labels of foreground pixels. Finally, assume that we want to determine the convex hull for every distinctly labeled set of points.

We have discussed the general convex hull problem for a variety of models in a preceding chapter. Clearly, the image input considered in this section can be simply and efficiently converted to the more general form of 2-dimensional point data input. From such input, the algorithms of the previous chapter can be invoked in a straightforward fashion. Our goal in this section, however, is to introduce some

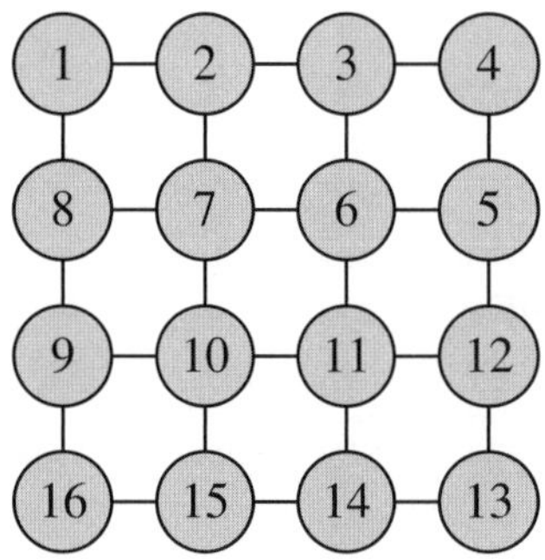


**FIGURE 11-6** *Snake-like indexing of the processors of a mesh, shown for a mesh of size* 16. *Processors are numbered consecutively in consecutive rows, with the direction of the numbering alternating by row.*

new techniques, which will result in a greatly simplified routine for a lattice of labeled points imposed on a mesh.

Initially, we determine the extreme points for each labeled set as restricted to each row. Once this is done, we note that there are no more than 2 possible extreme points in any row for any labeled set. Within each such set, every row-restricted extreme point can consider all other row-restricted extreme points of its set and determine whether or not it is contained in some triangle formed by the remaining points, in which case it is not an extreme point. Further, if no such triangle can be found, then it is an extreme point. The algorithm follows.

Initially in every row, we wish to identify the extreme points for every labeled set as restricted to the row. So, in a given row, the extreme points of a set are simply the, at most two, outermost nonzero points of the set. This identification can be done by a simple row rotation, simultaneously for all rows, so that every processor $P_{i,j}$ can view all of the data within its row and decide whether or not its point at $(i, j)$ is a row-restricted extreme point for its labeled set.

Next, sort all of these row-restricted extreme points by label so that after the sort is complete, elements with the same label are stored in consecutively indexed processors according to the snake-like indexing. Although there are $O(n^2)$ such points, it is important to note that for any label, there are at most $2n$ such points, *i.e.*, at most two points per each row. Since we use snake-like indexing of the processors, all of the row-restricted extreme points for a given set are now in a set of consecutively indexed processors. Therefore, we can perform rotations within such ordered intervals. These rotations are similar to row and column rotations but work within intervals that might cover fractions of one or more rows. Thus, simultaneously for all intervals, *i.e.*, labeled sets, rotate the set of row-restricted extreme points. During the rotation, suppose a processor is responsible for lattice point $X$.

Then as a new lattice point $Y$ arrives, the processor responsible for $X$ performs the following operations.

- If no other point is stored in the processor, then the processor stores $Y$.
- Suppose the processor has previously stored one other point, say, $U$. Then the processor will store $Y$. However, if $X$, $Y$, and $U$ are on the same line, then the processor eliminates the interior point of these three.
- Suppose the processor has previously stored two other points, $U$ and $V$, before $Y$ arrives.
  - If $X$ is in the triangle determined by $U$, $V$, and $Y$, then the processor determines that $X$ is not an extreme point.
  - Otherwise, if $Y$ is on a line segment determined by $X$ and either $U$ or $V$, then of the three collinear points, $X$ is not interior. This is because if $X$ were interior, the previous case would apply. Discard the interior of the three collinear points.
  - Otherwise, the processor should eliminate whichever of $U$, $V$, and $Y$ is inside the angle formed by $X$ and the other two, with $X$ as the vertex of the angle. Note the "eliminated" point is not eliminated as a possible extreme point, just as a determiner of whether $X$ is an extreme point.

If after the rotation, the processor responsible for row-restricted extreme point $X$ has not determined that $X$ should be eliminated, then $X$ is an extreme point.

A final concurrent read can be used to send the row-restricted extreme points back to their originating processors and the extreme points can then be marked for every labeled set of pixels.

#### Running Time

The analysis of running time is straightforward since we need not solve a recursive relation. The algorithm consists of a fixed number of $\Theta(n)$ time rotations and sort-based operations. Therefore, the running time of this algorithm is $\Theta(n)$. Notice that the cost of the algorithm is $\Theta(n^3)$ and we know that the problem can be solved sequentially in $\Theta(n^2 \log n)$ time by the traditional convex hull algorithm on arbitrary point data.

## Distance Problems

In this section, we consider problems of determining distances between labeled sets of pixels. Specifically, we consider the following.

1. Given a labeled set of, not necessarily connected, pixels, determine for every labeled set, a nearest distinctly labeled set.
2. Given two labeled sets of, not necessarily connected, pixels, determine the distance between the two sets using the Hausdorff metric as the distance measure.

### All-Nearest Neighbor between Labeled Sets

In this section, we consider the *all-nearest neighbor between labeled sets problem.* Assume that the input consists of a labeled set of pixels. That is, assume that every processor $P_{i,j}$ is associated with the lattice point $(i, j)$ on a mesh of size $n^2$. As we did in a previous section, assume that every processor contains a label in the range of $0 \ldots n^2$, where the interpretation is that 0 represents the background and that values in the range of $1 \ldots n^2$ represent labels of foreground pixels. Recall pixels in the same labeled set are not necessarily connected.

The problem we are concerned with is that of determining for every labeled set of pixels, the label of a nearest distinctly labeled set of pixels. We first determine, for every pixel, the label and distance to a nearest distinctly labeled pixel. We then determine the minimum of these pixels' nearest-pixel distances over all pixels within a labeled set. Details of the algorithm follow.

The first step is to find, for every labeled processor $P$, a nearest distinctly labeled processor to $P$. To do this, we take advantage of the fact that the pixels are laid out on a grid and that we are using the Euclidean distance as a metric. Suppose that $p$ and $q$ are labeled pixels that are in the same column. Further, let $r$ be a nearest distinctly labeled pixel to $p$ in the same row as $p$, as shown in Figure 11-7. Since we have made no assumption about the labels of $p$ and $q$, *i.e.*, they could be identical or distinct, then with respect to $p$'s row, either $p$ or $r$ is a nearest distinctly labeled pixel to $q$. We refer to this observation as "work-reducing." An algorithm to solve the all-nearest neighbor between labeled sets problem follows.

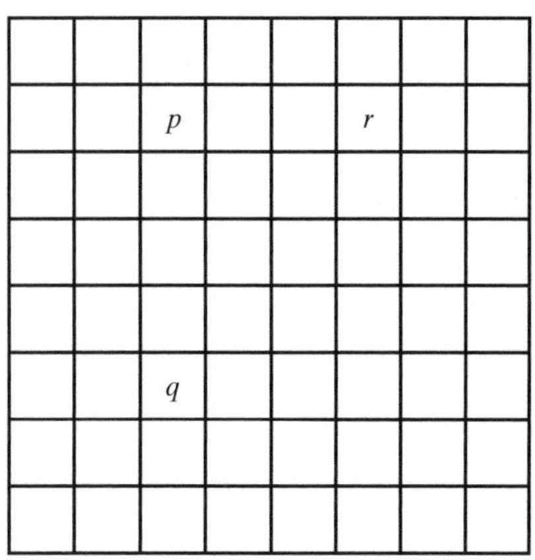


**FIGURE 11-7** *The all-nearest neighbor-between-labeled-sets problem. Suppose p, q, and r are labeled pixels. If r is a closest distinctly labeled pixel in row two to p, then either p or r is a closest distinctly labeled pixel to q among those in row 2.*

1. Perform row rotations simultaneously in every row so that every processor $P_{i,j}$ finds at most two distinctly labeled nearest processors in its row, if they exist. With respect to processor $P_{i,j}$, we denote these nearest distinctly labeled processors as $P_{i,j_1}$ and $P_{i,j_2}$, where either $j_1$ or $j_2$ is equal to $j$ if $P_{i,j}$ is a labeled processor. We need two such processors if the row has foreground pixels with distinct labels, as one of them may have the same label as a processor in column $j$.
2. Perform parallel column rotations simultaneously in every column, where every processor $P_{i,j}$ circulates its information, labels and positions, and the information associated with its row-restricted nearest distinctly labeled processors $P_{i,j_1}$ and $P_{i,j_2}$. During the rotations, every processor is able to determine its nearest distinctly labeled processor, using the work-reducing observation.
3. Sort all of the near neighbor information by initial pixel label.
4. Within every labeled set of data, perform a semigroup operation, using the operation of minimum as applied to the nearest distinct label distances, and a broadcast so that every pixel knows the label of a nearest distinctly labeled set to its set.
5. Finally, use a concurrent read so that each labeled pixel can bring the final result back to its initial processor.

### Running Time

The algorithm just presented is dominated by a row rotation, column rotation, semigroup operation, and sort-based operations. Therefore, given an $n \times n$ mesh, the running time of this algorithm is $\Theta(n)$. Notice that the cost of this algorithm is $\Theta(n^3)$, which is suboptimal, as the problem can be solved in $O(n^2 \log n)$ time on a RAM.

### Hausdorff Metric for Digital Images

Let $A$ and $B$ be nonempty, closed, bounded subsets of a Euclidean space $\mathbb{R}^k$. The *Hausdorff metric, $H(A,B)$*, is used to measure how well each of these sets approximates the other. In general, the Hausdorff metric has the following properties.

- $H(A,B)$ is small if every point of $A$ is close to some point of $B$ and every point of $B$ is close to some point of $A$.
- $H(A,B)$ is large if some point of $A$ is far from every point of $B$, or some point of $B$ is far from every point of $A$.

Formally, we can define the Hausdorff metric as follows. Let $d$ be the Euclidean metric for $\mathbb{R}^k$. For $x \in \mathbb{R}^k$, $\phi \neq Y \subset \mathbb{R}^k$, define $d(x,Y) = \min\{d(x,y) \mid y \in Y\}$. Let $H^*(A,B) = \max\{d(a,B) \mid a \in A\}$, where $H^*(A,B)$ is called the "one-way" or "nonsymmetric" Hausdorff distance. Note that $H^*(A,B)$ is not truly a "distance" in the sense of a metric function. The Hausdorff metric, which is indeed a metric function when applied to sets $A$ and $B$ that are nonempty, bounded, and closed, is defined by $H(A,B) = \max\{H^*(A,B), H^*(B,A)\}$. This definition is equivalent to the statement that $H(A,B) = \varepsilon$ if $\varepsilon$ is the minimum of all positive numbers $r$ for which each of $A$ and $B$ is contained in the $r$-neighborhood of the other, where the $r$-neighborhood of $Y$ in $\mathbb{R}^k$ is the set of all points in $\mathbb{R}^k$ that are less than $r$ distant from some point in $Y$. See Figure 11-8 for an example of $H(A,B)$.

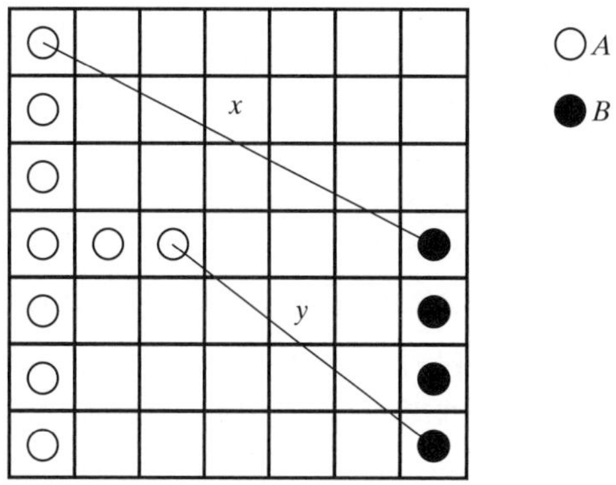


**FIGURE 11-8** *An example of the Hausdorff metric. The distances x and y respectively mark a furthest member of A from B and a furthest member of B from A.* $H(A,B) = \max\{x,y\}$.

Suppose that $A$ and $B$ are finite sets of points in $\mathbb{R}^2$ or $\mathbb{R}^3$. Further, suppose that these points represent black pixels corresponding to digital images. That is, suppose $A$ and $B$ represent distinct digital images in the same dimensional space. Then in order to determine whether or not the probability is high that $A$ and $B$ represent the same physical object, one might consider the result of applying a rigid motion $M$, *e.g.*, translation, rotation, and/or reflection, to $B$ and evaluating the result of $H(A,M(B))$. If for some $M$, $H(A,M(B))$ is small, then in certain situations, there is a good chance that $A$ and $B$ represent the same physical object. However, if no rigid motion translates $B$ close to $A$ in the Hausdorff sense, it is unlikely that $A$ and $B$ represent the same object. Of course, in some contexts a generalization provides a more satisfying conclusion. That is, instead of trying to approximate $A$ by $M(B)$, we might try approximating a magnification or shrinking $S(A)$ by $M(B)$ with respect to the Hausdorff metric.

It is interesting to note that two sets in a Euclidean space can occupy approximately the same space and yet have very different geometric features. Although better image recognition might result from a metric that reflects geometric as well as positional similarity, such metrics are often much more difficult to work with, both conceptually and computationally.

A simple, although inefficient, algorithm for computing the Hausdorff metric for two digital images $A$ and $B$, each contained in an $n \times n$ digital picture, is described below. The algorithm is a straightforward implementation of the definition of the Hausdorff metric as applied to digital images. As we outline a more efficient algorithm in the Exercises, we will only discuss the current algorithm's implementation for a RAM.

1. For every black pixel $a \in A$, compute the distance $d(a,b)$ from $a$ to every point $b \in B$ and compute $d(a,B) = \min\{d(a,b) | b \in B\}$. For a RAM, this step runs in $O(n^4)$ time, since each of the $O(n^2)$ black pixels of $A$ is compared with each of the $O(n^2)$ black pixels of $B$.
2. Compute $H^*(A,B) = \max\{d(a,B) | a \in A\}$ by a semigroup operation. This step runs in $\Theta(n^2)$ time on a RAM.
3. Interchange the roles of $A$ and $B$ and repeat steps 1 and 2 to compute $H^*(B,A)$.
4. Compute $H(A,B) = \max\{H^*(A,B), H^*(B,A)\}$. This step runs in $\Theta(1)$ time.

The algorithm above has a running time dominated by its first step, which runs in $O(n^4)$ time on a RAM. Clearly, the running time of the algorithm leaves much to be desired. Indeed, a simple and more efficient algorithm for computing the Hausdorff metric between two digital images on a RAM can be given using techniques presented in this chapter. This problem appears in the Exercises.

## Image Processing on a Cluster

Clusters are typically targeted at solving problems involving large data and/or large computation. In general, compared to the storage and computation available, problems involving images are often relatively small. That is, it typically does not make sense to solve problems on a cluster for an individual image in terms of spreading the image across a cluster and using the cluster to solve a problem in parallel. The reason for this is that the communication time significantly dominates the computation time, rendering such a solution strategy unreasonable. However, a cluster would make sense given a situation where one is interested in using a cluster as a high-throughput network of processors in order to solve problems simultaneously on multiple images.

In terms of utilizing parallel computing to solve problems for individual images, it often makes sense to use a computing system that involves an individual processor, *i.e.*, a standard multi-core processor, with an attached computational unit. For example, experimentation shows that it is often effective to solve a series of problems on an individual image on a single processor system with an attached GPGPU (General Purpose Graphics Processing Unit). Therefore, an efficient solution to many an image processing problem requires a combination of medium-grained and fine-grained processing. That is, a combination of computing on the multi-core system combined with fine-grained SIMD computing on the GPGPU. Note that the GPGPU typically contains several orders of magnitude more processors, where each of the processors is quite simple, but where groups or blocks of such simple processors can operate in a synchronous fashion.

## Summary

In this chapter, we examine several fundamental problems involving digitized pictures. These problems typically fall into the broad field of image processing. Problems examined include component labeling, determining the convex hulls of figures, and problems of distances between sets of pixels, including that of computing the Hausdorff distance between two digital images, a tool for image pattern matching. We present both RAM and mesh solutions in this chapter. In particular, the mesh is a natural architecture for implementing efficient algorithms on images because of the natural mapping of an image to a mesh.

## Chapter Notes

This chapter focuses on fundamental problems in image analysis for the RAM and mesh. These problems make up a nice vehicle to present interesting paradigms. Many of the mesh algorithms presented in this chapter are derived from algorithms presented by R. Miller & Q.F. Stout in *Parallel Algorithms for Regular Architectures* (The MIT Press, 1996). These algorithms include the component-labeling algorithm, the all-nearest-neighbor-between-labeled-sets algorithm, and the minimum internal distance within connected components algorithm. The book by R. Miller and Q.F. Stout also contains details of some of the data movement operations that were presented and utilized in this chapter, including rotation operations based on ordered intervals and so on. The ingenious algorithm used to compute the transitive closure of an $n \times n$ matrix on a RAM was devised by S. Warshall in his paper "A theorem on Boolean matrices," in the *Journal of the ACM* 9 (1962), 11–12. Further, in 1980, F.L. Van Scoy ("The parallel recognition of classes of graphs," *IEEE Transactions on Computers* 29 (1980), 563–570) showed that the transitive closure of an $n \times n$ matrix could be computed in $\Theta(n)$ time on an $n \times n$ mesh.

A classic reference concerning the Hausdorff metric is *Hyperspaces of Sets*, by S.B. Nadler, Jr. (Marcel Dekker, New York, 1978).

The paper that introduced the notion of digitally continuous functions (used in the exercises) is A. Rosenfeld, "'Continuous' functions on digital pictures" in *Pattern Recognition Letters* **4** (1986), 177–184.

## Exercises

1. Given an $n \times n$ digitized image, give an efficient algorithm to determine both *i*) the number of black pixels in the image, and *ii*) the number of white pixels in the image. Present an algorithm and analysis for both the RAM and mesh.
2. Let $A$ be the adjacency matrix of a graph $G$ with $n$ vertices. For integer $k > 0$, let $A^k$ be the $k^{\text{th}}$ power of $A$, as discussed in the chapter.

a. Prove that for $i \neq j$, $A^k(i,j) = 1$ if and only if there is a path in $G$ from vertex $i$ to vertex $j$ that has at most $k$ edges, for $1 \leq k \leq n$.

b. Prove that $A^{n+c} = A^n$ for any positive integer $c$.

**3.** Given an $n \times n$ digitized image in which each pixel is associated with a numerical value, provide an efficient algorithm that will set to zero (0) all of the pixel values that are below the median pixel value of the image. Present analysis for both the RAM and mesh.

**4.** Given an $n \times n$ digitized image for which each pixel is associated with a real number, give an efficient algorithm that will compute for each pixel the average of its number and those of its eight (8) nearest neighbors. Present analysis for both the RAM and mesh.

**5.** Given a labeled $n \times n$ digitized image, give an efficient algorithm to count the number of connected components in the image. Present analysis for both the RAM and mesh.

**6.** Given a labeled $n \times n$ digitized image and a single "marked" pixel somewhere in the image, give an efficient algorithm that will mark all other pixels in the same connected component as the "marked" pixel. Present analysis for both the RAM and mesh.

**7.** Given a labeled $n \times n$ digitized image, give an efficient algorithm to determine the number of pixels in every connected component. Present analysis for both the RAM and mesh.

**8.** Given a labeled $n \times n$ digitized image and one "marked" pixel per component, give an efficient algorithm for every pixel to determine its distance to its marked pixel. Present analysis for both the RAM and mesh.

**9.** Given a labeled $n \times n$ digitized image, give an efficient algorithm to determine a minimum-enclosing box of every connected component. Present analysis for both the RAM and mesh.

**10.** Give an efficient algorithm for computing $H(A,B)$, the Hausdorff metric between $A$ and $B$, where each of $A$ and $B$ is an $n \times n$ digital image. *Hint*: the algorithm presented in the text may be improved upon by using row and column rotations similar to those that appeared in our algorithm for the all-nearest-neighbor-between-labeled-sets problem, modified to allow that a pixel could belong to both $A$ and $B$. Show that your algorithm can be implemented to run in worst-case $\Theta(n^2)$ time on the RAM and in worst-case $\Theta(n)$ time on the mesh.

**11.** Suppose $A$ and $B$ are sets of black pixels for distinct $n \times n$ digital pictures. Let $f: A \rightarrow B$ be a function, *i.e.*, for every (black) pixel $a \in A$, $f(a)$ is a (black) pixel in $B$. Using the 4-adjacency notion of neighboring pixels, we say $f$ is *(digitally) continuous* if for every pair of neighboring pixels $a_0, a_1 \in A$, either

$f(a_0) = f(a_1)$ or $f(a_0)$ and $f(a_1)$ are neighbors in $B$. Prove that the following are equivalent:

- $f: A \to B$ is a digitally continuous function.
- For every connected subset $A_0$ of $A$, the image $f(A_0)$ is a connected subset of $B$.
- Using the Euclidean metric (in which 4-connected neighboring pixels are at distance one apart and non-neighboring pixels are at distance greater than one), for every $a_0 \in A$ and every $\varepsilon \geq 1$, there is a $\delta \geq 1$ such that if $a_1 \in A$ and $d(a_0, a_1) \leq \delta$, then $d[f(a_0), f(a_1)] \leq \varepsilon$.

**12.** Refer to the previous exercise. Let $A$ and $B$ be sets of black pixels within respective $n \times n$ digital pictures. Let $f: A \to B$ be a function. Suppose the value of $f(a)$ can be computed in $\Theta(1)$ time for every $a \in A$. Present an algorithm to determine whether or not the function $f$ is digitally continuous. In the case of the mesh, the algorithm should let every processor know the result of this determination. Give your analysis for the RAM and for the $n \times n$ mesh. Your algorithm should run in $\Theta(n^2)$ time on the RAM and $\Theta(n)$ time on an $n \times n$ mesh.

**13.** *Conway's Game of Life* can be regarded as a population simulation that is implemented on an $n \times n$ digitized picture $A$. The focus of the "game" is the transition between a "parent generation" and a "child generation." The child generation becomes the parent generation for the next transition. In one version of the game, the transition proceeds as follows:

- If in the parent generation $A[i, j]$ is a black pixel and exactly two or three of its nearest 8-neighbors are black, then in the child generation $A[i, j]$ is a black pixel. This simulates life propagated under favorable living conditions. However, if in the parent generation $A[i, j]$ is a black pixel with less than two black 8-neighbors or more than three black 8-neighbors, then in the child generation $A[i, j]$ is a white pixel. This simulates life not propagated due to isolation or overcrowding, respectively.
- If in the parent generation $A[i, j]$ is a white pixel, then in the child generation $A[i, j]$ is a black pixel if and only if exactly three of its nearest 8-neighbors are black. As above, this simulates life propagated or not propagated according to whether conditions are favorable.

Present and analyze an algorithm to compute the child generation matrix $A$ from the parent generation matrix for one transition, for the RAM and the mesh. Your algorithm should run in $\Theta(n^2)$ time for the RAM and in $\Theta(1)$ time for the mesh.

# 12

# Graph Algorithms

In this chapter, we focus on algorithms and paradigms to solve fundamental problems in graph theory, where the input consists of data representing sets of vertices and edges. We present efficient solutions to traditional problems from graph theory, including determining the connected components of a graph, constructing a minimal-cost spanning tree of a connected graph, and determining shortest paths between vertices in a connected graph. The algorithms will be presented for the RAM, the PRAM, and the mesh.

Many important problems can be expressed in terms of graphs, including problems involving power grids, water flow, line-of-sight coverage, relationships between objects, as well as problems involving communication, including telephone land lines, cellular phones and towers, and satellite communications, to name a few. In addition, problems involving general scheduling and routing that are critical to a variety of industrial and governmental concerns can be expressed in terms of graphs, including land and air transport, local and global delivery services, Internet- and cable-based services, and so forth. Tasks for which graphs are often used include the following.

- Given a set of locations, determine the cost between locations, where the cost can be distance, time, or money, to name a few metrics.
- Given a set of objects, determine connectivity between the objects. The resulting graph can represent a network that is internal to devices such as computer chips, cell phones, and gaming systems. Such a graph can also represent networks involving telephone, cable, and satellites, among more macroscopic interconnections.
- Given a set of objects and the network flow between a subset of pairs of the objects, determine the network flow capacity between the objects. This is an important problem in a variety of industries, including those involving water, gas, electric, cable, and Internet.
- Determine an ordered list of tasks. For example, one might create an ordered list of the tasks necessary to build a guitar.

## Terminology

Let $G = (V, E)$ be a graph consisting of a set $V$ of vertices and a set $E$ of edges. The edges, which connect members of $V$, can either all be directed or all undirected, resulting in either a *directed graph* or an *undirected graph*, respectively. That is, given a directed graph $G = (V, E)$, an edge $(a, b) \in E$ represents a directed connection *from* vertex $a$ to vertex $b$, where both $a$, $b \in V$. Given an undirected graph, an edge $(a, b) \in E$ represents an undirected connection, or bidirectional connection, *between* vertices $a$ and $b$. Problems in graph theory typically do not include *i*) *self-edges*, in which an edge connects a vertex to itself, or *ii*) multiple occurrences of an edge. See Figure 12-1 for examples of directed and undirected graphs.

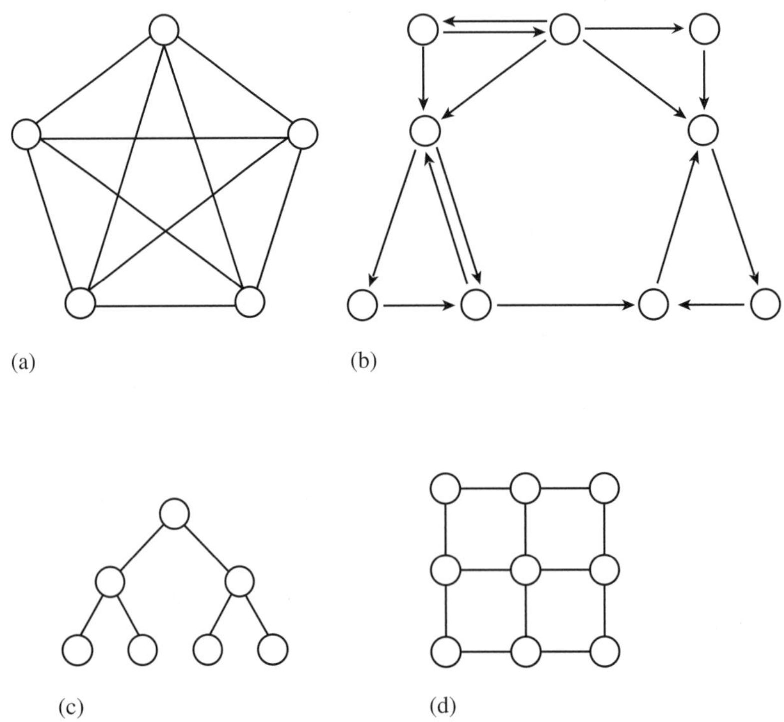


**FIGURE 12-1** *Four sample graphs.* (a) *shows a complete undirected graph of 5 vertices.* (b) *is a directed graph with pairs of vertices* $(u, v)$ *such that the graph has no directed path from u to v.* (c) *is an undirected tree with 7 vertices.* (d) *is an undirected mesh of 9 vertices.*

The number of vertices in $G = (V, E)$ is written as $|V|$ and the number of edges is written as $|E|$. However, for convenience, whenever the number of vertices or number of edges is represented inside of asymptotic notation, we will typically avoid using the absolute value signs since there is no ambiguity. For example, an algorithm that runs in time linear in the sum of the vertices and edges will be said to run in $\Theta(V + E)$ time.

In any description of a graph, we assume that there are unique representations of all vertices and edges. That is, no vertex will have more than one identity and no edge will be represented more than once. Given a directed graph, the maximum number of edges is $|V|(|V|-1)$, while for an undirected graph, the maximum number of unique edges is $|V|(|V|-1)/2$. Therefore, the number of edges in a graph $G=(V,E)$ is such that $|E|=O(V^2)$.

A *complete graph* $G=(V,E)$ is one in which all possible edges are present. That is, in a complete graph, there is an edge between every pair of distinct vertices. A *sparse graph* is one in which there are "relatively few" edges, while a *dense graph* is one in which a "high percentage of possible edges" is present. Alternately, a graph may be termed *sparse* if $|E|/|V|^2$ is "small," while a graph may be referred to as *dense* if $|E|/|V|^2$ is at least of "moderate" size.

Vertex $b$ is said to be *adjacent* to vertex $a$ if and only if $(a,b)\in E$. At times, adjacent vertices will be described as *neighbors.* An edge $(a,b)\in E$ is said to be *incident* on vertices $a$ and $b$. In a *weighted graph*, every edge $(a,b)\in E$ will have an associated weight or cost (see Figure 12-2).

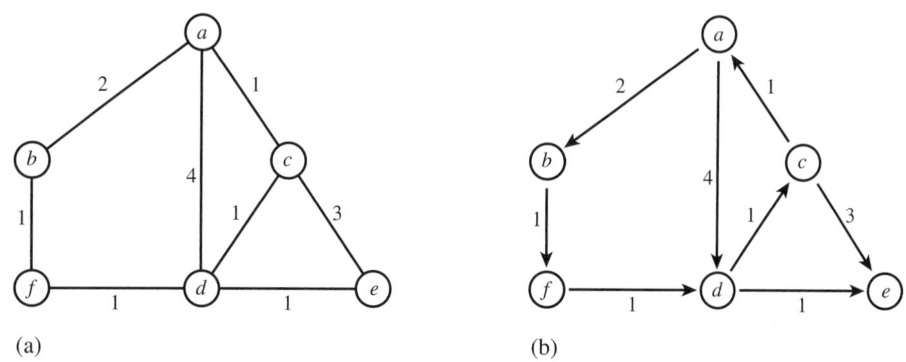


**FIGURE 12-2** *An undirected weighted graph is given in* (a) *that consists of* 8 *pairs of adjacent vertices. Notice in* (a) *that the entire graph is connected since there is a path between every pair of vertices. A directed weighted graph is given in* (b)*, in which paths are not formed between every pair of vertices. In fact, notice that vertex e is isolated in that e does not serve as the source of any nontrivial path. Notice in* (a) *that a minimum-weight path from a to e is* $\langle a,c,d,e\rangle$*, which has a total weight of* 3*, while in* (b) *minimum-weight paths from a to e are* $\langle a,d,e\rangle$ *and* $\langle a,b,f,d,e\rangle$.

A *path* in a graph $G=(V,E)$ is a sequence of vertices $v_1,v_2,\ldots,v_k$ such that $(v_i,v_{i+1})\in E$ for all $1\le i\le k-1$. The *length* of such a path is defined to be the number of *edges* in the path, which in this case is $k-1$. A *simple path* is a path in which all vertices are unique. A *cycle* is a path of length 3 or more in which $v_1=v_k$. A graph is *acyclic* if it has no cycles. Note that a *tree* in which all edges point away from the root is a directed acyclic graph.

An undirected graph is *connected* if and only if there is at least one path from every vertex to every other vertex. Given a graph $G = (V, E)$, a subgraph $S$ of $G$ is a pair $S = (V', E')$, where $V' \subset V$ and $E'$ is a subset of those edges in $E$ that contain vertices only in $V'$. The *connected components* of an undirected graph $G = (V, E)$ are the maximally connected subgraphs of $G$ (see Figure 12-3).

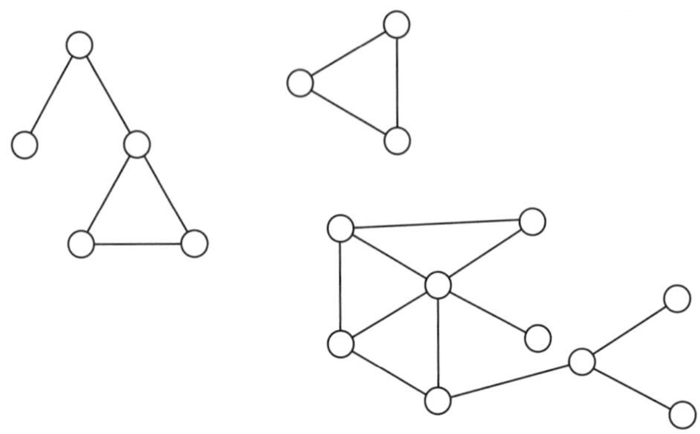

**FIGURE 12-3** *An undirected graph with three connected components.*

A directed graph is called *strongly connected* if and only if there is at least one path from every vertex to every other vertex. If a directed graph is not strongly connected but the underlying graph in which all directed edges are replaced by undirected edges is connected, then the original directed graph is called *weakly connected* (see Figure 12-4).

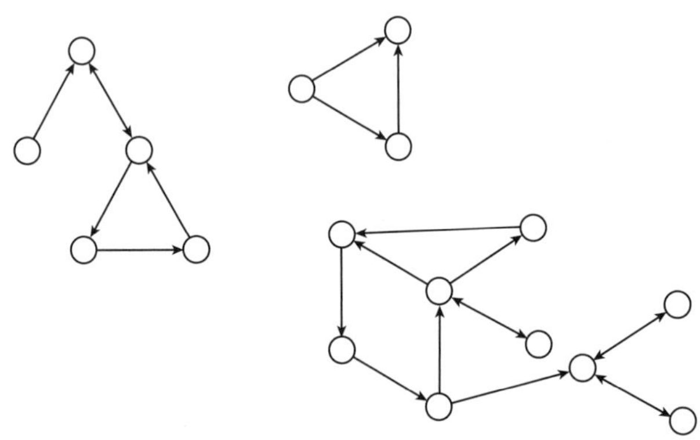

**FIGURE 12-4** *A directed graph with three weakly connected components and seven strongly connected components.*

Let $G = (V, E)$ be a connected graph. We say $e \in E$ is a *bridge edge* of $G$ if the graph $G_e = (V, E \setminus \{e\})$ is disconnected. It is easy to see that if $G$ represents a traffic system, its bridge edges represent potential bottlenecks. We define an *articulation point* of $G$ to be a vertex $v \in V$ with the property that its removal would leave the resulting graph disconnected. That is, $v$ is an articulation point of $G$ if and only if the graph $G_v = (V\setminus\{v\}, E_v)$, where $E_v = \{e \in E \mid e \text{ is not incident on } v\}$, is a disconnected graph. Thus, an articulation point plays a role among vertices analogous to that of a bridge edge among edges. See Figure 12-5 for examples of bridge edges and articulation points.

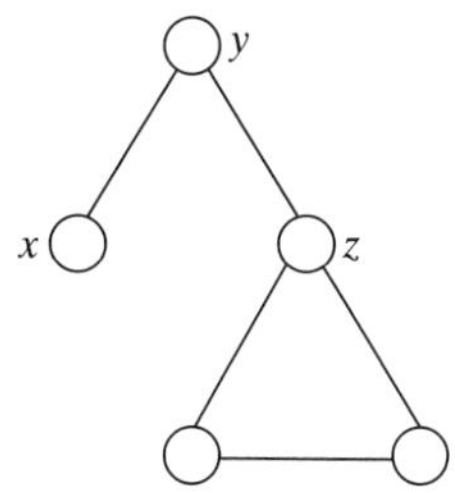


**FIGURE 12-5** *In this graph, $(x,y)$ and $(y,z)$ are bridge edges. The vertices y and z are articulation points.*

In an undirected graph, the *degree of a vertex* is the number of edges incident on the vertex, and the *degree of the graph* is the maximum degree of any vertex in the graph. In a directed graph, the *in-degree* of a vertex is the number of edges that terminate at the vertex and the *out-degree* of a vertex is the number of edges that originate at the vertex (see Figure 12-6).

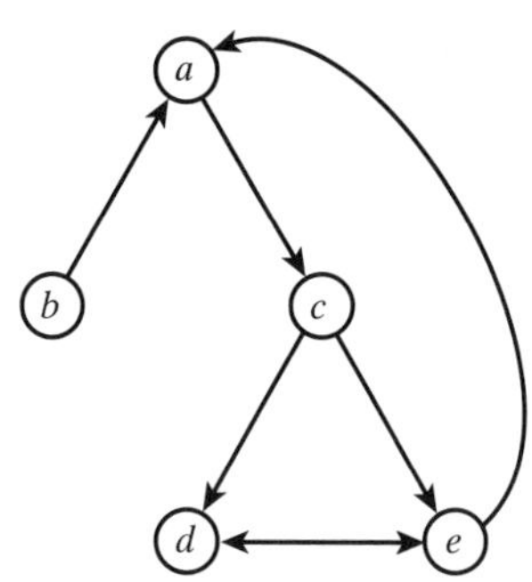


**FIGURE 12-6** *A directed graph. The in-degree of $\langle a,b,c,d,e\rangle$ is $\langle 2,0,1,2,2\rangle$, respectively, and the out-degree of $\langle a,b,c,d,e\rangle$ is $\langle 1,1,2,1,2\rangle$, respectively.*

For some problems in graph theory, it makes sense to assign weights to the edges or vertices of a graph. A graph $G = (V,E)$ is *edge-weighted* if there is a weight $W(v_i, v_j)$ associated with every edge $(v_i, v_j) \in E$. In the case of edge-weighted graphs, the *distance*, or *minimal-weight path*, between vertices $v_i$ and $v_j$ is the sum over the edge weights in a path from $v_i$ to $v_j$ of minimum total weight. The *diameter* of such a graph is the maximum of the distances between all pairs of vertices.

For many applications, it makes sense to consider all edges in an unweighted graph as having a weight of 1.

## Representations

There are several ways to represent a graph. In this book, we will consider three of the most common, namely, *i*) a set of adjacency lists, *ii*) an adjacency matrix, and *iii*) a set of arbitrarily distributed edges. It is important to note that in some cases, the user may have a choice of representations and can therefore choose a representation for which the computational resources may be optimized. In other situations, the user may be given the graph in a particular form and may need to design and implement efficient algorithms to solve problems on the structure.

### Adjacency Lists

The *adjacency-list representation* of a graph $G = (V, E)$ typically consists of $|V|$ lists, one corresponding to each vertex $v_i \in V$. For each such vertex $v_i$, its list contains an entry for every edge $(v_i, v_j) \in E$. To navigate efficiently through a graph, the headers of the $|V|$ lists are typically stored in an array or linked list, which we call *Adj*, as shown in Figure 12-7. In this chapter, unless otherwise specified, we will assume an array implementation of *Adj* so that we can refer to the adjacency list associated with vertex $v_i \in V$ as $Adj(v_i)$. It is important to note that we do not assume the adjacency lists are ordered.

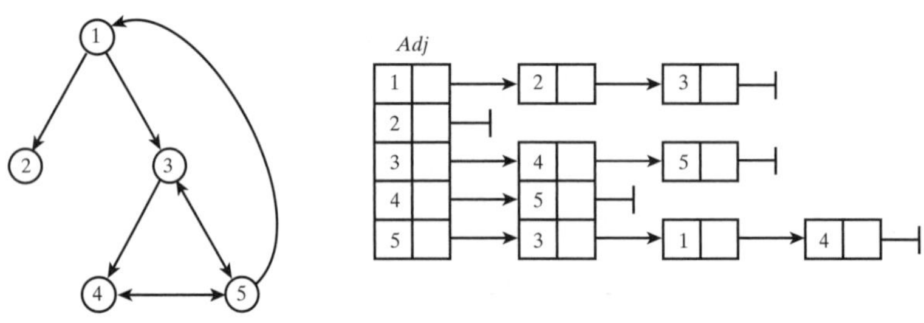


**FIGURE 12-7** *A directed graph and its adjacency-list representation.*

If the graph $G = (V, E)$ is a directed graph, then the total number of entries in all adjacency lists is $|E|$, since every edge $(v_i, v_j) \in E$ is represented only in $Adj(v_i)$. However, if the graph $G = (V, E)$ is an undirected graph, then the total number of entries in all adjacency lists is $2|E|$, since every edge $(v_i, v_j) \in E$ is represented in both $Adj(v_i)$ and $Adj(v_j)$. Notice that, regardless of the type of graph, an adjacency-list representation has the feature that the space required to store the graph is $\Theta(V + E)$. Assuming that one must store some information about every vertex and about every edge in the graph, this is an optimal representation with respect to the space used.

Suppose the graph $G = (V, E)$ is weighted. Then the elements in the individual adjacency lists can be modified to store the weight of every edge or vertex, as appropriate. For example, given an edge-weighted graph, an entry in $Adj(v_i)$ corresponding to edge $(v_i, v_j) \in E$ can store the identity of $v_j$, a pointer to $Adj(v_j)$, the weight $W(v_i, v_j)$, other miscellaneous fields required for necessary operations, and a pointer to the next record in the list, all in $\Theta(1)$ space.

While the adjacency-list representation is robust, in that it can be modified to support a wide variety of graphs and is asymptotically efficient in storage, it does have the drawback of not allowing quick detection of whether or not an edge $(v_i, v_j)$ exists. In the next section, we consider a representation that will overcome this deficiency.

### Adjacency Matrix

An adjacency matrix is presented in Figure 12-8 that corresponds to the adjacency list presented in Figure 12-7. For a graph $G = (V, E)$, the adjacency matrix $A$ is a $|V| \times |V|$ matrix in which entry $A(i, j) = 1$ if $(v_i, v_j) \in E$ and $A(i, j) = 0$ if $(v_i, v_j) \notin E$. Thus, row $i$ of the adjacency matrix contains all information in $Adj(v_i)$ of the corresponding adjacency list. Notice that the matrix contains a single bit at each of the $\Theta(V^2)$ positions. Further, if the graph is undirected and $i \neq j$, there is no need to store both $A(i, j)$ and $A(j, i)$, since $A(i, j) = A(j, i)$. That is, for an undirected graph, one only needs to maintain either the upper triangular or lower triangular portion of the adjacency matrix. More generally, for an edge-weight graph, each entry $A(i, j)$ will be set to the weight of edge $(v_i, v_j)$ if the edge exists and will be set to 0 otherwise. Given either a weighted or unweighted graph that is either directed or undirected, the total space required by an adjacency matrix is $\Theta(V^2)$.

| | 1 | 2 | 3 | 4 | 5 |
|---|---|---|---|---|---|
| 1 | 0 | 1 | 1 | 0 | 0 |
| 2 | 0 | 0 | 0 | 0 | 0 |
| 3 | 0 | 0 | 0 | 1 | 1 |
| 4 | 0 | 0 | 0 | 0 | 1 |
| 5 | 1 | 0 | 1 | 1 | 0 |

**FIGURE 12-8** *An adjacency matrix representation of the graph presented in Figure 12-7.*

The adjacency matrix has the advantage of providing direct access to information concerning the existence or absence of an edge. Given a dense graph, the adjacency matrix also has the advantage that it requires only one bit per entry, as opposed to the additional pointers required by the adjacency-list representation. However, for relatively sparse graphs, the adjacency list has the advantage of requiring less space and providing a relatively simplistic manner in which to traverse a graph. For an algorithm that requires the examination of all vertices and all edges, an adjacency-list implementation can provide a sequential algorithm with running time of $\Omega(V + E)$, while an adjacency matrix representation would result in a sequential running time of $\Omega(V^2)$. Thus, the algorithm based on the adjacency list might be significantly more efficient.

#### Unordered Edges

A third form of input that we mention is that of unordered edges, which provides the least amount of information and structure. Given a graph $G = (V, E)$, *unordered edge* input is such that the $|E|$ edges are distributed in an arbitrary fashion throughout the memory of the machine. On a sequential computer, one will typically restructure this information in order to create adjacency-list or adjacency-matrix input. However, on parallel machines, it is not always economical or feasible to perform such a conversion.

## Fundamental Algorithms

In this section, we consider fundamental algorithms for traversing and manipulating graphs. It is often useful to be able to visit the vertices of a graph in some well-defined order based on the graph's topology. We first consider sequential approaches to this concept of *graph traversal.* The two major techniques we consider, breadth-first search and depth-first search, both have the property that they begin with a specified vertex and then visit all other vertices in a deterministic fashion. In the presentation of both of these algorithms, the reader will notice that we keep track of the vertices as they are visited. Following the presentations of fundamental sequential traversal methods, we will review the fundamental problem of computing the transitive closure of a binary matrix, for the RAM, PRAM, and mesh.

#### Breadth-First Search

The first algorithm we consider for traversing a graph is called *breadth-first search* (*BFS*). The general flow of a BFS traversal is first to visit a predetermined "root" vertex $r$, then visit all vertices at distance 1 from $r$, then visit all vertices at distance 2 from $r$, and so on. This is a standard technique for traversing a graph $G = (V, E)$. On a RAM, the search procedure is as follows.

- Start the search at a *root* vertex $r \in V$.
- Add all neighboring vertices of the vertex under consideration to a queue.
- Process the queue in a standard first-in, first-out (FIFO) order.

So, initially all vertices $v \in V$ are marked as *unvisited*, and the queue is initialized to contain only a root vertex $r \in V$. The algorithm proceeds by removing the root from the queue, leaving us with an empty queue, determining all neighbors of this root vertex just removed from the queue, and placing every neighbor of the root into the queue. In general, each iteration of the algorithm consists of the following.

- Remove the next vertex $v \in V$ from the queue.
- Examine all neighbors of $v$ in $G$ in order to determine those that have not yet been visited during the search.

- Mark each of these previously unvisited neighbors as visited.
- Enter these previously unvisited neighbors of $v$ into the queue.

This process of removing an element from the queue and entering its unvisited neighbors into the queue continues until the queue is empty and the last vertex removed from the queue has no unvisited neighbors. Once the queue is empty at the conclusion of a remove-explore-enter step, all vertices reachable from the root vertex $r \in V$, *i.e.*, all vertices in the same component of $G$ as $r$, have been visited. Further, if the vertices are output as they are removed from the queue, the resulting list corresponds to a breadth-first search tree over the graph $G = (V, E)$ with root $r \in V$ (see Figure 12-9).

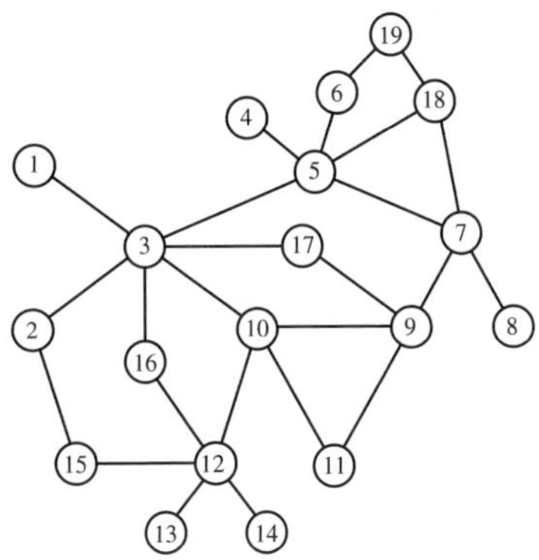


(a) A given graph *G*.

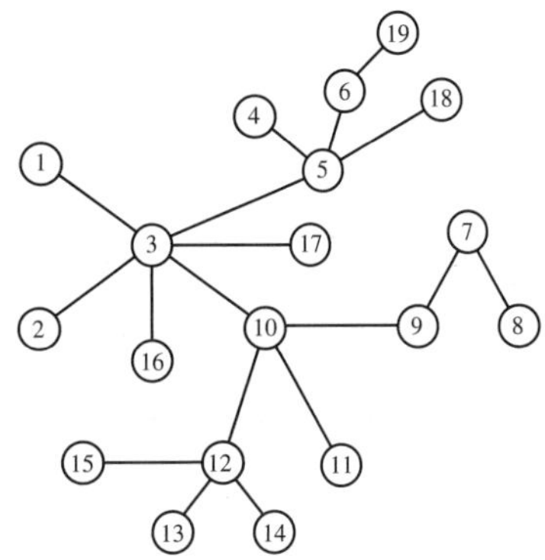


(b) This tree is associated with a traversal <10, 3, 12, 11, 9, 5, 17, 16, 2, 1, 15, 13, 14, 7, 4, 6, 18, 8, 19> of *G*, though other traversals of *G* would also yield this tree.

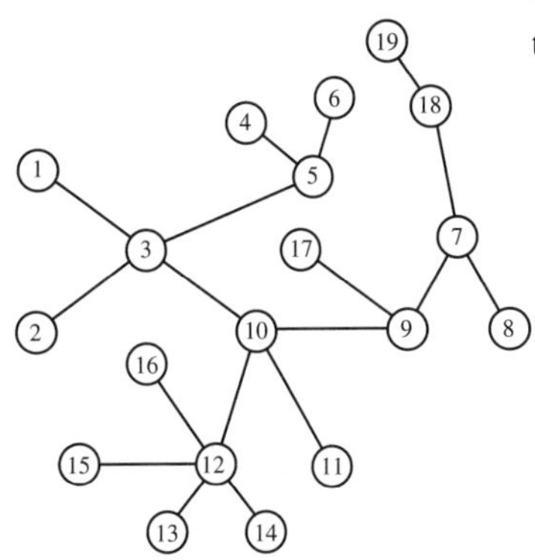


(c) This tree is associated with a traversal <10, 9, 12, 11, 3, 17, 7, 13, 14, 15, 16, 2, 1, 5, 18, 8, 6, 4, 19> of *G*, though the traversals of *G* would also yield this tree.

**FIGURE 12-9** *An example of a breadth-first search traversal. Depending on the order in which the vertices of a graph are stored, a breadth-first search could yield a variety of breadth-first search trees.*

We now present an algorithm for the RAM that will implement a breadth-first search of a graph and record the distance from the root to every reachable vertex (see Figure 12-10). That is, every vertex that can be reached by a path from the root. The reader should note that our algorithm is presented as a graph traversal. That is, this procedure will visit every vertex of the root's component. Such a procedure is easily modified to solve the query problem by returning to the calling routine with the appropriate information when a vertex is reached that is associated with the requested key.

```
    BFSroutine (G, r)
    CreateEmptyQueue(Q)                         {Initialize the queue}
    For all vertices v ∈ V, do
      visited(v) ← false                    {Initialize vertices to
                                                       "unvisited"}
      dist(v) ← ∞                          {Initialize all distances}
      parent(v) ← null                     {Initialize parents of
                                                     all vertices}
    End For
{*} visited(r) ← true                  {Initialize root vertex - it
    dist(r) ← 0                      is visited, it has distance 0
    PlaceInQueue(Q, r)               from itself, and it goes into
                                                         the queue}
    While NotEmptyQueue(Q), do
      v ← RemoveFromQueue(Q)              {Take first element from
                                                         queue: v}
      For all vertices w ∈ Adj(v), do  {Examine all neighbors
                                                             of v}
        If not visited(w) then {Process unvisited neighbors}
            visited(w) ← true          {Mark neighbor as visited}
            parent(w) ← v              {The BFS parent of w is v}
            dist(w) ← dist(v) + 1     {Dist. fr. w to r is 1 more
                                          than distance from its
                                                  parent, v, to r}
          PlaceInQueue (Q, w)          {Place w at end of queue}
        End If
      End For
    End While
```

Notice that the steps that compute the parent of a vertex $v$ and the distance of $v$ from the root are not necessary to the graph traversal. We have included these steps as they are useful to other problems we discuss below. Also note that what we have described as "$v \leftarrow$ RemoveFromQueue($Q$)" may involve not only dequeuing a node from the queue, but also processing the node as required by the graph traversal.

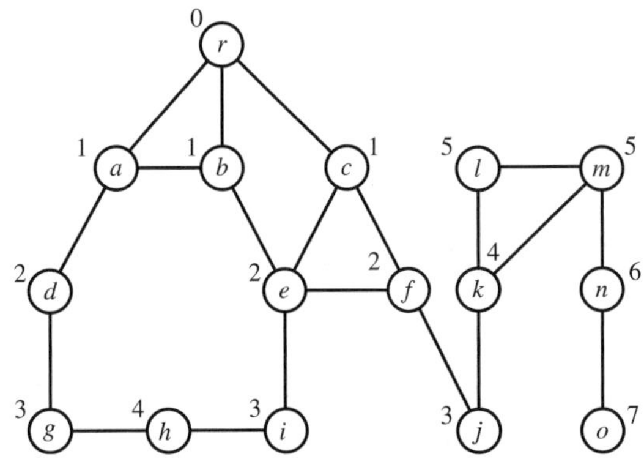


**FIGURE 12-10** *An undirected connected graph with distances from the root vertex r recorded next to the vertices. One possible traversal of the vertices in this graph by a breadth-first search is* $\langle r,c,b,a,e,f,d,i,j,g,h,k,l,m,n,o \rangle$.

Given a connected undirected graph $G=(V,E)$, a call to BFSroutine($G$, $r$) for any $r \in V$ will visit every vertex and every edge. In fact, a careful examination shows that every edge will be visited exactly twice and that every vertex will be considered at least once. Further, each vertex is visited only once. Every other consideration of a vertex is part of the consideration of an edge incident on the vertex. Therefore, assuming that entering and removing items from a queue are performed in $\Theta(1)$ time, the sequential running time for this BFSroutine on a connected undirected graph is $\Theta(V+E)$.

Now, suppose that the undirected graph $G=(V,E)$ is not necessarily connected. We can extend the BFSroutine in order to visit all vertices of $G$. See Figure 12-11 while considering the algorithm below.

```
BFS-all-undirected (G= (V, E))
CreateEmptyQueue(Q)                    {Initialize the queue}
For all vertices v ∈ V, do
  visited(v) ← false   {Initialize vertex to "unvisited"}
  dist(v) ← ∞                        {Initialize distance}
  parent(v) ← nil                      {Initialize parent}
End For
For all v ∈ V, do    {Consider all vertices in the graph}
  If not visited(v), then
    BFSroutine(G, v) at line {*}  {Perform a BFS starting
                            at every vertex not previously
                         visited—call BFSroutine, but jump
                                   immediately to line {*}}
End For
```

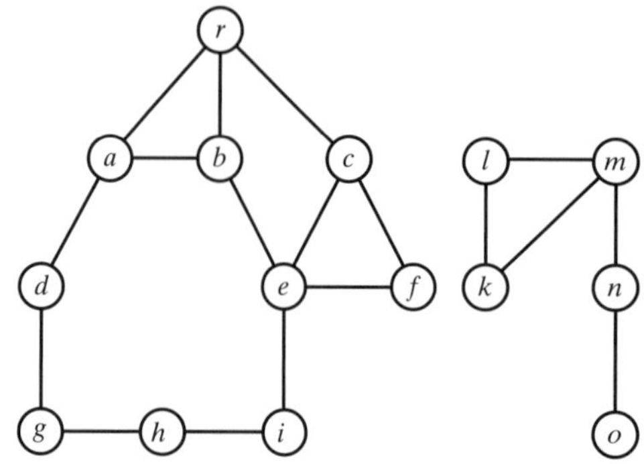


**FIGURE 12-11** *An undirected graph that is not connected. The two connected components can be labeled in time linear in the number of vertices plus the number of edges by a simple extrapolation of the breadth-first search algorithm.*

Analysis similar to that given above for BFSroutine yields that given an undirected graph $G = (V,E)$, the procedure BFS-all-undirected will visit all vertices and traverse all edges in the graph in $\Theta(V + E)$ time on a sequential machine.

### Depth-First Search

The second algorithm we consider for traversing a graph is called *depth-first search* (*DFS*). The philosophy of DFS is to start at a predetermined "root" vertex $r$ and *recursively* visit a previously unvisited neighbor $v$ of $r$. These vertices are visited one by one, until all neighbors of $r$ have been visited. As we remarked earlier, BFS and DFS are standard techniques for traversing or presenting a graph. Algorithmically, the DFS procedure on a RAM follows.

1. Start at a *root* vertex $r \in V$.
2. Determine a previously unvisited neighbor $v$ of $r$.
3. Recursively visit $v$. That is, consider $v$ as $r$ when performing step 1 of the recursion.
4. If not all neighbors of $v$ have been visited, then go to step 2.

The algorithm is recursive in nature. A more detailed description follows. Given a graph $G = (V,E)$, choose an initial vertex $r \in V$, which we again call the *root*, and mark $r$ as visited. Next, find a previously unvisited neighbor of $r$, say, $v$. Recursively perform a depth-first search on $v$ and then return to consider any other neighbors of $r$ that have not been visited (see Figure 12-12). A simple recursive presentation of this algorithm is given below.

```
                          {Assume that visited(v) ← false
        for all v∈ V prior to this routine being called}
DFSroutine(G, r)
visited(r) ← true                 {Mark r as being visited.}
For all vertices v∈ Adj(r), do               {Consider all
                                   neighbors of r in turn.}
  If not visited(v) do              {If a given neighbor has
                                  not been visited, mark its
    parent(v) ← r                parent as r and recursively
                                   visit this neighbor. Note
    DFSroutine (G, v)            the recursive step causes v
                                      to be marked visited.}
  End If
End For
```

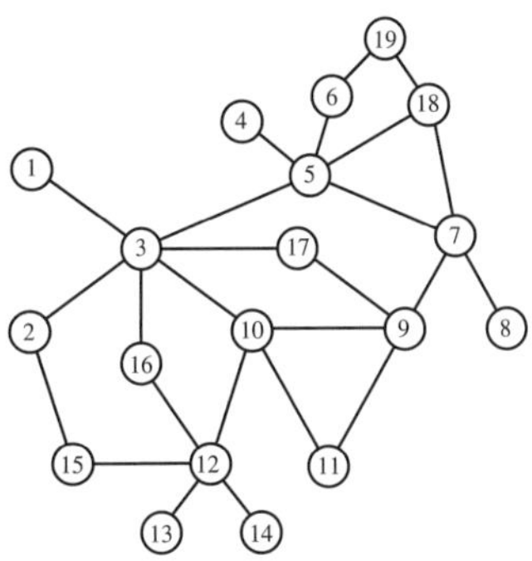

(a) A given graph *G*.

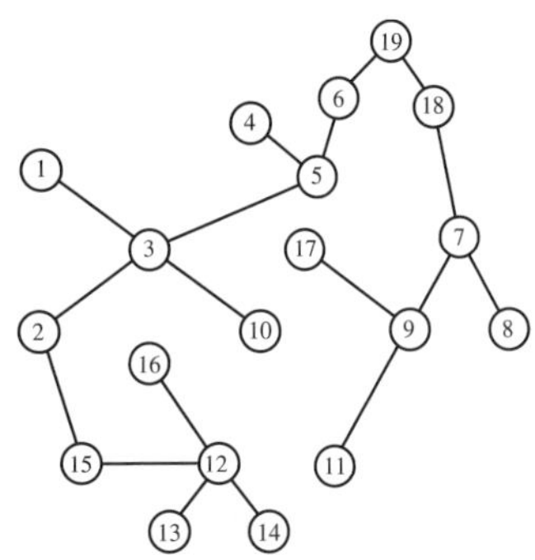

(b) This tree is associated with a traversal <10, 3, 1, 2, 15, 12, 13, 14, 16, 5, 4, 6, 19, 18, 7, 8, 9, 11, 17> of *G*, though other traversals of *G* would also yield this tree.

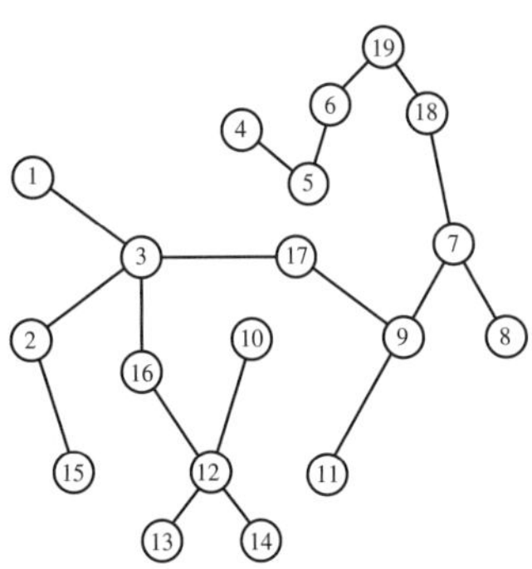

(c) This tree is associated with a traversal <10, 12, 16, 3, 17, 9, 11, 7, 18, 19, 6, 5, 4, 8, 1, 2, 15, 14, 13> of *G*, though other traversals of *G* would also yield this tree.

**FIGURE 12-12** *An example of a depth-first search traversal. Notice that the graph given in* (a) *is identical to the graph G utilized in Figure 12-9a.*

As in the breadth-first search graph traversal, the step that computes the parent of a vertex is not necessary to perform a depth-first search graph traversal, but it is included for its usefulness in a number of related problems. The step we have described as "*visited*($r$) ← *true*" is typically preceded or followed by steps that process the vertex $r$ as required by the graph traversal. Also, as with a breadth-first search, we have presented depth-first search as a graph traversal algorithm that can be modified by the insertion of a conditional exit instruction if a traditional search is desired that stops upon realizing success.

The RAM implementation of depth-first search, as presented, is an example of a "backtracking" algorithm. That is, when considering a given vertex $v$, the algorithm considers all of $v$'s "descendants" before backtracking to the parent of $v$ in order to allow its parent to continue with the traversal. Now, consider the analysis of DFSroutine on a sequential platform. Notice that every vertex is initialized to unvisited and that every vertex is visited exactly once during the search. Also, notice that every directed edge in a graph is considered exactly once. Note that every undirected edge would be considered twice, once from the point of view of each incident vertex. Therefore, the running time of DFSroutine on a graph $G = (V, E)$ is $\Theta(V + E)$, which is the same as the running time of BFSroutine.

### Discussion of Depth-First and Breadth-First Search

A *depth-first search tree* $T = (V, E')$ of a graph $G = (V, E)$ is formed during a depth-first search of the graph $G$, as follows. An edge $(u, v) \in E$ is a member of $E'$ if and only if one of its vertices is the parent of the other vertex. Given a depth-first search tree $T = (V, E')$ of $G$, it should be noted that if an edge $(u, v) \in E$ is not in $E'$, then either

- $u$ is a descendant of $v$ in $T$ and $v$ is not the parent of $u$, or
- $v$ is a descendant of $u$ in $T$ and $u$ is not the parent of $v$. See Figure 12-13.

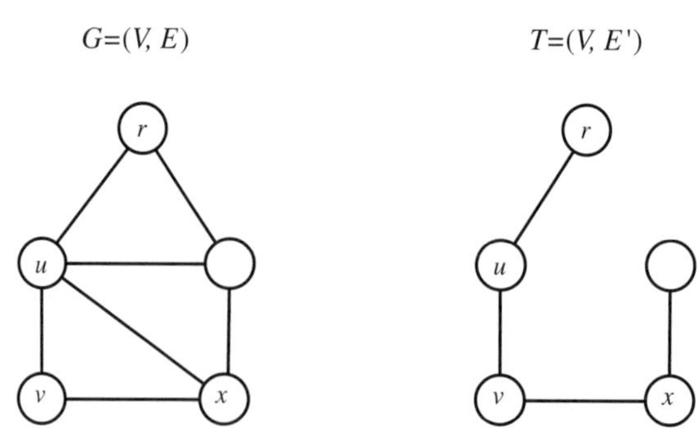


**FIGURE 12-13** *A depth-first search tree $T = (V, E')$ of a graph $G = (V, E)$. An edge $(u, v) \in E$ is a member of $E'$ if and only if one of its vertices is the parent of the other vertex. Edge $(u, x) \in E$ is not in $E'$, corresponding to the fact that one of its vertices is an ancestor but not the parent of the other.*

Each vertex $v$ in a depth-first search tree of $G$ can be given a time stamp corresponding to when the vertex was first encountered and another time stamp corresponding to when the search finished examining all of $v$'s neighbors. These time stamps can be used in higher-level graph algorithms to solve interesting and important problems. Problems typically solved through a depth-first search include labeling the strongly connected components of a directed graph, performing a topological sort of a directed graph, determining articulation points and biconnected components, and labeling connected components of undirected graphs, to name a few.

A *breadth-first search tree* is similarly formed from the edges joining parent and child vertices in a BFS of a graph $G = (V, E)$. Given a breadth-first search tree $T = (V, E')$ of $G$, it should be noted that if an edge $(u, v) \in E$ is not in $E'$, then $u$ is not a descendant of $v$ in $T$ and $v$ is not a descendant of $u$ in $T$ (see Figure 12-14).

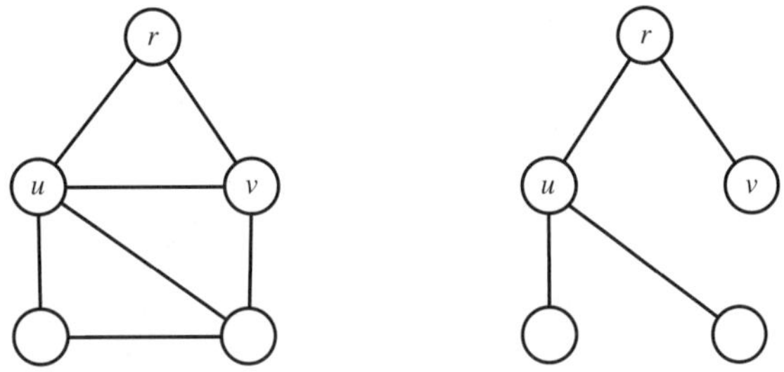


(a) $G=(V, E)$ (b) $T=(V, E')$

**FIGURE 12-14** *A breadth-first search tree $T = (V, E')$ of $G = (V, E)$. If an edge $(u, v) \in E$ is not in $E'$, then u is not a descendant of v in T and v is not a descendant of u in T.*

The vertices in a breadth-first search tree $T = (V, E')$ of $G = (V, E)$ are at minimum distance from the root $r \in V$ of the tree. That is, the distance of $u \in V$ in $T$ from $r$ is the length of a shortest path in $G$ from $u$ to $r$. This is a useful property when we consider certain minimal path-length problems, including the *single-source shortest-path problem.* Such searches, however, are not useful when one is considering weighted paths, which occurs, *e.g.*, when solving the minimal weight spanning tree problem. A breadth-first search of a graph can be used to solve a number of problems, including determining whether or not a graph is bipartite.

## Computing the Transitive Closure of an Adjacency Matrix

In this section, we review both the sequential and mesh implementations of a transitive closure algorithm. The algorithm to compute the transitive closure of a matrix is a critical component in terms of developing efficient algorithms to solve a variety of fundamental graph problems. We assume that we are given a directed graph $G = (V, E)$, where $n = |V|$, represented by an $n \times n$ adjacency matrix. In such a representation, $A(i,j) = 1$ if and only if there is an edge from $v_i$ to $v_j$ in $E$. Otherwise, $A(i,j) = 0$.

The transitive closure of $A$ is represented as a binary matrix $A^*_{n \times n}$ in which $A^*(i,j) = 1$ if and only if there is a path in $G$ from $v_i$ to $v_j$. Therefore, $A^*(i,j) = 0$ if no such path exists. As we have previously discussed, one way to obtain the transitive closure of an adjacency matrix $A$ is to multiply $A$ by itself $n$ times. This is not very efficient, however. Alternatively, one could perform $\lceil \log_2 n \rceil$ operations of squaring the matrix. That is, we could perform the computations $A \times A = A^2$, $A^2 \times A^2 = A^4$, and so on until a matrix $A^m$ is obtained, where $m \geq n$. Sequentially, this squaring procedure would result in a $\Theta(n^3 \log n)$ time algorithm, while on a mesh of size $n^2$, the procedure would run in $\Theta(n \log n)$ time.

Consider the binary matrix $A_k(i,j)$ representing $G$, with the interpretation that $A_k(i,j) = 1$ if and only if there is a path from $v_i$ to $v_j$ that only uses $\{v_1, \ldots, v_k\}$ as intermediate vertices. Notice that $A_0 = A$ and that $A_n = A^*$. Further, notice that there is a path from $v_i$ to $v_j$ using intermediate vertices $\{v_1, \ldots, v_k\}$ if and only if either there is a path from $v_i$ to $v_j$ using intermediate vertices $\{v_1, \ldots, v_{k-1}\}$ or there is a path from $v_i$ to $v_k$ using intermediate vertices $\{v_1, \ldots, v_{k-1}\}$ and a path from $v_k$ to $v_j$ also using only intermediate vertices $\{v_1, \ldots, v_{k-1}\}$. This observation forms the foundation of *Warshall's algorithm*, which can be used to compute the transitive closure of $A$ on a sequential machine in $\Theta(n^3)$ time. The sequential algorithm follows.

```
For k = 1 to n, do
  For i = 1 to n, do
    For j = 1 to n, do
      A_k(i, j) ← A_{k-1}(i, j) ∨ [A_{k-1}(i, k) ∧ A_{k-1}(k, j)]
    End For j
  End For i
End For k
```

Now, consider an implementation of Warshall's algorithm on a mesh computer. Suppose $A$ is stored in an $n \times n$ mesh such that processor $P_{i,j}$ stores entry $A(i,j)$. Further, suppose that at the end of the algorithm processor $P_{i,j}$ is required to store entry $A^*(i,j) = A_n(i,j)$. This can be accomplished with some interesting movement of data that adheres to the following conditions.

1. Entry $A_k(i,j)$ is computed in processor $P_{i,j}$ at time $3k + |k-i| + |k-j| - 2$.
2. For all $k$ and $i$, the value of $A_k(i,k)$ moves in a horizontal lock-step fashion in row $i$ away from processor $P_{i,k}$.
3. For all $k$ and $j$, the value of $A_k(k,j)$ moves in a vertical lock-step fashion in column $j$ away from processor $P_{k,j}$.

See Figure 12-15 for an illustration of this data movement. Notice from condition 1 that the algorithm runs in $\Theta(n)$ time. The reader is advised to spend some time with small examples of the mesh implementation of Warshall's algorithm in order to be comfortable with the fact that the appropriate items arrive at the appropriate processors at the precise time that they are required. Therefore, there is no congestion or bottleneck in any of the rows or columns.

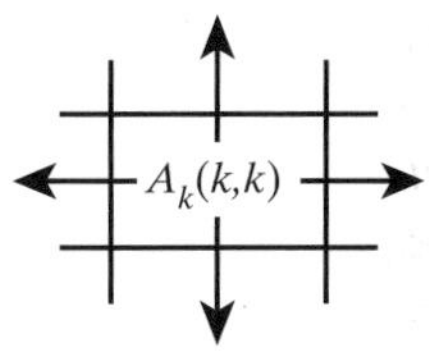


(a) At time $t = 3k - 2$, $A_k(k, k)$ is computed in processor $P_{k,k}$.

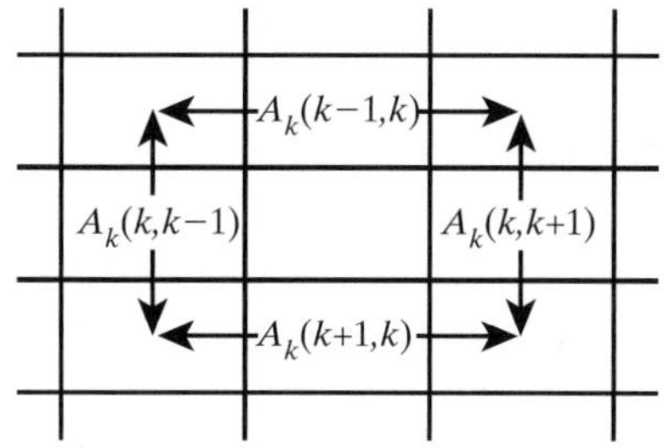


(b) The values $A_k(k-1, k)$, $A_k(k, k+1)$, $A_k(k+1, k)$, and $A_k(k, k-1)$ are computed in processors $P_{k-1,k}$, $P_{k,k+1}$, $P_{k+1,k}$, and $P_{k,k-1}$, respectively.

**FIGURE 12-15** *Data movement of van Scoy's implementation of Warshall's transitive closure algorithm on a mesh. $A_k(k,k)$ is computed at time $t = 3k - 2$, in processor $P_{k,k}$. During the next time step, this value is transmitted to processors $P_{k,k+1}$, $P_{k,k-1}$, $P_{k+1,k}$, and $P_{k-1,k}$, as shown in* (a). *At time $t + 1 = 3k - 1$, the values $A_k(k-1, k)$, $A_k(k, k+1)$, $A_k(k+1, k)$, and $A_k(k, k-1)$ are computed in processors $P_{k-1,k}$, $P_{k,k+1}$, $P_{k+1,k}$, and $P_{k,k-1}$, respectively, as shown in* (b). *The arrows displaying data movement in* (b) *show the direction that this information begins to move during time step $t + 2 = 3k$.*

The mesh algorithm for the generalized transitive closure can be used to solve the connected component labeling problem, the all-pairs shortest-path problem, and to determine whether or not a graph is a tree, to name a few. The first two algorithms will be discussed in more detail later in the chapter.

## Connected Component Labeling

In this section, we consider the problem of labeling the connected components of an undirected graph. The labeling should be such that if vertex $v$ is assigned a label *label*($v$), then all vertices to which $v$ is connected are assigned the same component label of *label*($v$).

### RAM

A simple sequential algorithm can be given to label all of the vertices of an undirected graph. Such an algorithm consists of applying the breadth-first search procedure to a given vertex. During the breadth-first search, the label corresponding to the initial vertex is propagated. Once the breadth-first search is complete, a search is made for any unlabeled vertex. If one is found, then the BFS is repeated, labeling the next component, and so on. An algorithm follows. The reader should observe that this is a modification of the BFS-all-undirected algorithm presented earlier in the chapter.

```
1. Given a graph G = (V, E), where V = {v_1, v_2, ... v_n}.
2. Assign label(v) = null for all v ∈ V          {Initialize
                                          labels of all vertices,
                                          representing each vertex
                                          as currently unvisited}
3. For i = 1 to n, do
4.    If label(v_i) = null, then          {If vertex hasn't been
                                          visited/labeled so far,
                                          then initiate a search,
5.         BFSroutine(G, v_i)              during which we set
                                          label(v) = i for every
                                          vertex visited}
6.    End If
7. End For
```

The algorithm is straightforward. Since the graph is undirected, every invocation of BFSroutine will visit and label all vertices that are connected to the given vertex $v_i$. Due to the For-loop, the algorithm will consider every connected component. The running time for the step that calls BFSroutine in aggregate is $\Theta(V + E)$ since every vertex and every edge in the graph is visited within the context of one and only one breadth-first search. Hence, the running time of the algorithm is $\Theta(V + E)$, which is optimal in the size of the graph.

### PRAM

The problem of computing the connected components of a graph $G = (V,E)$ is considered a fundamental problem in the area of graph algorithms. Unfortunately, an optimal parallel strategy for performing a breadth-first search or a depth-first search of a graph on a PRAM is not known. For this reason, a significant amount of effort has been applied to the development of an efficient PRAM algorithm to solve the graph-based connected component problem. Several efficient algorithms have been presented with slightly different running times and on a variety of PRAM models. The basic strategy of these algorithms consists of processing the graph for $O(\log V)$ stages. During each stage, the vertices are organized as a forest of directed trees, where each vertex is in one tree and has a link, *i.e.*, a directed edge or pointer, to its parent in that tree. All vertices in such a tree are in the same connected component of the graph. The algorithm repeatedly combines trees containing vertices in the same connected component. However, until the algorithm terminates, there is no guarantee that every such tree represents a maximally connected component.

Initially, there are $|V|$ directed trees, each consisting of a vertex pointing to itself. (Refer to the example presented in Figure 12-16.) During the $i^{\text{th}}$ stage of the algorithm, trees from stage $i-1$ are *hooked* or *grafted* together and compressed by a pointer-jumping operation so that the trees do not become unwieldy. Each such compressed tree is referred to as a *supervertex*. When the algorithm terminates, each supervertex corresponds to a maximally connected component in the graph and takes the form of a *star*, *i.e.*, a directed tree in which all vertices point directly to the root vertex. It is the implementation of hooking that is critical to designing an algorithm that runs in $O(\log V)$ stages. We will present an algorithm for an arbitrary CRCW PRAM that runs in $O(\log V)$ time using $\Theta(V+E)$ processors.

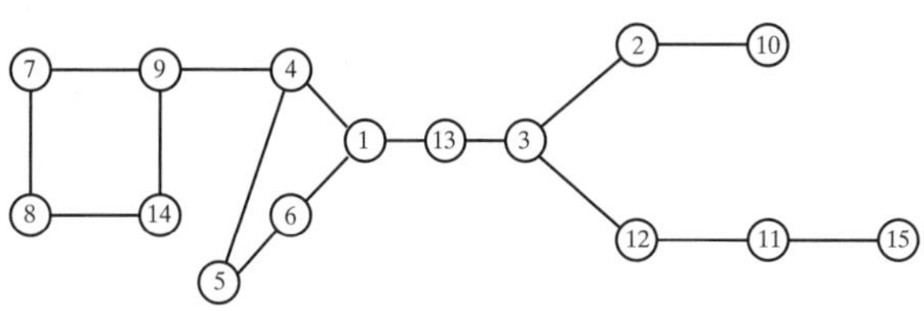


(a) The initial undirected graph $G=(V,E)$.

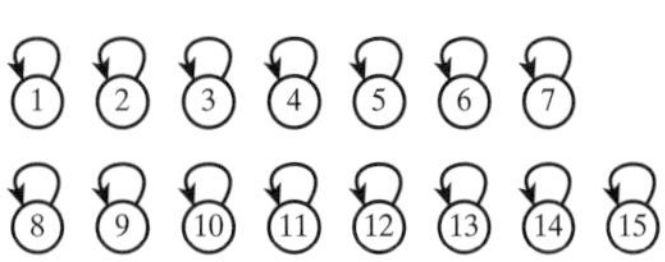


(b) The initial forest consisting of a distinct tree representing every vertex in $V$.

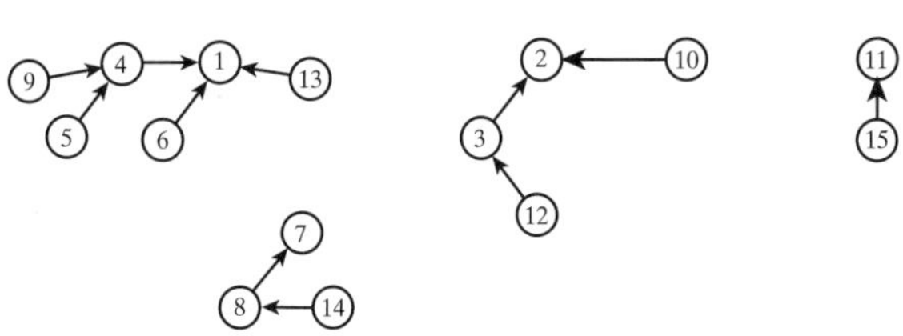


(c) The result of every vertex in $V$ attaching to its minimum-labeled neighbor.

(d) The four disjoint subgraphs resulting from the compression given in (c).

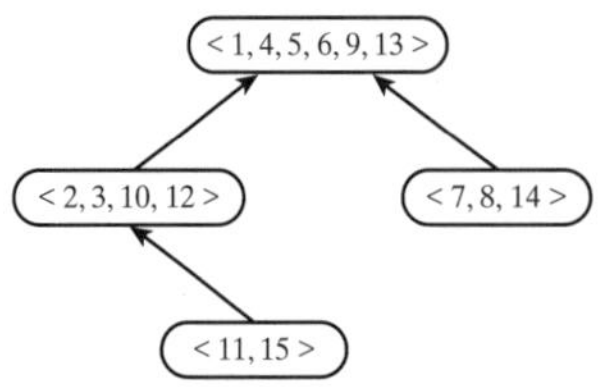


(e) The result from each of these four supervertices choosing its minimum-labeled neighbor.

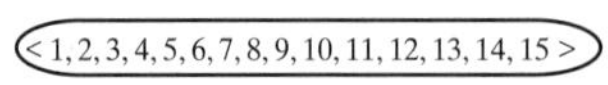


(f) The final stage of the algorithm in which all vertices in the connected graph have been compressed into a single supervertex.

**FIGURE 12-16** *A general description of a parallel component labeling algorithm. Note that when we present supervertices, the first vertex in the list will serve as the label for the supervertex.*

Define $index(v_i) = i$ to be the index of vertex $v_i$. Define $root(v_i)$ as a pointer to the root of the tree, or supervertex, that $v_i$ is a currently a member of. Then we can define the hooking operation $hook(v_i, v_j)$ as an operation that attaches $root(v_i)$ to $root(v_j)$, as shown in Figure 12-17.

We can determine, for each vertex $v_i \in V$, whether or not $v_i$ belongs to a star, by the following procedure.

```
1. Determine the Boolean function star(vᵢ) for all
   vᵢ ∈ V, as follows.
2. For all vertices vᵢ, do in parallel
3.     star(vᵢ) ← true
4.     If root(vᵢ) ≠ root(root(vᵢ)), then
5.       star(vᵢ) ← false
6.       star(root(vᵢ)) ← false
7.       star(root(root(vᵢ))) ← false
8.     End If
9.     star(vᵢ) ← star(root(vᵢ))
10. End For
```

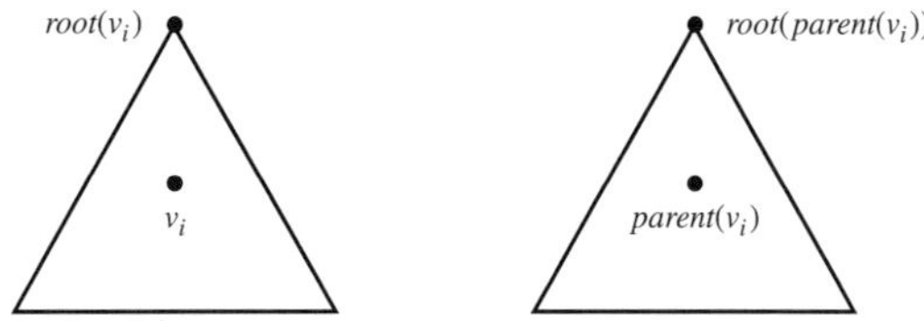


(a) $v_i$ and *parent*($v_i$) are in different supervertices.

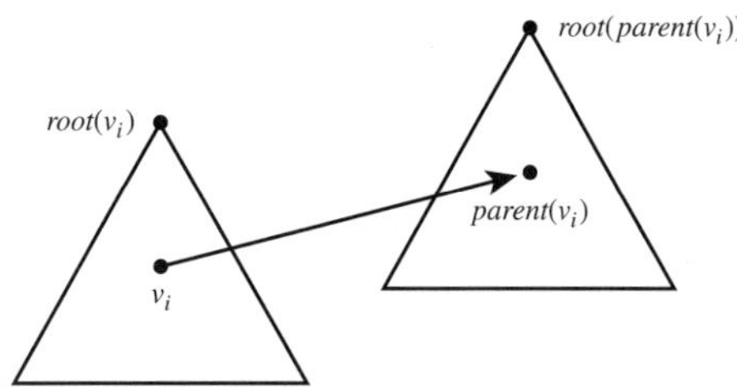


(b) The supervertex that $v_i$ is a member of chooses to hook to the supervertex containing *parent*($v_i$) since since *root*(*parent*($v_i$)) is a minimum label over all of the supervertices to which members of the supervertex labeled *root*($v_i$) are connected.

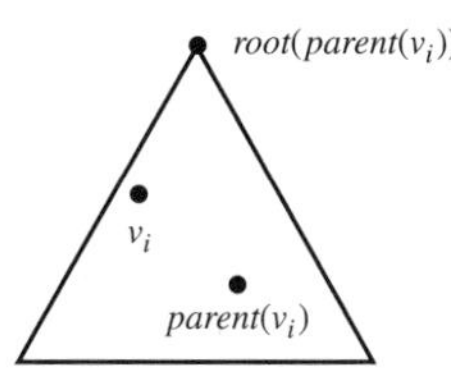


(c) The two supervertices are merged.

**FIGURE 12-17** *A demonstration of the hooking operation.*

See Figure 12-18 for an example that shows the necessity of Step 9. It is easily seen that this procedure runs in $\Theta(1)$ time.

The basic component labeling algorithm follows.

- The goal is to label the connected components of an undirected graph $G = (V, E)$.
- Assume that every edge between vertices $v_i$ and $v_j$ is represented by a pair of unordered edges $(v_i, v_j)$ and $(v_j, v_i)$.
- Recall that we assume an arbitrary CRCW PRAM. That is, if there is a write conflict, one of the writes will arbitrarily succeed.

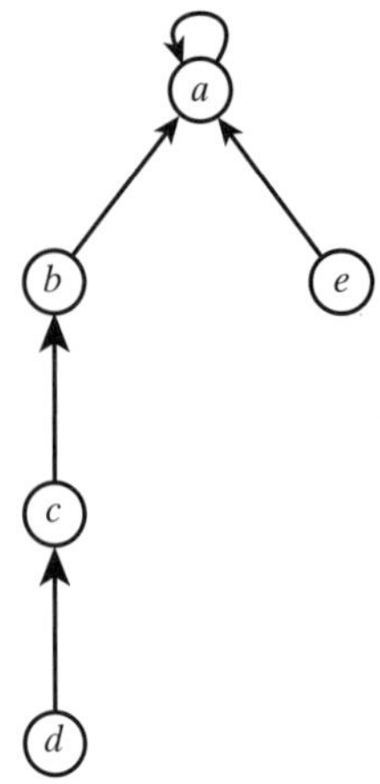


**FIGURE 12-18** *Computing the star function in parallel. Arrows represent root pointers. Step 3 initializes star($v_i$) ← true for all vertices. Steps 5-7 change star(a), star(b), star(c), and star(d) to false. However, we require Step 9 to change star(e) to false.*

```
For all vi ∈ V, set root(vi) = vi                {Initialize
                                                 supervertices.}
For all (vi, vj) ∈ E, do                   {Loop uses arbitrary
                                                 CRCW property}
  If index(vi) > index(vj), then hook(vi, vj)
                          {Hook larger indexed vertices into
                                   smaller indexed vertices.}
End For all (vi, vj) ∈ E
Repeat
   Determine star(vi) for all vi ∈ V
   For all (vi, vj) ∈ E, do
     If vi is in a star and
     index(root(vi)) > index(root(vj)), then
       hook(vi, vj)                      {Hook vertices in star
                                               to neighbors with
                                            lower-indexed roots}
   Determine star(vi) for all vi ∈ V
   For all vertices vi, do
     If vi is not in a star, then
       root(vi) ← root(root(vi))             {pointer jumping}
Until no changes are produced by the steps of the Repeat
loop
```

While it is beyond the scope of this book, it can be shown that the algorithm above is correct for an arbitrary CRCW PRAM. Critical observations can be made, including the following.

- At any time during the algorithm, the structure defined by the set of root pointers corresponds to a proper upward-directed forest, as no vertex ever has a root with a larger index.
- When the algorithm terminates, the forest defined by the root pointers consists of stars.

Given an arbitrary CRCW PRAM with $\Theta(V+E)$ processors, every computational step in the algorithm defined above runs in $\Theta(1)$ time. Therefore, we only need to determine the number of iterations required for the main loop before the algorithm naturally terminates with stars corresponding to every connected component. It can be shown that each pass through the loop reduces the height of a non-star tree by a fixed fraction. Therefore, the algorithm will terminate after $O(\log V)$ steps, yielding an algorithm with total cost of $O((V+E)\log V)$, which is not optimal. In fact, slightly more efficient algorithms are possible, but they are beyond the scope of this book.

### Mesh

Recall that a single step of a PRAM computation with $n$ processors operating on a set of $n$ data items can be simulated on a mesh of size $n$ in $\Theta(n^{1/2})$ time by sort-based associative read and associative write operations. Therefore, given a graph $G=(V,E)$ represented by a set of $|E|$ unordered edges, distributed arbitrarily one per processor on a mesh of size $|E|$, the component labeling algorithm can be solved in $\Theta(E^{1/2}\log E)$ time. Notice that this is at most a factor of $\Theta(\log E)$ from optimal on a mesh of size $|E|$. However, it is often convenient to represent a dense graph by an adjacency matrix. So consider the situation in which a $|V|\times|V|$ adjacency matrix is distributed in a natural fashion on a mesh of size $|V|^2$. Then, by applying the time-optimal transitive closure algorithm followed by a simple row or column rotation, the component labeling algorithm can be solved in $\Theta(V)$ time, which is optimal for this combination of architecture and graph representation.

## Minimum-Cost Spanning Trees

Suppose we want to install an Internet backbone at an office park so that there is at least one *path* between every pair of buildings. Further, suppose we want to minimize the total amount of "cable" that we lay. Viewing the buildings as vertices and the cables between buildings as edges, then this cabling problem is reduced to determining a spanning tree covering the buildings in which the total length of cable that is laid is minimized. This leads to the definition of a minimum-cost spanning tree.

Given a connected undirected graph $G = (V,E)$, we define a *spanning tree* $T = (V,E')$, where $E' \subseteq E$, as a connected acyclic graph. The reader should verify that in order for $T$ to have the same vertex set as the connected graph $G$, and for $T$ not to contain any cycles, $T$ must contain exactly $|V| - 1$ edges. Suppose that for every edge $e \in E$, there exists a *weight* $w(e)$, where such a weight might represent, for example, the cost, length, or time required to traverse the edge. Then a *minimum-cost spanning tree* $T$ is a spanning tree over $G$ in which the weight of the tree is minimized with respect to every spanning tree of $G$. The weight of a tree $T = (V,E')$ is defined intuitively to be

$$w(T) = \sum\nolimits_{e \in E'} w(e).$$

Note that a minimum-cost spanning tree is sometimes referred to as a *minimal spanning tree*, *minimum-weight spanning tree*, *minimum spanning tree*, or *MST.*

### RAM

In this section, we consider three traditional algorithms for determining a minimum-cost spanning tree of a connected, weighted, undirected graph $G = (V,E)$ on a RAM. All three algorithms use a *greedy* approach to solving the problem by repeatedly making the best local choice in an effort to obtain the global solution. At any point during these algorithms, a set of edges $E'$ exists that represents a subset of some minimal spanning tree of $G$. At each step of these algorithms, a "best" edge is selected from those that remain, based on certain properties, and added to the working minimal spanning tree. One of the critical properties of any edge that is added to $E'$ is that it is *safe*, *i.e.*, that the updated edge set $E'$ will continue to represent a subset of the edges of some minimal spanning tree for $G$.

#### *Kruskal's Algorithm*

The first algorithm we consider is *Kruskal's algorithm.* In this greedy algorithm, $E'$ is a forest over all vertices $V$ in $G$. Furthermore, this forest will always be a subset of some minimum spanning tree. Initially, we set $E' = \phi$, which represents the forest of isolated vertices. We also sort the edges of the graph into increasing order by weight. At each step in the algorithm, the next smallest weight edge from the ordered list is chosen and that edge is added to $E'$ so long as it does not create a cycle. The algorithm follows.

#### *Kruskal's MST Algorithm*

In 1956, J.B. Kruskal proposed a greedy algorithm for determining the minimal spanning tree of a graph. Kruskal's approach was to assume initially that every vertex of a graph $G = (V, E)$ is an independent connected component of a graph $G' = (V, \phi)$, which will morph into the minimal spanning tree $G' = (V, E')$ by adding edges to $E'$ in a greedy fashion. Specifically, at each iteration of the algorithm, an edge of minimal weight that does not create a cycle in $G'$ will be added to $E'$.

The algorithm terminates when there are no edges left to add to $G' = (V, E')$, the minimal spanning tree of $G = (V, E)$.

The resources required by the algorithm are dependent on the data structures chosen. We choose data structures that balance *i*) the time to perform an operation to sort the edges $E$ by weight, *ii*) the time to determine the component label of a vertex, and *iii*) the time to combine two components of the graph $G'$ as it is being constructed. In addition, the data structures we use to implement the graph do not use an unreasonable amount of space.

The algorithm that we provide will utilize two critical data structures. The first data structure will provide easy access for determining the component label of a vertex. It takes the form of a set of upward directed trees. There is direct access to each node. The label of the root of a component will serve as the label of the component and can be determined for any vertex by following the unique path of upward directed links to the root of the tree. The second data structure will be used to keep track of the edges as they are being added to $E'$ to form the minimal spanning tree $G' = (V, E')$. This second data structure can be a simple bag, unordered list, stack, or queue, to name a few. However, since a MST algorithm is typically used in the middle of a larger solution, we will use a set of adjacency lists to store the edges of the MST under the assumption that this will make these edges more easily accessible upon completion of Kruskal's algorithm.

```
The input consists of a connected, weighted, undirected
graph G=(V,E) with weight function w on the edges e∈E.
E' ← φ              {E' will become the edge set of the MST.}
For each v∈V, create Component(v)={v}. That is, every
vertex is initially its own connected component in G'.
This means, for each v∈V, set v.parent=null and
v.vertex_count=1.
Sort E into nondecreasing order by the weight
function w.
For each (u,v) ∈ E considered by sorted order, do the
following.
  Let r_u=Component(u) and r_v=Component(v) be the root
  vertices of the components of u and v, respectively.
  If r_u≠r_v then
    E' ← E' ∪ (u,v)              {update the edges of the MST}
    If r_u.vertex_count ≤ r_v.vertex_count then
    r_u.parent ← r_v and add r_u.vertex_count to
    r_v.vertex_count else r_v.parent ← r_u and add
    r_v.vertex_count to r_u.vertex_count.        {This step
                                   combines components of G'.}
  End If r_u≠r_v
End For
```

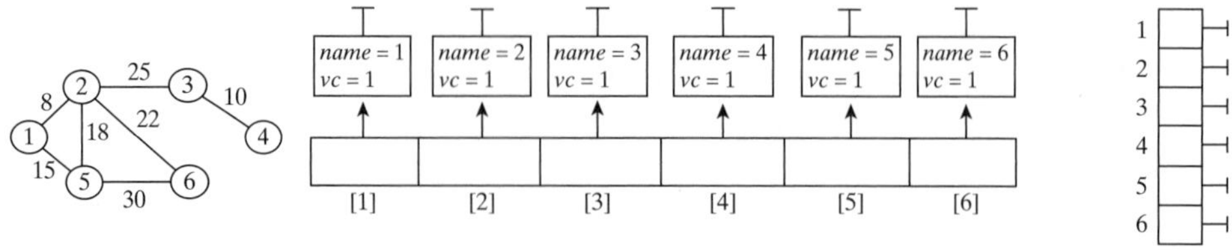


(a) On the left, the graph $G$ with both vertex labels and edge weights shown. In the middle, the initial forest of $G$ with vertices accessed through an array of pointers. In this initial forest, each vertex is an isolated tree. We use *vc* for the vertex count of a tree-like component in this graph. On the right, the initial adjacency lists in which no edges have yet been determined for $G'$, the minimal spanning tree (MST) of $G$.

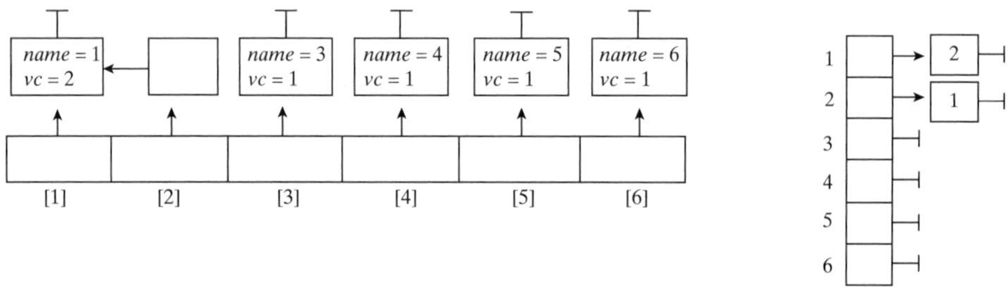


(b) The edge of $G$ between $v_1$ and $v_2$ is the smallest-weight edge. It is used to combine two components of $G'$ and is added in the adjacency lists.

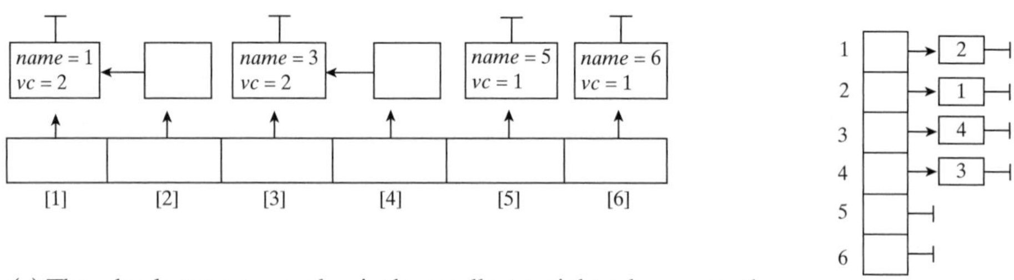


(c) The edge between $v_3$ and $v_4$ is the smallest-weight edge currently available. It is used to combine two components of $G'$ and is added in the adjacency lists.

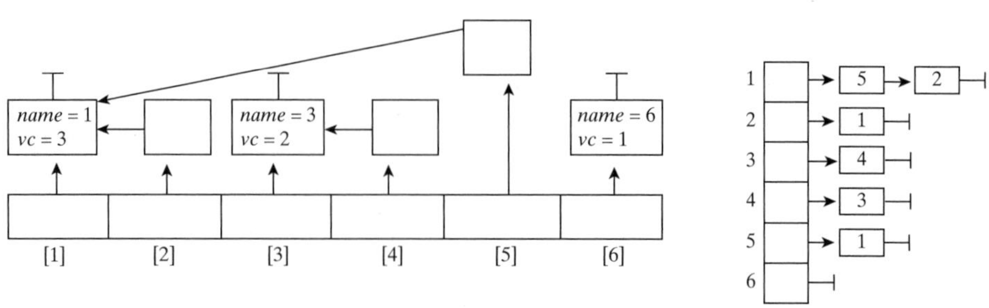


(d) The edge between $v_1$ and $v_5$ is the smallest-weight edge currently available. It is used to combine two components of $G'$ and is added in the adjacency lists.

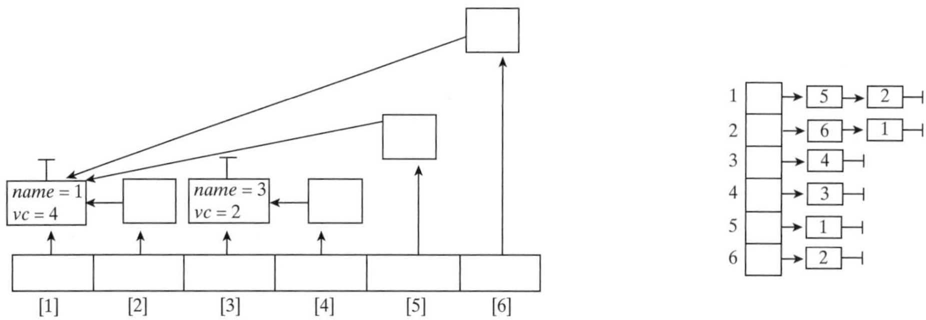


(e) The smallest-weight edge now available, between $v_2$ and $v_5$, is not added since these vertices were already in the same component of $G'$. Instead, the next smallest-weight edge, between $v_2$ and $v_6$ is added to the adjacency lists. Notice that in the connectivity graph to the left, the parent pointer of $v_6$ indexes $v_1$ rather than $v_2$, since $v_1$ is the root vertex of the component of $G'$ containing $v_2$.

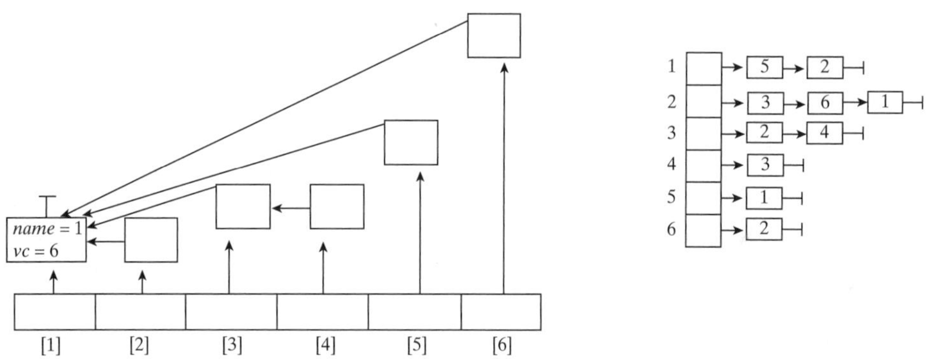


(f) The next smallest-weight edge, between $v_2$ and $v_3$, is added to the adjacency lists. As before, in $G'$ the parent pointer of $v_3$ indexes $v_1$ rather than $v_2$, since $v_1$ is the root vertex in its component of $G'$ before the union of the components of $v_2$ and $v_3$. The edge between $v_5$ and $v_6$ is not added, since these vertices are already in the same component of $G'$.

**FIGURE 12-19** *Our implementation of Kruskal's algorithm involves two data structures. The first is an auxiliary graph that shows the connectivity of the emerging Minimal Spanning Tree (MST). In this graph, all components are upward-pointing trees that will eventually be combined into a single tree-like graph. During the algorithm, this structure is used to keep track of the component of each vertex at each stage of the algorithm. The second data structure is an adjacency list structure that is built up and will eventually contain the edges corresponding to the MST. E', the edge set of the eventual MST, is initially empty. We add one edge to E' during every stage of the algorithm, while simultaneously combining the components of each vertex of the edge added. When there are no more edges to add, the algorithm is done and we have the final E', which represents the final MST G'.*

Given the data structures described, the statement $E' \leftarrow \varphi$ is equivalent to creating the initial graph $G'$, represented by empty adjacency lists in the structure that eventually will represent $G'$, the MST of $G$. The initialization of the adjacency lists and of $G'$ as a set of isolated vertices is performed in $\Theta(V)$ time. Sorting the edges takes $\Theta(E \log E)$ time.

Suppose that edge $(u, v) \in E$ is added to $E'$ in the algorithm given above. Let $r_1$ and $r_2$ be the root vertices of the components of $G'$ containing $u$ and $v$, respectively. Without loss of generality, assume the component rooted at $r_2$ has fewer vertices than the component rooted at $r_1$. Then the two components are combined by assigning $r_2$ to point to $r_1$, and updating the number of vertices in the combined component by adding together the number of vertices in the two original components. This step is performed in $\Theta(1)$ time.

When two components of $G'$ are combined, the identity of the smaller of the two components takes on that of the larger component. Notice that every vertex is updated $O(\log V)$ times since a vertex of $G'$ is only updated when its component in $G'$ is combined with a larger component. Further, the combine operation increases by at most 1 the number of edges of a vertex from the root of its component in $G'$. Thus, the number of edges between any vertex and the root of its component in $G'$ is $O(\log V)$. Hence, each call of the *Component* function is performed in $O(\log V)$ time. Since a component in $G'$ has connectivity properties of a tree, and a tree of $|V|$ vertices has $\Theta(V)$ edges, there are $\Theta(V)$ combine operations performed in a total of $\Theta(V)$ time. Since every edge in $E$ generates $\Theta(1)$ calls to the *Component* function, it follows that the time to perform all *Component* operations is $\Theta(E \log V)$. Therefore, the running time of the algorithm, as described, is $\Theta(E \log E)$, which is $\Theta(E \log V)$.

An alternative implementation to our presentation of Kruskal's algorithm follows. Suppose that instead of initially sorting the edges into nondecreasing order by weight, we place the weighted edges into a heap, and that during each iteration of the algorithm, we simply extract the minimum weighted edge left in the heap. Note that such a heap can be constructed in $\Theta(E \log E) = O(E \log V)$ time, and a heap extraction can be performed in $\Theta(\log E) = O(\log V)$ time. Therefore, the heap-based variant of this algorithm runs in $O(E \log V)$ time to set up the initial heap and $O(\log V)$ time to perform the operation required during each of the $O(E)$ iterations. Therefore, a heap-based approach results in a total running time of $O(E \log V)$, including the operations that combine components.

### *Prim's Algorithm*

The second algorithm we consider is *Prim's algorithm* for determining a minimum-cost spanning forest of a weighted, connected, undirected graph $G = (E, V)$, with edge weight function $w$. The approach taken in this greedy algorithm is to add edges continually to $E' \subset E$ so that $E'$ represents a tree with the property that it is a subtree of some minimum spanning tree of $G$. Initially, an arbitrary vertex $r \in V$ is chosen to be the root of the tree that will be grown. Next, an edge $(r, u)$ is used to initialize $E'$, where $(r, u)$ has minimal weight among edges incident on $r$. As the algorithm continues, an edge of minimum weight between some vertex in the current tree, represented by $E'$, and some vertex not in the current tree, is chosen and added to $E'$. The algorithm follows.

***Prim's MST Algorithm***

```
 1.  The input consists of a connected, weighted,
     undirected graph G = (E, V) with weight function w
     on the edges e ∈ E.
 2.  Let vertex set V = {v1, v2, . . . , vn}.
 3.  Let the root of the tree be r = v1.
 4.  Initialize NotInTree = {v2, . . . , vn}.
 5.  For all v ∈ NotInTree, initialize smalledge(v) ← ∞.
 6.  Set smalledge(r) ← 0 since r is in the tree.
 7.  Set parent(r) ← null since r is the root of the
     tree.
 8.  For all v ∈ Adj(r), do
 9.    parent(v) ← r
10.    smalledge(v) ← w(r, v)
11.  End For all v ∈ Adj(r)
12.  While NotInTree ≠ ϕ, do
13.    u ← ExtractMin(NotInTree)     {Member of NotInTree
                                    with minimal-weight edge
                                    to a member of the tree}
14.    Add (u, parent(u)) to E' and remove u from
       NotInTree.
15.    For all v ∈ Adj(u) do
16.      If v ∉ NotInTree and w(u, v) < smalledge(v), then
                         {If v is already in the tree, update}
17.        parent(v) ← u
18.        smalledge(v) ← w(u, v)
19.      End If
20.    End For
21.  End While
```

The structure *NotInTree* is most efficiently implemented as a priority queue since the major operations include finding a minimum weight vertex in *NotInTree* and removing it from *NotInTree*. Suppose that *NotInTree* is implemented as a heap. Then the heap can be initialized (lines 4-11) in $\Theta(V \log V)$ time. The While-loop (lines 12-21) is executed $|V| - 1$ times. Therefore, the $O(\log V)$ time *ExtractMin* operation is invoked $\Theta(V)$ times. Thus, the total time to perform all *ExtractMin* operations is $O(V \log V)$.

The test at line 16 can be performed in $\Theta(1)$ time. This follows from the observation that to see if a vertex is in the tree, *i.e.*, is not in *NotInTree*, it suffices to check whether or not the parent of the vertex is *null.* Now consider the time required to perform the operations specified in lines 17 and 18. Since every edge in a graph is determined by two vertices, lines 17 and 18 of the procedure can be invoked at most twice for every edge. Therefore, these assignments are performed at most $\Theta(E)$ times. However, notice that line 17 requires the adjustment of an entry in the priority queue, which runs in $O(\log V)$ time. Therefore, the running time for the entire algorithm is $O(V \log V + E \log V)$, which is $O(E \log V)$, since the graph is assumed to be connected. Notice that this is the same asymptotic running time as Kruskal's algorithm. However, by using Fibonacci heaps instead of traditional heaps, it should be noted that the time to perform Prim's algorithm on a RAM can be reduced to $\Theta(E + V \log V)$.

**Sollin's Algorithm**

Finally, we mention *Sollin's algorithm.* In this greedy algorithm, $E'$ will always represent a forest over all vertices $V$ in $G$. Initially, $E' = \phi$, which represents the forest of isolated vertices. At each step in the algorithm, every tree in the forest nominates one edge to be considered for inclusion in $E'$. Specifically, every tree nominates an edge of minimal weight between a vertex in its tree and a vertex in a distinct tree. So during the $i^{\text{th}}$ iteration of the algorithm, the $|V| - (i - 1)$ trees represented by $E'$ generate $|V| - (i - 1)$ not necessarily distinct edges to be considered for inclusion. The minimal weight edge will then be selected from these nominees for inclusion in $E'$. The sequential algorithm and analysis is left as an exercise.

## PRAM

In this section, we consider the problem of constructing a minimum-cost spanning tree for a connected graph represented by a weight matrix on a CREW PRAM. Given a connected graph $G = (V,E)$, we assume that the weights of the edges are stored in a matrix $W$. That is, entry $W(i, j)$ corresponds to the weight of edge $(i, j) \in E$. Since the graph is not necessarily complete, we define $W(i, j) = \infty$ if the edge $(i, j) \notin E$. Since we assume that self-edges are not present in the input, we should note that $W(i, i) = \infty$ for all $1 \le i \le n$. Notice that we use $\infty$ to represent nonexistent edges since the problem is one of determining a *minimum*-weight spanning tree.

The algorithm we consider is based on Sollin's algorithm, as previously described. Initially, we construct a forest of isolated vertices, which are then repetitively merged into trees until a single tree, *i.e.*, a minimum spanning tree, remains. The procedure for merging trees at a given stage of the algorithm is to consider one candidate edge $e_i$ from every tree $T_i$. The candidate edge $e_i$ corresponds to an edge of minimum weight connecting a vertex of $T_i$ to a vertex in some $T_j$ where $i \neq j$. All candidate edges are then added to the set of edges representing a minimum weight spanning tree of $G$, as we have done with previously described minimum spanning tree algorithms. Note that some of the added edges may be removed later.

During each of the merge steps, we must collapse every tree in the forest into a virtual vertex, *i.e.*, a supervertex. Throughout the algorithm, every vertex must know the identity of the tree that it belongs to so that candidate edges can be chosen properly during each iteration of the algorithm. We will use the component labeling technique, described earlier in this chapter, to accomplish this task.

Without loss of generality, we assume that every edge has a unique weight. Notice that in practice, ties in edge weight can be broken by appending unique edge labels to every weight. The basic algorithm follows.

The input consists of a connected, weighted, undirected graph $G = (V, E)$ with weight function $w$ on the edges $e \in E$. Let weight matrix $W$ be used to store the weights of the edges, where $W(i, j) = w(i, j)$

```
Let vertex set V={v1, . . . , vn}.
Let G' = (V, E') represent a minimum spanning tree
of G that is under construction.
Initially, set E' = ϕ.
Initially, set the forest of trees F={T1, . . . , Tn}
where Ti = ({vi}, ϕ). That is, every vertex is its
own tree.
While |F|>1, do
  For all Ti ∈ F, determine Candi, an edge of
  minimum weight between a vertex in Ti and
  a vertex in Tj  where i≠j.
  For all i, add Candi to E'.
  Combine all trees in F that are in the same connected
  component with respect to the edges just added to E'.
  Assuming that r trees remain in the forest, relabel
  these virtual vertices, i.e., connected components, so
  that F={T1, . . . , Tr}.
  Relabel the edges in E so that the vertices correspond
  to the appropriate virtual vertices. This can be ac-
  complished by reducing the weight matrix W so that it
  contains only information pertaining to the r virtual
  vertices.
End While
```

Consider the running time of the algorithm as described. Since the graph $G$ is connected, we know that every time through the While-loop, the number of trees in the forest will be reduced by at least half. That is, every tree in the forest will hook up with at least one other tree. Therefore, the number of iterations of the While-loop is $O(\log V)$. The operations described inside of the While-loop can be performed by invoking procedures to sort edges based on vertex labels, perform parallel prefix in order to determine candidate edges, and apply the component-labeling algorithm in order to collapse connected components into virtual vertices. Since each of these procedures can be performed in time logarithmic in the size of the input, the running time for the entire algorithm as given is $O(\log^2 V)$.

### Mesh

The mesh algorithm we discuss in this section is identical in spirit to that just presented for the PRAM. Our focus in this section is on the implementation of the specific steps of the algorithm. We assume that the input to the problem is a weight matrix $W$ representing a graph $G=(V,E)$, where $|V|=n$. Initially, $W(i,j)$, the weight of edge $(i,j) \in E$, is stored in mesh processor $P_{i,j}$. Again we assume that $W(i,j)=\infty$ if the edge does not exist or if $i=j$. We also assume, without loss of generality, that the edge weights are unique.

We define the forest $F=\{T_1,\ldots,T_n\}$, where $T_i=(\{v_i\},\phi)$. During each of the $\lceil \log_2 n \rceil$ iterations of the algorithm, the number of virtual vertices, *i.e.*, supervertices, in the forest is reduced by at least half. The reader might also note that at any point during the course of the algorithm, only a single minimum-weight edge needs to be maintained between any two virtual vertices. We need to discuss the details of reducing the forest during a generic iteration of the algorithm. Suppose that the forest $F$ currently has $r$ virtual vertices. Notice that at the start of an iteration of the While-loop, as given in the previous section, every virtual vertex is represented by a unique row and column in an $r \times r$ weight matrix $W$. As shown in Figure 12-20, entry $W(i,j)$, $1 \le i,j \le r$, denotes the weight and identity of a minimum-weight edge between virtual vertex $i$ and virtual vertex $j$.

| | 1 | 2 | 3 | ... | $r$ |
|---|---|---|---|---|---|
| 1 | $(\infty,-)$ | $(W(1,2),e_{1,2})$ | $(W(1,3),e_{1,3})$ | ... | $(W(1,r),e_{1,r})$ |
| 2 | $(W(2,1),e_{2,1})$ | $(\infty,-)$ | $(W(2,3),e_{2,3})$ | ... | $(W(2,r),e_{2,r})$ |
| 3 | $(W(3,1),e_{3,1})$ | $(W(3,2),e_{3,2})$ | $(\infty,-)$ | ... | $(W(3,r),e_{3,r})$ |
| | ⋮ | | | | |
| $r$ | $(W(r,1),e_{r,1})$ | $(W(r,2),e_{r,2})$ | $(W(r,3),e_{r,3})$ | ... | $(\infty,-)$ |

**FIGURE 12-20** *The $r \times r$ matrix $W$, as distributed one entry per processor in a natural fashion on an $r \times r$ submesh. Notice that each entry in processor $P_{i,j}$, $1 \le i,j \le r$, contains the record $(W_{i,j}, e_{i,j})$, which represents the minimum weight of any edge between virtual vertices, i.e., supervertices, $v_i$ and $v_j$, as well as information about one such edge $e_{i,j}$ to which the weight corresponds. In this situation, the "edge" $e_{i,j}$ is actually a record containing information identifying its original vertices and its current virtual vertices.*

In order to determine the candidate edge for every virtual vertex $v_i$, $1 \le i \le r$, simply perform a row rotation simultaneously over all rows of $W$, where the rotation is restricted to the $r \times r$ region of the mesh currently storing $W$. The edge in $E$ that this virtual edge represents can be conveniently stored in the rightmost column of the $r \times r$ region since there is only one such edge per row, as shown in Figure 12-21. Based on the virtual vertex indices of these edges being added to $E'$, an adjacency matrix can be created in the $r \times r$ region that represents the connections being formed between the current virtual vertices, as shown in Figure 12-22. Warshall's algorithm can then be applied to this adjacency matrix in order to determine the connected components. That is, an application of Warshall's algorithm will determine which trees in $F$ have just been combined using the edges in $E'$. The rows of the matrix can now be sorted according to their new virtual vertex number. Next, in a similar fashion, the columns of the matrix can be sorted with respect to the new virtual vertex numbers. Now within every interval of rows, a minimum weight edge can be determined to every other new virtual vertex by a combination of row and column rotations. Finally, a concurrent write can be used to compress the $r \times r$ matrix to an $r' \times r'$ matrix, as shown in Figure 12-23.

Notice that each of the critical mesh operations working in an $r \times r$ region can be performed in $O(r)$ time. Since the size of the matrix is reduced by at least a constant factor after every iteration, the running time of the algorithm is $\Theta(n)$,

| | 1 | 2 | 3 | 4 | 5 | 6 |
|---|---|---|---|---|---|---|
| 1 | $\infty$ | 98 | 17 | 36 | 47 | 58<br>$17, e_{1,3}$ |
| 2 | 98 | $\infty$ | 38 | 89 | 21 | 39<br>$21, e_{2,5}$ |
| 3 | 17 | 38 | $\infty$ | 97 | 27 | 73<br>$17, e_{3,1}$ |
| 4 | 36 | 89 | 97 | $\infty$ | 18 | 9<br>$9, e_{4,6}$ |
| 5 | 47 | 21 | 27 | 18 | $\infty$ | 47<br>$18, e_{5,4}$ |
| 6 | 58 | 39 | 73 | 9 | 47 | $\infty$<br>$9, e_{6,4}$ |

**FIGURE 12-21** *A sample $6 \times 6$ weight matrix in which, for simplicity's sake, only the weights of the records are given. Notice that the processors in the last column also contain a minimum-weight edge and its identity after the row rotation.*

| | 1 | 2 | 3 | 4 | 5 | 6 |
|---|---|---|---|---|---|---|
| 1 | 0 | 0 | 1 | 0 | 0 | 0 |
| 2 | 0 | 0 | 0 | 0 | 1 | 0 |
| 3 | 1 | 0 | 0 | 0 | 0 | 0 |
| 4 | 0 | 0 | 0 | 0 | 0 | 1 |
| 5 | 0 | 0 | 0 | 1 | 0 | 0 |
| 6 | 0 | 0 | 0 | 1 | 0 | 0 |

**FIGURE 12-22** *The $6 \times 6$ adjacency matrix corresponding to the minimum-weight edges selected by the row rotations as shown in Figure 12-21.*

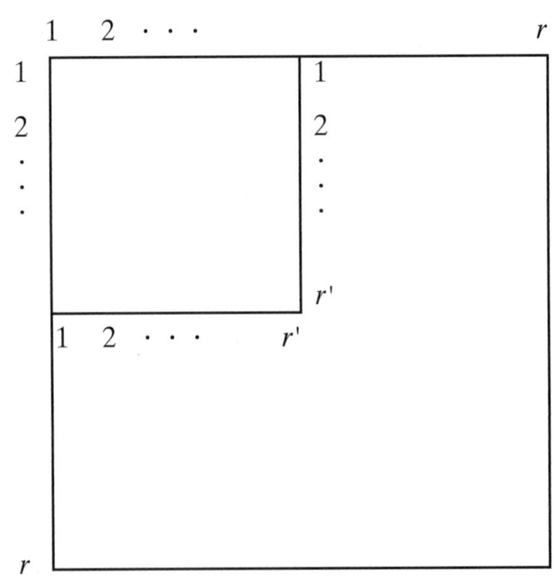


**FIGURE 12-23** *A concurrent write is used within the $r \times r$ region of the mesh to compress and update the $r'$ rows and columns corresponding to the $r'$ supervertices. This results in the creation of an $r' \times r'$ weight matrix in the upper-left regions of the $r \times r$ region so that the algorithm can proceed to the next stage.*

which includes the time to perform a final concurrent read to mark all of the edges in the minimum spanning tree that was determined.

## Shortest-Path Problems

In this section, we consider problems involving shortest paths within graphs. Specifically, we consider two fundamental problems, defined below.

1. **Single-Source Shortest-Path Problem:** Given a weighted, directed graph $G = (V, E)$, a solution to the *single-source shortest-path problem* requires that we determine a shortest, *i.e.*, minimum-weight, path from *source vertex* $s \in V$ to every other vertex $v \in V$. Notice that the notion of a minimum-weight path generalizes that of a shortest path in that a shortest path, *i.e.*, a path containing a minimal number of edges, can be regarded as a minimum-weight path in a graph in which all edges have weight 1.
2. **All-Pairs Shortest-Path Problem:** Given a weighted, directed graph $G = (V, E)$, a solution to the *all-pairs shortest-path problem* requires the determination of a shortest, *i.e.*, minimum weight, path between every pair of distinct vertices $u, v \in V$.

For problems involving shortest paths, several issues must be considered, such as whether or not negative weights and/or cycles are permitted in the input graph. It is also important to decide whether the total weight of a minimum-weight path will be presented as the sole result or if a representation of a path that generates such a weight is also required. Critical details such as these, which often depend on the definition of the problem, have a great effect on the algorithm that is to be developed and utilized. In the remainder of this section, we consider representative variants of shortest-path problems as ways to introduce critical paradigms.

### Single-Source Shortest-Path RAM Algorithm

For the RAM, we will consider the single-source shortest-path problem, for which we need to determine the weight of a shortest path from a unique source vertex to every other vertex in the graph. Further, we assume that the result must contain a representation of an appropriate shortest path from the source vertex to every other vertex in the graph. Assume that we are given a weighted, directed graph $G = (V, E)$, in which every edge $e \in E$ has an associated weight $w(e)$. Let $s \in V$ be the known source vertex. The algorithm that we present will produce a *shortest-path tree* $T = (V', E')$, rooted at $s$, where $V' \subset V$, $E' \subset E$, $V'$ is the set of vertices reachable from $s$, and for all $v \in V'$, a simple path from $s$ to $v$ in $T$ that is a minimum-weight path from $s$ to $v$ in $G$. It is important to emphasize that "shortest" paths, *i.e.*, minimum-weight paths, are not necessarily unique and that shortest-path trees, *i.e.*, trees representing minimum-weight paths, are also

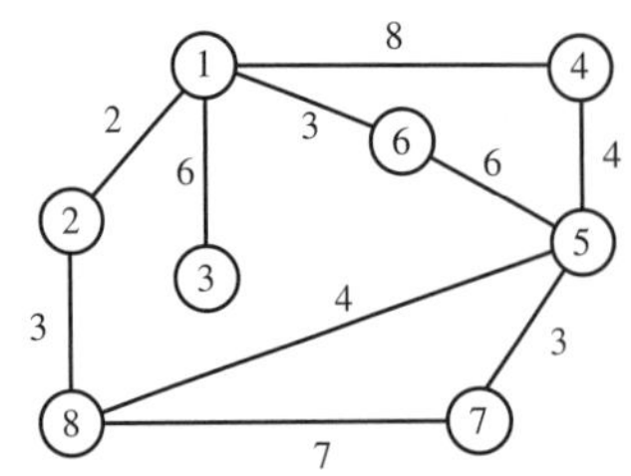

(a) A weighted, undirected graph $G = (V, E)$.

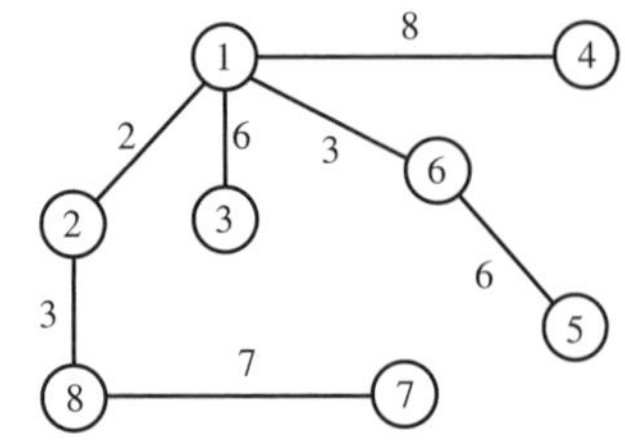

(b) A shortest-path tree. Notice the path <1, 2, 8, 7> of weight 12 chosen between source vertex 1 and sink vertex 7.

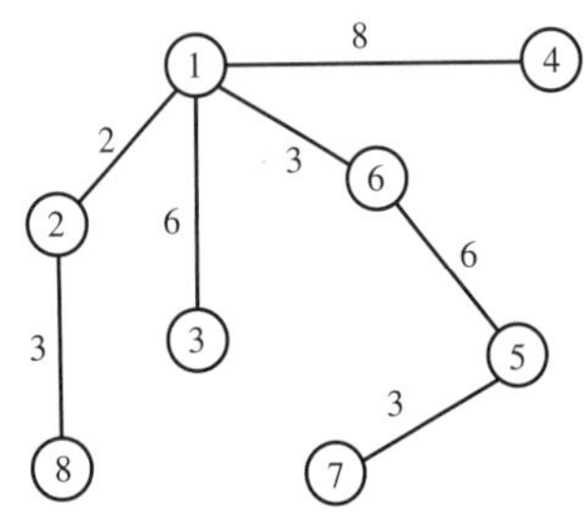

(c) A different shortest-path tree. Notice that the path <1, 6, 5, 7> chosen between vertices 1 and 7 is also of total weight 12.

**FIGURE 12-24** *A demonstration that shortest paths and shortest-path trees need not be unique.*

not necessarily unique. See Figure 12-24, which shows two shortest path trees for the given graph $G$.

We consider *Dijkstra's algorithm* for solving the single-source shortest-path problem on a weighted, directed graph $G = (V, E)$ where all of the edge weights are nonnegative. Let $s \in V$ be the predetermined source vertex. The algorithm will create and maintain a set $V'$ of vertices that, when complete, is used to represent the final shortest-path tree $T$. When a vertex $v$ is inserted into $V'$, it is assumed that the edge $(parent(v), v)$ is inserted into $E'$.

Initially, every vertex $v \in V$ is assumed to be at distance $dist(v) = \infty$ from the source vertex $s$, with the exception of all vertices directly connected to $s$ by an edge. Let $u$ be a neighboring vertex of $s$. Then, since $(s, u) \in E$, we initialize the distance from $s$ to $u$ to be $dist(u) = w(s, u)$, the weight of the edge originating at $s$ and terminating at $u$.

The algorithm consists of continually identifying a vertex that has not been added to $V'$, which is at minimum distance from $s$. Suppose the new vertex to be added to $V'$ is called $x$. Then after adding $x$ to $V'$, all vertices $t$ for which $(x, t) \in E$,

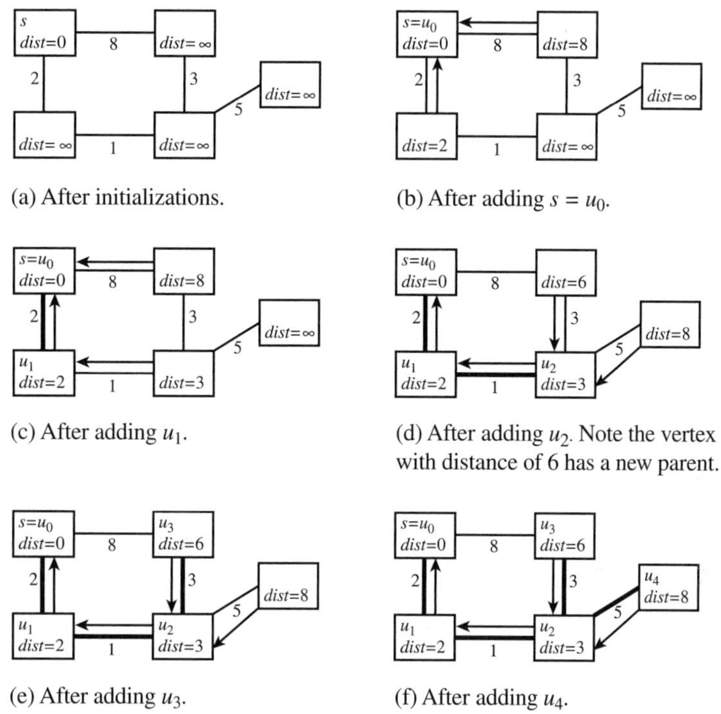


**FIGURE 12-25** *A demonstration of the progress of Dijkstra's algorithm, through the iterations of its While-loop, for constructing a shortest-path tree. The vertices are numbered $u_0, u_1, \ldots,$ in the order in which they are inserted into the tree. Arrows represent parent pointers. Dark edges are those inserted into the tree.*

are examined. If the current minimum distance from *s*, which is maintained in *dist*(*t*), can now be improved based on the fact that *x* is in *V*', then *dist*(*t*) is updated, and *parent*(*t*) is set to *x* (see Figure 12-25).

The algorithm follows.

- The algorithm takes a weighted, directed graph $G = (V, E)$ as input.
- Initialize the sets of vertices and edges in the shortest-path tree $T = (V', E')$ that this algorithm produces to be empty sets. That is, set $V' \leftarrow \phi$ and $E' \leftarrow \phi$.
- Initialize the set of available vertices to be added to $V'$ to be the entire set of vertices. That is, set $Avail \leftarrow V$.

```
For every vertex v ∈ V, do
  Set dist(v) ← ∞. That is, the distance from every
  vertex to the source is initialized to be infinity.
  Set parent(v) ← null. That is, the parent of every
  vertex is initially assumed to be nonexistent.
End For
```

```
Set dist(s) ← 0. That is, the distance from the source
to itself is 0. This step is critical to seeding the
While-loop that follows.
GrowingTree ← true
While Avail ≠ ϕ and GrowingTree, do
  Determine u ∈ Avail, where dist(u) is a minimum over
  all distances of vertices in Avail. Notice that the
  first pass through the loop yields u = s.
  If dist(u) is finite, then
    V' ← V' ∪ {u} and Avail ← Avail\{u}. That is, add u to
    the shortest-path tree and remove u from Avail.
    If u ≠ s, then E' ← E' ∪ {(parent(u), u)}. That is, add
    (parent(u), u) to the edge set of T.
    For every vertex v ∈ Adj(u), do           {Check to see
                                        if neighboring vertices
                                           should be updated.}
      If dist(v) > dist(u) + w(u, v), then             {Update
                          distance and parent information since
                              a shorter path is now possible.}
        dist(v) ← dist(u) + w(u, v)
        parent(v) ← u
      End If dist(v) > dist(u) + w(u, v)
    End For
  End If dist(u) is finite
  Else GrowingTree ← false           {(V', E') is the finished
                                     component of source vertex.}
End While
```

The algorithm is greedy in nature in that at each step the best local choice is taken and that choice is never undone. Dijkstra's algorithm relies on an efficient implementation of a priority queue, since the set *Avail* of available vertices is continually queried in terms of minimum distance. Suppose that the priority queue of *Avail* is maintained in a simple linear array. Then a generic query to the priority queue will, on average, run in $\Theta(V)$ time. Since there are $\Theta(V)$ such queries, they run in a total of $\Theta(V^2)$ time. Since each vertex is inserted into the shortest-path tree exactly once, this means that every edge in $E$ is examined exactly twice in terms of trying to update distance information to neighboring vertices. Therefore, the total time to update distance and parent information is $\Theta(E)$. It follows that the running time of the algorithm is $\Theta(V^2 + E)$, or $\Theta(V^2)$, since $E = O(V^2)$.

Notice that this algorithm is efficient for dense graphs. That is, if $E = \Theta(V^2)$, then the algorithm has an efficient running time of $\Theta(E)$. However, if the graph is sparse, then this implementation is not necessarily efficient. In fact, for a sparse graph, one might implement the priority queue as a binary heap or a Fibonacci heap in order to achieve a slightly more efficient running time.

### All-Pairs Shortest-Path Parallel Algorithm

For the PRAM and the mesh, we consider the all-pairs shortest-path problem, given a weight matrix as input. Specifically, suppose we are given a weighted, directed graph $G = (V, E)$ as input, where $|V| = n$ and every edge $(u, v) \in E$ has an associated weight $w(u, v)$. Further, assume that $G$ is represented by an $n \times n$ weight matrix $W$, where $W(u, v) = w(u, v)$ if $(u, v) \in E$ and $W(u, v) = \infty$ otherwise.

Let $W_k(u, v)$ represent the weight of a minimum-weight path from vertex $u$ to vertex $v$, assuming that the intermediate vertices traversed on the path from $u$ to $v$ are indexed in $\{1, 2, \ldots, k\}$. Then the matrix $W_n$ will contain the final weights representing a directed minimum-weight path between every pair of vertices. That is, $W_n(u, v)$ will contain the weight of a minimum-weight directed path with source $u$ and sink $v$, if such a path exists. $W_n(u, v)$ will have a value of $\infty$ if a $u \rightarrow v$ path does not exist.

Notice that we have recast the all-pairs shortest-path problem as a variant of the transitive closure problem discussed earlier in this chapter in the section "Computing the Transitive Closure of an Adjacency Matrix". Given a mesh of size $n^2$ in which processor $P_{i,j}$ stores weight information concerning a path from vertex $i$ to vertex $j$, we can represent the computation of $W$ as

$$W_k(i, j) = \min\{W_{k-1}(i, j), W_{k-1}(i, k) + W_{k-1}(k, j)\}.$$

Therefore, we can apply van Scoy's implementation of Warshall's algorithm, as described earlier in this chapter, in order to solve the problem on a mesh of size $n^2$ in optimal $\Theta(n)$ time. Notice that if the graph is dense (that is, $E = \Theta(V^2)$), then the weight matrix input is an efficient representation.

On a PRAM, notice that we can also implement Warshall's algorithm for computing the transitive closure of the input matrix $W$. Recall that two matrices can be multiplied in $\Theta(\log n)$ time on a PRAM containing $n^3/\log n$ processors. Given an $n \times n$ matrix as input on a PRAM, $W_n$ can be determined by performing $\Theta(\log n)$ such matrix multiplications. Therefore, given an $n \times n$ weight-matrix as input, the running time to solve the all-pairs shortest-path problem on a PRAM with $n^3/\log n$ processors is $\Theta(\log^2 n)$.

Notice that the algorithms we have presented for the all-pairs shortest-path problem give as output the total weight for every shortest path, but do not give shortest paths. Minor changes in the algorithms would enable us to have the shortest paths as part of the output, although the algorithms would become computationally more expensive as a result of doing so.

## Summary

In this chapter, we study algorithms to solve a variety of problems concerned with graphs. We present several methods, *i.e.*, adjacency list, adjacency matrix, and unordered edges, of representing a graph. We introduce efficient RAM solutions to fundamental problems such as breadth-first search and depth-first search. Warshall's efficient algorithm for computing the transitive closure of the adjacency matrix is discussed for the RAM, and van Scoy's efficient adaptation of the algorithm to the mesh is also presented. Connected component labeling algorithms are given for several models of computation. Several sequential and parallel algorithms for computing minimal-cost spanning trees are discussed. Solutions to shortest-path problems are given for multiple models of computation. These problems remain interesting open research problems for large-scale machines, including NOWs, clusters, and grids.

## Chapter Notes

In this chapter, we consider algorithms and paradigms to solve fundamental graph problems on a RAM, PRAM, and mesh computer. For a more in-depth treatment of sequential graph algorithms, please refer to the following sources:

- *Graph Algorithms* by S. Even (Computer Science Press, 1979).
- *Data Structures and Network Algorithms* by R.E. Tarjan (Society for Industrial and Applied Mathematics, 1983).
- "Basic Graph Algorithms" by S. Khuller and B. Raghavachari, in *Algorithms and Theory of Computation Handbook*, M.J. Atallah, ed., CRC Press, Boca Raton, FL, 1999.

For a survey of PRAM graph algorithms, complete with an extensive citation list, please refer to

- "A survey of parallel algorithms and shared memory machines" by R.M. Karp and V. Ramachandran, in the *Handbook of Theoretical Computer Science: Algorithms and Complexity*, A.J. van Leeuwen, ed. (Elsevier, New York, 1990, pp. 869–941).

The depth-first search procedure was developed by J.E. Hopcroft and R.E. Tarjan. Early citations to this work include

- "Efficient algorithms for graph manipulation" by J.E. Hopcroft and R.E. Tarjan, *Communications of the ACM* (16:372–378, 1973), and
- "Depth-first search and linear graph algorithms" by R.E. Tarjan, *SIAM Journal on Computing*, 1(2):146–160, June, 1972.

Warshall's innovative and efficient transitive closure algorithm was first presented in "A theorem on Boolean matrices" by S. Warshall in the *Journal of the*

*ACM* **9**, 1962, 11–12. An efficient mesh implementation of Warshall's algorithm is discussed in detail in *Parallel Algorithms for Regular Architectures* by R. Miller and Q.F. Stout (The MIT Press, Cambridge, 1996).

*An Introduction to Parallel Algorithms* by J. Já Já (Addison Wesley, 1992), contains details of PRAM algorithms for problems discussed in this chapter, including component labeling and minimum spanning trees. The PRAM component-labeling algorithm presented in this chapter comes from a combination of the algorithms presented in these sources:

- "A survey of parallel algorithms and shared memory machines" by R.M. Karp and V. Ramachandran, cited above, and
- "Introduction to Parallel Connectivity, List Ranking, and Euler Tour Techniques" by S. Baase in *Synthesis of Parallel Algorithms*, J.H. Reif, ed. (Morgan Kaufmann Publishers, San Mateo, CA, 1993, pp. 61–114).

The sequential minimum spanning tree algorithm presented in this chapter combines techniques presented in *Data Structures and Algorithms in JAVA* by M.T. Goodrich and R. Tamassia (John Wiley & Sons, Inc., New York, 1998), with those presented in *Introduction to Algorithms* by T.H. Cormen, C.E. Leiserson, R.L. Rivest, and C. Stein (3rd ed.: The MIT Press, Cambridge, MA, 2009). The minimum spanning tree algorithm for the PRAM was inspired by the one presented in *An Introduction to Parallel Algorithms* by J. Já Já (Addison Wesley, 1992), while the MST algorithm for the mesh was inspired by the one that appears in *Parallel Algorithms for Regular Architectures* by R. Miller and Q.F. Stout (The MIT Press, Cambridge, 1996).

For additional problems involving shortest paths, as well as techniques and algorithms for solving such problems, see the following sources.

- *Introduction to Algorithms* by T.H. Cormen, C.E. Leiserson, R.L. Rivest, and C. Stein (3rd ed.: The MIT Press, Cambridge, MA, 2009).
- *An Introduction to Parallel Algorithms* by J. Já Já (Addison Wesley, 1992).
- *Parallel Algorithms for Regular Architectures* by R. Miller and Q.F. Stout (The MIT Press, Cambridge, 1996).

## Exercises

1. Suppose a graph $G$ is represented by unordered edges. Give an efficient algorithm, as well as an analysis of its running time, to solve each of the following problems.
   a. Construct an adjacency-list representation of $G$ on a RAM. Provide an analysis of the running time of your algorithm.
   b. Construct an adjacency-list representation of $G$ on a PRAM with $|V| + |E|$ processors. Provide an analysis of the running time of your algorithm.

c. Construct an adjacency matrix representation of $G$ for the RAM, for a PRAM with $\Theta(V^2)$ processors, and for a mesh of size $\Theta(V^2)$ For the mesh, assume an initial distribution so that no processor has more than one edge, and include appropriate data movement operations in your algorithm.

**2.** Give an efficient RAM algorithm, along with an analysis of its running time, to compute the height of a nonempty binary tree. The *height* of a tree is the maximum number of edges between the root node and any leaf node. *Hint*: consider a recursive solution to the problem.

**3.** Prove that if $v_0$ and $v_1$ are distinct vertices of a graph $G = (V, E)$ and a path exists in $G$ from $v_0$ to $v_1$, then there is a simple path in $G$ from $v_0$ to $v_1$.

**4.** Recall that a graph $G = (V, E)$ is *complete* if an edge exists between every pair of vertices. Given an adjacency-list representation of $G$, describe an efficient algorithm to determine whether or not $G$ is complete. Analyze the algorithm for the RAM and for a CREW PRAM with $n^2 = |V|^2$ processors.

**5.** Suppose the graph $G = (V, E)$ is represented by an adjacency matrix, where $n = |V|$. Give an efficient algorithm to determine whether or not $G$ is complete, as defined in the previous exercise. Provide an analysis of your algorithm for the RAM, for an arbitrary CRCW PRAM with $n^2$ processors, and for an $n \times n$ mesh. Note for the mesh, at the end of the algorithm, every processor should know whether or not $G$ is complete.

**6.** Let $v_0$ and $v_1$ be distinct vertices of a graph $G = (V, E)$. Suppose we want to determine whether or not these two vertices are in the same component of $G$. One way to answer this query is to perform a component-labeling algorithm and then compare the component labels of $v_0$ and $v_1$. Give a "simple" search-based algorithm for the RAM and provide an analysis of its running time.

**7.** The *distance* between two vertices of a graph is the number of edges in a shortest path connecting the vertices. The distance between two vertices that are not connected is defined to be $\infty$. The *diameter* of a connected graph is the maximum distance between a pair of vertices of the graph. Give an algorithm to find the maximal diameter of the components of a graph. Provide an analysis of the running time of your algorithm for a PRAM of size $n^3/\log n$ and a mesh of size $n^2$.

**8.** Let $G = (V, E)$ be a connected graph. Suppose there is a Boolean function *hasTrait*(*vertex*) that can be applied to any vertex of $G$ in order to determine in $\Theta(1)$ time on a RAM whether or not the vertex has a certain trait.

- Given a graph represented by adjacency lists, describe an efficient RAM algorithm to determine whether or not there are adjacent vertices with the trait tested for by this function. Give an analysis of your algorithm.

- Suppose instead that the graph is represented by an adjacency matrix. Describe an efficient RAM algorithm to determine whether or not there are adjacent vertices with the trait tested for by this function. Give an analysis of your algorithm.

**9.** A *bipartite graph* is an undirected graph $G = (V, E)$ with nonempty subsets $V_0, V_1$ of $V$ such that $V_0 \cup V_1 = V$, $V_0 \cap V_1 = \phi$, and every member of $E$ joins a member of $V_0$ to a member of $V_1$. Let $T = (V, E')$ be a minimum spanning tree of a connected bipartite graph $G$. Show that $T$ is also a bipartite graph.

**10.** Suppose $G$ is a connected graph. Give an efficient algorithm to determine whether or not $G$ is a bipartite graph, as defined in the previous problem. Analyze the running time of the algorithm on the RAM.

**11.** Let $S = \{I_i = [a_i, b_i]\}_{i=1}^{n}$ be a set of intervals on the real line. An *interval graph* $G = (V, E)$ is determined by $S$ as follows. $V = \{v_i\}_{i=1}^{n}$, and for distinct indices $i$ and $j$, there is an edge from $v_i$ to $v_j$ if and only if $I_i \cap I_j \neq \varphi$. Give an efficient algorithm to construct an interval graph determined by a given set $S$ of intervals and analyze the algorithm's running time for a RAM. *Note*: there is a naïve algorithm that runs in $\Theta(n^2)$ time, where $n = |V|$. You should be able to give a more sophisticated algorithm that runs in $\Theta(n \log n + E)$ time.

**12.** Suppose $T = (V, E)$ is a tree. Explain the asymptotic relationship between $|E|$ and $|V|$.

**13.** Let $G = (V, E)$ be a connected graph. Recall we say $e \in E$ is a *bridge edge* of $G$ if the graph $G_e = (V, E \setminus \{e\})$ is disconnected.

a. A naïve algorithm may be given to identify all bridge edges as follows. Every edge $e$ is regarded as a possible bridge edge, and the graph $G_e$ is tested for connectedness. Show that such an algorithm runs in $O(E(V + E))$ time on a RAM.

b. Let $T$ be a minimal spanning tree for $G$. Show that every bridge edge of $G$ must be an edge of $T$.

c. Use the result of part b to obtain an algorithm for finding all bridge edges of $G$ that runs in $O(V^2 + E \log V)$ time on a RAM. *Hint*: use the result of Exercise 12.

**14.** Let $G = (V, E)$ be a connected graph. Recall an *articulation point* is a vertex of $G$ with the property that its removal would leave the resulting graph disconnected. That is, $v$ is an articulation point of $G$ if and only if the graph $G_v = (V \setminus \{v\}, E_v)$, where $E_v = \{e \in E \mid e \text{ is not incident on } v\}$, is a disconnected graph.

a. Suppose $|V| > 2$. Show that at least one vertex of a bridge edge of $G$ must be an articulation point of $G$.

b. Let $v \in V$ be an articulation point of $G$. Must there be a bridge edge of $G$ incident on $v$? If so, give a proof; if not, give an example.

c. Let $G$ be a connected graph for which there is a positive number $C$ such that no vertex has degree greater than $C$. Let $v \in V$ be a vertex of $G$. Give an algorithm to determine whether or not $v$ is an articulation point. Discuss the running time of implementations of your algorithm on the RAM, CRCW PRAM of size $|V| + |E|$, and mesh of size $|E|$.

**15.** Let $\otimes$ be an associative binary operation that is commutative and that can be applied to data stored at the vertices of a graph $G = (V, E)$. Assume a single computation of $\otimes$ runs in $\Theta(1)$ time. Suppose $|V| > 1$. Suppose $G$ is connected and represented in memory by unordered edges. Give an efficient RAM algorithm for a semigroup computation based on $\otimes$, on the vertices of $G$. Give the running time of your algorithm.

**16.** Suppose it is known that a graph $G = (V, E)$ is a tree with root vertex $v_* \in V$, but the identity of the parent vertex *parent*($v$) is not known for $v \in V \setminus \{v_*\}$. How can every vertex $v$ determine *parent*($v$)? What is the running time of your algorithm on a RAM?

**17.** Give an efficient RAM algorithm to determine the number of descendants of every vertex of a binary tree $T = (V, E)$ with root vertex $v_* \in V$. What is the running time of your algorithm?

**18.** Analyze the running time of Sollin's algorithm, as described in the text.

**19.** Given a labeled $n \times n$ digitized image, and one "marked" pixel per component, provide an efficient algorithm to construct a minimum-distance spanning tree within every component with respect to using the "marked" pixel as the root. Present analysis for the RAM.

# 13

# Numerical Problems

With the exception of Chapter 6, "Matrix Operations," most of this book has been concerned with "non-numerical" problems and algorithms. That is not to say that we have avoided doing arithmetic. Rather, we have concentrated on problems in which algorithms do not require the intensive use of floating point calculations or the unusual storage required for large integers or highly precise floating point numbers. It is important to realize that a stable, accurate, and efficient use of numerically intensive calculations is critical to scientific and technical computing.

As we have mentioned previously, the emerging discipline of *computational science and engineering* is now accepted as the third science, complementing both theoretical science and laboratory science. Computational science and engineering is an interdisciplinary subject that unites computing and mathematics with disciplinary efforts in chemistry, biology, physics, and other scientific and engineering fields. In terms of computing, major components include high-end computing systems, state-of-the art networking, high-end visualization, and high-end storage. In order for these systems to perform at their fullest, they require advanced paradigms, fundamental algorithms, middleware, and disciplinary applications. Computational science and engineering focuses on problems that require simulation and modeling in order to make significant advances to efforts in scientific and engineering fields. In this chapter, we examine algorithms for some fundamental numerical problems.

In most of our previous discussions, we have used $n$ as a measure of the size of a problem, in the sense of how much data is processed by an algorithm or how much storage is required by the data processed. This is not always the case for the problems discussed in this chapter. For example, the value of $x^n$ is based on a constant number of data items. However, the value of $n$ will still play a role in determining the running time and memory usage of the algorithms discussed. The focus of this chapter is on RAM algorithms, but several of the exercises consider the design and analysis of parallel algorithms to solve numerical problems.

We also call the reader's attention to the fact that *we make an important change in the focus of our analysis in this chapter.* Rather than analyzing the running time of a RAM algorithm, we analyze the number of operations performed by an algorithm. That is, we consider an asymptotic evaluation of the number of high-level operations utilized. These operations include addition, subtraction, multiplication, division, and the computation of square roots. This is because for some of the problems we consider, we can no longer assume that these are constant-time operations. When operands are not restricted to representations of a fixed number of bits, the number of bits in the operands impacts the running time of these operations.

## Primality

Given an integer $n > 1$, suppose we want to determine whether or not $n$ is a *prime number*. That is, we want to determine whether or not the only positive integer factors of $n$ are 1 and $n$. This problem, from the area of mathematics known as *Number Theory*, was once thought to be largely of theoretical interest. However, modern data encryption techniques depend on factoring large integers, so there is considerable practical value in the primality problem.

We recall that $n$ is prime if and only if the only factorization $n = u \times v$ of $n$ with integers $1 \le u \le v$ is $u = 1$ and $v = n$. This naturally suggests a RAM algorithm in which we test every integer $u$ from 2 to $n - 1$ to see if $u$ is a factor of $n$. Such an algorithm utilizes $O(n)$ operations.

We can improve the performance of the algorithm by observing that any factorization $n = u \times v$ of $n$ with integers $1 \le u \le v$ must satisfy $1 \le u \le n^{1/2}$. To prove this claim, notice that otherwise, we would have $n^{1/2} < u < v$, which implies $n = n^{1/2} \times n^{1/2} < u \times u \le u \times v = n$. Therefore, we would have the contradictory conclusion that $n < n$. Thus, we obtain the following RAM algorithm.

**Procedure Primality(*n, nIsPrime, factor*)**
**Input:** $n$, an integer greater than 1.
**Output:** *nIsPrime*, true or false according to whether $n$ is prime.
*factor*, the smallest prime factor of $n$ if $n$ is not prime.
**Local variable:** *Root_n*, integer approximation of $n^{1/2}$.

**Action:**

```
factor = 2
Root_n = ⌊n^{1/2}⌋
nIsPrime ← true
Repeat
  If n/factor = ⌊n/factor⌋, then nIsPrime ← false
  Else factor ← factor + 1
Until (not nIsPrime) or (factor > Root_n)
```

This algorithm utilizes $O(n^{1/2})$ operations. In fact, when $n$ is prime, $\Theta(n^{1/2})$ operations are utilized. This asymptotic worst-case scenario also occurs if $n$ is not prime and the smallest prime factor of $n$ is $\Theta(n^{1/2})$, since in this case a prime factor is not detected until $\Theta(n^{1/2})$ iterations of the loop have occurred.

Notice that exploring non-prime values of *factor* in the algorithm above is unnecessary, since if $n$ is divisible by a composite integer $u \times v$, it follows that $n$ is divisible by $u$. This has the following implications.

- With only minor modifications to the algorithm above, we can reduce the number of operations utilized by a constant factor if we consider only 2 and odd numbers as possible factors of $n$.

- If we have in memory a list $L$ of the prime integers that are no greater than $n^{1/2}$ and use only these values for *factor* in the algorithm above, we obtain a more efficient algorithm. It is known that the number $\pi(n)$ of prime numbers that are less than or equal to $n$ satisfies $\pi(n) = \Theta(n/\log n)$. This follows from the *Prime Number Theorem,* which states that

$$\lim_{n\to\infty}\left[\frac{\pi(n)}{n/\ln n}\right] = 1.$$

Thus, we can modify the previous algorithm, as follows.

**Procedure Primality(*n, L, nIsPrime, factor*)**
**Input:** $n$, a positive integer.
$L$, a list in which consecutive entries are successive primes including all primes $\leq n^{1/2}$, and the next prime.
**Output:** *nIsPrime*, true or false according to whether $n$ is prime.
*factor*, the smallest prime factor of $n$ if $n$ is not prime.
**Local variables:** $i$, an index.
*Root_n*, integer approximation of $n^{1/2}$.

**Action:**

```
i ← 1                      {set index for first entry of prime}
Root_n ← ⌊n^{1/2}⌋
nIsPrime ← true
Repeat
  factor ← L[i]
  If n/factor = ⌊n/factor⌋, then nIsPrime ← false
  Else i ← i + 1
Until (not nIsPrime) or (L[i] > Root_n)
Return nIsPrime, factor
```

In light of the asymptotic behavior of the function $\pi(n)$, it is easily seen that this RAM algorithm utilizes $O(n^{1/2}/\log n)$ operations.

In the Exercises, the reader is asked to devise a parallel algorithm for the primality problem.

## Greatest Common Divisor

Another problem concerned with factoring integers is the *greatest common divisor* (*gcd*) problem. Given nonnegative integers $n_0$ and $n_1$, we wish to find the largest positive integer, denoted $(n_0, n_1)$, that is a factor of both $n_0$ and $n_1$. We will find it useful to define $\gcd(0, n) = \gcd(n, 0) = n$ for all positive integers $n$.

The greatest common divisor is used in the familiar process of "reducing a fraction to its lowest terms." This can be important when calculations originating with integer quantities must compute divisions without roundoff error. For example, we would store 1/3 as the pair $(1,3)$ rather than as $0.333\ldots33$. In such a representation of real numbers, for example, we would have $(5,60) = (3,36)$, since each of the pairs represents the fraction 1/12.

The *Euclidean algorithm*, a classical solution to the gcd problem, is based on the following observation. Suppose there are integers $q$ and $r$, *i.e., quotient* and *remainder*, respectively, such that

$$n_0 = q \times n_1 + r.$$

Then any common factor of $n_0$ and $n_1$ must also be a factor of $r$. Therefore, if $n_0 \geq n_1$ and $q = \lfloor n_0/n_1 \rfloor$, we have $n_1 > r \geq 0$ and

$$\gcd(n_0, n_1) = \gcd(n_1, r).$$

These observations give us the following recursive algorithm.

**Function *gcd(n0, n1)*** {greatest common divisor of arguments}
**Input:** nonnegative integers *n*0, *n*1
**Local variables:** integer *quotient, remainder*

**Action:**

```
If n0 < n1, then swap(n0, n1)   {Thus, we assume n0 ≥ n1.}
If n1 = 0, return n0
Else
  quotient ← ⌊n0/n1⌋
  remainder ← n0 − n1 × quotient
  return gcd(n1, remainder)
End else
```

In terms of the variables discussed above, the number of operations utilized by this algorithm, $T(n_0, n_1)$, satisfies the recursive relation

$$T(n_0, n_1) = T(n_1, r) + \Theta(1).$$

It is perhaps not immediately obvious how to solve this recursion, but we can make use of the following.

### Lamé's Theorem

The number of division operations needed to find $\gcd(n_0, n_1)$, for integers satisfying $n_0 \geq n_1 \geq 0$, using the Euclidean algorithm, is no more than five times the number of decimal digits of $n_1$.

It follows from our solution to the primality problem that our implementation of the Euclidean algorithm on a RAM utilizes $T(n_0, n_1) = O(\log(\min\{n_0, n_1\}))$ operations for positive integers $n_0, n_1$.

The Euclidean algorithm seems inherently sequential. In the exercises, a very different approach is suggested that can be parallelized efficiently.

## Integral Powers

Let $x$ be a real, *i.e.*, floating point, number and let $n$ be an integer. Often we consider that computing $x^n$ utilizes $\Theta(1)$ operations. This is a reasonable assumption to make if the absolute value of $n$ is bounded by some constant. For example, we might assume that the computation of $x^n$ utilizes $\Theta(1)$ operations for $|n| \leq 100$. However, one can assume that the number of operations utilized in computing $x^n$ is related to the value of $n$.

We can easily reduce this problem to the assumption that $n \geq 0$ since an algorithm to compute $x^n$ for an arbitrary integer $n$ can be constructed as follows.

1. Compute $temp = x^{|n|}$.
2. If $n \geq 0$, return *temp* else return $1/temp$.

Notice that step 2 utilizes $\Theta(1)$ operations. Therefore, the number of operations utilized by the algorithm is dominated by the computation of a nonnegative power. Thus, without loss of generality in the analysis of the algorithm to solve this problem, we will assume that $n \geq 0$. A standard, brute-force, algorithm is given below for computing a simple power function on a RAM.

**Function power(*x*, *n*)** {return the value of $x^n$}
**Input:** $x$, a real number.
$n$, a nonnegative integer.
**Output:** $x^n$.
**Local variables:** *product*, a partial result.
*counter*, the current power.

**Action:**

```
product = 1
If n > 0, then
  For counter = 1 to n, do
    product = product × x
  End For
End If
Return product
```

The reader should verify that the number of operations utilized by the RAM algorithm given above is $\Theta(n)$, and that this algorithm requires extra space for $\Theta(1)$ data items.

Now let's consider computing $x^{19}$ for any real value $x$. The brute-force algorithm given above utilizes 19 multiplications. However, by exploiting the concept of recursive doubling that has been used throughout the book, observe that we can compute $x^{19}$ much more efficiently, as follows.

1. Compute and save $x^2 = x \times x$.
2. Compute and save $x^4 = x^2 \times x^2$.
3. Compute and save $x^8 = x^4 \times x^4$.
4. Compute and save $x^{16} = x^8 \times x^8$.
5. Compute and return $x^{19} = x^{16} \times x^2 \times x$.

Notice that this procedure utilizes a mere six multiplications, although we pay a small price in requiring extra memory.

In order to generalize from our example, we remark that the key to our recursive doubling algorithm is in the repeated squaring of powers of $x$ instead of the repeated multiplication by $x$. The general recursive doubling algorithm follows.

**Function power(*x*, *n*)** {return the value of $x^n$}
**Input:** $x$, a real number.
$n$, a nonnegative integer.
**Output:** $x^n$.
**Local variables:** *product*, a partial result.
*counter*, *exponent*: integers.
$p[0 \ldots \lfloor \log_2 n \rfloor]$, an array used for certain powers of $x$.
$q[[0 \ldots \lfloor \log_2 n \rfloor]$, an array used for powers of 2.

**Action:**

```
product = 1
If n > 0, then
  p[0] = x
  q[0] = 1
  For counter = 1 to ⌊log₂ n⌋, do
    q[counter] = 2 × q[counter − 1]  {= 2^counter}
    p[counter] = (p[counter − 1])²  {p[i] = x^q[i] = x^(2^i)}
  End For
  exponent = 0
  For counter = ⌊log₂ n⌋ downto 0, do
    If exponent + q[counter] ≤ n then
      exponent = exponent + q[counter]
      product = product × p[counter]
    End If exponent + q[counter] ≤ n
  End For
End If n > 0
Return product
```

The reader should be able to verify that this algorithm utilizes $\Theta(\log n)$ operations on a RAM, using extra space for $\Theta(\log n)$ data items. The reader will be asked to consider parallelizing this RAM algorithm as an exercise.

## Evaluating a Polynomial

Let $f(x)$ be a polynomial function,

$$f(x) = a_n x^n + a_{n-1}x^{n-1} + \cdots + a_1 x + a_0$$

for some set of real numbers $\{a_i\}_{i=0}^{n}$, with $a_n \neq 0$ if $n > 0$. Then $n$ is the *degree* of $f(x)$. As was the case in evaluating $x^n$, a straightforward algorithm for evaluating $f(t)$, for a given real number $t$, does not yield optimal performance. Consider the following naïve algorithm.

```
evaluation = 0
For i = 0 to n, do
  If a_i ≠ 0, then evaluation = evaluation + a_i × x^i
Return evaluation
```

Notice that we could, instead, use an unconditional assignment in the body of the For-loop. However, the calculation of $x^i$ utilizes $\omega(1)$ operations, so it is often useful to omit this calculation when it isn't necessary, *i.e.*, when $a_i = 0$.

It is clear that the For-loop dominates the work of the algorithm. If we use the naïve algorithm given above to compute $x^n$, then the algorithm presented above for evaluating a polynomial utilizes

$$\Theta\left(\sum_{i=1}^{n} i\right) = \Theta(n^2)$$

operations on a RAM in the worst case. Even if we use our recursive doubling algorithm for computing $x^n$, this straightforward algorithm for evaluating a polynomial utilizes

$$\Theta\left(\sum_{i=1}^{n} \log i\right) = \Theta(n \log n)$$

operations on a RAM in the worst case. However, we can do better than this.

Let's consider a 3rd-degree polynomial. We have

$$a_3x^3 + a_2x^2 + a_1x + a_0 = \big((a_3x + a_2)x + a_1\big)x + a_0.$$

For example,

$$10x^3 + 5x^2 - 8x + 4 = \big((10x + 5)x - 8\big)x + 4.$$

This illustrates a general principle, that by grouping expressions appropriately, we can reduce the number of arithmetic operations to a number that is linear in $n$, the degree of the polynomial. This observation is the basis for *Horner's Rule* and a corresponding algorithm, given below.

**Function Evaluate($a$, $x$)**
{evaluate the polynomial represented by the coefficient array $a$ at the input value $x$}
**Input:** Array of real coefficients $a[0\ldots n]$, real number $x$.
**Output:** Value $f(x) = \sum_{i=0}^{n} a[i] \times x^i$.
**Local variables:** $i$, an index variable, and *result* to accumulate the return value.

**Action:**

```
result = a[n]
If n > 0, then
  For i = n downto 1, do
    result = result × x + a[i − 1]
  End For
End If
Return result
```

The reader should verify that the algorithm given above implements Horner's Rule on a RAM while utilizing $\Theta(n)$ operations. Alternately, one can construct an algorithm based on a parallel prefix calculation that runs in a linear number of operations, but also uses a linear amount of additional memory. By contrast, Horner's algorithm requires only a constant amount of additional memory. In the Exercises, the reader is asked to consider constructing an efficient parallel algorithm to evaluate a polynomial.

## Approximation by Taylor Series

Recall from calculus that a function that is sufficiently differentiable may be approximately evaluated by using a *Taylor polynomial*, *i.e.*, a *Taylor series*. In particular, let $f(x)$ be continuous everywhere on a closed interval $[a, b]$ and $n$ times differentiable on the open interval $(a, b)$ containing values $x$ and $x_0$. Let $\{p_k\}_{k=0}^{n-1}$ be the set of polynomial functions defined by

$$p_k(x) = \sum_{i=0}^{k} \frac{f^{(i)}(x_0)}{i!}(x - x_0)^i,$$

where $f^{(i)}$ denotes the $i^{\text{th}}$ order derivative function and $i!$ denotes $i$ factorial. Then the *error term* in approximating $f(x)$ by $p_{n-1}(x)$ is

$$\varepsilon_n(x) = f(x) - p_{n-1}(x) = \frac{f^{(n)}(\tau)}{n!}(x - x_0)^n,$$

for some $\tau$ between $x$ and $x_0$.

The expression $\varepsilon_n(x)$ is defined to be the *truncation error*, which is used when replacing an exact value of an infinite computation by the approximation obtained by using truncating to a finite computation. By contrast, as we mentioned in Chapter 6, a *roundoff error* occurs whenever an exact calculation yields more non-zero decimal places than can be stored. In the remainder of this section, we will consider only truncation errors.

Often, we do not know the exact value of $\tau$ in the error expression. If we knew the value of $\tau$, we could compute the error and adjust our calculation by its value to obtain a net truncation error of 0. However, we can often obtain a useful upper bound on the magnitude of the error. Such a bound may provide us with information regarding how hard we must work to obtain an acceptable approximation.

For example, we may have an *error tolerance* $\varepsilon > 0$. This means we wish to allow no more than $\varepsilon$ of error in our approximation. The value of $\varepsilon$ may give us a measure of how many operations are necessary in order to compute an acceptable approximation. Therefore, we may wish to express our number of operations utilized as a function of $\varepsilon$. Notice that this is significantly different from the analysis of algorithms presented in previous chapters. We are used to the idea that the larger the value of $n$, the larger the number of operations performed by an algorithm. However, in a problem in which error tolerance determines running time, it is usually the case that the smaller the value of $\varepsilon$, the larger the number of operations performed. That is, the smaller the error we can tolerate, the more we must work to obtain a satisfactory approximation. It is difficult to give an analysis for large classes of functions. This is due to the fact that the rate of convergence of a Taylor series for the function $f(x)$ that it represents depends on the nature of $f(x)$ and the interval $[a, b]$ on which the approximation is desired. Of course, the analysis also depends on the error tolerance. Below, we present examples to illustrate typical methods.

**EXAMPLE**

We show how to give a polynomial of minimal or nearly minimal degree that will approximate the exponential function $e^x$ to $d$ decimal places of accuracy on the interval $[-1, 1]$, for some positive integer $d$.

Let's take $x_0 = 0$ and observe that $f^{(i)}(x) = e^x$ for all $i$. Our estimate of the truncation error then becomes

$$\varepsilon_n(x) = \frac{e^\tau}{n!} x^n.$$

Notice that $e^x$ is a positive and increasing function since its first derivative is always positive. Therefore, its maximum absolute value on any interval is at the interval's right endpoint. Thus, on the interval $[-1, 1]$, we have

$$|\varepsilon_n(x)| \le \frac{e^1}{n!} 1^n = \frac{e}{n!} < \frac{2.8}{n!}.$$

Note the choice of 2.8 as an upper bound for $e$ is somewhat arbitrary as we could have used 3 or 2.72 instead. The requirement of approximation accurate to $d$ decimal places means we need to have $|\varepsilon_n(x)| \le 0.5 \times 10^{-d}$. Therefore, it suffices to take

$$\frac{2.8}{n!} \le 0.5 \times 10^{-d} \Leftrightarrow \frac{2.8 \times 10^{d}}{0.5} \le n! \Leftrightarrow$$

$$5.6 \times 10^{d} \le n! \qquad (13.1)$$

in order that the polynomial

$$p_{n-1}(x) = \sum_{i=0}^{n-1} \frac{x^i}{i!}$$

approximate $e^x$ to $d$ decimal places of accuracy on the interval $[-1, 1]$.

We would prefer to solve inequality (13.1) for $n$ in terms of $d$, but a solution does not appear to be straightforward. However, it follows from inequality (13.1) that $n = o(d)$ (see the Exercises), although for small values of $d$, as shown below, this claim may not seem to be suggested. The assertion is important because we know from an Exercise that on a RAM, evaluating a polynomial by an optimal algorithm utilizes $\Theta(n)$ operations, where $n$ is the degree of the polynomial.

For a given value of $d$, let $n_d$ be the smallest value of $n$ satisfying inequality (13.1). Simple calculations based on inequality (13.1) yield the values shown in Table 13-1.

**Table 13-1** *Values of d, i.e., decimal places, and $n_d$, i.e., number of terms, for the Taylor series for $e^x$ expanded about $x_0 = 0$ on $[-1, 1]$.*

| $d$ | $n_d$ |
|---|---|
| 1 | 5 |
| 2 | 6 |
| 3 | 8 |
| 4 | 9 |
| 5 | 10 |

Thus, if $d = 3$, the desired approximating polynomial for $e^x$ on $[-1, 1]$ is

$$p_{n_3-1}(x) = \sum_{i=0}^{7} \frac{x^i}{i!}.$$

**EXAMPLE**

We show how to give a polynomial of minimal or nearly minimal degree that will approximate the trigonometric function sin $x$ to $d$ decimal places of accuracy on the interval $[-\pi, \pi]$ for some positive integer $d$.

Let's take $x_0 = 0$ and observe that $f^{(i)}(0) \in \{-1, 0, 1\}$ for all $i$. If the latter claim is not obvious to the reader, it is a good exercise in mathematical induction. Our estimate of the truncation error then becomes

$$|\varepsilon_n(x)| \leq \left|\frac{1}{n!}x^n\right| \leq \frac{\pi^n}{n!} < \frac{3.2^n}{n!}.$$

As in the previous example, accuracy to $d$ decimal places implies an error tolerance of $|\varepsilon_n(x)| \leq 0.5 \times 10^{-d}$. Hence, it suffices to take

$$\frac{3.2^n}{n!} \leq 0.5 \times 10^{-d} \Leftrightarrow$$

$$2 \times 10^d \leq \frac{n!}{3.2^n}. \tag{13.2}$$

If we take the minimal value of $n$ that satisfies inequality (13.2) for a given $d$, we have $n = o(d)$ (see the Exercises), although for small values of $d$, this claim may not seem to be suggested, as shown below.

For a given value of $d$, let $n_d$ be the smallest value of $n$ satisfying inequality (13.2). Simple calculations based on inequality (13.2) yield the values shown in Table 13-2.

**Table 13-2** *Values of d (decimal places) and $n_d$ terms for the Taylor series for sin x expanded about $x_0 = 0$ on $[-\pi, \pi]$.*

| $d$ | $n_d$ |
|---|---|
| 1 | 10 |
| 2 | 12 |
| 3 | 14 |
| 4 | 15 |
| 5 | 17 |

Thus, for $d = 2$ we can approximate $\sin x$ on the interval $[-\pi, \pi]$ to two decimal places of accuracy by the polynomial

$$p_{n_2-1}(x) = 0 + \frac{1x}{1!} + \frac{0x^2}{2!} + \frac{-1x^3}{3!} + \frac{0x^4}{4!} + \frac{1x^5}{5!}$$

$$+ \frac{0x^6}{6!} + \frac{-1x^7}{7!} + \frac{0x^8}{8!} + \frac{1x^9}{9!} + \frac{0x^{10}}{10!} + \frac{-1x^{11}}{11!}$$

$$= x - \frac{x^3}{6} + \frac{x^5}{120} - \frac{x^7}{5{,}040} + \frac{x^9}{362{,}880} - \frac{x^{11}}{39{,}916{,}800}.$$

## Trapezoidal Integration

A fundamental theorem of Calculus is that if $F'(x) = f(x)$ for every $x \in [a, b]$, then

$$\int_a^b f(x)dx = F(b) - F(a).$$

Unfortunately, for many important functions $f(x)$, the corresponding antiderivative function $F(x)$ is difficult to evaluate for a given value of $x$. As an example, consider the function $f(x) = x^{-1}$ with

$$F(x) = \ln x = \int_1^x f(t)dt.$$

For such functions, it is important to have approximation techniques in order to evaluate definite integrals.

One of the best-known approximation techniques for definite integrals is *Trapezoidal Integration*, in which we use the relationship between definite integrals and the area between the graph and the $x$-axis to approximate a slab of the definite integral with a trapezoid. We will not prove the following statement, as its derivation can be found in many Calculus or Numerical Analysis textbooks.

**Theorem:** Let $f(x)$ be a function that is twice differentiable on the interval $[a, b]$ and let $n$ be a positive integer. Let

$$h = \frac{b - a}{n}$$

and let $x_i$, $i \in \{1,2,\ldots,n-1\}$, be defined by $x_i = a + ih$. Let

$$t_n = h\left[\frac{f(a)+f(b)}{2} + \sum_{i=1}^{n-1} f(x_i)\right].$$

Then $t_n$ is an approximation to

$$\int_a^b f(x)dx,$$

with the error in the estimate given by

$$\varepsilon_n = t_n - \int_a^b f(x)dx = \frac{(b-a)^3 f''(\eta)}{12n^2}, \tag{13.3}$$

for some $\eta \in (a,b)$.

The reader should consider Figure 13-1 in order to recall the principles behind Trapezoidal Integration.

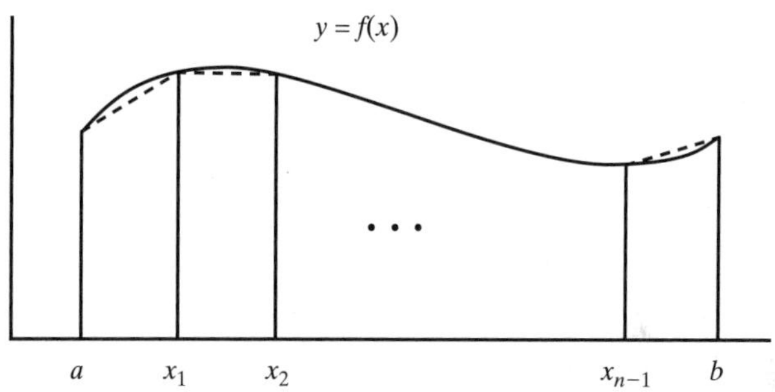


**FIGURE 13-1** *Trapezoidal Integration. The dashed lines represent the tops of the trapezoids. The area under each small arc is approximated by the area of a trapezoid. It is often much easier to compute the area of a trapezoid than the exact area under an arc. The total area of the trapezoids serves as an approximation to the total area under the curve.*

The value of $\eta$ in equation (13.3) is often unknown to us, but an upper bound for $|f''(\eta)|$ is often sufficient, as what we seek is for $|\varepsilon_n|$ to be small.

If we assume that for $x \in [a,b]$, each value of $f(x)$ can be computed on a RAM with $\Theta(1)$ operations, then it is easy to see that $t_n$ can be computed on a RAM with $\Theta(n)$ operations (see the Exercises). We expect that the number of operations performed by an algorithm will be a function of the quality of the approximation, much as was the case of computing the Taylor series to within a predetermined error.

**EXAMPLE**

For some positive integer $d$, we sketch how to compute $\ln 2$ to $d$ decimal places by using Trapezoidal Integration, and we give an analysis of the number of operations performed in terms of $d$. Recall that $\ln 2$ is $\log_e 2$, where $e \approx 2.7182818$ is the "Euler number." As mentioned previously in the text, "ln" is typically referred to as the "natural logarithm." Since

$$\ln 2 = \int_1^2 x^{-1}dx,$$

we take $f(x) = x^{-1}$, $f'(x) = -x^{-2}$, $f''(x) = 2x^{-3}$, $f^{(3)}(x) = -6x^{-4}$, and $[a, b] = [1, 2]$. Notice $f''(x) > 0$ on $[1, 2]$, and $f''$ is a decreasing function since its derivative, $f^{(3)}(x)$, is negative for all $x \in [1, 2]$. Therefore, $f''$ attains its maximum absolute value on $[1, 2]$ at the left endpoint. It follows that

$$|\varepsilon_n| \leq \frac{(2-1)^3 f''(1)}{12n^2} = \frac{1 \times 2(1)^{-3}}{12n^2} = \frac{1}{6n^2}.$$

Since we wish to attain $d$ decimal place accuracy, we want $|\varepsilon_n| \leq 0.5 \times 10^{-d}$, so it suffices to take

$$\frac{1}{6n^2} \leq 0.5 \times 10^{-d} \Leftrightarrow \frac{10^d}{3} \leq n^2 \Leftrightarrow$$

$$\frac{10^{d/2}}{3^{1/2}} \leq n. \tag{13.4}$$

We leave to the reader as an exercise the computation of $\ln 2$ accurate to a desired number of decimal places by Trapezoidal Integration, as discussed above.

If we choose the smallest value of $n$ satisfying the inequality (13.4), we conclude that the number of operations performed by our approximation of $\ln 2$, using Trapezoidal Integration as discussed above, is exponential in the number of decimal places of accuracy, $\Theta(10^{d/2})$.

We remark that it is not unusual to find that the amount of work required is exponential in the number of decimal places of accuracy required. In these situations, Trapezoidal Integration may not be a very good technique to use for computing approximations that are required to be extremely accurate. Another way of looking at this analysis is to observe that using an error tolerance of $\varepsilon = 0.5 \times 10^{-d}$, we have $d = -\log_{10}(2\varepsilon)$. Further, if we substitute this into inequality (13.4), we conclude that the minimal value of $n$ satisfying the inequality is $\Theta(\varepsilon^{-1/2})$.

Notice also, for example, that for $d = 6$, the minimum value of $n$ to satisfy inequality (13.4) is $n = 578$. While this indicates an unreasonable amount of work for a student in a calculus class using only pencil, paper, and a non-programmable calculator, it is still a small problem for a modern computer.

Other methods of "numerical integration" such as Simpson's Method tend to converge faster to the definite integral represented by the approximation. Fortunately, for many purposes, only a small number of decimal places of accuracy are required. Also, it may be that another technique, such as using a Taylor series, is more efficient for computing the value of a logarithm.

## Approximate Solution of an Equation

Suppose we have an equation of the form $f(x) = 0$, where the function $f(x)$ is continuous on an interval $[a, b]$ , and we wish to find a solution, or perhaps all solutions to this equation, *i.e.*, one or all values of $x \in [a,b]$ that satisfy the equation. It is often difficult to find an exact solution, and in such a case, a sufficiently accurate approximate solution will often serve our purposes well.

This problem is often made simpler if we happen to know that the function $f(x)$ is monotone on $[a, b]$, *i.e.*, either $f(x)$ is an increasing function on $[a, b]$ or $f(x)$ is a decreasing function on $[a, b]$. In the case of a monotone function, a Binary Search type of procedure yields an efficient sequential solution, as follows. For simplicity, we assume the value of $f(x)$ can be computed in a constant number of operations for any $x \in [a,b]$. Notice that since $f(x)$ is continuous and monotone on $[a,b]$, if $f(a)f(b) > 0$ then $f(a)$ and $f(b)$ have the same sign, and there is no solution in $[a, b]$. Clearly, the problem is trivial if $f(a) = 0$ or $f(b) = 0$. Therefore, we assume below that $f(a)$ and $f(b)$ have opposite signs, *i.e.,* one is positive and the other is negative.

**Algorithm for approximate solution of $f(x) = 0$ on $[a, b]$, where $f(x)$ is monotone on $[a, b]$ and $f(a)$ and $f(b)$ have opposite signs.**

**Function Solution($[a,b]$, $\varepsilon$)**
**Inputs:** $[a, b]$ is the interval considered.
$\varepsilon > 0$ is the error tolerance of the solution, *i.e.*, if the approximate value returned is denoted by $x_0$, then there is an exact solution $x'$ such that $|x' - x_0| < \varepsilon$.
**Local variable:** *mid*, used as the midpoint of the current interval.

**Action:**

```
mid ← (a + b) / 2
If b − a < ε or f(mid) = 0 then return mid
Else {b − a ≥ ε and 0 ∉ {f(a), f(b), f(mid)}}
  If f(a) × f(mid) < 0 then return Solution([a,mid],ε) {*}
  Else return Solution([mid, b],ε)
End Else {b − a ≥ ε and 0 ∉ {f(a), f(b), f(mid)}}
End algorithm
```

It is easily seen that if the condition at the line marked {*} is true, then there is a solution in the interval $[a, mid]$, and otherwise, there is a solution in the interval $[mid, b]$, so in either case the algorithm performs correctly.

At each level of recursion, the length of the current interval is decreased by a factor of ½. It follows that the number of levels of recursion, $n$, before a solution is returned, satisfies $(b-a)/2^n < \varepsilon \Rightarrow \log_2[(b-a)/\varepsilon] < n$. It follows that our algorithm utilizes $\Theta(\log[(b-a)/\varepsilon])$ operations.

**EXAMPLE**

How many levels of recursion are necessary in using the algorithm above to estimate a value for $\sqrt{10}$ that is accurate to 3 decimal places?

The question isn't entirely well defined, as we have not directed the reader concerning what function and what interval to use. It is reasonable to assume that we seek an approximate solution to the equation $x^2 - 10 = 0$. We note that $f(x) = x^2 - 10$ is an increasing function for $x > 0$, which is easily seen since $f'(x) = 2x > 0$ for $x > 0$. Further, $f(3) < 0$ and $f(4) > 0$, so we can take our interval to be [3,4]. Accuracy to 3 decimal places means we can take $\varepsilon = 0.5 \times 10^{-3} = 5 \times 10^{-4}$.

For such choices, the discussion above shows that the number of levels of recursion beyond the initial call upon the algorithm is

$$\left\lceil \log_2 \frac{4-3}{5 \times 10^{-4}} \right\rceil = \lceil \log_2 2{,}000 \rceil = 11.$$

## Summary

In contrast with most previous chapters, this chapter is concerned with numerical computations. Many problems in computational science/scientific computing/numerical methods perform operations in numbers that do not depend on the volume of input to be processed, which is often constant. Rather, problems in these areas typically rely on the values of a constant number of parameters, or, in some cases, on an error tolerance. Such problems come from core areas in science and engineering and involve solution techniques from branches of mathematics, such as Algebra, Number Theory, Calculus, and Numerical Analysis or Numerical Methods, as well as methods from computer science. In this chapter, we consider prime factorization, greatest common divisor, integral powers, evaluation of a polynomial, approximations by using a Taylor series, Trapezoidal Integration, and approximate solutions of equations. The solutions we present are all for the RAM, though readers will be asked to consider parallel models of computation in the Exercises.

## Chapter Notes

The primality problem and the greatest common divisor problem are taken from Number Theory, a branch of mathematics devoted to fundamental properties of numbers, particularly, although not exclusively, integers.

We use the Prime Number Theorem concerning the asymptotic behavior of the function $\pi(n)$, the number of primes less than or equal to the positive integer $n$. This theorem is discussed in the following sources.

- T.M. Apostol, *Introduction to Analytic Number Theory*, Springer-Verlag, New York, 2001.
- W. Narkiewicz, *The Development of Prime Number Theory*, Springer-Verlag, Berlin, 2000.
- K.H. Rosen, *Elementary Number Theory and its Applications*, Addison-Wesley Publishing, Reading, MA, 1993.

The latter also discusses the Euclidean algorithm for the greatest common divisor problem and contains a proof of Lamé's Theorem.

Other problems we discuss in this chapter are taken from *Numerical Analysis*, an area of applied mathematics and computing that is concerned with computationally intensive problems involving numerical algorithms, approximation, error analysis, and related issues. Problems in Numerical Analysis have applications in branches of mathematics that derive from Calculus, *e.g.*, Differential Equations, Probability, and Statistics, as well as Linear Algebra, including matrix multiplication, solution of systems of linear equations, and linear programming, and their application areas. For an introduction to the field, we refer the reader to the following.

- N.S. Asaithambi, *Numerical Analysis: Theory and Practice*, Saunders College Publishing, Fort Worth, 1995.
- R.L. Burden and J.D. Faires, *Numerical Analysis*, PWS-Kent Publishing Company, Boston, 1993.
- R. Butt, *Introduction to Numerical Analysis Using MATLAB*, Infinity Science Press, Hingham, MA, 2008.
- S. Yakowitz and Ferenc Szidarovszky, *An Introduction to Numerical Computations*, Prentice Hall, Upper Saddle River, NJ, 1990.

We discuss approximation problems with regard to the algorithmic efficiency of our solutions in terms of error tolerance, sometimes expressed in terms of the number of decimal places of accurate calculation. It is tempting to say this is rarely important, that most calculations require only a small number of decimal places of accuracy. One should note, however, that there are situations in which very large numbers of accurate decimal places are required. As an extreme example, some mathematicians are interested in computing the value of $\pi$ to millions of decimal places. While these examples involve techniques beyond the scope of this book, the point is that interest exists in computations with more than "ordinary" accuracy.

## Exercises

In several of the exercises, we ask the reader to construct a parallel version of a RAM algorithm presented in the chapter. Notice that the number of operations of a parallel algorithm is typically more than the number of operations of its sequential analog, since communications issues may come into play. When we discuss a parallel algorithm and its sequential analog, we are typically interested in comparing running times. Rather than use an awkward *ad hoc* expression such as *the time equivalent of* $\Theta(f(n))$ *sequential operations*, we will abbreviate with expressions of the form $\Theta(f(n))$ *parallel operations* throughout the exercises.

**1.** Devise a parallel algorithm to solve the primality problem for the positive integer $n$. At the end of the algorithm, every processor should know whether or not $n$ is prime. Further, if $n$ is not prime, every processor should know the smallest prime factor of $n$. Also, assume that no list of primes is initially stored in memory. Assuming $\lfloor n^{1/2} \rfloor$ processors, provide an analysis of the number of parallel operations used by your algorithm on the following.

a. CREW PRAM

b. EREW PRAM

c. Mesh

d. Hypercube

**2.** Suppose we modify the previous problem so that we include the assumption that a list $L$, consisting of all the primes $p_i$ satisfying $p_i \le \lfloor n^{1/2} \rfloor$, is initially distributed one prime per processor, where $p_i$ is initially stored in processor $P_i$. Analyze the number of processors required as well as the number of parallel operations utilized by your algorithm for each of the following models.

a. CREW PRAM

b. EREW PRAM

c. Mesh

d. Hypercube

**3.** Consider the problem of computing $\gcd(n_0, n_1)$ for nonnegative integers $n_0, n_1$, where $n_0 \ge n_1$. Assume a list $L$ of all primes $p_i$ satisfying $p_i \le \lfloor n^{1/2} \rfloor$ is kept in memory. For a parallel model of computation, assume these primes are distributed one prime per processor. Devise an algorithm for computing $\gcd(n_0, n_1)$ efficiently based on finding, for each prime $p \in L$, the maximal nonnegative integer $k$ such that $p^k$ is a common factor of $n_0$ and $n_1$. For parallel machines, at the end of the algorithm, every processor should have the value of $\gcd(n_0, n_1)$. Analyze the number of parallel operations utilized by such an algorithm for the following.

a. CREW PRAM

b. EREW PRAM

c. Mesh

d. Hypercube

*Hint*: consider using the efficient sequential algorithm for computing $x^n$ that was presented in the chapter.

**4.** Decide whether or not the $\Theta(\log n)$-operation algorithm for computing $x^n$ presented in the chapter is effectively parallelizable. That is, either give a version of this algorithm for a PRAM that utilizes $o(\log n)$ parallel operations and show that it does so, or argue why it is difficult or impossible to do so.

**5.** Show that a RAM algorithm to evaluate a polynomial of degree $n$ utilizes $\Omega(n)$ operations, which implies that Horner's algorithm is optimal.

**6.** Devise an algorithm for evaluation of a polynomial of degree $n$ on a PRAM. This will be somewhat easier on a CREW PRAM than on an EREW PRAM, but in either case, you should be able to achieve an algorithm that utilizes $\Theta(\log n)$ parallel operations using $\Theta(n/\log n)$ processors, which results in an optimal cost of $\Theta(n)$.

**7.** Modify your algorithm from the previous exercise to run on a mesh or hypercube of size $n$. Assume the coefficients of the polynomial are distributed $\Theta(1)$ per processor. Analyze the number of parallel operations for both of these architectures.

**8.** Devise an efficient algorithm for evaluation of a polynomial of degree at most $n$ on a $CGM(n,q)$. Assume that the coefficients $\{a_i\}_{i=0}^{n}$ of the polynomial $f(x)$ are distributed $\Theta(n/q)$ per processor and the value $x_0$, such that $f(x_0)$ is to be computed, is initially in just one processor. Derive an algorithm that utilizes $\Theta(n/q)$ parallel operations, either by modifying Horner's algorithm or by using an algorithm based on parallel prefix computation (Chapter 7, exercise 11).

**9.** Show that for any $x \in [-1, 1]$, the value of $e^x$ can be computed to within $0.5 \times 10^{-d}$ for positive integer $d$, *i.e.*, to $d$-decimal place accuracy, in $o(d)$ operations on a RAM. You may use inequality (13.1).

**10.** Show that inequality (13.2) implies $n = o(d)$ and use this result to show that the function $\sin x$ can be computed for any $x \in [-\pi, \pi]$ to $d$-decimal place accuracy by utilizing $o(d)$ operations on a RAM.

11. Show that if we assume the value of $f(x)$ can be computed by utilizing $\Theta(1)$ operations for all $x \in [a, b]$, the Trapezoidal Integration estimate $t_n$ can be computed on a RAM by utilizing $\Theta(n)$ operations.
12. Under the same assumptions as in the previous problem, provide an asymptotic analysis in terms of the number of parallel operations utilized for the efficient computation of the Trapezoidal Integration estimate $t_n$ as a function of $n$ on each of an EREW PRAM, hypercube, and mesh of size $n$. In addition, give the asymptotic number of parallel operations as a function of $n$ and $q$ on a $CGM(n, q)$. *Hint*: state one parallel algorithm that can be implemented efficiently on all of these architectures.
13. Analyze the number of operations utilized by of using Trapezoidal Integration to compute $\int_0^1 e^{-x^2} dx$ to $d$ decimal places on a RAM, as an asymptotic expression in $d$. To simplify the problem, you may assume that for all $x \in [0, 1]$, $e^x$ can be computed with sufficient accuracy in $\Theta(1)$ time.

# Appendix 1

## Proof of the Principle of Mathematical Induction

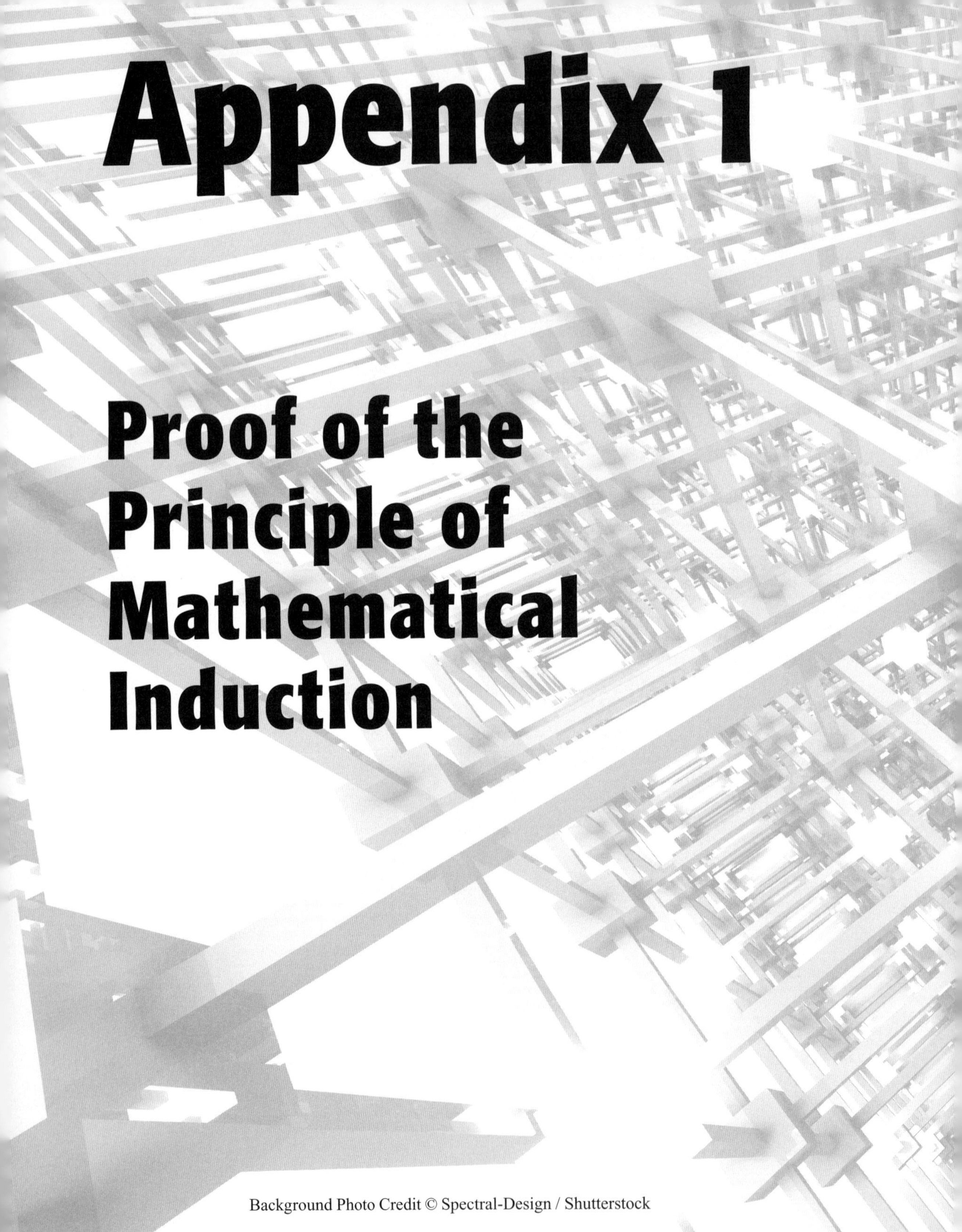

Background Photo Credit © Spectral-Design / Shutterstock

In this appendix, we provide a proof of the Principle of Mathematical Induction. We initially discuss induction in Chapter 2. We consider proofs of correctness of algorithms based on induction throughout the text. Recall from Chapter 2 that a predicate is a statement that is true or false. Some readers might find it useful to think of a predicate on the positive integers as a function $P\colon \mathbb{N} \rightarrow \{\textit{true}, \textit{false}\}$, where $\mathbb{N}$ is the set of natural numbers, *i.e.*, the set of positive integers.

**Principle of Mathematical Induction:** Let $P(n)$ be a predicate, where $n$ is an arbitrary positive integer. Suppose we can accomplish the following two steps.

1. Show that $P(1)$ is *true.*
2. Show that whenever $P(k)$ is *true*, it follows that $P(k + 1)$ is also *true.*

If we can achieve these two goals, then it follows that $P(n)$ is *true* for all positive integers $n$.

The proof we give of Mathematical Induction depends on an interesting and somewhat intuitive axiom, namely, the *Greatest Lower Bound Axiom*, given below.

**Greatest Lower Bound Axiom:** Let $X$ be a nonempty subset of the real numbers such that the members of $X$ have a lower bound. That is, suppose there exists a constant $C \in \mathbb{R}$ such that for every $x \in X, x \geq C$. Then a greatest lower bound for $X$ exists. That is, there exists a constant $C_0 \in \mathbb{R}$ such that $C_0$ is a lower bound for the members of $X$ and such that $C_0$ is greater than any other lower bound for $X$.

**Proof of the Principle of Mathematical Induction:** The proof is "by contradiction." Suppose the Principle of Mathematical Induction is false. That is, suppose there exists a predicate $P$ that yields a counterexample. Such a predicate $P$ would have to satisfy the following.

1. $P(1)$ is *true.*
2. Whenever $P(n)$ is *true*, $P(n + 1)$ is also *true.*
3. For some positive integer $k$, $P(k)$ is false.

Define a set

$$S = \{n \mid n \text{ is a positive integer and } P(n) = \textit{false}\}.$$

For the integer $k$ of statement 3, $k \in S$, so $S \neq \varnothing$. It follows from the Greatest Lower Bound Axiom that $S$ has a greatest lower bound $k_0 \in S$. It is easy to see that $k_0$ must be a positive integer. That is, $k_0$ is the first value of $n$ such that $P(n)$ is false. From statement 1, $P(1) = \textit{true}$, so $k_0 > 1$. Therefore, $k_0 - 1$ is a positive integer. Notice that by choice of $k_0$, we must have $P(k_0 - 1) = \textit{true}$. It follows from statement 2 that $P(k_0) = P((k_0 - 1) + 1) = \textit{true}$, contrary to the fact that $k_0 \in S$. Since the contradiction results from the assumption that the Principle is false, the proof is established.

# Appendix 2

## Proof of the Master Theorem

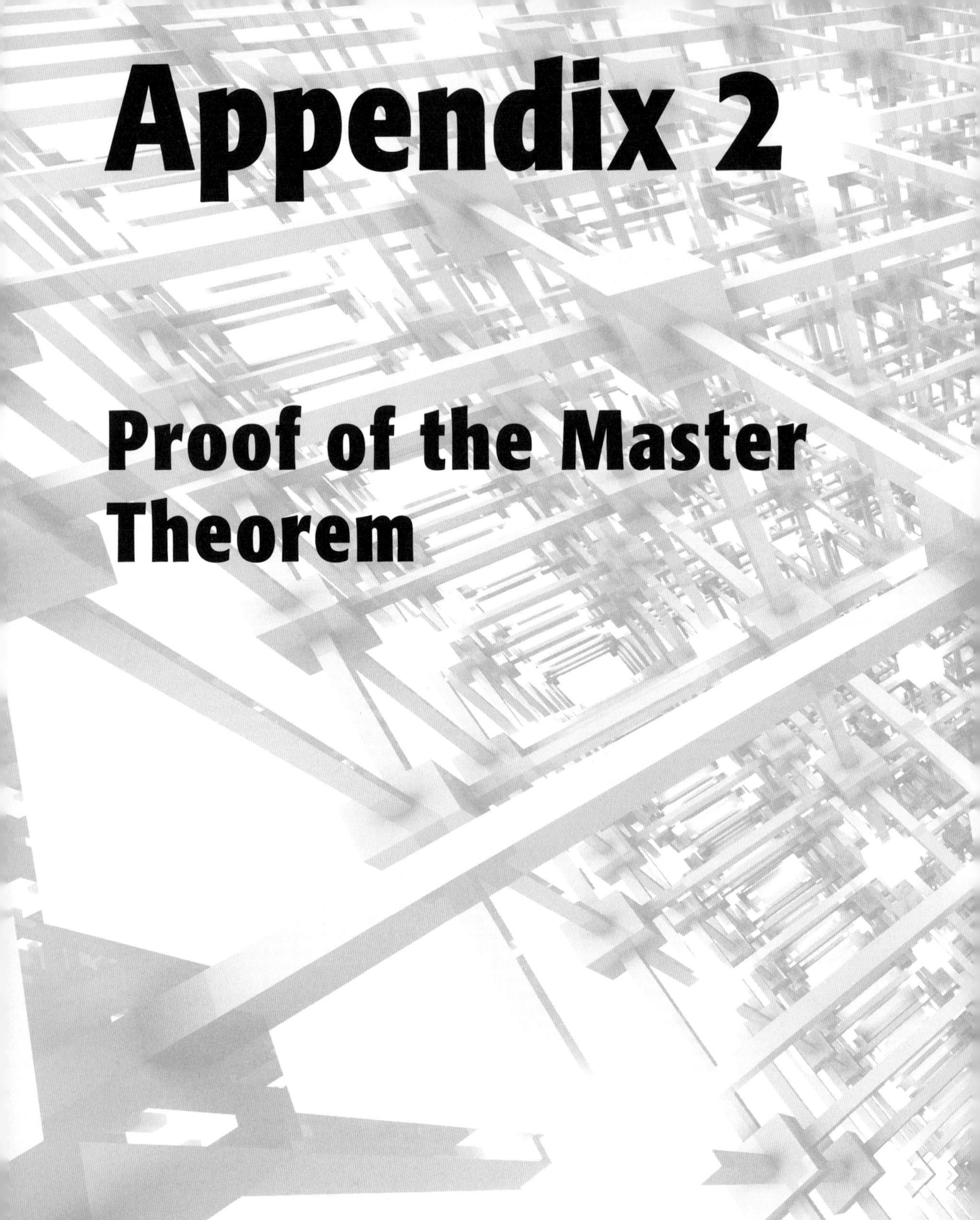

Background Photo Credit © Spectral-Design / Shutterstock

In this appendix, we give a proof of the Master Theorem, which was stated in Chapter 3. Recall this theorem is concerned with the resolution of recurrence relations.

**Master Theorem:** Let $a \geq 1$ and $b > 1$ be constants. Let $f(n)$ be a positive function defined on the positive integers. Let $T(n)$ be defined on the positive integers by

$$T(n) = aT\left(\frac{n}{b}\right) + f(n), \tag{3.1}$$

where we can interpret $n/b$ as meaning either $\lfloor n/b \rfloor$ or $\lceil n/b \rceil$. Then the following hold.

1. If $f(n) = O(n^{\log_b a - \varepsilon})$ for some constant $\varepsilon > 0$, then $T(n) = \Theta(n^{\log_b a})$.
2. If $f(n) = \Theta(n^{\log_b a})$, then $T(n) = \Theta(n^{\log_b a} \log n)$.
3. If $f(n) = \Omega(n^{\log_b a + \varepsilon})$ for some constant $\varepsilon > 0$, and there are constants $c$ and $N$, $0 < c < 1$ and $N > 0$, such that $n/b > N \Rightarrow af(n/b) \leq cf(n)$, then $T(n) = \Theta(f(n))$.

## Proof of the Master Theorem

We start under the simplifying assumption that the values of $n$ are nonnegative integral powers of $b$. The advantage of this assumption lies in the fact that at every level of recursion, $n/b$ is an integer. Later, we show how to handle the general case.

### Lemma 1

Let $a \geq 1$ and $b > 1$ be constants, and let $f(n)$ be a nonnegative function defined on integral powers of $b$. Let $T(n)$ be defined on integral powers of $b$ by the recurrence

$$T(n) = \begin{cases} \Theta(1) & \text{if } n = 1; \\ aT(n/b) + f(n) & \text{if } n = b^i \text{ for some positive integer } i. \end{cases}$$

Then

$$T(n) = \Theta\left(n^{\log_b a}\right) + \sum_{k=0}^{\log_b n-1} a^k f\left(\frac{n}{b^k}\right).$$

***Remarks***

We create a hypothesis of the pattern by simplifying an iterated expansion of the recurrence, as follows.

$$T(n) = f(n) + aT\left(\frac{n}{b}\right) = f(n) + af\left(\frac{n}{b}\right) + a^2T\left(\frac{n}{b^2}\right) = \cdots =$$

$$f(n) + af\left(\frac{n}{b}\right) + a^2 f\left(\frac{n}{b^2}\right) + \cdots + a^{\log_b n-1} f\left(\frac{n}{b^{\log_b n-1}}\right) + a^{\log_b n}T(1).$$

Since $a^{\log_b n} = n^{\log_b a}$ and $T(1) = \Theta(1)$, the last term in the expanded recurrence is $\Theta(n^{\log_b a})$, while the initial terms yield

$$\sum_{k=0}^{\log_b n-1} a^k f(n/b^k),$$

as asserted above. We provide a proof of our hypothesis by mathematical induction.

***Proof of Lemma 1***

We establish our claim by showing that

$$T(n) = n^{\log_b a}T(1) + \sum_{k=0}^{\log_b n-1} a^k f\left(\frac{n}{b^k}\right),$$

where we consider $n = b^i$ for nonnegative integers $i$. Therefore, the base case is $i = 0$, which is equivalent to $n = 1$. In this case, the

$$\sum_{k=0}^{\log_b n-1} a^k f(n/b^k)$$

term of the assertion is an empty sum, which by convention has value 0. Therefore, the assertion is true since the right side of the asserted equation is

$$1^{\log_b a}T(1) + \sum_{k=0}^{\log_b n-1} a^k f(n/b^k) = T(1) + 0 = T(1).$$

Thus, the base case of the induction is established.

Suppose the assertion is true for integer powers $i$ of $b$, where $0 \le i \le p$. In particular, suppose the assertion is true for $n = b^p$. Then, we have

$$T(b^p) = b^{p\log_b a}T(1) + \sum_{k=0}^{p-1} a^k f\left(\frac{n}{b^k}\right) = a^p T(1) + \sum_{k=0}^{p-1} a^k f(b^{p-k}).$$

Now, consider $n = b^{p+1}$. By the hypothesized recurrence, we have

$$T(b^{p+1}) = aT(b^p) + f(b^{p+1}) =$$

(using the inductive hypothesis)

$$a\left[a^p T(1) + \sum_{k=0}^{p-1} a^k f\left(b^{p-k}\right)\right] + f\left(b^{p+1}\right) =$$

$$a^{p+1}T(1) + \left[a\sum_{k=0}^{p-1} a^k f\left(b^{p-k}\right)\right] + f\left(b^{p+1}\right) =$$

(since $b^{\log_b a} = a$)

$$b^{(p+1)\log_b a}T(1) + \sum_{k=0}^{p} a^k f(b^{p+1-k}) = n^{\log_b a}T(1) + \sum_{k=0}^{p} a^k f\left(\frac{n}{b^k}\right),$$

which is the desired result, since $p = \log_b n - 1$. This completes the induction proof.

Next, we give asymptotic bounds for the summation term that appears in the conclusion of the statement of Lemma 1.

**Lemma 2**

Let $a \ge 1$ and $b > 1$ be constants, and let $f(n)$ be a nonnegative function defined on nonnegative integral powers of $b$. Let $g(n)$ be a function defined on integral powers of $b$ by

$$g(n) = \sum_{k=0}^{\log_b n-1} a^k f\left(\frac{n}{b^k}\right). \tag{3.2}$$

1. If $f(n) = O(n^{\log_b a - \varepsilon})$ for some constant $\varepsilon > 0$, then $g(n) = O(n^{\log_b a})$.
2. If $f(n) = \Theta(n^{\log_b a})$, then $g(n) = \Theta(n^{\log_b a} \log n)$.
3. If there are positive constants $c < 1$ and $N > 0$ such that $n/b > N \Rightarrow af(n/b) \le cf(n)$, then $g(n) = \Theta(f(n))$.

***Proof***

For case 1, substituting the hypothesis of the case into the definition of the function $g(n)$ yields

$$g(n) = O\left[\sum_{k=0}^{\log_b n - 1} a^k \left(\frac{n}{b^k}\right)^{\log_b a - \varepsilon}\right] = O\left[n^{\log_b a - \varepsilon} \sum_{k=0}^{\log_b n - 1} \left(\frac{ab^{\varepsilon}}{b^{\log_b a}}\right)^k\right] =$$

$$O\left[n^{\log_b a - \varepsilon} \sum_{k=0}^{\log_b n - 1} (b^{\varepsilon})^k\right] =$$

(using the formula for the sum of a geometric series)

$$O\left[n^{\log_b a - \varepsilon}\left(\frac{b^{\varepsilon \log_b n} - 1}{b^{\varepsilon} - 1}\right)\right] = O\left[n^{\log_b a - \varepsilon}\left(\frac{n^{\varepsilon} - 1}{b^{\varepsilon} - 1}\right)\right] =$$

(since $b$ and $\varepsilon$ are constants) $O(n^{\log_b a})$, as claimed.

For case 2, it follows from the hypothesis of the case that $f(n/b^k) = \Theta[(n/b^k)^{\log_b a}]$. When we substitute the latter into (3.2), we have

$$g(n) = \Theta\left[\sum_{k=0}^{\log_b n - 1} a^k \left(\frac{n}{b^k}\right)^{\log_b a}\right] = \Theta\left[n^{\log_b a} \sum_{k=0}^{\log_b n - 1} \left(\frac{a}{b^{\log_b a}}\right)^k\right] =$$

$$\Theta\left(n^{\log_b a} \sum_{k=0}^{\log_b n - 1} 1\right) = \Theta(n^{\log_b a} \log n),$$

as claimed.

For case 3, observe that all terms of the sum in (3.2) are nonnegative, and the term corresponding to $k = 0$ is $f(n)$. Therefore, $g(n) = \Omega(f(n))$. The hypothesis of the case, that there are constants $0 < c < 1$ and $N > 0$ such that $n/b > N \Rightarrow af(n/b) \le cf(n)$, implies by a straightforward induction argument that $n/b^k > N \Rightarrow a^k f(n/b^k) \le c^k f(n)$. When we substitute the latter into (3.2), we get

$$g(n) = \sum_{k=0}^{\log_b n - 1} a^k f\left(\frac{n}{b^k}\right) =$$

$$\sum_{\substack{0 \le k \le \log_b n - 1, \\ n/b^k \le N}} a^k f\left(\frac{n}{b^k}\right) + \sum_{\substack{0 \le k \le \log_b n - 1, \\ n/b^k > N}} a^k f\left(\frac{n}{b^k}\right).$$

The first summation in the latter expression has a fixed number of terms, so this summation satisfies $\sum_{\substack{0 \le k \le \log_b n-1, \\ n/b^k \le N}} a^k f\left(\frac{n}{b^k}\right) = \Theta(1)$. Therefore, our asymptotic evaluation of $g(n)$ depends on the second summation,

$$g(n) = \Theta\left[\sum_{\substack{0 \le k \le \log_b n-1, \\ n/b^k > N}} a^k f\left(\frac{n}{b^k}\right)\right].$$

The summation on the right side satisfies

$$\sum_{\substack{0 \le k \le \log_b n-1, \\ n/b^k > N}} a^k f\left(\frac{n}{b^k}\right) \le \sum_{\substack{0 \le k \le \log_b n-1, \\ n/b^k > N}} c^k f(n) = f(n) \sum_{\substack{0 \le k \le \log_b n-1, \\ n/b^k > N}} c^k.$$

Since the latter summation is a geometric series with decreasing terms, it follows that

$$g(n) = O\left(f(n)\left(\frac{1}{1-c}\right)\right) = O(f(n)).$$

Since we previously showed that $g(n) = \Omega(f(n))$, it follows that $g(n) = \Theta(f(n))$, as claimed.

Now we prove a version of the *Master Method* for the case in which $n$ is a non-negative integral power of $b$.

**Lemma 3**

Let $a \ge 1$ and $b > 1$ be constants, and let $f(n)$ be a nonnegative function defined on integral powers of $b$. Let $T(n)$ be defined on integral powers of $b$ by the recurrence

$$T(n) = \begin{cases} \Theta(1) & \text{if } n = 1; \\ aT\left(\frac{n}{b}\right) + f(n) & \text{if } n = b^i \text{ for some positive integer } i. \end{cases}$$

Then we have the following.

1. If $f(n) = O(n^{\log_b a - \varepsilon})$ for some constant $\varepsilon > 0$, then $T(n) = \Theta(n^{\log_b a})$.
2. If $f(n) = \Theta(n^{\log_b a})$, then $T(n) = \Theta(n^{\log_b a} \log n)$.
3. If $f(n) = \Omega(n^{\log_b a + \varepsilon})$ for some constant $\varepsilon > 0$, and if $n/b > N \Rightarrow af(n/b) \le cf(n)$ for some positive constants $c < 1$ and $N$, then $T(n) = \Theta(f(n))$.

***Proof***

First, we observe by Lemma 1 that $T(n) = \Theta(n^{\log_b a}) + g(n)$, where

$$g(n) = \sum_{k=0}^{\log_b n-1} a^k f\left(\frac{n}{b^k}\right).$$

In case 1, it follows from case 1 of Lemma 2 that

$$T(n) = \Theta(n^{\log_b a}) + g(n) = \Theta(n^{\log_b a} + n^{\log_b a}) = \Theta(n^{\log_b a})$$

In case 2, it follows from case 2 of Lemma 2 that

$$T(n) = f(n) + g(n) = \Theta(n^{\log_b a} + n^{\log_b a} \log n) = \Theta(n^{\log_b a} \log n).$$

In case 3, it follows from case 3 of Lemma 2 that $g(n) = \Theta(f(n))$, and (by Lemma 1)

$$T(n) = \Theta\left(n^{\log_b a}\right) + g(n) = \Theta\left(n^{\log_b a} + f(n)\right).$$

Since $f(n) = \Omega(n^{\log_b a+\varepsilon})$, it follows that $T(n) = \Theta(f(n))$.

### The General Case

Lemma 3 states the *Master Method* for the case that $n$ is a nonnegative integral power of $b$. Recall that the importance of this case is to guarantee that at every level of recursion the expression $n/b$ is an integer. For general $n$, however, the expression $n/b$ need not be an integer. We can therefore substitute $\lceil n/b \rceil$ or $\lfloor n/b \rfloor$ for $n/b$ in the recurrence (3.1) and attempt to obtain similar results. Since

$$\frac{n}{b} - 1 < \left\lfloor \frac{n}{b} \right\rfloor \le \left\lceil \frac{n}{b} \right\rceil < \frac{n}{b} + 1,$$

this will enable us to demonstrate that a small discrepancy in the value of the independent variable often makes no difference in asymptotic evaluation. In the following, we develop a version of the *Master Method* using the expression $\lceil n/b \rceil$ for $n/b$ in the recurrence (3.1). A similar argument can be given if, instead, we use $\lfloor n/b \rfloor$ for $n/b$ in (3.1).

Consider the sequences defined by the recursive equations

$$m_i = \begin{cases} n & \text{if } i = 0; \\ \left\lfloor \dfrac{m_{i-1}}{b} \right\rfloor & \text{if } i > 0, \end{cases}$$

and

$$n_i = \begin{cases} n & \text{if } i = 0; \\ \left\lceil \dfrac{n_{i-1}}{b} \right\rceil & \text{if } i > 0. \end{cases}$$

Since $b > 1$, these are nonincreasing sequences of integers. We have

$$m_0 = n_0 = n,$$

$$\frac{n}{b} - 1 < m_1 \le n_1 < \frac{n}{b} + 1,$$

$$\frac{n}{b^2} - \frac{1}{b} - 1 < m_2 \le n_2 < \frac{n}{b^2} + \frac{1}{b} + 1,$$

and more generally, based on simple inductive arguments for the lower bound for $m_i$ and the upper bound for $n_i$,

$$\frac{n}{b^i} - \frac{b}{b-1} =$$

$$\frac{n}{b^i} - \sum_{k=0}^{\infty} \frac{1}{b^k} < \frac{n}{b^i} - \sum_{k=0}^{i-1} \frac{1}{b^k} < m_i \le n_i < \frac{n}{b^i} + \sum_{k=0}^{i-1} \frac{1}{b^k} < \frac{n}{b^i} + \sum_{k=0}^{\infty} \frac{1}{b^k} =$$

$$\frac{n}{b^i} + \frac{b}{b-1}.$$

Thus,

$$i \ge \lceil \log_b n \rceil \Rightarrow b^i \ge n \Rightarrow n_i < 1 + \frac{b}{b-1}.$$

Since $n_i$ is integer-valued, we have

$$i \ge \lceil \log_b n \rceil \Rightarrow m_i \le n_i \le \left\lfloor 1 + \frac{b}{b-1} \right\rfloor = \Theta(1).$$

Suppose, then, that we use the recurrence

$$T(n) = aT\left(\frac{n}{b}\right) + f(n) \qquad (3.3)$$

and expand this recurrence iteratively in order to obtain

$$T(n) = f(n_0) + aT(n_1) = f(n_0) + af(n_1) + a^2T(n_2) = \ldots$$

The reader can prove by induction that for $0 \le i \le \lceil \log_b n \rceil - 1$,

$$T(n) = \left[ \sum_{k=0}^{i} a^k f(n_k) \right] + a^{i+1}T(n_{i+1}).$$

In particular, for $i = \lceil \log_b n \rceil - 1$,

$$T(n) = a^{\lceil \log_b n \rceil} T\left(n_{\lceil \log_b n \rceil}\right) + \sum_{k=0}^{\lceil \log_b n \rceil - 1} a^k f(n_k).$$

Now,

$$a^{\log_b n} \le a^{\lceil \log_b n \rceil} < a a^{\log_b n} \Rightarrow a^{\lceil \log_b n \rceil} = \Theta\left(a^{\log_b n}\right) = \Theta\left(n^{\log_b a}\right).$$

Since $n_{\lceil \log_b n \rceil} = \Theta(1)$, we have $T\left(n_{\lceil \log_b n \rceil}\right) = \Theta(1)$. Substituting these last two results into the last equation for $T(n)$, we have

$$T(n) = \Theta(n^{\log_b a}) + \sum_{k=0}^{\lceil \log_b n \rceil - 1} a^k f(n_k).$$

This is an equation much like that of the conclusion of Lemma 1.

Similarly, if we modify (3.3) to obtain the recurrence

$$T'(n) = aT'\left(\left\lfloor \frac{n}{b} \right\rfloor\right) + f(n), \tag{3.4}$$

then we similarly obtain

$$T'(n) = \Theta(n^{\log_b a}) + \sum_{k=0}^{\lceil \log_b n \rceil - 1} a^k f(m_k).$$

Let

$$g(n) = \sum_{k=0}^{\lceil \log_b n \rceil - 1} a^k f(n_k),$$

$$g'(n) = \sum_{k=0}^{\lceil \log_b n \rceil - 1} a^k f(m_k).$$

We wish to evaluate $g(n)$ and $g'(n)$ asymptotically.

In case 1, we have the hypothesis that $f(n) = O(n^{\log_b a - \varepsilon})$ for some constant $\varepsilon > 0$. Without loss of generality, we have $\log_b a - \varepsilon \ge 0$. There is a constant $c > 0$ such that for sufficiently large $n_k > N$,

$$f(n_k) \le c{n_k}^{\log_b a - \varepsilon} \le c\left(\frac{n}{b^k} + \frac{b}{b-1}\right)^{\log_b a - \varepsilon} = c\left[\left(\frac{n}{b^k}\right)\left(1 + \frac{b^k}{n} \times \frac{b}{b-1}\right)\right]^{\log_b a - \varepsilon}$$

$$= c\left(\frac{n^{\log_b a - \varepsilon}}{a^k b^{-k\varepsilon}}\right)\left[1 + \left(\frac{b^k}{n} \times \frac{b}{b-1}\right)\right]^{\log_b a - \varepsilon} \le c\left(\frac{n^{\log_b a - \varepsilon}}{a^k}\right)\left(1 + \frac{b}{b-1}\right)^{\log_b a - \varepsilon}$$

$$= \frac{d n^{\log_b a} b^{k\varepsilon}}{a^k},$$

where

$$d = c\left(1 + \frac{b}{b+1}\right)^{\log_b a - \varepsilon}$$

is a constant.

For such $k$, $a^k f(n_k) \le d n^{\log_b a} b^{k\varepsilon}$. It follows that

$$g(n) = \sum_{\substack{k\in\{0,\ldots,\lceil \log_b n\rceil -1\},\\ n_k\le N}} a^k f(n_k) + \sum_{\substack{k\in\{0,\ldots,\lceil \log_b n\rceil -1\},\\ n_k> N}} a^k f(n_k)$$

$$\le \Theta(1) \sum_{\substack{k\in\{0,\ldots,\lceil \log_b n\rceil -1\},\\ n_k\le N}} a^k + d n^{\log_b a-\varepsilon} \sum_{\substack{k\in\{0,\ldots,\lceil \log_b n\rceil -1\},\\ n_k> N}} b^{\varepsilon k}.$$

The former summation, a geometric series, is $O(a^{\log_b n}) = O(n^{\log_b a})$. In the latter summation, there are $\Theta(1)$ terms, as $n_k > N$ corresponds to small values of $k$. It follows that

$$g(n) \le O\left(n^{\log_b a}\right) + d n^{\log_b a-\varepsilon}\Theta(1) = O\left(n^{\log_b a}\right).$$

Hence, $T(n) = \Theta(n^{\log_b a}) + g(n) = \Theta(n^{\log_b a})$, as desired. A similar argument shows $T'(n) = \Theta(n^{\log_b a})$.

In case 2, the hypothesis that $f(n) = \Theta(n^{\log_b a})$ implies there are positive constants $c$ and $C$ such that for sufficiently large $m_k$ and $n_k$, say, $m_k, n_k > N$,

$$f(n_k) \le c n_k^{\log_b a} \le c\left(\frac{n}{b^k} + \frac{b}{b-1}\right)^{\log_b a} = c\left(\frac{n^{\log_b a}}{a^k}\right)\left[1 + \left(\frac{b^k}{n} \times \frac{b}{b-1}\right)\right]^{\log_b a}$$

$$\le c\left(\frac{n^{\log_b a}}{a^k}\right)\left(1 + \frac{b}{b-1}\right)^{\log_b a} = \frac{d n^{\log_b a}}{a^k},$$

where $d = c\left(1 + \frac{b}{b-1}\right)^{\log_b a}$ is a constant, and similarly, there is a constant $D > 0$ such that

$$f(m_k) \ge \frac{D n^{\log_b a}}{a^k}.$$

Therefore, for such $k$, $a^k f(n_k) \le d n^{\log_b a}$ and $a^k f(m_k) > D n^{\log_b a}$. So,

$$g(n) = \sum_{\substack{k\in\{0,\ldots,\lceil \log_b n\rceil -1\},\\ n_k\le N}} a^k f(n_k) + \sum_{\substack{k\in\{0,\ldots,\lceil \log_b n\rceil -1\},\\ n_k> N}} a^k f(n_k).$$

In the first summation, the values of $f(n_k)$ are bounded, since $n_k \le N$. Thus, the summation is bounded asymptotically by the geometric series

$$\sum_{k=0}^{\lceil \log_b n\rceil -1} a^k = O\left(a^{\log_b n}\right) = O\left(n^{\log_b a}\right).$$

The second summation in the expansion of $g(n)$ is simplified as

$$\sum_{\substack{k\in\{0,\ldots,\lceil\log_b n\rceil-1\},\\ n_k>N}} a^k f(n_k) \le \sum_{k=0}^{\lceil\log_b n\rceil-1} dn^{\log_b a} = O\left(n^{\log_b a}\log n\right).$$

Substituting these into the previous equation for $g(n)$, we obtain

$$g(n) = O(n^{\log_b a}) + O(n^{\log_b a}\log n) = O(n^{\log_b a}\log n).$$

Hence, $T(n) = O(n^{\log_b a}\log n)$. Similarly,

$$\begin{aligned} g'(n) &= \sum_{\substack{k\in\{0,\ldots,\lceil\log_b n\rceil-1\},\\ n_k\le N}} a^k f(m_k) + \sum_{\substack{k\in\{0,\ldots,\lceil\log_b n\rceil-1\},\\ n_k>N}} a^k f(m_k) \\ &= \Omega(1) + \Omega\left(n^{\log_b a}\log n\right) = \Omega\left(n^{\log_b a}\log n\right). \end{aligned}$$

Notice that

$$\left\{(m_k \le n_k) \text{ and } \left[f(n) = \Theta\left(n^{\log_b a}\right)\right]\right\} \Rightarrow$$

$$\sum_{\substack{k\in\{0,\ldots,\lceil\log_b n\rceil-1\},\\ m_k>N}} a^k f(m_k) = O\left(\sum_{\substack{k\in\{0,\ldots,\lceil\log_b n\rceil-1\},\\ n_k>N}} a^k f(n_k)\right).$$

Therefore,

$$\begin{aligned} g'(n) &= \sum_{\substack{k\in\{0,\ldots,\lceil\log_b n\rceil-1\},\\ n_k\le N}} a^k f(m_k) + \sum_{\substack{k\in\{0,\ldots,\lceil\log_b n\rceil-1\},\\ n_k>N}} a^k f(m_k) \\ &= O\left(\sum_{k=0}^{\lceil\log_b n\rceil-1} a^k\right) + O\left(\sum_{\substack{k\in\{0,1,\ldots\lceil\log_b n\rceil-1\},\\ n_k>N}} a^k f(n_k)\right) = O(g(n)). \end{aligned}$$

It follows that $g(n) = \Theta(n^{\log_b a}\log n)$ and $g'(n) = \Theta(n^{\log_b a}\log n)$. Therefore,

$$T(n) = \Theta(n^{\log_b a}\log n) \text{ and } T'(n) = \Theta(n^{\log_b a}\log n).$$

In case 3, an analysis similar to that given for case 3 of Lemma 2 shows $g(n) = \Theta(f(n))$, as follows. Recall the hypotheses of this case: $f(n) = \Omega(n^{\log_b a+\varepsilon})$ for some constant $\varepsilon > 0$, and there are constants $0 < c < 1$ and $N > 0$ such that $n/b > N \Rightarrow af(n/b) \le cf(n)$. As above, it follows by a simple induction argument that for

$$\frac{n}{b^k} > N, \text{ or, equivalently, } k < \left\lfloor \log_b\left(\frac{n}{N}\right)\right\rfloor,$$

we have

$$a^k f\left(\frac{n}{b^k}\right) \le c^k f(n).$$

Therefore,

$$g(n) = \sum_{k=0}^{\lfloor \log_b (n/N) \rfloor} a^k f\left(\frac{n}{b^k}\right) + \sum_{k=\lfloor \log_b (n/N) \rfloor+1}^{\lceil \log_b n \rceil - 1} a^k f\left(\frac{n}{b^k}\right) \le$$

$$f(n) \sum_{k=0}^{\lfloor \log_b (n/N) \rfloor} c^k + a^{\lceil \log_b n \rceil - 1} (\log_b N) \max_{k \ge \lfloor \log_b (n/N) \rfloor + 1} f\left(\frac{n}{b^k}\right) <$$

$$f(n) \frac{1}{1-c} + \Theta\left(a^{\log_b n}\right) = O\left(f(n) + a^{\log_b n}\right).$$

Since $f(n) = \Omega(n^{\log_b a + \varepsilon})$ and $a^{\log_b n} = n^{\log_b a}$, we have $g(n) = O(f(n))$, and therefore $T(n) = \Theta(n^{\log_b a} + g(n)) = O(f(n))$.

Since equation (3.3) implies $T(n) = \Omega(f(n))$, it follows that $T(n) = \Theta(f(n))$, as desired. A similar argument shows $T'(n) = \Theta(f(n))$.

Thus, in all cases, whether we use $\lceil n/b \rceil$ or $\lfloor n/b \rfloor$ as our interpretation of $n/b$ in (3.1), we have obtained the results asserted in the statement of the **Master Theorem.** Therefore, the proof of the **Master Theorem** is complete.

# Appendix 3

# Efficient Gather and Scatter Operations

In this appendix, we present algorithms to implement gather and scatter operations efficiently on coarse-grained parallel computers. These operations were discussed in Chapter 4. Typically, a *gather* operation collects data that is distributed across a group of processors. The data is typically moved to one of the processors of the group where it is reassembled. A *scatter* operation is typically used to partition data in one processor of a group and send one partition to each of the remaining processors in the group. Think of the gather as a group-based read by a distinguished processor in the group and a scatter as a group-based write from a distinguished processor in the group.

For example, we showed in Chapter 4 that using gather and scatter operations, an efficient algorithm to perform a semigroup operation over a set $X$ of values on a $CGM(n, q)$ can be performed as follows.

1. In parallel, every processor $P_j$ computes a partial result $m_j$ by sequentially computing a semigroup operation on the processor's portion of $X$.
2. Gather the set of partial results $S = \{m_j\}_{j=0}^{q-1}$ to processor $P_0$.
3. Processor $P_0$ performs a sequential version of the semigroup operation on $S$.
4. Processor $P_0$ writes the result of the semigroup calculation into a record associated with each of the $q$ members of $S$.
5. Scatter the $q$ members of $S$, so the result of the semigroup operation is sent to their original processors.

## Building a Tree of Processors

Efficient gather and scatter operations can be implemented by making use of a logical tree rooted at processor $P_0$ in the graph of processors of a parallel computer. Often, such a tree is known or easily determined. For example, in a mesh, we might use all the row edges and, among the column edges, only those of the column containing $P_0$. If it is necessary to determine such a tree, we can do so using the algorithm described below. This algorithm can be used for a parallel computer of arbitrarily many processors. However, we have in mind its use on a $CGM(n, q)$, where $q$ represents the number of processors. Thus, the problem can be stated as follows. Given a parallel computer $C$, regarded as a connected graph of processors, and a particular processor $R$, determine the edges representing a tree $T$ rooted at $R$ by identifying, for each processor in $C$, its parent and its children in $T$.

The algorithm we give may be regarded as a parallel breadth-first search (see Chapter 12).

**Algorithm for determining the edges of a tree *T* rooted at *R* containing all processors as vertices**
**Input:** Each processor knows its neighboring processors.
**Output:** Each processor knows its parent and its children in a tree rooted at $R$.

**Action:**

```
1. In parallel, each processor creates an ID record
   with the following.
   a. A field for the processor's ID.
   b. A field for the ID of the parent processor that
      is initially null.
   c. An initially empty list of children processors.
   This step runs in Θ(1) time.
2. R sends its ID record to all its neighbors. In the
   worst case, this requires R to send messages
   sequentially to individual neighbors. Thus, the
   time for this step is O(q).
3. In parallel, each processor P does the following.
   a. If P≠R, then perform the following.
           i. Receive a neighbor's ID record. This requires
              some time to wait for the first neighbor's
              message to arrive, as well as Θ(1) time to
              read the first neighbor's message. The wait
              time will be discussed below.
          ii. Set the processor's parent component equal
              to the processor ID contained in the first
```

```
            message received from a neighbor. This step
            runs in Θ(1) time.
        End If
    b. Send the processor's own ID record to each
        neighboring processor. This step runs in O(q)
        time. Note that except for R, no processor sends
        its ID record until it has marked its own
        parent.
    c. From every neighboring processor Q such that Q
        is not the parent of P, receive the ID record of
        Q. If Q's parent has been marked as P then P
        adds Q to its list of children. As in step a.i.
        above, there is some wait time, in addition to
        the O(q) time to read the neighbors' messages.
End of algorithm
```

If we can show that the wait time mentioned above is $O(q)$, it will follow that the algorithm's running time is $O(q)$. Note that this analysis is somewhat difficult, and perhaps should be skimmed or skipped by readers who do not have a deep mathematical background.

A processor other than $R$ waits for a message from its parent, *i.e.*, the first neighbor from which a message is received, and all processors wait for messages from their non-parental neighbors. First, let's analyze the time that a processor waits until it receives its parent's record. Note that if $P$ and $Q$ are neighboring processors, then their distances from $R$ in the graph $C$, $d_P$ and $d_Q$, respectively, satisfy

$$|d_P - d_Q| \le 1. \tag{1}$$

Let

$$d_{\max} = \max\{d_P | P \in V(C)\},$$

where $V(C)$ is the vertex set, *i.e.*, the set of processors, of $C$. For $i \in \{-2, -1, 0, 1, \ldots, d_{\max} + 1\}$, let

$$A_i = \{P \in V(C) | d_P = i\}.$$

Notice $A_{-2} = A_{-1} = A_{d_{\max}+1} = \varnothing$ and

$$\sum_{i=-2}^{d_{\max}+1} |A_i| = q. \tag{2}$$

Let's call the time required for a processor to send its ID record to a neighbor a *unit time step.* For $i > 0$, let $n_i$ be the maximum number of unit time steps until a member of $A_i$ receives its parent's ID record, and let $n_0 = 0$. We will show that for $i \in \{0, 1, \ldots, d_{\max}\}$,

$$n_i \leq 3\left(\sum_{j=-2}^{i-2} |A_j|\right) + 2|A_{i-1}| + |A_i|. \tag{3}$$

Inequality (3) is trivial for $i = 0$. Suppose, for some integer $k$ such that $0 \leq k < d_{\max}$, inequality (3) is true for $i \leq k$. Let $P \in A_{k+1}$. There exists $Q \in A_k$ such that $P$ and $Q$ are neighbors in $C$. Then the number of unit time steps until $P$ receives its message from its parent is less than or equal to the number of unit time steps until $P$ receives its message from $Q$. From inequality (1), all neighbors of $Q$ belong to $A_{k-1} \cup A_k \cup A_{k+1}$. In the worst case, $P$ is the last neighbor of $Q$ to receive a message from $Q$. It follows that

$$n_{k+1} \leq n_k + |A_{k-1}| + |A_k| + |A_{k+1}| \leq$$

(by the inductive hypothesis)

$$3\left(\sum_{j=-2}^{k-1} |A_i|\right) + 2|A_k| + |A_{k+1}|,$$

as desired. This completes the induction.

From equation (2) and inequality (3), $n_i \leq 3q$. Thus, the waiting time for all processors to receive their parents' ID records is $O(q)$.

We determine the time spent by a processor $P$ waiting for messages from non-parental neighbors as follows. Suppose $Q$ is a neighbor of $P$. After $P$ receives its parent's ID record, $P$ sends its own ID record to all its neighbors. In the worst case, $Q$ is the last of the neighbors of $P$ to receive the ID record from $P$. Therefore, $Q$ will wait for $O(q)$ time steps. Similarly, in the worst case, $P$ is then the last neighbor of $Q$ to receive the ID record from $Q$, waiting another $O(q)$ unit time steps. Thus, in $O(q)$ unit time steps, $P$ and $Q$ exchange their ID records. Taking the maximum over all neighbors $Q$ of $P$, we conclude that $P$ waits $O(q)$ unit time steps between receiving the first and the last of its neighbors' ID records.

Therefore, we can conclude that the algorithm performs in $O(q)$ time.

In order to obtain a lower bound for the running time of our algorithm, consider a linear array implementation of a *CGM*($n$, $q$), for which it is easily seen that the running time is $\Omega(q)$. Therefore, our time estimate of $O(q)$ yields optimal $\Theta(q)$ running time in the worst case.

## Gather and Scatter Algorithms

We can now derive efficient gather and scatter algorithms for a set $S$ of data items distributed among the processors of a *CGM*($n$, $q$), as follows. Note we limit $S$ to size $N = O(n/q)$ since we must be able to fit $S$ into a single processor.

Assume the processors are numbered $0,\ldots,q-1$. We use, in each processor, an array *from*$[0,\ldots,q-1]$ in order to route data efficiently in a scatter. In every processor $P_i$, the entries of this array will be defined by

*from*$[j] = k$ if data originating in $P_j$ reached $P_i$ from the latter's neighbor $P_k$.

By keeping track of which neighbor a data item came *from*, we can execute a scatter by reversing the flow of data used by a gather.

**Algorithms for Gather and Scatter**
**Input:** A set $S$ of $N$ data items distributed among the processors of a $CGM(n, q)$ $G$, where $N = \Omega(q)$ and $N = O(n/q)$, and each processor knowing whether it is the processor $R$ to which $S$ is gathered.

**Gather Algorithm**
**Output:** A copy of each member of $S$ in processor $R$.

**Action:**

1. In parallel, each processor $P_i$ sets its *from*$[i] = i$. This step runs in $\Theta(1)$ time.
2. In parallel, each processor $P_i$ tags each of its members $s$ of $S$ by $s.processorOrigin = i$. This step runs in $O(N)$ time.
3. If a spanning tree for $G$ with $R$ as the root isn't already known, use the algorithm above to determine a spanning tree $T$ of $G$ so that $R$ is the root processor and every processor $P$ knows its parent processor *parent*($P$) and its child processors in $T$. This step runs in $O(q)$ time.
4. In parallel, each processor $P$ sends members of $S$ to *parent*($P$) and receives members of $S$ from its child processors until there are no members of $S$ for $P$ to send. As $P$ receives $s \in S$ from a neighbor $P_k$, $P$ makes the assignment

$$from[s.processorOrigin] = k.$$

   Each processor handles $O(N)$ data with $O(N+q)$ waiting time, so this step runs in $O(N+q) = O(N)$ time.

End gather

Clearly, this algorithm runs in $O(N)$ time.

**Scatter algorithm**

**Action:**

1. The root processor $R$ does the following. For each $s \in S$, if $s.processorOrigin$ is not $R$ then send $s$ to the neighboring processor $P_{from[s.processorOrigin]}$. This step runs in $O(N)$ time.
2. All other processors $P_i$ in parallel do the following. For at most $N$ members $s$ of $S$, receive $s$ from $parent(P_i)$. If $s.processorOrigin \neq i$ then send $s$ to $P_{from[s.processorOrigin]}$. Since waiting for data to arrive from the parent processor requires a total of $O(N+q) = O(N)$ time, this step runs in $O(N)$ time.

End scatter

Clearly, our scatter algorithm runs in $O(N)$ time.

Note we presented our scatter algorithm above with the assumption that the appropriate values of each processor's *from* array are known. Thus, our presentation assumes that the scatter operation has been preceded by a gather operation. Sometimes, however, it is necessary to perform a scatter operation that has not been preceded by a gather operation. When this is the case, we can precede the first step listed in the scatter algorithm above by a gather of dummy records, one from each processor, to the root processor $R$, in order to establish the entries of each processor's *from* array. We know that such a gather operation runs in $\Theta(q) = O(N)$ time, so this additional step does not change the asymptotic analysis of our scatter algorithm.

In the worst case, our gather and scatter algorithms run in $\Omega(N)$ time. This is because in the worst case, the root processor must sequentially receive, for a gather, or send, for a scatter, $N$ data items. Therefore, our algorithms run in worst case optimal $\Theta(N)$ time.

## Appendix Notes

Gather and scatter operations have been presented in *Parallel Algorithms for Regular Architectures: Meshes and Pyramids* by R. Miller and Q.F. Stout (The MIT Press, Cambridge, Mass., 1996), and in "Coarse Grained Gather and Scatter Operations with Applications," by L. Boxer and R. Miller, *Journal of Parallel and Distributed Computing*, 64 (2004), 1297–1320. These presentations are not entirely consistent; we have followed the latter presentation. The algorithms presented here are taken from the Boxer and Miller paper. (There is an error in this paper that is corrected in "Efficient Coarse Grained Data Distributions and String Pattern Matching," by L. Boxer and R. Miller, *International Journal of Information and Systems Sciences* 6 (4) (2010), 424–434; the error does not affect the material presented here.)

# Appendix 4

# Expected-Case Running Time of Quicksort

In this appendix, we consider the expected-case running time of Quicksort. The analysis is intricate and is suitable only for a reader who has a solid mathematical background. We will make a variety of assumptions, most of which serve only to simplify the analysis. Our first major assumption is that we consider Quicksort on an **array** that consists of $n$ **distinct keys, randomly distributed.** In terms of fundamental notation, we let $k(i)$ be the expected number of key comparisons required to sort $i$ items. Quicksort is a comparison-based sort, and our analysis will focus on determining the number of times Quicksort compares two elements during the sorting procedure. The reader should note that $k(0) = 0$, $k(1) = 0$, and $k(2) = 3.5$. That is, an array with no more than one element is already sorted and does not require any keys to be compared. An array of size 2 requires 3.5 comparisons, on average, to be sorted by the array version of Quicksort that we have presented. The reader can verify this by considering the code as applied to two options for an array of size 2. Recall that the keys are distinct. Therefore, the options for an array of size two are a smaller key followed by a larger key and a larger key followed by a smaller key.

We now consider some assumptions that apply to the partition routine. Assume that we are required to sort $A[1 \ldots n]$.

- According to the partition routine, we will use $A[1]$ as the partition element.
- Since we assume distinct keys, if this partition element represents the $i^{\text{th}}$ largest of the $n$ elements in $A[1 \ldots n]$ and $i > 1$, then at the end of the partition routine, the smallest $i - 1$ elements will be stored in $A[1 \ldots i - 1]$. We will assume that a simple modification is made to the code so that at the end of the partition routine, the splitter is placed in position $i$, and *partitionIndex* is set to $i$. Notice that this modification to the partition routine increases the running time of the routine by $\Theta(1)$.
- Therefore, notice that it suffices to have the recursive calls performed on $A[1 \ldots i - 1]$ and $A[i + 1 \ldots n]$.

Consider the number of comparisons that are made in the partition routine.

- Notice that it takes $\Theta(n)$ comparisons to partition the $n$ elements.
- Based on our notation and the recursive nature of Quicksort, we note that, on average, it takes at most $k(i - 1)$ and $k(n - i)$ comparisons to sort $A[1 \ldots i - 1]$ and $A[i + 1 \ldots n]$, respectively.

We should point out that since we assume unique input elements and that all arrangements of the input data are equally likely, then it is equally likely that the *partitionIndex* returned is any of the elements of $\{1, \ldots, n\}$. That is, the *partitionIndex* will wind up with any value in the range of $[1 \ldots n]$ with probability $1/n$. Finally, we present details for determining the expected-case running time of Quicksort.

Notice that the definition provides that

$$k(n) = (n+1) + \frac{1}{n}\sum_{i=1}^{n}[k(i-1) + k(n-i)], \text{ where}$$

- $k(n)$ is the expected number of key comparisons,
- $(n + 1)$ is the number of comparisons required to partition $n$ data items, assuming that Partition is modified in such a way to prevent $i$ and $j$ from crossing,
- $1/n$ is the probability of the input $A[j]$ being the $i$-th largest entry of $A$, $j \in \{1, \ldots n\}$,
- $k(i - 1)$ is the expected number of key comparisons to sort $A[1 \ldots i - 1]$, and
- $k(n - i)$ is the expected number of key comparisons to sort $A[i + 1 \ldots n]$.

So, $k(n) = (n+1) + \frac{1}{n}\sum_{i=1}^{n}[k(i-1) + k(n-i)]$

$$= n + 1 + \frac{1}{n}\begin{bmatrix} & k(0) & + & k(n-1) \\ + & k(1) & + & k(n-2) \\ + & \ldots & & \\ + & k(n-1) & + & k(0) \end{bmatrix}$$

$$= n + 1 + \frac{2}{n}\sum_{i=1}^{n-1} k(i).$$

(Note that we used the fact that $k(0) = 0$.)

Therefore, we now have

$$k(n) = n + 1 + \frac{2}{n}[k(n-1) + k(n-2) + k(n-3) + \ldots + k(1)].$$

This gives us

$$k(n-1) = n + \frac{2}{n-1}[k(n-2) + k(n-3) + \ldots + k(1)].$$

In order to simplify the equation for $k(n)$, let's define

$$S = [k(n-2) + k(n-3) + \ldots + k(1)].$$

By substituting into the previous equations for $k(n)$ and $k(n - 1)$, we obtain

$$k(n) = n + 1 + \frac{2}{n}[k(n-1) + S] \text{ and}$$

$$k(n-1) = n + \frac{2}{n-1}S.$$

Therefore, $S = \frac{n-1}{2}[k(n-1) - n]$.

So,

$$k(n) = n + 1 + \frac{2}{n}\left[k(n-1) + \frac{n-1}{2}(k(n-1) - n)\right]$$

$$= \frac{n+1}{n}k(n-1) + 2.$$

Hence, $\frac{k(n)}{n+1} = \frac{2}{n+1} + \frac{k(n-1)}{n}$.

In order to simplify, let's define

$$X(n) = \frac{k(n)}{n+1}.$$

Therefore,

$$\frac{k(n-1)}{n} = X(n-1).$$

So,

$$X(n) = \frac{2}{n+1} + X(n-1) = \frac{2}{n+1} + \frac{2}{n} + X(n-2) = \frac{2}{n+1} + \frac{2}{n} + \frac{2}{n-1} + X(n-3) = \ldots.$$

An induction argument can be used to show that

$$X(n) = \frac{2}{n+1} + \frac{2}{n} + \frac{2}{n-1} + \cdots + \frac{2}{4} + X(2) = 2\left(\frac{1}{4} + \frac{1}{5} + \cdots + \frac{1}{n+1}\right) + C$$

$$\left(\text{where } C = X(2) \text{ (a constant)} = \frac{k(2)}{3} = \frac{3.5}{3} = \frac{7}{6}\right)$$

$$= C + 2\sum_{i=4}^{n+1}\frac{1}{i} = \Theta(\log n).$$

So, $k(n) = (n+1)X(n) = \Theta(n \log n)$ expected-case number of comparisons.

It is easily seen that the expected-case number of data moves, *i.e.*, swaps, is $O(n \log n)$, as the number of data moves is no more than the number of comparisons. Therefore, the expected-case running time of the array version of Quicksort is $\Theta(n \log n)$. The argument given above requires little modification to show that our queue-based implementation of Quicksort also has an expected-case running time of $\Theta(n \log n)$.

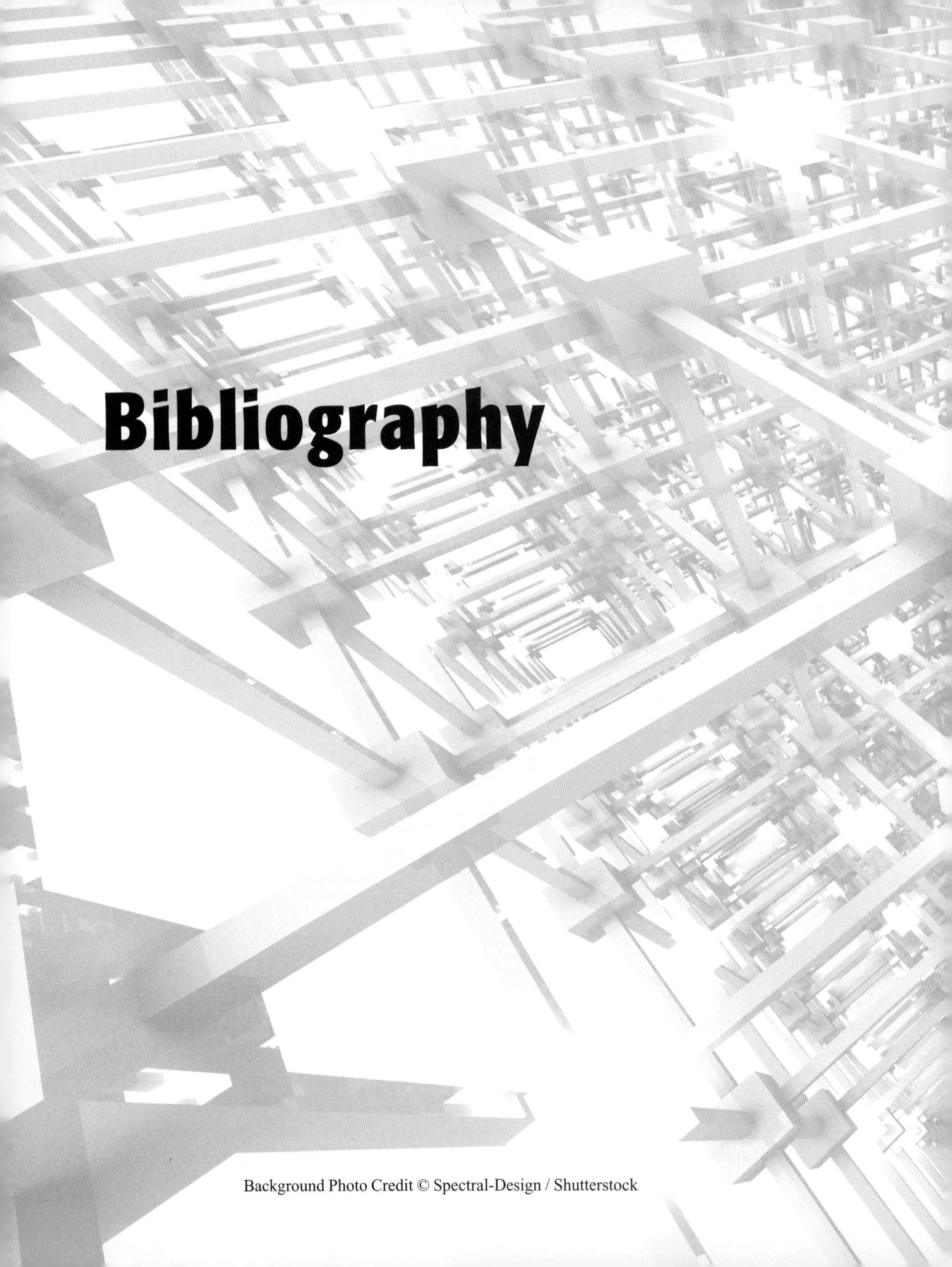

# Bibliography

1. A.V. Aho, J.E. Hopcroft, and J.D. Ullman, *The Design and Analysis of Computer Algorithms*, Addison-Wesley, Reading, Massachusetts, 1974.
2. S.G. Akl and K.A. Lyons, *Parallel Computational Geometry*, Prentice Hall, New Jersey, 1993.
3. G.S. Almasi and A. Gottlieb, *Highly Parallel Computing*, The Benjamin/Cummings Publishing Company, New York, 1994.
4. G. Amdahl, "Validity of the single processor approach to achieving large scale computing capabilities," *AFIPS Conference Proceedings*, vol. 30, Thompson Books, 1967, 483–485.
5. T.M. Apostol, *Introduction to Analytic Number Theory*, Springer-Verlag, New York, 2001.
6. N.S. Asaithambi, *Numerical Analysis: Theory and Practice*, Saunders College Publishing, Fort Worth, TX, 1995.
7. M.J. Atallah, ed., *Algorithms and Theory of Computation Handbook*, CRC Press, Boca Raton, FL, 1999.
8. M.J. Atallah and D.Z. Chen, "An optimal parallel algorithm for the minimum circle-cover problem," *Information Processing Letters* **32**, 1989, 159–165.
9. M. Atallah and M. Goodrich, "Efficient parallel solutions to some geometric problems," *Journal of Parallel and Distributed Computing* **3**, 1986, 492–507.
10. S. Baase, "Introduction to parallel connectivity, list ranking, and Euler tour techniques," in *Synthesis of Parallel Algorithms*, J.H. Reif, ed., Morgan Kaufmann Publishers, San Mateo, CA, 1993, 61–114.
11. K.E. Batcher, "Sorting networks and their applications," *Proc. AFIPS Spring Joint Computer Conference* **32**, 1968, 307–314.
12. J.L. Bentley, D. Haken, and J.B. Saxe, "A general method for solving divide-and-conquer recurrences," *SIGACT News* **12**, 1980, 36–44.
13. A.A. Bertossi, "Parallel circle-cover algorithms," *Information Processing Letters* **27**, 1988, 133–139.
14. G.E. Blelloch, *Vector Models for Data-Parallel Computing*, The MIT Press, Cambridge, Massachusetts, 1990.
15. G. Brassard and P. Bratley, *Algorithmics: Theory and Practice,* Prentice Hall, New Jersey, 1988.
16. L. Boxer, "Efficient Coarse Grained Permutation Exchanges and Matrix Multiplication," *Parallel Processing Letters* **19**, 2009, 477–484.
17. L. Boxer and R. Miller, "A parallel circle-cover minimization algorithm," *Information Processing Letters* **32**, 1989, 57–60.

18. L. Boxer and R. Miller, "Parallel algorithms for all maximal equally-spaced collinear sets and all maximal regular coplanar lattices," *Pattern Recognition Letters* **14**, 1993, 17–22.
19. L. Boxer and R. Miller, "A parallel algorithm for approximate regularity," *Information Processing Letters* **80**, 2001, 311–316.
20. L. Boxer and R. Miller, "Coarse grained gather and scatter operations with applications," *Journal of Parallel and Distributed Computing* **64**, 2004, 1297–1320.
21. L. Boxer and R. Miller, "Efficient Coarse Grained Data Distributions and String Pattern Matching," *International Journal of Information and Systems Sciences* **6**, 2010, 424–434.
22. L. Boxer, R. Miller, and A. Rau-Chaplin, "Scalable Parallel Algorithms for Geometric Pattern Recognition," *Journal of Parallel and Distributed Computing* **58**, 1999, 466–486.
23. R.L. Burden and J.D. Faires, *Numerical Analysis*, PWS-Kent Publishing Company, Boston, Massachusetts, 1993.
24. R. Butt, *Introduction to Numerical Analysis Using MATLAB*, Infinity Science Press, Hingham, Massachusetts, 2008.
25. R.J. Cole, "An optimally efficient selection algorithm," *Information Processing Letters* **26**, 1987/88, 295–299.
26. Condor High Throughput Computing, http://research.cs.wisc.edu/condor/, accessed August 24, 2012.
27. T.H. Cormen, C.E. Leiserson, R.L. Rivest, and C. Stein, *Introduction to Algorithms*, 3rd ed., The MIT Press, Cambridge, Massachusetts, 2009.
28. M. DeBerg, O. Cheong, M. van Kreveld, and M. Overmars, *Computational Geometry: Algorithms and Applications*, Springer, Berlin, 2010.
29. F. Dehne, ed., special edition of *Algorithmica* **24**, no. 3–4, 1999.
30. F. Dehne, A. Fabri, and A. Rau-Chaplin, "Scalable parallel geometric algorithms for multicomputers," *Proceedings 9th ACM Symposium on Computational Geometry,* 1993, 298–307.
31. S. Even, *Graph Algorithms*, Computer Science Press, New York, 1979.
32. M.J. Flynn, "Very high-speed computing systems," *Proceedings of the IEEE* **54**, 1966, 1901–1909.
33. M.J. Flynn, "Some computer organizations and their effectiveness," *IEEE Transactions on Computers* **21**, 1972, 948–960.
34. M.T. Goodrich and R. Tamassia, *Data Structures and Algorithms in JAVA*, John Wiley & Sons, Inc., New York, 1998.
35. R.L. Graham, "An efficient algorithm for determining the convex hull of a finite planar set," *Information Processing Letters* **1**, 1972, 132–133.

36. R.L. Graham, D.E. Knuth, and O. Patashnik, *Concrete Mathematics*, Addison-Wesley, Reading, Massachusetts, 1989.
37. C.A.R. Hoare, "Quicksort," *Computer Journal* **5**, 1962, 10–15.
38. J.E. Hopcroft and R.E. Tarjan, "Efficient algorithms for graph manipulation," *Communications of the ACM* **16**, 1973, 372–378.
39. E. Horowitz, S. Sahni, and S. Rajasekaran, *Computer Algorithms in C++*, Computer Science Press, New York, 1997.
40. *The IEEE/ACM International Symposium on Cluster, Cloud and Grid Computing (CCGrid),* http://www.cloudbus.org/, accessed August 24, 2012.
41. *IEEE Cloud: International Conference on Cloud Computing*, http://www.thecloudcomputing.org/, accessed August 24, 2012.
42. *IEEE Cluster*, http://www.ieeecluster.org/, accessed August 24, 2012.
43. *IEEE Cluster Computing: TCSC Annual Conference*, http://www.clustercomp.org/, accessed August 24, 2012.
44. J. Já Já, *An Introduction to Parallel Algorithms*, Addison-Wesley, Reading, Massachusetts, 1992.
45. R.A. Jarvis, "On the identification of the convex hull of a finite set of points in the plane," *Information Processing Letters* **2**, 1973, 18–21.
46. A.B. Kahng and G. Robins, "Optimal algorithms for extracting spatial regularity in images," *Pattern Recognition Letters* **12**, 1991, 757–764.
47. R.M. Karp and V. Ramachandran, "A survey of parallel algorithms for shared memory machines," in *Handbook of Theoretical Computer Science: Algorithms and Complexity*, A.J. van Leeuwen, ed., The MIT Press, Cambridge, Massachusetts, 1990, 869–941.
48. P. Kacsuk, T. Fahringer and Z. Nemeth, eds., *Distributed and Parallel Systems: From Cluster to Grid Computing*, Springer Science+Business Media, New York, 2007.
49. S. Khuller and B. Raghavachari, "Basic graph algorithms," in *Algorithms and Theory of Computation Handbook*, M.J. Atallah, ed., CRC Press, Boca Raton, FL, 1999.
50. D. B. Kirk and W.-m. W. Hwu, *Programming Massively Parallel Processors: A Hands-on Approach (Applications of GPU Computing Series)*, Morgan-Kaufmann Publishers, Burlington, Massachusetts, 2010.
51. D.E. Knuth, *Fundamental Algorithms*, Volume 1 of *The Art of Computer Programming*, Third Edition, Addison-Wesley, Reading, Massachusetts, 1997.
52. D.E. Knuth, *Seminumerical Algorithms,* Volume 2 of *The Art of Computer Programming*, Third Edition, Addison-Wesley, Reading, Massachusetts, 1997.
53. D.E. Knuth, *Sorting and Searching*, Volume 3 of *The Art of Computer Programming*, Third Edition, Addison-Wesley, Reading, Massachusetts, 1998.

54. D.E. Knuth, *Combinatorial Algorithms*, Part 1, Addison-Wesley, Upper Saddle River, New Jersey, 2011.

55. D.E. Knuth, "Big omicron and big omega and big theta," *ACM SIGACT News* **8** (2), 1976, 18–23.

56. J. Kurzak, D.A. Bader, and J. Dongarra, *Scientific Computing with Multicore and Accelerators*, CRC Press, Boca Raton, FL, 2010.

57. C.C. Lee and D.T. Lee, "On a cover-circle minimization problem," *Information Processing Letters* **18**, 1984, 180–185.

58. F.T. Leighton, *Introduction to Parallel Algorithms and Architectures: Arrays, Trees, Hypercubes*, Morgan Kaufmann Publishers, San Mateo, CA, 1992.

59. F. Magoules, J. Pan, K.-A. Tan and A. Kumar, *Introduction to Grid Computing,* CRC Press, London, England, 2009.

60. S.B. Maurer and A. Ralston, *Discrete Algorithmic Mathematics*, Addison-Wesley, Reading, Massachusetts, 1991.

61. R. Miller and Q.F. Stout, "Efficient parallel convex hull algorithms," *IEEE Transactions on Computers* **37**, 1988, 1605–1619.

62. R. Miller and Q.F. Stout, *Parallel Algorithms for Regular Architectures: Meshes and Pyramids*, The MIT Press, Cambridge, Massachusetts, 1996.

63. R. Miller and Q.F. Stout, "Algorithmic techniques for networks of processors," in *Algorithms and Theory of Computation Handbook*, M. Atallah, ed., CRC Press, Boca Raton, FL, 1999.

64. S.B. Nadler, Jr., *Hyperspaces of Sets*, Marcel Dekker, New York, 1978.

65. W. Narkiewicz, *The Development of Prime Number Theory*, Springer-Verlag, Berlin, 2000.

66. J. O'Rourke, *Art Gallery Theorems and Algorithms*, Oxford University Press, New York, 1987. http://maven.smith.edu/~orourke/books/ArtGalleryTheorems/Art_Gallery_Full_Book.pdf, accessed August 24, 2012.

67. M.H. Overmars and J. van Leeuwen, "Maintenance of configurations in the plane," *Journal of Computer and Systems Sciences* **23**, 1981, 166–204.

68. F.P. Preparata and M.I. Shamos, *Computational Geometry*, Springer-Verlag, New York, 1985.

69. M.J. Quinn, *Parallel Computing Theory and Practice*, McGraw-Hill, Inc., New York, 1994.

70. T. Rauber and G. Rünger, *Parallel Programming for Multicore and Cluster Systems*, Springer-Verlag Berlin Heidelberg, New York, 2010.

71. S. Ranka and S. Sahni, *Hypercube Algorithms for Image Processing and Pattern Recognition,* Springer-Verlag, New York, 1990.

72. G. Reese, *Cloud Application Architectures: Building Applications and Infrastructure in the Cloud*, O'Reilly Media, Sebastopol, CA, 2009.

73. G. Robins, B.L. Robinson, and B.S. Sethi, "On detecting spatial regularity in noisy images," *Information Processing Letters* **69**, 1999, 189–195.
74. K.H. Rosen, *Elementary Number Theory and its Applications*, Addison-Wesley, Reading, Massachusetts, 1993.
75. A. Rosenfeld, "'Continuous' functions on digital pictures," *Pattern Recognition Letters* **4**, 1986, 177–184.
76. J. Sanders and E. Kandrot, *CUDA by Example: An Introduction to General-Purpose GPU Programming*, Addison-Wesley, Reading, Massachusetts, 2011.
77. D. Sarkar and I. Stojmenovic, "An optimal parallel circle-cover algorithm," *Information Processing Letters* **32**, 1989, 3–6.
78. B. Sosinsky, *Cloud Computing Bible*, Wiley Publishing, Inc., Indianapolis, IN, 2011.
79. G.W. Stout, *High Performance Computing*, Addison-Wesley, Reading, Massachusetts, 1995.
80. V. Strassen, "Gaussian elimination is not optimal," *Numerische Mathematik* **14** (3), 1969, 354–356.
81. R.E. Tarjan, "Depth-first search and linear graph algorithms," *SIAM Journal on Computing* **1**, 1972, 146–160.
82. R.E. Tarjan, *Data Structures and Network Algorithms*, Society for Industrial and Applied Mathematics, 1983.
83. F.L. Van Scoy, "The parallel recognition of classes of graphs," *IEEE Transactions on Computers* **29**, 1980, 563–570.
84. B. Wagar, "Hyperquicksort: a fast sorting algorithm for hypercubes," in *Hypercube Multiprocessors 1987*, M.T. Heath, ed., SIAM, 1987, 292–299.
85. S. Warshall, "A theorem on Boolean matrices," *Journal of the ACM* **9**, 1962, 11–12.
86. B. Wilkinson, *Grid Computing: Techniques and Applications*, Chapman & Hall/CRC, Boca Raton, FL, 2010.
87. S. Yakowitz and Ferenc Szidarovszky, *An Introduction to Numerical Computations*, Prentice Hall, New Jersey, 1990.

# Index

## Special Characters



## A



## B



## C

## Q



## R